EveryWoman's
LEGAL
GUIDE

EveryWoman's ®
LEGAL
GUIDE

Protecting Your Rights at Home, in the Workplace, and in the Marketplace

BY 28 LAWYERS AND RIGHTS EXPERTS

Barbara A. Burnett, Esq., Consulting Editor

Doubleday & Company, Inc., Garden City, New York

Library of Congress Cataloging in Publication Data
Main entry under title:
EveryWoman's legal guide.   Includes index.
1. Women—Legal status, laws, etc.—United States.
2. Law—United States. 3. Women—United States—Handbooks, manuals, etc.
I. Burnett, Barbara A.
KF390.W6E83   1983   349.73'088042   82-45476
ISBN 0-385-18523-5   347.30088042

Contributors

Consulting Editor

BARBARA A. BURNETT, Professor, Syracuse University College of Law, Syracuse, New York

Authors

MARILYN YARBROUGH AINSWORTH, Professor of Law, University of Kansas College of Law

JANE N. BARRETT, Bureau of Consumer Frauds and Protection, New York State Department of Law

REBECCA J. COOK, Attorney; former Director, International Planned Parenthood, London

JAMES CRAWFORD, Editor, *Survival Kit,* newsletter of the Massachusetts Coalition for Occupational Safety and Health

PHYLLIS L. CROCKER, student, Northeastern University School of Law; formerly a legal worker in the New Haven Law Collective.

LETITIA DAVIS, doctoral candidate, Harvard School of Public Health; co-chair, Massachusetts Coalition for Occupational Safety and Health

JUDIANNE DENSEN-GERBER, J.D., M.D., President Odyssey Resources Inc., Bridgeport, Conn.

CLARENCE DITLOW, Attorney; Director, Center for Auto Safety, Washington, D.C.

JANE L. DOLKART, Attorney; former Assistant General Counsel, Equal Employment Opportunity Commission, Washington, D.C.

RONA F. FEIT, Attorney; former head, Office of Women's Business Enterprise, U.S. Small Business Administration

HENRY H. FOSTER, Professor of Law Emeritus, New York University School of Law

BEATRICE S. FRANK, Clinical Assistant Professor of Law, New York University School of Law

AMY M. HESS, Associate Professor of Law, University of Tennessee

MARTHA KEYS, former member of the U.S. House of Representatives

KAREN KULP, Public Information Coordinator, Women Organized Against Rape, Philadelphia, Pennsylvania

ANN W. LAKE, Professor of Law, Salem State College, Massachusetts

JOAN LENNINGTON, Attorney, member of the Legal Committee of the Massachusetts Coalition for Occupational Safety and Health

JEAN LOTHIAN, Vice-president for Public Information, Odyssey Institute, New York City

LYNN A. MARKS, Attorney; Executive Director, Women Organized Against Rape, Philadelphia, Pennsylvania

COLQUITT L. MEACHAM, Attorney; former Associate Dean, Amherst College, Amherst, Massachusetts

EMILY NOVICK, Attorney; member of the Legal Committee of the Massachusetts Coalition for Occupational Safety and Health

JULIE E. O'CONNOR, Attorney; member of the Women's Criminal Defense Bar, San Diego, California

AMY R. PIRO, Attorney; Assistant Counsel to the Governor, State of New Jersey

THERESA J. PLAYER, Attorney; member of the Women's Criminal Defense Bar, San Diego, California

ALICE QUINLAN, Government Relations Director, Older Women's League, Washington, D.C.

TONDA F. RUSH, Attorney; Director, Freedom of Information Service Center, Washington, D.C.

GERALDINE S. RUSSELL, Attorney; member of the Women's Criminal Defense Bar, San Diego, California

ROBERT SCHWARTZ, Attorney; member of the Legal Committee of the Massachusetts Coalition for Occupational Safety and Health

ANNE E. SIMON, Attorney, NOW Legal Defense and Education Fund

SARAH VOGEL, Attorney, Grand Forks, North Dakota; former Federal Trade Commission Program Advisor

Contents

PART TWO:
WOMEN AS FAMILY MEMBERS:
YOUR RIGHTS IN DOMESTIC RELATIONS

WHAT IS ESTATE PLANNING? • Property and Family Considerations
• Who Gets Property if the Owner Dies Without a Will • Automatic Transfer of Property at Death • MECHANICS OF TRANSFER:
PROCEDURES FOR THE ADMINISTRATION OF ESTATES • TAX CONSIDERATIONS • Gift Taxes • Death Taxes •

PART THREE:
WOMEN AS WORKERS:
   YOUR RIGHTS IN THE WORKPLACE

WHY OUR SCHOOLS PLAY FOLLOW-THE-LEADER • NEW LAWS
THAT HELPED EQUAL EDUCATION FOR WOMEN • SEX DISCRIMINATION IN EDUCATION • WOMEN AS STUDENTS • Title IX • VOCATIONAL EDUCATION • WOMEN REENTERING EDUCATIONAL PROGRAMS • Age Discrimination • FEDERAL FINANCIAL AID
PROGRAMS FOR STUDENTS • The Pell Grant Program • The Supplemental Educational Opportunity Grant Program • The College
Work Study Program • The National Direct Student Loan Program
• Guaranteed Student Loan Program • Other Federal Funding
Sources • STUDENTS' RIGHTS REGARDING EDUCATIONAL RECORDS
• Right to Review • Right to Correct • Right of Nondisclosure •

LAWS PROHIBITING DISCRIMINATION AGAINST WOMEN WORKERS
• TITLE VII • Title VII Coverage • Common Discriminatory
Practices and Relief • Filing a Charge with the EEOC • EEOC
Processing • Right to File a Lawsuit • Time Limitations • How to
Find a Lawyer and Finance a Title VII Lawsuit • Title VII Procedures for Federal Employees • THE EQUAL PAY ACT • Whether to
File a Charge with the EEOC • Time Limitations • Kinds of Discrimination Forbidden by the Equal Pay Act • Limitations of the
Equal Pay Act as Compared with Title VII • Violations of the Equal
Pay Act • Title IX of the Education Amendments • Executive
Order 11246 • The ADEA • Disability and Sexual Preference Discrimination •

Introduction

BARBARA A. BURNETT, CONSULTING EDITOR

The women and men of this country have experienced a revolution in law and culture over the past several generations that is unparalleled in world history. Not long ago, any legal manual purporting to advise women focused exclusively upon the rights of wives, ex-wives, and widows. This book starts with the premise that women today participate fully in the marketplace and the workplace as well as in the home. Most of the topics discussed in this work are not exclusively of interest to women. As many laws prohibiting gender discrimination are written in sex-neutral terms, men are entitled to the same protections given women. This book was conceived as a resource for anyone who wishes to be better informed about the law.

Much of this guide could not have been written even ten years ago; many of the laws discussed here did not exist. Employment discrimination, sexual harassment, and joint custody are just a few of the areas of the law that have developed rapidly in the recent past. The contributors were chosen for their professional expertise in these new and often complex disciplines as well as for their ability to explain the law in readable and accurate language.

Certainly there would have been fewer women lawyers and law professors to contribute to a legal guide for women ten years ago. When I graduated from law school, in 1972,[1] 7 percent of the law graduates nationwide were women. In 1981 the figure was 33 percent, and every year the percentage increases. No matter what the political fortunes of the Equal Rights

[1] I was able to go to law school because I received a scholarship which had only the year before I applied been available to men exclusively. I am grateful to the Root-Tilden Scholarship Program and New York University School of Law. I thank the feminist women in the classes just preceding mine who worked for the change in eligibility requirement which has now benefited women law students and NYU for over a decade.

Amendment,[2] women have earned the right to, and have accepted the responsibility for, fashioning law into a tool for social justice. We believe that all women and men, not just those trained in the law, may contribute to that goal.

The law has been called by legal scholars a vast, seamless web. It is complex, wide-ranging, and constantly in flux. New interpretations are regularly expanding or limiting the impact of existing statutes. New legislation is constantly being considered, debated, and enacted. Often regulations supplement rules and give them new meaning. Federal laws sometimes conflict with state laws. One state may provide a completely different solution to a legal problem from its neighbor.

Therefore, we have not provided specific references to statutes and decisions on a state-by-state basis. Particular problems usually require individual solutions. The contributors have unraveled only the most basic and durable features of the law. We provide a format for understanding general systems and for orienting the nonlawyer. The important questions and the common pitfalls are discussed. For any particular rights violation, individual legal representation is often necessary. We hope this guide will help the reader avoid mistakes, ask pertinent questions, choose the appropriate professional help, and make informed choices. We believe the law is a tool that is useful only when honed by intelligent application and sensitive interpretation. We hope that by knowing your rights you will be encouraged to enforce them. Only through their exercise are rights given meaning.

[2]The Equal Rights Amendment says:
EQUALITY OF RIGHTS UNDER THE LAW SHALL NOT BE DENIED OR ABRIDGED BY THE UNITED STATES OR ANY STATE ON ACCOUNT OF SEX.
Frequently those who oppose its passage do not know what it provides.

Part One

WOMEN AS CONSUMERS AND HOMEMAKERS

Your Rights in the Marketplace

1
Contracts and Credit

SARAH VOGEL

Sarah Vogel is an attorney in private practice in North Dakota currently specializing in defending farm foreclosures. Before returning to North Dakota, she was special assistant for consumer affairs for the Secretary of the Treasury; program adviser for Equal Credit Opportunity Act enforcement at the Federal Trade Commission; assistant counsel at Chesebrough-Pond's; assistant counsel for consumer credit at Manufacturers Hanover Trust Co.; and assistant counsel of the New York City Department of Consumer Affairs. Ms. Vogel is a graduate of New York University School of Law and the University of North Dakota. She is a member of the bars of New York and North Dakota.

WOMEN AND CONTRACTS

"Law" does not have to be a mystery. People engage in legal transactions every day and do not usually need a lawyer to do so. Writing checks, purchasing merchandise, signing rental leases, and many other everyday occurrences are legal transactions. When you make a deal with someone to paint your house, you are involved in a legal transaction—a contract.

What Is a Contract?
A contract is an agreement that involves at least one promise that has legal consequences. Usually the legal consequence is that performance of the promise can be enforced in court. Generally, it is a promise, or a set of promises, that create a duty to perform. Failure to perform is called a breach.

The author wishes to thank Leslie Johnson Soetebier for her help in preparing this chapter.

What Are the Basic Elements?

The basic elements of a contract are an offer and an acceptance. Both are necessary to create an agreement. For example, Ms. X agrees to buy Ms. Y's television set for $75. The parties must agree as to the subject of the agreement. If Ms. Y is talking about her 12-inch black-and-white television set and Ms. X is talking about Ms. Y's 26-inch color television set, there is a basic lack of agreement. Where there is such a material, or major, difference in what the parties are bargaining for, there is no agreement. There must be a "meeting of the minds."

A contract usually consists of an offer; e.g., "I will sell you my black-and-white television set for $75." An offer is a promise: a commitment to do or refrain from doing some specified thing in the future. An offer must be distinguished from an opinion ("I think my television is worth at least $75"), which is not binding.

Another essential part of a contract is an acceptance: "Yes, I will pay you $75 for your television." The acceptor has just promised to pay for the television and will be performing the request of the offeror.

Another basic element of a contract is "consideration." Consideration is something of value given by each party to the agreement. For example, "I will give you an apple if you give me an orange." If she agrees, then there is a contract. Each party has given up something and received something. Consideration is often hard to define, as it is not necessarily the same as equal value. Generally, courts will not consider the adequacy of the value of the consideration unless the disparity between what the parties give is so great that to enforce such a contract would be unconscionable. For example, a creditor obtaining a mortgage on a poor woman's home to secure a $50 loan.

Does It Make a Difference If a Contract Is Oral or Written?

Yes, it makes a big difference. Consider the situation in which Alice and Betty go into a catering business together and nothing is written down to define their roles or their expectations. Betty gives more money than time and Alice gives more time than money. The business goes well, but after a few months personal problems develop. This kind of situation often escalates into a real mess. If their rights and obligations had been put in written form before the business was started, the parties would have known where they stood. A written contract also helps focus the issues and encourages the parties to say what they expect from each other. If there are disagreements, it is better to know before major commitments are made.

If you are considering a business partnership or some other major transaction, an attorney is probably worth the money. She will draft a clear contract at the beginning and minimize the risk of an expensive and emotionally exhausting battle at the end.

With certain major exceptions, such as real estate sales or long-term employment contracts that are set by state law, oral contracts are generally binding. But an oral contract may disintegrate in conflicts between what the two parties believe the agreement to be. Proof of what was agreed to is often a problem. The best bet when entering an agreement is to negotiate a written contract.

Are There Any Basic Rules That I Should Know About the Interpretation of Contracts?

Yes, there are several basic rules that are valuable to know. The purpose of the written language of a contract is to govern its interpretation. If the language is clear, that language will govern. One cannot safely come into court and say, "But that is not what I meant!" If the language is not ambiguous, the court will hold the parties to it.

The intention of the parties is to be ascertained from the writing alone, if possible. However, when there is fraud, mistake, or accident, a written contract fails to express the real intentions of the parties. The court may then try to ascertain the real intentions of the parties and disregard the erroneous parts of the written part. If Jane and Sue make a contract for Jane to paint Sue's apartment for $250 but the contract says $25, the court may disregard the $25 figure. Obviously, it is prudent to check all contracts before you sign them, to make sure that you are signing a document that is accurate and says what you mean it to say.

Another rule of interpretation that is generally accepted is that when a contract has both preprinted or typewritten parts and handwritten parts, the handwritten parts will control if there are inconsistencies. Yet another rule states that where there is an ambiguity in a contract, that ambiguity or uncertainty will be interpreted against the party who drafted the contract.

What Is the Uniform Commercial Code?

The Uniform Commercial Code (UCC) governs commercial transactions. The UCC has been adopted, with minor variations, throughout the United States by the state legislature of every state except Louisiana. The UCC does not change all the traditional rules of contracts but does create a uniform, systematic way of dealing with commercial transactions. The Uniform Commercial Code contains nine articles, which deal with topics from the sale of goods to letters of credit.

Are There Laws That Protect Me in the Area of Contracts?

Yes. You'll have to check the law in the state you live in, however. Some states have adopted laws that protect people in certain areas, for example those who invest in franchises. If you feel you have been cheated, a good first place to start inquiring may be your state attorney general's office.

The rule concerning how long you have a right to sue for breach of contract (this is called a statute of limitations) varies from state to state. Don't wait too long to file a breach-of-contract suit. If the statute of limitations runs out, you are out of luck.

The Uniform Commercial Code also contains some guidelines for fair dealing. Some states have adopted higher standards applicable within their own borders.

What Kinds of Contracts Are There?

Every kind: Contracts are created to deal with multimillion-dollar mergers of huge companies, and rentals of lawnmowers on a daily basis.

In terms of classifying contracts, it is sometimes helpful to distinguish between negotiated, "arms-length" contracts, in which the parties sit down and express their agreement in writing, and "form contracts," in which the contract is presented by one party on a take-it-or-leave-it basis.

In this day of centralized and automated business, a woman is commonly faced with form contracts. *Beware of form contracts.* Beware also of the tendency to skip over and not read form contracts.

The law assumes that people read and understand the contracts that they sign. When a woman is faced with five pages of fine print loaded with "Whereas the party of the first part" and "Therefore the party of the second part," her eyes may glaze over, and in understandable bewilderment she may sign the contract hoping that it says what she thinks it says.

Sometimes special rules of interpretation will be applied to what the courts call "contracts of adhesion." These contracts arise when one party is in a vastly superior bargaining position. The contract is invariably preprinted and no negotiation is allowed. The party being asked to sign may be in a necessitous position, poorly educated, or ill equipped to understand what it is that she is signing. In these cases, the court may reform the contract to make the bargain more fair and equitable. Cases successfully challenging the plain language of "contracts of adhesion" are not common. The rarity of such cases is probably due to the unavailability of legal assistance to poor and middle-income persons, rather than to the merits of the individual cases.

When faced with a form contract, especially one involving substantial sums or commitments, read it first and understand it. If it has objectionable features and is completely one-sided, shop elsewhere if you can. Also let the company know how you feel about the contract you were asked to sign.

Is a Lease a Contract?

Yes, leases are contracts. These are generally on printed forms and leave little room for bargaining. You will generally be held to the terms of a lease.

As with all contracts, read the lease carefully and try to meet its terms in order to avoid liability. In this area, as in many others, there may be local housing codes or laws that provide you with certain protections that are not printed in the contract but apply nevertheless. If you believe your landlord or the leasing company is treating you unfairly, the general law may still provide a remedy.

Sometimes leases are written to give you the option of buying the leased product at the end of the contract. Be sure you understand the terms and that the lease fairly expresses those terms.

> Example: A freelance secretary wanted to lease a modern word processor. The salesperson promised her that at the end of a three-year term she could buy it for 10 percent of the original retail value. When the contract was presented for her signature, it had no buy-out term at all. She refused to sign. The next version of the lease simply said she could buy it for 10 percent. The obvious question was 10 percent of what? Without a better definition, the 10 percent figure could have been 10 percent of the total lease payments! She again refused to sign. Finally, the contract said what the bad salesperson promised her it would say and what she wanted. Only then did she sign the lease. Throughout the whole process, the salesperson kept saying that the company would honor her verbal promises; however, the would-be purchaser knew that the written terms would control and that a court would assume that she had agreed to the contract that she had signed.

Are There Protections Available to Women Who Enter into Leases?

There is a federal Consumer Leasing Act, which applies to personal property leased by an individual for a period of more than four months for personal, family, or household use. It covers long-term rentals of furniture, cars, and other personal property. It does not cover leases for apartments or houses, or leases for business purposes.

The Consumer Leasing Act requires the lessor to give you a written statement of lease costs before you sign the lease. You must also be told certain terms of the lease such as express warranties, the insurance you will need, the penalties for default, and so on.

What Is a Balloon Payment in a Lease?

A balloon payment term in an open-end lease is a term to watch out for. It may result in your owing more money at the end of the lease depending on the value of the property when you return it. The Consumer Leasing Act limits a balloon payment at the end of an open-end lease to no more than three times the average monthly payment, unless you explicitly agreed to pay more or you have used the property more than average.

Are There Terms and Conditions to Watch Out for in Contracts?

The law creates a duty to read a contract. A person who signs an instrument manifests assent to it and may generally not later complain that she did not read the instrument or did not understand its content. There are many things to look out for in a contract. We will touch upon a few of these.

Should I Just Take the Word of the Other Party as to What Is in the Contract?

No. Demand adequate time to read and review the contract. If there is any language that you do not understand, ask someone else to explain it to you. When you are reading over the contract, it is a good idea to outline what is in it. That way, you know what the contract calls for and whether there are any parts that you don't understand.

What if an Offer Sounds Too Good to Be True?

It may sound trite, but offers that sound too good to be true often have hidden features or missing terms that give the other party an out. Be careful, especially when the salesperson says, "Sign right now; this is a once-in-a-lifetime deal; don't bother reading the contract—it's only fine print."

"Fine-print," or "boilerplate," contractual terms are plenty important if the company later decides to come after you for enforcement! Read the whole contract and ask yourself some basic questions about the contract. If it is carpeting that you want to buy from a door-to-door salesperson, does the contract specify that the carpet that you will get will be the same quality as the sample?

What if the Salesperson Promises Me Something That Is Not in the Written Contract?

Get any additional promises or terms in writing. The "parol-evidence" rule in contract interpretation states that a contract made by the parties supersedes tentative terms made in earlier negotiations. If the salesperson said, "We won't bill you for three months," but the contract says: "To be paid in full on delivery," the contract terms will govern. A court may not listen to your argument that the salesperson told you otherwise.

I Simply Can't Understand a Lot of the "Legalese" in the Promissory Note and Security Agreement That I've Been Asked to Sign in Order to Get a Loan. What Does It All Mean?

You are in good company. Many of these documents are difficult even for lawyers to understand. One sometimes suspects that contracts are written obscurely in order to confuse and bewilder the other party. A few illustrations of typical credit contract terms and a "plain English" translation prepared by the staff of the Federal Trade Commission's Division of Credit Practices follow:

ACCELERATION CLAUSE

Legalese version: "Default in the payment of any installment of the principal balance or charges hereof or any part of either shall, at the option of the holder hereof, render the entire principal balance hereof and accrued charges thereon, at once due and payable."

Plain English version: "If I miss a payment, you can make me repay the whole loan immediately."

CONFESSION OF JUDGMENT CLAUSE

Legalese version: "To secure payment hereof, the Undersigned jointly and severally irrevocably authorize any attorney of any court to appear for any one or more of them in such court in term or vacation, after default in payment hereof and confess a judgment without process in favor of the creditor hereof for such amount as may then appear unpaid, to release all errors which may intervene in any such proceedings, and to consent to immediate execution upon such judgment, hereby ratifying every act of such attorney hereunder."

Plain English version: "If you ever sue me because I haven't paid, I agree, in advance, that you should win—even if I have a good reason for not paying. In fact, YOUR lawyer can represent me."

BLANKET SECURITY INTEREST CLAUSE

Legalese version: "This note is secured by a security interest in all of the following described personal property and proceeds thereof: If checked at left, Consumer goods consisting of all household goods, furniture, appliances and bric-a-brac, now owned and hereafter acquired, including replacements, and located in or about the premises at the Debtor's residence (unless otherwise stated) or at any other location to which the goods may be moved. In addition, all other goods and chattels of like nature hereafter acquired by the Debtor and kept or used in or about said premises and substituted for any property mentioned. Proceeds and Products of the collateral are also covered."

Plain English version: "If I don't pay, you can take all the household goods I own."

WAIVER OF STATE PROPERTY EXEMPTION CLAUSE

Legalese version: "Each of us hereby both individually and severally waives any or all benefit or relief from homestead exemption and all other exemptions or moratoriums to which the signers or any of them may be entitled under the laws of this or any other State, now in force or hereafter to be passed, as against this debt or any renewal thereof."

Plain English version: "If I don't pay, you may come take even the personal belongings state law would allow me to keep."

RIGHT TO COLLECT DEFICIENCY CLAUSE

Legalese version: "The Creditor may retain the goods as its property or may sell or otherwise dispose of the item pursuant to the (State) Uniform Commercial Code, whereupon Debtor shall be liable for and shall pay any deficiency on demand."

Plain English version: "If you repossess what I bought from you and you don't get a good resale price for it, I'll still owe you the difference. (For example, if you take back a perfectly good $500 TV and can get only $150 for it, I lose the TV and still owe you $350.)"

WAIVER OF RIGHT TO PRIVACY CLAUSE

Legalese version: "The undersigned, jointly and severally, waive any right of privacy of any nature in connection with this instrument, regardless of whether or not the debt evidenced thereby may be contested, and agree that the lender may at its option communicate with any persons whatsoever in relation to the obligation involved, or its delinquency, or in an effort to obtain cooperation or help relative to the collection or payment thereof."

Plain English version: "If I don't pay, you can tell all my friends and relatives and my boss that I'm a deadbeat."

WAGE ASSIGNMENT CLAUSE

Legalese version: "For value received, the undersigned jointly and severally hereby assign, transfer, convey and set over unto the

Assignee, named above, ten per centum (10%) of all salary, wages, commissions and other compensation for services severally earned or to be earned severally by us in the employ of the employer specified under our names set forth below by whom we are severally now employed or any future employer, until the loan secured hereby and described below shall have been fully discharged.

"We severally hereby authorize and direct our said employers or any future employers or either of them to pay said part of our salary, wages, commission or other compensation for services to the said Assignee and release such employers or any future employers from all liability to us on account of any and all monies paid in accordance with the terms hereof. We severally give and grant unto the said Assignee full power and authority to demand, receive and receipt for the same or any part thereof in any of our names."

Plain English version: "If I don't pay, just have my boss deduct the money from my paycheck. I won't argue about it— even if I have a good reason for not paying."

COSIGNER GUARANTY CLAUSE

Legalese version: "In consideration of the making and acceptance of the within note by the Debtor and Creditor named therein, respectively, undersigned jointly and severally unconditionally guarantees to the said Creditor and to any Assignee of said Creditor, the payment of all monies due or to become due under said note, in accordance with the terms thereof, and also the full performance by the said Debtor of all the promises and covenants on his or their part therein contained, and Undersigned does hereby expressly agree that anything in said note to the contrary notwithstanding any lack of capacity or liability on the part of the Debtor.

"The Undersigned (cosigner) hereby consents to all extensions of time for the making of any or all payments by the Debtor and further guarantees the payment of all said payments due by reason of said extensions. Notice of acceptance of this Guaranty, notice of nonpayment and nonperformance, notice of amount of indebtedness outstanding at any time, protest, demand, and prosecution of collection, foreclosure and possessory remedies are hereby expressly waived."

Plain English version: "If I don't pay, you may collect from my cosigner without trying to collect from me first. You don't even have to warn my cosigner I've fallen behind in my payments."

ATTORNEY'S FEE CLAUSE

Legalese version: "In addition, if this agreement is referred to any attorney for collection due to any default or breach of any promise or provision hereunder by Debtor, Debtor agrees to pay an attorney's fee of 15% of the Total of Payments then due, plus the court costs."

Plain English version: "It's a real hassle for you to sue me to collect, so I'll pay for your lawyer."

LATE FEE CLAUSE

Legalese version: "In the event Debtor defaults for 15 days in making any of the aforementioned payments when the same become payable hereunder, creditor may charge the debtor a delinquency or collection charge of 5% of the amount of payments in default or the sum of $5.00, whichever is less."

Plain English version: "You can charge me a late fee if I'm 15 days late, and if I don't pay on time just once, my state law may let you charge me a late fee on all my other payments too."

CONTINUING-COSIGNER GUARANTY CLAUSE

Legalese version: "The undersigned hereby guarantees the payment of the indebtedness or any balance thereof owing by the Purchaser to the Merchant as seller under such Retail Installment Credit Agreement and does further guarantee the payment of any future indebtedness or balance thereof hereafter contracted by such Purchaser upon purchase of goods, wares and merchandise by such Purchaser singly or jointly with others, from the merchant, if made within a period of two years from the date of the execution of this guarantee, provided, however, the maximum amount for which the undersigned shall be liable hereunder as to such future purchases shall in no event exceed $5,000 at the time it is sought to enforce this guarantee, but the extension of credit either at any one time, or in the aggregate, of any amount in excess of said sum, shall not operate to release the undersigned from liability as to said sum."

Plain English version: "If you finance any other purchase for me in the next two years (up to $5,000), the cosigner on this credit purchase guarantees payment on that purchase, too."

INSECURITY CLAUSE

Legalese version: "If the Debtor(s) fail(s) to pay any installment of any advance secured hereby or part thereof or if there is a breach of any of the covenants, agreements or warranties contained herein or in the Credit Agreement or if the Secured Party shall feel insecure, all sums then owing under said Credit Agreement shall immediately become due and payable without demand or notice."

Plain English version: "If you start to feel insecure about getting paid back, you may demand that I pay the entire amount at any time."

Not all these clauses are legal in all states. Your contract may contain one or more of them, however. If it does, you may wish to look for a different source of credit. You may also wish to check your state law to see if the clauses that appear in your contract are legal. Sometimes, a creditor will leave the illegal clauses in the contract either because of carelessness or because the creditor finds them a useful threat to enforce collection.

Why Don't Companies Just Write These Contracts So I Can Understand Them?

Good question. Sometimes the contract forms are overly wordy, as the seller or lender is trying to protect herself and give herself every edge possible at your expense.

A "plain English" movement is slowly developing. Some banks and other companies are writing their contracts in easy-to-understand language. They have found that business has improved and that their customers appreciate their efforts. You might mention this to companies with which you are doing business. Some state regulatory bodies have started to require plain English (for example, in insurance contracts). There are still too many obscure and misleading contracts in existence.

What Can I Do About The Promise That Was Not Fulfilled by the Other Party?

There may be a number of options, depending on the amount of damages that you suffered. You might consider reporting the violation to the consumer protection agency or assistant attorney general in charge of consumer protection in your area. (Just check the directory for the state capitol.) You might also consider reporting it to the Better Business Bureau, which does not have enforcement power but sometimes is able to negotiate a fair solution.

A small claims court may be available in your area. If it is, you could take the company or person who did you wrong to small claims court.

What Is a Small Claims Court?

A small claims court, or "people's court," is where a person can bring a claim against another person for a wrong done by that person. The party bringing the claim is called the "plaintiff" and the party against whom it is brought is called the "defendant." There is usually a dollar limit as to how much you may claim. The dollar limit will vary from court to court. You may either represent yourself or obtain help from an attorney. For example, Ms. T. V. Fixit comes to your house to repair your television. She turns some knobs and charges you $50. One week later, the television has the same problem. Ms. T. V. Fixit will neither repair it nor refund your money. You may file a claim against her in small claims court.

Forms and advice on how to file a claim are usually available at the small claims court. There will be a filing fee, which often will be refunded if you win your case.

The best tip for going into small claims court is be prepared. Bring in witnesses, photographs, documents, or anything that helps you tell your story. If the dry cleaner ruined your best suit by her negligence and she won't pay for it, bring the ruined suit into court with you.

When Should I See a Lawyer?

If someone has breached a contract with you or if you are in violation of the strict terms of a contract and the amount of money or the issue is significant, a lawyer may be needed.

It is probably also wise to see a lawyer when you are thinking of signing or negotiating a major contract. You may want to see a lawyer for a brief consultation when you just can't understand a contract clause or you feel that something is not right.

Sometimes a relatively small amount for legal advice before problems become major will save money in the long run.

Contact friends and neighbors for the name of a lawyer that they found to be good. Also contact the bar association to see if they have a legal referral service. Some legal referral services allow a free interview on the first visit. Whatever lawyer you choose, remember that she cannot do everything. Your clear exposition of the facts and what you want will facilitate the process and save you money. Attorneys have various fee arrangements. Negotiate the fee arrangement in advance, as you would negotiate any contract.

You will find that keeping good records (copies of all memoranda, letters, bills, etc.) will facilitate self-help efforts to resolve your problems and conserve your attorney's time.

Contracts are part of the life of every person. You may not even realize that plain, everyday transactions are contractual in nature. Contracts can help or hurt you, depending on how they are used. Read them and know what you are signing. When you don't understand your obligations or rights, get someone to help you.

WOMEN AND CREDIT CONTRACTS

What Is Credit?

Credit is a special variety of contract whereby one person or business (the "creditor") gives another person or business (the "debtor") the right to defer payment of a debt or to make purchases and incur debt and defer its payment. Sometimes credit will consist of a "loan"—for example, when a bank loans you $1,000. Sometimes, credit will consist of a purchase for which you do not have to make immediate payment—for example, when you buy a $100 chair and are allowed to pay for it over a year's time. Credit may also be a promise by a creditor to allow you to borrow money or defer payments in the future—for example, when you obtain a bank credit card, a department store credit card, or an "overdraft" line on your checking account.

What Are the Major Types of Credit?

It helps to think of credit as broken into two major kinds: open-end credit and closed-end credit.

An example of open-end credit is a charge-card account; an example of closed-end credit is an installment loan from a bank. Open-end credit generally allows you to borrow up to a certain amount of money and allows flexibility in repayment according to a formula that will appear in your credit contract. Closed-end credit is for a certain sum and will require steady payments of uniform amounts. In open-end credit you will almost always get a monthly bill. In closed-end credit, you may get a coupon book that gives the exact amount of your monthly payments.

What Does It Mean When a Loan Is "Secured"?

This simply means that you have promised the creditor that if you do not pay the loan according to the terms of the contract, the creditor may look to some property you own to enforce or "secure" payment. A classic example is a real estate mortgage. As long as you make payments, the creditor can't interfere with your right to live in and enjoy the house. But if you don't make your payments, the creditor could attempt to foreclose upon your house and force you to sell it to someone else. You may be surprised to see what loans are secured. Some department store credit contracts, for example, say that everything that you buy with the use of credit is security for the extension of credit. While there is little economic incentive to repossess used clothing, the threat of repossession can be used as a strong psychological club to force repayment!

If you are considering taking out a loan and your income is not adequate to justify it, some creditors will extend credit if you offer additional security. Be careful: If you fear being unable to pay out of your income, perhaps you should not borrow. Every state has adopted laws that govern security interests of real property and personal property. Every state but Louisiana follows the Uniform Commercial Code with respect to personal property. Real property law varies. Some states provide special rights, such as the right to cure default or the right to redeem after foreclosure. It may be worth asking your attorney to check.

How Can I Tell If I Can Afford to Use Credit?

In order to decide if you should use credit, you must balance many factors. You must ask yourself questions like these: What is my income? How much do I have to pay to use credit (this cost can be enormous when the interest rate is as high as it has been in the recent past)? What are my other monthly and yearly obligations? Am I better off saving money for the time being, then buying what I need with cash? Can I do without something that I would have to go into debt to buy? What will happen to me if I lose my job: will I have any means of repayment? If I have savings, should I take out my savings and pay cash or will I be better off if I borrow and repay later from future income?

Many of the basic guidelines on credit "affordability" must be modified to suit your own circumstances. If you live in a major city and have expensive housing and high taxes, you have less discretionary income than a person with the same salary who lives in a rural area with low rent and low taxes. Look to your discretionary income—not your gross income. Also remember that credit must be repaid and with interest. Even though it may be convenient to charge now and pay later, the paying-later phase does come and it often isn't pleasant.

Many women have encountered difficulties with credit because they simply have not observed the gradual increases in their debt due to many small purchases (e.g., dinners out, impulse purchases, gifts at holidays, gasoline charges) on open-end credit accounts. A number of small, seemingly innocuous purchases can mount up and become a major debt.

> Example: After college, Susan started work at a major insurance company. She applied for and received credit cards at a local bank, several department stores, and a gasoline company. Sur-

rounded by beautiful shops, she bought a blouse here, a dress there, theater tickets and music albums on impulse, and charged gas and car maintenance because it was more convenient than cash. She was earning so much more than she ever had before and felt "rich." Although she had the best of intentions to repay the charges in full at the end of the month, the end of the month came and she saw that she had only to pay a minimum of $10 or $20 on charges of $100. She simply deferred the day of reckoning. Six months later, Susan realized that her accumulated debts were $2,500. Had Susan been asked when she got her credit cards whether she could afford to spend that much money on clothes, entertainment, and transportation, she would have said, "No." Yet, by increments that she barely noticed, Susan was in a position in which repayment of the debt was a real strain. Her solution: no more impulse charging and a firm schedule to pay back the balances on each of her accounts. It took her nine months. When Susan was again debt free, she used the charge accounts rarely and then paid the balance due at the end of the month. She discovered that this saved her money, too. She not only had no major interest costs, several of her creditors did not charge interest during a thirty-day grace period. Susan could keep her cash in savings until the bill came, at the end of the month.

LAWS TO PROTECT WOMEN IN OBTAINING AND USING CREDIT

THE EQUAL CREDIT OPPORTUNITY ACT

In the preceding example, a young woman was faced with the problem of how to manage credit competently. Not too long ago, this was a problem that few women had, because women often could not get credit in the first instance. The reasons for sex and marital-status discrimination in credit were varied: women would have babies and stop paying their bills; women were poor credit risks (how did creditors know this if they had never tried to give women credit?); women only worked for "pin money" and didn't need credit; it was unfair to married men to allow their wives to obtain credit; a single woman could not get a housing loan, because she'd be unable to repair it and the house would shortly turn into a slum; or, the most frustrating reason of all, "just because."

When the author of this chapter graduated from law school, in 1970, she applied for credit from a women's clothing store. About two weeks later, a card came: in her husband's name! Ironically, he was still a student, but he was deserving of credit, not she! Because of this kind of absurd and economically destructive attitude by creditors, a movement arose in the early 1970s to pass a federal law to prohibit discrimination on the basis of sex or marital status in the extension of credit. The law was entitled Equal Credit Opportunity Act. It went into effect in October 1975.

What Does the Equal Credit Opportunity Act Say?

The language of the Equal Credit Opportunity Act (commonly abbreviated as ECOA) is deceptively simple and amazingly broad:

> It shall be unlawful for any creditor to discriminate with respect to any aspect of a credit transaction on the basis of sex or marital status.

The accompanying statement by Congress on the purpose of the Equal Credit Opportunity Act sets forth its basic purpose:

> The Congress finds that there is a need to insure that the various financial institutions and other firms engaged in the extensions of credit exercise their responsibility to make credit available with fairness, impartiality, and without discrimination on the basis of sex or marital status. Economic stabilization would be enhanced and competition among the various financial institutions and other firms engaged in the extension of credit would be strengthened by an absence of discrimination on the basis of sex or marital status, as well as by the informed use of credit, which Congress has heretofore sought to promote. It is the purpose of this Act to require that financial institutions and other firms engaged in the extension of credit make that credit equally available to all creditworthy customers without regard to sex or marital status.

To help women detect whether the reason they had been denied credit was legitimate or illegal, Congress also mandated—for the first time—that creditors provide the SPECIFIC REASONS for a rejection of credit or any other adverse action on a credit account. Moreover, creditors were not allowed to reject applications by "inaction." The Equal Credit Opportunity Act directed that all creditors take action on applications within thirty days of receipt of completed applications. Thus the practice of "round-filing" women's applications was barred.

I'm a Businesswoman. I Have No Trouble Getting Charge Cards, but I Need Credit for My Business, Too. Does the Equal Credit Opportunity Act Help My Business?

Yes. The Equal Credit Opportunity Act prohibits discrimination in business credit as well as consumer credit. Too few businesswomen are aware of this, because when business credit is denied, the creditor is under no obligation to inform the rejected applicant of the existence of the law or the proper agency to which a complaint may be directed.

If you are rejected for business credit, write (don't call) the creditor and ask for the *specific* reasons why you were turned down. The creditor must tell you or be in violation of the law. When you know the specific reasons for the rejection, you can better assess whether your sex played a role in the decision. If the reasons are valid or seem to be valid, you can make your business more creditworthy by remedying the deficiencies that the creditor pointed out to you.

I Want to Apply for My Own Credit Accounts. I'm Married, but I Have My Own Job. My Husband's Credit Rating Is Not Very Good. I'm Concerned That I May Be Disqualified Because of His Rating. Does the Equal Credit Opportunity Act Help Me?

Yes. If you are applying for an individual, unsecured account, if you are not relying on your husband's income, and if he will not be using the account, the creditor must not ask you for any information concerning him. The only exception arises when you live in a "community property state." The creditor will want to know whether you are liable on any other accounts. If you are jointly liable on your husband's accounts, his bad credit history is yours as well. The Act permits you the option, however, of showing that his credit history does not accurately reflect your creditworthiness.

I Am Married, but I Don't Use My Husband's Surname. Can I Get Credit in My Own Name?

Yes.

I Have a Well-paid Job, but It Is Only Part-time. Can I Obtain Credit?

Yes, if you otherwise meet the creditor's requirements. Because more women than men work part-time, the Equal Credit Opportunity Act prohibits the exclusion of part-time income.

I Was Turned Down for Credit Because My Income Was Too Low. The Creditor Said I Should Get My Husband to Be Cosigner. Do I Have to?

No. The creditor should have just told you that you needed a cosigner. You are free to obtain the person of your choice. But remember that the cosigner is just as responsible as you to repay the debt. Make sure that the cosigner knows this and is willing to enter into the transaction. Cosigning a debt is not a good bargain for the one who cosigns, since she doesn't get any benefit and may be obligated to pay for the whole debt if you don't.

I've Had Credit in My Own Name, But I'm About to Get a Divorce. I Want to Change the Name on the Accounts. Can My Accounts Be Canceled Because of the Divorce or Name Change?

No. According to the law, the creditor can't cancel just because of your divorce or because you are changing your name. If you got your accounts by relying on your husband's income, however, the story is somewhat different. If your income alone at the time of the application wasn't adequate, the creditor can require a reapplication based on your present circumstances.

I Have a Friend Who Receives Alimony and Child Support. She'd Like to Get Credit in Her Own Name. Is It Possible?

Yes. The law requires creditors to consider alimony and child support if it is likely to be consistently made. Factors that a creditor may consider include: whether the payments are received pursuant to a written agreement or court order; the length of time that they have been received; the regularity of receipt; the availability of procedures to complete payment, and the creditworthiness of the payor. If your friend can demonstrate consistent and reliable payment, her child support and alimony payments should be considered like any other income.

I'm Shopping for a House Mortgage. The Local Banker Seems Hesitant to Extend Us Credit Even Though Our Joint Income Meets All the Bank's Requirements. I'm 24 and My Husband Is 26.

What may be creating a problem is that the banker may be assuming that you will have children and you will stop working. Assumptions or aggregate statistics relating to the likelihood that any group of persons (i.e., young women) will bear or rear children, and for that reason will receive diminished or interrupted income in the future, are illegal. It is also illegal to ask you whether you plan on bearing or rearing children, whether you use birth control, and similar, intrusive questions.

As a practical matter, however, and in your own self-interest, plan wisely for periods of maternity and child-rearing leave in light of debt repayment obligations.

What Is a Credit-scoring System?

Credit-scoring systems are used by many major creditors. They are means of standardizing predictive factors by analysis of how persons with certain characteristics paid their bills in the past. It is illegal for a credit-scoring system to evaluate sex or marital status.

The credit-scoring system often settles on "criteria" that are surprising to the layperson. For example, a person's zip code, how long she has lived at a particular address, or the number of inquiries about her at the credit bureau may be more important than income.

If you are denied credit due to a low score on a credit-scoring system, the creditor can't just tell you that you have a low score but, rather, must give you the factor(s) on which you scored low or the factor(s) that most influenced your rejection.

If I Have Been Discriminated Against Because of My Sex or Marital Status, Does the Law Provide Any Remedies?

Yes. The Equal Credit Opportunity Act gives you the right to sue for actual and punitive damages. You may sue as an individual or as a representative of a class. Governmental agencies also fall under the Act, but they are not liable for punitive damages. The limitations on punitive damages are $10,000 in individual actions and the lesser of $500,000 or 1 percent of the creditor's net worth in class actions. As an aid to obtaining legal representation, the law says that if you are successful, the creditor must pay for your reasonable attorney's fees and court costs. A lawsuit under this Act must be commenced within a year of the violation.

OTHER CREDIT PROTECTION LAWS

THE FAIR DEBT COLLECTION PRACTICES ACT

Is There a Way I Can Stop a Collection Agency from Harassing Me?

Yes. The Fair Debt Collection Practices Act (FDCPA). This Act applies only to consumer credit and "debt collectors." Debt collectors are defined as those persons whose business's principal purpose is collection of debts owed or due to another. The act prohibits certain practices such as contacting the consumer at unusual times, using postcard communications, using abusive language, and so on.

The FDCPA prohibits a debt collector from further communication once the consumer notifies the collector in writing that she refuses to pay or that the collector should stop contacting her. The debt collector must cease all contacts, except that she may notify the consumer as to ordinary remedies being taken.

The FDCPA does not cover people or companies trying to collect on debts directly owed to themselves.

What Can I Do About Fair Debt Collection Practices Act Violations?

Under the FDCPA there is a right to individual and class actions. If a collection agency has been harassing you and using prohibited collection devices, you can sue for actual damages up to $1,000. If you win your case, the court must award you costs plus reasonable attorney's fees.

The court will look at the frequency and persistence of the violation, the nature of the violation, and the intent involved in the violation in deciding the case.

Congress realized when it passed the FDCPA that the primary causes of nonpayment of consumer obligations are unemployment, illness, and over-extension. The Act works toward the fair and ethical treatment of consumers.

I've Heard About the Truth in Lending Act. What Does It Do?

The Truth in Lending Act (TILA) was designed to promote "informed use of credit." The Act requires disclosure of credit terms, protects consumers against inaccurate and unfair billing in open-end accounts, and has a series of rules on credit card practices.

The TILA requires creditors to tell you how much the credit will cost you before you open an account or before credit is extended. The creditor must tell you the cost in writing and it must be expressed clearly and conspicuously. For example, two key terms—the *finance charge* and the *annual percentage rate*—must stand out over all the other credit terms.

The TILA helps you to shop for credit. Don't take the first contract that comes along. Other sources may be cheaper. TILA will help you find out.

Are There Means of Private Enforcement of the Truth in Lending Act?

Yes. As with the Equal Credit Opportunity Act and the Fair Debt Collection Practices Act, the Truth in Lending Act has teeth. One can get damages in a proper case through an individual lawsuit or a class action. There need not be a showing of actual damages before you can recover.

A lawsuit under the Truth in Lending Act must be brought within one year. Reasonable attorney's fees and court costs are awarded to successful applicants.

THE FAIR CREDIT REPORTING ACT

Do I Have Any Legal Rights with Respect to Practices of Consumer Credit Reporting Agencies?

Yes. The Fair Credit Reporting Act (passed in 1976) was intended by Congress to ensure that consumer credit reporting agencies act "with fairness, impartiality and a respect for the consumer's right of privacy." The act applies to those involved in furnishing consumer reports to third parties. A consumer report is any oral or written communication that bears on a consumer's credit standing, credit capacity, character, general reputation, personal characteristics, or mode of living. The Act does not apply to information collected for business purposes.

The basic protections provided by the Act are (1) privacy (the consumer report may be used only for permissible purposes such as legitimate requests in connection with credit, employment, and insurance that you are seeking); (2) accuracy; and (3) keeping the file current. Information that is more than 7 years old must generally be deleted. Bankruptcies, however, may be kept on file for 10 years.

How Do I Find Out if a Credit Report Played a Role in the Rejection of Credit?

The law says you must be told the name and address of the consumer reporting agency when you are rejected for credit, employment, or insurance based in whole or in part on the basis of a credit report.

Can I Get Access to My Consumer Credit Report?

Yes. You have the right of access to your file to learn the nature and substance of the information in your file, whether or not you have been rejected for credit. You are not necessarily entitled to see or handle the actual file (although the company may let you do so).

Will There Be a Charge?

No charge may be made if you were rejected for credit within the previous thirty days and the consumer credit report played a role in that rejection. Otherwise, the company may charge a reasonable fee. It must tell you the fee in advance.

What Can I Do if There Are Inaccurate Items in My Report?

You have the right to dispute items. The company must reinvestigate the disputed item and correct it if it is inaccurate. If you can't resolve the dispute, you have the right to put a brief statement of your version in the credit report.

Do I Have Any Legal Recourse if My Rights Were Violated?

Yes. You can bring a civil suit for willful noncompliance with the Act, with no ceiling on the amount of punitive damages. You can also sue for negligent (careless) noncompliance for whatever actual damages you suffered. Attorney's fees for both types of action are allowed and will be determined by the court. Cases must be brought within two years; however, you may have longer if the consumer reporting company intentionally misrepresented information essential to your successful prosecution of the suit.

THE "HOLDER IN DUE COURSE" RULE

I Bought a Couch from a Local Furniture Store. The Store Told Me a Short While Later to Make My Payments to a Finance Company. The Couch Is Broken, Even Though It Is Virtually New. The Furniture Store Has Gone Out of Business. May I Raise the Defect in the Couch if the Finance Company Sues Me for Payment?

A Federal Trade Commission trade regulation rule says that you may raise all the claims and defenses that you would have had against the furniture company against the finance company, up to the amount of the debt. The rule is often called the "holder in due course" rule, but its actual title is "Preservation of consumers' claims and defenses."

A notice summarizing your rights should appear in consumer credit contracts arising out of sales. The notice states: "Any holder of this consumer credit contract is subject to all claims and defenses which the debtor could assert against the seller of goods or services obtained pursuant hereto or with the proceeds hereof. Recovery hereunder by the debtor shall not exceed amounts to be paid by the debtor hereunder."

I've Gotten into Credit Trouble. What Can I Do to Help Myself Get Out of This Mess?

The first thing to do is to try to regroup. Figure out where you stand. Collect your bills and prepare a summary. Figure out how much money you can pay on these bills. Budgeting is hard but essential. Some people who are close to their credit limit or who have been prone to overextension, put their cards in a drawer for a few months.

There are also consumer credit counseling services to help you. (See Further Information, p. 517) Some are run for profit. Try to find a nonprofit group that has been set up by a governmental agency or an association of businesses. These services will help you create a budget and a schedule of repayment. Sometimes you can pay a set amount to them every month and they will pay your creditors for you. There are often charges for this service.

Is There Anything I Can Do When I Cannot Make a Payment?

Sure: you can pull down the blinds, stop opening the mail, and refuse to answer the door. That won't help. The best course of action is to call, write, or visit the credit manager. Tell her why it is impossible to keep the payment up to date. Discuss with her what you could pay in the future. It may be possible to renegotiate the payment schedule because of your change in circumstances.

If you are able to reach an agreement, make every effort possible to meet the terms of your temporary or permanent revised payment schedule. As long as the creditor believes you are cooperative and show an interest in making every effort to repay the obligation, other, more drastic collection efforts will be averted.

It may be prudent to slightly underestimate what revised payments you can make. That way you can show good faith by making extra payments. It won't help you if you overestimate your capabilities and don't meet the terms of the revised schedule or arrangement.

What Might Happen to Me if I Do Not Pay as Planned or Become Overextended?

First, your credit rating is sure to suffer. This will make it harder to get credit in the future, at a time you may really need it.

Second, if your loans are secured, the creditor may try to repossess the collateral in order to recoup part of the debt that you owe. Repossession sales generally bring in only a small amount of the value of the property, even though the Uniform Commercial Code sets basic standards for reasonable sale practices. In states that allow the creditor to pursue you for the "deficiency" (the amount that is still owed after the sale), you may still owe a substantial amount of money. Be businesslike. Approach the creditor *before* a repossession occurs. Most creditors would rather be paid eventually than have to repossess used merchandise.

Third, you might be sued. If this happens, you should immediately get in touch with a lawyer. Even at this late stage it may be possible to avoid a judgment if you reach a negotiated settlement with the lawyer for the creditor. If you have defenses or believe you have defenses, give your lawyer all the facts. The worst thing you can do is to ignore a complaint. If you fail to answer it, a default judgment will be taken against you. If a judgment is taken, the creditor may seek to garnish your wages, attach and sell your property, or put liens on your real estate. The judicial remedies available depend on state law. Some property is exempt from execution on a judgment, and you should find out what this property will be and file the appropriate exemptions.

I Think I'm in Really Bad Trouble. Should I Consider Bankruptcy?

Bankruptcy is a mixed blessing. There are many arguments for and against it. It is clear that it is a major step that should not be taken without competent counsel. Straight bankruptcy (commonly called Chapter 7) is designed to wipe out your debts and give you a fresh start; but there are some kinds of debts that are not wiped out—for example, federal taxes and debts that were incurred under false pretenses. "Wage-earner plans" are a different kind of "bankruptcy," in which you are given additional time (if you can qualify your plan) to make your payments. Compromise of debts can sometimes be arranged.

If you think that bankruptcy is your only or best way out of an impossible situation, find a lawyer who specializes in this area and obtain her advice on what you should do.

Women today are facing more of the stresses and demands of the commercial world. Familiarity with the basic concepts and principles of contracts and credit is essential to survive, let alone succeed. The vast increase in credit extended to women since the passage of the Equal Credit Opportunity Act has created a demand by women for help in managing credit and understanding its terms. Moreover, women are entering into business at an ever increasing rate as a result of the profound changes in the workplace over the past twenty years. Women, especially businesswomen, need to understand the role of contracts.

There are people who will seek to have women sign onerous contracts or contracts that fail to implement the terms of earlier negotiations. There are creditors who will seek to have women enter into credit transactions they cannot afford and credit contracts that are totally one-sided and unfair.

With some common sense, caution, a healthy willingness to trust your own instincts, and firm determination to go for competent help when it is needed, you will avoid the common pitfalls of contracts and credit and use these basic tools for further success and happiness.

FURTHER READING

Sylvia Porter's New Money Book for the 80's. Garden City, New York: Doubleday, 1980 (Chapter 16, "How to Borrow Cash and Use Credit"). Also available in paperback, Avon Books.

The following publications are available from the Consumer Information Center, Pueblo, Colo. 81009.

Consumer Credit Handbook

Consumer Protections and Electronic Banking

Do you Speak "Credit"?

2

Defective Products and Services

JANE N. BARRETT
BEATRICE S. FRANK

Jane N. Barrett (A.B., Vassar College; M.A., University of Michigan; J.D., New York University Law School) is a public-interest attorney and freelance author. As a New York State assistant attorney general, she litigates major cases of consumer fraud. Her work has appeared in several periodicals, including The Village Voice, *and numerous college texts in the social sciences.*

Beatrice S. Frank, a graduate of Sarah Lawrence College and Cornell University Law School, is a member of the faculty of the New York University School of Law, where she is director of the clinical program in consumer protection. She previously directed the Channel 13 / NYU Consumer Help Center. She has practiced law privately and has served as chair of the Association of the Bar of the City of New York's Committee on Legal Education and Admission to the Bar and as a member of its Committee on Professional Discipline. She served as reporter for the Association's Report on the Grievance System.

The toaster you bought three weeks ago turns bread into cinders, the slipcovers you ordered arrive in blue cotton instead of brown corduroy, the blow dryer blows sparks instead of hot air, the heel broke off your shoe after a few wearings, and your size 12 blouse becomes a size 6 after you wash it according to the manufacturer's instructions. What are your rights? What do you do? How do you complain so that someone will listen?

This chapter will discuss your legal rights when a product or service is defective. We will also suggest some practical methods of dealing with these problems without going to court; we will give you some pointers to keep in mind when shopping for goods and services; and we will list sources of help. (If you have a defective product that was purchased with a credit card, see Chapter 1 for the rules that apply to this type of transaction.)

If you have been injured or if the product or service was very expensive, you should consult a lawyer. Otherwise there are a number of steps you can take to resolve the problem. How do you begin?

THE COMPLAINT PROCESS

Start a File: The first items in the file will be your sales slip, receipt or contract, the bill if the item was charged, your canceled check if you paid by check, and any other papers (instructions, warranties, etc.) that you may have. If the item or service was advertised, include a copy of the ad if possible. *Note:* It is a good idea to keep a file with sales slips, warranties, etc., for all your purchases, so that these documents are available if you have to complain.

Go to the Store or Manufacturer's Service Center: Go armed with your file, and where possible the product, and ask for a replacement or a refund. (If the product is under warranty, you may be limited to repair, but see pp. 30–36 for a discussion of your rights under the warranty.) A telephone call may work in some cases. Whether you go in person or make a phone call, be sure to get the person's name, title, department, and extension number. If the store representative agrees to do what you want, write a letter to that person confirming your understanding (see sample letter at end of chapter). Keep a record of your phone calls and/or visits in the file.

Write a Letter: If you can't get to the store or can't get satisfaction when you have called or been there, a letter can be useful. An effective complaint letter does not have to be a legal document. A clear statement in your own words can do the job. (See the sample letter at the end of this chapter.)
Remember to include:
1. Your name and address
2. Your account number if the item was charged
3. The date of purchase and method of payment (check, cash, charge)
4. Any receipt, sales slip, or contract numbers
5. Any model or serial numbers
6. A clear description of the problem and any attempts you have made to solve it. Include the names of the persons you have spoken with
7. Whether you want repair or replacement of the item or a refund (see p. 33)

8. A copy of your sales check, receipt or contract, and canceled check if you paid by check. (Keep the originals for your file.)

Be sure to make a copy of this and all other letters you write concerning your complaint and keep them in your file.

If the letter is your first attempt to resolve the problem, send it to the place where you purchased the item. If you have tried without success to resolve the problem in person or on the phone, send the letter to the president of the company. (You can get the president's name by calling the main office of the store.) The same procedure applies when you are dealing with a manufacturer. It is often effective to note on the letter that you are sending a copy to your local consumer protection agency and the Better Business Bureau.

Contact Consumer Protection Agencies: Your local consumer protection agency may be your city or county department of consumer affairs or the state attorney general, depending upon where you live. Check your phone directory for the complaint number. These agencies usually have complaint departments staffed by trained mediators who will contact the merchant or manufacturer on your behalf and try to resolve the complaint. If your complaint involved a violation of federal, state, or local law, the mediator will advise the agency's legal staff, who will investigate the complaint. Copies of your complaint letter (see above) as well as copies of all your correspondence with the manufacturer and/or seller should be sent to these agencies, as well as to the Better Business Bureau (see the following paragraph).

Contact the Better Business Bureau and Industry Grievance Panel: Most communities have local offices of the Bureau which you can find by checking your phone book. They will contact the merchant and attempt to resolve the complaint. Many offices also provide free arbitration services for complaints that can't be solved by mediation. Your chances of success are greater if the merchant is a member of the organization. Some industries have their own complaint services, which you can contact (see "Industry Grievance Panels," p. 514).

Contact National or Local Consumer Groups: If your problem is one that affects many consumers, a local or national consumer advocate group may be interested in learning about it and possibly pursuing the case as a class action. Some of these groups are listed on p. 516, "Consumer Advocacy and Education Groups." Your local department of consumer affairs or state attorney general's office may be able to furnish the names of others in your area. Many newspapers, radio, and TV stations have consumer reporters. They usually do not handle individual complaints, but may be interested in a complaint about a problem that affects many consumers. If you feel that you have such a complaint, send them a copy of your complaint letter and all subsequent correspondence.

Go to Small Claims Court: If you have tried the complaint procedure without success, you may want to bring an action in small claims court. Check your phone book to find the number of your local small claims court and call the court to find out the procedure for filing a claim. Small claims court is a "people's court," where people can argue their own cases and don't need to hire a lawyer. The maximum amount you can sue for differs from place to place (in New York it is $1,500). The cost of filing a claim is generally under $5.00, and many communities have small claims court sessions at night to make it easier to use the court. If you go to small claims court, bring your file with all the documents. If it is possible, bring the item or a friend who saw the item.

If your claim is for more than the amount allowed by small claims court, you may want to consult a private lawyer. If you do not know a lawyer, the local bar associations in many communities have referral services where, for a small fee, you can meet with an attorney to discuss your case. The attorney will give you an estimate of the cost and your chances of success. See Chapter 21 for a discussion of things to consider when hiring a lawyer.

YOUR LEGAL ARSENAL

To some extent, your success in dealing with manufacturers and merchants will depend on your persistence, forcefulness, and persuasiveness. However, you should also arm yourself with a legal reason why you are entitled to win.

In this section we will look at the legal ammunition available to the consumer. Some of these laws are highly complex, and they often vary from state to state. Of course, whenever large sums of money or personal injuries are involved, you should consult a lawyer. But if you are arguing your own case, an understanding of these provisions can help you persuade a merchant or a judge that you are entitled to what you have asked for.

Warranties

A warranty is a valuable legal right. Most often it is the key to repairing or replacing defective consumer goods.

What is a warranty? It is a promise or guarantee about an item's quality, life-span, washability, etc. It doesn't have to be labeled "warranty" or "guarantee." In fact, it doesn't have to be written at all. Some warranties are oral, and arise from spoken promises. Other warranties don't have to be written or spoken; they exist in all consumer transactions simply because they are implied by law. The following warranties may exist separately or together. It will help you to know which ones are applicable to your situation.

Implied Warranties: Implied warranties give you the right to a lawn-mower that actually cuts grass, to a stereo that plays music, rather than merely rotating the record. They do not depend on registration cards or on what the salesperson told you.

The two most important warranties in this category are the warranty of merchantability and the warranty of fitness for a particular purpose. The warranty of merchantability is your guarantee of fair, average quality. In other words, it guarantees that the item you bought meets generally recognized standards and is not a lemon. For example, a vacuum cleaner should pick up pet hair off a rug. A blow dryer should dry the hair on your head. This warranty does not apply if you use the product in an unusual or abusive way. If you set the hair dryer down next to some wet stockings, it may melt the stockings, melt the counter, or burn itself out. The implied warranties do not cover this kind of loss. The warranty of fitness for a particular purpose is a promise that the product is suitable for a particular use. For example, indoor/outdoor carpeting must be more durable than indoor carpeting. A winter sleeping bag should be warmer than a summer-weight bag. The test here is as follows: (1) The seller knew or should have known of the particular way you planned to use the product, and (2) you relied on the seller's skill and judgment in selecting the item.

Sellers have to go a long way to deprive you of the protection of the implied warranties (legally, this is known as "disclaiming"). Most states hold that the implied warranties exist unless they are clearly disclaimed. A typical disclaimer is, "The seller disclaims all warranties, express or implied, including the warranty of merchantability." Another common way of negating implied warranties is to clearly label merchandise "seconds," "irregulars," or "as is."

Some states put even stricter limits on disclaimers of implied warranties. That is why you often see confusing variations such as: "The seller disclaims all implied warranties, including the warranty of merchantability. You may have additional rights under state law." So, don't be discouraged by a disclaimer that seems airtight; such disclaimers can be legally challenged on several grounds. For example, the disclaimer may be illegally buried in fine print; or the seller's loophole may not be permitted under your state law. If you're in doubt, check with a local lawyer or consumer agency. If an expensive product or personal injuries are involved, it is especially important to see a lawyer at once.

Written Warranties: When most of us refer to warranties, we're referring to the printed card that comes with most appliances. It may be simply worded: "This product is guaranteed free of defects in materials and workmanship for one year from the date of purchase." You may be surprised to learn that businesses are not required by law to give you any written warranty at all. These are promises of quality and service that sellers add to the deal they are offering in the hope that you will buy. Most reputable manufacturers do give express warranties, however, and you should consider warranty terms as part of the bargain when shopping for major items. It is often better to pay a higher price in a reputable store that will honor its own obligations and help you enforce the manufacturer's warranty, rather than buy a discounted item from a street vendor or door-to-door salesperson.

If a seller does give you a written warranty, it must comply with certain requirements of a federal law, the Magnuson-Moss Act.* Magnuson-Moss is applicable in every state, providing major legal protection in addition to whatever rights you have under your state law. It covers written warranties on items costing ten dollars or more.

One of the most important features of Magnuson-Moss is the requirement of full disclosure. All warranty terms must be clearly presented to you before sale. Warranties must be available for inspection in the store before sale. The merchant cannot just give you a factory-sealed carton with the warranty inside.

Magnuson-Moss divides written warranties into two categories: "full" and "limited." It also requires that warranties be clearly labeled either full or limited. The major differences between the two types are as follows:

FULL	LIMITED
If the product does not live up to the standard promised, it will be replaced or repaired at no cost to you. (N.B. This does not necessarily mean you will be reimbursed for losses suffered in connection with the product's failure, such as food spoilage, hotel bills, etc.)	The warrantor is guaranteeing coverage only to a particular extent. The limitation must be clearly stated. Limitations may vary for various parts of the product. For example: • Parts and labor for limited time • Parts only; you pay for labor • Labor only; you pay for parts • Service under the warranty will be done only at store or service center; you bear cost of transportation.

*15 U.S.C. §2301–2312

FULL	LIMITED
Service under the warranty will be performed within a "reasonable period" after notifying warrantor.	
Obtaining warranty service will not be "unreasonably" burdensome. All steps you must take to obtain service must be clearly disclosed.	
Warranty coverage includes not only you, but subsequent owners as well.	Warranty is made to the first buyers only and is not applicable to subsequent owners.
The warrantor can make a reasonable number of attempts to repair the defective product. If these fail, the product must be replaced or the purchase price refunded.	No such guarantee
You need not return a registration card to receive warranty coverage.	Return of registration card can be required, but this requirement must be clearly stated.
Implied warranties cannot be disclaimed or limited in time to the life of the full written warranty.	Implied warranties cannot be completely disclaimed; however, the life of the implied warranty can be limited to the life of the written limited warranty. (N.B. Is the time limitation so short as to be shockingly inadequate? See p. 31).

In most cases involving repair or replacement of a defective product, your rights will be those spelled out in the warranty itself. However, there are ways to escape the limits of the warranty and recover the full purchase price, lost wages, medical expenses, "pain and suffering," etc. To do this, you will have to sue the party offering the warranty. You must be able to show that your injury *directly* resulted from: (1) their refusal to honor the warranty; or (2) their failure to disclose all warranty terms before sale; or (3) their failure to designate the warranty as full or limited; or (4) their improper disclaimer of implied warranties. You may bring this suit in your local small claims court. However, if large sums of money or serious personal injury is involved, you definitely should consult a lawyer. If you win in court on a Magnuson-Moss-based legal theory (p. 32), you may also demand that the other side pay your lawyer's fees.

Oral Warranties: Remember that Magnuson-Moss governs only written warranties. What if the seller made verbal, unwritten promises? This may be an enforceable warranty, but there are some major obstacles to making it stick. Oral warranties are hard to prove; a witness may be helpful. Does it conflict with the provisions of the written warranty? Many written warranties contain a clause to the effect that the written warranty supersedes all oral representations made by the seller. These so-called "merger clauses" are usually upheld by the court. These complications highlight the necessity for examining written warranty material before leaving the store.

Be sure to distinguish enthusiastic sales pitching from oral warranties. Language such as "the greatest little vacuum cleaner in the world; you're gonna love it, I guarantee," is known as "puffing." The average person would not take it literally as a guarantee. Sometimes, however, the distinction between vigorous sales pitching and verbal promises of quality is a fine one indeed. If you have any question about what is being promised and the promise is important to you, ask the seller to put it in writing. If the merchant refuses, perhaps you should shop elsewhere.

Remedies

You have a defective product and you have a warranty, written or oral or implied. What good will it do you? Any lawyer will give you the infuriating answer: "It depends."

In theory, consumers have three types of recourse, or remedy. These are (1) rejection, (2) revocation, and (3) a suit for money damages. *Rejection* is your outright refusal to accept the merchandise, because it does not live up to the warranty. For example, you mail-ordered a camera guaranteed to be brand-new, but received a reconditioned model instead. You must (1) promptly notify the seller in writing that you are rejecting the item, (2) not use it, and (3) take care of it until it is returned. You are entitled to your money back. *Revocation* is often called "lemon-aid." It is the remedy you need if you've already accepted the camera and used it before discovering the defect. You can revoke your acceptance of the camera if you could not have discovered the defect sooner or if the seller at the time of sale promised to repair it and didn't. You must revoke before the merchandise has changed condition in any major way, and you must notify the seller in writing immediately.

A lawsuit for money damages is the type of remedy that can make merchants and manufacturers toss and turn at night. However, with the exception of small claims court (see p. 30), lawsuits are costly and time-consuming. Filing suit is most often worthwhile in the case of personal injury or expensive items. If, for example, an exploding bottle injures your eye, you may and should sue the bottler for breach of the warranties of merchantability and fitness for ordinary purpose.

Remember, however, that we said your rights in a particular situation "depend." Why? Because the law permits the limitation of remedies. This is seen most clearly in the warranties covered by Magnuson-Moss. In most cases, you will be limited to the rights spelled out in the warranty (see p. 30). For example, you have an appliance with a limited warranty guaranteeing parts and labor for ninety days. The appliance breaks within ninety days. You would prefer a full refund, but for some reason you can't meet the standards we outlined above for rejection or revocation. Your only real choice is to take it to the service center for repairs.

State law puts some restrictions on how far remedies under any warranty can be limited. If the remedy cannot possibly repair the product, you don't have to pursue it. You may choose one of the three standard remedies (rejection, revocation, or a lawsuit for damages). For example, if your limited warranty promises free parts and labor, but parts are not available at any service center, the remedy is useless and you are not limited by it. Demand your money back; go to small claims court if necessary.

Similarly, if the recourse offered in the warranty is so inadequate that it shocks the conscience, you are not bound by it and can choose one of the three main remedies. For example, a limited warranty for parts and labor for one month on a product with a 10-year life-span would probably fall into this category. In many states, a warranty that completely eliminates your right to sue for personal injuries caused by a consumer product is held to be grossly unfair and unenforceable.

Warranties can redress many wrongs suffered by consumers. But sometimes they may not be used at all. One problem is the time lapse between sale and injury. In most states, a lawsuit for breach of warranty must be started within four years of the date of sale. If your toaster blows up in its fifth year, you may not be able to sue on the warranty. Another legal barrier is the absence of a direct relationship between you and the warrantor. Was it secondhand? Did you burn yourself while using your friend's toaster? In the face of such technical problems as these, the courts have developed another theory for awarding damages for injury caused by a defective product.

Strict Liability in Tort

Simply stated, this theory holds that a person who uses a defective product in the normal manner and suffers injury may sue the manufacturer if (1) the defect existed when the product left the manufacturer's hands and (2) the defect caused the person's injury. Thus, many people who can't claim the protection of a warranty may use this approach. The product may be defective because it was improperly designed. A horrifying example is infant clothing with drawstrings at the neck that can catch on crib railings. Or the design may be perfectly safe, but one particular item may have been poorly made, such as a bottle that undergoes a statistically rare explosion at a stress point in the glass.

If you have suffered significant personal injury, consult a lawyer immediately. It is important to start compiling medical and technical evidence as soon as possible. Time limits on this type of lawsuit are usually two or three years from the date of the accident, but they may sometimes be shorter. Do not jeopardize your rights by delay.

Other Possibilities

Did the other side refuse to live up to some part of your written contract? You have the right to make them perform or pay you for your losses.

Did the other side mislead you about an important aspect of the product or service? You may have a right to recover damages for fraud.

PREVENTIVE STRATEGIES

Even though you have become an expert at resolving complaints for defective products and services, you would probably prefer not to have a reason to demonstrate your expertise. How can you avoid buying a "lemon"? Although there is no foolproof method, there are some things you can do to lessen the chances of ending up with a defective product or service.

If you are buying services:

1.   Get recommendations from people you know and respect, and don't be afraid to ask questions. Were the furnishings the decorator ordered delivered on time? Was she difficult to work with? Were the services the caterer provided the ones that were ordered?

2.   Ask to see examples of the work. Do you like the room the decorator designed? Are the wedding or baby pictures the kind you like?

3.   Check your local consumer protection agency and the Better Business Bureau for complaints.

4.   Read the contract carefully. Be sure you understand what is and what is not being promised. If you disagree with something in the contract, make sure that it reads the way you want it to before you sign it. In the case of custom services such as caterers, decorators, and photographers, try to have a liquidated-damages clause included. This is a provision that covers your losses in case the service is not performed or is performed poorly. Be sure that it provides for an amount that adequately covers your losses. If a contract is not provided, you and the merchant may draft one yourselves. You don't have to use legal language: just write out the terms of your agreement in your own language.

5.   Get a written estimate in the case of a repair, and make sure to limit the amount by which the final cost may exceed the estimate. If the estimate

is for the cost of a new carburetor, the estimate should give the cost of the carburetor, plus the estimated labor cost of installing it, and state that the final cost may not exceed the estimate by more than an amount or percentage specified by you. Some cities and states have regulations that require that the repairer give you a written estimate with such a statement. Check with your attorney general's office or your local department of consumer affairs. Be sure to get an itemized bill and a written guarantee that all replaced parts are new. Where possible, ask for the replaced parts.

If you are buying goods:

1.   Check your public library for publications such as *Consumer Reports* and *Consumers Research Magazine,* which compare brands of many items. The Government Printing Office publishes pamphlets that tell you what to look for when buying certain items. A list of available publications can be obtained by writing to Consumer Information Center, General Services Administration (see p. 514 for address).

2.   Check the terms of any written warranty, (see p. 32).

3.   Keep all receipts and accompanying literature, (see p. 28).

A note of caution: Service contracts (often referred to as extended warranties) are available for many products from cars to TV sets. In many cases they are not a good buy, since the cost of the contract is higher than the cost of any repairs you will ever need. You should check the item's repair record in publications like *Consumer Reports* before deciding whether it makes sense to purchase a service contract. If you are thinking about purchasing a service contract, be sure to read it carefully to determine what it does and does not cover. Find out who will do the repairs, where they will be done, and what happens if you move to another city. Finally, read your warranty to see whether the repairs covered by the service contract are already covered by the warranty.

SAMPLE COMPLAINT LETTER

Date

Big Department Store
2100 Main Street
Your city, state, zip

Attention: Ms. Mary Smith
      Adjustment Department
      Service Representative

      Re: Account #0000
        Order #0000
        Sales Check #0000

Dear Ms. Smith:

  This letter is written to confirm our telephone conversation today. When we spoke, I told you that I had ordered brown corduroy slipcovers, but the slipcovers you delivered to me were in blue cotton. You agreed to make new slipcovers according to the specifications written on your order #0000, a copy of which is enclosed. This will also confirm that the new covers will be made, delivered, and installed at no charge to me, and that delivery and installation will take place on January 5, 19

  Thank you for your assistance.

          Very truly yours,

          Your name
          address, zip code
          telephone number

SAMPLE COMPLAINT LETTER

Date

Ms. Mary Doe, President
Big Department Store
2100 Main Street
Your city, state, zip

Dear Ms. Doe:

Re: Account #0000
Sales Check #0000

On May 5, 1983, I purchased a blouse for $28.00 in Department #423. A copy of my sales check is enclosed. The blouse was a size 12. It contained washing instructions on the tag as well as on the blouse, which I carefully followed when washing it. Nevertheless, it shrank so that it is now totally unwearable.

On May 21, 1983, I went to the store with the blouse and spoke to Mr. Robert Jones, in the Adjustment Department. Mr. Jones offered to replace the defective blouse with another like it. I explained that this would not be satisfactory, since the material is clearly not washable as warranted, and asked to have the cost of the blouse credited to my account. Mr. Jones refused to credit my account.

Under the circumstances, I feel that I am entitled to a full refund for merchandise that is clearly defective. Please have my account credited at once and advise me that this has been done.

Very truly yours,

Your name
address, zip
phone number

cc. Department of Consumer Affairs
     Attorney General's Bureau of
        Consumer Frauds
     Better Business Bureau

FURTHER READING

Sylvia Porter's New Money Book for the 80's. Garden City, New York: Doubleday, 1980 (Chapter 28, "Know Your Rights and How to Use Them!"). Also available in paperback, Avon Books.

The following publications are available from the Consumer Information Center, Pueblo, Colo. 81009:

Consumer's Resource Handbook: A What-to-do, Where-to-go Manual for Resolving Consumer Problems

Direct Contacts for Consumers: Toll Free Numbers for Federal and State Services

Directory of Federal TDD Numbers

Dispute Resolution Services (lists 34 organizations handling complaints and publishing consumer education materials)

Mail Order Rights

3
Housing and Real Estate

AMY R. PIRO

Amy R. Piro, assistant counsel to the Governor of New Jersey, is a graduate of Fordham University School of Law and New York University. In her current position, she is responsible for reviewing for the Governor legislation and administration policies on housing, landlord-tenant relations, land use planning, condominium and cooperative regulation, and other matters involving real property law. Her work has spanned the administrations of two New Jersey governors. In 1981 she coordinated Governor Byrne's hearing on condominium conversions, which led to the development of ground-breaking state legislation protecting senior citizens and handicapped tenants in buildings undergoing conversions. She is now serving on Governor Kean's Housing Task Force.

The romance of real estate—a cabin nestled in the woods, a château on a rocky promontory, or a field of grass and flowers—has charmed people for generations. But land is a limited and unique resource. Each parcel of land is different from all others, and there is only a finite quantity of land on this earth. This limited resource is essential to human survival. All human beings need space in which to live, and in most cultures that space is found on land. As a result, rights to land are carefully laced with legal rules and restrictions to govern who may use it, when, and how.

Lawyers call the body of these rights and restrictions regarding land "real property law." Actually, the term "real property" goes beyond the land itself and also includes anything that is affixed to the land, whether it is a house, a telephone pole, or a tree; rights to air above the land; minerals below its surface; and water that may be situated on it. The terms "real property" and "real estate" as well as "realty" and "property" will be used interchangeably in this chapter.

In your private life, your major involvement with real property law will be in establishing your home. While most of your activities outside of your home also take place on real property, whether you are working, shopping, or walking down the street, the rights and restrictions involving those places are primarily the problems of others, such as your employer, the shopkeeper, or the municipality.

From a legal standpoint, you have three basic options available when establishing a home, each of which will give you a different kind of property interest in the real estate on which you make your home. You can (1) purchase a home, (2) rent a home, or (3) enter into the form of group ownership available in a condominium or a cooperative.

Many people do not realize the possible rights they may have, nor do they know how to protect themselves from liabilities they may face in connection with these options. For example, a woman whose home is in her husband's name alone may not realize that in most states the law gives her certain rights to the home anyway. A homeowner may not be aware that if she routinely permits people to trespass on her property she may eventually lose her rights to stop these people from doing so or that she may be liable if someone is injured on her property. A condominium owner may not realize that if the majority of owners agree to a major improvement, she may be required to contribute to it, even though she voted against the improvement and cannot afford the additional payments. State and federal laws protect women against discrimination in the renting and purchasing of real estate. Once a person becomes aware of these possibilities, then she can take the necessary steps to find out what her rights are and minimize her liabilities.

While a few principles of federal law apply to real estate law in all the states, for the most part each state may fix its own rules. As a result, real estate law varies from state to state, although many states recognize certain common principles of the law. Set forth below are general principles that apply in many places, but you cannot assume that they will necessarily apply to you in your particular situation. A unique factual aspect of your situation, or a differing rule of law or combination of rules of law in your state, can lead to very different results and mandate different actions from those which may be suggested from the discussion below. What the discussion is intended to do is to provide you with a framework for understanding real estate law; to alert you to pitfalls or unexpected rights that may exist; to help you to know when a lawyer is needed; to help you better understand the steps your attorney is taking; and, in general, to enable you to deal with your real estate transactions as an informed layperson.

BUYING, SELLING,
AND OWNING A HOME

From the time that settlers crossed the oceans and pioneers braved the western frontier, one of the great American dreams has been to own one's home. If you dream of owning a home, or if you already do, then you will want to understand *who* exactly owns it; *what* precisely you own; *what* rights and responsibilities are associated with the property; and *how* you go about buying and selling the realty and protecting your rights with respect to it. This section deals with these issues and is written with a single-family house on an average-size lot in mind.

WHO OWNS YOUR HOME

You can own a house in your name alone, in which case you would be its sole legal owner, or you can own it jointly with others. The three forms of joint ownership are tenants in common, joint tenants, and tenants by the entirety.

Tenancy in Common

The simplest form of joint ownership is a tenancy in common. It has the following characteristics:

1. Each of the joint owners has a fractional share in the property. Those shares may be equal or unequal. For example, you and your two friends can each own one third of the property, or you may own one half of it and they may each own a quarter. Commonly, the division will be made in proportion to your payments for the property (including down payments and mortgage, insurance, and tax payments). If your ownership shares are going to vary from the financial contributions of the parties, then check with an attorney or accountant to determine whether any of you will be liable for gift-tax payments. A co-owner who pays a portion of the costs of the house that is larger than her ownership share in the house is making a gift to the other co-owners and may have to pay a federal gift tax on the difference.

2. Each joint owner has the right to possession and use of the entire property. This means that you cannot claim half of the kitchen and relegate your two roommates to the remaining half. All three of you have an equal right to its use.

3.   At any time, a joint owner can bring an action to end the tenancy in common, in which case either the property is divided among the joint owners in proportion to their shares (not practical in the case of a single-family house) or the property is sold and the proceeds are divided among the tenants in proportion to their shares. Of course, the parties can always mutually agree that one will buy the others out.

4.   If one of the joint owners dies, her share in the property passes to her estate.

A tenancy in common is a form of ownership available to anyone, including friends, couples, relatives, married persons, and unmarried lovers. With the exception of married couples, who are protected by the law in other ways, if you decide to enter into a tenancy in common, it is advisable to retain a lawyer to draft a written agreement for you. The agreement should clearly set forth such things as the share each co-owner has in the property; the amount each is to contribute to the down payment, mortgage, insurance, and tax payments; what happens if a co-owner fails to contribute her portion of the payments (whether due to illness, unemployment, or irresponsibility); what happens if a co-owner decides to move out or dies; whether a co-owner can bring a husband, lover, or anyone else to live in the house. Appropriate provisions should be made for ending the tenancy.

Joint Tenancy

A joint tenancy is a tenancy in common coupled with a right of survivorship. This right of survivorship is its distinguishing feature. A joint tenancy shares the following characteristics with a tenancy in common:

1.   Each joint owner has a fractional share in the property; however, in the case of a joint tenancy the shares *must* be equal.

2.   Each joint owner has the right to possess and use the entire property.

3.   At any time, a joint owner may terminate the joint tenancy and compel division or sale of the property.

The right of survivorship provides that upon the death of one joint owner, the other owner(s) (rather than any heirs) receive(s) the property. This means that if you own property with a friend as joint tenants, then upon your death your share in the property does not pass to your heirs but goes to your friend, who is the surviving joint owner.

The right of survivorship in a joint tenancy often satisfies the desires of family members living together, such as two elderly sisters, a mother and daughters, or husband and wife, who want the property to go to the survivor. However, no federal estate taxes are necessarily saved by this device; in fact they could be increased.

Before entering into a joint tenancy, it is advisable to consult a lawyer to discuss the feasibility of having a written agreement govern the arrangement and to analyze the tax consequences.

Tenancy by the Entirety: A Special Option for Married Couples

Almost half the states recognize a tenancy by the entirety, which is exactly like a joint tenancy, with the following *exceptions:*

1.   A tenancy by the entirety can exist only between a husband and wife, and therefore terminates upon divorce.

2.   Neither party may terminate the tenancy by the entirety without the consent of the other. (This is an important protection, since it will prevent your husband from unilaterally terminating the tenancy and forcing a sale of the house or otherwise defeating your right of survivorship without your consent, unless you become divorced).

3.   In some states the property is protected to some extent from the claim of the creditors of either spouse (but still would be subject to joint creditors of both parties).

Due to these protections, a tenancy by entirety, if available, is usually preferred by married couples.

Special Concerns of Married Women

Historically, married women have faced legal limitations on their right to own real property. Under the old English common law imported to the colonies, upon marriage a woman lost control and management of her real property to her husband, although he could not sell or convey it. Upon her death, under the "estate by the curtesy" the husband had the right to control and use her property for the remainder of his life, provided a child had been born alive to the marriage. A wife had a counterbalancing "dower" right. If she survived her husband, for the remainder of her life she had an interest in one third of all the land her husband had ever owned during the marriage. In the nineteenth century, significant legislative reforms known as the "Married Women's Acts" gave married women more control over their property and protection from their husbands' creditors, thereby overturning the common law restrictions.

Nowadays, a married woman generally has the same rights as anyone else to own and control property. However, the rights of any married person to her/his property may be circumscribed by the rights of the spouse. For example, in a few states, known as "community property" states (Louisiana, Texas, California, Nevada, New Mexico, Arizona, Washington, and Idaho), all property acquired by either spouse during the marriage, except gifts and inheritances, is considered the property of both. Upon divorce, the community property is divided between the spouses.

In the other forty-two states, known as "common law" jurisdictions, a husband's or wife's separate ownership of property is recognized. However, in many of these states, upon divorce a court is empowered to divide assets between the parties irrespective of who holds title to the property (known as equitable distribution). In addition, upon the death of one party, the surviving spouse may have a right to a portion of the decedent's assets (known as the elective share), or dower and curtesy rights may exist in some form.

Due to the above rights, a married woman who discovers that title to the family homestead is in her husband's name alone may still be protected to some extent.

As a general rule, when buying a home as a married woman, you are best protected if title is put in your name alone or jointly with your husband. In this way your husband can not unilaterally sell the property. However, there are situations where overriding considerations of estate planning, taxes, or business may make it prudent to have the property placed in your husband's name alone. If title is being placed solely in your husband's name, make sure that you understand and agree with the necessity for doing so, that you have consulted with an attorney on the matter, that you understand your rights to the property in the event of divorce or death, and that you have other assets or income to rely upon.

Special Concerns of an Unmarried Woman Living with a Lover

If you and your lover are planning to buy a house together, you may take title as tenants in common or as joint tenants. Consult with a lawyer to discuss the ramifications of the arrangement in regard to death or a breakup, and consider having a written agreement made. Remember that as a partner you will *not* be protected by the rights of dower, elective share, community property, or equitable distribution accorded wives, although the evolving theory of palimony rights (see discussion below) may offer some protection.

If you own or buy a home and are considering having your lover move in with you, you should be aware that your lover (like Michelle Marvin) may claim an interest in your property. The development of "palimony" rights is in an early stage, so the law is not entirely clear. However, some basic rules that may help if you want to retain sole ownership are as follows:

1. Do not hold yourselves out as husband and wife.
2. Be careful to maintain your separate ownership of the home by making all mortgage payments on it yourself in your name.
3. Keep all other assets in your separate names, rather than jointly.
4. Make sure your partner remains employed, or he may claim he sacrificed his career for you.
5. Make no written or oral agreements to support or take care of him, or which may imply that you are giving him an interest in the house.
6. Maintain and make sure he acknowledges to others your separate ownership of the house.
7. If the relationship starts to become long-term, see a lawyer to discuss a written agreement clarifying your financial obligations to each other.

PURCHASING AND SELLING A HOUSE

The Broker

Generally, the first step when purchasing or selling a house is to contact a real estate broker. Although the broker may assist you in purchasing a house, it is important to remember that the broker is the agent for the *seller*. The broker and the seller will enter into a listing agreement, a legally binding contract that authorizes the broker to seek a buyer for the house and specifies the commission she will receive for her efforts.

Listing agreements fall into the following basic categories:

1. *Exclusive Right to Sell.* The broker has an exclusive right to sell the property and is entitled to a commission if anyone, *including the owner*, locates a buyer.

2. *Exclusive Agency to Sell.* The broker is entitled to a commission if anyone *other than the owner* locates a buyer.

3. *Open Listing.* The broker is entitled to the commission if she is the first broker to produce a buyer. While this type of listing permits the seller to use more than one broker, doing so can give rise to commission disputes.

4. *Multiple Listing.* The seller places an exclusive agency listing with a broker who belongs to a real estate board or multiple listing service. The property is listed with other members of the pool, and the commission is split between the listing broker and the selling broker.

Many state statutes require that the agreement between the seller and the broker be in writing in order to be enforceable. (In order to avoid the potential for fraud, ambiguity, and disagreements which are likely to arise with oral promises, the law requires that various types of agreements affecting realty be in writing. These laws, known as the "statute of frauds" and based on an old English statute, will be referred to throughout this chapter.) In states where a writing is not required, the prudent seller will have the listing agreement in writing anyway in order to avoid a commission dispute at a later date.

Usually, the real estate broker's commission is a percentage of the purchase price of the property. The broker is generally entitled to payment of the commission when she produces a buyer ready, willing, and able to purchase the property on the terms specified by the seller—*even if the property is never sold to the purchaser.* To avoid being liable for the commission in the event the sale is never closed, the seller can insist that the listing agreement provide that payment for the commission be contingent upon the closing actually taking place.

The Contract of Sale

Once the purchaser and the seller reach an agreement for sale of the property, they will enter into a "contract of sale." The statute of frauds requires that the contract of sale be in writing in order to be enforceable. One important exception to this principle is the doctrine of past performance, which will enforce an oral contract of sale where the parties have acted in reliance on the oral contract. In addition, once a written contract is made, it can usually be rescinded or modified verbally. However, it is much safer to do so in writing.

To assure protection of your interests, you definitely should have the contract of sale reviewed by your lawyer before signing it. This advice applies to both the buyer and the seller. A contract of sale is a binding legal document, and you can be held liable if you do not abide by its terms.

The following is a list of items generally found in contracts of sale:

1. The *seller and the purchaser* are *identified* by name and address.

2. The *contract must be signed* by the seller and the purchaser and their spouses.

3. The *property* to be sold must be *identified*.

4. The *sale price* must be set forth.

5. The amount of *deposit or "earnest" money* being put down by the purchaser will be set forth in the contract of sale. Generally, unless the contract provides otherwise, this sum will be forfeited to the seller if the buyer breaches the contract. Otherwise, it is applied against the purchase price when the transaction is completed.

6. If the seller is going to include any *items of personalty* in the sale such as appliances, carpeting, or furniture, these items should be specifically set forth in the contract.

7. The purchaser should make sure that the contract requires the seller to give her *marketable title* to the property.

8. The *form of the deed* that the seller gives to the purchaser may be specified in the contract. The kinds of deeds include a quitclaim deed, in which the seller makes no representations as to her ownership in the property. She merely gives to the purchaser whatever interest, if any, she has in the property. This form of deed is usually unsatisfactory to the purchaser. In a warranty deed, the seller makes full representations to the purchaser that she owns the property, that the property is not encumbered by undisclosed liens or easements, and that no one has a claim to the property. In the special warranty deed, the seller's warranties are more limited in that she promises that no defects to the title were created by or through her.

9. The *closing date* should be set forth in the contract. This is the day on which the seller transfers legal ownership of the property to the purchaser. Generally, if a party is not ready to close on the closing date, she

is given a reasonable time to do so. However, if time is made of the essence in the contract or otherwise, a party is deemed to be in breach of the contract if she does not close on the designated date.

10.   The contract of sale also will set forth various *contingencies* that must be met before the deal will close. The closing may be contingent upon: (a) the buyer obtaining mortgage financing within a specified time; (b) a satisfactory title search and survey; (c) the results of a professional inspection of the property covering such things as termites, fungus (dry rot), electrical and plumbing systems, construction, etc.; (d) the buyer selling her house; and any other requirements that the parties agree must be met before the deal closes.

11.   A complete contract of sale will also contain a *fire clause,* which determines the liabilities of the parties in the event the house is damaged by fire before the deal closes.

12.   The contract of sale may also enumerate those *items that must be prorated* between the buyer and the seller. Any time a house is sold, the seller may have paid in advance for utilities, taxes, and other expenses associated with the property. To the extent she has paid such expenses for the period after the sale (taxes, assessments) or materials that remain after the closing (oil, coal, etc.), she is reimbursed by the buyer. Similarly, to the extent the buyer may be billed for expenses occurring prior to the closing, she is reimbursed by the seller. The contract of sale or custom within your jurisdiction will generally dictate the extent and manner of the proration of these expenses.

The contract of sale is the guidepost that governs the parties until the closing, determining their rights and liabilities to each other. Both parties have an obligation to close the deal in accordance with the terms of the contract. Of course, the parties may mutually agree to end the deal and terminate the contract of sale; this is known as a "rescission." However, in the absence of something like fraud or mistake, you cannot terminate the agreement without the consent of the other party. If, on the other hand, the other party refuses to complete the sale when required, she is deemed to be in "breach" of the contract and you may sue her for damages or for an order compelling the sale.

If you are selling your home, you must purchase another principal residence within a specified time in order to avoid or minimize a capital gain on the sale of the house. However, senior citizens are given a special tax break on the sale of their homes even though they do not purchase a new residence.

The Mortgage

Note: Federal law prohibits lenders from discriminating on the basis of sex or marital status when making mortgage loans.

For most people, a mortgage is an essential element of purchasing a home. Since few are able to buy a house for cash, most purchasers must borrow much of the money. When lending large sums of money, a lender generally wants security; that is, she wants an interest in some property owned by the borrower, which she can apply toward the debt in the event the borrower fails to pay the loan. A mortgage is an interest in land that enables the lender to have the property as security for the loan. Coupled with a mortgage is the promissory note, or bond, that evidences the debt itself. In the note, the borrower agrees to pay back the loan on the terms provided. In the mortgage, the borrower (mortgagor) permits her land to be used as the lender's (mortgagee's) security for the loan.

Default: Should the borrower default on the loan—that is, fail to make payments as required in the promissory note—the lender may satisfy the debt with the land. In some states she may become the owner of the land. In other states she may force a sale of the land at public auction, the proceeds of the sale being used to satisfy the debt. Before the lender's right to take or sell the land is finalized, the borrower has a "right of redemption." This is the right to redeem her land by paying the balance of the debt. To terminate the borrower's "right of redemption," the lender must "foreclose" the borrower's right to redeem the land. Foreclosure procedures vary from state to state. In most places, a court proceeding is necessary. Sometimes the mortgage agreement will contain a "power of sale" clause, which permits the lender to sell the property without a court order. In some states, the right to redeem survives the foreclosure action for a fixed statutory period, after which it is forever barred. If the property is sold at public auction and the debt is not paid in full by the sale proceeds, the lender may seek payment of the balance of the debt from the borrower. The rules governing a foreclosure proceeding can be rigid and somewhat complex. Since the consequences can be dire, never ignore a notice involving a foreclosure action; see an attorney immediately.

The acceleration clause and the prepayment clause: These are two clauses that commonly appear in mortgage agreements. The acceleration clause provides that if the borrower misses a mortgage payment, the lender may declare the entire debt plus interest to be due. Such a provision enables the lender to foreclose on the entire mortgage after there has been a default (failure to make payments when required).

A prepayment clause permits the borrower to pay off the mortgage earlier than required by the terms of the promissory note. Such a provision is important to the borrower, since it enables her to refinance the mortgage if interest rates fall. Lenders sometimes charge a prepayment penalty if such an advance payment is made.

The seller's mortgage: When interest rates are high, many purchasers prefer to take the seller's mortgage, which is at a lower interest rate, rather than take a new mortgage at the prevailing higher interest rates. This can be done provided the seller agrees and the seller's mortgage agreement does not prohibit such an arrangement. To accomplish this, the purchaser may "assume" the seller's mortgage. This means that the purchaser becomes personally liable on the mortgage debt; that is, if in a foreclosure proceeding the value of the realty is insufficient to pay the debt, the lender can hold the purchaser personally liable for the balance due. If the mortgage is assumed by the purchaser, the seller still remains liable for the debt and, therefore, also could be held personally liable for the deficiency. If the seller wants to be relieved of her liability for the mortgage, she should demand a "novation," wherein the purchaser is substituted for the seller on the mortgage note. A novation requires the consent of the lender.

New types of mortgages: Traditionally, a mortgage debt is paid off by equal monthly payments due over a fixed period of time, usually twenty to thirty years, and is subject to a fixed rate of interest. Due to the recent fluctuations in interest rates, the financial community is experimenting with a variety of exotic mortgage arrangements. Mortgages have been developed in which the interest rate is keyed to an index that reflects market conditions, in which the rate is renegotiated periodically, in which payments increase periodically on a graduated basis, or in which the mortgage debt becomes due and must be renegotiated after a fixed period of time. If you are considering one of these new types of mortgage, make sure you understand exactly how the mortgage will operate, what index is being used for the interest rates, and what limits there are on the fluctuation in the interest rate. Project what will happen in future years if the interest rate goes up, if it goes down, if the property appreciates in value, or if it fails to appreciate. Project the monthly and total mortgage payments you will be making. Consider the risks you are running under the arrangement, and compare this mortgage offer with other alternatives. While the decision you make is essentially a financial one, it will become legally binding once you enter into the mortgage arrangement.

Title
Horrors! You have just paid the full price for your new home, have the deed in hand, and moved in when strangers appear at the door clutching a deed signed by the seller and asserting ownership in the house. Or the sheriff starts to auction the property off to satisfy claims of the seller's creditors. Or a mining company appears with all its rig and gear and advises you that it has the right to remove mineral ore from a portion of your land.

Protecting you from claims such as these is one of the main concerns of your attorney.

Conflicting claims: Where there are conflicting claims to property, the law applies various rules to determine whose claim prevails; that is, who has "priority." Which claim prevails depends on which claim arose first and the type of claim involved. For example, in the instance above, if the seller had first sold the property to the strangers appearing at your door and then purportedly sold it to you, the strangers would be the owners of the property. You would not be the owner of the property despite the fact that you paid for it, since the seller had already sold it. (Of course, you could sue the seller for your loss—if you can find her.) If the seller had sold mineral rights in the land to a mining company, you would take the property subject to the company's mineral rights.

Clearly, such rules can cause great hardship, since the purchaser may not know that the seller has already disposed of all or a part of her interest in the land. To ameliorate such hardship, the states have passed "recording acts," which permit deeds, mortgages, and other interests in land to be recorded in a public office (usually a county office). The interests that are recorded will have priority over unrecorded interests. Thus, the purchaser can search the public record and determine whether any interests in the property have been recorded. If the purchaser finds none, then she knows that so long as she records her deed she will take the property free and clear of any unrecorded interests. For example, in the hypothetical example given above, if the strangers appearing at your door had failed to record their deed, but you had recorded your deed, then you would be the owner of the house—even though they had the earlier deed.

Title search: This is a search of all public records that may reflect an interest in the land (tax liens, judgments and other court records, and recorded documents). The search may be conducted by an attorney, an abstract company, or a title company. The title search may also reveal various utility easements; these are customary and will not make the title unmarketable. The seller's mortgage and tax liabilities may be reflected in the search. However, if the seller pays off these and other undesirable liens on the land on or before the closing, you will have marketable title. For further assurance that title to the property is clear, it is customary in many places for the purchaser to obtain title insurance. In addition, the seller may warrant in the deed that title is marketable.

A title search will reveal only those interests in land that are reflected in public records. It will not alert you to such unrecordable interests as encroachment claims arising from adverse possession (see p. 59) or short-term leases. As a result, it is important to have a survey taken and to make a careful visual inspection of the property. If you discover anyone other than the seller regularly using the property, report this fact to your attorney.

The title search, the survey, visual inspection, title insurance, and the seller's deed covenants are all designed to ensure that you receive the interests in land bargained for and not something less.

The Closing

Once the purchaser has obtained financing and conducted a title search and survey; the parties have calculated prorated costs, disposed of old housing, or obtained new housing, as the case may be; and the deed and mortgage and other documents have been prepared; then the sale is ready to be completed, or "closed."

The closing is the meeting in which title to the house is transferred from the seller to the purchaser in exchange for the purchase price. Ownership of the property is transferred by the deed, a document in which the seller (grantor) conveys—that is, transfers—legal ownership of the property to the purchaser (grantee). The deed should be recorded to protect the purchaser's ownership rights under the recordation statutes.

A closing document is also prepared setting forth an itemization and adjustment of charges to the buyer and the seller at the closing. The purchaser must pay a number of charges at the closing, including such things as an appraisal fee, a credit-report fee, prorated costs, mortgage-insurance premium, title-insurance premium, survey cost, attorney's fees, as well as interest, insurance, and tax payments, to be placed in escrow according to the mortgage agreement. Federal law requires the lender to give the purchaser good-faith estimates of the closing costs associated with the mortgage prior to the closing and to provide her with a Department of Housing and Urban Development (HUD) guide on settlement costs.

The closing is attended by the seller and the purchaser and their attorneys, and representatives of the lender and the title-insurance company. At the closing, the purchaser is given her mortgage, the proceeds of the mortgage are given to the seller in payment of the purchase price, the seller in turn uses a portion of the proceeds to pay off her mortgage, deed and title insurance are delivered to the purchaser, and the broker receives her commission from the seller. In this flurry of signing papers and exchanges, legal ownership to the house is transferred.

WHAT DO YOU OWN WHEN YOU OWN LAND? RIGHTS ATTENDANT ON OWNERSHIP OF THE LAND

Now that you have purchased your property, what exactly is it that you own? Under the old common law, a landowner was recognized as owning not only the surface of her land, but the ground below it to the center of the earth, and the sky above it to the heavens. These grandiose rights have been reduced by modern law to ownership of so much below and above the earth as is usable in connection with the land.

Air Rights

A landowner has a right to the usable space above her land, and these air rights can be bought and sold separately from the land. For example, you may be interested in buying a neighbor's air space to prevent construction of a structure on her land that would obstruct your view or interfere with your solar heating system.

Mineral Rights

You as the landowner also own the minerals beneath the surface, and these also can be sold separately from the land.

Water Rights

As a landowner you also have rights in the water on your property. The nature of those rights will depend on the type of water involved, since differing rules apply to natural watercourses (rivers, streams), diffused surface water (rain or ice and snow runoff), and groundwater (under the land surface). In addition, the rules governing these categories of water rights vary from state to state. Without going into the details and complexity of water rights, I offer the following rule of thumb: If you intend to make an improvement on your land regarding water (such as changing location of drainpipes, damming a stream) and if that change will have a detrimental effect on the property of one or more of your neighbors (i.e., discharging runoff onto her land, drying up her pond), you may be in for trouble. If the court finds that your action was unlawful, you could be ordered to cease or undo the activity and be required to compensate your neighbor for her damages. Similarly, you may be protected from steps taken by your neighbor that detrimentally affect the water conditions on your land.

With respect to oceanfront property, the general rule is that the property owner owns the land to the high-water mark, and the state owns the land between the high-water mark and the low-water mark. However, in a tiny minority of states, the public is recognized as having an interest in the entire beach.

Trespass

As a landowner, you have the exclusive right to possess and use your land and any building situated on it. This gives you a general right to forbid others to enter upon your land (although public duty, emergency situations, and other special circumstances give others a limited right to enter your land without your permission). Any unauthorized person who enters your land unlawfully is a "trespasser." You may seek a court order to keep a trespasser off your property, and you may sue her for any damages the trespassing caused you.

Interference with Enjoyment of Your Property

Even though a neighboring landowner, whether resident or business, never enters your property, her activities can significantly interfere with your enjoyment of your land. The activities may generate loud noise or noxious fumes. Yet if you force her to terminate these activities, your neighbor's enjoyment of her land may be severely curtailed. The law attempts to balance these competing interests by applying a standard of reason. For example, you may not be able to prohibit your neighbor from practicing her trumpet an hour a day, no matter how much you hate the trumpet and how badly she plays. On the other hand, you should be able to prevent her from holding weekly hard rock marathons that involve many bands and the playing of music twenty-four hours a day in a residential area.

If you feel that a neighbor's activity is unreasonably interfering with the enjoyment of your property, then explore the possibility of obtaining relief from the police (your neighbor's activities may constitute breach of the peace); environmental law regulators (local, state, and federal authorities that enforce antipollution laws—including noise pollution); your municipal government (zoning laws may have been violated); or an attorney (you may be able to sue your neighbor for damages or an injunction on the basis that her activities constitute a nuisance).

Are You Liable if Someone Is Injured on Your Land?

Along with the rights and privileges attendant on ownership of land, come certain duties and responsibilities. Generally, as a homeowner you have a duty to exercise reasonable care not to injure those who enter upon your land, and you must warn them of hidden dangers. This duty extends to known trespassers, door-to-door solicitors, as well as friends and acquaintances invited to your house. Thus, if a project causes you to construct a ditch across a path often used by moped-riding trespassers or snowmobilers, you must put up a sign clearly warning them of this danger.

In many states, a special duty exists toward a child trespasser, under what is known as the "attractive nuisance doctrine." The landowner will be liable when a child trespasser is injured by a people-made condition such as a swimming pool if:

1.   The owner knew or should have known that young children were likely to trespass and that the artificial condition involved an unreasonable, serious risk to young children.

2.   The child did not realize the risk.

3. The risk to the child was great in comparison with the utility of the artificial condition.

In some states, a landowner may also be required to pay worker's compensation benefits to household employees, such as baby-sitters, handypeople, and gardeners, injured on her property.

In light of the liability exposure discussed above, the prudent landowner will take reasonable steps to assure that her property is safe and will obtain liability insurance coverage on the property.

Taxes and Assessments

Property taxes, an important source of revenues for local governments, are another liability associated with your land. Property taxes are generally used to help finance local school systems and local governments. They are usually assessed in accordance with the value of your land and become a lien on the land. If you fail to pay your property taxes, the local government can enforce the lien against the land in a procedure somewhat akin to a mortgage foreclosure. Any questions about property taxes should be directed to your local officials.

In addition, local governments also may impose assessments. Assessments are charges to local landowners to pay for municipal improvements, such as sewer pipes, which benefit their land.

RESTRICTIONS AND LIMITATIONS ON OWNERSHIP
OF LAND

Your right to use your land can be limited by private agreements. For example, the mineral rights in your property can be sold to another person separately from the land. The seller of land can impose a restriction, known as a "covenant running with the land," that restricts its use, such as by requiring that the land be used for residential purposes. In addition, the land may be burdened by an easement, discussed below.

Easements

Suppose that after reading this chapter you have a survey done of your property and discover that the property line between your house and your neighbor's is in the center of the alley that your neighbor has been using as a driveway. Can you use this discovery as an opportunity to expand your side yard by erecting a fence down the center of the driveway? Probably not, because your neighbor is likely to have already obtained an easement on the driveway.

An easement is an interest in land that gives its holder the right to use the land of another person for a specified purpose. It does not confer ownership of the land on the owner of the easement. Unlike adverse posses-

dustrial, and agricultural use. Zoning ordinances may specify minimum lot sizes, maximum height of buildings, and setbacks, and other requirements and aesthetic considerations may be imposed. To be constitutional, the classifications and requirements in the zoning ordinance must be reasonable. Before purchasing property, it is important to check the zoning law to find out what uses are permitted on your property and on neighboring land and to find out what requirements and limitations are imposed on structures built on the land.

If the zoning ordinance is changed so that your current use of the land is no longer zoned for the area, the municipality should permit you to continue as a nonconforming use. For example, suppose your office is attached to your house, and the land had been zoned as residential, light commercial. If the zone is changed to exclusively residential, you still should be able to continue your office indefinitely or for a period of time specified in the ordinance. If the municipality refuses to permit the use to continue, you may be able to challenge successfully its determination in a court action. A nonconforming use may not be increased; thus you may not transform the entire house into an office center. Once a nonconforming use is abandoned, the property must thereafter be used in accordance with the zoning ordinance.

Many times, a zoning ordinance is in accord with a master, or comprehensive plan that represents a broader, long-range land use planning projection for the area, often extending beyond the bounds of the municipality.

In addition to or in place of a local zoning law, your land may also be subject to regional or statewide land use regulations.

Environmental and Conservation Laws

Recognizing that we are custodians of our natural resources for future generations, the federal and state governments have passed various environmental and conservation laws to control pollution and to preserve natural resources. While the greatest impact of these laws is on industry and commercial development, homeowners in coastal areas and protected regions may find the use of their land affected by these laws. To find out if any environmental restrictions affect your property, check with a local attorney, a county or municipal official, your state offices dealing with environmental protection, or the public affairs office of the federal Environmental Protection Agency's regional office in your area.

Building and Construction Codes

States and municipalities often have building and construction codes that impose safety and construction standards on buildings in their jurisdictions. If you plan to build a structure or make an addition or structural change

sion (see p. 59) an easement acquired by a history of use gives the easement owner only the right to use the property in a particular way. In this case, your neighbor has the right to use your land in the alley as a driveway. After inquiry, you may discover that she was given this right in a written recorded document and that you purchased your property subject to that right. Even if she has no written document to establish the easement and in fact never received permission from anyone to use the alley, the law will recognize her easement if she has used the driveway, openly, regularly, and without objection for a period fixed by state statute, usually from 10 to 20 years. Thus, you must permit your neighbor to use the alley as a driveway. However, if your neighbor plows up the driveway and plants corn there, she has extinguished her easement, and since she is no longer using the land as a driveway, you may now build your fence.

Suppose the neighbor on the other side of your house, learning of the easement that your first neighbor has acquired, decides to use the space between your houses as a driveway and claims an easement on your land. Object! Build a fence; call the police; go to court and seek an injunction. Until the statutory period has run, she can have no easement without your permission. On the other hand, if you permit your neighbor to construct a driveway partly on your land, you may not thereafter change your mind and tell her to tear it up, even if the agreement is not in writing and the statutory period has not run. Under principles of estoppel, the law is likely to recognize her easement.

Easements are not limited to driveways, roadways, or paths. Your land may be riddled with numerous easements for utility, sewage, water lines, underground tunnels that, like harmless parasites, are scarcely noticeable. The right to enter upon the land of another to remove a fruit of the land (mineral, gravel, crop, timber) is also considered an easement.

Governmental Control over Land

Despite the landowner's sole right to control her property, many uses to which she puts the land will have side effects on neighboring land or community services and resources. A light industrial operation may generate noxious fumes; a new shopping center may generate traffic snarls; a gas station may mar the residential character of the neighborhood; unplanned development may leave a community with inadequate transportation facilities, schools, or utility services. In furtherance of the public health, safety, morals, and welfare, government usually seeks to regulate these issues with zoning and environmental laws.

Zoning and Land Use Planning

The zoning laws usually enacted by municipal governments regulate land use by limiting certain kinds of activities to designated parts of the municipality. Typically, areas will be designated for residential, commercial, in-

4

to an existing building, check with local authorities to obtain the necessary permits and inspections.

Condemnation

While she is a popular heroine, the hillbilly grandma rocking on the front porch, rifle in hand, refusing to leave her home to make way for a federal dam project, was breaking the law. The government does have the power to take private property from its owners and use it for a public purpose. The only limitations on this right of "eminent domain" are (1) that the property must be used for a public purpose, and (2) the private owner of the property must be given "just compensation" (the fair market value) for her land. Government regularly exercises its power of eminent domain when undertaking such activities as roads, buildings, and community development.

Government gains control of the property through a "condemnation" action, in which ownership of the land is transferred to the governmental entity and the owner is compensated. Condemnation actions are governed by procedural rules that must be followed meticulously by the governmental entity and by the landowners seeking to challenge the action or the compensation being offered. If you receive a notice that your property or a portion of it is being condemned, it is wise to review the matter with your attorney.

Inverse condemnation: If a government activity is interfering with your property to the extent that the realty is becoming unusable, you may be able to claim that a "taking" has occurred and that you should be given compensation for the value of your land. This is known as an "inverse condemnation," since the owner, rather than the government, is claiming that the land has been condemned. A typical case of inverse condemnation is where an airport is built so near to a residential area that the homes can no longer be adequately used as dwellings, due to the noise, lights, and vibrations of the planes.

Adverse Possession

The doctrine of adverse possession leads to sole ownership of the land of another and must be distinguished from easements, which involve merely the use of the land for a limited purpose. Suppose that your neighbor for the past twenty years has been using a portion of your land as though it were her own, extending a fence around it, gardening it, storing her car on it, and building a shed on it, and during that time you did nothing to stop her or to contest her ownership of the land. Under these circumstances, your neighbor will probably be able to claim successfully ownership of the land through "adverse possession." The law recognizes that if a person has treated land as though it were her own long enough, at some point it should become hers

To obtain ownership by adverse possession, one must have occupied the land without the owner's permission and with the intent of claiming ownership of it. It does not matter whether the person believes she owns the property or knows she does not. Not wanting to make the acquisition easy, the law requires that possession of the property be "hostile," "actual," "adverse," "open," "notorious," "continuous," "exclusive," or "peaceable," and must continue for a specified period of time, usually twenty years.

To avoid claims of adverse possession, the prudent landowner will have her property lines properly marked and will inspect her property regularly to ensure that no one is using it. If your neighbor claims that you have been using her land, have a survey done to verify the claim. If she is correct, you may be able to claim the land by adverse possession. To meet the statutory time period, you may be able to tack on the usage period of prior owners. See a lawyer to untangle this kind of problem.

RENTING AN APARTMENT

One of the great legal battlefields is the relationship between landlords and tenants. The origin of landlord-tenant law is in the English feudal system, and consequently tenants have fared poorly when disputes have arisen. However, recent times have seen a definite shift in favor of tenants. Tenants should be aware of the many rights they have.

A landlord-tenant relationship arises when one person—the landlord, or lessor—owns the property, and another person—the tenant, or lessee—has a right to possess it for a specified period of time in exchange for rent. The tenant's interest in the property is called a tenancy or leasehold. In addition, the tenant and the landlord exchange, either expressly or impliedly, a group of promises, called covenants, that govern their relationship. A leasing arrangement thus involves both an interest in property and a contract.

The discussion below addresses residential leases of apartment units in large multiple dwellings. Leases of single-family homes or units in small, owner-occupied dwellings are governed by many of the same rules. But often tenants in these units are not accorded many of the protections given tenants in larger apartment complexes.

KINDS OF LEASEHOLDS

The two common kinds of leasehold interests are "estate for years" and "periodic tenancy."

Estate for Years

An estate for years is a leasing arrangement in which specific dates are fixed for the lease to commence and to end. For example, if your lease provides that it is to begin on February 1 and will terminate December 31 you have an estate for years (even though it does not last a full year). In most states, the statute of frauds requires that if the lease extends beyond one year the agreement must be in writing to be enforceable. An estate for years terminates automatically at the end of the stated period unless a provision in the lease or a state law provides otherwise. The advantage of this kind of long-term lease is that the rent is fixed for the period of the lease and you are entitled to possession of the premises for that period. The disadvantage is that it may be difficult for you to terminate the lease if you decide to move out of the apartment before the end of the term.

Periodic Tenancy

In a periodic tenancy the leasehold will continue indefinitely from period to period until it is terminated. For example, in a month-to-month periodic tenancy the tenancy lasts for a month and is automatically renewed each month. State statutes often govern the procedure and notice requirements for terminating a periodic tenancy. Usually the notice period is identical to the period of the tenancy. Thus, a tenant with a month-to-month tenancy must be notified one month in advance that the lease will terminate. A landlord can easily increase the rent by terminating the tenancy and offering to renew at an increase in rent. The tenant must then either move out or pay the increased rent. While a periodic tenancy in which the period is less than a year need not be in writing, you should insist on a written lease as evidence of the agreement.

A periodic tenancy has an advantage for the mobile tenant, since she can terminate the lease and move out on relatively short notice. The disadvantage is that in the absence of any law to the contrary, the landlord can also terminate the lease or increase the rent on short notice.

STEPS TO TAKE WHEN ENTERING INTO A LEASE

Check the Landlord's Reputation

If you are planning to rent an apartment, try to rent from a reputable landlord. Avoid landlords who have a reputation for harassing tenants. Even if you win a controversy with such a landlord, it will hardly be worth the trouble.

Investigate the Premises

Before entering into a lease, inspect the premises carefully. If any repairs are needed or desired, discuss them with the landlord before entering into the lease or making a deposit on the apartment. If the landlord agrees to make any repairs, be sure to get that agreement in writing; otherwise you may have difficulty in enforcing it. Ideally the repairs should be made before the lease is signed or at least before you move in. Another precaution is to make a written inventory of the premises listing the condition of the premises and fixtures, and have it signed by the landlord or her representative.

Review the Lease

For your own protection, do not move in until you have received a signed, written lease. The lease is the agreement reached between the landlord and the tenant regarding their leasing arrangement. You should insist that the lease be in writing and signed by the landlord. Generally, a lease for a term in excess of one year will not be enforceable unless it is in writing.

The lease should be read carefully. It is a good idea to take it home and study it before signing it. The rent, security deposit, and duration of the lease should be correctly set forth. In long-term leases, be wary of escalation clauses that enable the landlord to increase the rent during the term of the lease to reflect her increased expenses for such items as fuel and taxes. Note the dates when rent is due and the provisions governing the return of your deposit. The lease should clearly set forth who is to pay for the fuel, gas, water, and electricity used in the unit. Pay particular attention to the assignment and subleasing clause (see section on subleasing, below). Note whether the lease contains a provision that automatically renews the lease on its expiration date unless the parties affirmatively terminate its provisions.

Provisions in the lease may limit your use of the apartment. Typically provisions may prohibit pets, installation of certain appliances, and structural changes to the apartment. Floor coverings or wall coverings may be subject to the landlord's consent. Provisions in the lease may cover such eventualities as nonpayment of rent, destruction of the premises, condemnation, accidents, or any other aspect of the landlord-tenant relationship.

In addition to the provisions in the lease, the relationship between a landlord and a tenant is governed by rules set forth in state and local laws. Many times, landlords insert provisions in the leases requiring tenants to waive the tenants' protections under the law. If possible, you may want to have such provisions deleted from the lease. In some cases, the inclusion of such provisions will constitute a valid waiver of rights; in other instances the law provides that the rights cannot be waived and the waiver is legally ineffective. Similarly, you might find that a provision in your lease conflicts with a rule of law. You must look to the law in your state to ascertain whether the provisions of the lease or the law prevails.

Any additions or deletions should be inserted or crossed out in the written lease and each change should be initialed by you and the landlord. Keep a signed copy of the lease for your records.

The Security Deposit

At the time the lease is signed, you are also generally required to give the landlord a security deposit. The security deposit is a sum of money, generally equal to one or two months' rent, which the landlord holds for the term of the lease. During that time, she may apply the security deposit to any rent you fail to pay, to the cost of repairing damages you caused to the apartment, or to compensate herself for harm caused by any violations of the lease on your part. Assuming the security deposit is not used for these purposes, it must be returned to you at the end of the lease. Whether you receive interest on the sum will depend on the provisions of the lease and state law.

RIGHTS AND OBLIGATIONS OF THE TENANT AND THE LANDLORD DURING THE TERM OF THE LEASE

The basic agreement between you, as tenant, and the landlord is that you have use and possession of the apartment for the term of the lease in exchange for the rent paid to the landlord. Both of you are obligated to abide by the terms of the lease and the applicable law. Problems develop when either a dispute arises as to what those obligations are or one party simply refuses to perform her part of the bargain.

What a Landlord Can Do if the Tenant Does Not Pay Her Rent or Otherwise Fails to Abide by the Lease.

A common problem for landlords is tenants who do not pay their rent. The usual remedy is to get rid of the tenant. To do this, the landlord will bring a court proceeding to gain possession of the apartment, called an eviction action or summary dispossess action (I will refer to all such actions as eviction actions). The tenant is served with a formal written notice of the action and is given an opportunity to defend the suit in a court hearing. Such a notice should *not* be ignored. If it is, the next thing you know, the sheriff may be at the door ready to move you out. If you do not attend the hearing, a default judgment will be entered in favor of the landlord. After that, even an attorney would have a difficult time preventing your eviction

If you receive an eviction notice and if, in fact, the rent has not been paid, one way to avoid eviction is to pay the rent. If you elect this alternative, get a receipt from the landlord that the rent was paid and, unless the hearing has been canceled, be sure to appear at the hearing to advise the court of the payment.

You may, however, decide to contest the eviction action, either because the rent was paid or because you believe you were justified in not paying the rent. In the former case, bring to the hearing written proof (a canceled check or the landlord's receipt) that the rent was paid. To establish such a fact, the rent should be paid by check or money order, rather than by cash. If the payment is in cash, the tenant should get a written receipt signed and dated by the landlord at the time the rent is paid.

If it is established that the rent has not been paid, the landlord will prevail and gain possession of the apartment in the absence of any ameliorating circumstances. Generally, the tenant has a few days after the hearing to pay the rent and avoid eviction. If the tenant refuses to leave the premises of her own accord as demanded by the court order, she can be physically removed from it by the sheriff. The whole process, from the day the rent was due and not paid until physical eviction by the sheriff, can take as little time as three weeks, although such speed is unusual in many places. Furthermore, in addition to regaining possession of the apartment, the landlord may obtain a judgment against the tenant in the amount of the rent due.

In addition to eviction for nonpayment of rent, the landlord may bring an eviction action if the tenant refuses to leave after the lease has expired. The landlord also may seek eviction "for cause"; that is, for the tenant's substantial breach of the terms of the lease. Such actions of the tenant as destruction of the premises, serious disturbance of neighbors, and illegal activities on the premises will generally enable the landlord to evict "for cause."

It is very important to realize that the above text gives the *general* framework for eviction actions. However, the laws and procedures differ from state to state in various ways. As a result, if at all possible, retain an attorney to represent you in the proceeding. If you are unable to do so, try to learn as much about your local law as possible.

What Can a Tenant Do if Premises Need Repair or Services Are Not Provided?

No heat in winter, a malfunctioning bathroom, and peeling paint are problems often faced by tenants. The extent of the landlord's duty to correct these conditions depends on whether the law in your state follows the traditional view or the new, progressive trend.

Traditional View—Action for Damages or Injunctive Relief: Under the traditional view, the landlord rents the premises "as is" and has no duty to repair it or maintain it unless she expressly agreed to do so in the lease. If the landlord had agreed to make the repairs or provide the service and refused to do so, you could bring an action against the landlord for breaching her duty to make the repair or provide the service. In such an action, you could seek an order directing her to make the repair or remedy the condition or could seek monetary damages to compensate you for the loss. For most tenants, such a suit is an expensive, unattractive alternative.

Code Enforcement: An alternative remedy is to seek correction of the problem through enforcement of the health or housing codes. These codes, developed by states or municipalities, often set forth in considerable detail the minimum health and safety standards a residential building must meet. The tenant may report the problem to the inspection agency that enforces the health, housing, or building code. Generally, this is the end of the tenant's self-help under the codes, since enforcement usually rests with administrative agencies.

Constructive Eviction: If the situation is bad enough and you can find alternative housing, your best solution may be simply to move out. If you have a periodic tenancy, the least troublesome way to do this is to terminate the tenancy, being sure to give the landlord proper written advance notice, in compliance with the terms of the lease and local law. If you have a lease for years and do not want to wait until the expiration of the lease, then your remedy, not without some risk, is to move out and claim constructive eviction.

Under the theory of constructive eviction, the tenant essentially claims that by permitting the condition to continue, the landlord is effectively forcing her to leave (evicting her), since the condition renders the premises uninhabitable. A tenant exercises this remedy at her peril. A court may not agree that the condition was serious enough to warrant constructive eviction. In such a case, the tenant could be found liable for breaching her lease.

Modern Trend—the Warranty of Habitability: The traditional tenant law discussed above is often unsatisfactory to the tenant, who must continue to pay the full rent for the apartment despite the defective conditions. The law in a growing number of states is moving away from this rigid view and is recognizing that the tenant's duty to pay rent is contingent on the landlord's duty to provide a habitable dwelling, irrespective of the terms in the lease. The modern view imposes upon the landlord a duty to provide housing that meets at least a minimum standard of adequacy. This duty is called the "implied warranty of habitability." If the housing does not meet the standards, the tenant may withhold all or a portion of her rent or may have the condition remedied herself and deduct the costs from the rent.

To utilize this approach, the tenant must first find out whether the warranty of habitability is recognized in her jurisdiction. If so, she then must determine whether the disrepair or loss of services in question constitutes a breach of the warranty in her jurisdiction. Usually, to constitute a breach the condition must be significant, such as no hot water, a broken window, or no heat in winter. Something like an unhinged closet door or chipped wall tile will not do. Generally, the landlord must have had notice of the condition and a reasonable opportunity to correct it before the rent can be affected. Thus, the tenant's next step is to give the landlord notice (keep a copy of your letter and postal receipt) that the problem exists and needs to be corrected.

The Repair and Deduct Remedy: Assuming the condition is not corrected, the tenant then may exercise her rent-related remedies. She has three choices: The first is to have the repair made herself and deduct the cost of the repair from her rent. The landlord should be advised that the repair was made and the cost deducted from the rent, and should be provided with copies of the receipts and bills for the work. This is an attractive remedy, since it results in the condition being corrected in a minimal period of time. However, it is not always available. Some conditions, such as a clogged drain or a broken lock, lend themselves to repair at the tenant's initiative. Other items, which affect the entire building, such as no heat or hot water, may not be corrected by a tenant on her own. In some places it may be possible for the tenants to combine their rents through an escrow arrangement and make major repairs to the building. This is a sophisticated operation and requires the advice of attorneys or experienced tenant representatives.

The Rent Abatement Remedy: The tenant's second alternative is to withhold all or a portion of the rent. Local law should be checked to determine what procedure applies. In some states, the withheld rent must be placed in an escrow account; in other states the tenant may keep the withheld rent. Determining the amount of rent that may be withheld is a subjective matter. The general theory is that the amount of rent withheld should be equal to the loss of rental value in the unit due to the condition or the percentage of the unit that is unusable due to the condition. Some authorities recommend that the entire amount be withheld and let the court decide how much should have been withheld.

The Landlord's Response—Eviction: Expect to be in court if you exercise either of these remedies. Unless the landlord agrees to the steps you have taken, chances are she will bring an eviction action against you for nonpayment of the rent. Your defense will be that she breached the warranty of habitability and therefore you were justified in withholding the rent or deducting the repair cost. In that action the court will decide whether the warranty was breached and whether the cost of repair or rent withheld was in the proper amount. If the court decides that the warranty was not breached or that the cost of repair or rent withheld was too much, you could be evicted. However, in most instances you would be given an opportunity to pay the rent due and avoid the eviction.

The Tenant's Lawsuit: In order to avoid an eviction action by the landlord, the tenant has another alternative. She may pay the full rent when due and sue the landlord for either the cost of repairs if made or an abatement of the rent and an order directing that the repair be made. In such an action she may be able to seek an abatement on back rents paid.

Due to the variations in policy and procedure among the states regarding the warranty of habitability, the safest course is to seek the advice of a lawyer. Note that you are almost certain to end up in court if rent is withheld. If you want to appear in court represented by counsel, do not put off retaining a lawyer until the landlord sues you, but do so before rent is withheld or the repair is made, in order to ensure that you proceed in a proper manner. You will save very little, if anything, in legal fees by waiting until the suit to hire the lawyer, and without her advice you may take steps detrimental to your case.

What to Do if Other Tenants Are Noisy or Otherwise Disturb You

A rock band gyrating in the apartment above you can transform your dear abode into a chamber of relentless noise. The noise and disturbances of outside parties, whether other tenants, their friends, or representatives of the landlord can be a source of constant annoyance and nuisance. The tenant's two basic protections against excessive noise and disturbances are the local "disturbing the peace" laws enforced by the police and the landlord's "covenant of quiet enjoyment."

The covenant of quiet enjoyment: This is an implied promise by the landlord that the tenant will have reasonably undisturbed use of the apartment. It may be breached by excessive disturbances to your use of the apartment.

In the case of noisy neighbors, you may complain to the landlord, who may be able to persuade them to quiet down or be able to evict them. If she refuses or is unsuccessful in these efforts, you may be able to negotiate with the tenants and landlord to have the tenants moved to another apartment, or you may request the landlord to move you to another apartment. (She may do so as an accommodation, but she has no duty to do so.)

If these efforts fail and the disturbance is making the apartment unlivable, you may want to move out. You may do so by properly terminating the lease of a periodic tenancy or by waiting until the leasing period expires, or you may use the constructive eviction remedy, discussed above.

What Protection Does a Tenant Have from Retaliatory Actions by a Landlord?

Occasionally, a landlord will harass or take harmful actions against a tenant because the tenant did something that was legal although detrimental to the landlord, such as reporting a housing code violation, organizing a tenants group, or exercising her repair and deduct remedy. The retaliatory steps the landlord takes may be illegal, such as locking the tenant out of her apartment or turning off the heat to her apartment. In these instances the tenant clearly has a remedy against the landlord for these wrongful steps. However, where the retaliatory step is otherwise legal, such as terminating a periodic tenancy or changing house rules, the tenant may have a remedy in only a few jurisdictions.

Who Is Liable if Someone Is Injured on the Premises?

The tenant should realize that as a general rule if someone is injured in her apartment, she, rather than the landlord, may be held liable for the injury. The prudent tenant will obtain liability insurance to insure against such claims. The landlord may be held liable for the injury if the accident is due to one of the following factors: (1) the accident was caused by a hidden danger that the landlord knew or should have known about, (2) the injury resulted from a condition that the landlord had a duty to correct, or (3) the injury resulted from a negligent repair made by the landlord. In addition, the landlord may be held liable for injuries caused by conditions in areas under her control, such as elevators, entry halls, stairways, and grounds.

SUBLEASING AND ASSIGNMENT: WHAT TO DO IF YOU WANT TO RENT YOUR APARTMENT TO SOMEONE ELSE

Many times, a tenant decides that she would like to rent her apartment to someone else. The tenant may plan to be away on a lengthy trip and seek to save money by renting out her apartment for a few months, or she may decide to move out before the lease expires.

Renting the apartment for the balance of the term in the lease is called an "assignment." The new tenant (the assignee) undertakes all the rights and duties of the old tenant (assignor) under the lease. In an assignment, your assignee (the new tenant) steps into your shoes and will have all the rights and duties under the lease that you had. However, the assignment does not relieve you of your duties under the lease. Thus, if your assignee (the new tenant) fails to pay rent or damages the apartment, you could eventually be held liable. In such a case, the landlord would seek a remedy against the new tenant and, if that failed, she would hold you responsible. While you could always seek reimbursement from the assignee, as a practical matter you may not be able to catch up with her. Of course, where there is an assignment, the landlord could agree to relieve you of your obligations under the lease and substitute the new tenant in your place. Such an arrangement is called a "novation" and is preferable from your point of view, but the landlord has little incentive to agree to this.

If you lease your apartment to another for only a portion of the unexpired term, say for six months, when two years remains on the lease, you have entered into a "sublease." (An assignment occurs when the *entire* unexpired term is rented; a sublease occurs when *only a portion* of the unexpired term is leased.) In a sublease arrangement, the rights and duties of your tenant (the subtenant) will be governed by the agreement between you and the subtenant. Such an agreement will generally mirror your lease, and it should require the subtenant to abide by the terms of your lease. As in an assignment, you remain liable for the lease and can be held liable if your subtenant does not abide by its terms.

Generally, you are free to assign or sublet *unless* there is a restriction or prohibition against assignments and sublets in your lease. Prohibitions against assignments and sublets are common and will be enforced. Often the lease will require the landlord's consent to an assignment or sublet. In such a case, the landlord's consent should be obtained in writing. Generally, unless the lease provides otherwise, the landlord may arbitrarily or unreasonably withhold her consent and prevent the assignment or sublet. However, some state laws provide that such consent may not be arbitrarily withheld.

In an assignment or sublet arrangement, you have duties to both your tenant and the landlord. You run the risk of being held liable on the lease if your subtenant or assignee fails to pay rent or otherwise abide by its terms. For example, if your tenant does not pay rent, you are liable for the rent to the landlord. Thus, you may be made to pay rent for an apartment you are not using and cannot use unless you bring an eviction action against your tenant. In addition, in a subtenancy you could be caught in the middle if your lease imposes duties on you that you neglected to impose on your subtenant.

Due to these risks and the practical difficulties in seeking recourse against a recalcitrant subtenant or assignee, assignments and subtenancies generally should be avoided. However, if you do decide to enter into one, consider the following rules:

1.   Check your lease to determine whether assignments or subleases are permitted and, if the landlord's consent is needed, get it in writing.

2.   Make sure your subtenant or assignee is responsible and trustworthy.

3.   Put your agreement with your subtenant or assignee in writing. In most states, the agreement must be in writing to be enforceable if the lease or sublease has more than a year to run.

4.   Make sure that all the duties and restrictions in your lease are imposed on your tenant.

5.   Take a security deposit.

6.   If possible, consult with a lawyer *before* entering into any arrangement. At the very least, check local law, using resources listed in the appendix (p. 540). The longer the time period involved, the more money involved, and the more unusual the situation, the greater the risk and hence the more important it is to retain a lawyer.

RENEWAL OF LEASE

In a periodic tenancy, the tenancy automatically renews at the end of the period on the same terms as the old lease. If the parties want to change the terms of the lease, they must in effect terminate the lease through the appropriate notice steps and then offer to renew the lease on the new terms. This is the mechanism the landlord would use to increase your rent in such a tenancy.

If you have a term for years, your tenancy will terminate automatically at the end of the term. Traditionally, at that time the landlord could require you to leave the apartment, and she could rent it to someone else. While this situation still prevails in most places, the modern trend is to require the landlord to permit the tenant to stay unless she has good cause for forcing the tenant to leave. Such good cause would include retiring of the unit from the rental market, and violations of lease by the tenant.

When renewing a lease at the end of the term, the provisions in the lease are open to negotiation. The landlord may condition renewal of the lease upon increased rent or changes in other terms in the lease.

If you are faced with a substantial rent increase, check with state or local authorities to determine whether you are protected by a rent control law, which places a limitation in the rent increases a landlord may charge.

TERMINATION OF A LEASE: HOW YOU CAN END A LEASING RELATIONSHIP

If you want to move out of your apartment, the simplest thing is to wait until your lease expires and then leave. In the case of a periodic tenancy, this will require that you give proper notice of termination. In the case of a term for years, you merely wait until the term expires, being sure to check the lease and local law to determine whether any notice is required. When moving out, be sure to demand in writing the return of your security deposit.

Unfortunately, often the time at which you need to move out does not coincide with the expiration of your lease. In such a case, you may be able to negotiate with your landlord for an early termination of the lease (be sure to get such an agreement in writing before moving out; a letter signed by the landlord will generally do). Assignment and subletting are other alternatives.

If you do none of these things, but merely move out, not only are you likely to lose your security deposit, but in many jurisdictions you could be held liable for all the rent due during the balance of the lease. In other jurisdictions, the landlord has a duty to cut her losses by making an effort to relet the premises. However, if the landlord relets the apartment for less than the rent you paid, you may be held liable for the difference for the balance of your term. Often, you can mitigate your damages by locating a tenant for the apartment.

OWNING A COOPERATIVE OR A CONDOMINIUM

Condominiums and cooperatives are enticing more and more Americans. When deciding whether to purchase a condominium or a cooperative, it is important to understand the legal aspects of the arrangement. While both condominiums and cooperatives give the owner the right to live in one unit and an interest in common facilities, from a legal standpoint the ways in which this is accomplished differ greatly.

CONDOMINIUMS

What Is a Condominium?

Condominium is a form of ownership in which you own outright your apartment or townhouse, and you own, as a tenant in common with the other apartment or townhouse owners, the rest of the project. In addition to referring to the form of ownership, the word "condominium" is also used to refer to the individual unit, as well as to the entire project.

In a condominium arrangement, you have sole ownership of your apartment or townhouse and may own it alone or with another, in the same manner as a single-family home; that is, you may own it as a tenant by the entirety, a tenant in common, a joint tenant, or solely. However, unlike a single-family home, various limitations may be placed on your use of the premises. For example, there may be restrictions on remodeling, owning pets, or renting the premises. Since the unit is treated as a single-family home, you may obtain a mortgage on your condominium unit, it is assessed separately for property taxes, and you may take interest on the mortgage and real estate taxes as deductions on your federal income tax return.

In addition to owning your unit, you own, as a tenant in common with other unit owners, all of the common areas. The common areas include those parts of the building not part of a unit, such as the hallways, lobby, basement, and grounds, and may include other facilities such as a club-house, a swimming pool, and other recreational areas. Your use of these facilities may be subject to various rules and restrictions, and you are required to pay a monthly maintenance fee toward the upkeep of the common areas. The ownership of the common areas and maintenance fees may be allocated equally among the unit owners, or may be allocated in proportion to the square footage or market values of the units.

The condominium project is governed by an association made up of all the owners. The association manages the common areas and assesses charges to the unit owners for the maintenance and operating costs. The owners' voting rights and responsibilities for charges are usually in proportion to their ownership rights in the common areas.

How Is a Condominium Organized?

Governance of a condominium is generally accomplished through the following documents:

DECLARATION, OR MASTER DEED

This document serves as the charter for the condominium organization. It identifies the realty that is subject to the condominium regime, describes each unit, identifies easements, sets forth the voting rights of the members and their shares in the common areas, provides the method of amending the declaration and the bylaws, and may deal with such issues as preemption rights on resale. Often, unanimous consent of all unit owners is needed to change the provisions in the declaration.

ARTICLES OF INCORPORATION AND BYLAWS

An association is organized to govern the condominium. The articles establish the association, and the bylaws adopted by the association are its rules. The bylaws will generally cover such issues as election, duties, powers, and qualifications of the board of directors; powers and duties of the officers; rules governing use and maintenance of recreational facilities and other common areas; and provisions for budgeting and maintenance of common areas. There may be other documents involved, such as a management agreement or an operating budget, which should also be studied.

Points to Consider When Buying a Condominium Unit

Within the above framework, the sponsor has significant latitude in establishing a condominium regime. As a result, the operations of various condominiums differ. You and your attorney will have to study the declaration, bylaws, and other legal documents governing the particular condominium you are considering in order to identify its peculiarities. (As in any purchase of realty, you should be represented by an attorney when purchasing a condominium unit.) Some items to pay particular attention to are noted below:

1.   What is owned solely by you and what is included in the common areas, subject to joint ownership.

2.   What fractional interest you have in the common areas.

3.   What enforcement mechanism the association has against a unit owner who fails to pay her share of the maintenance fees.

4.   How the monthly maintenance fee is determined.

5.   Whether the projected monthly assessment fee is realistic. The developer may try to "lowball" the figure in order to make the units more attractive to purchasers. However, if the costs are greater than her estimates, you will still have to pay your share of the increased assessments.

6.   Whether the developer has retained ownership or control of any recreational or other facility. If she has retained such control, what protection do you have from "legalized extortion" through escalating fees?

7.   Extent to which the association is bound by contracts made by the developer.

8.   What restrictions there are on your use of your unit.

9.   What restrictions there are on the renting or selling of your unit. Often the association is given a right of first refusal to purchase units.

10.   What restrictions there are on the use of recreational facilities and other common areas. How these can be changed.

11.   What provisions have been made for insurance. The association generally should have liability and casualty insurance covering the common areas, workers' compensation insurance for employees, and insurance to cover potential liability of directors and officers, who may also be bonded. As with the owner of a single-family house, you will want to obtain adequate casualty and liability insurance to cover your unit. However, unlike the owner of a single-family house, you have an interest in common areas, which may generate further liability exposure. A person who is injured in

a common area generally may sue the individual owners as well as the association. The association should have adequate coverage. However, in the event it does not, it is possible that individual unit owners would be held liable. As a result, a unit owner may want excess liability coverage for this contingency.

12. The condition of the building, particularly in the case of an older building. Are any major repairs likely to be needed? It is a good idea to get a report on the building from an independent construction engineer.

13. Whether there are adequate provisions for major repairs or renovations that may be needed in the future, to avoid having to raise a large sum of money at the time the repair is needed.

14. The manner in which any of the above items can be changed by the association in future years.

15. The provisions in your state and local law that may offer protection.

COOPERATIVES

What Is a Cooperative?

In a cooperative, the entire housing project is owned jointly by the occupants, and each occupant has a lease for her unit. Usually, in a cooperative the property is owned by a corporation and the shares in the corporation are divided among the cooperative owners. Coupled with the ownership of shares is the right to lease a unit in the project. Thus, cooperative owners will have shares in the corporation, which are evidence of their ownership in the project, and leases (called "proprietary leases"), which give them the right to occupy their units.

Unlike a condominium, in which each unit is owned separately, in a cooperative the project is owned as a whole by the corporation. As a result, taxes are assessed for the entire development and one mortgage can be obtained for the entire development. The cost of maintaining the building, and mortgage and property-tax payments, are assessed to the cooperative owners in the form of rent.

How Does a Cooperative Function?

A cooperative will operate in the same way as a corporation. It is established by a corporate charter or certificate of incorporation; a board of directors and officers is selected to run the corporation; and a set of bylaws will be adopted setting forth applicable rules and procedures. The cooperative owners participate in the management of the corporation through their votes as shareholders. However, as with other corporations, most of the management decisions and day-to-day operation of the corporation are left to the officers and directors. Shareholder control is exercised through election of these officials and through direct shareholder votes on certain specified matters.

The cooperative owner is also bound by the terms in her proprietary lease. The lease will identify the unit being rented and will set forth calculation of the rent.

Usually, the bylaws or other documents will place limitations on the right to sell shares or sublease the unit, and will establish grounds for terminating the lease for failure to pay rent or follow rules in the lease or bylaws. As with condominiums, there may be significant restrictions on your use of the unit covering such things as pets, remodeling, and so forth.

Points to Consider When Purchasing a Cooperative

Many of the points noted above regarding the purchase of a condominium are applicable to a cooperative as well. Pay careful attention to the provisions governing the calculation and collection of rent, voting rights, restrictions placed on your use, subleasing or sale of the unit, and the procedure governing changes in the bylaws, lease, and other governing documents and rules.

CONVERSIONS

More and more residential apartment buildings are being converted from rental dwellings to condominiums or cooperatives. The procedures governing the conversion and the rights of tenants in these situations are governed by state or local law.

The law usually provides a minimum period of time that the tenants must be permitted to remain in the apartment as tenants. In addition, tenants in the building have a right to remain in their apartments until their leases expire. (This does not necessarily prevent the sale of the unit, but the new owner of the apartment would have to wait until the tenant's lease expires before taking possession.)

The tenant usually has a first option to purchase her unit, often at a price below market value. This discount can be a substantial financial advantage. In fact, some tenants have been able to purchase their apartments at the discount price and turn around and resell it at market price, thereby making an easy tidy sum. However, purchasing tenants who do not resell their units may find that the monthly maintenance, mortgage, and tax costs on the unit significantly exceed the amount of monthly rent they had been paying for the unit.

The considerations noted above for purchasing a condominium or a cooperative apply equally here, when the purchase is after a conversion. In addition, the tenants may want to organize and hire a lawyer to ensure that their tenant rights are respected in the conversion process.

ADVANTAGES AND DISADVANTAGES OF OWNING A COOPERATIVE OR A CONDOMINIUM UNIT

Condominiums and cooperatives are forms of ownership that are suitable to many Americans today and present particularly viable forms of housing ownership in urban areas and in retirement and vacation communities. With today's life-styles, people often prefer smaller units that are free of maintenance care and offer recreational facilities that a single-family home-owner could not afford. Condominiums and cooperatives enable people who would otherwise be tenants to enjoy the security and financial benefits of home ownership. They have the opportunity to take the tax deductions enjoyed by homeowners, to build equity, to have a voice in the operation of their buildings, and to be free from dependence on a landlord for renewal of their leases and fixing rent. Condominiums and cooperatives are gener-ally more affordable than single-family houses and thus give people unable to finance a single-family house the opportunity of home ownership.

Condominium and cooperative owners have greater limitations on their use of their property than a single-family owner experiences. Limitations on leasing, selling, and using one's apartment are in effect when the unit is bought and may be changed anytime thereafter in accordance with proper procedure. In addition, the unit owner has much less control over the costs assessed to her unit. Group decisions on maintenance, major renovations, or improvements will be binding on all, and an owner who voted against the new expense and is financially unable to pay for it is still liable for her pro rata share.

A cooperative presents some particular disadvantages, since it is much more of a collective project. If one or more cooperative owners refuse to pay their share of taxes or mortgage payments, a lien can be placed on the entire project. The other owners would have to pay the unpaid share in order to remove the lien. If there were a significant number of such defaults, the entire project could be in jeopardy, and everyone's interests could be lost. As a result, the cooperative should be able to take strong and swift action against defaults. This problem is not as great in condominiums, because the lien would be placed on the defaulter's unit only, and the interests of the other owners would not be jeopardized. However, even in a condominium, if a unit owner defaults on her maintenance fees, the association would have to pay the maintenance costs with revenues from the other unit owners. Thus, it is important that the condominium association have a strong way to enforce payment of maintenance fees.

In addition to the administrative complexities attendant on condominiums and cooperatives, there are also some legal uncertainties. Since this is a new form of ownership for the United States, all the legal "bugs" have not yet been definitively resolved.   .

FURTHER READING

Blumberg, Richard E.; and Grow, James R. *The Rights of Tenants.* New York: Avon, 1979.

Bove, Alexander A., Jr. *Joint Property.* New York: Simon & Schuster, 1982.

Heatter, Justin W. *Buying a Condominium,* 3rd ed. New York: Scribner's, 1982.

Hemphill, Charles F., Jr. *A Practical Guide to Real Estate Law.* Englewood Cliffs, N.J.: Prentice-Hall, 1980.

Howell, John C. *The-Citizen's-Legal-Guide: The-Landlord-Tenant Relationship.* Englewood Cliffs, N.J.: Prentice-Hall, 1979.

Kiev, Phyllis. *The Woman's Guide to Buying Houses, Co-ops and Condominiums.* New York: Ballantine, 1981.

Kratovil, R. *Buying, Owning and Selling a Condominium in the 1980's.* Englewood Cliffs, N.J.: Prentice-Hall, 1982. .

———. *Buying, Owning and Selling a Home in the 1980s.* Englewood Cliffs, N.J.: Prentice-Hall, 1981.

Natelson, Robert G. *How to Buy and Sell a Condominium.* New York: Simon & Schuster, 1981.

Rejnis, Ruth. *Her Home: A Woman's Guide to Buying Real Estate.* New York: Ace, 1982.

4

Automobile Ownership: Consumers' Problems

CLARENCE DITLOW

Clarence Ditlow is director of the Center for Auto Safety, a consumer advocacy group founded by Ralph Nader and Consumers Union. Mr. Ditlow is an engineer and lawyer who has been active in automobile and consumer issues since 1971. Among his more noted accomplishments are the recall of 20 million Firestone 500 steel-belted radial tires and 1.8 million Ford Pintos for defective gas tanks.

When Dorothy Spicer, of Latonia, Kentucky, complained about the condition of the paint on her new car, in January 1979, she never suspected the legal nightmare that lay in store for her. The 60-year-old widow had bought a new Oldsmobile Omega and paid $200 extra for an extended warranty policy that included a free rental car for use when her own car was being repaired, so she would not be inconvenienced. Shortly after buying the car, she took it back to the dealership to correct a defective paint job. She left the car overnight with the understanding that the extended warranty would cover the cost of a rented car. But when she picked up her own car two days later, the dealership insisted that she pay $20 for the rental.

Mrs. Spicer paid the $20 charge, but then she wrote on the service order:

> To correct dealer's defective paint job. Charged 2 days' car rental at $10.00 per day for paint correction.

She was informed by an employee of the dealership that General Motors, the manufacturer of the car, would not honor a service order containing such a note. The employee told her that she must sign a new service order, but Mrs. Spicer refused to sign a new one and got in her car to leave. At that point, the employee ordered the garage door closed.

Mrs. Spicer got out of the car and pushed the "open" button. But by the time she got back in the car, the employee had closed the garage door. The door went up and down again in the same fashion. Meanwhile, Mrs. Spicer looked around and discovered:

> I was the only customer there, and all these big guys were standing around watching. I am a 60-year-old, crippled up Granny, and it was pretty darned scary, you can take my word for it. I warned the fellow that if he closed the door again, I would take the door with me. He closed it. I told them that I wanted out of there. I opened the door the third time, with the same warning. They closed it again. I opened the door again, but again they closed it, so I started taking the garage door right with me, for I had already paid them, had signed the work order, and they were without a doubt kidnapping this old woman, by holding me against my will, so I had no choice. By the time it was scraping across my hood and fenders, I heard Paul [an employee] yell to open the door, while the rest of them were just yelling.

When Mrs. Spicer returned home, she was informed that the dealer had sworn out a warrant for her arrest, claiming she had damaged the door. If convicted of the fourth-degree felony, she could have received a maximum $2,500 fine and five years in jail. When Mrs. Spicer appeared in court to answer the charges, the dealer refused to drop them unless she paid the alleged $500 damages to the door and agreed not to sue. But Mrs. Spicer, who had already been through such an unnecessary ordeal at the hands of the dealer, refused to pay a cent.

When she appeared before a grand jury on June 8, 1979, Mrs. Spicer was victorious. She was totally cleared of all criminal charges against her. Relieved, but not yet compensated for the emotional stress, which had put her in the hospital for two weeks, she sued the dealer and General Motors for malicious prosecution, false imprisonment, and libel. Although the judge granted a motion dismissing GM and its Oldsmobile Division as defendants, Mrs. Spicer accepted a $25,000 settlement offer from the dealer.

Very few of the 120 million car owners in the United States ever encounter the legal difficulties that Dorothy Spicer did. But when motorists do find themselves in legal hot water, it's far more likely to be with the auto company or a dealer over a defect than with the highway patrol over a speeding ticket

HOW BAD IS THE CONSUMER AUTO PROBLEM?

Automobile problems are a national epidemic affecting all socioeconomic groups. Almost every poll and survey, whether it's government- or industry-sponsored, shows that problems with the purchase and repair of automobiles are the number one consumer complaint across the country.

More and more consumers have become less and less willing to tolerate the failure of the auto industry to provide the public with reliable vehicles meeting minimum standards of quality, durability, and performance. When the consumer receives a lemon—an unsafe and unreliable car—topped off with poor warranty performance by manufacturer and dealer, and shoddy and expensive repair service, she wants to do something about it.

Resolving an auto complaint is frequently tedious and frustrating. If the car is a lemon, the dealer and the manufacturer invariably refuse the only good remedy: replacement, or refund of the purchase price. The reason has to do with pure economics. If car companies replaced defective cars as appliance companies replace defective toasters, it would cost car makers at least $100 million per year. So the owners of a lemon must be prepared for the frustration of the stonewall. No one gets a lemon replaced on the first or second trip to the dealer; but unless those trips are made, the lemon will never be replaced, nor will a refund be given.

WHAT SHOULD CONSUMERS DO ABOUT AUTO PROBLEMS?

There are many options open for consumers who wish to resolve auto problems short of filing a lawsuit. These include complaining in writing to all levels of the manufacturer, from the president on down; getting help from local and national consumer groups and agencies; using mediation or arbitration panels; and even picketing. But successful use of these avenues, as well as the courts, depends on documenting auto problems in the first instance.

Records That Must Be Kept and How They Should Be Kept

Besides persistence, the foremost key to success in getting a defective car repaired or replaced is to document everything that goes wrong with it.

Whenever a car owner visits the dealer, she should always obtain a legible copy of the repair order. Receipts for routine maintenance, particularly oil changes, should be saved. If a letter is sent to the manufacturer or the dealer, the consumer should always make a copy for her files.

Keep auto records together in an empty drawer or shoebox. They will be there when needed to document a complaint or prove that proper maintenance work was performed. Ultimately, the success or failure of any lawsuit depends upon being able to document the problem with a car and the manufacturer's failure to repair it.

Who Will Help Resolve a Complaint

All too frequently, consumers fail to take some simple steps that would help solve many auto problems. Instead, they give up, trade in their lemon car at a considerable economic loss, accept an excessive repair bill, or go to another garage to get a faulty repair corrected. Even where they sue and win, a simpler tactic might have succeeded.

Go to the Top: Whether it's a new car with a warranty problem or a complaint about a repair at the local service station, it pays to go to the top of the company. If the service manager shrugs off the consumer, she should see the owner of the dealership or the general manager. They can overrule a stubborn or errant subordinate or even authorize a free repair to retain the goodwill of a customer.

If a car dealer does not resolve a complaint, contact the manufacturer's regional office. (The names and addresses of these offices are often listed in the owner's manual which comes with a new car.) The manufacturer has more expertise in diagnosing complex defects, as well as the authority to approve goodwill repairs where the dealer refuses to do so. If a consumer is going to sue, contacting the manufacturer eliminates a common legal defense on the manufacturer's part, that they were not given a chance to repair the defect.

Consumer Groups and Agencies: Where a problem is particularly bad or widespread, state and local consumer agencies may be able to help the consumer. Their effectiveness and willingness to help consumers varies enormously from one area of the country to another, and from one year to the next. For example, Dade County, Florida, has its own consumer advocate, who successfully sued Ford Motor Company over rusting Fords. The Bureau of Automotive Repair, in California, and the Dallas Department of Consumer Affairs have both recovered hundreds of thousands of dollars for consumers victimized by faulty or fraudulent repairs.

Local consumer groups offer another alternative for consumers with auto problems. Some, like the Auto Owners Action Council in Washington, D.C., will directly negotiate with auto dealers and repair shops on behalf of consumers. Others, like the Consumers Education and Protective Association, in Philadelphia, and the Seattle Consumer Action Network will picket dealers and garages to resolve consumer complaints when negotiations fail.

National Agencies and Groups: Complaining to consumer groups and government agencies* is always a good idea when the consumer gets no action on the local level and has not decided to file a lawsuit. These groups and agencies use complaint letters they receive to generate broad relief, such as recalls, which benefit not only the individual who wrote initially but all others similarly affected. Even if these agencies or groups cannot act directly on an individual's behalf, they may send complaints on to the manufacturer, requesting the manufacturer to take action. When the manufacturer receives enough complaints from consumers and organizations, it may decide to repair the defective cars as the best means of quieting the uproar.

The most important agency to contact is the National Highway Traffic Safety Administration (NHTSA), of the U.S. Department of Transportation. (See p. 515 for the address and toll-free auto safety hot line, to register your complaint.) The NHTSA computerizes all the complaints it receives, so that it can spot defects quickly and order recalls. In the Firestone 500 steel-belted radial tire recall alone, consumers received $200 million in refunds and replacement tires from Firestone.

WHAT TO DO IF NO ONE LISTENS TO COMPLAINTS OR HELPS THE LEMON OWNER

If a consumer has taken all the above steps, with no satisfaction, then the only avenues left open are to file a lawsuit or to resort to public protest actions aimed at making someone listen. With the legal system's increased responsiveness to consumer protection laws, litigation may be the best course.

FILING A LAWSUIT

If the dealer and the manufacturer do not respond to the attorney's first few contacts, a lawsuit may be necessary. But this does not necessarily mean

*A list is provided on p. 515.

that a lengthy and expensive trial will result. Sometimes by filing a lawsuit an attorney can resolve a case without going to trial.

For example, when the law firm of Tydings and Rosenberg, in Baltimore, Maryland, filed a lawsuit against British Leyland on behalf of some 23 Jaguar, Triumph, and Austin car owners, the British auto company immediately negotiated a settlement, rather than defend the case.

At Trial

If the parties to a lawsuit do not settle before trial, the case usually will be heard in court. And it is in court that many consumers have been successful. One example is Giuseppe Ventura, of Edison, New Jersey, who was awarded $7,100 in damages and $5,100 in attorney fees. Ventura sued Ford Motor Company because his 1978 Mercury Marquis repeatedly overheated and stalled on the highway. This case is an excellent example of why it pays auto companies to resolve lemon cases quickly, rather than go through expensive trials and run up attorney fees both for their own lawyers and those of the successful consumer which they will also have to pay.

How to Find a Lawyer

If your case is too big for small claims court (in most states there is a limit of $1000–$1500 on the amount you may sue for in small claims court), and you cannot find a lawyer to go into regular court, you don't have to give up. Toby Cagan, a schoolteacher in Queens, New York, proved that when she took the giant Chrysler Corporation to court and won—without a lawyer. Cagan sued on her own because she couldn't find a lawyer willing to take on Chrysler over her defective 1977 Dodge Aspen. She had complained over and over again about her lemon to Chrysler dealers and the manufacturer, but Chrysler responded to her complaints with form letters and rude and reluctant service.

Before Cagan signed for her Aspen, she took a test drive and found many problems with the car, including difficult steering, sticky windows and doors, stalling, and dents. She complained to the salesperson but was told that "it was because it was a new car and that these problems would have to work themselves out." Trusting the salesperson's word, Cagan drove away in her new Chrysler. When the car developed more problems within one week, she took the car back to the dealership for service. For the next several months, Cagan tried to get six Chrysler dealerships to repair her car, but with no luck. The dealership where she purchased the car went out of business, so she tried five other dealerships only to receive more of the same treatment. She sent letters and made phone calls to Chrysler, but the company ignored her requests. At that point, Cagan was thoroughly angry and frustrated—"the car had been defective since the date of its purchase," she stated. "After three government recalls, numerous and multiple problems and defects, I am afraid to drive this car."

So Toby Cagan filed a lawsuit against Chrysler in Queens Superior Court. On March 9, 1979, Cagan presented her case in court. Fortunately, she had saved all the repair orders to document her "lemon" story. She was able to show how she had brought the car into numerous Chrysler service departments again and again with no success. Chrysler simply could not or would not repair her car. As her story unfolded in the courtroom, Chrysler's shabby treatment of Cagan was exposed. She brought in mechanics as well as a consumer-group witness with expertise in auto safety to testify on her behalf.

Chrysler brought in a high-priced corporate lawyer from New York City to oppose the courageous schoolteacher. Yet his objections were overruled and his witnesses were forced to admit that the car had all the defects that Cagan alleged. At that point in the trial, the court called for a recess to see if Chrysler wanted to admit defeat. The company gave in and offered to refund the consumer's purchase price minus $500.

Toby Cagan, who didn't give up easily, proved that you don't always need a lawyer to take a giant corporation to court and win.

What to Expect of a Lawyer

Lawyers can do many things for ripped-off or lemon car owners without filing a lawsuit. Indeed, many of these alternatives are far quicker and less expensive than litigation. For example, a short, threatening letter from an attorney is often enough to shock a hard-nosed dealer into repairing a car free.

It is hard to find a good lawyer who can handle this type of work effectively; but they are there. Get lawyer referrals from friends or local consumer groups. The Center for Auto Safety (1346 Connecticut Avenue N.W., Washington, D.C. 20036) keeps lists of attorneys from all around the country who are willing to take consumer auto cases. To expedite your request, send them a stamped self-addressed envelope. If a consumer cannot find an attorney any other way, local bar associations almost invariably run referral services.

Interview a lawyer before deciding to hire her. Many attorneys will give inexpensive or even free consultations for up to an hour to evaluate your case. While the lawyer is going over the facts and merits of your case, assess the attorney. Is she experienced and eager to take the case? Sometimes a younger attorney who is trying to develop a practice and who is familiar with all the new consumer laws is as good or better than an older lawyer who may consider a consumer case less important than her other, "bigger" ones.

When a Lawyer's Call or Letter Works

Many dealers and manufacturers rely on wearing out the consumer. They know that the vast majority of consumers will never get beyond the complaint-letter stage. So they wait to see if the consumer hires a lawyer. If she does, then the dealer or auto company will get serious about the problem. After all, if the consumer sues and wins, they may have to pay her attorney's fees as well as their own.

Thus a letter or a telephone call, alone, from an attorney to the dealer or manufacturer shows them that the lemon owner means business. Sometimes they will offer to repair the car, settle for money damages, or otherwise resolve a complaint. For example, J. Norris, of Washington, D.C., bought a new 1978 Oldsmobile diesel. The camshaft failed at 28,000 miles, well beyond the 12,000-mile written warranty. The cost of the camshaft replacement was over $1,000. When the consumer could not resolve the complaint on his own, his Washington attorney, Mark Steinbach, both called and wrote to the regional Oldsmobile office, which eventually offered to replace the camshaft free or resell the car at retail at the consumer's option. The legal cost to the consumer was about $200.

Mark Silber, one of the best-known "lemon lawyers" in the United States, uses the combined letter and telephone-call strategy to good success in his Metuchen, New Jersey, practice. His letters record the serious lack of cooperation and interest by the manufacturer in responding to the lawyer's phone calls on behalf of a consumer client with a warranty or other problem. Mr. Silber's letters take the following approach:

> This letter is a record of the fact that I called you on Tuesday and we discussed . . . and you refused to (do thus and so).
> This letter is a record . . . I have called you six times this week without your returning any of my calls.

A lawyer's letter to the dealer simply describing the remedies to which the consumer is entitled may have a great effect all by itself. In some cases, the dealer will give the customer a replacement car, rather than risk a lawsuit.

THE CONSUMER'S LEGAL RIGHTS

Consumers who know their legal rights get their auto problems resolved more quickly and fully than do consumers who are unaware of their rights. Consumers have a full array of legal rights, ranging from the warranty that comes with the sale of a new or used car, the right to a written repair estimate, treble damages if the dealer rolled back the odometer in a used car without disclosure, and many more. Indeed, if a consumer chooses to tell the world about a lemon, the U.S. Constitution would guarantee her freedom of speech to do so.

The New Car Written Warranty

The written warranty that comes with a new car is not what it appears to be. It is important to read it carefully and to understand that it limits the manufacturer's liability more than it protects the consumer's interests. The written warranty does not promise the consumer a working car, does not promise to replace the car if there are serious defects, and does not accept liability for any loss or damage as a result of defects.

Most written warranties provided by manufacturers are limited to certain parts and expire after a set period of time and mileage. The normal written warranty covers the entire car, with the exception of required maintenance. The manufacturer suggests that any paint or appearance defects be called to the attention of the dealer without delay, since normal deterioration due to use and exposure is not covered by the warranty. Manufacturers often offer longer warranties on the engine and transmission than on the rest of the car. Since 1980, most new cars come with a three- or five-year warranty against rust. Tires are frequently warranted by the tire manufacturer under a separate warranty included with the owner information brochures supplied with the vehicle.

The essential consumer right under the written warranty is that the dealer must replace or repair parts that, to the dealer's "reasonable satisfaction," are defective in workmanship or materials. The buyer has certain obligations under the warranty. The principal one is to follow specified service or maintenance schedules, which can be performed by the dealer or an independent garage or service-station mechanic.

Beyond this central right, the language of the warranty makes it clear that the manufacturer is limiting its liability. An example is the Buick Motor Division Limited Warranty on new 1982 Buicks. The warranty said: "Buick does not authorize any person to create for it any obligation or liability in connection with these cars." This means that advertising claims or promises made by the dealer's salespeople are not in the manufacturer's written warranty which will not be upheld by the manufacturer.

Beware of salespeople's *spoken* explanations of the warranty. What the dealership *says* about the warranty may not count when it comes time for warranty service. Check what is *written* in the manufacturer's warranty, because only there are the consumer's undisputed rights spelled out. If the dealership makes claims in an advertisement or gives a buyer a *written* explanation or addition to the manufacturer's warranty, then it is the dealership and not the manufacturer who may be obligated to make good on those additional promises.

The warranty states that "loss of time, inconvenience, loss of use of the vehicle or other matters not specifically included are not covered." If a consumer's car is tied up for a month at the dealership for repairs and a rental car costs $400, the manufacturer will not voluntarily reimburse the consumer. Although this is not necessarily so, it is what the dealer and the manufacturer will say when asked for reimbursement.

Other Warranty Rights

Because the manufacturer's written warranty is so limited, federal and state laws create or mandate additional warranties to protect the consumer. The most important of these are *express* and *implied* warranties that arise under state law. These apply to a car both during and after the manufacturer's written warranty period. In addition, certain vehicle components such as parts of the emission control system may have federal- or state-mandated warranties. Besides creating warranty rights, federal and state law may restrict how the manufacturers limit or honor their warranties.

In sum, a car may have *written* warranties (*express* warranties, *federal- or state-mandated* warranties) and *implied* warranties. Warranty problems are often the first and most frustrating problems faced by new-car owners, but knowing that protection exists in the following ways will encourage the owner to enforce her warranty rights.

Implied Warranties

Implied warranties are legal rights created by state law, not by the seller. In those states where they exist, implied warranties create legal rights above and beyond what is in the written warranty. Implied warranties can give consumers the right to get free repairs, a replacement, or a refund if the car is defective and does not work in the ordinary way a car is expected to work, provided the consumer takes the right steps in terms of use and maintenance. Thus, state law gives consumers rights that are similar to the rights given to car owners with a "full" warranty under federal law. (See p. 90 for an explanation of a full warranty under federal law.)

There are two kinds of implied warranties: an implied warranty of *merchantability* and an implied warranty of *fitness for a particular purpose.*

Warranty of Merchantability: This is the most common implied warranty. It means that the car must be fit for the reasonable and ordinary purposes for which a car is normally used. The car must be able to provide reasonably comfortable and safe transportation from one place to another. If it does not, the consumer has a legal right to get a refund or a replacement.

For example, after having driven $\frac{1}{10}$ of a mile from the dealer's showroom, Mrs. Smith's new Chevrolet stalled at a traffic light. It stalled again within another 15 feet, and again thereafter each time the vehicle was required to stop. When halfway home, about 2-½ miles from the showroom, the car could not be driven in "drive" gear at all. Mrs. Smith had to drive in "low" gear, at a rate of about 5 to 10 miles per hour. After Mrs. Smith finally arrived home, her husband immediately called the bank to stop payment on his check, and telephoned the dealer to inform him that the sale was canceled. The dealer sent a wrecker to the consumer's home, brought the vehicle in, and replaced the transmission. But Mr. Smith continued to refuse to accept the new car. Then the dealer sued Mr. Smith for the purchase price. The New Jersey Superior Court in *Zabriski Chevrolet* v. *Smith,* (1968) agreed with the consumer that the vehicle was substantially defective, that there was a breach of the implied warranty of merchantability; and upheld the Smiths' refusal to take and pay for the car.

Warranty of Fitness for a Particular Purpose: This less common warranty applies when a consumer buys a vehicle for a particular purpose, such as hauling a large trailer; informs the salesperson of the special use; and the salesperson states that the particular car will be good for that use. When the consumer buys that model in reliance on the salesperson's advice, an implied warranty of fitness for a particular purpose is created. If the vehicle cannot then perform the job for which it was bought, the consumer is entitled to a refund or a replacement.

Express Warranties

The manufacturer's written warranty that comes with a new vehicle is one form of an express warranty. However, there may be other express warranties, which are not in writing, that can apply to the sale of both a new and a used car by a dealer. Like implied warranties, express warranties are also created by state law and by what the seller (the manufacturer or the dealer) says about the car either orally or via various media such as advertisements, brochures, etc. Any (1) *affirmation* of fact, (2) *promise,* (3) *description,* (4) *sample,* or (5) *model,* advanced by the seller, which becomes part of the "basis of the bargain," creates an express warranty that the vehicle will conform to the affirmation, promise, description, sample, or model. Even where the seller does not use formal words such as "warrant" or "guarantee," an express warranty may still be given. But the seller's statements in which she is "puffing her wares" is not sufficient; that is, an affirmation merely of the *value* of the vehicle (and not of *fact*), or a statement purporting to be merely the seller's opinion or commendation of the vehicle, does not create a warranty. For example, the dealer who tells a buyer that she is getting "a great little car" has not created an express warranty as to the condition of the car. Advertising can be a source of an express warranty. Steve Lastovich, of Hibbing, Minnesota, saw a Ford Motor Company television commercial showing pickup trucks dashing over rough terrain and sailing through the air. He based his purchase of a Ford four-wheel-drive truck on claims made in that commercial. After the truck body was badly dented during a rough trip through mud and sand, he sued Ford for the $500 cost of repairs. Lastovich argued that Ford's ads constituted an express warranty on his pickup. Even though Ford stated in its written warranty that "there is no other express warranty on this vehicle," a jury agreed with Lastovich and ordered Ford to pay the $500 in actual damages plus $175 in costs. The court in *Lastovich* ruled that brochures the consumer had read, TV ads he had seen, promises made to him by the salesperson, and impressions he received from demonstrations of similar trucks (on TV) influenced him to purchase the vehicle. Ford was held liable for repairs when it allowed such an excessive amount of flex in its four-wheel-drive truck frames as to cause damage from box-with-cab contact.

Federal- or State-mandated Warranties

Certain components of the car, such as parts of the emission control system, may have federal- or state-mandated warranties. For example, Section 207(a) of the Clean Air Act requires the auto manufacturers to warrant for the first five years or 50,000 miles that the vehicle emission control system is free from defects in materials and workmanship that cause the vehicle to exceed the emission standards. Section 207(b) requires the manufacturer to warrant any component that causes the vehicle to fail a state-required emission test during the first 24,000 miles and any major component such as the catalyst for 50,000 miles. This warranty helps attain clean air while it protects the consumer's pocketbook.

Although the warranty is federally created, the manufacturer, not the federal government, is responsible for repairing cars that violate the warranty. A recent case illustrates how the emission-control warranty can work for the consumer. The Environmental Protection Agency (EPA) investigated certain 1977–79 models of Volkswagen vehicles when it suspected that those models had a valve-stem seal defect. The EPA concluded that this valve defect would lead to excessive emissions in those vehicles. Volkswagen then agreed not only to repair the affected 450,000 vehicles without charge to owners up to five years or 50,000 miles, whichever occurred first, but also to reimburse consumers who had already paid to have the valve-stem seals replaced.

The Clean Air Act makes it a crime for any manufacturer or dealer to refuse to honor a valid emission-control warranty claim. So if either the dealer or the manufacturer refuses to make a warranty repair on the emission-control system, remind them that there is a potential fine of $10,000, and then inform the Environmental Protection Agency, Mobile Source Enforcement Division, of the violation (see p. 525 for address and phone number).

What if the Manufacturer Keeps Working on a Car Without Success?

Under the written warranty, the manufacturer limits its obligation only to repairing or replacing defective parts. One of the most common complaints is that the consumer is forced to go back to the dealer again and again for unsuccessful repairs. The auto companies are so unabashed about repeated repairs that they say there is nothing wrong with requiring consumers to come back 20 or more times.

During hearings on a proposed California "lemon law" that would protect consumers against automobiles plagued with mechanical problems, a debate arose on the subject of how many attempts a dealer manufacturer should be allowed to repair a particular defect. While Assemblywoman Sally Tanner's bill allowed for a total of four tries or 20 days in which to remedy the defect, a representative from Ford Motor Company objected, testifying that "there are times when 30 visits might be required to solve the problem."

Contrary to what the manufacturer and the warranty say, consumers do not have to put up with endless repair trips to the dealer. Under the Uniform Commercial Code (Section 2-719), which is the law in every state except Louisiana, when an exclusive remedy "fails of its essential purpose," the consumer is entitled to other remedies, including revocation of acceptance and return of the purchase price.

For example, one consumer revoked acceptance of his new Saab after the car kept stalling and was plagued by a series of annoying minor defects. But the repeated stalling, which began five months after purchase, was never remedied, despite several attempted repairs by the dealer. When the consumer revoked acceptance, the manufacturer argued in part that the warranty limits a purchaser's remedies to repair or replacement of defective parts, and nothing more.

When the consumer in this case sued, the Supreme Court of Minnesota in *Durfee* v. *Rod Baxter Imports* (1977) held that revocation of acceptance was a remedy available to the purchaser. The court said:

An exclusive remedy fails of its essential purpose if circumstances arise to deprive the limiting clause of its meaning or one party of the substantial value of its bargain. So long as the seller repairs the goods each time a defect arises, a repair-and-replacement clause does not fail of its essential purpose. If repairs are not successfully undertaken within a reasonable time, the buyer may be deprived of the benefits of the exclusive remedy. Commendable efforts and considerable expense alone do not relieve a seller of his obligation to repair.

MAGNUSON-MOSS WARRANTY ACT

The single most important federal law protecting consumer rights in warranties is the Magnuson-Moss Warranty Act, passed by Congress in 1975. This Act makes it easier for consumers to get defective cars repaired and total lemons replaced, and to successfully sue the auto companies. For detailed information from the Federal Trade Commission on this law, read "Warranties: There Ought to Be a Law . . . ," which can be obtained by writing to the Consumer Information Center (see p. 514 for address).

The Act provides new remedies for consumers whose car warranties are not honored and makes it easier for lemon owners to find attorneys to represent them in breach-of-warranty lawsuits. The Act includes a "lemon" provision that may entitle a lemon owner to a full refund or a new replacement car if the manufacturer or dealer fails to remedy defects after a "reasonable number of attempts" to repair the car.

Under the Magnuson-Moss Act, all *written* warranties must be easy to read and understand. They must be written in ordinary language, not "legalese." Fine print is not allowed. The warranty must disclose the following in simple and readily understood language:

1. *Who* is covered by the written warranty. May only the first buyer enforce it or a subsequent buyer as well?

2. *Which parts* of the car the warranty does and does not cover.

3. *What* the seller or the manufacturer will and will not do in the case of a defect or a breakdown. At whose expense?

4. *When* the warranty period begins and ends. How long will the car be covered? Although the written warranty on a new car will invariably read that any implied warranty is good only for the length of the written warranty, this clause is invalid in some states and should be invalid in all. See number 7, on disclaimer of warranties, for further information about this.

5. What the consumer must do in order to get the manufacturer to meet its obligations. A *step-by-step* explanation of the procedure the consumer should follow in order to obtain performance of any warranty obligation. What are the buyer's responsibilities under the warranty? Who is authorized to perform warranty work—the selling dealer or any franchised dealer? This information must include the name of the manufacturer and an address or title of a representative responsible for the warranty performance. A toll-free number to use to contact the manufacturer or service person may take the place of an address.

6.   If any informal dispute-settlement procedures are available through the manufacturer, information about them must be provided.

7.   Any limitations on or disclaimers of the consumer's right to recover consequential or incidental damages—such as the cost of rental cars when a car breaks down. Once again, such conditions are invalid in some states, so that the consumer may have a right to collect these damages despite the limitation to the contrary in her car's written warranty. See the section on Limited Warranties for these states.

8.   The manufacturer's warranty must contain the following statements telling consumers of additional rights beyond what is in the written warranty:

> This warranty gives you specific legal rights, and you may also have other rights which vary from state to state. Some states do not allow limitations on how long an implied warranty will last or the exclusion or limitation of incidental or consequential damages, so the above limitations or exclusions may not apply to you.

Full Warranties

The Magnuson-Moss Act requires all written warranties to be labeled as either "full" or "limited" warranties. A full warranty is far better than a limited warranty in imposing specific obligations on the manufacturer and the dealer as well as giving consumers specific rights against them.

The label "full" on a warranty means:

1.   A defective car or part must be repaired or replaced free.

2.   A defective car or part must be repaired within a reasonable period of time after the consumer complains.

3.   A consumer cannot be required to do anything unreasonable to get warranty service, such as taking the car to the factory, 600 miles away.

4.   The warranty must cover anyone who owns the car during the warranty period.

5.   If the car cannot be or has not been repaired after a reasonable number of attempts, the consumer gets a choice of a new replacement car or her money back. This is the so-called "lemon provision."

One thing the word "full" does not promise: A full warranty does not have to cover the whole car. It may cover only selected components or systems such as the engine or drive train.

Limited Warranties

The loophole in the Magnuson-Moss Act is that auto companies are not required to give a full warranty. All other written warranties are limited and do not have to meet any federal standards, including the all-important lemon provision. A warranty must be labeled "limited" if it gives the consumer anything less than what a full warranty gives. A car may have both full and limited warranties. For example, it may have a full warranty on the engine and a limited warranty on the paint.

While the limited warranty does not give consumers additional substantive rights, manufacturers are prevented from denying certain warranty rights to consumers. Moreover, the Magnuson-Moss Act gives consumers major procedural rights, including the all-important right to seek reimbursement of attorney fees under both a full and a limited warranty.

Limitations on Implied Warranties

Under the Magnuson-Moss Act, if a written warranty is given, then the implied warranties may not be disclaimed. The only limitation of an implied warranty allowed (in limited but not full warranties) is a limit on how long it lasts. The implied warranty can be limited in duration only to the duration of the written warranty; for example, if a consumer has a one-year written warranty, the implied warranties may not be limited in duration to less than one year. Such a limitation must be "conscionable," which means that it may not be extremely unfair or harsh. Federal law also requires such limitations to be "set forth in clear and unmistakable language and prominently displayed on the face of the warranty."

The "unconscionability" argument will help a consumer who takes her lemon case to court. Usually an unconscionable act is one that is totally unfair or harsh to one party or is done in bad faith. If the court agrees that the consumer, as a new-car buyer, has been unconscionably treated by the manufacturer's warranty provisions, it may declare the warranty limitations unconscionable and therefore invalid. Thus, if the dealer refuses to repair a substantial defect that exists after the written warranty has expired, a consumer should claim in court that the manufacturer has breached the implied warranty and that any limitation of the implied warranty was unconscionable.

Most manufacturers do limit the duration of the implied warranties to the duration of the written warranty. That means that when the written warranty expires after, say, 24,000 miles or 24 months, the implied warranties expire along with it. Since most auto warranties are, in fact, "limited," most consumers will find themselves in this situation.

State law under the Uniform Commercial Code (UCC)—which has been adopted by all states except Louisiana—requires that a valid disclaimer of an implied warranty of merchantability must actually mention the word "merchantability." If the merchantability disclaimer is in writing, which it usually is in the case of auto warranties, it must be conspicuous or visible to the average reader. A valid disclaimer of an implied warranty of fitness must be in writing and must be conspicuous. A disclaimer of all implied warranties of fitness is valid if it states, for example, that "there are no warranties which extend beyond the description on the face hereof."

Even where a manufacturer has attempted to limit the duration of an implied warranty, implied warranty rights are still good if the consumer bought the car in a state that does not allow *any* limitations on the duration of implied warranties. These states include Kansas, Maine, Maryland, Massachusetts, Vermont, and West Virginia, which have specifically modified their state statutes or laws so that implied warranties may not be limited to a specific time period. More states are modifying their laws in this manner, so the consumer should check with the state attorney general and a local consumer group or agency to see whether her state has joined the above list.

Limitations on Remedies

The manufacturers and dealers try to limit not only their warranty liabilities and obligations, but the consumer's rights to a remedy as well. A remedy is a legal tool a consumer can use for the redress of a complaint. One remedy usually limited by auto manufacturers is the right to incidental or consequential damages—such as towing or hotel bills when a car breaks down.

Once again, the unconscionability argument may be used to strike down the limitation on recovery of such damages just as it can be used against the limitation on implied warranties. Moreover, where the exclusive written warranty of repair "fails of its essential purpose," as discussed above, the consumer is entitled to all remedies available under law, including payment of consequential damages. Thus if a consumer has paid for tow bills and rental cars, while the manufacturer has failed to repair the car in 20 attempts, the consumer is clearly entitled to payment of these bills in addition to a refund of the purchase price or replacement of the lemon car.

The right to incidental or consequential damages may not be limited in those states that have all modified their laws to invalidate any limitation on a consumer's legal remedies. The laws of Kansas, Maine, Maryland, Massachusetts, Vermont, and West Virginia thus make it easier for consumers to exercise this right.

Attorney Fees

Perhaps the most important provision of the Magnuson-Moss Warranty Act is the award of attorney fees and costs where the consumer prevails. Traditionally, even consumers with the world's worst lemon have been reluctant to sue, because attorney fees could be more than the court award of damages. In other words, Why sue and win ten thousand dollars if you have to pay the lawyer $3,000 (leaving $7,000), when you could sell the lemon for $8,000?

The Magnuson-Moss remedy of attorney fees and costs drastically changes the traditional economics. The Act provides for recovery, at the court's discretion and unless the court thinks an award inappropriate, of attorney fees "based on actual time expended" and costs "reasonably incurred." Thus the court has wide discretion to decide how much, if anything, to award for attorney fees. The purpose of the remedy of recovery of attorney fees was to encourage private attorneys to accept warranty cases and thus to make enforcement of warranty obligations more practical for consumers. Moreover, the consumer may recover costs and expenses "reasonably incurred for or in connection with the commencement and prosecution" of the action. This language is drawn broadly to encompass virtually all reasonable expenses, including expert-witness fees, filing fees, stenographic costs, mileage, and even lost wages for plaintiffs. Almost without exception, all the Magnuson-Moss decisions examined to date have allowed successful plaintiffs to recover for attorney fees, as well as court costs and expenses. In some cases, courts have awarded sizable attorney fees.

An excellent example is a decision in 1981 in which the Levine family, from Columbia, Maryland, sued to revoke acceptance of a 1978 Ford Granada, which at 109 miles broke a valve, which fell into a cylinder and damaged the engine, cylinder head, connecting rod, and piston. By the time the case went through a jury trial and appeal upholding the revocation, the Levines got a full refund of the $7,830 purchase price, while their attorney got over $20,000 in fees for the work he put into the case over two years.

PRACTICAL TIPS FOR GETTING RID OF A LEMON

Lemon owners who want to get rid of their lemons can follow either of two general routes: One is to trade the car in and then sue the dealer and the manufacturer for damages arising out of the resale of the lemon. The other strategy is to cancel the ownership of the car, return it to the dealer or manufacturer, and sue for a refund or replacement.

Revocation of Acceptance

Revocation of acceptance or ownership is usually the key to getting a refund on or replacement of a lemon. The legal procedures for revocation of acceptance must be carefully followed. Ownership must be revoked within a reasonable time after the defect is discovered and the dealer has had a reasonable opportunity to repair the car.

To revoke ownership, the car and the keys should be delivered to the dealer, and the license plates removed. The car must be returned without "substantial change," so original equipment (factory- or dealer-installed) should not be removed from the car; e.g., the radio. (Normal wear and tear is no problem.) The dealer must be given something *in writing* at that time notifying her of the consumer's intention to revoke acceptance, listing the specific reasons why the car is being returned, and stating that the consumer is also canceling the insurance and registration. Note the odometer reading at this time. A substantial increase in mileage on the odometer is evidence that the dealer accepted the revocation of ownership—that she no longer considered the consumer to be the owner of the car. After returning the car, the consumer must confirm with the dealer *in writing* that she is revoking ownership of the car. Registered mail helps prove that such notice was given.

Some consumers have used revocation of acceptance successfully, without hiring an attorney. If the dealer or manufacturer is close to taking the lemon back, this device may help. However, if the dealer does not respond favorably, the consumer should tell her that she will be retaining a lawyer to pursue the complaint. Often, hiring an attorney and filing a lawsuit are necessary in order to revoke acceptance successfully (receive the return of the purchase price).

Withholding Payments

In some cases, it may be easier to withhold payments on the car, rather than revoke acceptance—for example, if the car is not a total lemon and probably can be repaired, but the dealer has been giving the consumer the runaround. Stopping payments may be a good incentive to get the dealer finally to repair the defects. It may help to take the car to an independent mechanic to verify that the defects can indeed be remedied and that the car is worth keeping. The dealer should be shown the independent mechanic's diagnosis before payments are stopped. This will bolster the case. The consumer should consult a lawyer before withholding payments. If the consumer does stop paying, the bank will probably *sue her* for the balance on the loan. Thus, the decision to stop paying should be made with a lawyer's advice. Stopping payments is a last resort; it is not something to be done every time a small problem occurs.

Where acceptance is revoked, payment may be withheld. If the car was financed through the dealer, the bank or finance company to which payments are being made should be contacted. They should be informed that the consumer has revoked ownership of the car and will not be making further payments. They must be told that the dealer is responsible for the note, since the car is back at the dealership. In some instances, the dealer will then take the loan back from the bank, leaving the dispute between the consumer and the dealer.

The consumer may not withhold payments if the loan was obtained *directly* at a lending institution, without the dealer's assistance. If acceptance is revoked, the lending institution must be informed, but payments on the car must continue to be made. In the first instance, where the car was financed through the dealer, the consumer is legally protected if the dealer or bank sues her for the balance. In the second case, where the loan was obtained *directly* at a bank or a credit union, the consumer is not legally protected if the bank or credit union sues for the balance.

FTC HOLDER-IN-DUE-COURSE RULE

Car loans have traditionally been governed by the "holder-in-due-course" legal doctrine, which effectively required a consumer to continue car payments on even the world's worst lemon. A new rule issued by the Federal Trade Commission (FTC) substantially improves the consumer's position by permitting her to prove that the car is a lemon. The original rule allowed a bank to repossess a car and collect on the balance of the loan after deducting the value of the car when a buyer stopped making payments because the car was defective. However, as of May 14, 1976, under the FTC regulation on the Preservation of Consumers' Claims and Defenses, if the bank sues to collect on the loan balance, the car buyer now has a "lemon" defense in court. And where the *dealer* arranges the loan for the consumer on a car that is a lemon, the FTC rule also protects the consumer who stops making payments. (This FTC rule is commonly called the "Holder-in-due-course rule.")

The FTC rule protecting the withholding of payments does not protect the consumer who got a loan *directly* from a bank or a credit union. It applies only to loans that fall into certain categories. These include cases in which the dealer refers buyers to a lender, or the dealer is affiliated with the lender, or creditor. Affiliation may be created by contract or business arrangement. The arrangement need not be formal in any legal sense, but it must be ongoing and clearly related to the dealer's sales and sales financing. Referral means that the dealer cooperates with a lender to channel consumers to that credit source on a continuing basis. Unlike an affiliation, a referral relationship arises from a pattern of cooperative activity between the dealer and the lender directly relating to the arranging of credit. The fact that a dealer suggests credit sources or provides information to her customers does not alone invoke the FTC rule.

NONLEGAL STRATEGIES

If nothing else works and a lawsuit is out of the question, the consumer can always take her car problem to the court of public opinion. Dealers fearing adverse publicity from selling a lemon are particularly apt to reconsider their previous firm stance of no relief. Although public protest is a nonlegal strategy, it is not illegal, but is firmly grounded in the individual's constitutional rights.

The right of consumers to tell the world about their lemons is rooted in the First Amendment of the U.S. Constitution and in most state constitutions. The First Amendment protects an individual or group's freedom of expression, or "free speech." By making their lemon problems known to the public, consumers occasionally receive replacement cars or refunds from embarrassed dealers.

But picketing and the use of lemon signs, like other tactics that have proven effective against business interests, are controversial ones. Businesses claim a competing right: the right not to be injured in the conduct of their business. Thus, dealers have occasionally invoked the authority of the courts and the police in attempts to halt its use. The courts are divided in upholding the right of consumers to use lemon signs and picket dealerships. The cases frequently turn on a minor point such as whether the picketers were on dealer property or interfering with consumers trying to enter the dealership.

Lemon owners have used many techniques in informing the public about their lemons. The most frequently used tactics include picketing and lemon signs, classified advertisements in newspapers, and flyers handed out to prospective customers at the dealership. A few local consumer groups specialize in picketing dealers. Many successful consumers and groups who have used this tactic have encouraged others with similar complaints to organize "lemoncades," lines of cars covered with lemon signs, driving slowly around the block where the uncooperative dealer is situated.

How to Picket and Otherwise Protest Within the Law

There are certain guidelines the consumer should follow to remain within the law. These will help her defend her actions if the dealer requests a court order prohibiting the signs, picketing, demonstrations, or other activity, or simply calls the police. First, the lemon owner should not picket or otherwise protest until she has tried to negotiate with the dealer or the manufacturer. Picket only when this has failed.

The purpose of the protest is twofold: to announce to the public that the consumer has been treated unfairly, and to settle her complaint. If the goal is to interfere with the dealer's business activity or put her out of business, the demonstration, picketing, or lemon signs can be legally enjoined, or stopped by court order. Thus, it is important to avoid statements that might be interpreted as attempting to coerce the dealer into a course of action or into paying the consumer money. Disparagement should be directed at the vehicle, rather than at the dealer personally.

The key to legal picketing is to be nonviolent, nonobstructive, and honest. It is advisable to notify the local police and news media ahead of time. Do not interfere with the operation of the dealership's day-to-day activities. Be careful not to block traffic in the street or to prevent people from entering the showroom. Flyers or leaflets may be distributed to explain and clarify the message on the signs and car. Above all, it is essential *not* to interfere with the free flow of customers. They should be allowed to come to the protester or the display.

The location of the picketing is as important as the purpose. Generally, it must take place on public property such as city sidewalks. If the protester pickets or parks her car with lemon signs on the dealer's property, she can be thrown off for trespass.

FURTHER READING

Before you buy a new or used car, check *Consumer Reports.*

The following publications are available from the Consumer Information Center, Pueblo, Colo. 81009:

Auto Service Contracts

The Backyard Mechanic, Vols. I and II.

The Car Book

Car Care and Service

Cost of Owning and Operating Automobiles and Vans

Credit Cards: Auto Repair Protection

Self-Service: Gas Up and Go?

Warranties: There Ought to be a Law . . .

5

Your Health and the Law

REBECCA J. COOK

Rebecca J. Cook is a recent graduate of Georgetown University Law Center. As a legal adviser to the International Planned Parenthood Federation and the Commonwealth Secretariat, her interests lie in international comparative health law. She has written many articles, particularly on abortion in the common-law world and on therapeutic-drug law. She is active on the boards of directors of organizations concerned with women's health: the Pathfinder Fund, International Projects Assistance Service, and the Association for Voluntary Sterilization.

You are challenged throughout your life to preserve your health. As a woman, you face medical problems unique to your sex. You face other problems that are of special concern because the incidence is greater among women; for example, tranquilizers are prescribed for women at a much higher rate than they are for men. You also face the health problems of the total population; for example, the four leading causes of death for American men and women are heart disease, cancer, stroke, and accidents.

Health problems of special importance to you as a woman have broadened to include those long considered to affect primarily men, such as alcohol abuse, smoking, and exposure to occupational hazards. Until recently, occupational health hazards affecting women have been largely unexplored except for their impact upon pregnancy. Some women have special physical and mental health needs; for example, those women who are subject to domestic violence and rape, and women who have no or limited access to health care.

The law can't prevent illness or cure disease, but it can affect your access to medical care and its costs. This chapter attempts to advise you, as a

I would like to express my appreciation to Mary Cherrico, Judy Mears, Ruth Roemer, and Margery W. Shaw for their extensive comments on a draft of this article. The views expressed here are, of course, mine alone.

woman, about some mechanisms that the law uses to regulate the delivery of health care and approval of therapeutic drugs and devices. It also identifies some legal problems that might be likely to affect you because you are a woman, and it makes suggestions as to how you might solve them. It advises you as to how you might go about deciding to pay for your health care and getting appropriate tax deductions. This chapter does not try to comment on the advantages and disadvantages of the American health care system but, rather, to advise you as to how best you can use the present system to your advantage in order to preserve your health. It is hoped that this general advice about some of your health law problems will enable you to seek further local advice on specific state health laws and policies so that you can get high quality care at a low cost.

YOUR RIGHTS AS A HEALTH CARE CONSUMER

The law offers you as a health care consumer three general protections. First, it entitles you to a reasonable standard of care. Second, it requires that you be fully informed about the proposed care so that you can knowingly and voluntarily consent to or refuse diagnostic tests or treatments that are offered. Further, the law requires that the health care you choose be delivered in such a way as to protect your privacy and the confidentiality of your health records.

These three requirements are generally found in state and federal statutory and case law and also in hospital bylaws or in a Patients' Bill of Rights (see p. 120) often adopted as operative guidelines by hospitals and health facilities. It is important for you to remember that you are entitled to these three basic protections in all kinds of health care you may receive. For example, if you are mentally ill and have the legal capacity to choose care in a mental hospital, you are entitled to reasonable care under the circumstances, not, for example, to be overdosed with drugs or just to be there. You are also entitled to be informed as to the treatment and to give your voluntary informed consent, or to refuse consent, to the care you have chosen, and to the confidentiality of the records on that care.

Reasonable Standard of Care

You are entitled to a reasonable standard of care. If you receive care that is substandard or negligently given under the circumstances, you can usually sue the health care provider or the facility for malpractice to remedy the wrong that was done to you. Your health care provider has a duty to provide reasonable care that a practitioner with the same or similar level training or qualifications would provide under the same or similar circumstances. The duty of a qualified practitioner is to make a careful diagnosis and give reasonable treatment accordingly, but the duty does not necessarily ensure a favorable healthy outcome. The duty arises out of a contract relationship between you to provide compensation to your health care provider, and for that provider to render reasonable care under the circumstances. For example, reasonable care under the circumstances does not include an unnecessary hysterectomy. Further, if the circumstances are an emergency situation in a hospital emergency room, that hospital must provide care. Whatever the circumstances, if that duty is breached by the provider in rendering substandard care and you were harmed by that breach, you are entitled to a remedy from the health facility or provider, usually in the form of money damages.

It is often difficult to prove what is reasonable care under the circumstances. It is usually done through expert testimony by other health care providers with the same or a similar level of training and qualification at a hearing as to what in fact was reasonable under the same or similar circumstances. Fear of malpractice suits permeates the entire health care system, increasing the cost of health care, and affecting how health care is given and even the provider-patient relationship itself. Malpractice suits can provide needed remedies for those subject to medical negligence. It is unclear whether malpractice is the best way to improve the standard of care or whether it is more effectively done, for instance, by putting greater obligations on the health care professions to set and enforce higher professional standards.

Informed Consent

The informed consent doctrine requires that you be informed about the treatment and if you choose the treatment that you voluntarily give your consent to the treatment before it is provided. The doctrine grew out of the fear of committing a battery for an "unauthorized" (i.e., unconsented-to) touching. To knowingly and voluntarily give your consent, you have to be informed as to:

• *the purpose of the treatment:* for example, one purpose of a hysterectomy is to reduce the risk of uterine or cervical cancer;

• *the benefits of the treatment:* for example, a benefit of a hysterectomy may be the decreased risk of uterine or cervical cancer;

• *the known consequences:* for example, one known consequence of a hysterectomy is removal of the ovaries and the uterus, which results in sterility, or the inability to have children;

• *the possible risks:* for example, possible risks of a hysterectomy are the risks associated with general surgery such as postoperative infection;

    • *the mode of treatment:* for example, a hysterectomy requires major surgery;

    • *alternatives to the treatment if they exist:* for example, a noninvasive alternative to hysterectomy might be chemotherapy, depending on the nature and extent of the cancer;

    • *possible consequences of refusal:* for example, a possible increased risk of death from cancer from refusing a hysterectomy.

By voluntarily giving your informed consent, you are authorizing that the treatment be carried out. This is usually done by putting your signature on a voluntary informed consent form. It is important to remember that you may refuse treatment after being informed of the possible risks and benefits involved. If you do, the law considers that you have decided to take the risks involved in forgoing treatment.

Privacy and Confidentiality

You have a right of privacy in health care matters. Your right of privacy entitles you to privacy of your person and confidentiality of your health records and communications with health care providers. Your right of privacy encompasses several constitutional principles. Perhaps the most basic is the principle that prohibits the search of your house or your person without good cause. This prohibition against unwarranted searches thus implies a right of privacy concerning your body and your property. Therefore, in the health care context, intrusions of your person are permitted only in so far as they are necessary for proper diagnosis and treatment and done with your knowledge and consent.

Your privacy right also requires that your relationship with your health care provider be confidential. The provider may not disclose information on your condition to anyone who is not involved in your care, because such a disclosure would be a breach of your privacy. The law requires respect for your privacy by requiring that your relationship with your health care provider be kept confidential. If this relationship is not kept confidential, you might be reluctant to disclose information needed for proper treatment.

This privacy right requires, for example, that your hospital, health-insurance, and venereal-disease records be kept confidential. Disclosure of information about your medical condition may only be done according to your health care contract or, for instance, state public reporting statutes. Obviously, in order for your health insurance company to reimburse you for your health care costs, they need to know the medical reasons for which you sought that care. Health care providers and health insurance companies may not make disclosures contrary to any agreement you have made with them. State public reporting statutes require that health care providers report certain health conditions, particularly contagious diseases, to public authorities. These statutes are based on the state's police power to preserve public health and as a result take precedence over your privacy right in keeping your specified health conditions confidential.

Your remedy for unauthorized disclosure of information on your health condition may be a lawsuit for negligence or for an infringement upon your constitutional right of privacy, against the health provider, health facility, or health insurer. If you are successful in your suit, you could be entitled to money damages to remedy the wrong that was done to you.

YOUR SPECIFIC HEALTH NEEDS

Adolescent Health

Traditionally, women, usually those under 18 years of age, were considered by the law to be incapable of making medical decisions for themselves. As a result, the law required that parents consent to the care of their child. There were always some exceptions to this rule, and in recent years this rule has gradually been broadened to provide for additional exceptions allowing minors to consent. These legal changes can be particularly important for adolescent girls in enabling them to have access to needed health care. The exceptions include minors' rights to consent to their own medical care:

1. In emergency situations.
2. Where they are emancipated; for example, minors who are married, have served in the military, or live apart from their parents or are self-supporting.
3. Where an emancipated minors' statute has been passed allowing an emancipated minor, as defined by the law, to consent to her own medical care related to contraception, abortion, prenatal care, and delivery.
4. Where they are mature; that is, minors who are mature enough to understand the nature and the risks of a procedure and reach an informed consent about whether to undergo treatment.

A minor's rights to consent to her own health care vary from state to state. Some states have enacted statutes specifically dealing with medical care for minors. Generally either such statutes permit certain minors to consent to all kinds of health care or they specify the kinds of care to which minors may consent, such as venereal disease, contraception, abortion, prenatal care, and delivery.

Reproductive Health

Your constitutional right of privacy entitles you to voluntarily choose the means necessary to regulate your own fertility, whether it be contraception, voluntary sterilization, or abortion. As a result, neither state legislatures nor

6

the federal Congress may pass laws that deny you or unjustifiably intrude upon that right. They may not, for example, deny you access to contraceptives, prevent knowing and consenting adults from choosing or rejecting voluntary sterilization, prevent minority-age women from deciding whether or not to have an abortion, or allow a woman's spouse or partner to prevent, or require that she have, an abortion or a voluntary sterilization.

The Supreme Court in the landmark decision of *Roe* v. *Wade* (1973) extended the concept of the right of privacy derived from the due-process and the equal-protection clauses of the Constitution, to prevent state and federal government from infringing upon the woman's choice as to whether or not to have an abortion. Your decision to have an abortion, however, is not absolute. The 1973 decision outlined the conditions under which you may have an abortion. It depends on the stage of your pregnancy. Obviously, if you have decided to have an abortion it is best to have it as soon as possible, as it becomes legally more difficult to have an abortion as your pregnancy progresses. For the first three months of pregnancy, the first trimester, you, together with your doctor, may decide whether or not to have an abortion. For approximately the fourth, fifth, and sixth months of pregnancy, the second trimester, the state may regulate where and how the abortion is to be done, provided it is reasonably related to maternal health. For example, a state may pass legislation requiring that second-trimester abortions be done in a place where appropriate resources such as blood necessary for a transfusion are available. After the fetus reaches the stage of viability, the state may proscribe abortion except when it is necessary for the preservation of the life and health of the pregnant woman. The fetus becomes viable when it is able to survive outside the womb of the mother. The court reasoned that once the fetus becomes viable, the state has an interest in the potentiality of life and therefore could proscribe abortion except where it is necessary for the preservation of the life and health of the woman.

The U.S. Congress can not deny eligible women federal Medicaid funds for abortions necessary to save their lives. While the U.S. Congress may not eliminate your right of privacy, it has been able to limit the exercise of that right by, for example, denying federal Medicaid funds to eligible women for medically necessary or therapeutic abortions. This does not mean that you are necessarily denied state Medicaid funds for medically necessary abortions or even elective nontherapeutic abortions (see Medicaid section, p. 115 below).

Maternal Health

Maternal health care has a long history of regulation, some would argue overregulation. The United States Supreme Court, in *Muller* v. *Oregon* (1908), upheld an Oregon law limiting the numbers of hours women might work. One of the reasons the court used for upholding this protective labor legislation was the need to protect the health of expectant mothers. As the century progressed, working conditions improved and the hours declined for all workers, not just women. At the same time, it became increasingly apparent that antiquated protective labor laws were a basis for excluding women from the workplace or discharging pregnant women. Among the earliest sex-discrimination decisions under Title VII of the Civil Rights Act were those invalidating special state laws that purportedly protected women.

Today, however, you might be subject to policies which either limit your employment during pregnancy for fetal health reasons or eliminate your employment altogether to protect your reproductive capabilities. For example, you might not be eligible for a job in a chemical company or as an X-ray specialist. However, scientific evidence is now demonstrating that such exposure that is damaging to your reproductive capacity and to the fetus is probably equally damaging to the male reproductive system and, through the sperm, to the fetus. As a result, protective policies based on occupational exposure that affect only female employees may be subject to sex-discrimination challenges. They might discriminate against women's employment and against men's health. On the other hand, there might be legitimate biological differences that must be recognized by employers with respect to occupational hazards, but they should not be used as an excuse or a pretext to deny you, as a woman, your employment.

Where legitimate biological differences do not exist, employment policies might better be designed in a gender-neutral fashion. The policies, perhaps best called parental protection policies as opposed to maternal protection policies, should aim to protect both men and women by limiting the occupational exposure of both sexes. Where there are legitimate biological differences and where employment policies are accordingly designed, of course no legal challenges are possible. Where employment policies are not designed in a gender-neutral way and where legitimate biological differences do not exist, they are subject to sex-discrimination challenges. Do seek local advice to ensure that your employment policies are designed to accommodate legitimate biological differences and not just a pretext to deny women as a class their employment.

Maternity Care: Maternity care also has a long history of regulation, some would argue overregulation. At one time deliveries by midwives were common, and then they were prohibited. More recently, the laws governing midwifery licensing and scope of practice are changing to allow maternity care of healthy expectant mothers by certified nurse-midwives. This approach leaves more specialized care of high-risk women to obstetricians. Hospital regulations are also slowly changing to grant admitting privileges to certified nurse-midwives.

The reasons for these changes are many. The high and increasing cost of obstetrical care has forced health policy makers and health consumers to look at alternative, less expensive approaches. One such approach is some deregulation of the licensing and scope-of-practice laws to enable certified nurse-midwives to provide maternity care. This will increase the supply and in theory decrease the price. This approach is based on antitrust principles: If one group or type of health professionals has a monopoly, theoretically members of this group can set the price of health care higher than if two or more groups of professionals compete to provide the care. The argument is that obstetricians should not have a monopoly on the delivery of maternity care when certified nurse-midwives are equally qualified to provide many of the components of the care provided by obstetricians.

Another reason for the demand for nurse-midwife care could be that the obstetrical/gynecological profession is predominantly male, and the nurse/midwifery profession is almost exclusively female. This male predominance in the obstetrical/gynecological profession is gradually changing. But, for the present at least, if you want female maternity care, by and large you will have to get it from certified nurse-midwives. Nurse-midwifery laws and hospital admitting privileges vary from state to state and from hospital to hospital, respectively. As a result, if you want such care, you need to investigate the state laws and local hospital policies on certified nurse-midwives.

Therapeutic Drug and Device Regulation

Women are particularly affected by laws regulating the approval of therapeutic drugs and devices, in part because of women's contraceptive and reproductive-health needs. Recent history provides many examples of successes and failures of those laws whose objectives are to provide the public safe and effective drugs and devices for the purposes for which they are recommended. Contraceptive pills were welcomed by many as an improvement to the traditional contraceptive methods of withdrawal and diaphragms. Diethylstilbestrol (DES) was marketed as an antimiscarriage drug. When reports showed that it was ineffective for this purpose and also showed its connection with a rare form of cancer in exposed mothers and with precancerous conditions in daughters of exposed mothers, it was recalled from the market. Depo Provera, used among other purposes as a three-month injectible contraceptive, is another highly controversial drug, whose approval has been advocated and opposed at varying times by varying groups for varying reasons. There are other examples and no doubt will be other therapeutic drugs whose status will cause controversies.

In assessing the merits and demerits of such controversies to determine the value of therapeutic drugs and devices for your own purposes, it is important for you to understand the basic requirements for approval of the federal Food, Drug and Cosmetic Act (FDCA). The Food and Drug Administration's main enabling act, FDCA, was passed in 1938, with antecedents dating from 1906. Important amendments to the 1938 Act occurred in 1962, when premarket approval of drugs was required and the FDA was authorized to require proof of effectiveness for all "new drugs," and in 1976 when the FDA enlarged its authority to regulate medical devices.

The general factors that contribute to the decision to approve a new drug for marketing are summarized in the Schmidt equation:

authority to obtain information + needed for approval and marketing	authority to obtain information available after + approval and to require post-marketing surveillance	authority to control use in accordance with + labeling and provisional release	authority to withdraw approval = a constant. and recall a product

The FDA has a great deal of authority to require data for market approval but has disproportionately less authority to require post-marketing surveillance, provisional release, and recall authority. As a result, the FDA is cautious in approving drugs, in part because the FDCA doesn't adequately enable the FDA to require useful postmarketing surveillance, to enable provisional release in accordance with certain labels, or to recall drugs once new adverse information has become available.

Before a "new drug" or certain devices can be marketed, it has to be generally recognized by scientific experts as safe and effective. Since the use of a drug can never be absolutely safe, the decision to allow a new drug on the market involves a judgment that its potential benefit outweighs its potential risk. Such a judgment includes decisions based on questions of scientific fact and decisions based on scientific policy. Judgments based on science cannot deviate from scientific fact. For example, chemists seldom disagree about the scientific structure of a compound once it has undergone sufficient chemical analysis. Here the scientist is the fact finder.

Resolution of science policy questions, on the other hand, requires the regulator to decide scientific questions based on policy grounds that the scientist has not been able to resolve on grounds of scientific fact. An example of a science policy question is the extrapolation of carcinogenic effects at high dose levels to low dose levels. In these cases scientists can phrase the question in scientific terms and can even agree on an experiment to resolve it. However, scientists could never as a practical matter expose enough rats at low dosages, so they expose them at high dosages and extrapolate those findings to low dosages. Since it has not been proved that dose and response are linear, there has been much controversy about the validity of low-dose estimates.

Regulators cannot postpone their decisions indefinitely until definitive data are available. As a result, they have to make decisions based on inferences from the scientific data that are sometimes insufficient and/or subject to varying scientific interpretations. Drug regulators turn to policy to guide them in determining (1) whether to proceed, knowing the data are insufficient or uncertain, and (2) if the decision is to proceed, what kinds of inferences should be drawn from such data. The decision to proceed is dictated in part by estimates of the degree and probability of benefits and risks. One group might advocate approval of a therapeutic drug in the face of specific scientific uncertainties because of their special health needs, while another group might oppose approval because of what they perceive as unacceptable risks. FDA was instituted to find an acceptable balance between risks and benefits, which by necessity requires the resolution of questions of both scientific fact and scientific policy.

PAYING FOR YOUR HEALTH CARE

There are a variety of payment mechanisms available to you, depending on your circumstances, to help you pay for your health care (see chart p. 119). There are prepaid medical plans and health insurance policies. In a prepaid plan, you pay a fixed sum for a specified period, which entitles you to care unrelated to the amount of service you receive in that period. In a health insurance policy, you pay an annual or a monthly premium, which entitles you to reimbursement for all or part of specified health care costs that you obtain on a fee-for-service basis during that time. Reimbursement may be either to the consumer or to the provider. Further, oftentimes health insurance policies require that you pay deductibles or a certain portion of the cost for certain kinds of health care.

You may deduct from your federal income taxes a portion of your payments for those health care costs for which you aren't reimbursed or that aren't covered by your prepaid plan. You may also deduct a certain amount of your health insurance premiums or your fixed monthly payments.

When you choose a plan or policy, your rights and responsibilities under it are usually governed by a contract. You are contracting to pay money for a service under a plan, or reimbursement under a policy. As a result, the relationship with the insurance company can become an adversarial one for you as the insured. If that contract is breached by, for example, your health insurer canceling the policy contrary to the terms of the contract, your remedy is to sue for a breach of contract. Therefore it is important to read the contract carefully before you sign it, to determine the extent of your rights and responsibilities and what remedies either you or your insurer has if either one of you breaches that contract.

If you are on active military duty, you and your dependents get free health care. There are only a few such cases where the government provides health care directly free of charge. This country does not have a national health service similar to that of the United Kingdom. There the government provides health care directly to the consumer free of charge, in somewhat the same way that our government provides public education. For the time being at least, the U.S. Congress has failed to recognize the advantages of extending the insurance principle that we use for spreading risks in many other fields to health care costs. Individual states, however, might accord high constitutional priority to the preservation of health or even embrace a fundamental right to health and as a result be more accommodating in the public provision of health care and/or health insurance.

Prepaid Medical Plans

Prepaid medical plans offer health care services for a fixed sum either on a monthly, a quarterly, or an annual basis. Prepaid plans are also called group provider plans or health maintenance plans. Prepaid plans are available directly to the public in virtually all parts of the country. In some areas one might have a choice among prepaid plans. Employers often offer a prepaid medical plan as one of several types of health care payment or reimbursement plan. The Kaiser Plan is an example of a prepaid medical plan.

As was explained, fixed payments are unrelated to the amount of services provided in a particular month. They are often less than other forms of payment mechanism. This is due largely to the emphasis of most prepaid plans on preventative care; ambulatory service; effective use of nurse practitioners, certified nurse-midwives, and other, allied health personnel; and particularly, prudent use of costly hospitalization. Some consumers prefer prepayment because it is easier to budget for a fixed sum, rather than worry about the cost of a visit to the doctor if a medical problem arises. Studies have shown that illnesses are seen earlier and treated more effectively if payment is not an issue for each visit. On the other hand, some consumers do not choose prepaid plans, because of complaints about long waits and difficulty of seeing the health professional of one's choice.

Most prepaid plans are federally qualified. Federal qualification requires that such plans offer comprehensive benefits. These required benefits include basic hospital care, outpatient care, mental health care, alcoholism care, maternity care, reproductive health care, and laboratory and X-ray coverage. Within this comprehensive benefit framework, the level of benefits differs from plan to plan. It can also differ within one plan, depending on how extensive the coverage is. The copayments may vary by benefits and by plan. For example, you may be required to pay 15 percent of your X-ray costs while you pay 25 percent of your maternity-care costs.

As a result of this federal qualification, prepaid plans usually offer more-comprehensive benefits at a lower price than reimbursement plans. Further, they usually offer "one stop shopping," so that all one's medical care needs are met in one facility from a single group of providers. As a result, theoretically, a consumer isn't at risk for finding or getting other needed specialists.

In choosing whether and which prepaid plan to join, you will want to consider some of the following issues:

• What benefits does the plan cover? To what extent? (See Chart, p. 119, to estimate the extent and cost of coverage of your health care needs of alternative prepaid plans available to you.)

• How much are the fixed payments? What is the period of payment; monthly, quarterly, or annually?

• How much are the copayments for those benefits you will most likely require?

• Are the particular health facilities you need situated in a place convenient to you? Are they in one central facility or in many facilities in various locations?

• If you are married and both spouses are covered under either a prepaid plan or a health insurance policy, what are the provisions of this particular plan in determining which spouse's plan pays? For example, does this plan use a coordination-of-benefits principle that determines which spouse's plan or policy pays?

• What are the rules for out-of-plan services in, for example, emergency situations?

Prepaid medical plans are here to stay, but the government is phasing out its grant and loan programs for such plans. As a result, the cost to the consumer will probably increase, but the overall prepayment framework will not change.

Health Insurance Policies

Health insurance policies reimburse you for a portion or all of certain kinds of health services. These reimbursement policies are also called indemnity policies. They indemnify you against the risk of illness or disease somewhat as an insurance agency indemnifies you against the risk of your house burning down. Blue Cross/Blue Shield is an example of a health insurance policy.

Health insurance policies are offered in a variety of ways. For example, such policies are offered directly to the public or indirectly through your school, your work, your union, your professional organization, and often through organizations in which you volunteer. Group health insurance is generally cheaper than individual health insurance. Although married women can obtain single-person insurance coverage, it is cheaper for all members of a family with children to be covered as dependants of one employed spouse under work-based policies. Those women who are covered often find it necessary to supplement basic group coverage with individual coverage. If women covered under their husbands' policies divorce or are widowed, they may lose their coverage. If they do not lose their coverage, continuation of coverage usually entails higher charges for women than men in the same situation.

Health insurers will reimburse the costs of specified health care as agreed in a specific health insurance policy. The majority of health insurance policies cover only curative care provided by physicians. Even with curative care, coverage may vary. For instance, some health insurance policies refuse to pay for breast reconstruction after a mastectomy unless you provide them with a psychiatrist's letter saying it is essential. These policies generally do not cover preventive care. If you choose a policy that excludes preventive care, your cost of routine breast and cervical cancer screening and of reproductive health care will probably not be covered.

The majority of health insurers will not cover services provided by nurse practitioners and certified nurse-midwives. However, coverage of such providers varies from state to state. For example, Maryland requires health insurance to provide direct reimbursement to nurse practitioners. As the cost of physician care increases and as there are more nurse practitioners and certified nurse-midwives working on a fee-for-service basis in private practice, health insurance reimbursement for their services will become an increasingly significant issue.

Health insurance can raise questions of sex discrimination; for example, with respect to the kinds of benefits covered and in some cases the premiums charged. Health insurance prices for women can be considerably higher than for men, particularly for women in their thirties and forties. Some health insurance companies, albeit to a decreasing extent, develop their prices on sex-based data as opposed to health-based data. In so doing, the better health risks, for example fit women, subsidize the poorer health risks, for example overweight women. Such policies can be subject to sex-discrimination challenges because the grouping of risks is based on sex and not health. Other companies develop their health insurance prices based on health risks of both men and women. The grouping is based on health criteria such as weight and previous medical history. This grouping is fairer, because it relates directly to your healthiness, which is the basis for health insurance. Such health insurance policies that group both men and women on their degree of healthiness are fairer and don't require the fit woman to subsidize the unfit woman, but rather, allow you a premium based on your health irrespective of your sex. Turning to health insurance coverage for pregnancy, the U.S. Supreme Court decision in *Gilbert* v. *General Electric*

(1978) stated that an employer did not have to treat pregnancy as "other illnesses," since women were not thereby denied a benefit given to men. However the U.S. Congress reversed this decision in 1979 by the Pregnancy Discrimination Act. That 1979 Act requires that insurance policies that compensate employees for time missed due to illness or disability must compensate employees for time missed due to childbirth. Where maternity benefits are not required by the 1979 Act, they are optional. When they are offered, they usually require higher premiums. Women have to be enrolled in most health insurance policies for at least ten months, before they are entitled to maternity benefits. Reproductive health services account for a large proportion of women's greater use of health services. This may result in charging women higher premiums, a consideration that could discourage some companies from hiring women.

In choosing whether and which health insurance plan to join, you will want to consider some of the following issues:

• What benefits do the policies cover? To what extent? (see Chart p. 119 to determine the benefits a plan that you might join covers)

• What are the premium rates; that is, those amounts you have to pay to be part of the plan? Are the rates based on sex-based data or health-based data? What is the period of payment, monthly, quarterly, or annually?

• What are the deductibles; that is, those amounts you have to pay before coverage begins?

• What are the copayments; that is, your share of the cost of specified care? For example, you might have to pay 50 percent of your psychiatric care while the insurance policy pays 50 percent.

• What are the general rules for renewing your policy and the specific rules if you divorce or are widowed?

• What are the general rules for eligibility for health care providers? Are there any specific rules that govern the eligibility of your particular health care provider? For example, is your physician, nurse practitioner, or certified nurse-midwife eligible for reimbursement under this policy?

Does your health care provider, whether physician, nurse practitioner, or nurse-midwife, participate in the particular health insurance policy you are considering joining? Health insurance policies usually cover only participating physicians, according to a fixed schedule of allowances. If they are not participating, your health insurance policy might not cover them or will cover them only up to a specified amount, leaving you to pay the remainder, which may be a very high amount.

In situations in which you have a choice between health insurance policies, first establish what your health care needs are. Then determine which insurance policy best meets those needs at the lowest cost. For example, if you have dental problems that require continuing care, does a particular plan cover dental care? Usually dental care is covered under group plans, not individual plans. If it is not covered under any plan, investigate other health insurance policies that might. Also investigate dental services in your area. Frequently dental schools offer high quality dental care to the community at low prices. Using dental school services might cost you less than paying the additional premium to join a health insurance policy with dental care coverage.

If you are young and healthy, you might want a health insurance policy that is primarily a bolster against catastrophic illnesses or accidents. If you are older and you are advised that home care or hospitalization is reasonably foreseeable, you might want a health insurance policy that assures you home care and provides coverage for more hospital days and augments your coverage generally.

Having established your health needs and estimated the alternative costs of coverage of various health insurance policies, you are ready to sign a health insurance policy that best meets your health needs.

Medicaid

Medicaid is a government payment program established in 1965 to provide a source of payment for medical care for certain groups of people who could not pay for such care themselves. The federal government pays a percentage of the costs of Medicaid, and the state pays the remaining percentage. This federal/state cost sharing differs from state to state and depends in part on the arrangement each state has with the federal government.

Generally, those who are eligible for Medicaid are those people who are in the basic federal welfare categories. You are eligible for Medicaid if you receive money from, for example, the following welfare programs: Aid to Families with Dependent Children, aid to the aged, aid to the blind, or aid to the permanently and totally disabled, that is persons receiving supplemental security income. The law also permits states to enroll individuals who are "medically needy." Further, the law generally defines the "medically needy" as those people whose incomes are large enough to cover their daily living expenses but not large enough to cover their medical care as well. In addition, some states, for instance California, give exclusive coverage to medically indigent adults, in other words those that are poor but are not in any of the federal categories and therefore receive no federal contributions. Rules vary from state to state and keep changing for your eligibility, the benefits to which you are entitled, or your charges for specific services. As a result, it is best for you to discuss your eligibility for Medicaid with your own health care provider or a local Medicaid benefit representative.

Generally, Medicaid will reimburse the health provider for some of your medical expenses including essential drugs. Levels of payment and the services covered vary from state to state. Generally, Medicaid pays for medically necessary inpatient hospital care. A state may limit the number of days of hospital care that it will pay for under Medicaid. Medicaid usually pays for outpatient care. Outpatient care coverage also differs from state to state. Medicaid usually pays for the laboratory and X-ray services needed either on an inpatient or an outpatient basis. States may also provide other services, including dental care and physical therapy. Medicaid usually covers licensed nursing home care if skilled nursing is required, but not custodial care. In addition, every state that participates in Medicaid has a program to provide family planning services, including voluntary sterilization to Medicaid beneficiaries.

The U.S. Congress does not allow federal Medicaid funds to pay for abortions that aren't necessary to save the life of the woman. Whether a state will allow state Medicaid funds, as opposed to federal funds, to pay for therapeutic or nontherapeutic abortions varies from state to state. The New Jersey Supreme Court, for example, held that the equal protection clause of its state constitution required publicly funded abortions necessary to preserve the woman's life or health. The California and Massachusetts high courts, relying on their respective constitutions, have recognized a right to state-provided abortions, including elective abortions. As a result of these differing state holdings, it is important for you to seek local advice as to whether your state's constitution would also require public payment for therapeutic or elective abortions for women eligible for Medicaid.

Medicaid does not pay for care provided by all health care professionals. Medicaid will generally pay for physician and nurse-midwifery care. Medicaid will also make direct payments to nurse practitioners for their services.

If you apply for or receive Medicaid and then are denied it, you are entitled to a fair hearing and an explanation of the reason for the denial. Further if you, as a Medicaid recipient, have a complaint about the care you are receiving or about a health care provider you are entitled to an explanation about the care or the provider. Most states don't have specified procedures for asking for a fair hearing or filing a complaint about the care or a health care provider. A letter to the state department of health should be sufficient.

Medicare

Medicare is the nation's public health insurance program for the elderly and disabled. If you are 65 or older and eligible for Social Security or railroad retirement benefits, you are entitled to Medicare. Persons of any age on renal transplant or dialysis for kidney problems are entitled to Medicare. Further, if you have received Social Security for an extended period you might also be entitled to Medicare. However, these rules keep changing, so it is best for you to discuss your eligibility for Medicare with your own health care provider or a local Medicare benefit representative. Medicare is a health insurance reimbursement policy. The payment mechanism is similar to private health insurance. It reimburses you or your health care provider for some of your health care costs.

Medicare has two parts: Part A, hospitalization coverage, which all eligible beneficiaries get automatically, and Part B, medical and physician coverage, which is optional with each beneficiary. You get it only if you sign up for it and pay for it.

PART A

Medicare will reimburse for part of the cost of inpatient hospital services for up to a certain number of days and additional home care also up to a certain number of days. Medicare will pay for specified hospital services. Since the nature and extent of these services change, you should discuss specifics with your health care provider or local Medicare benefit representative. Medicare requires that you pay deductibles for each period of care. Further, copayments are required. They vary depending on the kind and extent of care.

PART B

Part B of Medicare is an insurance program that helps pay for inpatient physician services and some outpatient services. It is an optional program. You pay to join it and you may cancel at any time. The nature and extent of coverage changes, so, again, discuss the specifics with your health care provider or Medicare benefit representative. Generally speaking, Part B will help you pay for medical and surgical services provided by a doctor of medicine or of osteopathy, the services of a podiatrist, and dental surgery. It will also usually pay for services ordinarily furnished in a doctor's office. Part B will also usually help you pay for some outpatient services, including laboratory tests, X rays, emergency room services, and medical supplies. Part B will also help pay for a visiting part-time nurse in the home.

Part B will not pay for ordinary routine services such as dental services, routine physical checkups, eye and ear examinations, or immunizations. Further, it will not pay for certain kinds of health practitioners such as chiropractors and nurse practitioners.

Military Health Care

The government provides health care directly to certain individuals free of charge. For example, if you are on active military duty, you and your dependents will get health care free of charge. If you have retired from the military, you are entitled to reimbursement for your health care costs through a program called Civilian Health and Medical Program for the

Uniformed Service retirees and their dependents (CHAMPUS). This is a health insurance program whose payment mechanism is similar to Medicare. It allows you to use fee-for-service providers and then get reimbursed for those costs through CHAMPUS. Health care providers, including eligible doctors and nurse practitioners, may also obtain reimbursement for the care they provide you if you do not choose to get reimbursement yourself.

Tax Deductions

You, as a taxpayer, can get limited federal income tax deductions for your medical care costs and those of your dependents that aren't reimbursable or provided under a prepaid plan. You can also be sure that the tax law will keep changing and that the health care expenses you may deduct will also keep changing. A new tax law, passed in 1982, makes it more expensive to be sick. Under prior law, you subtracted 3 percent of your adjusted gross income (AGI) from your medical expenses to get your tax-deductible expenses. Now the nondeductible floor has been raised, requiring you to subtract 5 percent of your AGI, making your tax-deductible medical expenses less under the 1982 law.

Those expenses that qualify are payments you make to health care providers for diagnosis and treatment, costs of prescription drugs and insulin, and costs of transportation to and from the health facility. You may total the amount spent for yourself, your dependents, and your spouse if you file a joint return. You may deduct only those costs you pay and that are not reimbursable. For example, your copayment is deductible, but not the insurer's copayments. Further, those medical insurance premiums paid by your employer are not deductible, but they are not included in your taxable income.

Your medical expenses, including prescription drugs and insulin, are deductible as part of the total medical expenses that exceed 5 percent of your AGI. An example might help explain these deductions:

Assume your adjusted gross income (AGI) is $20,000 and you pay $280 for medical insurance premiums, $2,500 for doctor and hospital expenses (in excess of insurance recoveries) and $500 for prescription drugs. The amount deductible is computed as follows:

Prescription drugs	$500
Nonreimbursable medical expenses	2,500
Medical insurance premiums	280
Total	$3,280
Less 5% of AGI of $20,000	−1,000
Total deductible medical expenses	$2,280

YOUR HEALTH CARE NEEDS
A Chart to Check Your Coverage

Health Care Needs	Your Health Plan or Policy			
(Add your specific needs to this list.)	Prepaid Plans	Health Insurance Policies	Medicaid Medicare CHAMPUS	Tax Deductions

Hospital Benefits
(days covered are important here)
   For example:
   General nursing service
   Intravenous solutions and injections				

Surgical Benefits
(limitation on coverage is important here)
   For example:
   Hysterectomy
   Breast cancer and
   reconstruction surgery				

Major Medical Benefits
(generally outpatient care; deductibles and copayments are important here)
   For example:
   Psychiatric care
   Preventive health
     routine check-ups
     cancer screening (uterine)
     reproductive health
       contraceptive
       voluntary sterilization
       abortion
Home care
(important for older women)				

Maternity Benefits
(waiting periods, deductibles and copayments are important here)
   For example:
   Genetic counseling and
   amniocentesis
   (important to determine at what age
   it is available)
   Caesarean section delivery				

Drugs and Medical Supplies				

YOUR RESPONSIBILITY FOR YOUR HEALTH

The law accords you rights within the health care system, but along with rights come responsibilities. Traditionally, health care services have focused on treatment of disease. More recently, health care services have begun to concentrate on the prevention of illness and promotion of health. This approach concentrates more on developing your skills for proper care. Much of your general healthiness is your own responsibility; for example, a varied diet, appropriate exercise, abstinence from cigarettes, moderate alcohol consumption, and breast self-examination. As the health care system moves away from curative treatment of diseases in a paternalistic fashion, toward educating you as to disease prevention and health promotion, you are increasingly responsible for your own health care and for determining how best to meet your own health care needs.

A MODEL PATIENTS' BILL OF RIGHTS

Preamble: As you enter this health care facility, it is our duty to remind you that your health care is a cooperative effort between you as a patient and the doctors and hospital staff. During your stay, a patients' rights advocate will be available to you. The duty of the advocate is to assist you in all the decisions you must make and in all situations in which your health and welfare are at stake. The advocate's first responsibility is to help you understand the role of all who will be working with you, and to help you understand what your rights as a patient are. Your advocate can be reached at any time of the day by dialing _____. The following is a list of your rights as a patient. Your advocate's duty is to see to it that you are afforded these rights. You should call your advocate whenever you have any questions or concerns about any of these rights.

   1. The patient has a legal right to informed participation in all decisions involving his/her health care program.

From *The Rights of Doctors, Nurses, and Allied Health Professionals,* by George J. Annas, Leonard H. Clantz, and Barbara F. Katz. Reprinted by permission of the American Civil Liberties Union.

2.   We recognize the right of all potential patients to know what research and experimental protocols are being used in our facility and what alternatives are available in the community.

3.   The patient has a legal right to privacy regarding the source of payment for treatment and care. This right includes access to the highest degree of care without regard to the source of payment for that treatment and care.

4.   We recognize the right of a potential patient to complete and accurate information concerning medical care and procedures.

5.   The patient has a legal right to prompt attention, especially in an emergency situation.

6.   The patient has a legal right to a clear, concise explanation in layperson's terms of all proposed procedures, including the possibilities of any risk of mortality or serious side effects, problems related to recuperation, and probability of success, and will not be subjected to any procedure without his/her voluntary, competent and understanding consent. The specifics of such consent shall be set out in a written consent form, signed by the patient.

7.   The patient has a legal right to a clear, complete, and accurate evaluation of his/her condition and prognosis without treatment before being asked to consent to any test or procedure.

8.   We recognize the right of the patient to know the identity and professional status of all those providing service. All personnel have been instructed to introduce themselves, state their status, and explain their roles in the health care of the patient. Part of this right is the right of the patient to know the identity of the physician responsible for his/her care.

9.   We recognize the right of any patient who does not speak English to have access to an interpreter.

10.   The patient has a right to all the information contained in his/her medical record while in the health care facility, and to examine the record on request.

11.   We recognize the right of a patient to discuss his/her condition with a consultant specialist, at the patient's request and expense.

12.   The patient has a legal right not to have any test or procedure, designed for educational purposes rather than his/her direct personal benefit, performed on him/her.

13.   The patient has a legal right to refuse any particular drug, test, procedure, or treatment.

14.   The patient has a legal right to privacy of both person and information with respect to: the hospital staff, other doctors, residents, interns and medical students, researchers, nurses, other hospital personnel, and other patients.

15. We recognize the patient's right of access to people outside the health care facility by means of visitors and the telephone. Parents may stay with their children and relatives with terminally ill patients 24 hours a day.

16. The patient has a legal right to leave the health care facility regardless of his/her physical condition or financial status, although the patient may be requested to sign a release stating that he/she is leaving against the medical judgment of his/her doctor or the hospital.

17. The patient has a right not to be transferred to another facility unless he/she has received a complete explanation of the desirability and need for the transfer, the other facility has accepted the patient for transfer, and the patient has agreed to transfer. If the patient does not agree to transfer, the patient has the right to a consultant's opinion on the desirability of transfer.

18. A patient has a right to be notified of his/her impending discharge at least one day before it is accomplished, to insist on a consultation by an expert on the desirability of discharge, and to have a person of the patient's choice notified in advance.

19. The patient has a right, regardless of the source of payment, to examine and receive an itemized and detailed explanation of the total bill for services rendered in the facility.

20. The patient has a right to competent counseling from the hospital staff to help in obtaining financial assistance from public or private sources to meet the expense of services received in the institution.

21. The patient has a right to timely prior notice of the termination of his/her eligibility for reimbursement by any third-party payor for the expense of hospital care.

22. At the termination of his/her stay at the health care facility we recognize the right of a patient to a complete copy of the information contained in his/her medical record.

23. We recognize the right of all patients to have 24-hour-a-day access to a patient's rights advocate, who may act on behalf of the patient to assert or protect the rights set out in this document.

FURTHER READING

Annas, George J. *The Rights of Hospital Patients.* New York: Avon Books, 1975.

———; Clantz, Leonard H.; and Katz, Barbara F. *The Rights of Doctors, Nurses and Allied Health Professionals.* New York: Avon Books, 1981.

Ennis, Bruce J.; and Emery, Richard D. *The Rights of Mental Patients.* New York: Avon Books, 1978.

Guttmacher Institute. *Family Planning Perspectives* (monthly). Washington, D.C.: Alan Guttmacher Institute, 1220 19th Street, N.W., Washington, D.C. 20036.

Isaacs, Stephen L. "The Law of Fertility Regulation in the U.S.: A 1980 Review," *Journal of Family Law,* Vol. 19, pp. 65–96.

Latanich, T.; and Schultheiss, P. "Competition and Health Manpower Issues," in L. Aiken (ed.) *Nursing in the 1980s: Crises, Opportunities, Challenges.* Philadelphia: J.B. Lippincott, 1982.

Marieskind, Helen. *Women in the Health System, Patients, Providers and Programs.* St. Louis: C.V. Mosby, 1980.

Moore, Emily. "Women and Health United States, 1980." Supplement to the September/October 1980 issue of *Public Health Reports.* Washington, D.C.: Superintendent of Documents, U.S. Government Printing Office.

National Abortion Rights Action League newsletter, 825 15th Street, N.W., Washington, D.C. 20005.

Ross, Susan and Ann Barcher. *The Rights of Women.* New York: Bantam Books, 1983. See especially the chapter, "A Women's Right to Control Her Body."

U.S. Department of Health Education and Welfare, *Requirements of Laws and Regulations Enforced by the U.S. Food and Drug Administration,* Public Health Service FDA, 5600 Fishers Lane, Rockville, Maryland 20857. HEW Publication (FDA) 79-1042 (1979).

Williams, Wendy W. "Hiring the Woman to Protect the Fetus: The Reconciliation of Fetal Protection with Employment Opportunity Goals Under Title VII," *Georgetown Law Journal,* Vol. 69, pp. 641–704 (1981).

Part Two

WOMEN AS FAMILY MEMBERS

Your Rights in Domestic Relations

6

Marriage and Its Alternatives

HENRY H. FOSTER

*Henry H. Foster is professor of law emeritus, New York University, and
counsel to the firm of Gaffin & Mayo, P.C., New York City. Professor
Foster also is a past chairman of the Family Law Section of the American
Bar Association, and the editor of* Fair$hare, *a monthly newsletter of
divorce, alimony, and marital property law. He is coauthor, of H.H.
Foster & D.J. Freed,* Law and the Family—New York.

To a large extent, legal rights and duties depend upon the nature of the
relationship between people. This was true in feudal times, when the "peck-
ing order" was all-important, and it is still true today. For example it may
be murder or manslaughter for a woman to permit her husband or child to
starve to death, but no offense where she knowingly permits her lover or
a neighbor's child to die of starvation. In the absence of a *legal* relationship,
there may be no *legal* duty to be a Good Samaritan.

Not all social relationships are legal relationships. In the world of business, ordinarily it is permissible to drive a hard bargain or to seek an
advantage, even where you are dealing with a friend, but such behavior is
not permitted when the other party is a spouse or a minor. A fiduciary
relationship (a relationship of trust) is held to exist between engaged or
married couples, and the law requires the utmost good faith and full disclosure of assets, and condemns overreaching (sharp practice) or unfair advantage. Minors generally are protected from bad bargains entered into with
adults, and due to their presumed immature judgment, have an option to
call off the deal.

The common law is protective of wives, children, and the insane. The
other side of the coin is that until the middle of the nineteenth century,

wives were not legal persons, and even today minors and the mentally incompetent, are subject to guardianships. Moreover, to a great extent, common law and statute control and regulate the incidents of marriage and those of the parent-child relationship. In these cases, it is assumed that the state (society) has a great enough interest to justify governmental intrusion into the family's autonomy. There is no comparable assumption or policy outside the family relationship, and subject to public policy limitations, only private contracts or agreements control extralegal relationships.

Traditionally, the law refers to the special relationship of husband and wife as a "status." The parent-child relationship also is said to be a status. The term status is a shorthand way of saying that the law imposes or grants certain duties or rights in addition to, or regardless of, a private contract. If a particular relationship is extralegal (e.g., that between a man and a woman living together) rights and duties, if any, must usually come from a valid agreement between the concerned parties. The law, on its own, does not presume to interfere in such a case. For example, if a married woman owns a house and dies without making a will, her surviving spouse and children will be her heirs, according to the law. But if the woman is unmarried and dies intestate, her lover will not automatically inherit the property. In the latter case, the woman would need to name her lover as the inheritor of the property by making a will.

THE MARRIAGE RELATIONSHIP:
THE DEFINITION OF MARRIAGE

In the United States (and England) the generally accepted definition of marriage is "the voluntary union for life of one man and one woman, to the exclusion of all others." Marriage also is commonly referred to as a "civil contract" and as a status.

The words voluntary union in the above definition mean that there was a *matrimonial intent,* the parties were free to *consent,* and they *willingly* entered into the marital relationship. An English case illustrates the requirement of matrimonial intent. An Englishwoman, in the company of her Hindu suitor, visited India and participated in a religious ceremony that she believed converted her to the Hindu faith. In fact the foreign words and ceremony constituted a wedding. The English court annulled the purported marriage because of the absence of any matrimonial intent on her part. So too, numerous American cases have voided purported marriages in which the purpose was to circumvent immigration laws and not to live together as husband and wife. Similarly, the purported marriage of an insane person or a minor may be annulled because of lack of capacity to consent. There also is no true consent where a party is forced into marriage by coercion, or duress, as happened in a New York case in which the bridegroom threatened to kill the bride and blow up her home if she didn't go through with the ceremony.

Changing times and the increased frequency of divorce have forced some adjustment of the "for life" aspect of the accepted definition. That requirement, however, is met if the parties at the time of the ceremony intend or hope that it will be a permanent relationship, as distinguished from a "trial run," and such is true even though both were aware of the liberality of current divorce laws. However, a private agreement between the marital couple that either or both would immediately seek a divorce if the honeymoon was not satisfactory, undoubtedly would jeopardize the validity of the marriage.

The "one man and one woman" requirement currently is being challenged, but, to date, no American court has held that gay or lesbian couples may contract a valid *marriage,* and the Supreme Court has upheld statutes forbidding polygamous marriages. Although gay or lesbian couples may regard themselves as "married," and members of communes may undergo group "weddings," so far as the law is concerned this does not create the legal and social institution of marriage.

"To the exclusion of all others" remains the rule in our monogamous society. In all but a few states, marriage carries with it the mutual obligation of fidelity, and adultery is a criminal offense, albeit rarely punished. It also is a ground for divorce. There may be a common misunderstanding, at least in some circles, that physical or legal separation releases a married person from the marriage vows. Legally speaking, such is not the case, and until a marriage is terminated by divorce or dissolution, a spouse does not have the sexual freedom of a single person. Presumably, contracts for an "open marriage" are illegal and certainly unenforceable as against public policy, due to the state's concern over the integrity of marriage and the family.

A CIVIL CONTRACT

It is somewhat misleading to describe marriage as a "civil contract." Except for the Jewish *ketubah,* brides and grooms do not execute a formal agreement upon marriage, nor do they receive any written document from the state that sets forth their matrimonial rights and duties. What is meant by "a civil contract" is that, so far as secular law is concerned, marriage and its termination are subject to state regulation, even though particular religions may view marriage as a sacrament (since the fifteenth century) and as being indissoluble. There is no implication that the civil contract of marriage is subject to the law of commercial contracts. (The phrase "civil contract" came from the Protestant Reformation and its rejection of the religious doctrine of the indissoluble nature of a marriage.)

There are more differences than similarities between the marriage contract and commercial contracts. This is because it frequently is said that the state is a party to the marriage contract, which is merely another way of saying that statutory and court-made law sets limits on the freedom to contract regarding marriage and its incidents. The parties are not free to enter into an incestuous or polygamous marriage insofar as the law is concerned. Although the parties are free to call off an ordinary commercial contract, a marriage contract is terminated only by death or legal dissolution such as a divorce or an annulment. The law will sometimes grant what it calls "specific performance" in order to enforce commercial agreements, but an American court will not order a wife to "love, honor, and obey" her husband. The customary freedom to contract is impaired because of the state's claimed special interest in marriage and the family.

MARRIAGE AS A STATUS

The legal term "status," as previously mentioned, is a way of expressing the state's interest in marriage as a social institution. The state controls or regulates some of the incidents of the marital status. For example, it may impose reasonable and nondiscriminatory restrictions as to the age for marriage, as to the need for parental consent, and as to mental capacity. State statutes may require marriage licenses and a reporting of marriage ceremonies. Blood tests may be mandatory. Bigamous and incestuous marriages are uniformly prohibited in the Western world.

As we said earlier, since marriage law creates a status, the wife and husband are not free to rescind the marriage contract at will as they may an ordinary commercial contract. They must go to court and obtain a legal dissolution. This is so even though there is a mistaken belief that after five or seven years of separation the parties are free to remarry. The law also fixes certain duties and liabilities, rights and privileges, regardless of the wishes of the individual couple.

DUTY TO SUPPORT

From an economic standpoint, the most important incident of marriage is the duty to support. Until recently, the primary duty of support rested upon the husband/father. Only under unusual circumstances was there a secondary duty of support imposed upon the wife/mother; for example, where the husband/father was dead, was incapacitated, or his whereabouts was unknown. Even then, the secondary duty was imposed in accordance with the wife/mother's means, and had as its objective the saving of welfare expenditures. This policy dates from Elizabethan times. Once the husband/father was located, the wife/mother, or perhaps the parish, could seek to recover from him for support paid to or for the family.

Originally, there were sound economic reasons for placing the primary duty of support upon the husband/father, because at common law he controlled the family purse strings. Upon marriage, the husband ordinarily acquired most of his wife's personal property and gained control over her real estate, and was privileged to pocket any profits therefrom. But beginning around 1850, married women's property acts were passed by American legislatures, so that upon marriage the wife retained the ownership and control of her individual property. Nonetheless, the primary duty of support remained that of the husband/father. Justification for retention of the rule was then assumed to exist because typically the husband/father was the breadwinner and the wife/mother worked in the home. However, if the wife worked outside the home or earned "pin money" by selling eggs, produce or handicrafts, under married women's property acts, she was entitled to keep such income if she cared to do so rather than to contribute it to the family.

The courts rationalized that the "consideration" for the husband-father's primary duty of support was the wife's legal obligation to provide "services," and that it was a fair exchange. Of course, neither might be satisfied if he was a poor breadwinner or squandered his paycheck at the corner saloon, or if she was a slovenly housekeeper and an indifferent wife or mother. The only remedy for either, however, was separation or divorce.

The economic consequence of married women's property acts and similar legislation is that each party may own and retain her/his property and separate earnings as separate property. Such individual ownership, however, is qualified by child and spousal support laws, and by marital or community-property laws that apply where the marriage is dissolved by a court decree or death. In the latter event, the state laws relating to a surviving spouse's inheritance rights apply against the decedent's estate.

Feminists have made the point that the wife was expected to provide services "gratuitously," and hence she was "enslaved," but the same reasoning would support the assertion that the husband was subjected to a form of "peonage" or "involuntary servitude" because of his primary duty to support his wife and children. Moreover, the only remedy for the husband where the wife failed to fulfill her marital obligations was a possible suit for annulment or divorce if he could establish some statutory ground—for example, adultery—whereas the wife/mother in the nonsupport situation had and has a variety of criminal and civil remedies (which, unfortunately, often prove to be illusory). It is indeed ironic that the legal system, which in theory placed an unequal burden on the husband/father, has been so inept in the enforcement of the support obligation.

In some if not most states, there remains a vestige of the husband/breadwinner and wife/homemaker stereotypes. Usually it is difficult if not impossible for a wife to obtain a court order for wife and child support where the parties are still living together. A well-known Nebraska case, involving a wealthy but miserly farmer, held that the court would not write the family budget and give the wife an allowance as long *as they were living together.* The evidence showed that the wealthy farmer still maintained outdoor toilet facilities, had a broken-down wood-burning stove in the kitchen, and that there was no laundry equipment. The wife got a new gingham dress every five years but otherwise had to make do, and she had no money, despite his considerable means, to take trips to visit her relatives. Of course, the probable practical consequences of the decision would be to force a separation or divorce, which supposedly is to be discouraged by the law (see pp. 133–35, Public Policy Limitations).

Since the decision of the United States Supreme Court in *Orr* v. *Orr* (1979), it is held to be unconstitutional to impose primary support obligations on husbands/fathers and only a secondary obligation on wives/mothers. The general principle is that, depending upon *need and means,* either spouse may be required to contribute to the support of the other and that the parents have a mutual duty of child support, according to their respective means. Although alimony or support has been awarded to men but rarely, under proper circumstances wives may be ordered to pay alimony to husbands or child support for their children. Support, alimony, and maintenance statutes are now gender-neutral, and we may anticipate an increase in cases in which the wife/mother will be required to assume all or part of the support burden.

In fixing the amount or duration of alimony or maintenance, the courts consider factors such as the length of the marriage and the age and health of the parties, their future earning capacity, the presence of children in the home, tax consequences to each party, the customary standard of living, and the contributions of the party seeking maintenance as a spouse, parent, wage earner, or homemaker, and to the career or career potential of the other party. In the case of a long-term marriage, or of an older couple, future financial security, where possible, is an objective. Where it is a short marriage involving a young couple, the major objective may be to "wipe the slate clean" so that the parties may make a fresh start.

PUBLIC POLICY LIMITATIONS

In the past, marriage and divorce law in the United States reflected religious principles derived from conservative Protestantism. Divorce was to be discouraged, but available as a last resort to reward an innocent spouse and to punish a guilty one. In practice, however, the fault grounds for divorce were diluted in many states, and even in the nineteenth century there were migratory divorce Meccas, where divorce was readily available. Since the 1960s, there have been waves of divorce reform, and in the early eighties only two states (Illinois and South Dakota) do not have some form of no-fault divorce.

Despite the availability of no-fault divorce, which may result in divorce upon unilateral demand, the official public policy in many if not most states still condemns agreements or activities that are conducive to or promote divorce. A specific agreement to obtain a divorce or not to contest the divorce still offends public policy. The result is that lawyers draft agreements and settlements in language that merely covers the possibility of divorce, when in fact the parties intend that their agreement be operative to cover their prospective divorce. In New York, for example, the parties are forbidden to enter into an *express* agreement that requires dissolution of the marriage or the procurement of grounds for divorce.

There also is a public policy in most states against marriage brokerage contracts or any scheme that interferes with free choice of a marital partner. Thus, it has been held to be contrary to public policy to organize a pool of singles and to give a bonus to the first one who is married.

The law in numerous other ways seeks to protect and safeguard the marital as distinct from other relationships. Unless outlawed by statute or decision, there are several common-law tort actions or civil wrongs calculated to protect the family or its members. These include civil damage suits for the seduction or enticement of a child. The parent may recover damages for loss of services when without parental consent a daughter is seduced and moves out of the home or becomes pregnant. The circus may be liable to the parent where the young daughter leaves home and joins the entourage without parental consent. The parent (or custodian) is entitled to services from her children, and when a third party interferes, there is potential liability. To date, however, for constitutional reasons, this common-law doctrine has not been applied against religious cults.

The common law protected the marriage chances for women in two ways. First, it was held to be slander per se to impugn the chastity of a woman. This meant that there need be no proof of actual damages or financial loss, although the truth of the charges might be a defense. Second, a jilted female, in the absence of statute, may recover for breach of promise when the engagement is called off for no valid reason, as, for example, the man merely decides to marry someone else. In most states, except Louisiana and New York, she also is entitled to keep the engagement ring.

Breach of Promise

Breach of promise actions no longer enjoy their former popularity, and so-called "heart balm" acts in about one third of the states now outlaw or limit such actions. Charles Dickens's story about the hapless Mr. Pickwick and his landlady, Mrs. Bardell, and tabloid exploitation of such cases, brought them into disfavor. In its heyday, however, juries awarded substantial damages against wealthy men and in favor of attractive females, even in the case of a short-lived romance. In most but not all states, a jilting male has no legal right to demand the return of the engagement ring, but if the woman without good cause breaks the engagement, he is entitled to its return. With regard to gifts between engaged couples, ownership depends upon the giver's intent. If the gift is deemed to be conditioned upon the marriage taking place and the one who received the gift for no good reason calls off the wedding, the law may require the return of the gift. However, when a Diamond Jim Brady gives a trinket to Lillian Russell to "curry her favor," as distinguished from in contemplation of marriage, the gift is effective and the trinket may not be reclaimed. A prospective mother-in-law is entitled to the return of any gifts she gave on the assumption that the marriage would take place.

Alienation of Affections and Criminal Conversation

Two other common-law actions, in the absence of statute, protect the marriage relationship. Damages may be recovered for alienation of affections or for "criminal conversation," or both, against one who interferes with the marital relationship. Alienation-of-affections actions may permit recovery against a lover. Moreover, such suits also may be brought against intermeddling in-laws. In some states, a hostile mother-in-law (or father-in-law) may incur liability for unjustifiable intermeddling when a daughter is induced to leave a spouse and come home. It all depends upon whether or not there was justification.

Perhaps due to the general unpopularity of alienation-of-affection suits, which have been abolished in about 15 states, courts generally have refused to extend such actions to alienation of parental affections. Thus, although there are a few cases to the contrary, most states have held that a child may not recover damages against the lover who induces a parent to leave home and abandon the parental role.

"Criminal conversation" is quaint legal jargon meaning adultery. It entails more than mere talk, including "pillow talk." Some states, such as Pennsylvania, which have outlawed the other actions under discussion, have retained "criminal conversation" as a tort or civil wrong to discourage adultery. Moreover, where available, it may be no defense that the married couple had separated or that the marriage was on the rocks, because it is presumed that they might have been reconciled but for the extramarital relationship.

Loss of Consortium

This is yet another common-law action for damages. "Consortium" is a somewhat ambiguous term that covers spousal services, including those of a sexual nature. Originally it was available for a husband when his wife was injured by the intentional or negligent wrong of another. The wife was entitled to recover her own damages, and her husband in addition might be awarded damages for loss of her services. Although the cases are in conflict, the trend today is to extend to the wife a cause of action for damages for loss of her husband's services. A few years ago, a Pennsylvania court chauvinistically held that a wife had merely been relieved from carrying out her wifely duties, which may tell us something about the judges' marriages.

PROTECTION FROM CREDITORS

Homestead Protections

American statutes also protect the family from creditors, the most familiar example being "homestead," or marital-home, exemptions. In a "debtor state" such as Texas, the family residence, automobile, and "tools of the trade," may be out of reach of creditors. In a farm state, a team of mules or horses, a tractor and farm equipment, and other items may be immune from general creditors. Most western states have comparable exemptions, designed to protect family survival at the expense of creditors.

Family Liability

At the other extreme are family expense statutes which create a joint liability for the family expenses of the individual members. There also is the "family car" doctrine, which imposes liability on the insured parent when a child has an accident, and in some states, due to statute, parents are liable for their offspring's vandalism, even though they had no prior warning of the child's dangerous behavior. Contrary to popular belief, however, ordinarily a parent is not liable to pay for the neighbor's window when junior hits a home run, although good community relations may indicate payment.

Wage Attachment and Garnishment: Family creditors also are affected by wage-attachment and garnishment statutes. Support obligations usually take priority over the claims of general creditors. The federal Consumer's Protection Act, in order to provide protection against bankruptcy, limits general creditors to an attachment of 25 percent of "disposable income" (similar to take-home pay), but the percentage may rise to 50–60 percent where there are family support arrears. This federal law, in effect, places a ceiling on the amount of garnishment, regardless of state law. However, state law may stipulate a lower amount that is subject to attachment. If wages already are attached to satisfy support claims, general creditors may have to stand in line to wait their turn. Family support claims have priority.

If the marital home is owned by the married couple as tenants by the entirety (as distinguished from ownership as tenants in common) it is usually immune from individual creditors, although a mortgagee may be able to foreclose and a contractor may have a lien. Even foreclosure is inhibited, however, by statutes and by the equity of redemption, which protect homeowners from losing their homes. It should be noted that ownership by entireties is limited to married couples and was designed to protect the family home. If the parties are unmarried they do not receive the protection given by that form of co-ownership.

TAX ADVANTAGES

The status of marriage also carries with it certain federal, state, and local tax advantages, the best known of which is the privilege of filing joint income tax returns, which ordinarily lessens the tax burden for the family. In addition, there are dependency exemptions and "head of household" provisions, and the estate tax's "marital deduction." In the divorce situation, any or all of these tax law provisions may be important.

The Unlimited Marital Deduction
Generally the tax law seeks to protect the legal family and does not give the same break to extralegal families. Thus, a new, *unlimited* marital deduc-

tion was established by the Economic Recovery Act of 1981, which applies to spouses dying after 1981. Where the decedent's will contemplates the current instead of the former tax law, there is an unlimited marital deduction if the entire estate is left to the surviving spouse. Under former law, the federal ceiling was $250,000 or 50 percent of the adjusted gross estate, whichever was greater. Under the new law, if the estate is left to a non-spouse, there is a generous "equivalent exemption," which in 1982 is $225,-000 and which reaches $600,000 in 1987, as contrasted with the unlimited marital deduction for a surviving spouse.

The above changes have the practical consequence of encouraging the naming of the surviving spouse as sole heir, and where large sums are involved, not naming children or grandchildren. It should be noted, however, that when the surviving spouse dies, the children or other heirs will be subject to the "equivalent exemption," so in a sense the unlimited marital deduction merely postpones the estate tax where large inheritances are involved.

Gift Taxes

In addition, the 1981 law changed the rules as to gift taxes. The unlimited marital deduction applies to both federal estate and federal gift taxes, and in this regard gives spouses in common-law-property states* the same advantage previously enjoyed only in community-property states. In effect, husband and wife are treated as an economic unit for estate and gift tax purposes, as they are for income tax purposes when a joint return is filed.

With regard to gifts to children, the annual gift tax exclusion was raised from $3,000 to $10,000, and the tax was further reduced by a new uniform credit that was increased from $47,000 to $192,800, phased in over a six-year period. Gift and estate transfers up to $600,000 will be free of tax starting in 1987. It should also be noted that school tuition, medical care, and medical insurance are not treated as gifts subject to the gift tax, and that the husband and wife may elect to split gifts for a total of $20,000 annual exclusion per donee. The full impact of these new changes can best be explained by an expert in estate planning or a tax law specialist (see also Chapter 10).

The "Marriage Penalty"

A highly publicized anomaly of the former income tax law was the so-called "marriage penalty," which occurred where both husband and wife had substantial earnings and the second earner's income was taxed at a

*Most states continue to have the common-law property system. However, eight states and Puerto Rico have varying forms of the community-property system as it developed in France and Spain. The community-property states are: Arizona, California, Idaho, Louisiana, Nevada, New Mexico, Texas, and Washington.

higher rate than if she/he were single. In order to avoid that result, a few married couples over a period of several years obtained "quickie" divorces in December, remarried the next January, and paid lower aggregate federal income tax. Tax courts eventually ruled against such tax "avoidance," and the 1981 tax law partially plugs the loophole by giving a deduction (5 percent in 1982, 10 percent in 1983) to the spouse with the lower income.

The Capital Gain Advantage

A tax advantage that ordinarily works to the benefit of married couples but is not as limited as the deduction mentioned above, occurs with reference to the capital gain realized on the sale of a home. The tax may be deferred on the sale of the old principal residence when a new residence is purchased within twenty-four months (formerly eighteen months) if the cost of the new place is equal to the amount received for the house sold. This applies to the principal residence but not to a second house or a summer home; and the contract to purchase the new place must be made within the twenty-four-month period, although the closing need not have occurred. The tax deferment extends to mobile homes, cooperative apartments, and condominiums. In order to defer the tax, each party must file consent statements if title in the new place differs from the title to the old place.

In addition, there may be a tax-free sale of a home by owners age 55 or over, who may avoid the tax on the profits up to $125,000 (formerly $100,000) if the place was the principal residence for at least three of the five years preceding the date of sale. This means that when a couple is approaching age 55, the sale of the principal residence ordinarily should be postponed until after that age to obtain "one-time" benefits of the federal tax law and regulations. If the home is sold at age 54, the difference may be between paying a 20 percent capital gains tax on the amount paid over the original price, and paying no federal tax at all.

Capital gains taxes may also impinge where there is a transfer of stocks and securities that have increased in value since their original purchase. The transfer may be a taxable event subject to the 20 percent capital gains tax, and this is true even though the transfer occurs due to a separation agreement or a court decree. It is only when there is a preexisting ownership of the property in question, as in community-property states, that the federal capital gains tax is avoided under the so-called *Davis* rule. That case, in effect, held that where upon divorce the husband transferred to the wife $150,000 in stocks that had originally cost him $50,000, a capital gains tax was owed on $100,000. It made no difference that this transfer was made in relation to an agreement or decree. It is best to assume that the federal capital gains tax may be due whenever appreciated property is transferred in relation to a divorce, and it is important to know who is to pay the tax. If possible, a transfer of cash may save tax dollars.

The above brief discussion and few examples are the tip of the iceberg so far as complicated tax problems are concerned, but they should be sufficient to alert the reader to the problems. Remember, an expert tax adviser may be as important to the family as a friendly tax assessor.

Other Benefits

State and local tax laws also are structured to give advantages to legal families and may provide similar deductions or exemptions. Estate planning and a knowledge of tax law are extremely important to the family, because all marriages will be terminated, by either death or dissolution. The amazing current figures are that about 55 percent of marriages will be terminated by divorce and 45 percent by death (see Chapter 10, "Estate Planning").

OTHER LAWS THAT AFFECT THE LEGAL FAMILY

In addition to tax laws there are other federal, state, and local laws that are protective of or otherwise affect the legal family. A spouse who was married for ten years or more may qualify for Social Security benefits, which are not available where the marriage is of shorter duration. Obviously, this provision becomes crucial where divorce is secured during the ninth year of marriage. In terms of future financial security, it may be urgent to delay divorce until after ten years have elapsed.

Formerly, there were two provisions in our welfare laws that were detrimental to the legal family. Until the Social Security law was changed, elderly persons on Social Security who married received a reduced amount as a couple, rather than their former individual benefits. Thus, there was an economic incentive for such people not to marry. This untoward result now has been eliminated and each may marry and keep her/his full Social Security benefits. The Social Security Act, however, still denies an employed wife the benefit she otherwise would have if not married, and limits her to her share of the benefits her husband has earned.

Aid to Families with Dependent Children

The other provision that is to the family's detriment still remains. It occurs under the Aid to Families with Dependent Children (AFDC) program, which was designed mainly to protect mothers and children who had been abandoned. To qualify for full entitlement, the man must be absent, and the woman is supposed to cooperate with welfare authorities in helping to locate him so that he may be forced to contribute support. In practical operation, however, the welfare law provides practical incentives for a father to desert or to hide out so that his family may receive AFDC. (This is especially true in times of high unemployment.) If the father has little or no income, his family will be better off on AFDC, since it will be greater in amount than what he can pay, and the payments will be regular. Thus, existing federal law may encourage the breakup of the legal or de facto family.

Pension and Retirement Benefits

Pension and retirement benefits may accrue for the spouse of a retired worker. In the case of a nonmarital couple, however, entitlement will depend upon whether the particular pension or retirement plan permits the designation of a nonspouse as a beneficiary. Payments received from the federal government, including those from federal employers and the armed services, may be subject to garnishment or attachment in order to pay wife and child support obligations, provided the wife has taken legal action to get judgment against her husband. Civil Service employees and employees in the Foreign Service may have their pay docked to satisfy their support and alimony obligations. Formerly it was held that the retirement or disability pensions of service personnel were immune from state law regarding community or marital property distribution upon divorce. In 1982, however, Congress removed the immunity so that at present a state court may treat military retirement pay as marital or community property. Moreover, once the pension or retirement benefit is in the hands of the pensioner, it may be attached under the law of most states in order to satisfy any outstanding support or alimony arrears.

PROPERTY AND INHERITANCE

Historically, under the common law there were inheritance rights, obtained in each other's property upon marriage. The wife got a dower interest and the husband got curtesy. Dower was a life interest for the widow in all lands owned by the husband during their marriage if he died intestate, or one third of his lands if she rejected his will. Curtesy meant that the husband acquired a lifetime interest in all the lands she had owned during marriage, provided they had a child born alive who might have been capable of inheriting the estate.

In most states today there are statutory provisions that replace common-law dower and curtesy. Widows and widowers are treated the same, and there is a forced statutory share which automatically applies in the event the survivor elects to take against a will of the decedent. The estate of the decedent must provide the "statutory share" to the surviving spouse if he/she elects to take against the terms of the will. In New York State, for example, if there are no children, the surviving spouse has an elective share of one half of the property (real and personal) left by the deceased spouse, but the share is one third if there are children. Statutes in other states may stipulate different percentages or conditions for the right of election. In all states except Louisiana, children have no right to a forced share of their parents' estate and may be disinherited by either parent. Of course, they qualify as heirs if a parent dies intestate.

There is no claim to inheritance based upon a nonmarital relationship, although a party may be named as an heir subject to the statutory rights of a surviving spouse. Children born out of wedlock may be designated as heirs by will, and if the father died intestate they may qualify as heirs if paternity is established according to state law. Nonmarital children qualify as heirs of the biological mother unless they have been adopted.

Community Property and Common Law Property

Property consequences also occur upon divorce or dissolution of a marriage. In community-property states, there is equitable or equal distribution of the property held jointly by the couple. Formerly, in common law property states, upon divorce each kept her/his separate property and only marital property (jointly owned) was divided. Today, approximately 40 common law states make an equitable distribution of marital property upon divorce, Mississippi and Virginia retain the old common law, and Arkansas and Wisconsin provide for an equal distribution. The property that qualifies as "marital property" differs from one state to another, but a substantial majority of states include only property accumulated during the marriage, regardless of how title is held. A minority of states define "marital property" so as to include that owned before the marriage, but a majority treat such property as "separate" and usually add to that category individual gifts or inheritances from outside the marriage.

As we shall see, the above sketch of "marital property" is important for the purpose of comparing the situation of nonmarital partners.

SOCIAL ACCEPTANCE OF MARRIAGE AND DIVORCE

Marriage, divorce, mothers-in-law, and lawyers are favorite subjects for one-liners. Each of these targets is assumed to invite or deserve cheap shots, perhaps because they are viewed with some ambivalence.

Despite competition from alternative life-styles, marriage still enjoys an amazing popularity in America, and the number of marriages increases each year. In 1979, there were 26,000 more marriages than in any previous year, which was a 3 percent increase over 1978 and the fourth consecutive year of increase. The rate was 10.5 per 1,000 population, and in 1979 there were 2,317,000 new marriages. Currently, there are 50 million married couples in the United States.

What has also happened, however, is that for the past two decades the age of those first entering marriage has increased. The proportion of single women in the 20–24-year age bracket has risen by more than one half since 1960 (from 28 to 43 percent). The median age at first marriage in 1982 was 21.1 for females and 22.5 for males. There also has been an increase in remarriage, in every age group.

It is the increasing incidence of divorce that has been of greatest concern to students of social change. In 1979, there were 1,170,000 divorces, and a little under a million marriages were terminated by the death of one of the partners. Since 1973, more American marriages have been terminated by divorce than by death, and the current figure is 55 percent for the former as compared with 45 percent for the latter. There is approximately one divorce for every two marriages today, as compared with one divorce for every six marriages in 1930. The median length of marriages now being terminated by divorce is 6.6 years, and the median age of the wife around 29 and of the husband around 30 years of age.

Parties to divorce usually remarry within a few months or years, and a prior divorce is no handicap. Previously married persons, of whatever age, are more apt to get married than singles of the same age, and this is true even though there are children in the household. The psychological or economic explanation of this phenomenon will be left to the reader, but it should be noted that the divorced are not automatically eliminated from the marriage market. It was not always thus.

Before World War I, divorced people were excluded from many social circles and there was a stigma attached to divorce. The abdication and subsequent marriage of King Edward VIII of England in the late thirties, and the sympathy the couple invoked, may have contributed to the removal of the social stigma. Today, except in some religious circles, no stigma attaches to divorce.

It also should be noted that those marriages which endure last longer than formerly was the case. Medical progress has increased life expectancy and decreased deaths from childbirth. Married couples are exposed to tensions and strains over a longer period of time. For example, the expected duration of a marriage in 1900–2 between a man of 23 and a woman of 21 was 31.3 years. In 1969–71 the expected duration was 42.4 years. The chances that a bride and groom will survive the next 50 years of marriage are more than twice as great as in 1900–2—though not necessarily as a couple. Before 1900, about one third of all marriages did not last more than fifteen years, because of the high death rate. (One wag has suggested marital "sabbaticals" as a method of alleviating the stresses and strains of long marriages.)

Formerly, commentators or demographers point out, the divorce rate differed according to socioeconomic class, and educational attainment was a factor. Persons with lower incomes had more divorces in proportion, as did high school dropouts. Today since divorce has obtained middle-class acceptance, the socioeconomic and educational distinctions have become blurred. However, the fact remains that the incidence of divorce increases during prosperous times and decreases during a depression, and currently, if legal aid is not provided, the poor are priced out of the divorce market.

The increasing employment of married women and the independence engendered by the women's movement are significant factors in our current divorce rate. There are over 23 million wives in the workforce, and 40 percent of all households with a living husband and wife have a woman in the workforce. About 57 percent of married women with children work outside the home, and about 80 percent of all marriages with an annual income over $20,000 are two-earner marriages.

The old stereotype of the husband/breadwinner and the wife/ homemaker, which may have had validity in the nineteenth century, does not suit current conditions. Moreover, the average woman completes her childbearing by age 26 and her last child attains majority when she is in her mid-forties. She may become a grandmother in her early forties, when she has a life expectancy of almost 40 years.

As astonishing as some of the current statistics of marriage and divorce may be, the dramatic increase in cohabitants is a greater social phenomenon. The 1978 figures show that 2.2 million unmarried persons were "sharing a household with an unrelated adult of the opposite sex" (a 117 percent increase between 1970 and 1978), and it has been estimated that the actual figure probably is twice as great. Although about 42 percent of nonmarital couples are under age 25, and 59 percent are under 35, about 15 percent are between 45 and 64, and 11 percent over 65. Living together in a non-marital relationship no longer is limited to the young, poor, bohemians, and the very rich. That citadel of respectability, the middle class, now accepts cohabitation as normal.

Notwithstanding the number of people living together (cohabitation), it has not achieved the standing of status in the legal sense, although increasingly the law will have to consider what if any rights and duties flow from a nonmarital relationship. Eventually both contract law and principles of equity may establish the legal rights and wrongs of what formerly was dubbed a "meretricious relationship," i.e., immoral and illegal, and outside the pale of legal protection and a fit subject for criminal punishment.

ALTERNATIVE LIFE-STYLES

We have seen that marriage and the parent/child relationship involve a status and that certain legal rights, duties, privileges, and entitlements usually adhere to the status, independent of private agreement. In the case of nonmarital, lesbian, gay, or group relationships, rights, duties, etc., if any, ordinarily are based upon contracts. The contract, or agreement, however, must not violate public policy, including that expressed in criminal statutes.

Cohabitation

In over 20 states, cohabitation by unmarried couples is a criminal offense, and in all but a few states adultery is also a crime. Where the criminal code makes adultery, bigamous cohabitation, fornication, or cohabitation a criminal offense, the legislature has made a pronouncement of public policy even though such criminal statutes are rarely if ever enforced. As used in criminal statutes, "cohabitation" includes nonmarital relationships that formerly were called "meretricious." Thus, an agreement covering aspects of an illicit relationship in one of the above categories may be void because it may be against public policy to admit that such a relationship has sufficient validity to be the subject of a legal agreement. Certainly, that is what used to happen.

More recently, however, the rule has been emerging that if the agreement between cohabitants is supported by a quid pro quo or what the courts call a valuable "consideration" it may be sustained. "Consideration" means the reason or material cause of the contract and includes "an act or forbearance, or the promise thereof, which is offered by one party to an agreement, and accepted by the other as an inducement to that other's act or promise." Legal consideration is one recognized and permitted by the law as valid and lawful; it is an illegal consideration where the act if done, or a promise if enforced, would be prejudicial to the public interest.

The trend today is to sustain agreements between nonmarital partners if there is some valid consideration for the contract. Thus, most recent cases have held that where the parties agree that one will provide services in the home and the other will support the household, their agreement is valid because of the value of the contemplated domestic and nonsexual services. The illegal consideration (sexual services) is severed from the legal consideration (other domestic services) and the agreement is sustained. Oregon has gone even farther and holds that it no longer regards the contemplation of sexual services as against its public policy. A few states, however, retain the old rule and refuse to enforce or recognize any portion of nonmarital agreements even where services of a nonsexual nature were contemplated. Illinois and Georgia, in relatively recent cases, have had this point of view, saying that illegality taints the entire agreement.

The most obvious situation that invites enforcement of an agreement is where the female cohabitant performs valuable services outside the home. The New York case of *McCall* v. *Frampton* was one in which a married woman became the business manager of a rock star and moved in with him. She was held to be entitled to the agreed-upon compensation for her business services. Of course, in a case where there was no agreement, recovery would present additional problems.

The other appealing situation for recovery is where the unmarried couple hold themselves out to the community as husband and wife. In *Hewitt* v. *Hewitt,* the parties were college classmates, and when she became pregnant, they told their families that they had eloped. They had three children and lived together fifteen years, until the man left her for a younger woman. In their community they were known as husband and wife; the fact that there had been no ceremony was kept secret. In addition to bearing and raising three children, the ostensible wife helped to support the family while he worked for and secured a specialty in dentistry, and she also worked for him at his dental office. The Illinois court held that she was not entitled to support or to any of his property, and seized upon Illinois criminal and divorce statutes as the embodiments of a contrary public policy. The unfairness of the decision is obvious, and it is a safe prediction that the *Hewitt* case eventually will be reversed. New York, in *Morone* v. *Morone,* rejected the type of reasoning indulged in by the Illinois court.

In *Morone* the relationship lasted for 25 years and produced two children; then the man moved out and cut off all support. The New York court held that the woman was entitled to recover on the basis of an express agreement, written or oral, but that recovery could not be had on the basis of an implied agreement or on the theory of unjust enrichment. These terms require explanation.

An *express* agreement results from a verbalized agreement that may be either written or oral. The parties specify their understanding. An *implied* agreement is one inferred from behavior or conduct. The parties act or behave in such a way that it is reasonable to conclude that they must have reached an understanding. Unjust enrichment is the doctrine that one person should not be permitted to enrich herself inequitably at another's expense. If a defendant has received something of value, such as property or services, at the plaintiff's expense, the plaintiff may have an equitable remedy such as restitution or reimbursement.

The well-known case of *Marvin* v. *Marvin* involved a consideration of the concepts of express and implied agreements and unjust enrichment. The California court held that Michelle Marvin might recover from Lee Marvin on any one of the above concepts. The fact that Lee was still married to his former wife for the first three years of his relationship with Michelle was held to be no barrier. However, Michelle eventually lost the case. The court on rehearing held that Michelle had failed to prove her alleged express or implied "pooling and sharing" agreement; i.e., there was no express or implied contract. And she also failed to establish unjust enrichment, because she was generously provided for during the relationship. The trial court, however, did award Michelle $104,000 as "severance pay," which was based on two years' pay at the highest salary she had ever earned. An intermediate appellate court, however, canceled the $104,000, finding that there was no statutory basis to award that sum. It should be noted that none of the various decisions in the *Marvin* case held that Lee had any duty to support Michelle after their separation, and to date no state, with the possible exception of New Jersey, has imposed alimony in the cohabitant situation.

From our standpoint, the *Marvin* case is more interesting for its legal analysis than for its dénouement. The California court took judicial notice of the prevalence of nonmarital partnerships in contemporary society. It found that there was no public policy expressed in the California criminal or civil statutes, which precluded recovery by Michelle. If she could prove a "pooling and sharing" agreement in the form of an express (written or oral) contract, or an "implied" agreement resulting from Lee's behavior, she was entitled to recover per the terms of the agreement. For example, if he had deposited half of his earnings in her separate savings account, it would indicate that there was a "pooling and sharing" agreement. If she could prove that Lee was "unjustly enriched," she also could recover. Unfortunately for Michelle, her evidence failed to establish any agreement or unjust enrichment.

Many of the media accounts of *Marvin* v. *Marvin* were inaccurate or misleading. The term "palimony" was coined and frequently used, even though Michelle was claiming a "pooling and sharing" agreement, and gave up all claim to alimony (maintenance). The fact that other states previously had allowed comparable suits was ignored, and to this day the general public probably is unaware that the Oregon decision in *Latham* v. *Latham* is more radical than *Marvin*. Aside from the language of the decision, the only novel feature of the majority holding in *Marvin* was its endorsement of an unjust-enrichment theory (where warranted) as a basis for giving Michelle a share of Lee's property accumulated during their relationship.

One reaction to *Marvin* in other states was the introduction of legislation to limit recovery in such cases to instances where written contracts existed. New York in the *Morone* case limited recovery to the *express* (written or oral) agreement situation and rejected *implied* agreements and unjust enrichment, while Illinois in *Hewitt* would have no part of such shocking goings-on. The New York position probably represents the current majority position in the United States. It should be noted, however, that in New York a husband-wife agreement providing for maintenance and property distribution must be in writing and executed before a notary, whereas an express "pooling and sharing" agreement by cohabitants may be oral, which surely is an anomaly.

One of the difficulties inherent in the *Marvin* situation is that of determining the truth where there is no written contract. That difficulty also exists to a lesser extent under the New York, the majority, position. It may become her word against his. Each is tempted to lie. A nonmarital agreement, therefore, written and properly executed, provides the best protection against the hazards of potential litigation. In most states, such agreements will be sustained if supported by valid consideration apart from anticipated sexual services.

It is ironic that cohabitants, many of whom reject marriage because of their dislike of legal red tape, end up with legal problems comparable to those of married couples. They may have jumped from the frying pan into the fire. And on the human level, the hostility and bitterness when they "split" may be as great as or greater than that of married couples.

A recent book by Professor Lenore J. Weitzman, of Stanford University's Center for Research on Women, *The Marriage Contract: Spouses, Lovers, and the Law,* discusses at length what she calls "intimate contracts" between nonspouses. She also makes valuable comments regarding specific provisions for such agreements. Although we do not agree with some of Professor Weitzman's statements and conclusions, her book is provocative and a valuable reference source.

Lesbian and Gay Relationships

With regard to such relationships, whether called "marriage" or not, it is imperative to have any agreement as to the financial or economic aspects of the relationship in writing. A court is not apt to find a "pooling and sharing" agreement if it is not in writing, or any duty of support. There is no reason, except prejudice, however, why written terms covering matters that are not of a sexual nature should not be enforced. The same is true of group or commune arrangements.

De Facto Families

Regardless of the legal principles under discussion, the facts and equities of the individual case are of great importance. The strongest case for allowing a recovery and granting relief is where the cohabitants have had a de facto family relationship for an extended period of time and "are married except in name." In cases such as *Hewitt* and *Morone,* the man should not be permitted to allege and prove there was no legal marriage when it was a long-term relationship involving children and the reputation in the community that they were husband and wife. The fact situation is even more appealing to courts if the couple were unmarried and not guilty of adultery. What the law calls an "estoppel," or bar, should be invoked against a claim of no marriage, so that the woman will have the same rights and entitlements as a wife.

In some cases, de facto families are treated the same as legal marriages. For example, worker's compensation laws may provide for monetary awards to the *dependents* of injured or deceased workers. Proof that there was a nonlegal, or de facto, family relationship may be sufficient to qualify one as a dependent, especially if the relationship was of long duration.

Common Law Marriages

There is considerable confusion over the concept of common law marriage. It is sometimes regarded as an informal, "at will" relationship of uncertain duration. The term "common-lawing it" sometimes is used. This is *not* the legal meaning of common law marriage. Insofar as the law is concerned, a common law marriage, if valid at the place where it was entered into, entails the same legal consequences as a licensed marriage performed in St. Patrick's Cathedral. It may be terminated only by death or legal proceedings such as divorce or annulment. Today, about twelve states and the District of Columbia still permit common law marriages to be entered into within their borders. Usually, the couple must live together and have the reputation in their community of being husband and wife, and they both must have the capacity to marry as single persons. The remainder of American jurisdictions require a license and some sort of ceremony.

The situation is more complicated, however, because all states recognize the validity of common law marriages entered into at a place where they are still permitted. If valid at the place of celebration they are valid elsewhere. There is disagreement, however, as to what is required when an unmarried couple visits a common-law marriage state. Most states hold that the unmarried couple must become residents of the common law state or have some close and meaningful relationship with it. New York, however, in some cases has found that a common law marriage was contracted during a short visit to the common law state when both parties were free to marry. In effect, the New York rules as to the recognition of common law marriages serve as a *net* to protect the de facto marriage situation as if it were a regular marriage.

Successive Marriages

Another legal doctrine also serves as a net. Where there are successive marriages, the law presumes that the latest marriage was valid. The court will presume that a former marriage was terminated by death or court decree. Cases and states differ as to what must be shown to rebut this presumption. In addition, if the last relationship was "meretricious" at its inception, the court may refuse to presume that there was a valid marriage. The point is, however, that the common-law-marriage and presumption nets may serve as devices to protect ostensible marriages that in fact were never contracted.

The "Putative Wife" Doctrine

In community-property jurisdictions, there also is the "putative wife" doctrine, which is applied where the wife or both parties married in good faith but one or the other then lacked capacity to marry. For example, if the husband told his second wife he was validly divorced from his former wife, but in fact there was no divorce or the divorce decree was void, and the second wife reasonably relied upon his statement, she may qualify as a "putative wife" and will be accorded the same rights as if in fact it were a valid second marriage. A few common law states have reached the same result on various theories including that of a "quasi-partnership," in order to protect the so-called "putative wife."

In a sense, the nets described above and the "putative wife" doctrine operate to achieve equity and to protect some but not all deserving cohabitants. In many cases, the nets operate even though there was no marriage in fact, and none was intended, but as a matter of fairness the parties should be treated as if they were married. Valid agreements offer the only protection today where there was no matrimonial intent (hence no possible common law marriage), the relationship was "meretricious" (hence no presumption), and there was no honest mistake (hence no "putative wife" situation). Eventually, the law may come to distinguish the relatively long-term, de facto situation from a shorter, "at will" relationship and may determine the equities accordingly. At this writing, however, agreements, if valid, control the legal consequences emanating from a nonmarital relationship.

As we have seen, the law does not confer or impose the incidents of marriage and divorce upon cohabitants; the rights and duties implicit in the marital relationship do not apply; there are no common law actions that are protective of the relationship; there are no insulations from the reach of creditors, as in a legal marriage; there are no tax advantages or special concessions.

Having voluntarily chosen cohabitation without marriage, nonmarital partners are stuck with their choice. Under current law they are entitled to challenge discrimination and prejudice, but it does not follow that cohabitants have an entitlement to all of the incidents of marriage and divorce. It is one thing to object to punitive measures being imposed upon unmarried couples, lesbians or gays, or communes, but it is quite another thing to accord the benefits of marriage upon those who have deliberately rejected that relationship, for whatever reason.

There is one area, however, where there is a more legitimate claim to the entitlements of marriage. It is becoming quite common for cohabitants eventually to marry and later to undergo divorce. The question may arise, in determining alimony or distributing property, whether the nonmarital period of time should be considered by the court in reaching an equitable result. The duration of the overall relationship may be a significant factor if it is considered. It may be unfair but technically correct to make the date of marriage a cutoff point. If the court is granted discretion under applicable statutes, it should seek to achieve equity and to reach a fair decision.

The law's response to the current sexual revolution and the dramatic social changes of our times is a delayed reaction. There is a time lag between the formulation of a social consensus and a change of law. But eventually the law catches up or is only a step or so behind social change, and our system is flexible enough to undergo a mutation or to adapt to contemporary needs. If the reader of this chapter is tempted to quote Charles Dickens and say "the law is a ass," she should have patience, for in good time the law will reflect widely held views of the rights and wrongs of human relationships. It just takes time.

Since agreements in such large measure control the legal rights (if any) of cohabitants and spouses, it is important to know the basic rules that apply. People thinking of living together and making an agreement to cover economic or other considerations, as well as spouses contemplating divorce, should be aware of the following points:

1. Before marriage, the parties have a limited area of subject matter to bargain about, but that area is being extended. Most if not all states permit premarriage contracts waiving inheritance rights. The present legal trends also permit the parties to stipulate a fair and reasonable amount of alimony (maintenance)—or to waive alimony—in the event of divorce, and as to the ownership and distribution of property.

2. In many if not most states a waiver of support or alimony is not effective if the other party becomes a welfare case.

3. In most states the parties must be separated before they can execute a "separation agreement," but in a few states, such as New York, comparable agreements may now be entered into *during* marriage and before separation.

4. Agreements and provisions must be fair and reasonable when made and not unconscionable at the time of divorce. States differ as to whether or not there must be a full and complete disclosure of assets in order for an agreement to be valid, and whether or not each party must have independent counsel. It is best to meet those requirements, in any event. Remember, the obligation of the utmost good faith is imposed upon the parties.

5.   Public policy limitations apply to pre- and postmarital agreements. For example, an agreement having unreasonable and detrimental provisions as to child custody and visitation rights will not be upheld by the courts. Provisions requiring the procurement of a divorce also may violate public policy.

6.   Be wary of the distinction between alimony (maintenance) and property settlement. A lump-sum property settlement for tax purposes generally is not deductible by the husband or taxable to the wife, and a capital gains tax may be incurred. In addition, such settlements are not subject to modification, as are alimony (maintenance) awards, and the extraordinary remedies for the enforcement of support orders, e.g. contempt, do not apply.

7.   It is important to consult with a tax-wise matrimonial lawyer whenever substantial money or property is involved, and even where the parties have only modest means there may be a basis for a claim of a spousal interest in retirement or pension benefits, Keogh plans, etc. Generally it is to the advantage of both parties to take those tax advantages permitted by law, as under the rule of the *Lester* case.

8.   Agreements should be drafted and negotiated so that the final product is fair and reasonable for both parties. Otherwise the agreement is apt to be violated and it may be unenforceable. An overwhelming Pyrrhic victory is short-lived.

9.   Trust your lawyer or get another one. Do not conceal your future plans (if any) from your lawyer, because your lawyer's bargaining efforts will vary depending upon whether the lawyer should concentrate on alimony (maintenance) or property distribution.

10.   Don't sell the kids down the river in order to obtain some financial advantage for yourself, and remember that divorce and the post-divorce period are painful and difficult for them. If there are children, your misery *has* company. Don't try to get even by brainwashing the kids; they are entitled to know and communicate with both parents unless it is clearly shown that such an association would be detrimental to their welfare.

Admittedly, it is difficult to persuade indignant clients to take heed of the above points. Both spousal and cohabitant agreements are apt to occur within an emotional context, and the drafting and negotiation process may bring out the worst in human nature. Counseling or therapy may be indicated in many cases. Mediation or arbitration often are useful techniques that merit consideration, and they may cut down the legal costs.

A well-known California lawyer (Jerry Giesler) once said that there were two things that should not be done prematurely: embalming, and divorce. We would add a third: cohabitation and spousal agreements. Time and effort are essential if you care to write your own ticket and want to avoid the cost and uncertainties of litigation.

FURTHER READING

Clark, Homer H. Jr. *Law of Domestic Relations* St. Paul, Minn.: West, 1968.

Foster, H.; and Freed, D. J. *Law and the Family—New York* Rochester, N.Y.: Lawyers Co-op Pub. Co., rev. ed. 2 vols., annual supplement.

Glendon, Mary Ann. *The New Family and the New Property* Toronto: Butterworths, 1981.

Krause, Harry D. *Family Law in a Nutshell* St. Paul, Minn.: West, 1977.

Lindey, Alexander. *Separation Agreements and Antenuptial Contracts* New York: Matthew Bender, 2 vols. with annual supplements.

O'Donnell, William J. *The Law of Marriage and Marital Alternatives* Lexington, Mass.: D. C. Heath, 1981.

Rheinstein, Max. *Marriage Stability, Divorce & the Law* Chicago: Univ. of Chicago Press, 1972.

Weitzman, Lenore. *The Marriage Contract: Spouses, Lovers & the Law* New York: Free Press, 1981.

7
Children and Child Custody

Marilyn Yarbrough Ainsworth

Marilyn Y. Ainsworth, professor of law at the University of Kansas, is the divorced mother of two daughters, Carmen and Carla. She teaches courses in torts, race discrimination, intellectual property, and legal research and writing.

The children's rights movement, which has been compared to the movement for the rights of minorities and women, has accelerated greatly since the late sixties. Before 1967, a child had almost no "rights" and many disabilities. Some of these disabilities were in fact privileges bestowed on children by law. For example, a person who had not reached the age of majority (a minor) had, and still has, the right to disavow many contracts she makes. Many people date the beginning of the present children's rights movement to 1967, the year in which the United States Supreme Court first declared that children have constitutional rights in court proceedings. These rights include those usually accorded adults: the right to an attorney, the privilege against testifying against oneself, and the right to personally challenge the statements of witnesses. Since that decision, the Supreme Court has considered cases involving the right of a minor to seek an abortion or other medical services contrary to parental wishes, the rights of foster children to due process, the rights of children involved in proceedings regarding commitment to mental institutions, and the rights of children to freedom of expression. In the early eighties, the Court decided a case that has the effect of requiring states to have more proof of unfitness than previously required before taking a child away from her natural parents.

In all these cases, there has been a question of the child's rights as opposed to the parents' rights or as opposed to the rights of the government. These tensions continue. Legislators are attempting to solve many of these conflicts through statutes and agency regulations that would more clearly define the rights of children. This chapter addresses specific questions suggested by these conflicts.

Clarification of the term "child," or "minor," is necessary before considering those questions. Each state sets the age of majority or adulthood for its citizens in situations involving state law. In addition, federal law or regulations may prescribe the age of majority for special situations involving federal law or interstate activity. For example, the voting age for persons participating in a federal election is 18.

AGE OF MAJORITY

The charts entitled "Age of Majority" (p. 177–82) give, for each state, the age at which a person becomes an adult for some of the more common situations: voting, marrying, drinking alcoholic beverages, serving on a jury, obtaining a license to drive a motor vehicle, attending school, and suing someone.

What Is Meant by the Term "Age of Majority"?

The term usually designates the age at which one legally becomes an adult. As the charts indicate, age of majority may differ depending on the activity in which the child is engaged. Until 1971, when 18-year-olds were given the right to vote in federal elections, most states designated the age of majority as 21. Since that time, many states have lowered it to 18 for most activities. In 1975 the United States Supreme Court held that a different age of majority for boys and girls was unconstitutional, because it discriminated on the basis of sex.

When a Child Is "Emancipated," Does That Mean She Has Reached the Age of Majority?

When a child is emancipated, she may be released from some (partial emancipation) or all of the requirements for minors and thus be considered an adult even though that child has not reached the age of majority. Emancipation may also release the parents from their duties and responsibilities with regard to their child. A child may be partially emancipated and thus be free from the disabilities associated with minority for only a part of the period of minority, or from only a part of the parent's rights, or for some purposes and not others. Some of the most common situations in which a child seeks emancipation are when she is seeking outside financial aid for college, or credit for purchases independent of consideration of parental resources or creditworthiness.

How Does the Child Become Emancipated?

Emancipation involves an entire surrender of the right to care, custody, and earnings of a minor child by the parents and a termination of parental duties. It can be express, as by voluntary agreement between the parent and the child or by order of the court, or it can be implied by the fact that the child is supporting herself and living away from home.

What If My Child Is Not Emancipated and Has Not Reached the Age of Majority but Runs Away from Home?

Congress has passed a Runaway Youth Act, which increases and improves services for children who have left home, so that they may receive counseling and aid. Individuals and institutions have set up runaway hot lines so that minors who have left home can let their parents know that they are alive and well without having to communicate directly with them. (See p. 547 for runaway hot-line numbers.)

This is not much comfort to parents who would like to have their child home, but these measures at least ensure that children who cannot be found or who will not come home are receiving some support and can keep in touch. If a child does run away from home, reporting to the police and to state family and child service agencies is probably the best way to enlist help in finding the child. One publication, *Search,* an Englewood, New Jersey, catalog of missing children, is circulated nationally to police, hospitals, and social agencies. A parent may register a missing child with that publication.

The organization Child Find, Inc. has a similar purpose for children who are "stolen" (see p. 513 in the appendix for address; also see the section on child snatching in this chapter, p. 165).

RIGHTS AND DUTIES OF PARENTS

The primary children's right is to be cared for and supported by their parents. Although there is no legal requirement that parents give love and emotional support to their children, there are guidelines for more easily regulated items of support and care such as food, clothing, housing, etc. Special problems affecting single parents, adoptive parents, and foster parents will be discussed later.

Does the State Designate How a Child Should Be Supported by Her Parents?

The law usually indicates that a parent is responsible for providing a child with the "necessaries of life." These include the right to receive food, shelter, clothing, medical care, and in some instances education.

Am I Obligated to Provide My Child with a College Education?

A parent is obligated to provide a child with an elementary and a high school education. Traditionally, however, the duty to support does not require that a parent pay for a child's education beyond high school. Some states have required this type of support where the parent is financially able to provide the college education and the life situation of the child requires or suggests a need for such an education. At least one court declared that an agreement between a father and a child regarding a college education amounted to a legally enforceable contract.

Do Both Parents Have an Obligation to Support the Child?

At one time, the father had the duty to support, with no similar duty required of the mother of the child. Now children are entitled to look to both parents for support, although usually resort to the mother is had only if the father is unable to, or does not, support the child. Where the parents are divorced, there is usually an agreement or a court order indicating the duties of the respective parents for support of the child.

Do I Still Have to Support My Child Even Though She Is Working?

Even if your child is earning enough money to support or partially support herself, she is entitled to support from you until she either reaches the age of majority or becomes totally emancipated. This question will be addressed in the section below entitled "Children's Finances."

May I Take Some of My Child's Earnings to Help Pay for Her Support?

Just as children have the right to be supported by their parents, parents are entitled to the services and income of their children in exchange for their duty of support. Many states have regulated the amount of the child's earnings that the parent may take, but there still is this general right to the child's earnings as long as the child is being supported by the parents.

May I Still Claim My Child as an Exemption on My Federal Income Tax Return Even If She Works and Pays Taxes Herself?
You will still be able to claim your child as a tax exemption, no matter how much the child earns, if you can claim the child as a dependent, the child is a student for five months of the year, and the child is under age 19.

NEVER-MARRIED PARENTS AND THEIR CHILDREN

Legal problems concerning the rights of never-married biological parents most often concern the rights of fathers of children who have not been legitimated and the rights of the nonmarital children themselves. Although courts have recently begun to address questions of visitation and adoption by such fathers, the legal controversy surrounding "illegitimacy" has traditionally focused on property rights.

What Is an "Illegitimate," or Nonmarital, Child, and How Does This Affect Her Status?
The term "illegitimate" (here we use "nonmarital") is usually used to describe the legal status of a child whose parents were not married at the time of her birth. The term "putative" father is used to describe the father of the nonmarital child. The nonmarital child is at no disability outside the family situation, and increasingly is at little disability even inside the family. The United States Supreme Court has indicated that nonmarital children have the right to be supported by their parents in the same manner as any other child must be supported.

Nonmarital children also have the right to be supported by public assistance if family financial qualifications are met. They have the right to sue for damages for the wrongful death of their parents. They have the right to recover Social Security benefits due because of their relation to the deceased father, and the right to receive disability benefits as the children of disabled wage-earning parents. In each of these cases, however, there must be some proof of paternity, and in the case of Social Security benefits for the child of a deceased father, there must be proof of paternity and dependency.

How Can Paternity Be Proved?
Although more recent blood grouping tests (such as the HLA test) are quite accurate in proving nonpaternity, paternity can almost never be con-

clusively determined. When the mother is married, however, the presumption of legitimacy is so strong that it may rule out a determination of nonpaternity of a husband even when there is proof that the husband had no access to the mother at the presumed time of conception. Paternity may be established either by (1) a court order declaring such paternity, (2) a written declaration of paternity by the father, (3) payment of support in acknowledgment of paternity, or (4) some other public acknowledgment of the fact.

How Can the Nonmarital Child Prove That She Is Dependent on Her Father?

This requirement of proof of dependency can be met by proof by the nonmarital child either that (1) the father had been determined by a court to be the parent of the child; (2) the child was adopted by the deceased, or the child's parents married before the father's death (this usually serves to "legitimate" the child for all purposes); (3) the father had acknowledged in writing that the child was his; or (4) the child is entitled to inherit from the father under the state inheritance laws.

Can Nonmarital Children Inherit from Their Parents?

The Supreme Court has recently said that states may not discriminate against nonmarital children in their laws of inheritance unless there is some reasonable relationship between the fact of "illegitimacy" and the state's valid interest in regulating wills and inheritance. Since then, the Court has found no such relationship in any of the laws examined that prevented the nonmarital child from inheriting from her parents.

Does the Putative Father Have Visitation Rights or Adoptive Rights with Regard to the Nonmarital Child?

There is no definitive answer yet to questions regarding visitation or adoption rights of putative fathers as against the rights of third parties. These questions are still being addressed on a state-by-state basis.

What Is the Status of Children Conceived by Artificial Insemination or of Children Born to "Surrogate" Mothers?

Interesting legal questions occasionally appear regarding the status of children conceived by artificial insemination from a donor not married to the mother and of children born to "surrogate" mothers. Although there is a strong presumption of "legitimacy" for a child born to a married woman, courts have allowed medical evidence to be presented to support claims of "illegitimacy" by husbands (in one case, even when the husband had given consent to the artificial insemination). As discrimination against the nonmarital child is eliminated, this labeling becomes less important.

ADOPTIVE PARENTS AND THEIR CHILDREN

What Rights and Obligations Does a Biological Parent Have Once a Child Is Adopted?

Once a child has been legally adopted, the legal rights and obligations that formerly existed between the child and the child's biological parents are terminated and are replaced by similar rights and obligations of the adoptive parents. That termination may be either voluntary or involuntary.

When there is adoption by a stepparent (a person married to one of the child's biological parents), there is, of course, no termination of the rights of the biological parent. Although the other biological parent's rights are generally terminated, recently a biological father who voluntarily gave his consent to the adoption of his daughters by a stepfather was granted visitation rights after the adoption. Traditionally, however, adoption has been allowed only after the termination of all parental rights of both biological parents. This may include the removal of the biological parent's name from the birth certificate. Because of the issues involved, a decision to allow adoption by a stepparent is often a very difficult one. Psychological distress may be suffered by the terminated parent or by the child, each of whom loses a legal relationship with a loved one.

How Does Termination of Parental Rights Occur?

Voluntary termination of parental rights occurs when the biological parents consent in writing to the adoption of the child. If the decision to terminate the rights was against the parents' free will, there is a valid ground for challenging the legality of the consent and, therefore, the legality of the adoption if it has been completed.

The most common situations of involuntary termination occur when parents are determined to be unfit or to have abandoned their children. Resort to court action is necessary whenever there is an involuntary termination of the biological parents' rights.

Many states are considering utilization of the courts in every instance where biological parents' rights are being terminated, so that the court can be satisfied that the consent is indeed voluntarily given.

Do the Courts Need the Consent of the Putative Father of a Nonmarital Child Before the Child May Be Adopted?

In all states, termination of the biological mother's parental rights is required. Several states have attempted, however, not to require consent of a putative father when there is a nonmarital child. The United States Supreme Court has indicated that a law requiring the consent of the mother and not of the father of a nonmarital child is discriminatory as between the sexes. Most state statutes allow for notice in a newspaper or other public place for a short period of time. They assume that if the putative father does not come forward in response to the notice he does not object to the adoption.

When May the Court Terminate Parental Rights Without the Parents' Permission?

When there is involuntary termination of parental rights, there must be a court order for termination. Most states require that parents be shown to be neglectful or abusive, to suffer from some mental disability or habitual drunkenness, to be subject to extended imprisonment, or to have abandoned the child. Other states require that the parent provide "improper parental care" or some other such vague standard. There is no recognized right to counsel for the parents in these proceedings. Some jurisdictions provide, however, for a right to counsel for the *children* involved.

May Parents Who Are Minors Consent to the Termination of Their Parental Rights?

In some states, the consent of the parent of a biological parent who is a minor is required before the minor may voluntarily consent to termination of parental rights. In other states no such consent is necessary.

Does the Adoptive Child Have Any Say in the Adoption?

In many states where there is an older child (over 12) to be adopted, the consent of the child is necessary.

When Are Parental Rights Terminated, Before or After the Adoption?

Some states require that parental rights be terminated before the child is even eligible for adoption. In others, the biological parents' rights are not terminated until the adoption is final.

What Do Adoption Agencies Look for When Choosing Adoptive Parents?

In state-regulated adoptions, the adoptive parents are very closely regulated to assure their suitability as adoptive parents. In the past, agencies would examine, for example, the existence and stability of a marriage, the "atmosphere" of the home, the health of the parents, and the financial resources of the parents. They would require that indeed there were two parents, with the mother at home, engaged almost exclusively in homemaking and child-rearing responsibilities, and the father making enough money to support the family in what was then a traditional middle-class manner. They would require that the parents be young, that they have no other children, and that they be incapable of having biological children. They would further require that they be of the same race and religion as the adopted child and that they in fact meet some minimal standard of physical resemblance to the child.

Much of that is no longer required. Single parents and working parents are allowed to adopt children. Children are adopted into homes where other children are present and where the parents may in the future have other children. Racial, religious, and physical similarities are not required in the overwhelming majority of states.

Once the Investigation Is Over, May the Child Be Adopted Immediately?

Once the investigation is completed, adoptive parents are, when the child is available, given custody of the child—usually under a temporary, or interlocutory, decree. This is normally for a period of six months, after which the adoptive parents may petition the court for a final decree of adoption.

Why Is There This Waiting (Interlocutory) Period?

The interlocutory period allows either the adoptive parents or the court to determine that the adoption is not in the best interests of the child, or of the adoptive parents, and allows cancelation of the adoption agreement.

May I Adopt Privately Without Going Through All That Red Tape?

There are many independent ("gray" or "black" market) adoptions despite the existence of state agencies and state regulations regarding adoption. Gray-market adoptions are legal in just about every state. In these adoptions, arrangements are made directly between the biological and the adoptive parents. All necessary consents are obtained, all parties go to court to have the proper changes made in the birth certificate, and adoption decrees are issued, both interlocutory and final. Investigations that are made before placement of a child in state-regulated adoptions are also usually made in gray-market adoptions.

In black-market, or private-placement, adoptions, generally no legalities are observed. There is no court intervention in the process. This type of adoption can, like gray market adoptions, involve only the biological and adoptive parents, or can also involve doctors, lawyers, or other intermediaries. Birth certificates are forged in the name of the adopting parents and no investigation is done. These adoptions are illegal in every state.

Once the Child Is Finally Adopted, What Rights Does She Have?

Once the adoption is final, the adopted child stands in the same relationship to the adoptive parents as does a child in a nonadoption situation to her biological parents. There is a right to inherit from the adoptive parent, though usually there is no such right with regard to the biological parents. There is a right to inherit from relatives of the adoptive parents as any biological child of those parents would. Some states have held that these children also have the right to inherit from biological grandparents where the biological parents have predeceased the biological grandparents.

Can the Adopted Child Ever Find Out Who Her Biological Parents Are?

Lately the most controversial legal problem involving adoption has been the right of the adopted child to discover the identity of her biological parents and her right to reopen the files to discover information about her birth and family, not always including the identity of the biological parents. A few states give the adopted child the right to inspect the original birth certificate upon reaching the age of majority. In most states, however, original birth certificates are sealed and may not be unsealed without a court order based upon "good cause." Courts have recognized as "good cause" fraud in the adoption proceedings, the need for medical information, and the need for information about family background to prove inheritance. However, they balance the biological parents' rights to privacy, the adoptive parents' right to raise the child without undue interference, and the child's interests, when considering a court order to reopen or unseal a birth certificate. In a recent case a child who had reached the age of majority was denied the right to know his mother's identity even though that request was predicated upon the need for a close-relative donor for life-saving medical treatment.

GUARDIANSHIP AND FOSTER CARE

What Is the Difference Between Guardianship, Foster Care, and Custody?

Guardianship, foster care, and custody are often associated with or confused with adoption. "Guardianship" is designed to provide a minor with some means of overcoming the legal disabilities of minority, with regard to either property or personal rights. Parents are referred to as "natural" guardians for their children. "Legal" guardians may also be appointed to provide the child with independent, responsible representation in matters concerning property or personal rights. Where it is in the child's best interests, a legal guardian may be appointed even though the parents or some other person or agency has physical custody of the child. This most often occurs when there is a potential conflict of interest if the parents or the custodian were to represent the child in a particular matter; for example, where both parent and child are potential recipients of a disputed inheritance, or where the child has inherited stock in a concern and the parent is vying for control of that stock. The scope of the guardianship may be limited to fit each case.

"Foster care" is a temporary home placement for a child, with no rights of custody transferred. The standard is what is in the "best interest of the child." If the natural parents are temporarily unable to care for the child or if the child is awaiting adoption, foster care may be warranted. Foster parents have some duty to support their foster children, at least with respect to basic necessities. There is usually, however, no right of foster children to inherit or receive benefits because of their relationship to the foster parents unless there is some specific designation of the child as a beneficiary of a foster parent's will. These provisions differ from state to state.

DIVORCED PARENTS AND THEIR CHILDREN

As divorce becomes more and more a reality in American life, issues of child custody become more important. When parents are married, they generally share the responsibilities and decisions for raising their children. When there is no longer a two-parent home, there often must be new arrangements for that responsibility and those decisions. Until recently, the mother usually retained custody of small children, while the father was sometimes able to obtain custody of older children. In the early days of this country, the father was considered to have a superior right to custody of minor children. Fathers were regarded as more competent financially and to need the services of their children in their businesses or on their farms. As women began to exercise more rights—the right to vote, the right to own property, and the right to be gainfully employed—they also acquired rights to custody.

Originally there was a "tender years" presumption that stated that a mother was more capable of raising children and providing them with love and guidance while they were of "tender years." That was, in fact, a part of some state statutes until very recently. That presumption is probably still working, judicially and culturally, since in 90 percent of all contested custody cases, mothers still receive custody. There is a trend toward equality of parents' rights to custody nationwide as men assume more responsibilities while in the two-parent home and desire more responsibilities if the parents separate. Some courts have held recently that maternal preference in child custody cases deprives the father of his right to equal protection of the law under the Fourteenth Amendment to the U.S. Constitution. All courts, following the lead of the United States Supreme Court, indicate that the standard in awarding child custody should be what is "in the best interest of the child."

How Does a Court Determine What Is in the Best Interest of the Child?

The state of Michigan in 1970 set out ten specific criteria for determining the best interest of the child. This is considered by many to be model legislation with regard to child custody. The Michigan statute indicates that the "best interest of the child" is determined by considering, evaluating, and determining "the sum total of the following factors":

1. The love, affection, and other emotional ties existing between the competing parties and the child.

2. The capacity and disposition of competing parties to give the child love, affection, and guidance and continuation of the educating and raising of the child in its religion or creed, if any.

3. The capacity and disposition of competing parties to provide the child with food, clothing, medical care or other remedial care recognized and permitted under the laws of this state in lieu of medical care, and other material needs.

4. The length of time the child has lived in a stable, satisfactory environment and the desirability of maintaining continuity.

5. The permanence, as a family unit, of the existing or proposed custodial home.

6. The moral fitness of the competing parties.

7. The mental and physical health of the competing parties.

8. The home, school, and community record of the child.

9. The reasonable preference of the child, if the court deems the child to be of sufficient age to express preference.

10. Any other factor considered by the court to be relevant to a particular child custody dispute.

Does a Court Have to Make the Decision About Custody, or May Parents Just Agree Between Themselves?

Parents may work out custody arrangements by agreement. When there is no agreement, however, the decision will probably be left to the judge in the divorce case or in a separate child custody proceeding. When a child is considered old enough or mature enough, the preference of the child may be considered and may be the determining factor.

What Kinds of Custody Arrangements Are There?

Custody arrangements are usually described as one-parent (sole or exclusive), joint (shared), or split (divided).

What Is One-parent Custody?

One-parent custody usually means that the custodial parent takes care of the child on a daily basis and assumes responsibility for the child's needs and responsibility for decisions that are made about the child's welfare. The noncustodial parent usually has some rights to visit the child or to have the child visit the noncustodial parent.

When There Is One-parent Custody, How Do the Parent Without Custody and Her/His Family Keep Close to the Child?

Visitation rights are usually given to the noncustodial parent in a one-parent custody arrangement. Typically, the noncustodial parent has specific days and times, often weekends or summer and winter vacations, during which she/he may see the child. Recently, grandparents have been given similar rights. A problem often arises where the custodial parent is unwilling to allow the noncustodial parent the designated visitation rights; there is often no quick and viable solution. If the noncustodial parent defaults on child support payments, the custodial parent is generally afforded help from the prosecutor's (state attorney general's) office in enforcing the support provisions, but there is no corresponding public help to enforce visitation rights.

What Is "Child Snatching" and How Does That Differ from Kidnapping?

There are over one hundred thousand child-snatching cases each year, and the law in virtually every state indicates that the taking of a child by one of her parents is not kidnapping and not against the law. On July 1, 1981, the Parental Kidnapping Prevention Act of 1980 went into effect. Under this legislation, every state is under an obligation to recognize the custody ruling of every other state. This has not been required in the past. This law was passed specifically to deter the child snatching that has occurred as noncustodial parents have taken their children and either hidden them from the custodial parent with no attempt to litigate the question of custody, or moved to another jurisdiction and tried to get the new state's courts to appoint them the custodial parent. While courts could act independently "in the best interest of the child," there was no requirement that they honor another state's custody agreement.

When the parent snatches the child with no intent to petition for legal custody, there is little that can be done even with the enactment of the Parental Kidnapping Prevention Act. In those cases, the custodial parent is usually left to hire a private investigator or to investigate on her/his own, find the child, and in turn "snatch" her from the offending parent. At least one national organization has been formed to give parents and missing children a means of contacting each other. For a small fee (fifty dollars in 1982) parents may register their missing children. The child's picture and information will be released to television stations and newspapers. In addition, posters and literature have been sent to public libraries and schools telling children how to contact Child Find, Inc. Current information about that organization can be obtained from Child Find, Inc. (see p. 513 for address).

May a Noncustodial Parent Make the Parent with Custody Live Close Enough for Regular Visitation to Be Possible?

In 1981, a New York court decided that in fact there were considerations involving visitation that overrode the traditional rights of the custodial parent to determine the child's place of residence. In that case, the mother could not show extreme need to move based on either a job offer or new marital obligations. The court ordered that she accommodate the wishes of the father and her son, and remain in the vicinity. Although this case seems unique as an exercise of judicial prerogative, many separation agreements provide for the same type of restriction. Most would provide for not a blanket prohibition against moving, but at least for consultation with, if not permission of, the noncustodial parent, before such a move is made.

What Is Joint Custody?

In joint custody, each parent agrees to share in decisions and responsibilities regarding the children. The sharing does not have to be equal sharing. Some arrangements provide for the child's staying with one parent for part of the week and the other parent another part of the week. Other parents agree to have the child in one home for a week or a month and then the other home for a week or a month. Some parents even agree to leave the child in the family home and have the parents move in and out of the home during "on" or "off" weeks. In most arrangements, the parents agree to live in the same neighborhood, so that the child can move from one parent's house to the other easily and can attend school and associate with neighborhood friends without too much trouble. At least one court has ruled that joint custody is inappropriate where the parents are "persistently and severely embattled."

What Is Split Custody?

Split custody involves separating children so that each parent has custody of at least one child. Except in cases where there is great difference in ages of the children and a difference in the sex of the children, split custody is not usually practiced.

How Can I Tell Which Type of Custody Arrangement Is Best for My Child?

Suzanne Ramos, in her book *The Complete Book of Child Custody,* poses very detailed and pointed questions for parents considering various custody arrangements:*

If You're Thinking About One-Parent Custody:

1.   Do you believe that you are the "psychological parent" of your children? (Experts at the Yale Child Study Center now say that in almost every family, there is clearly one parent who is the psychological parent.)

2.   Are you and your spouse bitter toward one another or not on cooperative terms? (If so, joint custody would be unwise.)

3.   Do you like having children around, not just your own, but their friends too? Do you mind feeding them and cleaning up after them?

4.   Do you have the patience and the determination to discipline and train children so that they have a sense of order in their lives and so that they:

a.   learn to do things for themselves (bathe, brush their teeth, take care of their clothes, do their homework, practice the piano, handle money);

b.   learn acceptable, polite behavior and can handle themselves in social situations; and,

c.   learn to be considerate of and helpful to you, to each other, and to others? These may sound like simple tasks but they require years of perseverance on your part.

5.   Can you remove splinters, treat wounds, pull loose teeth, give tepid baths when fevers run high, give shampoos?

6.   More importantly, can you handle emotional wounds or problems? Do your children find you sensitive to their feelings and, therefore, trust you and confide in you? Essentially, do you connect with them emotionally?

7.   Can you allow them a certain amount of childish behavior —crying, being jealous of a sister or brother, bad dreams, anxiety —without becoming angry?

*From *The Complete Book of Child Custody,* © 1979 by Suzanne Ramos. Reprinted by permission of G. P. Putnam's Sons.

8. Are you affectionate and physical with your children?

9. Can you cook—fix breakfasts during the morning rush, pack lunches, and prepare nutritious meals offering more variety than hamburgers and spaghetti?

10. Are you willing to handle housework—laundry, marketing, cleaning kitchens and bathrooms, vacuuming, picking up after the children, sewing torn seams, replacing buttons, ironing a shirt or dress for a special occasion—and give up the eight to ten hours a week necessary to take care of these things?

11. If you work full-time, can you be home for a reasonable amount of time during the week when the children are home? For example, can you be with them for dinner on at least three out of five weekday evenings?

12. Do you have, or know where to find, someone reliable, kind and intelligent to be there when the children come home from school, someone who can stay if you have to work late?

13. Can you take time off from work if one of your children is sick, has a day off, or is on vacation from school? If not, do you have a good substitute?

14. Can you attend a fair number of PTA meetings and parent-teacher conferences? Can you get away for some daytime school events, such as class plays, field days, and the like? Will you volunteer occasionally for some of the many jobs parents are called upon to do to help make the school run smoothly?

15. Can you drop everything and leave work if the school calls and says your child has a temperature or just vomited in the classroom?

16. Are you willing to try and cope with a child saying to you, "If my parents hadn't gotten a divorce, maybe I would do better in school" ("maybe I would be happier") ("maybe I wouldn't be overweight") . . . ?

17. How do you feel about having your personal life secondary to your parental responsibilities: being able to meet fewer people socially; at times, having to cancel plans at the last minute because one of your children is sick or the baby-sitter can't make it; having a limited sex life?

18. Do you know that you will probably feel that you never have *enough* money, quiet, adult conversation, sex, *time*—time to be with your children, to concentrate on your work, to keep the house in order, to get out with friends?

19. Do you know that, in spite of all your work, you probably won't get much appreciation?

20. Do you feel that your children are special and irresistible? That having them with you will make all the sacrifices worthwhile?

21. Are you willing to take on whatever emotional problems your children may have in reaction to the separation, at a time when you, yourself, may not be feeling too strong?

22. Do you feel that you should assume exclusive custody because you are the more loving, more responsible, better parent?

23. Have you asked your children what living arrangement they would like? This is essential where children are approximately ten or older. Even younger children should be consulted, although their opinions should not be controlling.

If You're Thinking About Joint Custody:

1. Do you sincerely believe that both of you have an equally close emotional bond with your children? That you share the role of "psychological parent" and are not depriving them of being with the one parent who really is the closer to the children—the one they talk to, trust, love, and depend on more than the other? (Parents often report having overheard their children ask each other, "Who do you like better, Mommy or Daddy?" with the children giving thoughtful but very definite answers.) Many others feel that one parent should almost always be given the dominant role, because joint custody, with its dual living arrangements, puts too great a strain on children. It is often too disruptive for young children and frequently doesn't last long with teenagers, who generally want to live in one place—where their friends and social lives are, where they can bring friends, and where they have a calm, stable life during what are difficult years.

2. Do neither of you want full-time custody?

3. Do both of you work outside the home?

4. Do you have a good working relationship with your former spouse?

5. Are you prepared to talk to him/her as often as every day to discuss your mutual responsibilities regarding the children—school, health care, discipline, extracurricular activities, dates with friends?

6. Do you live within a few miles of your former spouse?

7. Are you prepared for the inconvenience of your child moving in and out every few days, every week, or every month?

8. Can you handle all of the responsibilities mentioned under one-parent custody? While you will not have the children full-time, you will have them enough of the time so that you will have to provide full parental services—physical, emotional, intellectual, social. If your children are with you for roughly 50 percent of the time, that time with you is part of their real life and should not have the off-schedule tone that is often the case when children "visit" a noncustodial parent for a day or weekend.

9. What living arrangement do your children say they would like?

If You're Thinking About Split Custody:

1. How will your children feel about being separated from one another and how difficult will it be for them? Remember,

children lend each other support and they can be especially help-ful to each other following a separation.

2. Have you thought about how many other adjustments this will involve for your child at the same time he must cope with your divorce? Will he have to:

    a. move to a new home? a new part of the country?

    b. change schools?

    c. give up most friends?

    d. learn a new language?

3. Have you explored other, less drastic arrangements and found them unworkable (such as split/joint custody—see 9.)?

4. Have you thought about the recommendations on split custody of some psychiatrists who say that:

    a. If there are three children in your family, you might consider separating the middle, sometimes more neglected, child and leave the oldest and youngest together;

    b. where there is an older boy and a younger girl, the boy might go with the father and the girl with the mother?

5. Are your children more than six years apart in age? (This would probably make the separation easier on them.)

6. Are you and your former spouse going to be separated by a great distance? If the distance between you would prohibit anything more than one trip a year, this strengthens the argument for split custody—provided the children are not very close.

7. Do you realize that children can provide help and support to a custodial parent, thereby improving the home atmosphere for all? Older children often help with and act as surrogate parents to younger children. Breaking up the children precludes this sup-port system.

8. Do you in any way think of your children as possessions? Could it be that, without realizing it, you feel that having custody of none of the children would be "giving" too much to your spouse, and for that reason, you want split custody?

9. If you're contemplating a variation of split custody, what we call split/joint custody, do the following criteria apply:

    a. Do you both want custody of one or more of the children with all the time, work, and responsibility that it entails?

Can I Lose Custody Once I Get It?

Courts always retain the right to modify custody agreements. Again, they look at what is in the best interest of the child. In situations involving lesbian or gay parents and parents who have live-in lovers, courts have taken children away from their parents. Lip service is given to the notion that the courts will look at the relationship between the parent and the child and not the life-style of the parent if it doesn't affect the child. However, judges still are willing to remove children from happy and stable home environments, often against the child's will, when homosexuality or other nontraditional life-styles are involved. Additionally, custody arrangements agreed to by parents or ordered by the court may be changed because the circumstances are changed, or because one of the parents changes her/his mind. This sometimes occurs too when the child asks for a change. In short, custody decisions are almost never final.

EDUCATION FOR CHILDREN

Although the United States Supreme Court has declared that there is no constitutional right to an education, all states have provided for the maintenance of public school systems and for compulsory school attendance. Since the states have undertaken to provide children with public education, the United States Constitution requires that that education be provided in a fair and equitable manner. Controversy over children's rights in the educational setting began in the 1960s. Most of the conflicts that arose between school officials and students during that time concerned political, rather than educational, matters. Unlawful search and seizure, dress and hair codes, First Amendment expression, suspensions and expulsions, and corporal punishment were some of the topics addressed. The confidentiality of student records, bilingual education, education of the handicapped, and vocational education were matters addressed by the federal government. Federal budget cuts in the eighties, which have returned much of the responsibility for and control of funds for education to the states, may have a profound impact on some of these gains in children's educational rights. In the conflict between federal and state government over these issues and programs, parental concerns have often been lost.

Does a Parent Have Any Control over a Child's Education?

The law has traditionally held that parental control over a child's welfare includes control over that child's education. Despite compulsory attendance laws, parents have been allowed to choose between public and private schools for their children. They have been allowed to withdraw their children from school when continued attendance would have a detrimental effect on an established religious community's way of life. They have also been allowed to provide home instruction for their children.

Withdrawing children from school for home instruction or even from particular courses within the school depends on state law. Some states require only that home instruction be equivalent to instruction received in the public schools. Other states may require that home instructors be teachers who meet all the requirements prescribed by law for private tutors, or even that they be certified teachers.

What Right Does a Parent or Child Have Regarding the Quality of the Child's Education?

By 1981, at least eight educational malpractice lawsuits had been filed. None of those suits resulted in recovery by the parent or child. Many lawyers believe, however, that recovery for educational malpractice, like recovery for medical or legal malpractice, may be recognized in the near future. At present, the only recourse a parent or child has regarding the quality of education received is through protest and lobbying actions with school administrations and school boards.

Who Has a Right of Access to a Child's School Records?

The Family Educational Rights and Privacy Act of 1974 (Buckley Amendment) gave parents the right of access to their minor children's records. This includes a right to review and correct any data directly related to a student that are maintained by an educational agency or institution that receives federal funds.

When a child reaches the age of 18 or is a student in a postsecondary educational institution, the student acquires the right of review and correction described above. Otherwise, the law requires that the parent of a dependent student (with dependency defined by the child's dependent tax status) is the person who acquires rights under the Act. This would seem to preclude a divorced parent who does not claim the child as a dependent under the tax laws from claiming the right of access to the student's records. Minor children have no right of access to their records.

The Buckley Amendment also provides for nondisclosure of any information except "directory information" to anyone except the persons mentioned above and educational personnel who have a legitimate educational interest to pursue. Directory information includes the student's name, address, telephone number, date and place of birth, major field of study, participation in officially recognized activities and sports, weight and height of members of athletic teams, dates of attendance, degrees and awards received, and the most recent previous educational agency or institution attended by the student. Students or parents who have the right of access also have the right to request that none of that directory information be released.

School Grounds: What Rights Does a Child Have?

Although school officials have the power to limit the substantive rights of students when it is necessary to maintain order on school grounds, some definite rights with regard to the areas mentioned in the introductory paragraph above continue to be recognized.

It is usually held that for a *search* to violate the Fourth Amendment of the United States Constitution, it must be conducted by a state official and there must be no probable cause for the search. In school cases, the United States Supreme Court has ruled that only reasonable suspicion is necessary for there to be a lawful search where the school official is acting so as to maintain order and enforce rules of the school, rather than for general law-enforcement purposes. School locker searches have almost uniformly been allowed under the theory that the student and the school jointly own the locker. It has also been held that the school has the duty to inspect the locker in the interest of the health and safety of the other students.

Dress and hair codes: These have not caused much controversy in the past few years. Most courts have supported the discretion of school administrators as long as regulations are reasonable and essential to the educational process. In determining whether this standard has been met, courts have balanced the student's rights to personal freedom against the school administration's duty to ensure adequate health and safety standards, maintain discipline, and prevent interference with the educational environment. Since the United States Supreme Court has indicated that this matter should be left to the states, the validity of school regulations has often depended upon state law.

Freedom of religion: This is guaranteed in the First Amendment of the United States Constitution, which requires that there be a separation of church and state in public education. This would require that schools do nothing to promote any religious instruction. This has been interpreted to prohibit prayer in schools and to prohibit the teaching of the "creationist" theory of human origin as scientific theory. As noted above, however, the Supreme Court has recognized an exception to the compulsory attendance law where that law would have a detrimental effect on an established religious community's way of life.

Freedom of expression: This has been upheld with regard to activities that do not materially and substantially interfere with school educational activities. These have included the right to wear armbands, the right to picket, the right of association, and free speech and press. Schools are allowed to impose reasonable restrictions with regard to time, place, and manner on the distribution of literature and on speech. Courts will no doubt continue to balance the rights of students against the duty of the school to maintain order. For instance, even though students may have the right to speak to classmates about political issues, the school may prohibit such speech during formal class periods or prohibit the use of loudspeakers on school grounds when either may disrupt the education process if allowed at that time or place.

Suspensions and expulsions: These require that students be accorded due process of law. Prior to a short-term suspension, a student is entitled to a basic due-process hearing. This can be met by telling the student orally or in writing what the alleged wrong-doing was and what the evidence is, and by giving the student a chance to tell the other side of the story. With regard to serious disciplinary matters which may result in long-term suspension or expulsion, there must be notice and a formal hearing. The accused student must be given the right to confront witnesses and the right to counsel. There must also be a statement of the findings, conclusions, and recommendations of the hearing officer(s). There must be a right to appeal.

Corporal punishment: Unless it is specifically prohibited by state or local law, corporal punishment is not illegal. Where excessive force is used, students may bring civil or criminal actions for battery against school officials, but there is no constitutional right to be free from corporal punishment.

Does My Child Have a Right to Participate in Extracurricular Activities?

Students have no absolute right to participate in extracurricular activities. If schools provide opportunities for such activities, however, they must be made available on a nondiscriminatory basis. There can be no discrimination based on race, sex, marital status, or even pregnancy.

Does My "Special" Child Have Special Rights?

Children who may be considered "special" (basically, handicapped, gifted, learning-disabled, bilingual, etc.) are entitled to an education suited to their special needs.

Congress has enacted the Education for All Handicapped Children Act, which requires that any school system receiving federal funds provide for the education of handicapped children according to those children's needs. The Act also provides for procedures to assure fairness in determining whether a child is properly placed in a special program when that child may be capable of performing in a regular classroom.

For bilingual children, the United States Supreme Court decided in 1974 that it was a violation of the Civil Rights Act of 1964 not to provide special instruction for non-English-speaking children whose educations were severely handicapped by a language barrier, where there are substantial numbers of such students in the district. Although some federal officials question the need for such a provision, there is at this writing continued funding for such bilingual programs.

MEDICAL CARE FOR CHILDREN

May a Doctor or Hospital Give Medical Care to My Children Without My Consent?

Although in some instances an older minor may receive medical care without a parent's consent, courts have generally required that a parent agree to the treatment of a minor unless there is danger to life and limb without immediate care *and* the parent is unavailable to give consent. Blanket written permission should be given routinely to a child's school, regular physician, or a baby-sitter.

When May an Older Minor Receive Medical Care Without Parental Consent?

Most states have statutes that allow a teenager to receive care for drug abuse and for contraception, venereal disease, pregnancy, and abortion. The legislatures (and the courts) have determined that it is important that teenagers concerned with these health areas be able freely to receive information and treatment without fear of parental interference or disapproval.

WORKING CHILDREN

Will the State Restrict My Child's Right to Work?

The state does have the right to protect minors from dangerous and unhealthful work, but will usually not interfere when children are engaged in work generally done by minors (for example, baby-sitting, packaging groceries, clerking in stores, or working in fast-food restaurants) that does not interfere with school attendance (see chart p. 177). Some states require that children have "working papers." Information about the existence and particulars of this requirement can be obtained from your state employment-services or human-resources office.

Also see Chapter 5 for further information on medical care for children.

Does my Child Have to Pay Taxes on What She Earns?

A minor must file a tax return if she earns more than $3,300 a year. If the minor can be claimed by someone else as a dependent and receives income from investments of more than $1,000 a year, she must file if her gross income is $1,000 or more. Gross income is that amount of income not exempt from or excluded from being taxed.

Any employee who had no income tax liability in the preceding tax year and anticipates none for the current year may file a "certification of nontaxability," claiming exemption from federal withholding tax. An employer may not withhold federal income tax from an employee who has properly filed this form.

Is My Child Eligible for All the Benefits an Adult Gets for Working?

Your child is eligible for fringe benefits if the employer pays them to similarly situated adult workers. Your child is entitled to worker's compensation if injured while working. The child also qualifies for unemployment insurance if she meets the requirements set forth for all similarly situated adults who are working. The child should have a Social Security card and is eligible for Social Security benefits based on the work done even while a minor.

CHILDREN'S FINANCES

If the Child Has Earnings of Her Own or Otherwise Has Money of Her Own, Does She Have the Right to Spend It or Manage It?

As indicated in the section on rights and duties of the parents, parents have some rights to the earnings of their children. Where the child is emancipated from the parent, however, either because she is living away from home or because she is married, or where it is understood either by formal agreement or by practice that the child has the right to her earnings, the parent has no right to the earnings.

Where the child has money through inheritance or a gift, this money may not be claimed by anyone except the child and then only under the conditions set forth by the inheritance or by the gift.

May a Child Open a Bank Account in Her Own Name?

The child may open a bank account and deposit or withdraw money without the consent of a parent. Again, however, where money is placed in bank accounts in trust for the child through the terms of inheritance or gift, the child is restricted from using the money by the terms of the gift or inheritance. Those accounts, however, may be managed by a trustee who may authorize the use of funds for special needs of the child such as for a college education.

Does a Child Have the Right to Make a Will or to Inherit Under a Will Because of a Relationship with the Deceased Person?

The child may not make a will. A person must reach the age of majority before making a valid will. If the child dies, any money or property she has will usually go to her parents or, if her parents are dead, to her sisters and brothers. Each state has its own rules as to what happens if there are no sisters or brothers. These sometimes complicated schemes attempt to distribute the child's property to the closest relatives that can be found. If the minor is married, the property and money will go to her spouse and children.

A child may inherit in the same ways in which adults inherit through will or because of their relationship with the person who died. If her parents have no will, the court will usually appoint someone to care for the child's money until she reaches the age of majority. If there is a will, it will usually designate a guardian or trustee for the child's inheritance. If the will doesn't, the court will appoint someone in that instance too.

May a Child Be Disinherited by Her Parents?

A child may be disinherited if there is specific mention of that fact in the will. If a child is simply left out of the will, she may usually contest the disinheritance.

AGE OF MAJORITY

STATES	VOTING	JURY SERVICE	WORKING FOR WAGES[1]	COMPULSORY SCHOOL ATTENDANCE[2]	SUING WITHOUT GUARDIAN	DISAFFIRM. OTHERWISE BINDING
Alabama	21	19	16	16	19	19
Alaska	18	19	18	16	19	18
Arizona	18	18	18	16	18	18
Arkansas	21	—	16	15	18	18
California	18	18	16	16	18	18
Colorado	18	18	18	16	18	18
Connecticut	18	18	16	16	18	18
Delaware	18	18	18	16	18	18
District of Columbia	18	18	—	16	—	—
Florida	18	18	18	16	18	18
Georgia	18	18	16	16	18	18

9

AGE OF MAJORITY (continued)

STATES	VOTING	JURY SERVICE	WORKING FOR WAGES[1]	COMPULSORY SCHOOL ATTENDANCE[2]	SUING WITHOUT GUARDIAN	DISAFFIRM. OTHERWISE BINDING
Hawaii	18	18	18	18	18	18
Idaho	18	18	16	16	18	18
Illinois	18	18	16	16	18	18
Indiana	18	18	18	16	18	18
Iowa	18	18	18	16	18	18
Kansas	18	18	18	16	18	18
Kentucky	18	18	18	16	18	18
Louisiana	18	18	18	16	18	18
Maine	18	18	18	16	18	18
Maryland	18	18	18	16	18	18
Massachusetts	18	18	18	16	18	18
Michigan	18	18	18	16	18	18
Minnesota	18	18	18	16	18	18
Mississippi	18	21	16	13	18	18
Missouri	18	21	16	16	21	18
Montana	18	18	16	16	18	18
Nebraska	18	19	16	16	20	19
Nevada	18	18	18	17	18	18
New Hampshire	18	18	18	16	18	18
New Jersey	18	18	21	16	18	18
New Mexico	18	18	18	18	18	18
New York	18	18	18	16	18	18
North Carolina	18	18	18	16	18	19
North Dakota	18	18	16	16	18	19
Ohio	18	18	18	18	18	18
Oklahoma	18	18	16	18	18	18
Oregon	18	18	18	18	18	18
Pennsylvania	18	18	18	—	18	18
Rhode Island	18	18	16	16	18	18
South Carolina	18	18	16	16	18	18
South Dakota	18	18	16	16	18	16
Tennessee	18	18	18	16	18	18
Texas	18	18	17	—	18	18
Utah	18	18	18	18	18	18
Vermont	18	—	18	16	18	18
Virginia	18	18	18	17	18	18
Washington	21	18	18	18	18	18
West Virginia	18	18	18	16	18	18
Wisconsin	18	18	18	18	18	18
Wyoming	18	—	16	16	19	19

1. General age at which person may be employed without restrictions because of age. States usually allow nonhazardous work at an earlier age.
2. States waive compulsory attendance if: 1) the student has graduated from high school or has completed a certain grade level; and 2) is employed.

AGE OF MAJORITY

Alcohol

STATES	BEER	WINE	LIQUOR	STATES	BEER	WINE	LIQUOR
Alabama	19	19	19	Montana	19	19	19
Alaska	19	19	19	Nebraska	19	19	19
Arizona	19	19	19	Nevada	21	21	21
Arkansas	21	21	21	New Hampshire	18	18	18
California	21	21	21	New Jersey	21	21	21
Colorado	18	21	21	New Mexico	21	21	21
Connecticut	18	18	18	New York	18	18	18
Delaware	20	20	20	North Carolina	18	18	21
District of Columbia	18	18	18	North Dakota	21	21	21
Florida	18	18	18	Ohio	18	21	21
Georgia	18	18	18	Oklahoma	18	21	21
Hawaii	18	18	18	Oregon	21	21	21
Idaho	19	19	19	Pennsylvania	21	21	21
Illinois	18	18	18	Rhode Island	18	18	18
Indiana	21	21	21	South Carolina	18	18	21
Iowa	19	19	19	South Dakota	18	21	21
Kansas	18	21	21	Tennessee	19	19	19
Kentucky	21	21	21	Texas	18	18	18
Louisiana	18	18	18	Utah	21	21	21
Maine	16	16	16	Vermont	18	18	18
Maryland	18	18	21	Virginia	19	21	21
Massachusetts	18	18	18	Washington	18	18	18
Michigan	18	18	18	West Virginia	18	18	18
Minnesota	18	18	18	Wisconsin	18	18	18
Mississippi	21	21	21	Wyoming	19	19	19
Missouri	21	21	21				

AGE OF MAJORITY

Driver's License

STATES	OPERATOR'S LICENSE	LEARNER PERMIT JR. LICENSE	WITH DRIVER EDUCATION	WITH PARENT PERMISSION
Alabama	16	15	16	18
Alaska	16	14	—	18
Arizona	16	15	—	18
Arkansas	16	14	—	18
California	16	15/14	18	18
Colorado	16	15.5	—	18
Connecticut	16	16	18	—
Delaware	16	—	18	18
District of Columbia	16	—	—	—
Florida	16	15	18	18
Georgia	16	15	—	18
Hawaii	17	15	—	18

AGE OF MAJORITY (continued)

Driver's License

STATES	OPERATOR'S LICENSE	LEARNER PERMIT JR. LICENSE	WITH DRIVER EDUCATION	WITH PARENT PERMISSION
Idaho	16	14	16	18
Illinois	18	15	18	18
Indiana	16 & 1 mo	15	16.5	18
Iowa	17	14	18	—
Kansas	16	14	—	18
Kentucky	16	—	—	18
Louisiana	15	—	17	18
Maine	15	15	—	18
Maryland	16	15.75	18	—
Massachusetts	18	16.5	17	18
Michigan	16	14	16	18
Minnesota	16	15	18	17
Mississippi	15	—	—	—
Missouri	16	15	—	18
Montana	16	13	—	—
Nebraska	16	14–15	—	18
Nevada	16	14–16	—	—
New Hampshire	18/16[1]	15	18	—
New Jersey	17	16.5	—	18
New Mexico	16	14	16	16
New York	18/17[2]	16	18	18
North Carolina	16	15	18	18
North Dakota	16	14	16	18
Ohio	18	14–16& 16–18	—	16
			—	—
Oklahoma	16	14	15.5	18
Oregon	16	14–15	—	18
Pennsylvania	17	16	18	18
Rhode Island	16	16	21	18
South Carolina	16	15	—	18
South Dakota	16	14	—	—
Tennessee	16	14	—	18
Texas	16	15	16	18
Utah	16	16	All[3]	17
Vermont	18	15	18	18
Virginia	16	15.66	18	18
Washington	16	15.5	18	—
West Virginia	18	16	—	18
Wisconsin	16	14	18	18
Wyoming	16	15	—	—

1. Sixteen if minor has completed driver's education.
2. Seventeen if minor has completed driver's education.
3. Utah requires every driver to complete driver's education.

AGE OF MAJORITY
Marriage

STATES	Without Parental Consent		Court Permission Required	
	MALE	FEMALE	MALE	FEMALE
Alabama	18	18		
Alaska	18	18	14–16	14–16
Arizona	18	18	16	16
Arkansas	21	18		
California				
Colorado	18	18		
Connecticut	18	18	16	16
Delaware	18	16		
District of Columbia	21	18		
Florida	18	18		
Georgia	18	18		
Hawaii	18	18	15–16	15–16
Idaho	18	18	16	16
Illinois	18	18		
Indiana	18	18		
Iowa	18	18		
Kansas	18	18	18	18
Kentucky	18	18		
Louisiana	18	18		
Maine	18	18	16	16
Maryland	18	18		
Massachusetts	18	18	18	18
Michigan		18		
Minnesota		18		
Mississippi	21	21	17	15
Missouri	18	18	15	15
Montana	18	18	16–18	16–18
Nebraska	19	19		
Nevada	18	18	16	16
New Hampshire	18	18	18	18
New Jersey	21	18	18	16
New Mexico	18	18	16	16
New York	18	18		14–16
North Carolina	18	18		
North Dakota	18	18		18
Ohio	18	18		18
Oklahoma	18	18		16
Oregon	18	18		
Pennsylvania	18	18	16	16
Rhode Island	18	18	18	16
South Carolina	18	18		
South Dakota	18	18		
Tennessee	18	18		

AGE OF MAJORITY (continued)

Marriage

STATES	Without Parental Consent		Court Permission Required	
	MALE	FEMALE	MALE	FEMALE
Texas	Repealed			
Utah	18	18		
Vermont	18	18	16	16
Virginia	18	18		
Washington	18	18	17	17
West Virginia	18	18	18	18
Wisconsin	21	18	18	
Wyoming	18	18	16	16

8
Divorce and Separation

ANN W. LAKE

Ann W. Lake is a professor of law at Salem State College, Massachusetts. She has practiced law privately since 1946 with specialization in family law and probate of estates. She served as president of the National Association of Women Lawyers (1980–81), president of the Massachusetts Association of Women Lawyers (1972–73), and as council member, American Bar Association GPS (1975–79). She chaired the Family Law Committee of the Massachusetts Bar Association for four years and that of the ABA General Practice Section for five years.

When a marriage takes place, a ceremony, or formal proceeding, customarily occurs, either before a clergyman or before a justice of the peace. This is a voluntary union, with both parties willingly and with intent entering the marriage. At that point, the intent in marriage is permanence: the "happy-ever-aftering" of Camelot. When that condition is not achieved and either one or both parties to a marriage wish to terminate it, there are a number of options available. It is through the formal marriage ceremony that the state acquires an interest in the relationship, since the marriage is recorded in the city or town where the ceremony took place, and in addition, in many states, it is also recorded in the secretary of state's office, division of vital statistics. The ceremony is a matter of public record available to everyone wishing to check the files or to receive a certified copy of the document recording it. Married partners cannot, on their own, act to dissolve a marriage; they must seek the approval of the state by filing for a divorce in the courts.

A marriage can be dissolved via (1) an annulment, when the court decides that for some reason at the time of marriage no valid or legal marriage ever existed (for example, one of the partners was already married to someone else); or (2) a divorce, which is based on the theory of a valid marriage but is granted for some cause that arose after the marriage (for example, one of the partners becoming a drug addict). A third procedure is a separation, or separate-support, petition, which does not dissolve the marriage, but, for cause similar to divorce grounds, the parties are adjudged to be living apart by court decree.

According to the 1981 United States Census Bureau statistics, fewer than three in every five United States households were headed by a married couple. One out of every two marriages ended in divorce. The prevalence of divorce reflects, among other factors, the improved financial independence of women, greater knowledge by both men and women of the legal remedies available to them as relief from unbearable or intolerable living conditions, and lessening of social pressures which had previously stigmatized divorced people.

The increase in divorce does not make it any less serious an undertaking today than it was historically. There can be pain, dislocation, financial strain, and unhappiness for children when divorce takes place. However, the worst problems can be avoided if both parties know their rights and obligations under the law and the services available from and to be expected of attorneys.

It cannot be said too often that the time to exercise the greatest possible care is at the time of contracting marriage. If you are careless at this critical time, it adds unnecessary and painful complications to the divorce process.

The validity of a marriage is determined by the laws of the state in which it took place. The United States Constitution provides that each state must honor the public acts, records, and judicial proceedings of every other state. Therefore, before entering either a formal marriage or a common law bond, parties should be particularly careful that the prospective spouse is free to contract the marriage.

Some divorces in other states or in foreign countries may be found to be incomplete or are not recognized in the jurisdiction where a subsequent marriage takes place. Expense, embarrassment, and frustration follow such an event as the couple attempts to define their marital status. Even if it is determined that no previous marriage ever legally existed, property rights, inheritance rights, and legitimacy of children can still loom as formidable issues for the court to resolve.

This is not to suggest that one should enter marriage with divorce in mind; rather, it is to emphasize that as a practical matter, every precaution should be exercised at the time one marries. Readers who are in the process of divorcing in order to marry again should acquire all written or certified assurances possible about the future spouse's marital history and background. For example, procure a copy of his divorce judgment, check with the probation department for a criminal record, inquire about mental illness, psychiatric evaluation, medical history including venereal disease, and operations such as vasectomy. If there are children from the prior marriage, find out about the support order; and also check if there are nonmarital ("illegitimate") children whom he may be supporting after acknowledging paternity. If he is from a foreign country, check his resident status and citizenship.

MARRIAGE COUNSELING

Before we talk about the options available to people who want to end a marriage, we should mention marriage counseling. Marriage counselors have increased significantly in both numbers and effectiveness in the past few years. Their training is better than it once was, and people today are more likely to make use of the "helping" occupations than they once were.

Even when marriage counseling is not successful in saving the marriage and avoiding divorce, it can be helpful in making the divorce process more efficient and less painful. For example, questions about the well-being of the children of the marriage can be better discussed somewhere other than the court (although those decisions will be incorporated into a later agreement meeting court approval).

Ambivalence of either party about the decision to divorce may be resolved in counseling, so that when the judicial process is entered into, there is no indecision, which may appear frivolous to the courts and which can be costly to both parties. In addition, some of the heightened hostility common to a failed marriage is frequently diffused by counseling, making both parties better disposed to negotiate settlements that are of mutual benefit.

COMMON-LAW AND "LIVE-IN" RELATIONSHIPS

Far less certain than established judicial procedures for divorce is the treatment of those who have been joined in a common-law marriage (i.e., one not solemnized in the ordinary way, but created informally by two people of opposite sexes, followed by cohabitation). Some 12 states and the District of Columbia permit common-law marriages, whereas the rest of the states demand a license and a ceremony. Similarly, there is little in the way of legal precedent to guide participants in a live-in arrangement when they wish to end the relationship.

In general, states that do permit common-law marriage do not provide for common-law divorce. In such cases, the resolution of jointly held assets and the custody of children from the union depend more heavily on the goodwill of the partners and the precedents that may exist in the individual states. (A precedent refers to an earlier case in which similar problems were solved by the courts in a particular way.)

As live-in arrangements continue to become firmly established as a contemporary American life-style, some pattern of disposing of such cases is likely to emerge, but at present, guidelines are far less clear than in the disposition of traditional marriages.

It should be noted that under present laws, women who consent to live-in arrangements sacrifice benefits and protections that accrue to wives, in such matters as social-security and pension rights, support, community property, and survivorships. While it is convenient to move in and move out of relationships and living arrangements, without the expense and burden of legal process, such mobility becomes disadvantageous to live-in women when child custody and division of jointly acquired assets are issues.

SEPARATION

What Is a Separation?

A separation occurs when a married couple stops living together, either by mutual agreement or under the decree of a court. If the separation takes place through court intervention, a separation, or separate-support, petition is filed and an order is entered by the court after a hearing for a cause usually similar to that for divorce proceedings. There is public documentation of a legal separation, which makes the parties subject to further orders and findings. If the separation is by mutual agreement, there is no signed or formal document and there is no public recording.

When a couple finds their marriage irreparably broken and it is impossible for them to live together, the wife (in 99 percent of the cases) files a separation, or separate-support, petition. Under temporary and final orders, the husband continues to support his wife and any minor children; his obligations remain the same, as do his rights, with the exception of cohabitation (conjugal rights, his right to have sexual intercourse with his wife).

A separation does not free either spouse to remarry, unless a divorce or an annulment takes place. A separation by decree of a court is also called a "limited divorce" or divorce *a mensa et thoro* (from bed and board). The marriage bond is not dissolved.

What Is the Procedure in Separation Actions?

The wife, as plaintiff or petitioner, is commonly the spouse who files a separation action. It is rare to see an action started by a husband.

The action—or "complaint"—states the date of marriage, the names of minor children, the date the parties last lived together, the grounds (cause), and the demands for a court order.

If the wife decides to act as her own attorney, she signs the complaint *pro se* (on behalf of herself or in her own behalf), and a copy is served on the husband either by certified mail or by a deputy sheriff.

If a wife has been physically abused, she may file an affidavit (a statement made under oath) alleging the specific details of abuse with dates, times, places, and police involvement, if that was the case. The court will issue a temporary vacate order with notice to the husband to appear within a period of time (such as three days) to give testimony on continuing the vacate order.

In some states, a husband who has an interest in the marital home— whether fee simple (sole owner), joint tenancy or tenancy by the entirety (survivorship rights of 100 percent interest to surviving spouse)—is ordered to leave the marital home for a period of time up to ninety days (a vacate order); and if, after a hearing, the health, safety, or welfare of the wife or any minor children would be endangered or substantially impaired, the order may be continued.

The court may issue an order to vacate although the husband does not reside in the marital home at the time of its issuance, or if the wife has left the home because of fear for her safety or for that of any minor children.

What Is at Risk in a Pro Se Proceeding?

Because a number of organizations have formed in recent years such as Fathers United for Justice, and Fathers for Custody of Children, a wife should review the facts of her case carefully with a competent lawyer specializing in domestic relations, to avoid being thwarted during a *pro se* proceeding. If she is serious about having her husband ordered from the marital home through court intervention, she should be prepared to accept the surprise of an order which might provide that both the parties vacate the marital home at alternate periods of time.

Why Is a Legal Separation Preferable to an Informal Separation by Mutual Agreement?

The problem with an informal separation arrangement, without court sanction, is that a husband may return to the marital home at any time and even request conjugal rights. Since there has been no court proceeding or restraining order barring him from interfering with the personal liberty of the wife, the husband who chooses on his own to end the separation may not be removed from the home. Unless the wife is physically attacked or abused (battered), the police are powerless to evict the husband at the wife's request. If, however, a separation complaint or petition has been brought in court, the wife will be protected.

What Are Grounds for Legal Separation?

Legal, or judicial, separations are given for causes (grounds) similar to those honored in divorce proceedings: cruel and abusive treatment, adultery, alcoholism, desertion, and nonsupport being most common, and others. It is not necessary to have a summons personally served upon the husband before a witness.

Before a final hearing on the separation is scheduled, the wife may ask for and receive temporary court orders for support, custody of minor children, and a restraining order.

Why Do People Sometimes Prefer Nonlegal (Mutual-agreement) Separations?

Often parties agree to live apart because of religious conviction and church affiliation that prohibit divorce. Sometimes people who are well known in the community wish to avoid the public record resulting from a court decree.

Frequently a married couple will live apart while trying to reconcile their differences in a serious dispute that threatens the marriage, do not wish the finality implied by a legal separation. Couples in marriage counseling may be advised to resort to a trial separation and may not wish to recognize the change in status in a formal way.

Finally, some couples feel that a nonlegal separation is preferable "for the children's sake." Such is not necessarily advantageous for the children, as their well-being may be better protected when the state becomes an active party to the family's negotiations.

How May Separated Persons Become Free to Remarry?

If a separation complaint has been filed, it does not bar the couple from later filing a divorce petition, even if there has been a final hearing on the separation case and agreements have been executed. Divorce supersedes a separation judgment. When the divorce action is final, then the parties are free to remarry.

Some difficulty may arise in cases where a final separation judgment is entered in one state and a divorce is entered in a different state without the appearance of both parties in both actions. Women should be alert to enter an appearance in the second action in such cases (i.e., the divorce action) to protect their interests in property, support, and any other references in the separation order that are advantageous and should be considered in the divorce settlement.

Should One Have a Separation Prior to a Divorce Action?

Because the expense and time period involved in processing a separation complaint equals, in most cases, that of a divorce proceeding, clients are often advised to bypass a court separation and instead have a trial separation to determine if there is a possibility of reconciliation. If no reconciliation is possible, only then would the matter come to court. As pointed out above, however, women are particularly vulnerable to the whim or initiative of the male spouse during trial separations without decree.

There are many separation complaints on file in the courts that have never been processed beyond temporary orders. Young couples who have a first fight or who are unduly influenced by interfering parents; young women who feel unbearably confined by young children, or young men who are not mature enough to accept the responsibilities of fatherhood and marriage; or vindictive spouses who use the courts to intimidate mates— all of these and others fill court files with temporary actions never pursued. Many of these actions have been brought *pro se* (on behalf of herself/himself), without an attorney.

This may seem like an abuse of the court system, but such possible abuse has to be tolerated so that the system can also be accessible to those for whom a quick response is supportive and often life-protecting.

What Becomes of Jointly Held Property in a Separation?

A legal separation does not usually involve an order that substantial assets, such as the marital home or the family car, be sold or transferred to the wife, or even that bank accounts or stocks be divided. Wives mistakenly anticipate that the court will distribute all assets of the marriage in a separation judgment.

There can be no final and complete distribution of marital assets unless it is specified in a separation agreement or if, after the separation order, one or other of the parties files for divorce.

If a husband wishes to marry another and is trying to encourage his wife to proceed to a divorce, he may agree willingly to a property settlement under a separation agreement. This, however, is not the general case, and more often the case proceeds into divorce where the major issue to be litigated is distribution of property. This issue in most states is guided by statutory provisions requiring evidence of specific criteria.

Many attorneys advise that the first action that should be started by a spouse who has no intention of continuing a marriage is more properly the divorce. In this way the major issues of property, support, custody, and visitation, medical and school expenses, even pet custody are more likely to be resolved quickly and fairly.

Does Legal Separation Prevent Reconciliation?

A separation ends when the wife and husband live together once again.

However, if a separation agreement relating to property division has been completed, parties may find themselves in an awkward position—especially if the reconciliation is tentative, or "trial." For example, suppose a wife obtains title to the marital home under a separation agreement by giving up (waiving) her interest in equivalent assets. If the reconciliation attempt fails after a reasonably long interval, the wife's fee-simple ownership of the home will be valued by the court in any new settlement, and she may find herself without leverage when it comes to dividing any assets the couple may have acquired during the reconciliation.

What Are the Defenses Available in Separation Cases?

A spouse may deny the allegations spelled out in a complaint, and during a hearing in court may as a witness prove that the allegations are not true, supported by evidence and other witnesses. Condonation (turning a blind eye to an offense or forgiving it) is a defense in some states. The spouse defending the action relates that the parties have lived together following the alleged misconduct and that the other party forgave the misconduct.

Connivance is available in some states as a defense, where it can be shown that a spouse deliberately plotted to create grounds for a complaint.

If a husband and wife are equally guilty of misbehavior, recrimination as a defense will bar an action. If they have conspired to give false evidence, collusion as a defense can cause dismissal of an action.

Because the states vary widely on the issue of defense in separation cases, an attorney should be consulted. In practice, very few cases offer defense other than general denial, since a separation complaint does not dissolve a marriage.

Are Alimony and Support Available?

Temporary alimony, support, and custody of minor children may be decreed by the court for validly married couples one or both of whom seek to live apart from the other. In general, the obligation to pay alimony to the wife and support for the minor children does not extend to persons who cohabit without formal marriage. (That is one of the disadvantages of living together without marriage.)

In determining the amount of a support order, if any, in a formal marriage within which the parties are separating, the court considers a number of factors: (1) the net income, assets, and earning *ability* of both; (2) expenses and necessities of life for the standard of living of the person to be supported; (3) capacity of any person seeking to be supported to obtain employment or to obtain skills necessary for employment.

In most states there are laws that say that the courts must protect children born of a marriage. The courts make judgments relative to care, custody, education, and maintenance of children and may alter judgments from other jurisdictions when the children come under the jurisdiction of any particular court.

Women who receive legal separation decrees with alimony and/or support awards should be aware that the awards can be changed even within signed agreements. Should a wife return to work, the husband may petition for release from payments. While the wife may return to court for an increase in the event of a substantial improvement in the husband's financial position, she cannot be certain of a favorable judgment.

It is advisable for formerly married or newly separated women to resume a career and reenter the working world quite promptly. This is not always an easy route, but it is the inevitable route in a life event that is not guaranteed to be easy. After all, the end of a marriage is not the end of life, and the sooner one gets on with living, the better.

DIVORCE

A divorce *a vinculo matrimonii* (a divorce from the bond of marriage) is a total divorce of husband and wife—dissolving the marriage tie, releasing parties wholly from matrimonial obligations, and freeing both parties to enter into subsequent marriages. It is a judicial proceeding and involves only those who have a valid, that is, legally binding, marriage.

The increase in divorce is in part attributable to changes in divorce laws, especially with respect to no-fault divorce.

Divorce laws in the 50 states vary widely and change frequently. It is important to choose an attorney who is informed and experienced in family law, assuring the best advice and representation in a sensitive major negotiation. See State Divorce Law Chart, pp. 213–16.

Grounds for Divorce

Causes (grounds) for divorce vary within the states, but as we have already mentioned, the United States Constitution provides that full faith and credit shall be given in each state to the public acts, records, and judicial proceedings of every other state. The increased mobility of the United States population makes it imperative that in entering into a divorce proceeding one establish a legal residence in the particular state. As was pointed out earlier, when considering marriage to a previously married partner, it is vital to seek assurances that any previous divorce met this requirement, or else the divorce may not have been final.

Grounds for divorce may include one or more of the following conditions: adultery, alcoholism, bigamy, desertion, mental cruelty, physical cruelty, impotency, nonsupport, insanity, conviction of a felony, or imprisonment for more than five years. Either spouse may institute a divorce proceeding.

A Summons Must Be Served

A basic requirement is that the defendant be served a summons or voluntarily accept a summons to make certain that notice of the proceeding and a copy of the complaint are given. The defendant has a specified period of time within which to reply to the complaint, on a date assigned by the court.

The Return Day: No final hearing on a divorce complaint may be requested until the return day on the summons has passed. The return day is the date by which the defendant has to respond to the statements in the complaint and file an appearance (that is, either by appearing in court personally, or being represented by an attorney). Due to heavy schedules and caseload, trial dates are not automatically available when requested. The delays can be nine months and longer for contested matters; three months is more typical for uncontested matters. The scheduling varies from jurisdiction to jurisdiction.

The Answer Period: During the answer period (usually twenty days), the plaintiff may request the court to enter temporary orders including support, custody of children, and a restraining order. Generally, no support or any money order will be entered by the court unless the defendant appears on record and has been personally served in the state where the action is being brought.

Serving Papers within the Proper Jurisdiction: A husband who has left the marital home and becomes a resident of another state may not be ordered to pay any money order by the court where the divorce is sought. Therefore, before a divorce complaint is brought by a nonworking wife who will be dependent on a money order, either a temporary or a final one, the strategy of making certain that the husband is served papers within the proper jurisdiction should be carefully planned.

As a further illustration of the necessity for service within a particular jurisdiction, consider the case of a married couple with children, in which both husband and wife are working, since this is now frequently the case. A Massachusetts husband is transferred to Illinois; the wife is a Massachusetts teacher. Wife and children visit the husband during the summer vacation to determine whether Illinois will become the permanent family residence. The wife is unaware that the husband has encouraged this familial visit in order to have divorce papers served using Illinois as the residence. The court now has jurisdiction over the wife and children with respect to questions of custody and support, and the wife's Massachusetts teaching income will be taken into account.

Taking this same case farther for illustration, the wife returns to her job in Massachusetts and files a divorce complaint asking for temporary orders for support and custody. Because the children are now in Massachusetts, the court has jurisdiction and will award temporary custody to the wife irrespective of the Illinois order, *but* the court cannot enter a support order, since the husband has not been personally served in Massachusetts.

The Illinois attorney representing the husband usually will advise the husband not to return to Massachusetts in order to avoid personal service, which would subject him to the jurisdiction of the court. In such a case, where children are involved, most likely service would take place during a visit by the father to the children, who would remain in Massachusetts, with service carried out by a sheriff or a disinterested person.

However, in a case such as this, in which some geographical distance is involved, it is probable that many months could intervene without a parental visit to children, and considerable financial hardship could occur that might have been avoided with some knowledge of this requirement by the plaintiff. Again, an attorney with considerable experience in such cases—certain aspects of which are far from unusual—is recommended.

What Is a No-fault Divorce?

Beginning in 1970, some states began to enact legislation providing for no-fault divorce on such grounds as irretrievable breakdown, irreconcilable differences, irremediable breakdown, incompatibility, breakdown of marriage relationship, or discord and conflict that destroys the legitimate ends of marriage. The terms under no-fault procedures in the various states are defined quite similarly and stress the fact that the parties consider the marriage problems impossible to resolve and not repairable under any circumstances. The prerequisite to entering such a divorce is an agreement of the parties to provide for distribution of property, support, alimony, custody, visitation, medical and life insurance, and other matters customarily included in court-sanctioned agreements, such as costs of children's education.

If the parties executed a separation agreement, and the court, upon review, accepted the document as a fair solution to the major issues of the divorce, the court would then grant a divorce *nisi* (a temporary judgment that will be valid and operative unless the party affected by it appears and shows cause against it), without the requirement of testimony as to the grounds for divorce.

Some jurisdictions require proof that parties to a no-fault divorce have been living apart for a stated period of time after the agreement has been presented and before the judgment *nisi* enters; others provide that living apart for a period of time, such as one year, is prima facie evidence that the marriage is irreparably broken, and in such a case the parties won't have to give evidence of continuing to live apart for a period of time before an order is entered.

Still other court jurisdictions—even in the case of no fault—will require the plaintiff to describe the cause of the breakdown of the marriage, even though the parties have filed an agreement and acknowledged mutually that the marriage is irretrievable.

The prevalence of no-fault divorces, which are now on the books in the majority of states, has been unjustly blamed for causing an excessive increase in the number of divorces. No-fault divorce has been an effective divorce procedure in some states for a decade, and became widely known usually through the "glamour" divorces of rich people or people in public life who had the resources and the mobility to establish residence in favorable jurisdictions. For such people, the financial settlements in no-fault divorces either were no problem or were preferred to the notoriety that can accompany contested divorces.

Therefore, the increased accessibility of no-fault divorce was simply a democratizing process, making the full remedies of the system available and useful to a greater number of people.

That is the good news; the bad news is that no-fault divorce can be very damaging to women who do not understand or have experience with the court system.

Many women, perhaps even most women, have their first and often sole encounter with the judicial system during divorce. Because of the emotional atmosphere of a divorce action, the uncertainty of property distribution, lack of personal income by the female plaintiff, perhaps problems of employability, and concern for immediate needs of small children, the woman does not take the long view. Often, in a no-fault divorce the wife too eagerly signs an agreement prepared by an attorney selected and paid by the husband. The wife is under the assumption that she and the children are being protected, and the contrary is likely to be the case. During a divorce hearing, a petition for counsel fees is always presented by the wife. She signs the petition and pleads that she has insufficient funds to pay for her counsel. If she is a nonworking spouse, she will receive reimbursement of the entire amount presented by her attorney, who will be required to file a time schedule showing work done, charges, and expenses.

Many bar associations have referral services whereby callers can be given the names of several attorneys who are on the list and who agree to charge a lower-than-usual hourly rate. They, too, will submit a petition for counsel fees during the divorce hearing and thus lessen the actual expense to the wife.

A woman should be very protective of her own and especially her children's interests in this situation. Nothing should be signed until she has retained and consulted her own attorney.

There is no bargaining ground once the no-fault grounds have been specified and an agreement has been signed. The preferred strategy is to file for a fault ground and place the burden of negotiation on the husband. This gives the plaintiff (wife) the advantage while the case is awaiting a hearing-date assignment. When the case is contested—and it should be, unless the husband generously assents to property settlement and all other major issues—it may take months before the case is assigned for hearing.

In the interim, the wife may request interrogatories. These are a set of questions, with a maximum of thirty in some states, to be answered by the husband under the penalties of perjury. The questions may inquire in depth as to the assets of the husband, documentation of account numbers, transfers for benefit of others (mother, child, sister, brother), tax-return information for a number of preceding years, corporate returns, debts and liabilities for five to ten years, proof of expenditures, etc. An order to produce all financial documents within thirty days or some other time period is mandatory, and the husband must obey it. This is an excellent strategy, as it frightens a husband, who may wish to avoid public disclosure of his personal finances and corporate records, into negotiating. In addition, oral depositions may be taken before a stenographer, who records and produces copies of the testimony taken. During oral discovery (cross-examination), the husband is questioned on all details relating to his financial records, his tax returns, his conduct during the marriage, and the history of his employment, activities (including extramarital), and inheritance bequests.

Interrogatories, production of documents, and depositions may be used later during court hearings to discredit testimony being given by the husband.

It is a misconception that no-fault divorce implies a pleasant and elusive domestic phenomenon referred to as the "friendly divorce." It is acceptable to be as forgiving of transgressions as one wants within the limits of one's personality and philosophy; people may be as civilized as suits them in their *personal* relationships with divorcing spouses—either for their own sake or for the well-being of children. However, divorce is an action of the *state* carried out by the courts at the request of citizens; it is not intended to be either affectionate or sentimental. It is intended to be just. Parties to any divorce action—no-fault or otherwise—should play for keeps and try to get as many of the marbles as feasible the first time around.

Play to Win

Renegotiation of agreements is costly and highly risky, and seldom worth the financial and emotional investment. It is better to do it right the first time through.

This position is not advocacy of an embittered, "take him for what he's worth" attitude. Rather, it is encouragement to play to win—a rational and acceptable goal in negotiation. Despite women's new and often successful demands for equality and liberation, it remains a fact of life that the woman is the more disadvantaged party in most divorce actions. This is not moderated in any way by the fact that the woman is more often the plaintiff and the man the defendant.

In some cases, women have interrupted a career or the chance for advancement in a job, or they have set it aside entirely, for marriage and childbearing. Sometimes there has been a tacit understanding between career partners who may be childless that within the marriage his career will have the emphasis, often at the expense of hers, as evidenced through choice of the marital home near a site that will nurture his career, and a social life that fosters contacts favorable to his advancement in business.

What About Children in Divorce?

In the majority of cases, women still do seek and receive custody of minor children, although shared custody and custody by the father are emerging as minor patterns. Custody of the children is an emotional comfort to the parent to whom it is awarded. However, children are not unaffected by parents' divorces, and it is the parent with custody who must be sensitive to this. Expert and realistic guidelines can be negotiated within divorce stipulations.

The wife may decide to be a "good sport," insofar as her own wishes and needs are concerned, when negotiating a settlement; but she should perform like an animal in the forest protecting her cubs against an aggressor when she is negotiating for support and amenities for her children. Women who perform this function well are performing in the highest traditions of motherhood in a modern setting, by defending their young.

Those items which a mother bargains away through being intimidated, ignorance, or "good manners" become her responsibility to provide for many long years ahead. Just as she once thought marriage would be forever, she now anticipates that she is embarking on a new, prosperous, and untroubled life, with perfect health and uninterrupted income. She should, from her experience with the fragility of marriage, know that nothing is certain, and she should not trade away any security and comforts for her children.

What About Renegotiating?

An additional hazard is that after having signed an agreement, a wife may learn that her husband has not disclosed his true financial worth. She has already negotiated away her opportunity for justice. Even today, many women do not have full knowledge of a husband's diverse sources of income. A deposition would reveal much of which she was not aware.

In negotiating, it is essential to know what size pie you are carving up. *That* is the point: not to connive for more than your share, but to be *sure* that you are fully aware of the total picture as a prerequisite to determining what your fair share might be, for yourself and the children.

There should not be fear or shame in deciding to go the route of some of the fault grounds. A number of grounds can be easily proved; for example, cruel and abusive treatment no longer requires evidence of a husband's having struck or beaten or marked a wife. It is sufficient to show mental and emotional distress, attributable to such diverse conditions as alcoholism, infidelity, drugs, or accusatory threats. Some evidence can be brought forth from the day-to-day conduct of most marriages; for example, return to parents or staying with friends for a few days, late hours, noncommunication, and the like.

Therefore, it can be concluded that no-fault divorce is not necessarily an easier or more advantageous route to follow, unless there is a willingness on the part of the defendant to surrender something of value in an agreement that is greater than the court would have been likely to order. It is also, in these days of premarital financial agreements, which provide for wife and children in the event of a breakup, the route of choice if the premarital agreement was especially beneficial and required no substantive change.

When Is a Divorce Final?

A divorce is entered as "divorce *nisi*" (which means "divorce—unless"). This indicates that the court's ruling will stand as valid unless the party affected by it (the defendant) seeks to have it revoked by appealing to a higher court within a specified period of time. Once the time period passes (30 days, six months, or other), a divorce absolute is entered. This time period varies from state to state.

During the period of waiting, the parties are still considered husband and wife for all purposes, including inheritance rights in the event either should die. If they wish to reconcile, a motion may be made to the court requesting that a permanent divorce not be entered.

What Is Meant by "Foreign Divorce"?

Foreign divorce refers to a spouse's going to another state or a foreign country, apart from that of the marital domicile, to file for a divorce. If the court obtains jurisdiction of *both* parties and the subject matter of the cause of action, the judgment rendered will be binding anywhere in the United States.

The difficulty of foreign divorce is its enforcement, since many states by statute provide that if an inhabitant of state A goes into state B to obtain a divorce for a cause occurring while the parties resided in state A, or for a cause that would not be grounds for divorce in state A, the divorce obtained in state B is not valid.

For example, if a wife who remains in a marital home in Idaho, say, receives notice that a husband is in Nevada, Iowa, or Haiti and has filed a divorce petition, she can protect her rights by not appearing in that foreign jurisdiction. ("Appearance" means either by personally filing a letter or card informing the court that she wishes to be entered in that divorce as a party and subject to the jurisdiction of the court or that her attorney is filing such a notice.) Such appearance binds the wife in all the findings of the court, which will be fully honored by other states. The appearance does not mean that the party has to be physically present in the foreign jurisdiction. Many divorces in foreign jurisdictions are granted with the presence of only one of the parties: the plaintiff. But the "appearance" of the defendant, either by her/his written notice or by an attorney, is sufficient authorization to enter a judgment subjecting both parties to the jurisdiction of the court.

It is important to know that while such an appearance allows the court to recognize that both parties consent to being subject to its jurisdiction, it also means that a divorce judgment binds both parties.

The wife who refuses to enter an appearance is at an advantage, since the divorce entered with only one party in appearance (the plaintiff) is subject to challenge in other states.

The fact that the Constitution forces all the states to honor each other's laws does not rule out an inquiry into the question of a particular state's jurisdiction over a particular case. No state court is the final legal authority on issues of jurisdiction. But when there is an agreement not to challenge, the state entering the divorce becomes, for all intents and purposes, the final authority.

The "full faith and credit" clause does require a sister state to accept at face value any and every judgment and decree that other states issue.

If the laws of the state where a plaintiff lives do not provide a cause that applies to the facts of the case, it is seldom a good idea to move secretly to establish a new residence in a more favorable jurisdiction. Such moves are likely to be challenged by defendants, causing delay and expense that might be greater than would have been involved in pursuing the case in the actual state of residence of the couple. (A plaintiff's lawyer might be able to file for divorce on other grounds than those that first come to the plaintiff's mind.)

What Is an Annulment?

An annulment decree reaches back to the time of the marriage and says it never occurred. If the validity of a marriage is in any way in question, either party may institute action for annulment.

The grounds for annulment vary from state to state. Competent legal counsel can define the current laws. All states, of course, declare marriages void where a prior marriage is proved to continue to exist.

In addition, fraud, duress, and incapacity of either party to consummate the marriage can be grounds for annulment. Incest and bigamy are prima facie grounds for annulment, as are marriages in which either party is found to have been insane at the time of the marriage.

At the initiative of the individuals concerned, marriages that are terminated in a civil divorce may also be subject to further review by church authorities in those faiths that do not recognize civil divorce. Roman Catholicism, Episcopalianism, and Judaism are among the faiths that have strictly defined procedures within their own rubrics for the dissolution of marriages.

It is important to distinguish between a civil annulment and an annulment granted within a particular religion or sect. Annulment granted by a religion or sect is not binding on the state unless a civil divorce has also taken place.

As in the case of the rapidly changing legislation for civil divorce or annulment, the church-related procedures are also undergoing study and reevaluation in efforts to conform with changing mores. For example, the Roman Catholic guidelines for annulment are expected to be modified when a modified Code of Canon Law is issued in 1983.

DIVISION OF PROPERTY AT THE TIME OF DIVORCE OR SEPARATION

Divorce and separation are matters of human relationships, but nothing takes place in a vacuum. Where a marriage exists, there are material considerations, and where a marriage exists for an extended period of time, there are questions based on the time the woman has spent out of the work force. Where there are children, there is the question of guarantees of their interest in the parents' properties.

The time of divorce is charged with emotion, and consequently it is a time when the primary parties are not always able to make the best and the fairest decisions. Advice of counsel and the protection of the courts are not luxuries; they are necessities.

Women, especially, are not well schooled about their rights as wives, custodians, property owners, beneficiaries, or any of the remote-sounding, but powerful, titles that husbands often know about in the day-to-day conduct of business. Women have a responsibility to become informed in their own interest and the interests of their children, and they should secure competent counsel to complement their own interests. Apart from career choice, for women who divorce, the purchase of a house and the negotiation of the separation agreement are the two most important transactions most encounter in a lifetime.

In separation cases, excepting those in which the parties are successful in negotiating an agreement, the courts do not determine ownership of the property or division of assets, since the relationship (although not the domicile) of the husband and wife remains intact. The value of the assets and the earnings of the husband (and the employability of the wife, among other facts) are considered to aid the court in establishing a support order to supplement the needs of the wife and children.

Divorce cases are different from separation complaints in that the division of property may be handled by the state and may vary from state to state.

In general, there are three techniques:

1. Community-property states California, Idaho, Louisiana, Nevada, New Mexico, Puerto Rico, Texas, and Washington provide for everything acquired by a husband and wife during a marriage to be divided equally.

2. Title states allocate property to the spouse in whose name it is listed (Michigan, Virginia, and West Virginia).

3. Equitable-distribution states distribute the property as property or as alimony at the discretion of the court. This is the practice in about forty states, some of which permit only property accumulated during marriage to be distributed, whereas other states include property that was separately owned before the marriage, or the increase in value of separate property.

It is in those states which follow the equitable distribution doctrine that the emphasis on equal rights for women has an impact on the issue of property division. In contested matters, the court follows specific criteria outlined in the respective statutes, and financial statements are required to be filed by the parties and executed under penalty of perjury.

Among the considerations are length of marriage, conduct of the parties during marriage, age, health, station, occupation, amount and sources of income, vocational skills, employability, estate, liabilities and needs of the parties, opportunity to acquire future capital assets and income, contribution of the parties in the acquisition, preservation, and appreciation in value of their estate, and most recently, contribution of each party as a home-maker to the family unit.

What About the Marital Home?

If negotiation between the parties is possible, the wife should ask to have the marital home transferred to her, so that the children will not be uprooted from their neighborhood, school, and friends. Some husbands argue that a wife who is not already self-supporting is incapable of carrying the house, and that the home should be sold and the net profits distributed.

Selling the marital home is not necessarily beneficial to women, since it is difficult and costly to obtain an apartment when there are children, and expenses could be higher than maintaining the home. Particular attention should be paid to interest rates for mortgages and to the incremental value of the real estate, before deciding on the appropriate course of action.

Wives who have not established a credit record, who do not have an already established career, and whose lives are in transition should be wary of hasty decisions about relocation, especially if the divorce is not their "fault."

Some courts have struck a workable compromise by ordering that the wife be allowed to continue living in the marital home until the youngest child reaches a certain age, and that the husband, in addition to child support, continue to pay for mortgage, taxes, and insurance, while the wife pays for utilities, repairs, and incidentals. This has the appeal of continuing the house as a real estate investment for the husband, and the wife's equal share continues to accrue to her interest.

Another option exists where personal and other assets are available, and the wife might consider relinquishing her equal share of joint savings or stock accounts as payment of the husband's share of the marital home. This has an appeal to the husband for its impact on his current cash profile, but when the wife acquires the sole ownership of the marital home, she also assumes responsibility for its upkeep and its taxes.

Both financial and legal advice are useful here, if the wife is in a position to negotiate and has the freedom to review alternatives. The advice must be current, however, as the factors affecting the decision are highly variable in today's economy.

If, during the marriage or the separation, the wife has used her money to pay for the home mortgage, taxes, or other expenses (either from wages or an inheritance or from premarital savings), she should substantiate this to prove her contribution, and thereby her equity.

For instance, if a woman paid the original deposit on the marital home out of her premarital resources, she should have the husband acknowledge the payment in writing and promise (also in writing) to repay the amount if the property is sold—and *before* the division of the net profits. Such contribution should, in effect, be considered a first lien on the property.

If, when property is acquired, the property is taken in one name and that is the wife's name, it guarantees and protects the wife in the event of domestic difficulties. Wives must be alert at the time of passing of the property that it is not, in fact, deeded to the husband. In such cases, should the husband elect to divest himself of the property during a dispute, the wife and children could find themselves evicted even without separation or divorce proceedings being in process, since most states permit a husband to transfer and sell property, when he is the sole owner, *without the wife's signature.* If the property is in the name of the wife solely, she, too, has the right to sell without the husband's signature.

What About Personal Property?

If the wife continues to live in the marital home and has physical custody of children, she should keep all of the personal property, furniture, and household effects. As goodwill, wives often give some of the property freely to husbands who are trying to establish separate domiciles.

If there is an inability between the parties to resolve these "pots and pans" issues, then an inventory must be made, and the courts, unwillingly and reluctantly, will intervene. It is far better to resolve this comparatively minor issue amicably, not only from an economic point of view but also with respect to the impact on the court of the integrity of the parties.

What About Assets of Special Value?

Where antiques, for example, may have been collected by the parties during the marriage, and there is disagreement over distribution, appraisers are frequently asked to submit evidence of value during a trial. Sometimes individual items are awarded (not always to the party with the greater interest); sometimes the order is to sell and divide proceeds. In either case, neither party is happy. Every effort should be made to reach a compromise in these matters.

The court will follow the same criteria in equitable-distribution states to determine contribution to stock and bond holdings and bank accounts. Other states follow the title or community-property concept.

The parties themselves may, in agreements, provide that accounts in the sole name of either husband or wife shall remain her/his property. A wife should always maintain a current check on the status of such accounts.

What About Gifts?

Gifts of a husband to his wife, or vice versa, are not property subject to division by the court. However, if such gifts are significant, they are often calculated as an asset of the wife by the court when determining her financial status.

Seldom does a divorce or separation action come as a total surprise to a wife. If it *is* a surprise, it is often because the wife has refused to accept the reality and inevitability of the impending action because it is not her first choice of action.

However, where an action is contemplated by the wife, or she has a suspicion it is forthcoming from the husband, it is prudent for her to secure a safe-deposit box, in which important records may be accumulated as a safeguard against confiscation.

As cited above, when a marriage is being dissolved, it is sensible to assume the other party is playing "for keeps," and it is both sensible and practical to take steps to safeguard one's interests. Insurance policies, deeds, stock certificates, bankbooks, jewels, and rare coins are examples of negotiable items that should be sequestered. They are "negotiable" in the sense that they can become leverage for other, less tangible but more desirable concessions that a wife may seek in litigation.

It is not unheard of for husbands to sweep joint accounts clean to frustrate just such strategies.

Are Debts Treated the Same as Assets?

The husband is required to pay for all necessaries required by the wife and children. Therefore, he is responsible for all debts incurred until there is a court order to provide support or there is a legally binding settlement agreement.

Clothing, housing, food, medical and dental care, utilities, mortgage, taxes, and car payments and expenses are considered "necessaries." In addition, courts take into consideration the status of the family and its customary style of living.

The wife is not required to and need not forgo the use of credit cards during a dispute. Until there is a court determination, she may continue to use them to acquire necessaries. Should the husband automatically suspend payment, the wife may refer creditors and collection agencies to the husband for him to meet his obligation.

It is neither wise nor fair, however, for the wife to make extraordinary use of credit cards during this period (e.g., for travel, redecoration, etc.), since these may become items for suit at a later time.

A word here about credit. During marriage, today's wives are encouraged to establish credit and use it sufficiently during marriage to have a credit rating. Store charges, Mastercard/Visa, and gasoline credit are most useful for women in transition. Husbands may close accounts if they are in joint names, and the wife's own cards would be useful while support questions are pending in the courts.

During this time, wives are not required to pay any bills for necessaries that the husband is required to pay by law. Bills for mortgage and utilities should continue to be forwarded to him.

Creditors often intimidate wives during this uncertain period, and frequently are able to collect from wives unfamiliar with the law. Wives should also be aware that public notice of not being responsible for debts, which husbands cause to be printed in newspapers, is not binding with regard to necessaries. Vulnerable wives should not be intimidated by this technique sometimes resorted to by angry, vengeful spouses to embarrass divorcing mates.

What About Nontangible Assets?

A new assessment value has entered the property settlement scene in recent years as a result of the practice of wives working in the early years of a marriage to finance the professional education of a mate—only to find themselves set aside when the degree or license is in hand. The court has responded affirmatively to women's inquiry, "Isn't my contribution to his future earnings worth something extra?"

Where education and training that the wife has contributed to by working or sacrificing will contribute significantly to the lifetime earnings of a separated or divorcing mate (e.g., dentist, lawyer, CPA, doctor, professor), the courts consider the professional license a marital asset. Also taken into consideration are retirement benefits, pensions, business interest, or any likely significant future earnings.

What Kinds of Records Are Useful in Division of Properties?

Due to the many and varied marital assets that the court accepts in considering agreements, it is wise for wives to keep copies of joint income tax returns for interest listed on tax returns (often revelatory of "secret" bank accounts); dividends (often revelatory of new or "secret" investments); any moonlighting or other occupations the husband undertakes; a schedule of sales and exchanges of securities to estimate value, to see if there are unusual reported items such as income from rental property, trusts, or royalties unknown to spouses.

How Can a Wife Acquire Knowledge of Her Husband's Business Affairs?

The marriage bond is the most intimate relationship civilized beings have yet conceived. It is almost unbelievable that women are willing to surrender their ultimate privacy to a husband but are unwilling to ask or are uninterested in having answered many basic questions about the financial structure of the union they have entered into.

A marriage is far more sensitive and certainly more intimate than a business, but historically women have been willing to enter into what they label a "full partnership" without access to a significant part of the "business."

A full partner in a store would not consider a partnership to exist where she had access only to inventory, but not cash records. A doctor would not consider herself in joint practice with a physician where she had access to patients but not to their records. (Such relationships would be those of little-trusted employees.)

Yet in many cases, wives continue, even today, to have a "Bob takes care of everything" attitude. This is archaic and inadvisable, not only in the frequently cited instances of sudden death of a spouse, but also for women who face dissolution of a marriage they had expected to last forever.

ALIMONY AND CHILD SUPPORT

Alimony and support payments come usually as payments from the husband to the wife. Here again, social changes result in occasional instances of wives' being obligated for alimony and support payments, for example, affluent professional women or women successful in business, or in cases in which fathers obtain legal custody of minor children. But such instances are so rare as to require only passing mention and no further discussion here.

Special care should be observed in the wording of alimony and support payments in the court order, because of the tax implications.

The husband pays alimony to the wife for personal support and maintenance until such time as she remarries or dies, whichever comes first; in cases in which the alimony continues while the wife gets job training, it would stop when she is employed. It is important that in the divorce settlement a clause is written specifying that if the former husband predeceases the former wife, his estate would continue to provide for the wife and children before creditors are satisfied.

With the drive for an equal rights amendment in the 1970s, the courts became sensitive to a number of new criteria as guidelines for determining if wives should receive alimony. These considerations included financial contribution of the wife as a wage earner and as a homemaker, the length of the marriage, the ability of the wife to be self-supporting, the educational background and work experience of the wife, the possibility of inheritance from her parents, etc.

If the marriage has not been of long duration and no children have been born, the court may not award alimony if the wife had been employed full time prior to marriage. As we have mentioned, some states award alimony for several years—"rehabilitative alimony"—to permit the wife to return to the work force, to retrain, and/or to study new skills.

Both parents are obligated to support minor children. Statutes provide separately for mother and father, but criminal sanctions are imposed on either parent who neglects or fails to provide support.

By common law, the father is held primarily responsible for the support of his children. If he is unable to or refuses to, the mother may turn to public assistance to supplement her own contribution. Such programs are known as Aid to Families with Dependent Children (AFDC).

In divorce proceedings, the court provides sufficient allowance so that children may be raised in an atmosphere that reflects the parents' standard of living. Usually the court states that payments will continue until the child reaches majority. In some states, statutes provide that if a child is physically disabled, mentally retarded, or attending undergraduate college, the parent is required to continue support even after majority age is reached.

Support payments for children are subject to modification at the discretion of the court. If circumstances change for the better, due to success in business ventures, inheritance, or increased earnings, then the court may increase the original award or stipulation in an agreement signed by the husband and the wife.

If a child who has not attained majority becomes emancipated or self-supporting, the support orders terminate. Emancipation includes marriage, military service, and full-time work.

How Does the IRS View Alimony and Support?

A divorce that includes alimony payments can produce a net tax savings for a couple with one wage earner. Alimony is deductible by the husband and taxable to the wife, but amounts paid as property settlements and child support are neither deductible by the husband nor taxable to the wife. Purely voluntary payments also do not qualify.

If the payments are for support and are made yearly over a period exceeding ten years, annual payments of up to 10 percent of the principal sum will be treated as alimony. Support payments subject to events such as death of either spouse, wife's remarriage, or a change in the economic circumstances of either spouse, may qualify as alimony without percentage limitations no matter how long they continue.

Payments fixed as support for minor children, although not taxable to the wife or deductible to the husband, should be specifically designated in the decree or judgment as child support; otherwise all payments to the wife would be taxable as alimony.

If alimony and child support were combined in an unallocated lump sum, the total amount might be treated as alimony if the agreement contained proper language. This would be an advantage for the husband/father but a disadvantage to the wife/mother, who, if she is employed, would be placed in a higher income bracket for tax purposes.

The wife/mother may be entitled to dependency deductions and the "head of household" rate if she has no other income. For this reason, a wife should carefully review with an expert the tax consequences of a settlement. Tax planning can decrease the costs of divorce and separate maintenance. It is imperative to resolve this favorably at the outset, before the divorce judgment is finalized or an agreement is signed.

For those who do not know what income taxes were filed by the husband, it is easy to obtain back copies by filing Form 4506 with the IRS and, as joint signer, to receive copies of all past returns. Also, records of payments made into Social Security by the wife may also be procured.

Is Support Available Without a Divorce Proceeding?

There are several alternatives available to the wife prior to filing a divorce or separation proceeding:

THE UNIFORM RECIPROCAL ENFORCEMENT OF SUPPORT ACT (1950)

This act is recognized by all the states. It is a lower-court proceeding in which a wife may petition for an order of support, detailing expenses, income, assets, and debts.

The order is then forwarded to the court with jurisdiction over such matters in the state where the husband is situated. Without the necessity of appearing in the husband's state, the wife is protected under the Act and incurs no costs in the receiving state.

The husband will be served and will be required to submit a detailed financial statement, which the receiving state will compare with the forwarding state's report. The court will then enter either the same amount or a different amount based on its own evaluation.

Such an order will be enforceable where the husband works and resides.

THE PARENT LOCATOR ACT

This is used when the wife is unable to locate her husband. It has several major provisions: to establish paternity, to locate an errant parent, and to collect support.

Each state was authorized to establish and name its own department for the purpose of implementing the Act. In some states, a new department was named; in others, the process is administered through the department of public welfare. However, one need not be on welfare in order to use the services of such an agency where this avenue has been designated. This procedure is available to all segments of society: professional wives, blue-collar wives, traveling salesmen's wives, actors' wives, police wives.

In using this method of obtaining a support order, a wife avoids expenses and has the use of government staff and government records, such as Social Security, military, and IRS, to locate her husband. Since the Act was implemented, states report outstanding success in obtaining welfare reimbursement from husbands who, by their absence, avoided the responsibility for supporting their families. The state has a vested incentive to process such cases, and this works to the advantage of the wife and children.

What If a Husband Fails to Pay Under a Support Order or Agreement?

If a husband fails to make regular payments, either for alimony or support, there are a number of alternatives available to enforce any award, in addition to The Uniform Reciprocal Enforcement of Support Act (URESA) and The Parent Locator Act, both previously cited.

1. Contempt: The wife may file a complaint, which must be served personally on the husband. On the hearing date—which may take two or three months to schedule—the husband has the opportunity to testify as to his ability to pay.

There is now a new direction seen in a number of states. Inquiry is made as to the current financial status of a husband at the time of the contempt hearing, to determine if there is in fact an ability to pay the award previously entered. The findings from that inquiry determine if an order to pay arrearages will be made, or a compromise worked out.

2. Long-arm Statute: This is a statute adopted in many states which provides for personal jurisdiction over a spouse who has gone to another state; it is based upon acts or conduct within the marital domicile. The criteria for enforcement include domicile of both parties within the state for at least one year within the two years immediately preceding the commencement of the action, despite the subsequent departure of the husband from the marital state. If the wife continues to reside within the marital state, the court judgment will be valid as to all obligations or modifications of alimony, child support, custody, and property settlement, and it will be enforced by the receiving state, where the husband resides.

3. Garnishment: Some states provide for the attachment of a spouse's salary if support payments are more than one to four weeks in arrears. The employer is ordered to deduct a specified amount each week from the defendant's salary and to forward the monies either to a designated agency of the court or to the department of public welfare, if the wife is receiving aid. The employer receives a small sum as reimbursement for costs incurred in processing the support payments.

4. Imprisonment: Criminal statutes provide mandatory prison terms of up to two years or more if a spouse or parent deserts his spouse or minor child without making reasonable provision for her support and there is danger that the family will become a burden upon the public. In some states the sentence may be served during such hours as will permit the spouse to continue his employment, and the wife benefits from the resumption of regular support payments.

What About the Cost of Child Care?

The new 1982 tax credit increased both the child-care expenses a taxpayer may claim and the maximum amount of total expenses that may be applied.

The maximum credit for taxpayers earning $10,000 or less is now $720 for one child, or $1,440 for two or more children. For taxpayers earning between $10,000 and $28,000 the 30 percent credit is reduced one percentage point for each $2,000, with the maximum allowable deduction being $2,400 for one child and $4,800 for two or more children.

In addition, the tax law now permits payment to relatives, such as a grandmother, to qualify for the child-care credits, provided that the relative is not also a dependent claimed on the same return.

FINDING A LAWYER AND APPEARING IN COURT

There are many situations in which it is advisable for a woman to find the right answer to the question "How do I find a lawyer?"

These occur when (1) her husband initiates a divorce/separation action against her; (2) she wishes to initiate a divorce/separation action against her husband; and (3) she is battered, and getting protection is an immediate consideration (probably to be followed by a divorce/separation).

The most convenient and sometimes most favorable situation in all three cases exists when there is a friend who is an attorney. She need not be an expert in domestic relations at this point, but should be sufficiently informed to make some good immediate decisions with the wife and to assist her in reviewing qualifications of attorneys who will ultimately handle the details of the case.

The usefulness of the "friend" approach is that the friend will want what is best for the plaintiff because of the friendship bond; good friends will not use people in trouble to build a peer's practice. This recommending intermediary can be a very important advocate.

It is realistic to face the fact that almost no one can be equally and objectively friendly toward both sides of a domestic litigation. A friend of a couple is often unconsciously predisposed toward keeping the marriage intact and is not useful to a woman who has made important decisions about her own life and wants help in implementing them, not reversing them.

Local bar associations are also informative as to attorneys who specialize in domestic relations. In this kind of objective reference, it would be important to inquire how long the attorney has been active in family or domestic law. Experience is very important in this sensitive area. Human qualities of maturity, patience, fairness, charity, sympathy, and civility are not to be taken for granted. A divorce or a separation involves complicated emotions, disturbed lives of children, and often an overwhelming sense of failure, and an attorney who is also a "good person" is a pearl of great price.

If the parties to a divorce action have been attempting to reconcile differences in marriage counseling, often the end of the counseling process leads into the divorce or separation action. At that time, some advice on the selection of an attorney could be asked for.

Because divorce is so prevalent, some family member or close friend may also have gone through the divorce process, and through observation or inquiry, the name of a suitable lawyer may be found. A close bond often grows between lawyer and client, and clients are frank to recommend or warn, depending on the success of the relationship.

It may be necessary to "shop" for an attorney and to meet more than one before deciding which one is suitable. This may involve fees, but unless some substantial legal advice is transmitted, the cost of screening should not be exorbitant.

The investment of time, effort, and funds is worth it to find an attorney with whom you are comfortable. Ethical attorneys are usually willing to explore for rapport in an initial consultation without great expense being involved.

However, an attorney's time is a major part of her inventory, and a frivolous client who goes from firm to firm ventilating her case without a serious commitment—picking up tidbits of legal advice at each stop—is operating without scruple and is unlikely to find a serious attorney who will serve her interest well.

The process of selecting an attorney is an excellent circumstance for a wife contemplating divorce to become expert in the financial facts of life. There is no reason to be timid, or to be reluctant to inquire about the fee structure and the manner in which payment is expected by the attorney. Most assuredly, one should get the best kind of legal service one can afford, but this is not the time to add extra and uncalled-for expense for "name" counsel or flashy offices.

It is important for you to like your attorney. You should be comfortable with the person selected and feel assured of her competence. You should not be embarrassed at the lawyer's appearance or behavior in court, and you must feel that you can trust the lawyer to act in your behalf when you are not present, exactly as if you were there to observe.

It cannot always be arranged, but it is useful if one's attorney is happily married, with children, since this kind of experience brings its own appreciation of the full range of domestic relations. Happily married people tend to be empathetic and protective of people in marital trouble; unhappily married attorneys could unconsciously vent their own disillusionment in angry transference to the case at hand.

A very important criterion in selection is the lawyer's accessibility. Clients should be reasonable in their demands and expectations, but phone calls should be answered with some promptness, not only to transmit advice and instructions but also to allay fears and prevent valid concerns from becoming emotionally charged.

What About the Court Appearances?

Good and considerate attorneys prepare clients for court appearances where necessary and do not enter the courtroom with a totally uninitiated client supported only with: "Trust me; I'm your lawyer."

Remember that the lawyer is in court to help the client accomplish her business; the client is not there to help the lawyer.

Insist on a full description of what is to transpire. If you are to have a participatory role, ask to rehearse it, to "role play" with your attorney.

You have undergone considerable trauma to arrive at a court action; there is no need for unnecessary and avoidable suffering based on ignorance, fear, or refusal of an attorney to make you a partner in your own case.

Wives who are seeking redress and release from cruel, abusive, or dominant mates are especially vulnerable in this situation. It is often the first experience a wife has had in many years of being assertive in her own behalf, and it is important for the lawyer to help the wife become skillful in this behavior, rather than to thwart it to protect the lawyer's own ego.

A court appearance against an estranged husband can often be a very painful experience. Often this is the first meeting since the breakup. Despite the animosity present in the relationship and the sincere desire of the wife to be freed from the husband, there may be pain associated with public disclosure of the unacceptable behavior of a person with whom one has shared dreams, intimacies, and children.

This is an experience for which there can be no precise preparation, but it may be helpful to be aware of this potential discomfort.

For women who are totally unfamiliar with courtroom atmosphere and procedure, it is useful to visit a court one morning, even if not in the jurisdiction where the case will be heard. This transmits some feeling for the language, the procedures, the furnishings, the bearing of court personnel, and the general ambience of the scene.

FURTHER READING

Ramos, Suzanne. *The Complete Book of Child Custody.* New York: Putnam, 1979.

Sussman, Alan; and Guggenheim, Martin. *The Rights of Parents.* New York: Avon Books, 1980. (Includes information for natural and adoptive parents, grandparents, stepparents, gay parents, unwed, foster, minor, divorced, and separated parents.)

Sussman, Alan. *The Rights of Young People.* New York: Avon Books, 1977.

STATE DIVORCE LAW CHART

Reprinted by permission from the *Family Law Reporter*, copyright 1982, by the Bureau of National Affairs, Inc., Washington, D.C.

Legend

DIVORCE:
- UMDA — indicates adoption of the Uniform Marriage and Dissolution of Marriage Act or substantially similar law.

CHILD SUPPORT: URESA/RURESA
- ● — indicates adoption of the uniform act of 1951.
- R — indicates adoption of the revised uniform act.
- * — indicates a substantially similar statute.

PROPERTY: Equal/Equitable Distribution
- ● — denotes equitable division
- = — denotes equal division.
- N — denotes no statutory authority.

CUSTODY: UCCJA
- * — denotes substantially similar statute.

	ALABAMA	ALASKA	ARIZONA	ARKANSAS	CALIFORNIA	COLORADO	CONNECTICUT	DELAWARE	DIST. OF COLUMBIA	FLORIDA	GEORGIA	HAWAII	IDAHO
DIVORCE			UMDA			UMDA					UMDA		
Irretrievable Breakdown	●	●	●		●	●	●	●		●		●	●
No Fault	●	●										●	
No Fault & Traditional Grounds			●			●	●	●	●	●	●		●
Fault Abolished					●	●			●	●			
Proof of Separation				3 Yrs			18 Mo	6 Mo	6 Mos-1 Yr.			2 Yrs	5 Yrs
Incompatibility	●	●	●				●	●		●		●	●
Irreconcilable Differences	●	●											
ALIMONY													
None If Fault													
Rehabilitative		●	●		●	●	●	●	●	●	●		
Sunset Law													
Factors Listed		●	●	●		●	●	●	●	●	●	●	●
Homemaker Contribution				●		●		●	●	●	●	●	
"Financial Fault" Affects		●	●		●					●	●		
Termination for Open Cohabitation	●												
CHILD SUPPORT													
Factors Listed	●	●	●	●	●	●	●	●	●	●		●	●
Impound For Visit. Denial													
URESA/RURESA	●	●	R	R	R	R	●	●	●	R	R		R
PROPERTY													
Community			●		●								●
Equal/Equitable Distribution	●	●	●	●	=	●	●	●	●	●	●	●	●
Pensions Considered/Divisible		●	●	●	●	●	●	●	●				●
CUSTODY													
Joint Custody	●	●	●	●	●	●	●		●	●		●	●
Joint Custody - Presumption													●
Natural Parents Equal	●	●	●	●	●	●	●	●	●	●	●	●	●
Visit. Denial affects Custody													
Visit. Denial affects Alimony													
Grandparent Visitation	●	●	●	●	●		●	●	●	●	●	●	●
UCCJA	●	●	●	●	●	●	●	●	●	●	●	●	●

Reprinted by permission from the *Family Law Reporter*, copyright 1982, by the Bureau of National Affairs, Inc., Washington, D.C.

Legend

DIVORCE:
UMDA — indicates adoption of the Uniform Marriage and Dissolution of Marriage Act or substantially similar law.

CHILD SUPPORT: URESA/RURESA
● — indicates adoption of the uniform act of 1951.
R — indicates adoption of the revised uniform act.
* — indicates a substantially similar statute.

PROPERTY: Equal/Equitable Distribution
● — denotes equitable division
= — denotes equal division.
N — denotes no statutory authority.

CUSTODY: UCCJA
* — denotes substantially similar statute.

	ILLINOIS	INDIANA	IOWA	KANSAS	KENTUCKY	LOUISIANA	MAINE	MARYLAND	MASSACHUSETTS	MICHIGAN	MINNESOTA	MISSISSIPPI
DIVORCE												
Irretrievable Breakdown	UMDA	●	●		UMDA			●	●	●	UMDA	●
No Fault			●		●				●	●	●	●
No Fault & Traditional Grounds				●			●	●		●	●	●
Fault Abolished					●		●				●	
Proof of Separation					1 Yr	1 Yr		1 Yr–3 Yrs				
Incompatibility		●	●	●								
Irreconcilable Differences												
ALIMONY												
None If Fault	●					●						
Rehabilitative	●	●			●		●				●	
Sunset Law												
Factors Listed	●	●		●	●		●	●	●	●	●	●
Homemaker Contribution	●	●			●			●	●		●	●
"Financial Fault" Affects	●	●										●
Termination for Open Cohabitation	●											
CHILD SUPPORT												
Factors Listed	●	●			●						●	●
Impound For Visit. Denial												
URESA/RURESA	R	●		R	R	R	R	●	●	●	R	●
PROPERTY							●					
Community						●						
Equal/Equitable Distribution	●	●	●	●	●	=	●	●	●	●	●	N
Pensions Considered/Divisible	●	●			●						●	●
CUSTODY												
Joint Custody		●	●	●	●	●	●	●	●	●	●	
Joint Custody - Presumption											●	
Natural Parents Equal	●	●	●	●	●	●	●	●	●	●	●	
Visit. Denial affects Custody											●	
Visit. Denial affects Alimony		●										
Grandparent Visitation	●	●	●	●	●	●	●	●	●	●	●	●
UCCJA	●	●	●	●	●	●	●	●	●	●	●	●

Reprinted by permission from the *Family Law Reporter*, copyright 1982, by the Bureau of National Affairs, Inc., Washington, D.C.

Legend

DIVORCE:
UMDA — indicates adoption of the Uniform Marriage and Dissolution of Marriage Act or substantially similar law.

CHILD SUPPORT:
URESA/RURESA
• — indicates adoption of the uniform act of 1951.
R — indicates adoption of the revised uniform act.
* — indicates a substantially similar statute.

PROPERTY:
Equal/Equitable Distribution
• — denotes equitable division
= — denotes equal division.
N — denotes no statutory authority.

CUSTODY:
UCCJA
* — denotes substantially similar statute.

	MISSOURI	MONTANA	NEBRASKA	NEVADA	NEW HAMPSHIRE	NEW JERSEY	NEW MEXICO	NEW YORK	NORTH CAROLINA	NORTH DAKOTA	OHIO	OKLAHOMA	OREGON
	UMDA	UMDA											
DIVORCE													
Irretrievable Breakdown	•	•	•		•		•	•		•	•		•
No Fault	•	•	•	•	•							•	•
No Fault & Traditional Grounds													
Fault Abolished													•
Proof of Separation			1 Yr	2 Yrs	18 Mo	•		1 Yr		2 Yrs	2 Yrs		
Incompatibility							•		•			•	
Irreconcilable Differences	•				•					•		•	•
ALIMONY													
None If Fault	•	•						•					
Rehabilitative		•											
Sunset Law				•	•		•	•					
Factors Listed	•	•			•		•	•			•	•	•
Homemaker Contribution	•	•	•	•	•		•	•			•	•	•
"Financial Fault" Affects		•						•					
Termination for Open Cohabitation								•					
CHILD SUPPORT													
Factors Listed	•	•					•					•	•
Impound For Visit. Denial										•	•	•	
URESA/RURESA	R	R	R	R	R	R	R *	R	R	R	R	R	R
PROPERTY													
Community													
Equal/Equitable Distribution	•	•	•	•	•	•	=	•	•	•	•	•	•
Pensions Considered/Divisible	•		•		•	=	•	•				•	
CUSTODY													
Joint Custody		•	•	•	•	•		•			•	•	•
Joint Custody - Presumption	•	•	•	•	•	•		•			•		
Natural Parents Equal				•	•		•					•	
Visit. Denial affects Custody	•											•	
Visit. Denial affects Alimony													
Grandparent Visitation	•	•	•		•		•	•			•	•	•
UCCJA	•	•	•	•	•		•	•			•	•	•

	PENNSYLVANIA	RHODE ISLAND	SOUTH CAROLINA	SOUTH DAKOTA	TENNESSEE	TEXAS	UTAH	VERMONT	VIRGINIA	WASHINGTON	WEST VIRGINIA	WISCONSIN	WYOMING
DIVORCE										UMDA			
Irretrievable Breakdown	●			●	●	●				●	●	●	●
No Fault	●	●			●		●			●	●	●	●
No Fault & Traditional Grounds									●				
Fault Abolished		●											
Proof of Separation	3 Yrs	3 Yrs	1 Yr			3 Yrs		6 Mos	6 Mos	1 Yr			
Incompatibility											●	●	
Irreconcilable Differences		●		●						●			
ALIMONY													
None If Fault													
Rehabilitative	●	●		●									
Sunset Law													
Factors Listed	●	●	●		●			●	●	●	●	●	
Homemaker Contribution	●	●								●	●	●	
"Financial Fault" Affects	●										●	●	
Termination for Open Cohabitation	●			●			●						
CHILD SUPPORT													
Factors Listed								●					
Impound For Visit. Denial	●	●						●		●			
URESA/RURESA	R	R	R	R	●	●	●	R	R	R	R	R	R
PROPERTY													
Community						●				●			
Equal/Equitable Distribution	●	●	●	●	●	●	●	●	●	N	=	=	●
Pensions Considered/Divisible	●	●	●		●	●		●		●	●	●	
CUSTODY													
Joint Custody	●	●									●	●	
Joint Custody - Presumption													
Natural Parents Equal	●		●						●				
Visit. Denial affects Custody													
Visit. Denial affects Alimony													
Grandparent Visitation	●	●	●	●	●	●	●	●	●	●	●	●	●
UCCJA	●	●	●	●	*	●	●	●	●	●	●	●	●

9
Displaced Homemakers: Making the Transition to Independence

ALICE QUINLAN

Alice Quinlan is Government Relations Director for the Older Women's League, an advocacy organization that focuses on issues of concern to midlife and older women. She was a cofounder of the Displaced Homemakers Network and has provided technical assistance to displaced-homemaker programs throughout the United States. As an adult educator, she has worked with displaced homemakers and other reentry women, and has been especially interested in helping them overcome math anxiety, often a barrier to employment and to effective personal financial management.

Widowhood, divorce, separation, and abandonment are traumatic life experiences that have implications for women far beyond the need for legal services. A recent widow may need legal assistance to deal with her spouse's business matters, but she may need even more help coming to terms with her feelings of anger and grief, and developing an independent life. A woman whose husband has suddenly left her after many years of marriage has an immediate need for legal service, including where and how to get it, but may have an even more urgent need to learn that her world has not come to an end, and how to begin the long journey toward economic self-sufficiency. It is likely that both women need or will soon need jobs.

While other chapters in this handbook deal with many of the specific problems such women face—how to get a lawyer, what to expect during divorce, how to get credit in one's own name, what is involved in estate settlement—this chapter examines the problems of a special group of women who face them in a particularly acute form. As longtime homemakers, they were dependent on a spouse for economic support, and they lose their role, identity, and support when they lose that spouse through death, divorce, or abandonment.

The material that follows will outline who displaced homemakers are, what kinds of problems they face, where help can be found, how to prevent displacement, and additional suggested reading.

DISPLACED HOMEMAKERS:
A SPEAK-OUT

When groups of displaced homemakers get together, they often share their stories, concerns, and needs at a "speak-out." The following true stories came from letters, but they are all variations on the same theme: displacement.

"After 25 years of marriage, my husband abandoned us, leaving me with his business problems and a remaining dependent son. I'm not eligible for Social Security or unemployment."

"Though I was a capable wife, mother, and homemaker for over 20 years, I'm swallowed up in hopelessness. Widowed at 54, I have no identity now."

"I was married to an Air Force Sergeant. He left for no reason. I don't have a job, no training, don't drive, and am now living with my folks."

"My husband of 33 years passed away two weeks ago. I have some savings, but no income, and am lost and confused. My field was data processing, but after some years away, I'm obsolete."

"I'm one of those older women who have been divorced. I'm 63, and 3 years older than my former husband. Since he is still working, I'm ineligible for Social Security."

"My husband is totally disabled and we receive disability payments, but it's not enough. I have two children age 11 and 6, and haven't been employed for 12 years."

"After nearly 30 years of hard work and a good marriage, I now find myself alone, and may lose my home. I will soon be without health insurance because I can't afford $60 a month."

"I am a widow 51 years old, and I must work to keep my house and pay taxes. I don't know what kind of work would be suitable."

"My husband left after 35 years of marriage. Except as a volunteer, I haven't worked all these years. He didn't want me to."

"I am desperate, going through a divorce and depression with no help from anyone. I must find a way to take care of myself and somehow learn to live alone."

DISPLACED HOMEMAKERS:
THE TERM AND THE MOVEMENT

Sometimes people think "displaced homemaker" refers to persons who need housing, or to victims of domestic violence. Others think it applies to anyone who has been out of the job market for some time, and they suggest "reentry woman" or "woman in transition" as a more positive phrase. Still others get confused with "displaced worker," which refers to persons whose jobs have been lost due to technological or other changes in the paid labor force.

While some reentry women are displaced homemakers, and some displaced homemakers have experienced domestic violence, and all displaced homemakers could be considered "displaced workers" in the broadest sense, "displaced homemaker" had a specific and unique meaning to those who coined the term.

• First, displaced homemakers are *homemakers.* They are persons who chose homemaking and child rearing as their career, devoting many years to this unpaid occupation, rather than to developing a career in paid employment outside the home.

• Second, displaced homemakers are *displaced.* As Laurie Shields notes in her book *Displaced Homemakers: Organizing for a New Life,* the link with refugees was intentional. The dictionary definition, "forcibly exiled," aptly describes the predicament of dependent homemakers who lose their source of support and their primary identity through death, divorce, separation, abandonment, or disability of a spouse after many years of marriage.

Frequently people have an initial negative reaction to the term "displaced homemaker." But the term is harsh because the situation is harsh, and the effects of the displacement are greater the longer the homemaker has been in that role. Younger women have fewer difficulties making the transition, partly because they meet fewer obstacles such as the compounding effects of sex *and* age discrimination, and partly because they are more likely to have recent paid work experience.

Though "displaced homemakers" may sound harsh to others, there is often a first shock of recognition from those going through the experience and then the relief that comes from knowing that what they are experiencing has a *name* and that others are going through the same thing.

How many others? According to U.S. Department of Labor estimates, there are about 4 million displaced homemakers in this country, from every racial and ethnic background and prior economic status. Nearly 75 percent are over the age of 40, and all have lost their source of economic support through death, divorce, separation, disability of their spouse, or ineligibility for government assistance.

From a self-help employment project in California in 1974, an awareness of the problem spread across the country, primarily through the efforts of displaced homemakers themselves. By 1978, nearly half the states and the federal government had recognized displaced homemakers as a group facing special disadvantages in entering the paid labor force, and had begun to provide limited financial resources for special programs to help them. In the same year, displaced homemakers, service providers (often former displaced homemakers), and other advocates formed a national nonprofit organization, the Displaced Homemakers Network, to further develop the issue and the movement.

PROBLEMS DISPLACED HOMEMAKERS FACE

What kinds of problems do displaced homemakers have? Even a cursory reading of the letters at the beginning of this chapter will make clear the basic predicament and its implications. The woman who loses her job as homemaker has been hit by an earthquake, her entire life turned upside down, while those around her are untouched and, though sympathetic, cannot comprehend the extent of her devastation.

If you take a moment to reread those letters, you will easily see the central themes: a basic loss of role and identity; shock, grief, anger, and depression; a sense of confusion and loss, the fruits of a lifelong commitment forever beyond reach; an acute need for good legal advice and assistance with financial management; pressing and often immediate financial needs—how to pay for housing, food, health care, transportation, and taxes; the need to get a decently paying job and begin remaking retirement plans, however late; the lack of recent work history, and seeming lack of marketable skills with which the displaced homemaker begins the job search, and the indifference or overt age, sex, and race discrimination those efforts meet; a growing awareness that the system (courts, human services, Social Security, employment offices) is indifferent and must be changed.

Doing all this in the midst of discouragement and loneliness requires strength and a basic will to live. Some women turn to drugs or attempt suicide. As one displaced homemaker said: "Building when you are 20, energetic, and life is an adventure ahead of you is one thing; picking up the pieces and trying to rebuild at 50 or 60, when you are tired and should be enjoying what you worked for all your life is something else again." What is needed most is self-empowerment, tapping the sources of strength within each person. Programs and services that help displaced homemakers do this in a variety of ways, but the goal is always the same: to make the transition from dependence to independence through employment.

While displaced homemakers need jobs, most women aren't immediately ready for employment. Many have never spent much time on themselves, and have no idea what they can or want to do. Others carry such heavy loads of anger, grief, and depression that workshops on résumé writing are useless until the emotions are adequately heard. At special displaced home-maker programs, this happens in two ways: in individual sessions with program counselors (who are often former displaced homemakers, really do understand what the woman is going through, and know when to make referrals to mental health professionals), and most important, in support groups with peers. When a small group of displaced homemakers share their experiences, their hopes, and their fears with one another, the relief is palpable, the mutual support infectious, and the progress amazing. Un-derstanding one's emotions, and realizing that they are common and very appropriate reactions to a traumatic experience, is the first step toward dealing with the situation.

Closely related to acceptance of feelings is a willingness to face the reality of one's circumstances. Seeing clearly "this is where I am" usually leads to a period of self-searching, a resulting awareness of strengths and weak-nesses, likes and dislikes, and a clarification of values that is essential for decision making. Who am I? What do I want from the rest of my life? What do I bring to this stage of my development? Through workshops, exercises, and sharing, displaced homemakers begin to deal with these questions.

Soon the focus sharpens. What skills and abilities have I developed? How can they be transferred from homemaking to the paid labor force? What kind of work do I want to do, what is available, and is there a fit between the two? What additional training do I need and can afford that will make the fit a better one? Gradually the agenda shifts from personal coping to functioning in a larger world. Exploring the labor market, becoming job-ready through preparing a résumé, filling out applications, and practicing interview techniques usually comes next. While employment is, of course, the culmination of the job search, support groups often continue for a while after initial employment to help smooth the transition.

WHERE TO GO FOR HELP

If you suddenly become a displaced homemaker, where can you go for help? You may be fortunate enough to have a full-scale displaced-homemaker center in your community, with a wide range of services. Or you may be hundreds of miles from such a resource and have to piece together whatever help you can from what is at hand. But the basic process is probably the same. You have to go through the steps of:

- accepting what you feel and where you are
- learning about and liking yourself; understanding who you are and what is important to you
- assessing what you've done in the past, and what you want to do in the future
- exploring the job market, and learning what's out there
- getting additional education or skill training, if appropriate and possible
- becoming job-ready (such as preparing a résumé and developing interview skills)
- finding a job and adjusting to the paid labor force

Displaced-homemaker programs exist in a variety of settings. They can be found at YWCAs, community-based women's centers, voc/tech schools, community colleges, adult schools, and continuing-education divisions of colleges, to name the most common. To find out what's available, call these institutions in your community and ask if they have programs for displaced homemakers, women in transition, or reentry women. You could also try calling the "Women's" listings in the Yellow Pages, and your city, county, or state commission for women—check under "Government." Finally, you can contact the Displaced Homemakers Network, which will let you know the location of the nearest identified displaced-homemaker program or center. See p. 518 for the address.

If the nearest program is too far away, you will have to do it yourself. Perhaps you can join a widows or divorced persons support group, take some decision-making and assertiveness workshops at the local community college, pick up ideas on job readiness from such books as those suggested at the end of this chapter, and get some job leads from the local office of the state employment service. Good luck! And try to remember that you are not alone.

HOW DISPLACEMENT CAN BE PREVENTED

If you are currently a homemaker, should you consider the possibility that you might become displaced in the future? And is there anything you can do to prevent such displacement? The answer to both questions is YES. While death, divorce, or disability of a spouse, or other loss of economic support cannot be predicted individually, planning for such a possibility is wise. There are preventative steps that both full-time homemakers and married women who are now in the paid labor force can take to lessen the trauma associated with marital disruption. As indicated at the beginning of this chapter, however, the longtime homemaker who is economically dependent is most at risk.

Here are some specific steps that you can take to help prevent future displacement. If you take appropriate action now, you can develop your ability to handle finances, complete or update your education, and build on your experience as a volunteer and an advocate.

Develop Financial Management Skills
* How skilled are you in managing your personal and family finances?
* Do you have credit in your own name?
* Do you have and use a checking account?
* Are you directly involved in family budgeting?
* Does your family income allow for retirement planning, and are you and your spouse learning about your options and jointly making decisions?
* Does your family have adequate insurance?
* What decisions have been made regarding survivor benefits under your spouse's pension?
* Do you and your spouse have wills?

Through workshops, courses, and other presentations on financial management, you can develop your capacity to make informed decisions and take appropriate action, from learning how to use a checking account, to making long-range financial investments. Explore the learning opportunities available through your local women's center, community college, YWCA, adult and continuing education program, or women's organization. Your future economic security may be at stake.

Get Additional Education and Job Training
So you didn't graduate from high school! Or you quit college to get married. Or you graduated from a liberal arts college 20 years ago with a major in literature. And now you are 35, or 45, or 55. Take the time *now* to complete or further your education and/or to develop job skills. It is *never too late* to learn, or to gain the credentials or the skills that will help you become self-sufficient if you are suddenly displaced. Nor will you be "out of place"—untold thousands of mature women seeking education are changing what was a common public perception that education is only for the very young.

You can earn a high school diploma by passing an equivalency examination, and there are classes available through most school systems and community colleges to help you prepare. Don't overlook postsecondary vocational education as a way to develop or update job skills; occupational training is available at voc/tech schools and is relatively inexpensive. If you have the time and resources to pursue a college degree, begin now. But before you set out on a two-year or four-year program, spend some time assessing your interests and abilities and, *most important,* whether the additional education will *really* help you in later job seeking. If you are attracted to the traditional "helping" occupations, such as teaching, allow yourself the freedom to explore other options, including nontraditional careers in which there may be many more job opportunities at higher salaries, before making a decision. In the end, the most satisfactory decisions are based on relevant labor market information and forecasts, as well as on your past experience and current interests.

Make Your Volunteer Activities Count

As a full-time homemaker, you *do have* skills now. Through the years, you've developed abilities through your experiences as a homemaker and probably as a volunteer. Make the most of these experiences. If you don't already do so, start documenting the work you do in your community, church, school, or civic group. Keep records of your accomplishments, the skills you've developed, the activities you've been involved in. Ask the groups you work for—and it *is* work, even if you're not paid for it—if volunteer training, volunteer contracts, or evaluations are available. All this information becomes the raw material for a résumé when you decide—or need—to seek a job. And it helps *you* see the skills you've developed, which will make it easier for you to market your abilities to a potential employer.

Become a Knowledgeable Advocate

While personal preparation can help, the displaced-homemaker problem is based not on personal failure, but on societal failure. The root of displacement is a society that does not value homemaking (except on Mother's Day), a society that says homemaking isn't "work" and shouldn't count for Social Security or unemployment compensation or a pension. You can become a knowledgeable advocate concerned about the inequities that homemakers, especially older ones, face. For example, did you know that under current law:

• Your husband does not need to consult you, or even inform you, about his decision either to choose survivor benefit coverage under his private pension plan, *or forgo it.*

• As a displaced homemaker, unless you have dependent children, or are old enough for early Social Security (age 60 for widows and age 62 for other women, but with permanently reduced benefits), you are ineligible for nearly all other assistance.

• If you get a job (or return to the labor force after an absence of ten years or more) and become disabled before you've worked for five years, you don't qualify for disability benefits.

• If your husband dies, or you are divorced, you may not be able to get continued health insurance at comparable coverage and cost.

• Unless you have a legal document establishing your rights, your husband may be legally entitled to all the assets of the family business, even though you worked for years as his "partner," accountant, secretary, receptionist, and manager. Also there are variations in state laws.

• If you begin working the last five years before the normal age of retirement, you have no right to pay into your employer's private pension plan.

• It is extremely difficult for you to prove that an employer discriminated against you in the hiring process because of the combination of your age and sex.

• Every year you spend at home caring for dependents—children, a disabled spouse, elderly relatives—is a "zero year," which counts against you when your Social Security benefits as a worker are calculated, decades later.

You may want to learn more about these inequities in existing law, both for your own understanding and future planning, and to let your legislators know your concern and desire for change. The organizations listed on p. 518 can provide additional information about one or more of these issues.

Think the Unthinkable

The heart of personal preparation for displacement is to do what most displaced homemakers never did: think the unthinkable. What *would* happen to you, and to your children, if something happened to your husband? (Remember that the "something" may be his death, or it may be a bitterly contested divorce in which you are forced to depend on child-support payments that never arrive.)

Could you live independently? What areas do you think you couldn't manage? Make a list, including everything that comes to your mind, from the mundane to the very significant.

You don't drive?

You have never understood the tax return you signed each year?

You are deathly afraid of the furnace? Or of traveling alone?

You assume there would be enough money from savings and your husband's life insurance, or child support, to take care of you for a while, but you really don't know. . . . And how much *would* it take, really?

Make a second list. This time, think about the information, knowledge, skills, personal development, and other resources you would need to fill in the gaps, making it possible for you to be self-sufficient. Think the unthinkable—and DO SOMETHING ABOUT IT NOW!

FURTHER READING

Andre, Rae. *Homemakers: The Forgotten Workers.* Chicago: University of Chicago Press, 1981. Examines the status of homemaking and homemakers in American society.

Aspaklaria, Shelley; and Geltner, Gerson. *Everything You Want to Know About Your Husband's Money . . . and Need to Know Before the Divorce.* New York: Wideview Books, 1981. Practical information on how to provide for a better divorce settlement; Appendix includes an overview of state marriage and divorce laws.

Azibo, Moni; and Unumb, Therese. *The Mature Women's Back-to-Work Book.* Chicago: Contemporary Books, 1980. An easy-to-read book on preemployment skills for women with limited paid work experience and education.

Baker, Nancy C. *New Lives for Former Wives: Displaced Homemakers.* New York: Anchor Press (Doubleday), 1980. Traces the path to self-sufficiency through the stories of individual displaced homemakers.

Friedman, James T. *The Divorce Handbook: Your Basic Guide to Divorce.* New York: Random House, 1982. In Q and A format, walks the reader through the legal process of getting a divorce; useful work sheets and checklists.

Grollman, Earl A.; and Sams, Marjorie. *Living Through Your Divorce.* Boston: Beacon Press, 1978. Brief chapters on separation, grieving, decision making, and rebuilding to aid in self-exploration of feelings.

Loewinsohn, Ruth Jean. *Survival Handbook for Widows.* Chicago: Follett, 1979. Describes the phases of grief and suggests how to cope with immediate and long-term transitions.

Older Women's League. "The Disillusionment of Divorce for Older Women." *Gray Paper* No. 6. Oakland, Calif.: Older Women's League, 1980. Surveys the impact of divorce on older women and suggests ways to avoid victimization.

Robertson, Christina. *Divorce and Decision Making: A Woman's Guide.* Chicago: Follett, 1980. A self-help guide focusing on life choices, goal setting, values, and assertiveness; practical checklists for planning and decision making.

Shields, Laurie. *Displaced Homemakers: Organizing for a New Life.* New York: McGraw-Hill, 1981. The history of the displaced-homemaker movement, by one of its premier organizers and founders; Appendix includes list of programs and useful publications.

10
Estate Planning

AMY M. HESS

Amy M. Hess is an associate professor at the University of Tennessee College of Law. A graduate of Barnard College and the University of Virginia Law School, she practiced law in New York City and in Charlottesville, Virginia, prior to beginning teaching.

WHAT IS ESTATE PLANNING?

Estate planning is the process by which people provide for the orderly acquisition, management, and disposition of material wealth. It deals not only with planning and writing wills, but also with acquiring and managing property during life, and with gift giving.

The legal aspects of estate planning are rather complex, since they are affected by both state and federal laws. Frequently in these days of high mobility, the estate of one individual will involve the laws of several states, which may not be uniform. In addition, several substantive areas of the law may be involved, including property, decedents' estates, trusts, and taxation. Furthermore, the laws relevant to estate planning change frequently. Thus it may be impossible even for a person of relatively modest means to plan her estate entirely without the help of an attorney.

However, estate planning is also an area of the law in which there is great opportunity to tailor the plan to suit individual needs and preferences, provided the legal ramifications of each possible alternative are clearly understood. Thus, a knowledgeable consumer will be in a particularly good position to get exactly what she wants in this area of the law, by knowing what to ask for.

PROPERTY AND FAMILY CONSIDERATIONS

What Is a Will?

A will is a written document in which a person directs how and to whom her property is to be distributed after her death. A will does not take effect until the person whose will it is (the testator) dies; a will may be changed, or amended, as often as the testator wishes during her life. An amendment to a will is called a codicil.

In most states, any person over the age of 18 years and of sound mind may make a will or a codicil. There is no special language that must be used to write an effective will, but it must be clear from the words used that the testator intends the document to dispose of her property after her death and not before. In other words, it must be clear that the document is intended to be a *will*, and not something else, such as a deed which could be used to dispose of property *during* her lifetime.

Execution, or Signing Ceremony

Execution is the legal term for the signing of a document. All states have fairly strict statutory requirements concerning the procedure by which wills are executed. The requirements for the proper execution of a will are called "testamentary formalities." The most common of these requirements are that the testator, whose will it is, sign the will in the presence of several witnesses, usually two but sometimes more, to whom the testator declares that the document is her will and that she would like them to sign as witnesses. The witnesses then each sign in the presence of the testator and of the other witness or witnesses. The act of the witnesses in signing is called attestation. In some states, anyone over the age of 18 and of sound mind may be a witness. However, in a fairly substantial number of states, a person who is "interested" in the testator's estate may not be a witness. The word "interested" generally refers to anyone who is a beneficiary under the will and sometimes also includes spouses of beneficiaries.

Witnesses are important, because before the will can take effect, it must be shown in a court proceeding (probate) that the testamentary formalities required by the particular state where the probate takes place were complied with when the will was executed. Usually, the witnesses testify that these formalities did indeed take place.

Probate and estate administration are described in greater detail later in this chapter. But here it is important to stress that these formalities are strictly enforced, because they are designed to protect the testator, who is dead when the probate takes place, from those who might try by fraud or other nefarious means to have a document admitted to probate that is not the true will of the testator. If it is found that the formalities were not complied with, the judge is generally without power to admit the will to probate even though there is ample evidence that the document does, in fact, embody the testator's wishes concerning the disposition of her property. A will that is not admitted to probate has no effect, and the testator's property will be distributed as if she had died without writing a will.

There is a widespread belief today that probate is a highly complex, time-consuming, and expensive procedure, which ought to be avoided at all cost. Part of the reason for this belief is a confusion concerning the meaning of the word probate. Technically, probate refers only to the court proceeding in which a will is proved to be the true last will and testament of the decedent. This is the only sense in which it is used in this chapter. However, since the same court usually hears the probate proceeding and oversees estate administration and is often called the probate court, the entire process of administration is sometimes colloquially referred to as probate.

In most cases, the probate of the will is an inexpensive and quick proceeding, which may not even require a formal hearing before a judge. For a description of the typical probate proceeding, see p. 248. It is true that administration of the estate may take some time, even a few years in some cases. (A description of the administration of an estate begins on p. 248.) However, there are two points to keep in mind concerning probate and administration: First, not all estates require lengthy administration, even though they involve the probate of a will. Second, a will is often the simplest and least costly way for an individual to dispose of her property after death. And in order to be effective to dispose of the testator's property, the will must be probated.

There are, to be sure, reasons why an individual may wish to provide for the disposition of her property after death other than by means of a will. These reasons and several of the other means of disposing of property after the death of the owner will be discussed in greater detail in the section of this chapter on Testamentary Substitutes, see p. 242.

Testamentary formalities vary from state to state. Although most states allow probate of a will executed in another state if the formalities of that other state (that is, the place of execution) were complied with, it is best to have your will reviewed by a lawyer when you move to a new state, to make sure it can be probated there if you die there.

Unwitnessed Wills

Some states have laws allowing wills written entirely in the testator's handwriting and dated to be probated, even though they are not witnessed and do not comply with the testamentary formalities. This seems to be an area of the law in which state legislatures make rapid changes. Therefore, before deciding to write out your will in this way, it would be wise to find

out the details of the current law in your state. However, a few generaliza-
tions can be made about the law in those states which allow unwitnessed
wills to be probated.

An unwitnessed will written entirely in the handwriting of the testator
is called a "holograph" or a "holographic will." Those states which allow
holographs to be probated usually require that, before the will may be
declared valid, at least two people must appear at the probate proceeding
to testify that the handwriting is that of the testator. Since a holograph is
not witnessed at the time it is signed, there is a greater chance for fraud,
and thus a greater likelihood that the document is not really the testator's
will. Therefore, judges tend to be somewhat chary of admitting holographic
wills to probate unless the evidence in favor of the will's validity is beyond
question. Furthermore, the statutes concerning admission of holographic
wills are generally read quite narrowly. Thus, "entirely in the handwriting
of the testator" means literally what it says; wills that are typewritten by
the testator, wills dictated by the testator to another so that the will is
written in another person's handwriting, and wills that consist of a printed
form on which blank spaces have been filled in by the testator in her own
handwriting are *not* holographic wills and cannot be admitted to probate
unless they are witnessed and the testamentary formalities are complied
with.

A Note About "Homemade" Wills

It would be inaccurate to conclude from our discussion so far that a will,
other than a holographic will, must be written by an attorney. You may
write your own will. This is true even if you live in a state that does not
allow unwitnessed holographic wills to be probated or if you choose to type
your will, rather than write it longhand. However, you should bear in mind
two points before deciding to write your own will: First, unless the will you
write is a holographic will and you live in a state that recognizes the validity
of unwitnessed holographic wills, you must comply with the testamentary
formalities described in the section on execution (page 228), including
having the will witnessed by the number of witnesses required in the state
where the will is to be probated. If you fail to comply with these requirements, the will cannot be probated and will never be given effect as your
will. Since, as was stated above, these formalities vary from state to state
and tend to be rather technical, it is generally risky to attempt to execute
a will without the help of an attorney. Second, legal language tends to be
quite precise, and this is especially true with respect to the language used
to direct the disposition of property in a will. If you write a will in your own
words, you run the risk of writing something which, although it seems quite
clear to you, is capable of several legal interpretations. Even though an
ambiguous will can be probated, it may be necessary for your beneficiaries

to engage in a lawsuit called a "construction proceeding" to have a court determine what you meant, before your property may be distributed. Obviously, this litigation could cost substantially more in time and money than having the will drawn up by an attorney.

Why Should I Have a Will?

Transfer of Property at Death: With the exception of the "testamentary substitutes" described on p. 242, a will is the only effective means of directing to whom and under what conditions your property will pass after your death. If you do not leave a will, any property you own on the date you die will be distributed in accordance with the laws of "intestate succession," discussed on p. 241. However, if you do leave a will, you may dispose of your property in any way you choose, and your wishes will be respected as closely as possible.

Perhaps, then, the most important reason to leave a will is to direct that some or all of your property pass to someone other than the person to whom it would pass under the laws of intestate succession.

For example, as we shall see on p. 241, in most states, when a married person with children dies, her property is divided among the surviving spouse and children. Many people would prefer that all their property pass to the surviving spouse.

There are various reasons for this: If you are a married woman with grown children, you might leave all your money and property to your husband, because you believe that your children are now capable of providing for themselves, while your husband, who is now getting older and perhaps living on a fixed income such as a pension, could use your assets to pay for increased medical costs or other living expenses. On the other hand, if your children are young, you might want a part of your assets to be used for their benefit, such as to help raise them, or to pay for their education, or for summer vacations. However, you would want your husband to manage the money and property for them, since they are not old enough to handle it wisely themselves. In the second situation, you would want to leave all or part of your property to your husband "as trustee" for the benefit of your children. Trustees are discussed in greater detail on p. 233. The point here is that if you want your husband to have control over that portion of your money and property that you intend to be used for your children's benefit, you must write a will. If you die without writing a will, a portion of the money and property you own at your death will automatically belong to your children under the laws of intestate succession. This will be true even if they are adults and better able to provide for themselves than is your husband, and it will also be true even if they are too young to be able to handle it wisely.

Similarly, if you are a single parent of young children, you must write a will to designate the person who will manage your property for the benefit of your children after your death.

Other, similar reasons for writing a will are as follows:

1.   To provide that specific assets go to specific persons.

2.   To make a deliberately unequal distribution among close relatives, such as children, because their personal financial resources are unequal, or you have provided for them unequally before and now wish to give more to the one who got less earlier, or because one is handicapped.

3.   To leave property to a relative who would not receive the property under the laws of intestate succession, for example, a sister, brother, or parent if you are a married person with children; or to a friend; or to make a contribution to charity, for example, your church or the college you attended.

It is important to note here that the laws of intestate succession are written and interpreted exclusively in terms of traditional family relationships. Therefore, if you are not legally married to your life partner, he or she will not receive any part of your property as your "surviving spouse" under the laws of intestate succession. You must write a will in order to give your property to that person at your death.

Even if you have very little property of your own, if you are married and expect your husband to leave you his property, or if you own property jointly with him that you would own alone if he died before you, you should have a will. This assures that the property will pass as you wish it to in the event your husband dies leaving the property to you and you die shortly thereafter without having had a chance to write another will.

Appointment of Executor: Another reason to write a will is to specify your personal representatives, that is, those who will carry out your wishes. The personal representative is the person responsible for finding all of the property, inventorying it, selling any that might need to be sold to raise money for debts, expenses, and taxes, and distributing the rest among the persons entitled to receive it under the deceased person's will or under the laws of intestate succession.

A personal representative named in a will is generally called an executor. If a person dies without a will, the law of the state of her domicile (permanent home) at the time of death will determine who her personal representative will be. The person designated by state law to be a personal representative is often called an administrator and is generally a close relative; for example, surviving spouse, child, etc. By writing a will the property owner can choose the person she thinks will do the job best, or can choose more than one in which case they would act jointly.

In most cases, anyone over the age of 18 years and of sound mind may act as executor. In addition, some banks and trust companies licensed to do business in the state of the deceased person's domicile may also act as executors. Some states require that at least one executor be a resident of that state. The laws of those states generally give the probate court judge authority to appoint a resident executor in the event none is named by the testator in her will.

Executors generally receive compensation for their work (commissions). The money to pay these commissions comes out of the estate assets of the deceased person. In a few states, the amount of these commissions is set by statute, but in most states it is set by the judge of the probate court that oversees administration of the estate. Most banks and trust companies have printed schedules of the commissions they charge to serve as executor, and these schedules are generally respected by the probate court. Commissions are generally figured in terms of a percentage of the value of the estate assets, but the percentage may vary with the extent and difficulty of the work the executor must do to complete the administration of the particular estate.

You may specify in your will the amount of the commissions to be paid to your executor, and this specification will generally be respected by the probate court. However, no one is required to serve as executor simply because he, she, or it is nominated in another person's will. Therefore, before you write a will nominating someone, you should ask your nominee whether he, she, or it will be willing to act as executor for the commission you want your estate to pay. If the person has never been an executor before, it might also be wise to review with her the duties of the executor as described in this chapter; see p. 249. Anyone may serve as executor without compensation if she chooses to do so. Close relatives of the deceased person often do.

Provision for the Care of Children and Other Dependent Relatives (Guardians and Trustees):   A third reason for writing a will is to provide for the care of minor children and the management of property to be distributed to children and other people who might be unable to handle it themselves.

In most states, a parent who dies leaving orphaned minor children (that is, the second parent to die) may designate someone (a guardian of the person) to raise and care for the children until they attain the age of majority, currently age 18 in most states. The duties of a guardian of the person are different from those of a guardian of the property, discussed below. The same person might but need not be guardian both of the person and of the property of a particular child. A guardian of the person is responsible for the physical custody and upbringing of the child, while a guardian of the property is responsible for managing the property owned by the child.

In some states, the parent's designation of a guardian of the person of her minor children is binding; in others, the court may designate someone other than the person named by the parent upon a showing that the best interests of the child require it to do so. In a number of states, the court may consider the personal preference of a child over a certain age, usually 14. If the parent dies without having made such a designation, the court will appoint a guardian of the person.

The designation of a trustee to manage property for those who cannot handle it themselves is one of the most important things that can be done in a will.

The decedent's property will not be held in trust for a beneficiary, even a minor child, unless it is specifically placed in trust by the terms of the will. Since, in most states, any contract made during minority may be disaffirmed by the minor upon attaining majority, property given to a minor child will have to be handled by an adult until the child reaches 18 if she is to receive the economic benefits of it. In any event, it is obviously undesirable to entrust substantial sums of money or other property of considerable value to a child.

If property passes outright to a minor under a will or by intestate succession, an adult may be appointed by the appropriate court to handle the property (a guardian of the property). In most states, the guardian may serve only until the minor reaches 18 and will have relatively little discretion concerning use and investment of the money or property. Generally, state law requires the guardian to get prior court approval before expending the funds on the child's behalf. Like executors and administrators, guardians of the property are entitled to compensation (commissions) for their services. In some states, these commissions are prescribed by state law; in others, the law requires the court to set the amount of the commission.

Substantially greater flexibility can be achieved by directing in the will that the property be held in trust by a named trustee who will manage the property for the child. A trust is a device by which legal title to property is transferred to one person (the trustee), who must manage the property for the benefit of another (the beneficiary) upon specific terms set out by the testator in her will. The property can be held in trust for longer than it would be possible for a court-appointed guardian of the property to hold it. Indeed, it can remain in trust for the entire lifetime of the beneficiary. The trustee can also be given wide latitude in the choice of investments and in determining how the trust fund will be used for the benefit of the minor. Conversely, the testator may narrowly circumscribe the uses to which the trust fund may be put; for example, the trustee could be required to use the trust fund only for the beneficiary's education. Thus a trust can be tailored to the specific needs and desires of the testator. The express directions of the testator concerning the operation of the trust are generally enforceable in court against the trustee by the beneficiary.

Furthermore, since an adult can be the beneficiary of a trust, trusts are often used to provide for management of property for the benefit of adults who are unable or simply unwilling to handle it themselves due to advanced age, physical or mental impairment, lack of financial expertise, or lack of interest.

In general, the rules concerning nomination and compensation of trustees are the same as those concerning nomination and compensation of executors. Any person over the age of majority and of sound mind can be a trustee, and certain banks and trust companies can be trustees as well. The trustees ordinarily receive compensation for their services, called commissions. These commissions are usually payable annually and are determined principally by the value of the property held in trust, the amount of income it earns during the year, and the amount of work the trustee must do to comply with the terms of the trust. In some states, commissions are set by statute; in others, they are set by the probate court. Banks and trust companies generally have a set schedule of commissions which will be respected by the court.

As is the case with executors, a trustee's commissions may be set by the testator in the will, and this direction will generally be respected by the court. However, as is also the case with executors, no one is required to serve as trustee merely because of the testator's nomination. Therefore, it is wise to ask if your nominee will be willing to serve before you include his, her, or its name in the will. A trustee may consent to serve without compensation, and close relatives of the testator often do.

Since there may be more than one trustee, it is fairly common for a testator to appoint two or more, each of whom has a different area of knowledge. For example, one might appoint a bank for its knowledge of financial matters to serve jointly with a close relative who is personally acquainted with the beneficiary and knows her particular needs.

In a number of states, property may be left in a will to a custodian under the state's version of the uniform gifts to minors acts. A custodianship is another statutory means of providing adult management of property intended to be used for the benefit of a minor. A custodian has somewhat more discretion in managing the property than has a guardian of the property, but somewhat less than a trustee.

If I Already Have a Will, When Should I Think About Writing a New One?

As was stated at the very beginning of this chapter, a will does not take effect until the testator dies, and a will can be changed by amendment (codicil), or revoked and replaced by a new will whenever the testator wishes. Once you have executed a will, you should reread it at least once every three years, to be sure that it still embodies your wishes, even if no major changes have taken place in your family situation. At the time you do these periodic reviews, it is a good idea to make a list of your assets with their approximate current values. This will encourage you to consider whether the distribution of your assets should change because their relative values have changed. It will also enable you to determine whether your estate has gotten large enough so that transfer taxes may be due at your death. (For a description of federal and state gift and death taxes, see the last portion of this chapter, pp. 251–58.)

You may wish to check with your lawyer while you are doing your periodic review to see if your will should be changed because of changes in the federal or state tax laws, or in the state laws concerning decedents' estates. It cannot be emphasized often enough that the laws relevant to estate planning are constantly changing. This chapter can provide you with knowledge of general trends and with some guidance as to the questions that you might ask concerning the state and federal laws relevant to your particular estate, but it cannot completely substitute for accurate, up-to-the-minute knowledge of the laws themselves.

In addition to these periodic reviews, you should consider rewriting your will if any one of the following events occurs:

1. Your marital status changes;
2. You give birth to a child or adopt one;
3. You move to a new state; or
4. There is a substantial increase in the value of your assets.

In the paragraphs that follow, we will explore the reasons why these changes might cause you to change your will.

Your Marital Status Changes: If you marry, you might want to leave much of your property to your new husband. Conversely, if you become divorced, you would probably want to delete your former husband from your will. There are statutes in a number of states that will treat as revoked any part of a will written prior to the date of the divorce, that leaves property to a former spouse. The effect of the statute will be that the former spouse will not receive the property. However, the identity of the beneficiary who will receive it instead will depend on the particular state statute and the wording of the will. Should you become divorced and still want to leave property to your former husband, you must write a new will after the date of the divorce to provide for him.

In the special case in which you do *not* want your new husband to receive your property after your death, merely writing a will may not be sufficient. This is because most states allow a surviving spouse to receive a certain share of the deceased spouse's property by filing an "election against the will" (see the section on statutory share p. 239). The only way to obtain the result you desire in such a case may be to enter into a prenuptial agreement with your prospective husband prior to the marriage. In a prenuptial agreement, each party agrees not to demand a greater share of the other's estate than is left to her/him in the will.

It seems pertinent to note here that these rules do not apply to changes in relationships between people who live together but are not legally married. Therefore, if you want to leave property to a life partner who is not legally your husband under state law, you must provide for that person in your will. Conversely, if you terminate such a relationship and no longer wish the former partner to receive property, you must write a new will to leave the property to someone else.

You Give Birth to a Child or Adopt One: As was discussed before, even though you have a child, you might want all your property to go to your husband. However, there are still a number of reasons for rewriting your will when a child is born. First, a number of states have statutes that will allow the child to take her intestate share of your estate unless it can be shown, by reference to some language in the will, that you intended to disinherit the child. Ordinarily, a will written before the child was born will give no indication of how the testator would have wanted the property distributed if a child were born. If you write a new will after the child is born, you can make explicit that you want your husband (or some other person) to receive your assets even though you have a child.

Second, your will should designate a guardian of the person for the child in the event you and your husband die simultaneously (for example, as the result of an airplane crash) or he dies and you die very shortly thereafter without having had time to write a new will.

Third, your will should provide for a trustee of your property for the child's benefit, if you are going to leave property to the child.

Fourth, if you adopt a child, in most states the child will be treated the same way as a natural child for purposes of interpreting your will, unless you specifically provide otherwise. Thus, anytime you use the word "children" to describe a group of beneficiaries, in most states the adopted child will receive a share of the property. This will likely be the result you intend in most cases. However, you should check to be sure that adopted children do, in fact, share in such a gift in the state where your will will be probated, as the rule is not uniform in all states. Furthermore, if the adopted child is your husband's child by a previous marriage, you may not wish the child to share equally with your own children. In that case you should provide explicitly in a new will or a codicil to your old will for how this adopted child is to be treated in the division of your assets.

You move to a new state: Since the laws concerning testamentary formalities, intestate succession, and the interpretation of language used in wills is not uniform among the 50 states, you should check with a lawyer to be sure your will can be probated in the new state and that it will be interpreted the same way in the new state as it would have been in the state you lived in when you executed it.

There Is a Substantial Increase in the Value of Your Assets: One of the most important reasons to review your will if there is a substantial increase in your assets is that your estate may now be large enough to cause transfer taxes to be due at your death. If this is the case, you may wish to consult a lawyer to find out if there are ways of rewriting your will or making transfers during your life that will reduce the total taxes to be paid. Other reasons to consider in these circumstances include placing property in trust for a beneficiary who could have handled a relatively small amount of property but will be unable to manage a larger amount successfully, changing the designated trustee from an individual to a bank to assure expert investment management of the larger trust fund, or adding gifts to new beneficiaries to whom you could not have afforded to leave property when your estate was smaller.

The increase in value we are referring to here could be due either to an increase in the value of the assets you have always owned, your purchase of new assets over time, or your receipt of a gift or an inheritance.

What Are the Rights of One Spouse in the Property Owned by Another?

Historically, governments have granted to a surviving spouse certain rights in the estate of the deceased spouse which cannot be defeated by the provisions of the deceased spouse's will. Their purpose is to provide for the support of the survivor. The most common of these are dower and curtesy, statutory share, family support allowance, and homestead allowance.

In other words, in most states, it is impossible for one spouse to completely disinherit the other. As a general rule, there are not similar restrictions on disinheriting a child, except that the number of dependent children a person had at the time of death is often taken into consideration in determining the amount of the support allowance.

Remember as you read this section the comment made earlier in the section on why you should have a will: The phrase "surviving spouse" in these laws refers only to someone who was legally married to the decedent at the time he or she died. If you and your life partner are not legally married under state law when one of you dies, the survivor will have no claim under the laws discussed in this section.

Dower and Curtesy: Dower and curtesy are the oldest of these spousal property rights, having their origins in feudal land ownership laws of medieval England. Originally, dower referred to a surviving wife's right upon the death of her husband to a one-third interest for life in all real property owned outright by her husband at any time during their marriage. The words dowager, meaning an elderly widow, and dower house, referring to what we might now call a mother-in-law cottage, are derived from the widow's right to dower.

Curtesy referred to a surviving husband's interest for life in all real property owned by his deceased wife at any time during their marriage provided they had a child born alive.

Today, dower and curtesy have been abolished in many states. In others, although the terms dower and curtesy may still be used, the rights of the survivor have been extended to include personal property, and have become outright interests instead of life interests.

Statutory Share: In most states today, a surviving spouse has the right to elect to take a fraction, usually one third, but sometimes one half, of her deceased spouse's estate in lieu of what the deceased spouse leaves the survivor by will. The election is made by filing a paper with the probate court.

To give an example: Suppose you are a married woman living in a state in which the elective share is one third of the decedent's estate. Your husband dies owning property worth $600,000. In his will, he left you property worth $50,000 and left the rest of his property to his brothers and sisters. Since one third of $600,000 is $200,000, you would be entitled to file a paper "electing against the will," and the probate court would direct the executor of your husband's estate to distribute $200,000 worth of your husband's property to you and the remaining $400,000 to your husband's siblings.

In some states, the election applies only to property owned outright by the deceased spouse at the time of death. In those states, the first spouse to die can render the election worthless and successfully disinherit the survivor by giving away all of the property during her lifetime. In our example in the preceding paragraph, suppose your husband had owned $600,000 worth of property, but one year before his death, he gave his sister a gift of $300,000 worth of property. Now, when he dies, his estate is worth only $300,000. Since your right of election applies only to those assets he still owned at death, you will now only receive $100,000 (one third of the $300,000 left in your husband's estate) when you elect against the will. His sister will be allowed to keep all of the $300,000 your husband gave her the year before his death.

The laws of a growing number of states include in the property to which the election applies certain lifetime transfers, such as transfers made shortly before death (usually within two years prior to death) and transfers in which the deceased spouse retained some interest in the property, such as the power to revoke the transfer or the right to receive the income from the property. To continue our example, in a state that follows this rule, since your husband made the $300,000 gift to his sister one year before he died, it would be added to the assets remaining in his estate for purposes of determining the amount of property you would be entitled to if you elected against his will. Thus, you would once again be entitled to $200,000 worth of property, or one third of $600,000. Since the gift to your sister-in-law is equal in value to one half of all the property to which your election applies, the probate court would probably be required by state law to direct the executor of your husband's estate to pay one half of your share, or $100,000, out of estate assets, and to direct your sister-in-law to give you the other $100,000.

In other states, the law requires that the deceased spouse's lifetime gifts be included in the pool of property to which the surviving spouse's election applies if the survivor can show that the deceased spouse made the gift for the purpose of defrauding the survivor of the property. Thus, in our example, if it could be shown that the transfer to your sister-in-law was a sham, that your husband still had all the rights of an owner with respect to the property until he died, and that he transferred title to the property into his sister's name only so that you would not be able to obtain it after his death, your right to elect might again entitle you to $200,000 worth of property, since the gift to your sister-in-law would be considered a "fraud on the statutory share."

Support Allowance and Homestead Rights: These rights are designed for the maintenance of the family while the property constituting the estate of the deceased spouse is in administration. Often, particularly in smaller estates, during the early stages of administration, property may not be distributed to the beneficiaries without a court order, because it cannot be ascertained immediately how much will be needed to pay the decedent's debts, estate administration expenses, and taxes. The probate court is therefore given authority to allow payment out of the estate to the surviving spouse of a monthly allowance to support the spouse and any dependent children for a specified length of time, usually a year. Often, the surviving spouse is also entitled to receive a specified amount of property, called exempt property, and to live in the family home for a specified time. This last right is often called the "homestead" right, although the reader should be aware that it is not necessarily the same right as the homestead right referred to in the bankruptcy laws and the real estate and divorce laws of a number of states (for information on *those* laws see Chapter 6). The support allowances and homestead rights usually have priority over the rights of the deceased spouse's creditors and are in addition to the surviving spouse's rights under the will, the intestacy laws, and the statutory elective share.

To Whom Does Property Go if the Owner Does Not Leave a Will?

A person who dies without a will is called an intestate decedent, and such a person's property is distributed according to the laws of intestate succession. Each state has its own law of intestate succession. Usually the intestate succession law of the state where the person was domiciled at death governs the distribution, except that if one dies owning real estate or tangible personal property in another state, the law of that state will govern the distribution of that property.

Although the laws of intestate succession vary from state to state, these laws are quite similar and generally follow this basic format:

If the intestate decedent was married and had children, half of the property is distributed to the surviving spouse and half to the children. In some states, if there is more than one child, the spouse receives one third, and the children receive two thirds. If there is a surviving spouse but no children, the spouse may receive all the property, but in a number of states, the property is divided between the surviving spouse and the deceased spouse's parents.

If there is no surviving spouse, the children generally receive all the property; if any child has predeceased the parent, that child's children (the decedent's grandchildren) receive the child's share.

The laws of intestacy are written only in terms of the beneficiary's relationship to the decedent, without regard to the beneficiary's age or financial need. Thus, children will receive their shares even though they are adults and financially independent when one of their parents dies intestate, and even though some other person, such as the decedent's spouse, needs the property more. And a person who was not legally married to the decedent will not receive the surviving spouse's share under the laws of intestacy, since the word "spouse" is always given its traditional meaning in this body of law. As was noted earlier in this chapter, these are good reasons to write a will. If a person leaves a validly executed will, the property will always pass to those named in the will, rather than those who are named in the laws of intestate succession.

If an intestate decedent leaves neither spouse, children, nor descendants of children, the property will generally be distributed to the decedent's parents, or if they are dead, the decedent's brothers and sisters and their descendants.

In most states, the law provides for distribution to more remote relatives if the decedent left no close relatives. Ultimately, however, all states provide that the property will become the property of the state if a person who dies intestate leaves no relative within a stated degree of kinship. This is called the law of escheat.

At one time, the rules governing intestate succession to real estate on the one hand and to personal property on the other were different within each state. This is no longer generally the case, although there may still be some states that preserve the distinction. In those states which do, real estate will generally pass directly to the children of the intestate decedent even if her/his spouse is alive. The property will, however, generally be subject to the spouse's dower or curtesy rights. Thus, in such a state, if the legal title to the family home were in a husband's name alone, and he died survived by his wife and children, the home would pass to the children, subject to the wife's dower rights.

Lifetime Transactions That Result in Property Transfer at Death (Testamentary Substitutes)

There are a number of fairly common property transactions that people enter into during their lives that result in automatic transfer of property to someone else upon their deaths. Since a will disposes only of property not otherwise disposed of during the testator's life, the property acquired in these transactions will be disposed of in accordance with the specific provisions of the contract, deed, or other document executed in connection with the transaction, rather than by the terms of the testator's will.

In this section, we will discuss three of the most common types of property in this category: life insurance, jointly owned property, and living trusts. Another common type of property that also belongs in this group is employer-created retirement benefits, such as pensions, and the related benefits payable to an employee's survivors after the employee's death. These benefits are discussed in Chapter 16.

Among the principal advantages to the transactions discussed in this section are that the property is not part of the deceased's estate for administration purposes, and the documents creating the interests do not have to be probated. A probated will is a matter of public record that anyone may read at the county courthouse. Thus these lifetime transactions have two advantages: They expedite receipt of the property by the survivors, and they allow the family to keep its financial affairs private.

Life Insurance: A life insurance policy is a contract whereby the insurance company agrees to pay a stated sum, usually called the face amount, to a designated beneficiary upon the death of the insured person in exchange for a payment or a series of payments of money called premiums paid during the insured person's life.

Usually the insured person is also the owner of the policy, but the owner may be another person. The owner has a number of contract rights, such as the right to borrow against the policy, change the beneficiary, cancel the policy, direct that the proceeds be paid to the beneficiary in installments rather than in one lump sum, and transfer ownership of the policy to someone else.

Upon the death of the insured person, the proceeds are paid directly to the named beneficiary. They need not be held by the personal representative of the decedent's estate subject to administration.

There are many kinds of life insurance, providing the owner with various rights. It is important to understand exactly which rights you are buying in a particular policy, so that you can be sure you get the best policy for yourself and your family. One of the most common such differences is that between whole life insurance and term life insurance. The exact differences are rather technical and may vary somewhat depending on the life insurance company. Basically, however, whole life insurance provides coverage for the entire life of the insured in exchange for a series of equal premiums paid over the life of the insured. The owner can terminate a whole life policy at any time and receive the "cash surrender value" or can continue the policy in force and borrow against the cash surrender value. The cash surrender value of a life insurance policy is an amount roughly equal to the premiums paid, plus interest on them since their payment, less administrative costs.

Term life insurance, on the other hand, provides that the company will pay the face amount if the insured dies within the "term," a stated number of years, usually between one and five. The price of a term life insurance policy is ordinarily a single premium paid at the beginning of the term. The premiums for such policies are often lower than the premiums for the same face amount of whole life insurance. This is because the policy, and therefore the risk, is for a relatively short term, and because the policy has no cash surrender value nor any loan value.

Jointly Owned Property: It is quite common for a married couple to take title to their major assets (the family home, checking and savings accounts, and often stocks and other securities) in the names of both spouses as joint tenants with right of survivorship. In most states, the spouses are treated as co-owners of the property. At the death of the first spouse, jointly held property becomes the sole property of the surviving spouse, regardless of the provisions of the will of the deceased spouse. The jointly held assets do not have to go through administration in the estate of the first spouse to die.

Of course, it is not required that a wife and husband own their property as joint tenants with right of survivorship. They are free to decide for themselves how to own each asset, and they could own some or all of the family property individually, or as tenants in common, rather than as joint tenants with right of survivorship.

In deciding how to take title to any particular asset, it is important to know exactly what the words "joint tenancy" mean in the state whose law will govern the transaction. In some states, a joint tenancy has no survivorship feature unless the words "with the right of survivorship" or a similar phrase is used. Thus half the property might be subject to the terms of the will of the first spouse to die. In some states, a joint tenancy with right of survivorship in certain bank accounts and savings accounts may be considered for convenience only and will not automatically create survivorship rights in the survivor, especially if the first spouse to die has made all the deposits into the account.

It is also important to distinguish between joint tenancies with right of survivorship and tenancies in common. A tenancy in common is a form of co-ownership that allows each tenant to dispose of her share of the property during life without the consent of the other, and to dispose of that share at death by will. There is no survivorship feature.

Some states allow spouses to own real estate in a special kind of joint tenancy called a tenancy by the entirety. The rights of the surviving spouse at the death of the first spouse are essentially the same whether the spouses owned the property as tenants by the entirety or as joint tenants with right of survivorship. However, the spouses' rights are somewhat different during life. If they own the property as joint tenants, either spouse may generally dispose of her/his half of the property without the consent of the other. The person who receives this half of the property then owns this property as a tenant in common with the other spouse. There is no longer any survivorship feature. Further, the creditors of one spouse can bring a lawsuit called a partition proceeding to have the debtor spouse's half of the property transferred to them to satisfy the debts due. If the property cannot be easily divided in half, the judge in the partition proceeding generally has power to require the entire property to be sold. If this is necessary, the debtor spouse's half of the proceeds will then be paid to her/his creditors to satisfy the debts, and the other half of the proceeds will be paid to the other spouse. On the other hand, if the spouses owned the property as tenants by the entirety, neither could convey her/his half of the property without the consent of the other, and the property could not be partitioned or sold to satisfy the creditors of one spouse.

Joint tenancies with or without right of survivorship and tenancies in common may be created between people who are related but are not spouses (for example, sister and brother, or parent and child), between people who arc unrelated, and between more than two people.

Living Trusts: As was noted earlier in this chapter, the trust is a highly useful means of transferring property.

In our earlier discussion, we dealt with trusts created in a will (testamentary trusts). A trust may also be created by transferring property to a trustee during the owner's lifetime. Such trusts are called living trusts, or *inter vivos* trusts. The terms of a living trust are usually written in a document called a trust instrument or trust agreement signed by the property owner (grantor or settlor) and the trustee. All comments concerning trustees and beneficiaries of testamentary trusts in our earlier discussion are also true of trustees and beneficiaries of living trusts.

Living trusts may be either revocable or irrevocable, and may last for either a stated term of years or until the death of a certain named person.

If a trust is revocable, the settlor may revoke it entirely or in part and take back the property. In most states, the settlor may also change the terms of a revocable trust. An irrevocable trust is one that cannot be changed, nor can the property be taken back. Under the law of most states, a trust is irrevocable unless the settlor expressly reserves the right to revoke it as part of the provisions of the trust agreement.

Use of Trusts as "Will Substitutes":   Since a trust may continue beyond the death of the settlor, it is quite common for a person with a moderate to large estate to put much of her property in a revocable living trust, providing in the trust agreement that she receive the income for life and that, upon her death, the property continue in trust for others. A common disposition after the settlor's death provides for income to be paid to the settlor's spouse for life together with so much of the principal property as he might need for support and health expenditures in excess of the income, and for the remainder of the principal to be distributed to the children at the spouse's death. There are usually also provisions for retention in trust of property that might otherwise pass to a minor child.

The terms of a living trust insofar as they refer to disposition of the property after the settlor's death could, of course, be put in her will. The advantage to the living trust is that, like life insurance and jointly held property, these assets avoid administration, and the trust assures privacy, since the trust agreement need not be probated.

A common estate-planning device combines life insurance and a living trust to create what is called a revocable unfunded life insurance trust. The terms of such a trust can be varied to meet the needs of the individual settlor. The general format is as follows: The settlor creates a revocable trust and makes the trustee the beneficiary of life insurance on the settlor's life. The settlor continues to own the policies and, usually, to pay the premiums during her life. The trust agreement directs the trustee to pay any income to the settlor during her life, and then to collect the proceeds at death and manage them in accordance with the terms of the trust agreement, usually for the benefit of the spouse and children of the settlor. The terms of such a trust following the death of the settlor may be any terms that would be permissible for any other trust. For example, the trust agreement might provide that after the death of the settlor, the trustee should invest the life insurance proceeds and pay the income from the investment to the settlor's surviving spouse for life. After the spouse's death, the trustee might be directed in the trust instrument to divide up the principal (the investment) among the settlor's children.

Lifetime Uses: Trusts are often used for the benefits the settlor may enjoy during her life. Indeed, trusts are sometimes created only for those benefits and terminate on the settlor's death or after a stated number of years. The property then passes back to the settlor's estate for disposition under her will, or if the settlor is still alive, it passes back to her as owner.

Two such benefits are property management and income tax savings.

Trusts are often created to shift responsibility to the trustee for the day-to-day management and investment decisions which a property owner must make, such as checking that dividends, interest, or rent are paid on time and deciding when and upon what terms to sell and purchase such assets as stocks, bonds, and real estate. A property owner might decide to shift this burden for a number of reasons, including lack of financial expertise or interest, preoccupation with other family or business matters, ill health, or advancing age.

A common estate-planning device for people with relatively high taxable incomes who are supporting relatives, particularly aged or infirm adult relatives, is the creation of a short-term trust called a Clifford Trust. This is a trust that is irrevocable by the settlor for a term of not less than ten years (or until the death of the income beneficiary) and provides that the income be paid to someone other than the settlor or the settlor's spouse for that term. If the trust agreement is properly drafted, the income of such a trust will be taxable to the beneficiary, rather than to the settlor, during the term of the trust. This can result in considerable tax savings if the income beneficiary is in a lower income tax bracket than the settlor.

To assure the income tax benefits, care must be taken in drafting the terms of the trust to avoid giving the settlor any discretionary control during the ten-year term, either as trustee or otherwise, and to avoid making the beneficiary someone the settlor is legally obligated to support, such as a minor child.

Is It Always Better to Have a Living Trust Instead of a Will?:   While a living trust may be desirable in many estate plans, it is important to understand that it is not the best plan in all cases. Therefore, it seems appropriate here to summarize the principal advantages and disadvantages of using a living trust as compared to a will as the main vehicle for disposing of your estate after death.

The major advantages of using a living trust to transfer property after the death of the settlor are (1) privacy, since the trust agreement does not have to be probated; and (2) speed, since the trustee simply continues to manage the property for the designated beneficiaries without having to wait while the deceased settlor's estate goes through the procedures of administration described on p. 248. In some cases, it may also save money, since, as will be seen in the section on probate, p. 248, some states have probate court fees (sometimes called probate taxes) based upon the amount of property passing under a will (but not under a living trust), and in a few special circumstances the probate proceeding itself may be complicated or costly. However, there are also situations in which the living trust may be the more expensive or time-consuming alternative, and having a will is preferable.

The most common such situation is that of the estate which is small enough and involves beneficiaries capable enough so that no asset management is really necessary after the death of the settlor. Trustees are entitled to commissions. There is no reason to pay commissions when the trustee's services are not needed, especially if, because of the particular provisions of the state's law, the probate fees or taxes are less than the trustee's commissions would be, and it can be predicted with reasonable certainty that the settlor's will would not require a costly or complicated probate proceeding.

There are two basic categories of wills that might require costly or lengthy probate: (1) those which might be contested because of unusual provisions or disharmony among family members; and (2) those for which state law will require a more formal probate proceeding than is ordinarily necessary because some of the decedent's intestate beneficiaries (those who would receive the decedent's property if she died without a will) are minors; for example, if the decedent is survived by minor children.

Thus, a woman who wishes to manage her own affairs while she is alive and plans to leave all her property outright to her adult children when she dies is probably better off writing a will rather than creating a living trust. On the other hand, a woman who wants to employ a trustee to manage her assets during her life and will leave the property in trust for her minor grandchildren after she dies is probably better off creating a living trust. A woman who prefers to manage her property herself during her life, but expects to leave it in trust for her minor children at her death, might be better off with a will or a living trust depending upon the particular state laws likely to govern the probate of her will and the administration of her estate, the extent of her assets, and her particular family situation.

MECHANICS OF TRANSFER: PROCEDURES FOR THE ADMINISTRATION OF ESTATES

Probate

The probate proceeding is conducted in the probate court for the county where the decedent was domiciled; that is, where she made her permanent home at the date of her death. Sometimes there will have to be additional probate proceedings, called ancillary probate proceedings, in each additional state where the decedent owned real estate or tangible personal property that passes by the terms of her will.

Many states have a probate court fee (sometimes called a probate tax), which must be paid before the probate proceeding may be commenced. The probate fees of most states are based upon the total value of all the property that will pass to the beneficiaries under the will.

There are two kinds of probate in many states, common form, or informal, probate and solemn form, or formal, probate. Common form probate is a simple, short proceeding, usually held before the probate clerk, rather than the judge. In the common form proceeding, it is usually unnecessary for the beneficiaries named in the will or the intestate beneficiaries to receive formal notice of the hearing. Wills admitted to probate in common form have the same legal force as those admitted to probate in solemn form, except that the former are subject in most states to contest and revocation of probate by a proceeding in solemn form brought within a statutory length of time, usually one year, but sometimes longer.

A solemn form probate proceeding is a formal court hearing before a judge and, often, a jury. Legal notice of the hearing must be given to all interested parties who could come in to contest the validity of the will, usually the potential intestate beneficiaries and all beneficiaries under earlier known wills of the testator. Solemn form probate is generally not used except in cases of contest, due to the additional delay and expense of a formal trial. Will contests are relatively rare, and most wills are probated without formal litigation.

There are some states in which somewhat more formal procedures (though not necessarily solemn form probate) are required when there are minors who might receive some of the testator's property, either under the will or under the laws of intestate succession (see p. 241) if the will were denied probate. The laws of those states generally require a guardian *ad litem* to be appointed to represent the minors' interests during the probate proceeding. The guardian *ad litem* will be a lawyer chosen by the probate court judge. The guardian *ad litem* is entitled to a fee, which is payable out of estate assets.

The inquiry in all probate proceedings is the same: Is the document under examination the true last will and testament of the testator? Testimony will be heard as to whether the testator was of sound mind, was over the age of 18, and intended that this writing dispose of her property after her death, and whether the testamentary formalities (see p. 228) were complied with. If all requirements are met, the will is "admitted to probate," that is, declared to be the true last will and testament of the testator.

Many states today have statutes allowing for what is referred to as a self-proved will. This is a will to which an affidavit is attached during the life of the testator, usually at the time the will is executed, which states that the testator is of sound mind, over the age of 18 years, and intends the document to be her will, and that all of the testamentary formalities of execution were complied with. The affidavit is signed and sworn to before a notary public by the testator and the witnesses. In most states that have such a statute, a self-proved will can be admitted to common form probate without the witnesses testifying.

The fact that a witness dies before the testator and is therefore unable to testify is not fatal to probate.

The reader has probably noticed that nowhere in this section is there any mention of the family gathering at the decedent's lawyer's office for a reading of the will. The reason for this omission is simple: In modern practice, wills are almost never formally read in this manner. Although it might be an efficient way of acquainting all family members with the terms of the will, a reading is certainly not required by law.

Functions of the Executor

Immediately after the will is admitted to probate, the executor named in the will is asked to qualify, that is, to take an oath promising to carry out the duties of the office, and if required by state statute, to post bond in case she should cause a loss to the estate by mishandling it. If no executor is named in the will, or if the named executor is dead or refuses to qualify, an administrator will be appointed and be required to take a similar oath and post bond. Since the duties of executor and administrator are generally the same in most states, the term personal representative will be used throughout the rest of this chapter to refer to one holding either office.

The personal representative must now administer the estate, a job consisting of five main categories of functions: marshaling the assets, payment of debts, preparation of tax returns, accounting, and distributing the assets to the beneficiaries.

Marshaling Assets: This function consists mainly of two tasks: first, ascertaining all of the property that belonged to the decedent, and second, bringing it within the personal representative's control. In most states, the personal representative must file an inventory, that is, a list of all of the decedent's assets. The inventory may also be required to include a statement of the fair market value of each asset. The fair market value of an asset is the price it would bring if offered for sale publicly.

Traditionally, a decedent's real estate is not subject to administration by the personal representative, but passes directly to the beneficiary named to receive it in the decedent's will or by the laws of intestate succession. Thus the personal representative marshals and administers only personal property. However, real estate is often made subject to the decedent's debts in the event the personal property is insufficient to satisfy them, and to the payment of a proportionate share of the federal and state death taxes.

Payment of Debts: Within a statutory period after qualification, the personal representative must publish notice to creditors of the decedent. Usually this means placing a legal notice in a local newspaper for a specified number of issues and posting a notice at the courthouse. Thereafter, the creditors will have a statutory period of time to present their claims. The personal representative is entitled to ask for court direction concerning the payment of any questionable claim.

Tax Returns: The personal representative is charged with the responsibility to prepare returns required by the federal estate tax laws and any state death tax laws. In addition, since an estate is treated as a separate taxpayer for federal (and most state) income tax purposes, the personal representative may also have to prepare income tax returns.

Accounting: The personal representative is required to submit to the court a log showing all items received and disbursements paid out on behalf of the estate, and a proposed plan for distribution of the remaining property in the estate to the beneficiaries. This log is called an accounting. It is examined by the probate judge, or in some states, by the commissioner of accounts, and if it is found to be in order, the personal representative is awarded commissions and discharged. Customarily, the personal representative is required to notify all beneficiaries when she presents the accounting to the appropriate official. Any beneficiary who has grounds to object to any aspect of the personal representative's handling of the estate must make her objections known within a certain period following notification. The objections may necessitate a court hearing before the personal representative may be discharged.

Distribution of Assets to Beneficiaries: After all assets have been marshaled, and all debts, expenses of administration, and taxes have been paid, the personal representative may make distribution of the remaining assets to the beneficiaries in accordance with the directions of the testator's will or the laws of intestate succession.

It may take several years for an estate to be fully administered and the decedent's property to be finally distributed, depending on how difficult the personal representative's duties are to accomplish in a particular case. For example, there may be questions concerning the decedent's title to certain property which require protracted negotiations or litigation to resolve. In many states, it is unwise for a personal representative to distribute any of the decedent's assets without court approval until these issues are resolved, since she may be personally liable for any loss to a beneficiary or creditor caused by distributing property to the wrong person.

TAX CONSIDERATIONS

GIFT TAXES: FEDERAL GIFT TAX

What Property Is Taxed?

The federal tax laws impose a gift tax on each lifetime transfer of property in which the giver receives from the beneficiary less than the full value (in money or other property) of the property transferred. For example, a "sale" of land worth $20,000 to one's son for $10 is not a sale but, rather, a gift of $19,990 worth of property. The tax is imposed on all types of property, including real estate, tangible personal property such as jewelry or furniture, and intangible personal property such as stocks and bonds, savings accounts, and life insurance policies.

Annual Exclusion from Tax: Each person may give up to $10,000 per year to as many beneficiaries as she wishes without incurring gift tax. Thus, in the example in the preceding section the total gift was $19,990, but if the mother had made no other gifts to that son that year, she would be entitled to exclude $10,000 of the gift and pay tax on only $9,990. She could also give up to $10,000 each to as many other people as she wished this year without incurring gift tax.

Many readers may be familiar with a $3,000-per-beneficiary annual exclusion from federal gift tax. Until January 1, 1982, the maximum annual exclusion was $3,000; it was increased to $10,000 as part of federal tax legislation passed in August 1981 and effective for all gifts made on and after January 1, 1982.

It seems appropriate to insert a warning at this point: The federal tax laws, like any other federal statutes, can be changed by Congress at any time, and in fact are amended quite frequently. Thus, although this chapter accurately reflects the state of the law as it existed at the time the chapter was written, it could suddenly become outdated by an act of Congress.

Therefore, before doing any actual estate planning, the reader would have to check that the law has not changed.

Split Gifts: A married person may agree to treat one half of the gifts made by her spouse as her own gifts for gift tax purposes. Thus, the mother in our previous example and her husband could elect to treat the gift for tax purposes as if each of them had made a gift of $9,995 to the son. Since each of them may exclude the first $10,000 of gifts to any beneficiary, the effect of this gift splitting is to allow the entire transfer to escape federal gift tax.

Marital Deduction: A married person may make unlimited gifts to her spouse without incurring federal gift tax.

Here, again, the reader may be familiar with a federal gift tax marital deduction that exempted from tax only a portion of the gifts made to one's husband or wife. The unlimited federal gift tax marital deduction is another change made in August 1981 and is effective for gifts made on or after January 1, 1982.

The federal tax laws, like the state decedents' estates laws, only treat legally married people as "married." Therefore, gifts made to a life partner to whom you are not legally married are fully taxable, except, of course, for the $10,000 annual exclusion.

How Is the Tax Computed?:

Federal gift tax is computed annually on the total amount of gifts made in that year in excess of $10,000 per beneficiary. The tax is cumulative; that is, in the second year in which one makes gifts, one computes the tax by adding the two years' gifts together, determining the tax on the total, and subtracting the tax on the first year's gifts. This has the effect of taxing succeeding years' gifts at higher and higher tax rates.

In 1976, the federal estate and gift taxes were "unified" so that the tax rates are now the same. The federal gift and estate tax rates are graduated like the federal income tax rates. In 1982 they ran from 18 percent on transfers under $10,000 to 65 percent on those over $4 million but they are scheduled to be reduced under current law so that the highest rate will be 50 percent in 1985.

Also as part of the unification of the federal estate and gift taxes, a "unified credit," which can be used against the two taxes, was adopted. The "unified credit" has the effect of allowing each person to transfer a certain amount of property tax-free either during life, at death, or partly at each time. The total amount of property that a person may transfer tax-free is $225,000 in 1982 and is scheduled under current law to increase annually until it reaches $600,000 for transfers made on or after January 1, 1987.

The way these tax provisions work can be illustrated as follows:

Suppose you have assets with a total fair market value of $500,000 and make a gift worth $100,000 to your daughter in 1982, and you and your husband elect to treat the gift as a split gift. The federal gift tax would be figured as follows: First, you and your husband would each be considered to have made a gift of $50,000 worth of property, one half of the gift, by virtue of the split gift election. From this total gift, each of you may subtract one annual exclusion of $10,000, so you would therefore each have made a taxable gift of $40,000. If neither of you had ever made any taxable gifts before, you would each have all of your unified credit available. Since the unified credit allows each of you to transfer $225,000 tax-free, neither of you would pay any gift tax in 1982. Now, suppose you were to die in 1983. At your death, you still owned the rest of your assets and they still had a fair market value of $400,000. In your will, you leave all these assets to your children. As stated above, the unified credit is increasing annually; the unified credit for 1983 allows one to pass $275,000 worth of property tax-free. Since you have used up $40,000 of your unified credit by making the gift of $40,000 in 1982, your estate will escape estate tax on $235,000 (that is, the $275,000 total unified credit less the $40,000 prior gift). The estate will owe tax on the remaining $165,000 worth of property.

You may use as much of the unified credit as you wish to give property tax-free during your lifetime, or, if you prefer, you may refrain from making gifts entirely during your lifetime and the entire amount of the unified credit will be available to allow property to pass tax-free to your beneficiaries at your death.

State Gift Taxes

Some states' gift taxes are assessed approximately the same way as the federal gift tax. A few have a gift tax that is assessed the way the inheritance tax is assessed. Inheritance taxes are discussed in greater detail below. Basically, a gift tax that is assessed in the way that an inheritance tax is assessed would involve varying rates and exemptions, depending on the familial relationship between each beneficiary and the giver. Such a gift tax is not ordinarily cumulative from year to year. Some states have no gift tax.

DEATH TAXES: FEDERAL ESTATE TAX

What Property Is Taxed?

The federal tax laws require that estate tax be paid on the total fair market value of all property in which the decedent had an interest, to the extent of her interest on the date of her death. As was noted in the discussion of estate administration, the term fair market value means the price that an item of property would sell for on the open market in a transaction between a willing buyer and a willing seller. As with the federal gift tax, the federal estate tax is imposed on both real estate and personal property and on both tangible items, such as jewelry and furniture, and intangible items, such as stocks and bonds, savings accounts, and life insurance policies. Furthermore, the federal estate tax is assessed not only on property that is administered as part of the decedent's estate and that passes under her will or by the law of intestate succession, but also on certain property in which the decedent had an interest during her life and which passes to another at her death by the terms of some other instrument. For example, the property in a revocable living trust created by the decedent, and life insurance on her life that the decedent owned, are subject to federal estate tax at the decedent's death.

The tax is paid out of the estate, usually by the personal representative.

The reader will undoubtedly notice the number of times that the phrase "under current law" appears in the discussion of federal estate tax. The warning given in the section on the federal gift tax is important enough to bear repeating here: The federal estate tax can be changed by Congress at any time. It has, in fact, undergone three fairly substantial revisions in the five years immediately preceding the writing of this chapter. Therefore, it would be unwise to treat the statements made in this chapter as any more than a guide. Before doing any actual estate planning, the reader should consult an attorney to find out the current specific provisions of the law.

There are special rules governing the federal estate taxation of a number of types of property. Among the most commonly encountered of these special categories of property are jointly held property, life insurance, and family-run farms.

The rules concerning estate taxation of *jointly held property* are rather complex. Therefore, the following is necessarily an oversimplification designed to summarize the general rules. For a comparison of the types of joint ownership from the standpoint of property law rights, see p. 243 of this chapter.

Property held in a tenancy in common or in a joint tenancy without right of survivorship is taxed in the estate of a decedent only to the extent of the fractional interest the decedent had during life. Thus, if a person owns property as an equal tenant in common with her brother and sister, when she dies only one third of the fair market value of the property is taxable.

On the other hand, if the property is held in joint tenancy with right of survivorship, the estate of the first tenant to die is generally taxed on that portion of the fair market value of the property that corresponds to the portion of the purchase price paid by that tenant. Thus, if the decedent in the previous example owned the property as a joint tenant with right of survivorship with her brother and sister, and paid one third of the price when they bought it, one third of the fair market value at her death would be subject to estate tax. On the other hand, if she paid for the whole property, the whole property is subject to federal estate tax at her death.

There is a special rule that covers situations in which the only two joint tenants with right of survivorship are husband and wife. In that event, not more than one half of the property will be taxed to the estate of the first spouse to die even if she paid the entire purchase price for the property. This rule also applies to tenancies by the entirety.

Naturally, the entire property will be subject to federal estate tax in the estate of the survivor, since the property will have been solely owned by that person at the time of his or her death.

Life insurance is generally taxed to the owner of the policy at her death, regardless of whether the owner is also the insured, unless the proceeds are payable to the estate of the insured. Thus if a person died owning a policy of insurance on her own life, the proceeds would be subject to federal estate tax at her death no matter who the beneficiary was. On the other hand, if her husband owned the policy, the proceeds would be subject to federal estate tax on the insured's death only if the beneficiary of the policy was her estate. If the beneficiary was anyone else, such as her husband or children, the proceeds would not be taxable in the insured's estate.

If the owner of a policy dies before the insured, an amount roughly equal to the cash surrender value of the policy will be subject to estate tax at the owner's death.

As a general rule for federal estate tax purposes, all property is valued at its "highest and best use" fair market value, rather than at its fair market value for the use to which it is actually put by the decedent and his or her family. Thus, if a decedent owned farmland that would have a higher fair market value for sale to a developer to build residential housing, under the general rules of valuation the farmland would be taxed at its development value, rather than at its value as a farm, even though the decedent farmed the land and the beneficiaries intended to continue to do so when they inherited it.

To reduce the hardship this causes to farm families, Congress passed an amendment to the federal estate tax laws in 1976 which allows the personal representative of a decedent who owned a working farm to elect to have it valued for estate tax purposes at its farm value, even if that is lower than its highest and best use value, under certain conditions. Again, as with much of the tax law, the rules are too lengthy and technical to admit of complete explanation here. Basically, however, the election is available only if the farm makes up the major part of the decedent's estate, the decedent or a member of her immediate family has been active in the operation of the farm for a certain number of years immediately prior to the decedent's death, and a member of the decedent's family continues to run the farm as a farm for a certain number of years after the decedent's death. The special use valuation cannot be used, under current law, to reduce the value of the farm by more than $750,000 below its highest and best use fair market value. If the family sells the farm, even to another farmer, within a certain number of years after the death of the decedent, all or part of the estate tax saved may become due and payable.

Can the Federal Estate Tax Be Avoided by Making Transfers During Life?

The answer to this question is, "Yes, and no." Since the federal estate tax is payable only on property in which the decedent had an interest at the time of death, any property that is completely disposed of during life will not be taxed at death. However, any transfer that does result in complete disposition during life will be a taxable gift under the federal gift tax, unless the person who receives the property pays the transferor the full fair market value for the property. The gift tax rates and the estate tax rates are the same. Thus, the tax on the property will be the same whether it is subject to gift tax or to estate tax. However, the fair market value of the property for gift tax purposes is determined as of the date of the gift. If the property increases in value after the gift is made, the result of the gift will be to save the tax on the increase in value between the date of the gift and the date of the transferor's death.

Perhaps an illustration will make this clearer: Suppose you make a gift of property worth $200,000 in 1982, and then die in 1985, when the property is worth $300,000. The federal gift tax would be assessed in 1982 on $200,000, that is, on the fair market value of the property on the date the gift was made. (For a more detailed description of how the gift tax is computed, see the example on p. 251). At your death, in 1985, this property would not be subject to estate tax at all, since the property would then belong not to you, but to the person you gave it to in 1982. On the other hand, if you had kept the property until your death in 1985 and left it in your will to the same beneficiary (or that beneficiary received it under the laws of intestate succession), the property would be valued at $300,000 for federal estate tax purposes, since that is its fair market value on the date of your death, and federal estate tax would be assessed at that time.

In order to prevent tax avoidance, Congress and the courts have adopted very strict definitions of the terms "completely disposed of" and "interest" to determine whether the property should be taxed as a gift during the life of the giver, or should be included in her estate and subjected to federal estate tax. The retention of any rights in transferred property may cause the property to be fully taxable at the transferor's death, even though she would not ordinarily be thought of by a layperson as the owner of the property. Examples of rights or interests that will result in the federal estate taxation of transferred property are as follows: the right to revoke the transfer; the right to change the terms of the transfer, such as the right to modify the terms of a trust agreement; and the right to use the property or to receive the income from it during life, even though the rights to the property after the transferor's death are irrevocably transferred during her life.

The Marital Deduction: Special Treatment for Property Transferred to a Spouse

Under current law, all property that a decedent leaves to the surviving spouse is relieved of federal estate tax. In other words, if you leave all your property to your husband, there will be no federal estate tax due at your death, no matter how much property you own at your death. The property may pass to the spouse by the decedent's will, under the law of intestate succession, or by virtue of the terms of a lifetime transaction such as the survivorship provisions of a joint tenancy. The property may pass to the surviving spouse outright or it may be held in any one of several qualifying trust arrangements.

The reader may be familiar with a federal estate tax marital deduction provision that allows a portion of the decedent's estate to pass tax-free to the surviving spouse, but not the entire estate. That was the law prior to the passage of the August 1981 tax legislation referred to several times previously in this chapter. The 1981 law grants an unlimited marital deduction for the estate of anyone who dies on or after January 1, 1982. Again, you must be legally married to take advantage of this deduction.

How Is the Tax Computed?

As was stated in the discussion of the gift tax, the federal estate and gift taxes were "unified" in 1976. The actual computation of the estate is rather complex. The law requires that an estate tax be computed on the total of the taxable estate and all gifts made during life to arrive at the estate tax due. The gift tax previously paid is then subtracted from the amount of estate tax computed in the first part of the calculation. The taxable estate is the total of the fair market values of all the interests in property the decedent owned at death, less certain debts, and expenses such as mortgages and medical bills of her last illness, executors' commissions, probate filing fees, etc., and deductions for charity and for property passing to a surviving spouse. There are credits against the federal tax for state death taxes and the unified credit. As was mentioned in the section on the federal gift tax, the unified credit has the effect of allowing each person to give away tax-free a certain amount of property, either during life or at death or partly at each time. Under current law, this amount is increasing annually. Those who die in 1982 may pass $225,000 of property without incurring any federal estate tax, and the amount increases to $600,000 for those dying on or after January 1, 1987.

The tax rates are graduated like the federal income tax rates. In 1982 they ran from 18 percent on transfers under $10,000 to 65 percent on those over $4 million but are scheduled to be reduced under current law so that the highest rate will be 50 percent by 1985. The gift tax rates and the estate tax rates are the same.

STATE DEATH TAXES

Estate Tax

Many states have an estate tax which is computed roughly the same way as the federal estate tax. The interests in property which are subject to tax, and the method of valuing them, may differ, as may the amount of allowable deductions and credits. Thus, for example, a state might allow more or less property to pass free of state estate tax than passes tax-free by virtue of the federal estate tax unified credit, and it might allow a marital deduction for a certain fraction of the estate passing to the surviving spouse but tax the excess.

Inheritance Tax

The total tax base of a state inheritance tax is generally the same as that of a state estate tax, that is, all the interests in property that pass to others by virtue of the decedent's death.

The main difference between an estate tax and an inheritance tax is in the ways they are computed. The inheritance tax is computed separately on the total property passing to each beneficiary, less certain debts and expenses allocable to that beneficiary's interest. The rates of tax and the amount of property that passes free of tax depend on the relationship of the beneficiary to the decedent. In general, the decedent's spouse and children enjoy the highest exemptions and the lowest rates of tax; the exemptions get lower and the rates higher as the familial relationship between the decedent and the beneficiary gets more remote. Each beneficiary is responsible for paying her tax.

FURTHER READING

The best source of additional material on the topics considered in this chapter is your local or state bar association. Many have pamphlets on such topics as Wills, Estate Administration, the Laws of Intestate Succession, and Estate Taxation, which they will provide free or at a nominal charge to the public.

Part Three

WOMEN AS WORKERS

Your Rights in the Workplace

11
Education

COLQUITT L. MEACHAM

Colquitt L. Meacham is an attorney in private practice in Boston. She is a former Associate Dean of Amherst College, Amherst, Massachusetts.

Since 1972, federal laws such as Title IX and amendments to the civil rights acts have outlawed discrimination in education on the basis of sex. As you will see in Chapter 12, all these laws have led to only a minuscule increase in the numbers of women doing nontraditional jobs. However, more women *are* getting academic and athletic scholarships to colleges, and at the kindergarten level primers are beginning to be changed so that women and girls do not automatically appear in stereotypically female roles. The changes in the law have had an effect.

It cannot be emphasized too strongly how much discrimination in *education* can affect a woman's whole working life. If girls are discouraged from the start from being physically active, discouraged from taking shop, discouraged from the demanding disciplines of competitive sports and academic subjects, and encouraged to be passive, "polite," and unassertive, they do not so much choose a career as drift into the type of work for which they have been educated: traditional "women's" work, rather than the more demanding jobs that may require assertiveness, physical strength, and self-assurance.

Recent changes in the law have mandated that girls and women be treated equally in all aspects of an educational program and that this treatment occur at all levels.

The first congressional hearings on sex discrimination in education were held in 1970. These hearings documented an extensive pattern of discrimi-

The author wishes to acknowledge the publications of the project on the Status of Education of Women of the Association of American Colleges as the source of much of the information contained in this chapter.

nation against female students and teachers in educational institutions. For example:

> A school district with 19,000 students maintained a full inter-scholastic program for boys in seven sports. Girls were allowed only informal games of tennis. The school district allowed $250,-000 annually for boys' athletics and $970 for girls' tennis. Except for tennis balls, girls were prohibited the regular use of athletic properties, including stadiums, athletic fields, equipment, and gymnasiums.

> The head of the physics department in a large public university told HEW officials who were inquiring why the department lacked women faculty, that "women were not adaptable to science, and further that where women in science were concerned, they were only good as lab technicians to clean test tubes."

> Elementary readers with biased material that perpetuated sex-role stereotypes were used in most school systems.

WHY OUR SCHOOLS PLAY FOLLOW-THE-LEADER

Schools are minisocieties that mirror the greater society. If the greater society treats women one way, the school will, in most cases, simply mimic that behavior. Stereotypical masculine and feminine behavior will be rewarded in each sex. Girls are still often counseled into traditional, frequently overcrowded fields such as nursing, secretarial work, teaching, and home economics, rather than encouraged to study science and math. Boys are guided into the traditional male areas of engineering, science, and the mechanical trades, for which they are encouraged to study as much math as possible. In short, the individual student's abilities, needs, and preferences may not be considered.

Therefore, discrimination in education can affect a woman's whole working life, by channeling her into subjects that can lead only to low-paying, low-status, unsatisfying work. Because women have been denied equal opportunity in education, they are not so well prepared as men when they look for a job, or in terms of achieving personal independence. By keeping down the number and quality of skilled women, inequality in educational opportunities has resulted in the waste of a large proportion of our nation's natural resources. Thus, sex discrimination in education harms the entire nation as well as individuals who happen to be female.

NEW LAWS THAT HELPED EQUAL
EDUCATION FOR WOMEN

In 1972, Congress took several actions to ensure that women will have the same opportunities as men in almost all phases of education. First, Title VII of the Civil Rights Act of 1964, which prohibits discrimination in employment practices on the basis of sex as well as of race, religion, national origin, or color was amended to include educational institutions. Next, the Equal Pay Act of 1963, which requires equal pay for men and women doing substantially equal work (work requiring equal skill, effort, and responsibility under similar working conditions in the same workplace), was extended to cover executive, administrative, and professional employees, including teachers and faculty. Finally, Title IX of the Education Amendments of 1972 was enacted to forbid sex discrimination in any educational program or activity receiving federal financial assistance (which includes almost all public and private elementary, secondary, and postsecondary institutions).

Other federal laws and regulations that affect women's rights in relation to educational institutions include Title VII and Title VIII of the Public Health Service Act, which prohibits discrimination against students in admissions by medical and nursing schools and other schools where health workers are trained; Executive Order 11246, as amended by Executive Order 11375, which prohibits federal contractors from discriminating on the basis of sex in employment; the Age Discrimination Act of 1975; and Title II of the Education Amendments of 1976 (to the Vocational Education Act of 1963).

In recognition of the inequities women have experienced in educational institutions, and the need to eradicate sexism in the schools, Congress passed the Women's Educational Equity Act in 1974. The purpose of the Act was to fund activities that promote equity for women at all levels of education: preschool, elementary and secondary, higher, and adult education. Projects funded under the Act must be designed to promote systematic or institutional change in regard to sex equity in education.

SEX DISCRIMINATION IN EDUCATION

Some discrimination is overt and consists of specific acts of ill will or policies and practices that clearly exclude one sex or treat people differently on the basis of sex. An example would be where a school demanded higher academic achievements from women before they could be admitted than from men; or where young boys were excluded from a dance class and girls could not take shop. Although overt acts of ill will do still exist, particularly in the area of employment, most discrimination is so pervasive, subtle, and complex that it is hard to pin down. Men, and even women, often do not recognize it. For example, a vocational school that had stated in its brochure that certain courses were open only to males and others only to females attempted to comply by inserting a page at the beginning of the old brochure stating that all courses were open to all students regardless of sex and that the school "would continue its nondiscriminatory policy."

Often policies and practices that are clearly discriminatory were developed to exclude girls and women for reasons that seemed plausible at one time. Admission quotas for women in schools and colleges were rationalized on the assumption that most women would not need career or technical training, or on the grounds that there was an optimum "social mix" for women and men at a liberal arts college. Some courses have been restricted to one sex because they were not considered "suitable" for the other. All such instances are to be regarded as discrimination regardless of the motivation of past policymakers.

A more subtle application of discriminatory treatment of the sexes occurs when a uniform standard of conduct for all students is enforced unfairly. Often girls are more severely punished than boys for committing such offenses as swearing or hitting, because girls are supposed to have better deportment than boys. Similarly, an officially sex-neutral policy for awarding of scholarships or assistantships may become discriminatory in practice when male students receive a larger proportion of such awards than equally qualified female students on the assumption that the male students, being breadwinners, need more financial aid and will make better use of such support by making a greater contribution to the field than the females.

An even more subtle, often unrecognized type of discrimination occurs when policies or practices appear to be nonbiased, yet have a disproportionate effect on one sex or the other. The requirement that in order to be graduate students degree candidates must be in full-time residence for a certain period discriminates against women with family responsibilities, who may find this requirement difficult or impossible to fulfill. Whether or not there was an intent to discriminate is irrelevant. It is the result that counts. The Supreme Court decision in the case of *Griggs* v. *Duke Power* held that practices that appear fair but have a disproportionate effect on minorities may be considered discriminatory regardless of intent. While the *Griggs* case involved racial employment discrimination, the principle can be extended to sex discrimination.

WOMEN AS STUDENTS

TITLE IX

The statute states, "No person . . . shall, on the basis of sex, be excluded from participation in, be denied the benefits of, or be subjected to discrimination under any education program or activity receiving Federal financial assistance."

Most elementary and secondary schools are covered as well as colleges, universities, and vocational institutions; religious institutions are exempt if Title IX provisions are not consistent with their religious tenets. Military schools are exempt if their primary purpose is to train people for the U.S. military services or merchant marine.

Title IX and its implementing regulations apply to all aspects of all education programs or activities of a school district, institution of higher education, or other entity that receives federal funds for any of those programs. Some of the important areas covered by the statute and regulations are discussed below.

Physical Education and Athletics: The regulation states that no person may be subjected to discrimination based on sex in any scholastic, intercollegiate, club, or intramural athletics offered by a recipient of federal education aid.

The regulations *do* allow separate teams for girls and boys in physical education classes for wrestling, boxing, basketball, football, and other sports involving body contact. Other athletic benefits, opportunities, and treatment must be "equivalent" in availability, quality, and kind for both sexes. While programs need not be identical, "the effect of any difference must be negligible."

When there is a team for only one sex, and the excluded sex is interested in the sport, the school may be required to permit members of the excluded sex to try out for the team, provided it is not a contact sport; or sponsor a separate team for the previously excluded sex. For example, a school with a boys-only basketball team would have to set up a girls' team, and spend an equivalent amount of effort and money on it.

The question of equality for women in intercollegiate sports caused considerable controversy and was strongly contested by schools, coaches, and athletic associations such as the National Collegiate Athletic Association. It took the Department of Health, Education and Welfare (HEW) eight years to develop a "policy interpretation" to define what schools must provide for women in varsity collegiate athletics. The final policy was issued in 1979 and provides the following guidance:

SCHOLARSHIPS. The total amount of athletic scholarship money a college spends on women and men must be proportional to the number of females and males participating in intercollegiate sports at that institution. If women are 30 percent of the athletes, they should receive 30 percent of the scholarship dollars.

ATHLETIC BENEFITS AND OPPORTUNITIES. Women and men must receive equivalent treatment in athletic programs. Factors to be considered are equipment and supplies, scheduling of games and practices, compensation of coaches, housing and dining services for athletes, publicity of team activities, and travel and per diem costs.

ACCOMMODATION OF STUDENT INTERESTS AND ABILITIES. The athletic interests and abilities of female and male students must be effectively accommodated by the institution in regard to the types of sports offered and the levels of competition.

ENFORCEMENT PROCESS. The Department of Education and the Department of Health and Human Services have responsibility for enforcing Title IX. Under the 1979 guidelines a school which is found to be in violation of the regulations regarding intercollegiate athletics may avoid a finding of noncompliance if it can demonstrate both: a history and continuing practice of upgrading the deficient program, and an acceptable plan showing that the program will be corrected within a "reasonable" period of time.

Admissions: With respect to admission to educational institutions, Title IX applies only to vocational, professional, and graduate schools, and to public undergraduate institutions (except those that have been continuously single-sex).

Under the regulations, covered schools may not limit the number of persons of either sex who may be admitted, or give preference to someone because of sex. The school may not consider a person's marital or family status in making admissions decisions, nor may it discriminate against an applicant who is pregnant. The schools may ask an applicant's sex if the information is not used in a discriminatory way.

Schools must make equal efforts to recruit female and male students, unless special efforts to recruit members of one sex are needed to remedy the effects of past discrimination.

Admission to preschools, elementary and secondary schools, private undergraduate institutions, and public undergraduate institutions that have been continuously single-sex is not covered, and these schools may select students for admission on the basis of sex. It is important to note that these schools whose admission policy is exempt under the statute may not discriminate against students on the basis of sex once the students are admitted. For example: A college that has traditionally been all-male does not have to change its admission policy and admit women. But if it decides to go co-ed, it then must treat its women students exactly like its men students.

Single-sex Organizations and Programs: Membership practices of the following organizations are exempt under Title IX:

YMCA, YWCA, Girl Scouts, Boy Scouts, Camp Fire Girls

Social sororities and fraternities

Voluntary youth service organizations whose membership has traditionally been limited to one sex and to people less than 19 years of age.

Also not covered under the statute are any programs or activities of the American Legion or educational institutions undertaken in connection with the operation or promotion of Boys State, Girls State, Boys Nation, or Girls Nation conferences.

In addition, the statute does not preclude father-son, mother-daughter activities as long as comparable activities are offered for students of both sexes. For example the football team may have a banquet for the male players and their fathers, as long as similar activities are offered for the female soccer players and their mothers.

Programs designed to address the special needs or interests of women are allowed, as long as they are open to men who wish to participate.

Any organization that receives "significant assistance" from a school district, college, or university may not discriminate on the basis of sex in any way, including membership, programs, services, or benefits. Such assistance may include such things as faculty sponsors, use of facilities, or access to clerical assistance. Organizations operating off campus and without significant assistance from the schools are not covered by Title IX.

Courses and Other Educational Activities: School courses and other educational activities may not be segregated on the basis of sex, and students may not be excluded on that basis, except for the following:

1. Elementary and secondary classes dealing with human sexuality may be separated by sex.

2. Membership in a choral group may be based on vocal range, which may result in a single-sex chorus.

If a class or course of study has a disproportionate number of students of one sex, the school must check to be sure it is not the result of sex bias in counseling or testing.

Financial Aid: All forms of financial aid offered by a school are covered by Title IX and must be distributed without regard to sex, except for the following:

Discriminatory scholarships for study abroad may be awarded provided the school makes similar opportunities available to members of the excluded sex. For example, a school may have a scholarship for study in England that is limited to men students, as long as there are a sufficient number of other such scholarship opportunities open to women.

A school may distribute financial aid from a bequest of a will or trust that limits its use to one sex, as long as the overall effect on the opposite sex is not discriminatory; in other words, as long as members of the excluded sex receive equal benefits from other . sources. For example: The John Smith Fund may be used to benefit male students only, so long as female students similarly situated receive an equal amount of financial aid from other sources. If there is not enough money from other sources to assist women equally, the discriminatory bequest may not be used.

Health and Insurance Benefits: In providing a medical, hospital, accident, or life-insurance benefit, service, policy, or plan to any of its students, a school may not discriminate on the basis of sex. The regulation does not prohibit a school from providing a benefit or service that may be used by a higher proportion of students of one sex than of the other, including family planning services. A school that provides full-coverage health service must provide gynecological care.

A pregnant student, one who has just given birth, or one who is recovering from an abortion or a false pregnancy may not be discriminated against or excluded from a school's education program or activities, including any class or extracurricular activity. But a student may request voluntarily to take part in a separate portion of the program or activity, for example in a school that has a separate and voluntary program for pregnant students.

A school may require a student in the categories mentioned above to obtain a doctor's certificate that she is physically and emotionally able to continue to take part in the normal education program or activity, so long as such a certificate is required of *all* students for all other physical or emotional conditions requiring a doctor's care. A separate program for pregnant students must be comparable in every way to that offered to nonpregnant students.

A school shall treat pregnancy, maternity leave, and recovery from false pregnancy or abortion in the same way and under the same policies as any other temporary disability with respect to any medical or hospital benefit, service, plan, or policy that such school offers or participates in with respect to students admitted to the school's educational program or activity.

In the case of a school that does not maintain a leave policy for its students, or in the case of a student who does not otherwise qualify for leave under such a policy, a school receiving federal funds shall treat pregnancy, maternity leave, and recovery from false pregnancy or abortion as justification for a leave of absence for as long a period of time as the student's doctor decides is medically necessary. And at the conclusion of the leave the student must have the same status she held when the leave began. (For example, a student who has been accepted into a doctoral program may not be demoted to candidacy for a master's degree.)

Sexual Harassment: While Title IX does not explicitly prohibit sexual harassment, the implementing regulations issued by the Department of Education provide a number of points at which such coverage can be readily construed.

Judicial interpretation of Title IX also indicates that sexual harassment constitutes a violation of that statute. The Supreme Court has ruled that an individual may sue a school in federal court to get redress for a violation of Title IX. Such a case was initiated by a student against Yale University. She charged that she had been the victim of sexual harassment by a professor at the institution and had therefore suffered discrimination under Title IX. The Federal District Court allowed the lawsuit to proceed, finding that "academic advancement conditioned upon submission to sexual demands constitutes sex discrimination in education. . . ."

The definition of illegal sexual harassment of students has been stated as follows:

> Objectionable emphasis on the sexuality or sexual identity of a student by (or with the acquiescence of) an agent of an educational institution when (1) the objectionable acts are directed toward students of only one gender, and (2) the intent or effect of the objectionable acts is to limit or deny full and equal participation in educational services, opportunities or benefits on the basis of sex; or (3) the intent or effect of the objectionable acts is to create an intimidating, hostile, or offensive academic environment for the members of one sex.

In addition to Title IX, students who are victims of sexual harassment have a wide range of options for legal redress. Criminal charges may be appropriate under certain circumstances, such as rape, or civil suits against the school and the harassing party (see chart, p. 520).

Employment

The Supreme Court has recently ruled that the employment practices of educational institutions are covered by Title IX. This means that women *employees* of schools and colleges as well as students must be treated equally with male employees. Clerical and food-service workers, graduate-student research assistants, as well as lecturers and faculty members are included in the Title IX protection. Therefore, if a chemistry department, for example, persists in giving tenure only to male faculty members, a Title IX complaint might be in order. Such a complaint could be brought by a female member of the faculty who is denied tenure by the chemistry department, or by the students who perceive such discriminatory treatment of female faculty as detrimental to their learning environment.

Employees of educational institutions are also protected against discriminatory treatment by Title VII of the Civil Rights Act of 1974 and may seek redress under its procedures as well. (See Chapter 12.) The remedies and the enforcement procedures under the two laws differ, so it is probably wise to file a complaint under both. A complaint alleging a Title IX violation would be filed with the regional office of the Department of Education, while a complaint under Title VII must be filed with the Equal Employment Opportunity Commission and/or a comparable state anti-discrimination agency.

Enforcement: While Title IX may be enforced through private litigation, enforcement is usually initiated by a complaint to a federal agency. The Department of Education is the agency that handles most of the complaints involving students.

Complaints filed by individuals or groups must be filed with the Department of Education within 180 days of the date of the violation or discriminatory act. The Department must promptly investigate the charge, and if it finds that discrimination exists, it must attempt to get voluntary compliance by the school. Should this not succeed, the Department may start administrative proceedings that could lead to termination of federal financial assistance.

Title IX regulations also require educational institutions to keep records documenting their compliance with the law. The Department of Education may initiate broad-based investigations of school districts and institutions of higher education to ensure compliance with the law.

VOCATIONAL EDUCATION

The 1976 amendments to the Vocational Education Act were enacted as a response to the growth in women's employment and the fact that women's wages were approximately 59 cents to every dollar earned by men. Statistical analyses of the labor-force data indicated that unless major changes occurred that would prepare women for the work force, they would continue to hold low-paying, dead-end jobs. The economic differences between male and female workers were well documented and increased congressional interest in vocational education as a means to narrow the gap.

The 1976 amendments represented the first federal legislation to address the need for equal access to vocational education for women and girls. The implementation of the legislation is carried out by the states, usually through the state board of education.

The numerous programs in vocational education prepare individuals for a wide range of opportunities, many in expanding fields with substantial salary potential. Congress intended the 1976 amendments to direct efforts toward developing and providing programs to overcome sex bias, sex discrimination, and sex stereotyping, and promote equal educational opportunity. The specific provisions are clear:

Federally assisted state vocational education programs are subject to both Title IX and the Vocational Education Act mandates to eliminate sex discrimination and stereotyping—for example, women being excluded from an electrician training course but not from a secretarial course.

Advisory councils on vocational education, national and state, must have women and minority women members knowledgeable about sex discrimination in employment and training.

Each state must hire full-time sex-equity personnel; duties of that person are clearly outlined, and $50,000 of federal funds are provided to the states for this purpose.

State plans must describe in detail how equal access to vocational education will be ensured for both sexes.

Public hearings on state plans must be held, involving a wide range of agencies and individuals, to develop each state's vocational education goals and programs.

Displaced homemakers and other special groups—women and men who are single heads of household, homemakers seeking employment, part-time workers seeking full-time jobs, and persons seeking nontraditional jobs—must have opportunities for program participation.

Support services, day-care services, vocational guidance and counseling, as well as grants to overcome sex bias, may be funded.

The desperate need for these services is underscored by the fact that in the early eighties 50 percent of working women are employed in low-paying clerical or service jobs.

WOMEN REENTERING EDUCATIONAL
PROGRAMS

Women going back to school after time away, or women going to college for the first time, whether in their mid to late twenties or in their sixties and seventies, often find they have problems arising from inflexible school policies. For example, a college may demand that all freshmen live in the dormitories. This may prove impossible for women with families, and be unacceptable to those who do not have families. Inflexible schedules can make it very difficult or impossible for working women to attend college.

However, Title IX does not prevent schools from offering special services and programs for reentry students as long as the programs are open to members of both sexes. But schools are not *required* to offer such special programs, nor are they required to make special efforts to overcome the effects of conditions (such as inflexible scheduling) that lead to fewer women than men, say, taking part in a particular course.

Age Discrimination

Age discrimination affects all people, but older women receive a "double dose" of discrimination—once because of their age and once again because of their sex. If the older woman is a member of a minority group or handicapped, the problem is intensified. In education, age discrimination is not limited solely to senior citizens; it can begin as early as the mid-twenties, when a student may be labeled "too old" for a particular program or activity. The Age Discrimination Act of 1975 prohibits "discrimination on the basis of age in programs or activities receiving federal financial assistance." The Act, which contains some exemptions, is unique in that it does not define "age" to limit coverage to a particular group, such as those 65 or older. It simply prohibits unreasonable discrimination on the basis of age at any age. Thus, workshops, courses, and programs may not be restricted to students on the basis of age, and an applicant's age may not be taken into consideration in admissions decisions.

Because of the competition for admission to graduate and professional programs, some schools have been reluctant to admit older applicants. Women who have delayed or interrupted their education sometimes find it difficult to gain admittance to such programs. There are many problems of *attitude* that work against admission of older women to education programs at all levels. The stereotypes in our society that, most unrealistically, make youth the "ideal" state, also couple age with the stereotypical notion of a loss of "brainpower." And while scientists such as Alex Comfort have found that the majority of people can continue to live a full life into their eighties, and sometimes beyond (both physically *and* mentally), the stereotypes remain. Indeed so strong are they that even women in their late twenties who want to enter college may find that their age is a strike against them. It may be necessary, therefore, for "older women" from their mid-twenties on to make legal challenges to school policies that are based on illegal considerations of age.

FEDERAL FINANCIAL AID PROGRAMS FOR STUDENTS*

The purpose of financial aid programs is to assist those students who without such assistance would be unable to attend postsecondary educational institutions—two- and four-year colleges, or vocational schools. The primary responsibility of financing higher-education costs falls upon the family. Parents will be expected to contribute to their children's educational expenses as long as the children are listed as dependents on the parents' tax return. If a child is self-supporting and no longer dependent, many institutions will consider the child "emancipated" and will not require a contribution from parents. The woman living with her husband will be required to report his income, and he will be expected to make a contribution. When a family is unable to meet the costs of higher education, funding is available from federal, state, institutional, and private sources. Essentially, two forms of resources are available: gift aid and self-help. The former is referred to as gift aid because it does not have to be repaid or worked for. The latter must be earned through employment or repaid after the completion of studies. Most financial aid awards to students are offered in the form of a financial aid package consisting of both gift aid and self-help.

The following programs are available:

THE PELL GRANT PROGRAM

The Pell Grant is a federally sponsored entitlement program designed to assist students who demonstrate exceptional financial need. By the federal formula, the award is tied to the cost of the education budget and may not

*Financial aid laws are changing, so it is best to check with the financial aid officer of the school you are attending, for the most up-to-date information.

exceed more than half of the calculated cost of education. Grant awards may range as high as $1,800 during an academic year of undergraduate study. The Pell award is considered the "floor," or base, of a financial aid package. All students applying for other forms of financial aid are required to apply for the Pell Grant.

THE SUPPLEMENTAL EDUCATIONAL OPPORTUNITY GRANT PROGRAM

The Supplemental Educational Opportunity Grant Program (SEOG) is a federally funded program designed to assist those students who demonstrate extreme financial need. The federal government awards a sum of SEOG funding to the school, and it in turn decides which students show the most extreme need and make awards to assist them.

THE COLLEGE WORK STUDY PROGRAM

The College Work Study Program is a federally funded program designed to provide students with an opportunity to work part time either on campus or off campus at a nonprofit organization. To qualify for College Work Study, students must evidence financial need. Students may gain valuable experience in an area of their career choice to complement their academic concentration. Generally, a guide of ten hours per week is used to ensure that the student's academic schedule and academic preparation are not adversely affected. The federal government provides 80 percent of the funding. The remaining 20 percent is a matching contribution from the institution.

THE NATIONAL DIRECT STUDENT LOAN PROGRAM

The National Direct Student Loan Program is a long-term, low-cost loan designed specifically for educational purposes. The federal government provides federal capital contributions to institutions, which are required to provide a ⅑ contribution to maintain the program. Additional funds are provided through a revolving account supported by student repayments. The college acts as a lending institution throughout the entire loan process. The interest in 1982 was 5 percent, but changes occur from time to time. The program is restricted to those students who demonstrate financial need.

GUARANTEED STUDENT LOAN PROGRAM

The Guaranteed Student Loan Program is another long-term, low-cost educational loan designed to assist both undergraduate and graduate students. Students may borrow up to $2,500 for undergraduate education and $5,000 for graduate education from local lending institutions; i.e., banks and credit unions. The interest rate in 1982 was 9 percent for new borrowers and 7 percent for old borrowers.

OTHER FEDERAL FUNDING SOURCES

In addition to the programs indicated, there are other forms of special financial assistance. Among these programs are veterans educational benefits, Social Security education benefits, and Army ROTC scholarship awards. It is essential to remember that the total financial aid package may never exceed the cost of the education budget.

STUDENTS' RIGHTS REGARDING EDUCATIONAL RECORDS

The Buckley Amendment to the General Education Provisions Act provides for parental or student review, correction, and control over the release of education records maintained by an educational institution.

Three basic rights given to students by the law must be recognized in a school's institutional policy:

Right to Review
A student or a dependent student's parent has the right to inspect and review her education records. For purposes of the Act, the following are not considered "educational records":
1. personal notes
2. law-enforcement records
3. personnel records
4. medical records
5. alumni records

Applicants to a school who are not admitted and are therefore not in attendance are not students and have no rights regarding school records.

Letters of recommendation may remain confidential if they were received by the school prior to January 1, 1975. After that date, the student will have the right to review all letters of recommendation unless the right is explicitly waived, in writing, by the student.

Right to Correct

A student or her parent has the right to challenge the contents of her education record on the grounds that they are "inaccurate, misleading, or otherwise in violation of the privacy or other rights of the student." The school may amend the record or it may refuse to do so. If it refuses, the student has a right to a hearing. If the school still refuses to amend the record, the student or parent may place a statement in the file as to her interpretation of or objection to the offending information.

Right of Nondisclosure

The school may not disclose information from education records to other than certain specified individuals or entities without prior *written* consent of the student or her parent.

Although the passage of Title IX has resulted in some significant improvements in educational opportunities for women and girls, the task of providing full equality in education has not been completed. "Older" women continue to be excluded from graduate programs that lead to lucrative professions such as medicine. Women continue to be underrepresented in the tenure ranks of faculties and to be paid less than male colleagues. Women athletes are still denied the full range of support services provided their male counterparts at major universities.

Because Title IX is enforced by a federal agency, it can be only as effective as that agency's enforcement efforts. Despite the congressional mandate that Title IX represents, the entire Act can be sabotaged and rendered useless by ineffective enforcement. In other words, unless the executive branch of government is dedicated to a vigorous and effective enforcement effort, Title IX and the promise it offers future generations of women will be of little value.

FURTHER READING

Levine, Alan H. and Eve Cary. *The Rights of Students.* New York: Avon Books, 1977.

12
Discrimination on the Job

JANE L. DOLKART

*Jane L. Dolkart has her own law practice and is of counsel to Liotta &
Finkelstein, in Washington, D.C. Formerly, she held several positions at
the Equal Employment Opportunity Commission, including assistant
general counsel and executive assistant to Eleanor Holmes Norton, then
chair of the agency. She was also a law professor for five years, teaching
in the areas of employment, sex-discrimination, family, and property
law.*

The price of discrimination for women can be measured in jobs and
money. Conversely, continuing sex discrimination saves companies money.
Fortune magazine has estimated that an increase in the total compensation
of full-time female workers to the median pay level of full-time male workers would cost approximately $150 billion per year. Because correcting sex
discrimination in employment is a costly proposition for employers, many
will not do so unless pushed by means of effective law enforcement.

This chapter gives women the basic information necessary to attack
discriminatory employment practices and patterns by explaining the meaning and operation of the laws that make discrimination illegal.

Federal, state, and local laws that prohibit employers from discriminating
against women workers have existed since the sixties. These laws provide
the tools from which to attack discriminatory employment patterns and
practices in a concerted and systematic way throughout the nation, in
virtually all jobs, and against almost all employers whether they are public
(federal, state, or local) or private. These laws, however, are only as good
as the enforcement of them.

The inferior status of women in the workplace has remained remarkably
intransigent in the face of over 15 years of litigation. Legal attacks on
discriminatory employment practices that maintain this status have pro-

duced substantial victories and remain a potent weapon. However, although this chapter focuses on legal means of redress, it is important to remember that other strategies that give women greater power in the workplace must be used in conjunction with legal pressure in order to produce effective change. These include organizing efforts, greater participation and power within existing unions, lobbying, and further legislative efforts on the federal, state, and local levels.

The implication in economic terms, for women and their families, of ending job discrimination is overwhelming and can be illustrated with a brief profile of the place of women workers in the labor force. Since World War II, the labor participation of women has risen dramatically so that today more than 51 percent of women 16 years of age and older (43 million) are in the labor force. Married women with children have entered the labor market in increasing numbers. Approximately one third of all married women with children under age 6, and 50 percent of those with children 6 to 17, are in the labor force.

Women are in the work force because their wages are critical to their families' support. Nearly two thirds of all women in the labor force in 1978 were single, widowed, divorced, or separated, or had husbands who earned ten thousand dollars or less a year. Female-headed households account for 12 percent of all families and 39 percent of all minority families; among all poor families, nearly half were headed by women in 1978.

In spite of the increase of women in the work force and the economic need that motivates a majority of them, the position of women in the labor market has changed little over the years. The overwhelming fact is that the work force is sex-segregated, and women are concentrated in a few low-paying, dead-end jobs. Female workers have continued, since the 1950s, to earn only about fifty-nine cents for every dollar a man earns.

In the early sixties, 52 percent of all working women were employed in just four occupations: clerk, waitress, saleswoman, and hairdresser. Today, 47 percent of all working women are still found in these same categories. Over 90 percent of all secretaries, nurses, household workers, bank tellers, and bookkeepers are women. In contrast, only 5 percent of engineers, welders, and police are women, only 7 percent of mail carriers, 26 percent of computer specialists, and 29 percent of college and university teachers.

If current trends continue, the Department of Labor estimates that by 1985, male-intensive occupations, such as truck driver, auto mechanic, and administrator, will earn an average annual salary of $16,000 to $26,000. Female-intensive occupations, such as retail sales clerk, secretary, and nurse, will earn an average salary of $9,400 to $12,000.

In a society in which an individual's worth and economic well-being are determined, to a large degree, by her/his paycheck, women's work is less valued than men's work. The belief is that specific occupations have been traditionally undervalued and underpaid precisely because they are held by women. Thus, job segregation and wage discrimination are related. Most women do not work the same jobs as men, and "women's" jobs are undercompensated in comparison to "men's" jobs requiring similar skills, responsibilities, effort, and work experiences. And women continue to work for lower wages, because the opportunities for women to earn more are limited.[1]

These structural forms of sex discrimination suggest two enforcement strategies: First, women must attempt to move out of "women's jobs" into nontraditional and higher-paying jobs and must challenge barriers to their increased employment in these nontraditional jobs. Second, since the majority of women will remain in "women's jobs," we must look for ways to challenge employers whose wage scales compensate women less than men for work of similar skill, responsibility, and effort.

In maximizing the effectiveness of these two strategies, one important concept in employment law must be kept in mind: More often than not, the discrimination that you are personally experiencing from a given employer is being experienced by large numbers of other women employees and applicants for employment. By definition, most of the kinds of employment practices that are discriminatory affect whole classes of persons, not just individuals. The law recognizes this fact and therefore allows lawsuits to be brought by one or more individuals as representatives of or on behalf of a defined class of individuals. For instance, if an employer has two, sex-segregated assembly-line jobs, one paying $4.08 per hour called light packer (female) and one paying $5.20 per hour called heavy packer (male), you and all other women are denied initial assignment or transfer to the heavy packer job. If you file suit only on your own behalf, you may be given a job as a heavy packer, but the two job categories will remain substantially sex-segregated, and other women will not be given the same opportunity. If instead you file a class action on behalf of yourself and all other women who have been denied or want jobs as heavy packers, you may gain relief for many more women and change the employer's general policy. It is even possible to attack all of a single employer's discriminatory policies in one class action, thereby attempting to restructure the entire employment environment so as to eradicate all discriminatory patterns and practices at once. Thus one lawsuit may attack recruitment, hiring, assignment, promotions, and terms and conditions of work throughout the employer's workplace. A few individuals willing to file charges can end up helping many women who are afraid to risk their jobs or who do not understand that they are being discriminated against.

There are certain requirements that must be met before a court will permit a class action, but it is important to examine discrimination in the workplace with an eye toward ferreting out policies or systems that operate against women as a group and to phrase charges of discrimination in class-wide terms. It is generally much easier to prove discrimination against a group of women than against just one woman. Employers can often find a reason why one particular woman was not hired or promoted. It is much harder to find reasons why all or most women were not hired or promoted. It is class-wide lawsuits that provide the most effective legal tool for change.

LAWS PROHIBITING DISCRIMINATION AGAINST WOMEN WORKERS

There are seven major federal laws and a myriad of state and local laws that forbid discrimination against women workers. The federal laws include:

1. Title VII of the Civil Rights Act of 1964, as amended by the Equal Employment Opportunity Act of 1972 and the Pregnancy Discrimination Act of 1978, 42 U.S.C. §§2000c et seq.
2. The Equal Pay Act of 1963, 29 U.S.C. §206(d)
3. Title IX of the Education Amendment of 1972, 20 U.S.C. §1681–86
4. Executive Order 11246 (as amended by Executive Order 11375)
5. Executive Order 11478, 44 F.R. 1053
6. The Age Discrimination in Employment Act of 1967 as amended, 20 U.S.C. §§621–34
7. The Rehabilitation, Comprehensive Services, and Developmental Disabilities Amendments of 1978

Of these, Title VII is by far the most comprehensive and widely used. It is the law under which most of the concepts defining employment discrimination have been litigated. It is also the law that provides the greatest access for women workers themselves to challenge, individually or on behalf of a class, discriminatory employment practices. Title VII created the Equal Employment Opportunity Commission (EEOC), which has responsibility for enforcement of the Act. The President's Reorganization Plan No. 1 of 1978[2] also gave the EEOC responsibility for enforcing the Equal Pay Act, the Age Discrimination in Employment Act, and Executive Order 11478, which provides equal employment opportunity for federal employees. This makes the EEOC the principal federal agency for fair-employment enforcement.

TITLE VII

Theories of Discrimination Under Title VII
Title VII prohibits discrimination based upon race, color, religion, sex, or national origin with respect to hiring, discharge, promotion, compensa-

tion, terms, conditions, or other employment opportunities. Individuals who may use the act include current, discharged, or former employees, applicants for employment, union members or applicants for union membership, and apprentices or other on-the-job trainees or applicants. Covered employers include private employers with 15 or more employees, state and local governments, the federal government, and labor unions. Employment agencies are also prohibited from discriminatorily referring individuals for employment; for example, referring a woman to a traditional "woman's job" when she is qualified for other work.

Under traditional Title VII law, there are three frameworks in which discriminatory employer policies are analyzed. Each framework applies to a distinct kind of employer action, each requires a distinct type of proof of discrimination, and each allows for a distinct kind of employer defense.

Facial, or Overt, Discrimination: The first kind of employer discrimination is facial, or overt, discrimination, which occurs when an employer adopts a policy or practice of overtly treating women differently from men on the basis of their sex. Most early cases of sex discrimination involved issues of facial discrimination such as refusing to hire women for certain jobs that allegedly required the lifting of heavy weights or were too dangerous, refusing to hire men for jobs such as flight attendant, or refusing to hire women on the ground that state protective laws forbade women from working in that job or on that shift.

The employer's defense to an allegation of facial discrimination is that, because of the nature of the job, men are required. This is called the bona fide occupational qualification (BFOQ) defense and is expressly recognized by Title VII. This defense has been interpreted very narrowly by the courts and the EEOC, and is available to an employer only where women (or men) are shown to be unable to perform the essence of the job. The defense has been allowed where an employee of one gender is necessary for purposes of authenticity or genuineness (e.g., actor, actress, sperm donor, wet nurse) or to preserve privacy. For instance, a maximum-security male prison that made no provision for inmate privacy and where conditions were so bad they were found to be unconstitutional, was permitted to exclude women from employment as correction officers because their mere presence in such an environment was found to pose a security threat;[3] while a medium-security prison was forbidden to continue to exclude women correction officers, because it was found that the privacy of male prisoners could be preserved by exempting female officers from a few duties.[4]

Because of the narrowness of the BFOQ defense, whenever an employer has a policy of overtly and admittedly excluding women from particular jobs or shifts, there is a strong likelihood that the employer's policy violates Title VII.

Discriminatory Impact: The second framework applies to those employer practices or job requirements that are truly neutral but have a disproportionately adverse effect on women. It is important to remember that even employment policies that appear fair may be illegal.[5] A classic example of this kind of policy is an employee height and weight requirement, which, while it excludes all men, as well as women, below the required height and weight, will clearly exclude a greater percentage of women. Also important is the fact that a showing of employer intent to discriminate is not required. It is enough if the plaintiff establishes a discriminatory effect on women. Then the employer must show that the rule is justified by business necessity, that is, the practice is substantially related to the actual essence of job performance and that the employer could not meet its legitimate business needs in a way that had less of an impact on women.

A recent example of a successful attack on an employer practice with a discriminatory impact on women involved a state prison system that required prison guards to be at least 5 feet 2 inches tall and weigh 120 pounds. The evidence showed that while only 1.28 percent of the male population between 18 and 79 failed to meet these qualifications, 33.2 percent of the women in that age group were excluded. The Supreme Court rejected the state's defense that the height and weight requirements were job-related, finding that the state had not proved that there was a correlation between the height and weight requirements and the amount of strength necessary for good job performance.[6]

Discriminatory Treatment: The third framework applies in those situations in which the employer's policy or practice, on its face, treats male and female workers the same, but in which the employer *in fact* treats one or more women in a less favorable manner because of their sex. Disparate-treatment cases may be individual or involve class/pattern and practice allegations of discrimination. The crucial factor in any disparate-treatment case, however, is that it is necessary to prove discriminatory intent or motive on the part of the employer. While intent may be inferred from the fact of differences in treatment, the courts have been getting stricter in their requirement that the employee prove actual intent to discriminate. If the employee or applicant offers evidence indicating that the employment decision was based on sex discrimination, the employer's defense will be to show some legitimate nondiscriminatory reason for the employee's (applicant's) rejection or other employment decision.

Discriminatory-treatment cases are the hardest for plaintiffs to win. Most individual, and some class, actions are treatment cases, and frequently the issue boils down to who is more or equally qualified, and an evaluation of what are frequently subjective employment criteria. It is often easy for an employer to come up with some plausible nondiscriminatory reason for the employment decision. In this regard, statistics or other evidence of a pattern and practice of discrimination is useful to support even an individual claim of sex discrimination.

One area of discriminatory treatment on the basis of sex in which women have begun to fight back successfully is sexual harassment in the workplace. This topic is discussed in greater detail in Chapter 13.

Common Discriminatory Practices Under Title VII

Segregation of Jobs by Sex

It is almost never legal for a company to segregate jobs according to sex.

State Protective Laws: During the 1900s, many states passed a series of "protective laws," which purported to protect women from undesirable working conditions, e.g., long hours, heavy lifting, or night shifts, or from jobs such as bartending, which were considered undesirable for women to hold. These laws were used by many companies to deny women better-paying and more-desirable jobs, and were, at first, used as a defense to comply with Title VII. Federal courts have consistently rejected this defense and have ordered companies to stop discriminating against women on the basis of state protective laws. At this time there are few such statutes remaining in effect, since most have been invalidated by the courts under Title VII, or repealed by state legislatures.

Sex-segregated Help-wanted Ads: It is illegal for an employer or an employment agency to place help-wanted ads in sex-segregated newspaper columns. It is also discriminatory for an ad itself to either specify or suggest that only men or only women should apply for a particular position. It is also illegal for an employment agency to send only men or women to fill a certain job, even if the company has requested the agency to do so.

Sex-segregated Labor Unions: It is illegal for a labor union to limit its membership either to males or to females. It is also illegal for a labor union to refer only male members for most jobs. It remains true that most blue-collar skilled craft unions are predominantly male. It is not true that only men can perform these jobs, and since most of them are highly paid, skilled blue-collar jobs, it is important that women attack discriminatory practices of unions and employers.

It is also illegal for unions to negotiate collective-bargaining agreements that discriminate against women. One way to prevent this, and also to get unions working for women in protecting and advancing their job opportunities, is for women to get more involved in the union, where there is one.

Company Practices That Discriminate Against Subgroups of Women:
Many employers have had policies that discriminated on the basis of "sex plus." Two particularly well-known examples of this kind of discrimination are a company refusing to hire or promote mothers of preschool-age children while hiring and promoting fathers of preschool-age children,[7] and companies firing women when they get married while not firing men who get married. Courts have consistently held that men and women in the same position must be treated in the same way. In this regard, airlines that used to fire stewardesses when they got married were told that these policies were illegal under Title VII.[8] Another possible example of this kind of discrimination, which is just now being tested in the courts, relates to some company policies that prohibit pregnant women or women of childbearing age from working in certain jobs with exposure to hazardous substances that allegedly pose health hazards in fetuses while allowing men, whose health might also be affected by the hazardous substances, to continue to work. This issue is discussed further in Chapter 14.

Common Neutral Policies that Have a Discriminatory Effect on Women

Companies frequently have substantially sex-segregated work forces even though they do not have overt policies of excluding women from certain jobs. This is especially true in nontraditional jobs, jobs classified as "heavy" work, and higher-level professional and managerial jobs. If you have applied at or work for a company that appears to have sex-segregated jobs, there are a number of specific areas in the employment process that you should look at to determine if the company is discriminating on the basis of sex. These areas include recruitment, hiring, assignment, training, compensation, and promotion.

Recruitment: A company has an affirmative obligation to correct sex segregation and therefore must take affirmative steps to ensure a sufficient number of both male and female applicants for every job. This may mean changing advertising and recruiting methods, and educating company personnel. For instance, if jobs in the company have previously been segregated by sex, it would be illegal to engage entirely in word-of-mouth recruiting. This would mean that male employees would recruit their male friends for jobs and women would never hear of these particular jobs. The same would happen in all-female jobs: women would tend to recruit other women for these jobs. Or if a company's advertising has previously shown men and women performing in differing typically sex-segregated kinds of jobs, the company would have to change its advertising materials to show women in nontraditional jobs and men in nontraditional jobs.

Hiring: Ensuring a sufficiently integrated pool of applicants for each job is only the first step. It is then necessary to ensure that hiring is done in a nondiscriminatory manner. The company must employ the same job qualifications for all applicants, male and female. A company may give a whole range or variety of employment tests or face-to-face interviews. These tests are not illegal per se. However, if the proportion of women who pass the test is less than the proportion of men who pass the test, the test may well be illegal, because it has a disparate impact. In that case, the company must show that the test validly predicts who will perform the job better and that there is no less-discriminatory way to determine job qualification. The EEOC definition of a test is extremely broad and includes any formal or informal scored or unscored technique to assess job qualifications.[9] The kinds of tests that women should be particularly wary of include any test or qualification involving height or weight, or tests of mathematic, scientific, or mechanical aptitude. Likewise, tests or interviews that require the subjective evaluation of the grader or interviewer should be examined for sex bias.

Apprenticeship Programs: One way to gain entry into a number of blue-collar construction and craft jobs is to gain acceptance into an apprenticeship program, which may be run either by the employer or the union, or jointly by the employer and the union. Women remain vastly underrepresented in such apprenticeship programs. The method of recruitment, qualifications for admission, and hiring procedures for such programs should be carefully scrutinized for possible sex discrimination.

Job Assignment / Transfer: Once hired, there may be discrimination in the assignment of employees to jobs. For instance, in a manufacturing job it is possible that women are being assigned to light-work assembly lines while men are being assigned to heavier-work assembly lines. It is illegal to take two similarly qualified individuals and assign them to differing jobs on the basis of sex. Women may also be assigned to jobs from which it is harder to transfer to more-upwardly mobile or better-paying jobs.

Promotion: Initial hiring is not always the problem in sex discrimination. Frequently women are able to get their foot in the door, particularly if they are willing to be hired into traditionally "female" jobs. However, time and time again women are to be found at the bottom of the company hierarchy and infrequently or not at all in higher-level supervisory, managerial, and professional jobs. It is therefore important to examine the procedures followed by an employer in making promotions. Particularly suspect are promotions that are made primarily through supervisory recommendation, especially when almost all the supervisors are male. Also it should be determined if an employer has established employee training and education programs for women to train them for positions in which there are currently few women. Another common employer practice is to place women in jobs that have traditionally been dead-end jobs, with few opportunities for promotion, or to refuse to accept the experience women have as valuable for higher-level jobs. Each of these practices may constitute illegal discrimination.

The Seniority-system Exception: Seniority, or length of time with a company or a department or in a job, is an essential component of industrial organization, particularly in blue-collar, unionized industries. In companies that employ seniority systems, seniority is often used to determine a worker's right to bid for a better job; to determine shifts, overtime, and vacation and other fringe benefits; and to determine who may continue to work during a layoff period. Those persons who have the highest seniority will have the first chance to bid for a new and usually better-paying job, and those persons who have the least seniority will be the first laid off during a period of layoff. Wage scales and pension pay may also be determined by seniority. Many employees measure seniority by department or job lines of progression, rather than within the whole company. What this means is that once an employee begins to work in a given department, she/he builds up seniority within that department or line of progression. However, any time that worker wants to transfer into a new department or a new line of progression, she/he will lose all the seniority built up in the former department. Thus, if you have a company that previously segregated jobs into men's departments and women's departments and then is forced under Title VII to integrate those departments, for a woman to transfer to a new department means that she will have to give up all the seniority she has built up in her former department and go to the bottom of her new department in terms of her chance to bid for better jobs—possibly even at reduced wages. She will also then be in a position to be laid off first. Needless to say, most workers are hesitant to move into a new department and give up rights that they have built up over years. Likewise, if a company that previously refused to hire women for certain jobs, and must now do so, operates on a last-hired, first-fired principle, it will lay off newly hired women first during a period of layoffs. What this means is that seniority systems lock women into the less-well-paying departments and jobs that they were relegated to during a period of discriminatory hiring and assignment.

This would seem like a classic case of a neutral employment policy (departmental seniority) that operates to discriminate against women, and it should be illegal under Title VII. However, the Supreme Court has specifically held that Title VII provides an exception for bona fide seniority systems that were not created with the intent to discriminate.[10] Thus, even though seniority systems have a substantial adverse impact on women's employment rights, particularly given the extensive sex segregation of most jobs in this country, they have been left immune from attack under Title VII and employers are not required to change their seniority policies even though they lock women into lower-paying, less-desirable jobs. The only possible way to attack a seniority system that adversely impacts on women is to argue that it is not bona fide or that it was specifically set up with the intent to discriminate, i.e., lock women into specific jobs. While it is difficult to show that a seniority system is not bona fide, since the courts have said that so long as it is a system that to some extent determines job rights on the basis of length of service it is bona fide, it may be easier to show that some seniority systems were created with an intent to discriminate. In this regard it is necessary to examine the circumstances surrounding the creation and continuation of the seniority system. Any information that can be gleaned that shows an intent to create the system to preserve discrimination, including statements made during collective bargaining, prior treatment of women employees, etc., will be helpful in showing an intent to discriminate.

Examples of Disparate Treatment of Women

Often it is not possible to identify specific employer practices or policies that appear to be the cause of discrimination against women. Sometimes the problem lies in the fact that the company is simply treating women differently from men even though its employment policies themselves do not treat women differently from men. Particular examples of disparate treatment that may affect women include taking disparate disciplinary action when men versus women engage in the same infractions, differing compensation for the same or similar work, differences in the quality of job assignments, differences in performance evaluations, and harassment from fellow workers and/or supervisors.

Pregnancy Discrimination

The move toward equal treatment of women has been measured in legal terms in relation to, or as an integration into, a preexisting white male middle-class world. Therefore it is hardly surprising that the move toward equality in employment has had its greatest difficulties when faced with issues and concerns surrounding the treatment of pregnancy and maternity in the workplace. Pregnancy lies at the center of the entire ideology of separate spheres for men and women, the separation of the public man and the private woman. True gender equality cannot be achieved without examining rules concerning pregnancy which set women apart from men. And yet, the biological capacity to bear children remains an immutable difference between men and women. The question of how to treat the sexes equally with respect to characteristics they do not share has been at the heart of the dilemma.

In 1976 the Supreme Court ruled in *General Electric Company* v. *Gilbert*[11] that discrimination on the basis of pregnancy was not sex discrimination under Title VII. In that case, challenging the exclusion of pregnancy-related disabilities from an otherwise comprehensive disability program, the court held that pregnancy classifications were not sex-based but, rather, based on a physical condition, and that, further, the employer's rule did not have a disparate impact on women, because both men and women received coverage for the disabilities they had in common. Because pregnancy is unique to women, its treatment cannot be compared for equality purposes. Since the standard of equality is measured against the man, not the woman, women were bound to lose out.

In reaction to *Gilbert,* Congress overturned the Supreme Court's decision and in 1978 amended Title VII to provide expressly that discrimination on the basis of pregnancy, childbirth, or related medical conditions is a form of sex discrimination prohibited by the Act. The law specifically states that

> women affected by pregnancy, childbirth, or related medical conditions shall be treated the same for all employment-related purposes . . . as other persons not so affected but similar in their ability or inability to work . . .[12]

The Pregnancy Discrimination Act (PDA) rejects the presumption that pregnancy is unique and instead states that a woman employee's pregnancy must be viewed in the same way as all other physical conditions that may affect an employee's ability to do her/his job. This means that a woman may not be fired or forced to take unpaid leave because she is pregnant. She must be allowed to work as long as she is able. If an employee becomes sick or disabled because of her pregnancy, the same sick-leave or disability-leave policies and practices must be applied to her as are applied to all other types of disabilities or illnesses. For instance, if other employees who take sick leave or disability leave continue to accumulate seniority, she must also be allowed to continue to accumulate seniority. Similarly, health insurance coverage may not have special provisions or conditions applicable to the medical costs of pregnancy. This means that pregnancy is covered in the same way that other disabilities are covered under company health insurance plans. It remains unclear whether, if an employer's health insurance policy provides health insurance coverage for women employees who are pregnant, it must also provide health insurance coverage for spouses of male employees who are pregnant.

The Pregnancy Discrimination Act applies only to women affected by pregnancy, childbirth, or related medical conditions. A pregnant woman who is able to work is not entitled to sick-leave benefits. It also means that if a woman chooses to take leave when she is no longer disabled from work, that leave will be treated in the same way as other voluntary leaves of absences are treated by the employer. Thus, she must be reinstated on the same conditions, but not on any better conditions than would be granted for other leaves of absence. If a company has a policy of personal leaves of absence, or if the company chooses to institute a policy that gives child-rearing leave, the policy must be applicable to both men and women, and both must be given the opportunity to take a leave of absence for child rearing.

A new conflict in the debate on the appropriate treatment of pregnancy has arisen because several states have passed legislation that, instead of placing pregnant women at a disadvantage, entitles them to greater protection. An example of such a statute is a Montana law that forbids employers to fire women who become pregnant and requires them to give women reasonable maternity leave.[13] A possible conflict with the equality principle of the PDA arises in the following situation. An employer in Montana has a sick-leave policy in which employees in their first year of employment are entitled to no leave and only five days per year thereafter. A pregnant employee who misses several days of work because of morning sickness is fired. She asserts her rights under the Montana statute. The question is whether the special treatment accorded pregnancy is contrary to the equality principle of the PDA.[14] The debate in this instance is not led by men attempting to justify disadvantaging women in the workplace, but by feminists grappling with the question of what women's equality means. Some feminists feel that statutes like the Montana statute are incompatible with the equality principle of Title VII and the PDA, that the approach that would allow statutes which create special benefits for pregnancy is the same approach that has permitted pregnancy to be treated worse than other disabilities. Others argue that pregnancy is a problem unique to women, an extra source of workplace disability, and that women cannot compete equally with men in the workplace unless pregnancy is taken into account in special ways. Thus such laws reflect the material reality of women's lives.

In the particular conflict discussed above, it might be possible to harmonize the equality principle of the PDA and the Montana statute by arguing that the employer's sick-leave policy, while neutral and equal on its face, had a discriminatory impact on women. Because two thirds of all women in the work force will become pregnant during their working lives, women are subject to most of the disabilities men are subject to, plus the additional disability of pregnancy. If statistics show that this difference results in the fact that many more women than men are fired under the employer's sick leave policy, a classic Title VII disparate-impact claim exists. However this specific issue is resolved, the fundamental issue of the meaning of women's equality within the workplace, particularly in relation to pregnancy and maternity, is likely to remain unresolved for some time. Litigation involving employer policies excluding women of childbearing age from jobs involving exposure to substances that may cause fetal harm is likely to raise this issue. (See Chapter 14.)

Pension Plans

It has been a common practice to give women lower monthly pension benefits than men, or to require that women make higher monthly contributions than men in order to receive the same monthly benefits upon retirement. This is based on the theory that, because the average woman lives longer than the average man, it is appropriate for insurance companies to use sex-segregated mortality tables in calculating the benefits and payments for men and women. Courts have consistently held, however, that this concept of determining individual benefits on the basis of sex-based averaging fails to follow Title VII's fundamental concept that individuals are to be treated separately as individuals. The concept of averaging in determining pension benefits prejudices and penalizes any individual woman who does not fit the average. The Supreme Court has already held, in *Manhart v. Department of Water Power of the City of Los Angeles,*[15] that a requirement that women contribute higher monthly payments into pension plans was illegal under Title VII. A number of federal circuit courts of appeals have also determined that paying women lower monthly benefits is likewise illegal.[16] One federal circuit court of appeals recently determined that such a practice does not violate Title VII.[17] This issue is now before the Supreme Court for decision.

Fighting Employment Discrimination in Higher Education and Other Highly Skilled Professions

Recently there have been an increasing number of lawsuits filed by women against institutions of higher education, alleging sex discrimination in hiring, promotion, tenure decisions, and compensation. These cases reflect an increased focus on attempting to end sex discrimination in the more-complex, best-paying, and most-powerful professional jobs. Unfortunately these cases have met with mixed success and reflect the difficulty encountered in applying principles of Title VII law to extremely complex and sophisticated jobs in which each individual, her qualifications, and her job duties may be seen by the courts as unique. The problems in higher education are exacerbated by an unwillingness on the part of judges to interfere in the time-honored tradition of academic freedom. Frequently courts have been unwilling to certify these cases as class actions, arguing that the claim of each individual woman is unique, different from that of any other woman. The failure to certify a case of this nature as a class action leaves one to fall back on the murky waters of comparative qualifications of one individual against another. Statistical evidence of a pattern of failure to hire or promote women, or of a pay disparity between comparable male and female faculty members, is helpful. However, it is difficult to quantify certain elusive qualitative standards such as teaching ability, quality of publications, contribution to the university, national or international reputation, etc. Therefore, courts have been less willing to accept standard statistical analyses as demonstrating proof of discrimination. Particularly difficult are cases involving denial of tenure. These cases are almost always, by their nature, individual, since each tenure decision is made separately for each individual faculty member. While most colleges and universities have some kind of written standards for determining tenure, there is always some subjective evaluation on the part of the faculty member's peers involved. Whereas in other areas of Title VII discrimination, the fact of subjective evaluation would in and of itself raise a suspicion of discrimination, particularly where the evaluators were almost entirely men, in the area of higher education it raises instead the question of overruling or second-guessing the decision of an academic institution. Courts are loath to do this and have often failed to find discrimination in tenure cases.

While other lawsuits challenging discrimination in highly sophisticated professions will not have the added problems presented by the hallowed halls of academia, they, too, can expect to meet with judicial reluctance to second-guess the decisions of managers and professionals. For instance, in a recent case, a federal district court held that a decision whether or not to make an attorney at a law firm a partner was not subject to Title VII review, because a partnership was not an employer but, rather, an association.[18]

Comparable Worth or Pay Equity

As has previously been noted, the wage gap between men and women is one of the most persistent signs of sex discrimination. The single most important source of the wage gap between men and women is job segregation, the concentration of women in a narrow range of low-paying occupations. Pay equity involves correcting the practice of paying women less than men for work that requires comparable skill, effort, responsibility, and working conditions. A recent Supreme Court case, *County of Washington v. Gunther*,[19] made clear that if a disparity between the salary for a woman's job and the salary for a man's job can be shown to be caused by discrimination on the basis of sex, it may violate Title VII. It is unclear exactly how far the holding in the *Gunther* case will be extended. The law does not require equal pay for comparable worth in the sense that if you show that the job of nurse in New York is worth the same or more than the job of janitor in California it will be necessary to pay nurses in New York more than janitors in California. What it does require is that, within a given employment establishment, wages must be set without taking sex into account.

One of the main tools used in determining whether the wages set for female-dominated jobs accurately reflect their value to an employee is the use of job-evaluation studies. Briefly, job-evaluation studies attempt to develop composite job descriptions for the positions to be evaluated, then assign points to each job, based on the categories of skill, effort, responsibility, and working conditions. Then jobs that have similar numbers of points are compared to see whether their salaries are similar, and if not, to determine whether the difference is related to the genders of those filling the jobs.

There are four types of cases that can presently be identified as providing good bases for bringing a pay-equity claim under Title VII. Each of these situations involves proof of intentional discrimination on the part of the employer. Therefore, in evaluating situations in which women are paid less than men for doing different but comparable jobs, it is necessary to look at all of the circumstances for evidence of discrimination. Indications that the company has set women's salaries lower because they are not the primary support of their families, that companies have used differing procedures for evaluating and setting wages for men's and women's jobs, etc., would all support a finding of intentional discrimination.

The first case, *I.U.E.* v. *Westinghouse Electric Corporation,* [20] involved a company that in the 1930s actually did a gender-neutral job-evaluation study, although all jobs in the plant at the time were sex-segregated. After completing the study and assigning points to various jobs, the employer then deliberately set lower wage rates for jobs occupied by women than for those held by men, even though the male and the female jobs were rated equal. Thus, one key practice to examine if a company has actually employed job-evaluation studies in the past is to determine whether those studies were actually applied differently for men's and women's jobs. If they were, this would support a wage-discrimination claim under Title VII.

In the second case, *Taylor* v. *Charley Bros. Company,* [21] plaintiffs worked at a wholesale grocery supply warehouse. All the women workers were in one division, while the other division was all-male. The majority of the jobs in the two divisions were comparable in that they were all entry-level jobs that required no formal training. The company not only refused to consider women applicants for the men's jobs and vice versa but also maintained a wage differential between the two departments of from $1.70 to $1.45. The court found that the wage differential could not be justified by the differences between the jobs but could be attributed only to intentional sex discrimination. The court inferred this intent to discriminate from the company-wide practice of sex segregation, the lack of any job evaluation to justify the wages, and the fact that plaintiffs hired an expert who did a job-evaluation study supporting the conclusion that women were assigned lower wages because they were women and not because of the worth of their job content. Thus, where there has been substantial evidence of other discriminatory employment practices by the employer, and where these practices have led to sex-segregated departments, where the jobs are at least substantially similar in content, and a substantial difference in pay is found, a wage-discrimination claim under Title VII is possible.

In another case, a class of women who held nonacademic jobs at a college were classified and paid as clerical employees, even though their duties were managerial.[22] The court found that the college discriminated on the basis of sex by failing to pay salaries commensurate with job responsibilities. This case can be categorized as a misclassification case. It is not the employer's entire system that is at fault but, rather, the choice of classifying a particular job held by women as clerical instead of managerial in nature, leading therefore to paying them a lower salary.

The fourth type of case can best be illustrated by looking at an academic institution. There, salaries are frequently set on an individual basis, although within certain types of guidelines, and readjusted each year based on a whole variety of subjective and some objective factors. No two individuals perform precisely the same job, and yet, everybody, for instance in the law school, performs a similar type of job. This is not a situation in which either job classifications or job-evaluation studies are likely to be very helpful. However, what would be helpful in a situation like this is to use a multiple-regression statistical analysis in which all other factors are held constant and a determination can then be made as to whether as a group women in comparable positions to men are receiving lower salaries than men.[23] Such a finding would also support a wage discrimination claim under Title VII.

Comparable worth or pay equity is a newly emerging concept. Litigation under Title VII is likely to occur slowly and cautiously. However, there are a variety of other ways in which to attack problems of comparable worth or pay equity, some of which have had substantial success in recent years. These include legislation, organizing, collective bargaining, research, and public education. For instance, in the past several years over twenty-five state and local governments have taken comparable-worth action including the funding of job-evaluation studies to identify the extent of wage discrimination in female-dominated jobs. These studies have been triggered in many ways, including collective bargaining, legislation, executive order, budget appropriation, and personnel-department action. California, Hawaii, and

Minnesota have passed laws establishing a policy or commitment to comparable worth. In addition, many states have equal-rights laws that prohibit unequal compensation rates for comparable worth. These states include Alaska, Arkansas, Georgia, Idaho, Kentucky, Maine, Maryland, Massachusetts, North Dakota, Oklahoma, Oregon, South Dakota, Tennessee, and West Virginia. Labor unions are winning comparable-worth settlements in both the private and the public sectors. For instance, in San Jose, California, the municipal employees represented by Local 101 of the American Federation of State, County and Municipal Employees won pay-equity raises of 5–10 percent for employees in predominantly female jobs. The settlement came after the employees were forced to strike for nine days because bargaining failed to produce appropriate comparable-worth adjustments.

Thus, pay-equity initiatives need to be taken in the legislative, bargaining, and organizing arenas as well as through litigation.

Relief

Once a violation of Title VII has been found, courts have broad discretion in granting whatever relief is necessary under the equities of the case. The basic principle under Title VII is that a victim of unlawful discrimination is to be made whole or restored to the place she/he would have been had the discrimination never occurred. Thus the employer may be ordered to hire, reinstate, promote, or transfer the plaintiff. The court may also order that the plaintiff's seniority rights, if any, be restored to the level at which they would have been had the discrimination not occurred.

Title VII also expressly authorizes the award of back pay. Back pay may not extend more than two years prior to the filing of the EEOC charge. Courts have defined back pay broadly to include (in addition to lost salary) fringe benefits, overtime pay, raises, retirement contributions, and leave and vacation pay. Interest may also be awarded. Any interim earnings will be deducted from the back-pay award.

Courts may also require that the employer take affirmative steps in the future to ensure that further violations of Title VII do not occur and to compensate for past discrimination through "catch-up" policies. Affirmative actions include increased efforts to hire and/or promote women into jobs from which they have been excluded, usually accomplished through the setting of goals and timetables for the hiring and promotion of women, the establishment of training programs for women, the alteration of recruitment, hiring, or job-posting practices, and the establishment of mechanisms to prevent the harassment of women employees.

It should be noted that where the parties negotiate a settlement during the course of a lawsuit or an investigation of a charge with the EEOC, their settlement agreement may include relief of all types described above. Compensatory, punitive, and liquidated damages are not available under Title VII.

Filing a Charge with the EEOC: Private and Nonfederal-Public Employers

In order to set into motion the EEOC procedures that may resolve your complaint of discrimination or allow you to bring a Title VII lawsuit in federal district court, it is absolutely necessary that you file a timely charge with the EEOC. There are 22 district offices and 27 area offices throughout the country, each of which has an intake unit set up to receive individual charges of discrimination. Check your local phone book for the office nearest to you. An intake equal opportunity specialist (EOS) will conduct an intake interview and obtain the information necessary to fill out a charge form. If you are unable to come into the district or area office for an interview, the intake EOS will conduct the interview by telephone (you may call collect). The EOS will draw up a charge and mail it to you for your signature. In either case, the information will include your name and address, the employer's name and address, a statement of the facts you believe to be an unlawful employment practice, the number of employees the employer has, and whether you have filed a charge within an appropriate state or local agency. You must then swear to the charge to meet the oath requirement of the statute. While you may request anonymity if you are afraid to let the employer know you have filed a charge, Title VII does protect you from employer retaliation, and it will be difficult to get appropriate relief without eventually revealing your name. You may also have the charge filed on your behalf by a labor organization or a women's or civil rights group of which you are a member. Sometimes the EEOC intake person will try to discourage you from filing your charge. Remember that the agency must take your charge, and if you believe that you have been discriminated against you should insist that the charge be filed. To help the intake officer and later the EEOC investigation, you should come prepared with all the facts and examples of ways in which you believe the employer has discriminated, and with as much information on how hiring and promotion decisions are made as you can find out. In order to attack employment discrimination as broadly as possible, you should insist that the charge cover more than your specific case if you believe the problem is broader. For instance, if the employer refuses to promote you to a foreman's job but you also know that there are no women foremen, then you should state the problem as failure to promote all women to the job of foremen. If you also know that women are not hired for certain departments or jobs, include hiring discrimination in your charge as well.

However, you should be aware that during the charge intake interview, the intake EOS has been instructed to define the scope of the charge narrowly and to cover only those issues that directly affect you. The emphasis on limiting the scope of investigations is based on the necessity of allocating limited Commission resources. While a limited investigation should not

FLOW CHART: EEOC PROCEDURES*

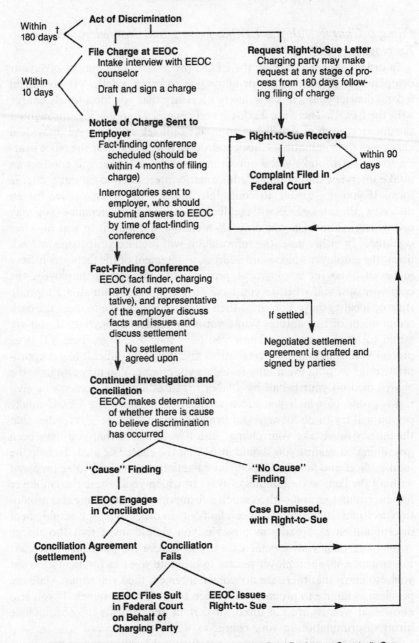

Act of Discrimination

Within 180 days †

File Charge at EEOC
Intake interview with EEOC counselor
Draft and sign a charge

Request Right-to-Sue Letter
Charging party may make request at any stage of process from 180 days following filing of charge

Within 10 days

Notice of Charge Sent to Employer
Fact-finding conference scheduled (should be within 4 months of filing charge)
Interrogatories sent to employer, who should submit answers to EEOC by time of fact-finding conference

Right-to-Sue Received

within 90 days

Complaint Filed in Federal Court

Fact-Finding Conference
EEOC fact finder, charging party (and representative), and representative of the employer discuss facts and issues and discuss settlement

If settled

Negotiated settlement agreement is drafted and signed by parties

No settlement agreed upon

Continued Investigation and Conciliation
EEOC makes determination of whether there is cause to believe discrimination has occurred

"Cause" Finding

"No Cause" Finding

EEOC Engages in Conciliation

Case Dismissed, with Right-to-Sue

Conciliation Agreement (settlement)

Conciliation Fails

EEOC Files Suit in Federal Court on Behalf of Charging Party

EEOC Issues Right-to-Sue

*This chart applies to the procedures that are used by the federal Equal Employment Opportunity Commission (EEOC) for charges under Title VII of the Civil Rights Act of 1964. Local agencies, such as the District of Columbia Office of Human Rights, follow similar procedures.

†In jurisdictions where there are state or local laws prohibiting employment discrimination such as the District of Columbia, this period will be longer.

preclude a private suit that covers all discriminatory practices like or related to those in the charge, it is best for you to write the charge in broad terms. This will give information that will encourage the EEOC to conduct the broadest possible investigation into the employer's practices. This will later make it easier for you to file a class action, which will aim at correcting systemic sex discrimination in the work place.

Employer Notification and Protection from Retaliation

If you file a charge with the EEOC, it will send a notice of the charge to the employer or union within ten days. The notice will include the name of the person filing the charge unless you have an organization file on your behalf. Even then your name will usually have to be revealed for the EEOC to discuss a remedy. However, Title VII specifically protects you from retaliation for filing a charge of discrimination. If your employer retaliates by firing, demoting, or reassigning you, by making your working conditions unbearable, or in any other way, you should file another charge, claiming retaliation, with the EEOC. If some action is needed immediately, the EEOC may bring a lawsuit for temporary or preliminary relief pending a final decision on your original charge.

EEOC Processing of Your Charge

In many states there are state or local antidiscrimination laws and enforcement agencies (Fair Employment Practices, or FEP, agencies). As to these states, Title VII requires that the EEOC not proceed with or assume jurisdiction over your charge until the state/local agency has had jurisdiction over the charge for sixty days. If you file a charge with an EEOC office in a state with a deferral agency, the EEOC will automatically defer your charge to that agency for sixty days and may then assume jurisdiction over the charge. Most state/local agencies will not automatically refer charges to the EEOC. Therefore in order to meet Title VII's filing requirements, which will be discussed below, it is necessary to file your charge with the EEOC. The best way to avoid problems is to file your charge with the EEOC and the state/local agency at the same time and to request on your EEOC charge form that the EEOC automatically assume jurisdiction sixty days from the date of filing. Under work-sharing agreements between the EEOC and some state/local agencies, some charges will be processed exclusively by the state/local agency. The EEOC will, however, have resumed jurisdiction after sixty days.

Once the EEOC has jurisdiction over your charge, the agency has exclusive control over it for one hundred eighty days. Your charge will enter the agency's Rapid Charge Processing system, which is designed to expedite the handling of charges by narrowly defining the issues to be resolved and attempting to reach a settlement between the parties quickly and with a limited expenditure of time and resources.

The EEOC may ask a charging party for information concerning the alleged discriminatory practices, may conduct a fact-finding conference, and may visit the employer, talk to other employees, or request documentary evidence from the employer. The first thing that is likely to happen is that the agency will hold a fact-finding conference. A date will be set for the charging party and the employer to come to the agency office. It is important that you cooperate with the EEOC, since otherwise your charge may be administratively closed for failure to cooperate. The conference will be conducted by an EOS. The EOS may have contacted you or the employer and requested information from you or asked that you bring certain documents to the conference. The purpose of the conference is to narrow the issues, get out all the facts and, ideally, to resolve the problem through a written settlement agreement. The EOS acts as an impartial mediator in this process, but emphasis is placed on resolving the charge at this stage, and a charging party may feel some pressure to take what the employer offers. This will almost never be more than relief for an individual case of discrimination. For instance, you may be offered a promotion to that supervisor's job, or your wages may be raised to the same level as the men in your office, but you will not reach an agreement that gives all the qualified women in your plant or department a chance to become supervisors or increase their wages. That is, you may be faced with the following dilemma: whether to accept a solution to your individual problem or to pursue a lawsuit to correct systemic problems, which may be expensive and time-consuming. As part of this decision, you should know that there is an incentive for some attorneys to take your case if it is good. Under Title VII a court may award attorney's fees and court costs to the successful party, which means that if you win, your employer will have to pay the fees. You may want to try to find an attorney who will agree to take your case on the basis that she will collect a fee from the employer if you win and nothing if you lose, and who can give you advice on the strength of your case before the fact-finding conference. This way you will be better able to decide whether to take the relief offered at the conference, if any, or to refuse the relief and continue with your charge. Each charging party will have to make that decision for herself.

After the fact-finding conference, if your charge has not been resolved the agency will either decide that there is no cause to believe that discrimination has occurred and issue you a right-to-sue notice, or it will refer your charge for further investigation in the Continuing Investigation and Conciliation Unit (CIC Unit). After completing the investigation, the EEOC will write a final decision on whether there is reasonable cause to believe there is discrimination. Where the agency finds reasonable cause, it will make a final effort at settlement, called conciliation. If conciliation fails because, again, you cannot accept what the employer offers or the employer makes no offer, the commission will issue you a notice of right to sue.

Right to File a Lawsuit in District Court

Once the EEOC has found cause and issued you a notice of right to sue, you may take the employer to federal district court. Also, at any point in the process, if the EEOC issues a finding of no cause, you may file suit. But, it will be harder to find a lawyer in this case. In a very few cases the EEOC will bring a lawsuit on your behalf (or the Justice Department will do so for state and local employers) instead of issuing you a notice of right to sue, but you should not count on this happening.

If you wait for the entire agency process to be completed, it will probably take anywhere from three months to two years, because of the large volume of charges the EEOC gets.

You may shorten this process by requesting your notice of right to sue to bring your own lawsuit. You are entitled to do this anytime at least 180 days after the EEOC takes control of your charge. You should not do this unless you have already found a lawyer to take your case, because the lawsuit must be started within 90 days of your receipt of the notice. It is sometimes better to wait longer and allow the EEOC to collect the information you will need during its investigation. A 1982 Supreme Court case *(EEOC* v. *Associated Dry Goods Corp.)*[24] makes clear that you are entitled to information relating to your charge gathered during the investigation.

Time Limitations and Requirements

There are a number of time requirements under Title VII that you must comply with or lose your lawsuit.

The first has to do with the time within which you must file your charge with the EEOC. This depends upon whether you are in a state or locality with a certified Fair Employment Practices (FEP) deferral agency. (Check your phone book for your nearest office, or call the local office of the EEOC.) If there is no deferral agency, you must file within 180 days from the date of the discriminatory act. If there is a deferral agency, you must file within 300 days. However, a recent case has made it clear that in a deferral state your charge may not be filed with the EEOC until either the state/local agency has had the charge for 60 days or termination of its processing, whichever is sooner. This means that, in a deferral state, if you file with the EEOC 250 days after you have been discharged and the state keeps your charge for 60 days, the EEOC will not be able to take it over until 310 days after your discharge and you will have your charge dismissed. Therefore, if there is a deferral agency you should always file within 240 days.

The safest thing to do is to file your charge as soon as possible. Filing as soon as possible will also increase the amount of back wages (money you would have earned if you had not been discriminated against) that you can get in a settlement or a lawsuit. Under Title VII you can collect back wages only for the period of time starting two years prior to filing a charge up to the date of settlement or the end of your lawsuit. The time for filing a charge begins to run from the date you knew or should have known of the discriminatory act. For instance, if on May 1 you receive a notice of termination as of June 1, your time runs from May 1, the date you knew of the discrimination, not June 1, the date you were actually terminated.

Even if you think you have missed the time deadline, you may be timely in certain circumstances. The courts have said that some kinds of discrimination are continuing violations, and so long as the policy continues, a charge is always timely, because the discriminatory act continues. The following actions have generally been held to be continuing violations: promotion—where, for instance, many men have been promoted over time and you have not been promoted; continued dissemination of adverse references causing problems for former employees; discriminatory health, pension, and maternity policies; and discriminatory and harassing work environment. The following actions have usually been held not to be continuing violations: refusal to hire, discharge, termination, layoff, denial of tenure, demotion, transfer, or job reclassification. Again, the safest thing to do is to file your charge as soon as you believe you have been discriminated against.

The second important time requirement involves going to court. Under Title VII you have only ninety days after you receive your notice of right to sue to file a complaint with the district court, starting your lawsuit. If you do not file within the time period, you will lose your case. That is why you should never request your right to sue until you already have a lawyer and she is ready to file your lawsuit.

Title VII Procedures for Federal Employees

Federal employees are also covered by Title VII, and their rights are also enforced by the EEOC, but they must follow different procedures, as laid out in Section 717 of Title VII. Although the procedures differ, the same definitions of discrimination apply to federal employees as apply to other employees.

Procedures and Time Limits to Be Followed by Federal Employees:
Briefly, you must first consult with your agency's Equal Employment Opportunity (EEO) counselor and attempt to resolve the complaint informally. This consultation must occur within thirty days of the discriminatory act. Within fifteen days following the final interview with the EEO counselor, you may file a formal written administrative complaint with your agency's director of EEO or another person the agency has designated to receive complaints.

The administrative complaint may be submitted either by yourself or by your representative. You may be represented by someone else at any stage of the administrative proceeding. While your representative need not be a lawyer, a lawyer may be advisable. As in the case of charges filed with the EEOC, you should frame your complaint broadly, to include all agency practices you believe to be discriminatory. Your complaint will be investigated by someone who does not work for your agency.

Within fifteen days after receipt of a notice of disposition of your complaint from the EEOC office, you have a right to request a hearing, which will be conducted by a complaints examiner who is not an employee of the agency. Following the hearing or, if you choose not to have a hearing, following the investigation, the findings and recommendations in your file will be sent to the head of the agency for a final agency decision. You then have a right to appeal this decision to the EEOC Office of Review and Appeals (ORA) within twenty days after the final agency decision. There is no right to a hearing before the ORA. This is the end of the administrative process.

Right to File an Action in District Court

You may file an action in district court at a number of points in the administrative process. You may choose to wait until the end of the process, following a decision from the EEOC. You must then file within 30 days after receipt of notice of the final Commission decision. It takes federal agencies an average of 407 days to resolve complaints. If the process is taking too long, or you do not believe you will get the relief you want from the administrative process, and you have a lawyer ready to file a lawsuit for you, you may go to court sooner. You may go to court after 180 days after the date of filing of your original written complaint with the agency if no final agency decision has been reached; or within 30 days of receipt of the notice of final agency decision; or after 180 days from the date of filing an appeal with the EEOC if no decision has been reached.

If you go to court, you should know that a class action may be brought even though you are the only plaintiff who has exhausted your administrative remedies. If you file a successful suit against the federal government, the court may award attorney fees and court costs as in a suit against a private employer.

How to Find a Lawyer and Finance a Title VII Lawsuit

Title VII provides for an award of attorney fees and costs by the court to the winning party. This provision is in the statute to encourage attorneys to take Title VII cases on a contingency fee basis where if they win, the court will order their fee paid by the losing employer or union. If they lose, the attorney won't get a fee. Courts almost always award costs and fees to a successful plaintiff. Some awards have been very large, including a number over $1 million. You should not agree to an arrangement with a lawyer in which the fee comes out of your earnings from winning the lawsuit, because Title VII allows the court to award a separate fee to the lawyer based on hours worked. Many attorneys are requiring some payment of fees in advance. You will have to pay costs as you go along and get reimbursed after the court award. Because the standard is much stricter, courts rarely require plaintiffs to pay the fees of successful defendants. However, recently there have been several cases in which this has happened, and you should know there is a slight risk of being assessed fees if you bring a lawsuit that is really frivolous.

Title VII litigation has become increasingly more complex and costly. This is in part because the defense bar has become more sophisticated in defending employers against discrimination suits and in part because the case law on proof of discrimination has become increasingly complex. Discrimination suits are proved through the use of several types of evidence. These include documents obtained from employers, anecdotal evidence or testimony of other employees, job evaluations and, most important, statistical evidence. These latter two types of evidence frequently require the hiring of experts, including labor-market economists, industrial psychologists, and statisticians. Complex multiple-regression analyses must be run on computers, necessitating the hiring of data processors and computer time. Large class actions can cost well into the hundreds of thousands of dollars and even more-modest ones can cost between $50,000 and $100,000 to litigate.

Obviously, neither a few charging parties nor small practitioners can afford this kind of cost. Increasingly, the civil rights bar has turned to large law firms, which can carry these costs for a few years, to take on a small number of meritorious class actions for plaintiffs. Another approach is to request EEOC intervention in a lawsuit filed by private attorneys. The government will usually pay a substantial share of the costs if it intervenes. A third alternative is for plaintiffs to set up defense funds and start raising money early on in the litigation to help finance it. This is a good way to generate interest and organize women workers, as well as raise money.

Where none of these avenues is available, private attorneys are finding that they are sometimes unable to expand their clients' charge into a large class action that can attack systemic discrimination. This is an unfortunate result of a body of law meant to provide financial incentives to private attorneys to litigate cases on behalf of discriminated-against workers.

If you want help in finding a lawyer to handle your case, the best source is your local EEOC office, which maintains a lawyer referral list. You can also try human rights organizations, Fair Employment Practices offices (which also have lawyer referral lists) and local women's organizations.

THE EQUAL PAY ACT

The Equal Pay Act (EPA) prohibits companies from paying women less than men for the same work. The Act covers most private employees and federal, state, and local governmental employees, including executive, administrative, and professional employees. Technically, companies covered by the Equal Pay Act are those "engaged in commerce" or "engaged in the production of goods for commerce." This definition has been interpreted broadly to cover almost all employers. Labor unions are also covered by the Act.

Enforcement responsibility for the EPA is with the EEOC. If you wish to file an EPA charge with the EEOC, you should follow the procedures outlined on pp. 295–302 for filing a Title VII charge. Generally, the EEOC will process your charge the same way it will process a Title VII charge. See pp. 297–98. Unlike Title VII, it is not necessary that you file a charge with the EEOC and go through the agency's administrative process before you may file a lawsuit in court. Under the EPA, you may file a suit directly in court. However, if the EEOC files suit on your behalf, your right to bring a separate lawsuit is cut off.

Should You File a Charge with the EEOC?

There are a number of advantages to filing a charge with the EEOC. The agency will conduct the investigation and collect evidence on your charge. If the agency files a lawsuit, you will not have the expense of an attorney to worry about. Most important, the EEOC can get relief for you that you cannot get in your own lawsuit. If you yourself sue and win, you may recover the amount of underpaid wages going back two years from the date you filed the lawsuit, plus the same amount as liquidated damages (double wages), plus attorney fees and court costs. If you can show that the employer discriminated willfully, you may recover three years' back wages, doubled. However, if the EEOC sues for you, it can get the same back pay and liquidated damages but can also get an order from the judge requiring the company to raise your salary to the legal amount for the future. Also, the EEOC may file a lawsuit on behalf of all women who, like you, are being paid less, whereas if you file a private lawsuit you may only file on behalf of individual women who have given you specific authorization to file on their behalf.

Time Limitations and Requirements

A suit under the EPA must be brought within two years from the time the discrimination takes place, or three years if the violation is willful. The fact that you have filed a charge with the EEOC will not stop the time from running (unlike a Title VII charge), and if the EEOC has not yet filed suit and the two years is near an end, you will have to decide whether to get your own attorney and file a lawsuit. However, as in Title VII, continuing violations are allowed. If your employer continues to underpay women workers the time will not run.

Time is also important for back-pay purposes. You can collect back pay for only the two years prior to filing a lawsuit (unlike Title VII, under which it is two years prior to filing a charge). Therefore you should try to sue as quickly as possible.

Kinds of Discrimination Forbidden by the Equal Pay Act

The EPA forbids only a very narrowly defined kind of wage discrimination. It forbids companies from paying women less money than men for the same work. While this is a simple idea, determining what is the "same" work is very complicated. The law has set down standards that must be met in order to win an equal-pay case. You must compare the work performed by the men and women in order to determine if it is equal. Three specific factors must be examined: The jobs of both must require equal skill, equal effort, and equal responsibility. Also, the work must be performed under similar working conditions, and both the men and the women must work in the same establishment or physical place. For instance, you cannot compare a man's job of lineman in an AT&T facility in Pennsylvania with a woman's job of lineman in an AT&T facility in Arizona. This requirement is in the Act because differing market factors in differing geographic locations may account for differences in wages, rather than the factor of sex. Lastly, the work performed must be the same or equal, meaning that individual tasks performed in the woman's job must be the same as the tasks performed in the man's job. The courts have interpreted this standard to mean that the job must be the same or *substantially similar,* not identical.

Each of the criteria listed must be met in order to win an equal-pay case.

This requires conducting a thorough comparison of the men's and women's work and the identification of each of the tasks that make up the work and the amount of time spent on each task. EPA cases tend to revolve around the presentation of and disputes over the technical facts concerning the definitions of each job.

Limitations of the Equal Pay Act as Compared with Title VII

The Equal Pay Act has only limited value in attacking wage discrimination. It is premised on the notion that part of the wage gap is caused by women's weak bargaining power vis-à-vis men for the same jobs, and that by requiring employers to pay women wages based on the stronger bargaining power of men you will close the wage gap. This would be true if most women were in jobs that were substantially the same as those of most men. However, as shown earlier, this is not the situation. In fact, it is occupational segregation that is responsible for most wage discrimination. Remember, the EPA will help you only if you are earning less than a man who is performing a virtually identical job.

Title VII, on the other hand, is much broader than the EPA. Many employment practices involving wage issues that are legal under the EPA are illegal under Title VII. For instance, take an insurance company that hires men as claims adjusters and women as clericals and pays the men more than the women. The jobs of claims adjuster and clerical are not substantially the same, so this is not an equal-pay case. However, the employer is assigning men and women to differing jobs based on sex. A Title VII lawsuit to make the employer assign women as claims adjusters would be the appropriate route. This would raise the wages of women by integrating the work force and would also give women clericals back pay for the wage differential between clerical and claims-adjuster jobs.

Another wage issue in which Title VII is broader than the EPA involves salary discrimination in similar but not identical jobs. For instance, if the women professors at a particular college or university receive salaries that are on the average lower than those received by men who are similarly qualified, a Title VII salary discrimination suit could be brought. It would be almost impossible under the EPA's highly technical requirements to show that the job of any given female professor is the same as the job of any given male professor, but under Title VII, statistics can be used to show a pattern of paying equally qualified female professors lower salaries than male professors. Title VII's greatest potential advantage for providing relief for wage discrimination lies in the area of pay equity or comparable worth. This is discussed on p. 291.

These examples illustrate the importance of including a Title VII claim along with an EPA claim, even where you think you have a good EPA case. Because Title VII is much broader than the EPA, even if you lose your EPA claim on a technicality you may have a valid Title VII wage-discrimination claim.

Practices Found to Violate the Equal Pay Act

The Equal Pay Act has been used most successfully on behalf of blue-collar workers. This is because blue-collar work tends to have clearly defined job requirements, with little variation from worker to worker. It is extremely difficult to prove that jobs are identical in the professional, white-collar area, where individual variation in job content and subjective evaluation of workers' abilities are frequent.

Types of jobs that have been found to be equal in successful Equal Pay Act challenges include aides and orderlies in hospitals, maids and janitors, salespersons in department stores working in different departments and selling different merchandise, bank tellers and management trainees, various kinds of assembly-line workers, and night-shift versus day-shift workers.

Employers have engaged in various strategies to avoid complying with the Equal Pay Act, usually involving redesigning or reassigning jobs. Courts have rejected these strategies. For instance, a company may try to avoid complying with the Act by giving men extra weight-lifting duties. The courts have inquired as to how important these extra duties are, whether all men perform them, what percentage of the workday is spent performing these duties, etc., and have concluded that in spite of such extra duties the work of men and women workers was "substantially equal." Companies have also attempted to avoid liability by removing tasks from the women's work, but courts have found the jobs were still equal.

Employers have also moved to segregate their work forces to avoid compliance by transferring all the men, who received higher wages, into another job, so that only the women, who are paid at a lower rate, are left doing the first job. However, once the company has established a higher rate for men, it must raise the women's wages.

In situations in which a company operates both a day and a night shift in which women have historically worked for less during the day and men have worked on the higher-paid, night shift, it is not sufficient to merely open the higher-paid, night-shift jobs to women. The mere existence of differing shifts does not make the work unequal, and to cure the violation the company must raise the pay for day-shift work.

Note that one of the provisions of the Equal Pay Act is that a company may not comply with the Act by lowering the wages of the men, but must always raise the wages of the lower-paid sex.

TITLE IX OF THE EDUCATION
AMENDMENTS OF 1972

Title IX of the Education Amendments of 1972 constitutes a small part of the Education Amendments of 1972, which deal with federal involvement in a wide range of activities of educational institutions at all levels. The Supreme Court has recently held that Title IX provides protection against sex-based employment discrimination for employees of such educational institutions.[25] This includes all institutions that receive federal funds earmarked for educational purposes, including some libraries, museums, etc., as well as traditional educational institutions.

Enforcement

If you want to file a private lawsuit under Title IX, it is not necessary to first exhaust any administrative remedies. You may file directly in federal district court. If you wish to file a complaint with the federal government, the proper place to file is with the office of civil rights in the agency that has funded the school. While this will usually be the Department of Education, it may in some instances be the Health and Human Services Department or some other agency. Once a complaint has been filed, the agency must investigate the complaint and may refer it to the Department of Justice for enforcement. Such referrals are rare, however. Under Title IX, the government may cut off federal contract funds to a discriminatory school. It is unclear whether a fund cutoff may be ordered in a private lawsuit.

When Should You File Under Title IX?

Because the Supreme Court has held only recently that Title IX covers employment discrimination, there have been few lawsuits determining what the substantive law or appropriate remedies are under Title IX. It is unlikely that either the substantive rights or the available relief in a private action will be broader than those available under Title VII. In fact there is some indication that the courts may require a showing of intent to discriminate to prove a Title IX violation and that the relief available to plaintiffs will not be as broad as under Title VII.

Therefore, there are probably only a few instances when you would file a private suit under Title IX instead of Title VII. These would include: (1) When you have missed a time requirement under Title VII. Because there is no administrative process precedent to filing a suit under Title IX, the only time requirement you must comply with is the general state statute of limitations. This will often be longer than the time within which you must file a charge under Title VII. (2) When you wish to go immediately into federal district court without waiting for a right to sue under Title VII. This must be balanced against forgoing the benefit of allowing an administrative investigation of your complaint and the advantage of including the possibly broader coverage of Title VII. (3) When you wish to combine a Title IX employment claim along with other Title IX discrimination. For instance, there may be discrimination against the women's athletic program in a given university that affects both the rights of women students and the salaries and status of women coaches.

It is always possible to file a claim under both Title VII and Title IX. It may also be advisable to file a Title IX complaint with the federal government even if you do not intend to file your own lawsuit, since the statute requires that the agency conduct an investigation. This means that the government may be able to gain the relief you seek without the necessity of your filing your own lawsuit.

EXECUTIVE ORDER 11246, AS AMENDED

Executive Order 11246 covers all companies and agencies that have contracts with the federal government of $10,000 or more yearly, their subcontractors, and recipients of federally assisted construction contracts. Most companies covered by the Executive Order are also covered by Title VII. Unions are not directly covered by the Executive Order.

The Executive Order and regulations promulgated pursuant to it require all covered contractors to agree in their government contract not to discriminate and to create an affirmative action plan. This means that a contractor must determine those jobs in which it underutilizes women or minorities, and set goals and timetables for increased minority and female employment. In theory, the requirement of an affirmative action plan provides the best opportunity for bringing about vast institutional change in employment patterns throughout the country. Unlike Title VII, which relies for its effectiveness on the filing of lawsuits, the Executive Order requires companies to examine their employment practices and institutionalize affirmative action before lawsuits have been filed. Unfortunately, the Executive Order has not produced the substantial change one may have hoped for. This is in part because the regulations promulgated thereunder have themselves allowed substantial loopholes and partly because enforcement has not been as vigorous as many would like.

Enforcement

An employee or applicant for employment may not file a lawsuit under the Executive Order. Enforcement is by government action only.

An investigation of a contractor may be started in one of three ways: First, a complaint of discrimination may be filed by an employee or any other person aware of such discrimination. However, complaints of discrimination on behalf of individuals will generally be referred to the EEOC. These complaints are filed with the Office of Federal Contract Compliance Programs (OFCCP), the office in the Department of Labor charged with enforcing the Executive Order. The OFCCP retains and investigates only those complaints that are filed on behalf of a class. Therefore, if you consider filing a complaint with the OFCCP, any class-wide aspects of discrimination should be emphasized.

The OFCCP may also initiate compliance reviews of contractors. This is the most common way in which a contractor may be investigated. Over 2,000 such compliance reviews are conducted each year. During a compliance review or complaint investigation, the OFCCP reviews the contractor's documents, may interview witnesses, and will attempt to get the contractor to comply voluntarily. If voluntary compliance fails, OFCCP, represented by the solicitor of the Department of Labor may file an administrative complaint, which is tried in a hearing before an administrative law judge. The judge's recommended findings may then be appealed to the Secretary of Labor, who may adopt, modify, or reject them. The Secretary's final decision may then be reviewed by the federal courts of appeal. The OFCCP may also refer cases to the Justice Department to bring a lawsuit against the company for breach of contract. This avenue of initiating an investigation of a contractor is rarely used.

Remedies Under the Executive Order

Under the Executive Order, the following remedies or sanctions may be recommended: the company may be debarred from eligibility for federal contracts; may be ordered to comply with the Executive Order, including the institution of affirmative action programs, etc.; and relief for the entire class affected by the discriminatory practices, including back pay, promotion, etc., may be recommended.

The threat of debarment from future federal contracts creates a substantial incentive for contractors to comply with the Executive Order. However, the threat of debarment is so powerful it has been carried out fewer than 30 times in the first 17 years of the Executive Order. Since the Executive Order's effectiveness depends almost entirely on the commitment of the Labor Department to enforce it, and since only the Department of Labor may sue for debarment and other remedies, compliance has been spotty.

EXECUTIVE ORDER 11478

Executive Order 11478 applies only to the federal government. It requires all federal agencies not to discriminate, and to create affirmative action plans and programs. In this sense it operates similarly to Executive Order 11246. (See p. 308, above.) It requires that agencies in the federal government examine their employment practices and set goals and timetables and eliminate barriers to employment where underutilization in any job is found. Under the Executive Order, the EEOC monitors the government's compliance. It is unclear how much enforcement authority the EEOC has.

There is no private right of action under the Executive Order, although Title VII provides a private right of action for the same kinds of discriminatory practices in the federal government. (See pp. 300, above.)

THE AGE DISCRIMINATION IN EMPLOYMENT ACT

The Age Discrimination in Employment Act (ADEA) prohibits age discrimination against individuals between the ages of 40 and 70. It prohibits discrimination in hiring, firing, or other terms and conditions of employment, in referrals for employment, or membership in a labor union, because of age. The law applies to employers of 20 or more persons engaged in an industry affecting interstate commerce, and employment agencies and labor unions of more than 25 members. It also covers public employers.

Enforcement responsibility for the ADEA lies with the EEOC. If you wish to file an ADEA charge with the EEOC, you should follow the procedures outlined on p. 295 for filing a Title VII charge. Generally, the EEOC will process your charge the same way it will a Title VII charge. Unlike Title VII, however, the ADEA does not require the EEOC to investigate charges or issue formal findings. In most instances, however, the EEOC will at least submit charges to a fact-finding process and may pursue more extended investigations in a limited number of cases.

In order to file a private suit under the ADEA, it is necessary for an employee to first file a charge with the EEOC, either (1) within 180 days of the alleged unlawful employment practice or (2) in a state with a law prohibiting age discrimination and establishing state authority to seek relief from such discrimination, within 300 days of the alleged unlawful employment practice, or within 30 days after receipt by the individual of notice of termination of proceedings under state law, whichever is earlier.

An employee may file a civil action in court after 60 days or more have elapsed since filing of a charge with the EEOC. It is not necessary to receive a right-to-sue letter from the EEOC before going to court.

A civil action in court must be brought within two years after the date of the unlawful employment practice. This time period is not tolled, or stopped, during the administrative processing with the EEOC. If the discriminatory act is "willful," a three-year time period for filing applies. However, since intent, or willfulness, may be hard to prove, it is advisable to file suit within the two-year period.

Kinds of Discrimination Forbidden by the Age Discrimination in Employment Act

The ADEA provides important protection for women. Because nowadays women frequently enter the labor market later in life and are seeking jobs later in life, discrimination in hiring on the basis of age is likely to have a greater impact on women than men. This also means that women often have fewer years of gainful employment available to them and smaller pensions upon retirement. Therefore, it is important that they remain in the labor market as long as they are willing and able to work.

An employer is prohibited from discriminating against older workers in hiring, discharge, promotions, training, compensation, or other terms and conditions of employment. An employer may not reduce the wages of employees to comply with provisions of the ADEA. Likewise, an employer may not discharge an older, more expensive worker in order to hire a younger worker who will cost the employer less money in salary and benefits. Employers may also not discriminate against older workers by virtue of refusing to count experience as a substitute for educational qualifications. And discriminatory conduct against, for instance, older persons in the 40–70-year-old, protected age group in favor of younger persons within the protected age group is also prohibited age discrimination.

The treatment of employee benefits under the ADEA is a particularly complex subject. Under the Act, the extension of additional benefits to older workers in the 40–70 age group is not prohibited. For instance, the extension of additional benefits such as longer vacations, increased severance pay, or more favorable shift differentials may be lawful in certain circumstances when made to older employees within the protected age bracket to promote and encourage opportunities for such individuals who might otherwise experience disproportionate hardships, so long as the extension of such benefits does not create an unreasonable hardship for the younger employees within the protected age bracket.

Employers are permitted to provide lesser fringe benefits to older workers in certain limited situations in which the cost of such benefits is greater for older workers and would otherwise discourage their employment. Likewise, it is not unlawful to observe the terms of a bona fide seniority system or any bona fide employee benefit plan. The ADEA expressly prohibits involuntary retirements of persons under age 70 unless required pursuant to the terms of a bona fide retirement plan and essential to the plan's economic survival or some other legitimate business purpose.

A major exception to coverage under the ADEA or, rather, a major defense by the employer is that it is not unlawful to discharge, refuse to hire, or promote older workers for a job for which age is a bona fide occupational qualification reasonably necessary to the normal operation of the particular business. BFOQ under the ADEA, as in Title VII, has been narrowly construed. The BFOQ has been found to be a valid defense in litigation involving mandatory retirement age for various employees of fire departments and police departments and for airline pilots. However, the courts have by no means been uniform in accepting a BFOQ defense in these cases. It is necessary for the employer to do a task analysis to establish the connection between age and ability to perform the job.

Another important exception to the ADEA is the exclusion of apprenticeship programs from its coverage. This means that many union and/or employer apprenticeship programs, which require that individuals be under a certain age for acceptance into the program, often 25, are exempt from ADEA coverage. This is particularly significant in the case of women, since they often consider entering such apprenticeship programs at a later age than men. Since apprenticeship programs are frequently among the main entrees into the higher-skilled blue-collar craft and construction jobs from which women have traditionally been excluded, the existence of an age requirement for entry into the apprenticeship program provides yet another barrier for women's entry into the skilled trades.

Relief Under the ADEA

Relief available under the ADEA includes an agreement to hire, reinstate, or promote; payment of any amounts deemed to be unpaid compensation, including fringe and related benefits; and in the case of a willful violation, liquidated or double damages. An individual suing under the ADEA is entitled to a jury trial. Courts are split on the issue of whether compensatory and punitive damages are available under the ADEA.

An important thing to remember about the ADEA is that class actions may not be brought under the statute. Instead, individuals must opt into an ADEA suit.

DISABILITY DISCRIMINATION

The Rehabilitation, Comprehensive Services, and Developmental Disabilities Amendments of 1978 provide that a "handicapped person," including one who is "regarded [as having] a physical or mental impairment which substantially limits one or more of such person's major life activities," may file a complaint alleging discrimination by the federal government in the hiring, promotion, or other treatment of federal employees or applicants for federal employment on the basis of handicap. The procedures for filing a complaint of discrimination in federal employment based on handicap are the same as the procedures for filing complaints of discrimination in federal employment under Title VII.

There are several other provisions in the Rehabilitation Act that are of use to certain individuals claiming discrimination. Section 504 of the Act provides that no otherwise qualified handicapped individual shall, solely by reason of her/his handicap, be excluded from participation in, be denied the benefits of, or be subjected to discrimination under any program or activity receiving federal financial assistance or under any program or activity conducted by executive agency or by the U.S. Postal Service. Private individuals may file suit under Section 504. However, a case of discrimination in employment on the basis of handicap may be filed under Section 504 only if the purpose of the federal assistance in question is to create employment or if the discriminatory employment practice would cause discrimination against primary beneficiaries of the federal aid who are handicapped.

Section 503 of the Act requires that government contracts for the procurement of personal property and nonpersonal services shall require that the government contractor take affirmative action to employ and advance "qualified handicapped individuals." There is no private right of action under Section 503. Complaints of violations of Section 503 may be filed with the Secretary of Labor, who has the responsibility for enforcing the section.

SEXUAL PREFERENCE DISCRIMINATION

There is not always legal recourse against discrimination in employment on the basis of sexual preference. Title VII has been held to refer only to gender-based discrimination and not to discrimination based on sexual preference. Therefore, the EEOC has refused to accept charges involving sexual preference discrimination, claiming that it lacks jurisdiction to address the problem.

In general, individuals working in the federal government are afforded the greatest amount of protection. Employees in regular civil service jobs are protected against inquiries into or action based upon nonjob-related conduct, including sexual orientation. For employees in military or national security positions, there is some indication that nonjob-related conduct may not be scrutinized. However, homosexuals are afforded less protection from discrimination where "high risk" positions are involved: individuals have been discharged from the armed services on the basis of their sexual orientation.

Two states, California and Pennsylvania, have adopted statewide executive orders prohibiting discrimination in public employment on the basis of sexual preference. There are also approximately 30 municipalities and counties that have passed local ordinances prohibiting sexual preference discrimination in employment. Some, like the one in the District of Columbia, cover discrimination in all employment, private and public, by reason of sexual orientation. The law in this area is still developing, and there are active groups on local, state, and federal levels attempting to expand legislation prohibiting discrimination in employment and in other areas on the basis of sexual preference.

FOOTNOTES

1. A landmark study by the prestigious National Academy of Sciences concludes that a significant portion of the national wage gap between the sexes is due to sex discrimination. The study claims that "the more an occupation is dominated by women, the less it pays" and that "only a small part of the earnings differences in education, labor force experience, labor force commitment, or other human or capital factors [are] believed to contribute to productivity differences among workers." D. S. Teriman and H. I. Hartmann, *Women, Work and Wages: Equal Pay for Jobs of Equal Value,* Washington, D.C., National Academy Press, 1981, p. 42.

2. 43 F.R. 19807.

3. *Dothard* v. *Rawlinson,* 433 U.S. 321 (1977).

4. *Gunther* v. *Iowa State Men's Reformatory,* 462 F. Supp. 952 (N.D. Iowa 1979).

5. In *Griggs* v. *Duke Power Co.,* 407 U.S. 424 (1971), a seminal case under Title VII, the Supreme Court struck down an employer requirement that as a condition of employment, employees have a high school diploma and pass a standardized general intelligence test, both of which requirements operated to disqualify blacks at a substantially higher rate than white applicants, holding that "practices, procedures, or tests neutral on their face, and even neutral in terms of intent, cannot be maintained if they operate to "freeze" the status quo of prior discriminatory employment practices." At p. 428.

6. *Dothard* v. *Rawlinson, supra.*

7. *Phillips* v. *Martin Marietta Corp.,* 400 U.S. 542 (1971).

8. See e.g. *Sprogis* v. *United Airlines, Inc.,* 444 F. 2d 1194.

9. Uniform Guidelines on Employee Selection Procedure, 29 C.F.R. 1607.

10. *U.S.* v. *Teamsters,* 431 U.S. 324 (1977).

11. 429 U.S. 125 (1976).

12. 42 U.S.C. 2000 e(k). The one exception is that employers are not required to provide health insurance benefits for abortions unless the life of the mother would be endangered if the fetus were carried to term or where medical complications arise from an abortion.

13. Montana Maternity Leave Act, Mont. Code Ann §9 39-7-201 through 39-7-209 (1981).

14. See *Miller-Wohl Co.* v. *Commissioner of Labor and Industry, State of Montana,* 515 F Supp. 1264 (1981).

15. 435 U.S. 702 (1978).

16. See e.g. *Spirt* v. *Teachers Insurance and Annuity Association,* 30 EPD §33,072 (2nd Cir. 1982), *Retired Public Employees' Assoc. of Ca.* v. *California,* 677 F.2d 733 (1st Cir. 1982), *Norris* v. *Arizona Governing Comm. for Tax Deferred Annuity,* 671 F.2d 330 (9th Cir. 1982), *E.E.O.C.* v. *Colby College,* 589 F.2d 1139 (1st Cir. 1978).

17. *Peters* v. *Wayne State Univ.,* 691 F.2d 235 (6th Cir. 1982).

18. *Hishon* v. *King & Spalding,* 29 EPD §32,840 (11th Cir., 1982).

19. 26 EPD §31,877 (U.S., 1981).

20. 23 EPD §31,106A (3rd Cir. 1981).

21. 25 FEP cases 602 (W.D. Pa. 1981).

22. *Evans* v. *Central Piedmont Community College,* 475 F. Supp. 114 (W.D. N. Car. 1979).

23. *See e.g. Sobel* v. *Yeshiva University,* awaiting decision in the District Court, S.D.N.Y.

24. 24 EPD §31,458 (U.S. 1981).

25. *North Haven Board of Education* v. *Bell,* 102 S. Ct. 1912 (1982).

FURTHER READING

The American Promise: Equal Justice and Economic Opportunity. Final Report, National Advisory Council on Economic Opportunity, 1981 (Washington, D.C.: Government Printing Office). (stock # 041-008-000-19-9)

Comparable Worth Project Newsletter (488 41st Street, No. 5, Oakland, Calif. 94609.

Employment Discrimination Laws: A Handbook (Women's Legal Defense Fund, 2000 P Street, N.W., Washington, D.C. 20036). The fund also publishes easy-to-understand handbooks in a number of other areas related to women's rights

Employment Practices Guide (Commerce Clearing House, Publications Department, 4025 West Peterson Avenue, Chicago, Ill. 60646).

Fair Employment Practice Cases Washington, D.C.: Bureau of National Affairs, 1231 25th Street, N.W., Washington, D.C. 20037. This is a law reporter which publishes in full all cases and laws in the field of employment discrimination.

The reporters send monthly updates on new cases and changes in the laws. While this reporter system, and the Employment Practices Guide, are meant primarily for lawyers working in the field of employment discrimination, they may also be helpful to laypersons. Both have indexes divided by subject matter.

U.S. Commission on Civil Rights, Affirmative Action in the 1980s. *Dismantling the Process of Discrimination,* January 1981 (Clearing House Publication 70, November 1981).

U.S. Department of Labor, Women's Bureau. A variety of fact sheets and information on women in the paid work force.

Subcommittee on Civil Service, Compensation and Employee Benefits and Human Resources of the House Committee on Post Office and Civil Service. *Hearings on pay equity or comparable worth,* September 1982 (Washington, D.C.: Government Printing Office).

Women, Work and Wages. Equal Pay for Jobs of Equal Value (Washington, D.C.: National Academy Press, 1981).

13
Sexual Harassment on the Job

ANNE E. SIMON
PHYLLIS L. CROCKER

Anne E. Simon is a staff attorney at the NOW Legal Defense and Education Fund in New York. Prior to taking that position, she worked as an attorney in the New Haven Law Collective, where she represented the plaintiffs in Alexander v. Yale, *which established that sexual harassment is sex discrimination in education. She has also represented numerous women experiencing problems of sexual harassment in employment.*

Phyllis L. Crocker is a student at Northeastern University School of Law. Before returning to school, she was a legal worker in the New Haven Law Collective, participating in the trial of Alexander v. Yale, *which established that sexual harassment is sex discrimination in education. She has also been a consultant, specializing in analyzing sexual harassment problems.*

This chapter would not have been written in the early seventies. In the mid-70s it might have been about five pages long and consisted largely of a discussion of three legal cases. Today, because of the efforts of many women across the country, it is possible to say a great deal more than that about sexual harassment, a pervasive problem for women in the workplace.

Although sexual harassment has been a serious problem for women for a long time, it has only recently been clearly identified and discussed. Like rape and wife beating, sexual harassment has flourished behind a wall of silence and disbelief. As more women have been able to name and talk about their experiences, the true contours of the problem of sexual harassment have begun to emerge. This chapter addresses some fundamental questions about sexual harassment: Whom does it happen to? What is it? Why does it happen? What can one do about it?

WHO IS SEXUALLY HARASSED?

Linda is an executive secretary. When her boss was transferred to another city, she was reassigned to a company vice-president. One night when they were working late, he called Linda into his office. When she came in, he closed the door, and put his arms around her. He informed her that they would be more productive if they got to know each other a lot better. Linda disagreed, got out of his grasp, and promptly left. During the next three weeks, he spoke to her only to give orders and remind her of her obligation to assist the company, as his other secretaries had done. Linda finally told him that the answer would always be no, and that if he did not stop his behavior she would be forced to tell the personnel office. Three days later, she was fired for "poor work performance."

Susan was a lathe operator in a small manufacturing company. The company issued coveralls to people on the shop floor, but the pair she received was too big. She told the foreman, and gave him her correct size. He told her to put on the coveralls, then moved his hands over her arms and chest, "checking to see where it didn't fit." After the new coveralls finally arrived, the foreman came by her work station every day to "check the fit" of the new pair. She asked him to stop; he didn't. She asked for a transfer, but he wouldn't approve it. After six weeks of being "checked," she quit.

Barbara's progress in the management training program was excellent. She was learning quickly, and her supervisor praised her work. Toward the end of the program, her supervisor invited Barbara out to dinner to discuss her future with the company. He suggested that if she would sleep with him, he could assure her rapid promotion. Flustered, Barbara declined. When Barbara finished the training program, she was placed in a low-level management position. She did not receive her first promotion until six months after everyone else in her program. When Barbara finally asked the head of her department why her progress was so slow, he told her that the training supervisor's written evaluation had characterized her as capable, but not a good "team player."

Renée is the only woman working in the drafting room of a large engineering firm. She came in one morning to find that the drawing she had left on her table the night before had been altered so that part of a bridge was now a penis. She redid the drawing, and stopped leaving her work out. Once a week, though, she arrives to find a life-size drawing of a penis on her desk.

Does any of this sound familiar? It's not surprising if it does. A number of studies have documented how widespread and how serious a problem sexual harassment is. In 1976, *Redbook* magazine asked its readers to send in their responses to a questionnaire about "sex on the job." Of the nine thousand women who answered, 88 percent reported that they had been sexually harassed. Almost half the respondents had been forced to leave their jobs because of sexual harassment, or knew another woman who had been forced to do so.[1] Working Women's Institute, a New York-based organization that provides a range of resources about sexual harassment, surveyed victims of sexual harassment in 1978 and found that 42 percent had quit jobs where they were being sexually harassed, either because they were unable to get the harassment to stop or because they were retaliated against for complaining about it. Another 24 percent had been fired as part of the harassment.[2] That means that two thirds of that group of women had been driven out of at least one job by sexual harassment.

These horrifying results are not, unfortunately, flukes due to small, self-selected pools of respondents. A carefully designed random-sample survey of federal government employees, released in 1981 by the Merit Systems Protection Board (formerly the Civil Service Commission), showed that 42 percent of the 10,648 women responding had been sexually harassed in a federal job in the two years immediately prior to the survey.[3]

WHAT IS SEXUAL HARASSMENT?

The Equal Employment Opportunity Commission (EEOC), the federal agency in charge of enforcing Title VII of the Civil Rights Act of 1964 (see Chapter 12), issued final guidelines regarding sexual harassment, in November 1980.[4] The opening section states:

> (a) Harassment on the basis of sex is a violation of Sec. 703 of Title VII. Unwelcome sexual advances, requests for sexual favors, and other verbal or physical conduct of a sexual nature constitute sexual harassment when (1) submission to such conduct is made either explicitly or implicitly a term or condition of an individual's employment, (2) submission to or rejection of such conduct by an individual is used as the basis for employment decisions affecting such individual, or (3) such conduct has the purpose or effect of unreasonably interfering with an individual's work performance or creating an intimidating, hostile, or offensive working environment.

This statement provides a good working definition of sexual harassment in employment. It condenses the results of years of litigation and research into basic precepts of sexual harassment in employment. It is worthwhile to look closely at this section, to draw out what is behind the terse statements of these official guidelines.

Sexual Harassment Is Based on "Unwelcome" Conduct

This important issue has been the subject of a great deal of misunderstanding. Many people believe that opposition to sexual *harassment* also means opposition to consensual office romances and interactions. In fact, a key element of sexual harassment is that the sexual conduct is not wanted by the recipient. Genuinely mutual relationships are not sexual harassment; unwanted and coerced relationships are.

Many men contend that they understand this concept but that it is impossible to know beforehand whether a woman will find an advance "unwelcome." This may be due to authentic uncertainty in a time of changing sexual mores, but it is also necessary to take into account part of the history of sexual interactions. Men have had the exclusive right to exercise sexual initiative, and women have had to accept or reject male advances. But women have rarely, in general, been in a position to refuse male sexual attention. One of the consequences of this situation is that men have not had to learn to distinguish between attention that women "wanted" and attention women "didn't want." Now that women are beginning to assert their rights in these matters, men who have not made the adjustment are confused. This does not mean that the definition is unworkable; rather, it means that men are going to have to pay more attention to women's responses.

But what about the relationship that begins as mutual and consensual, and then ends? Just because it is over, was the woman sexually harassed? No. But all too often, sexual harassment begins when the relationship ends, as the man (especially when he is her boss) takes out his negative feelings on her at work. Some people nevertheless feel that a woman who is sexually involved with her boss "assumed the risk" and ought to take the consequences. This attitude is similar to the view that a woman who is raped by a man on a date "consented" to it by going out with him. Neither attitude is justified. There is no reason to believe that the legal rights of a woman who is denied legitimate employment benefits because a sexual relationship has ended are any less than those of a woman denied employment benefits because a sexual relationship has not started.

Sexual Harassment Is a Work-related Problem

The claim that sexual harassment is employment discrimination is often met by the response that "this is merely a personal misunderstanding or problem; it has nothing to do with the job." Even many judges, faced with sexual harassment complaints for the first time, decided that a sexual harassment case was really "underpinned by the subtleties of an inharmonious personal relationship."[5] The legal understanding of sexual harassment has, fortunately, advanced from that point. It is now clear that on-the-job sexual harassment is not simply a problem between two individuals, but a danger to a woman's ability to do her job.

The EEOC guidelines, and many court decisions,[6] recognize a broad range of circumstances in which sexual harassment can threaten a woman's employment opportunities.

The Choice Between Submitting and Being Fired (or Not Hired): This is probably the most dramatic instance of sexual harassment, and is often the one that first comes to mind when people think about sexual harassment. Linda, the executive secretary discussed at the beginning of this chapter, was a victim of that kind of sexual harassment, colloquially characterized as "put out or get out." Her boss wanted her to sleep with him and had the power to fire her if she did not respond the way he wanted.

A similar situation can also be created before a woman gets a job. The man doing the hiring simply adds on "sleeping with me" as one of the "qualifications" for the job. This form of sexual harassment has been trivialized by numerous jokes and innuendos about the "casting couch" for actresses (who, like most women, are hired by men). It is, nevertheless, a real problem for actresses, waitresses, and other women in jobs in which hiring decisions are usually made by one man, without consultation and without review.

The Choice Between Submitting and Losing Out on Opportunities: Less dramatic, but also very important, is the form of sexual harassment in which the woman is not fired but still loses if she rejects a sexual advance. Barbara, the management trainee in the example, was caught in this situation. Her supervisor offered her the prospect of career advancement if she slept with him, an advancement that she had earned by her own efforts anyway. When she refused, he appeared to accept the refusal. Actually, however, he merely waited for his opportunity to characterize her as a "poor team player," thus ruining her chances as a manager.

It is hard to decide which possible interpretation of the supervisor's actions is more distressing: He gave Barbara a poor evaluation to punish her, or he really believed that a woman's willingness to sleep with her boss is an element of managerial capability. (Perhaps he even thought he was doing her a favor by introducing her to the realities of corporate life.) For Barbara, of course, his motivation made no difference. Her career had been damaged by her refusal of his sexual advances. It is worth noting that the guidelines make it clear that the harasser's state of mind—malign, ignorant, misguided, or merely vacant—is not the determining factor in concluding that a woman has been sexually harassed. It is his actions, and their effect on her and her job environment, that are at issue.

Having to Endure a Working Environment Made Offensive Because of Sexual Harassment: This is the element of the description of sexual harassment provided by the guidelines that probably meets the most resistance from people considering the issue for the first time. Getting fired for refusing to sleep with the boss is one thing—but should the law really be worrying about whether a woman's working environment is "intimidating, hostile, or offensive"? Susan and Renée, the lathe operator and the engineering drafter in the examples, help to show why it is important. Susan's foreman didn't take her away from her work, didn't fire her, didn't give her a poor work evaluation. Instead, he forced her to endure extremely unpleasant and intimidating personal contact. The man who left the drawings for Renée didn't ever touch her. He just made sure that every week she was reminded of the fact that she was the only woman in the department, that she was an outsider, and that she was sexually vulnerable.

Such hostility can take a great toll on women, especially women who work in occupations that have traditionally been virtually all-male. An analogous situation is presented by racial harassment and intimidation. It is clear how the two black workers in a shop would feel if, once a week at lunchtime, the white foreman made a short speech to all the workers about the genetic superiority of whites, and passed out swastika decals. The EEOC and the courts have recognized that those blacks are victims of race discrimination in employment, even though they were fairly hired and are being paid as much as their white co-workers. Similarly, a working environment that is hostile to women, separates them from men, and singles them out as inferior, is discriminatory.

A further aspect of the issue of discriminatory environment is beginning to be explored in the law: sexual harassment by co-workers. Co-workers do not have the same kind of power that supervisors do, but their actions are sufficiently important that they have been legally recognized. The EEOC guidelines provide that

> (d) With respect to conduct between fellow employees, an employer is responsible for acts of sexual harassment in the workplace where the employer (or its agents or supervisory employees) knows or should have known of the conduct, unless it can show that it took immediate and appropriate corrective action.

Basically, this interpretation of Title VII rests on the employer's control over the work environment. Employers have rules and work standards, employ supervisors, and discipline employees. With such control come legal responsibilities for exercising control in a nondiscriminatory manner. Tolerating the sexual harassment of women by their co-workers is an act of the employer, for which it can be held liable.[7]

Sexual Harassment in Employment Is Illegal

The guidelines describe general situations that the EEOC, following the lead of the federal courts, has concluded would violate Title VII. The guidelines generalize from the numerous specific cases of sexual harassment that have been decided by the courts. Specific circumstances can, and do, vary tremendously, but the basic principle is clear: Sexual harassment is illegal sex discrimination in employment. Since Title VII applies throughout the country, it provides a general basis for discussion and understanding of sexual harassment.

It is important to be aware, however, that sexual harassment can also be illegal under various state laws. Some state courts have followed a course similar to that of federal courts, interpreting their state antidiscrimination laws to include sexual harassment.[8] Some states have amended their statutes to make it clear that sexual harassment is one of the prohibited forms of employment discrimination.[9] In addition, women in some states have been successful in asserting legal theories other than employment discrimination as the basis of their sexual harassment claims.[10] The appropriate legal treatment of a particular claim can vary, and should be determined by consultation with a competent attorney.

TWO THINGS THAT SEXUAL HARASSMENT IS NOT

Although women are overwhelmingly the victims of sexual harassment, the legal definition of sexual harassment does not exclude men. The crucial issue is: Were you treated this way because of your gender? Would a woman have been asked to sleep with her boss, if she were a man? Would a man have been asked to escort his boss to a nightclub, if he were a woman? Since almost all bosses are heterosexual men, women are going to be almost all of the victims of sexual harassment, but they are not the only possible victims. Men can be sexually harassed too.

Claims of sexual harassment are not, as some people still insist, cases of "sour grapes" on the part of a woman who tried and failed to use her sexuality to her advantage on the job. This is a version of the myth that women "sleep their way to the top," manipulating well-meaning but susceptible men. The virtually complete absence of women from "the top" of any occupation suggests that this view is primarily wishful thinking, an attempt to believe that women want and/or solicit sexual attention at work because it really is advantageous for them. Perhaps the myth does, however, contain a kernel of melancholy truth: Men in positions of power tend to recognize ability and competence only in women with whom they have had a sexual relationship.

WHY DOES SEXUAL HARASSMENT HAPPEN?

It is, of course, impossible to give an answer that will be true for each particular case of sexual harassment. Two important facts of life in our society can be seen to contribute significantly to the existence of sexual harassment as a widespread problem. One is the fact that women are generally at an economic disadvantage in the workplace. As a group, they earn less than 60 percent of what men as a group earn.[11] They tend to be clustered in jobs that have little power and are considered to be of low status. For example, about 98 percent of all secretaries are women,[12] and the vast majority of them work for men.

Women's disadvantaged status has two effects that are particularly relevant to the phenomenon of sexual harassment. First, a woman in a low-paying job is extremely vulnerable to the threat of losing her job, since she will not have any financial cushion if she is out of work. Second, a woman in a job with little power or status is very likely to be viewed as expendable, whereas her harasser may be viewed as vital to the business. This aspect of the power differential tends to encourage harassment, since the harassers believe—on the whole accurately—that their superiors will not want to punish them.

In addition to women's lack of power in the workplace, there is a second major social fact: Women in general have less sexual power than men. In our society, men are expected to be sexually and personally aggressive, taking the initiative. Women, on the other hand, are expected to be receptive, responding to and supporting male initiative. Most ordinary social/sexual interactions, therefore, tend to conform to a pattern of male assertiveness and female responsiveness.

When they come together in the workplace, these two facts—men's greater economic power and their greater sexual power—can lead to sexual harassment. The harasser's more secure position at work can be used to emphasize his role as initiator of sexual advances. If his superior status does not induce willing acquiescence, then it can always be used to force the victim's compliance.

These general social patterns are expressed in various interactions between individuals. The apparently "personal" nature of sexual harassment can be difficult for a victim to come to grips with. Many women feel that they must be the only person ever to be in such a situation, when actually thousands of other women are experiencing similar feelings.

Women, who are used to being responsible for the emotional content of a relationship, sometimes believe that the harassment is the result of something they did, or failed to do: They must somehow have given the harasser a mistaken impression; perhaps they failed to manage the relationship correctly; perhaps he is only trying to be innocently affectionate.

The list of "personal" explanations can be almost endless. Against it must be put two clear facts: First, sexual harassment is a widespread social problem, with social causes. It is unlikely that a particular instance is an exception to the general rule. Second, many harassers are repeat offenders.[13] This strongly suggests that the harassment has little, if anything, to do with the personal characteristics or behavior of a particular victim but rather is a way that the harasser expresses his power.

WHAT CAN YOU DO IF YOU ARE SEXUALLY HARASSED?

This is a crucial question that does not have a simple answer. The specific details of individual situations must always be taken into account. Nevertheless, it is possible to point out some general elements of the process of reacting to being sexually harassed, and illustrate some particular responses.

The first, and undoubtedly most important, step is to understand what is happening. This generalization can take many concrete forms. At one level, it can mean trusting your own perception that your boss keeps the door closed during routine meetings with you but leaves it open during other conferences; realizing that he was not "just joking" when he said that he likes to sleep with his assistants; knowing that you should have been promoted, but were not, a month after you didn't go on that "ski weekend" with him. At another level (often more difficult), it can mean becoming convinced that the harassment is not "my fault"; that you are not the only woman who has ever been in such a situation; overcoming the feeling that he is behaving this way out of overwhelming personal affection.

Once a woman achieves a reasonably clear understanding of the situation (which may be almost immediate, or may take years), she is in a position to consider what she wants to do about it. Each individual situation is different, but some common elements may be discerned.

One consideration is whether to take any additional action at all, such as directly confronting the harasser, or going to his supervisor, or filing a formal complaint or grievance. Many women are concerned about escalating the situation by some kind of direct response. They hope that eventually the harasser will get the message and leave them alone. Even if they do not believe he will give up, they fear that the consequences of complaining will be worse than the harassment.

There may be some circumstances in which this is an accurate perception, but there are other considerations as well. One such consideration is the evidence that "ignoring" sexual harassment can lead to the harassment increasing, rather than decreasing or remaining about the same.[14] Another is the fact that a woman's reluctance to "make an issue" of the harassment is really reluctance to make it an issue for the harasser. It already is an issue for her, or she would not be trying to figure out what to do about it.

Another question faced by almost all victims of sexual harassment is whether to go outside the employer with their complaint. Most people are reluctant to go outside unless they are fairly sure that they will not get any result from an internal complaint or a union grievance. There are circumstances, however, in which going outside the company, at least for advice, may be appropriate early in the process of dealing with the harassment. (Of course, if a woman is fired as part of the harassment, she has much less reason to try to work the problem out with the employer.) One such circumstance arises when the harasser is a high-ranking official of the company, whose superiors are inaccessible, and who outranks anyone else to whom the victim might reasonably complain. A second circumstance is to preserve the possibility of eventually taking legal action. Since most antidiscrimination statutes have strict time limits on complaints (see Chapter 12), outside advice may be needed to avoid inadvertently failing to adhere to them. A third circumstance is presented when the victim knows that almost all of her co-workers and supervisors will be hostile to a complaint. Outside advice and support can play a crucial role in overcoming the demoralizing effects of hostility in the workplace. There are many organizations, both local and national in scope, that provide assistance to sexual harassment victims. (A sample of them is listed in Further Information, p. 547.)

Many women who do complain are surprised and disappointed by other people's reactions to the complaint. Co-workers and supervisors who had been professionally respectful and personally friendly can become harshly critical of the decision to complain. It is important to accept this possibility and to understand that such criticism is more likely to spring from their own uneasiness about a woman actually publicly objecting to sexual harassment than from any error the victim made by complaining. Realistically, a woman should expect some opposition and be aware that the situation may get worse before it gets better. If it does get worse, it is important to remember that you complained because it was going to get worse—with no prospect for improvement—if you *didn't* complain.

Probably the most common first step for you to take once you have decided to act is to confront the harasser explicitly, telling him:

1. That he is harassing you;
2. What he has been doing;
3. That you don't like it;
4. That he had better stop—now.

It is wise to then say it again, in writing, and *keep a copy for yourself.* Never put anything in writing without keeping your own copy; it is amazing what can be "lost," even in an efficient company.

In general, it is useful to become very conscious about documenting what has happened. A woman who is being harassed through notes or pictures, like Renée in the example, should keep them—even if she does not yet know who sent them. Recording the date, time, and circumstances of receiving them is also a good idea. Although keeping track of such things is certainly unpleasant, it can be useful later on, either in confronting the harasser or in making a complaint to the employer or an outside agency.

Sometimes, confronting the harasser is not a good first step. He may be too powerful, too mean, or too obtuse to respond at all constructively to being confronted about his behavior. The victim then must go to someone else in order to complain. When she does so, she will, in all likelihood, immediately be confronted with one of the paradoxes of sexual harassment. Although she is speaking up for the first time, the person to whom she is complaining will want detailed "proof" of her allegations, before he (and it is generally he) even begins to investigate them. It is as though the police would only begin a burglary investigation if the victim came to the station with the burglar in tow.

The assumption that the victim is probably wrong pervades the treatment of sexual harassment. Despite the tremendous progress that has been made in a very short time, too many women are still faced with the necessity of convincing very skeptical people (usually men) that they are not "making it all up." This attitude puts an additional, very serious burden on victims. At the very time that they are in the process of being harassed—often a very upsetting and scarring experience—they are expected to have the courage, foresight, presence of mind, and information to keep detailed records of what is happening to them. Such an expectation is quite unrealistic. Many women, understandably enough, do not want to dwell on what is being done to them. Many women are simply not particularly literary; writing things down is not a natural response to trouble for them. Furthermore, many women are reluctant even to tell other people what is happening, whether through shame, fear, or reluctance to involve them.

Nevertheless, it is important to recognize that a high level of corroboration will probably be required at some point in the complaint process. One way to handle this, once you have decided to complain, is to try to reconstruct what has been happening, and make some written notes. That will at least help to preserve your memories as of the time you wrote your notes down. Two or three years later (a standard period of time before lawsuits come to trial), much may have faded away.

An important, and often unexpected, source of corroboration can be other women at your workplace. Women often find that talking about their problems with sexual harassment will lead other women to share their experiences, which are sometimes about the same man. In addition, female co-workers often notice odd patterns of behavior, overhear conversations, and generally are aware of sexual harassment. They can be a valuable source of emotional support, as well as of important evidence. In order to make best use of such conversations, it is, again, useful to keep written notes. However, in this situation it is extremely important not to do something that might compromise the confidentiality of what other women have told you. If they are still employed at the workplace, and even more if they are still under the harasser's supervision, they are in a vulnerable position. Therefore, their names and information about them should not be given to other people without checking carefully with them. Sometimes, for instance in a grievance investigation, other women may need to come forward, but they should not be forced to do so by accidental disclosure of the information they have shared.

Some employers have formal grievance procedures, whether through a union contract or company policy. These procedures can be a useful forum for sexual harassment victims, since they are substantially cheaper and quicker than suing. Almost all union contracts forbid sex discrimination in employment decisions. Since sexual harassment is sex discrimination, it is included by such contract language. Because many union contracts, as well as nonunion employer policies, provide for very short time limits for filing a grievance, it is important to be alert to the existence of the limits, and any other procedural requirements, for filing a grievance. Any formal procedure will involve some presentation of evidence, which can be a very trying experience for the grievant. Often, it feels as though she, not the harasser, is being accused of wrongdoing and having her motives and actions minutely scrutinized. This makes it especially important for a victim to seek sources of emotional and practical support, such as members of her union, co-workers, a local women's center, groups working on combatting sexual harassment, and/or an attorney.

This brings this discussion to what in many ways is the bottom line for a sexual harassment victim—taking legal action. As set out in Chapter 12, filing an employment discrimination complaint with the EEOC or a state human rights agency is not complicated, but there are time limits that are strictly enforced. Filing such a complaint might be all the legal action a victim wants to take. She can leave the investigation and processing of her complaint to the enforcement agency, and hope that the investigators are not too overworked or too indifferent to pursue her claim vigorously. Or, often a complaint to an enforcement agency can be the required first step to filing a lawsuit.

Suing is the most potent weapon available to victims. It has the potential for costing the employer a great deal of time and money, causing significant embarrassment, and generating unfavorable publicity, and leading to a legal judgment against the employer. On the other hand, it has the potential for costing the victim a great deal of time and money (and she usually has less of both than the employer), as well as energy and commitment. Lawsuits usually drag on for years and require the investment of much care and attention. Moreover, an employer faced with the high stakes in a lawsuit will be very likely to make every effort to attack and discredit the victim. Finally, although sexual harassment is clearly illegal, most courts do not have much, if any, experience with sexual harassment cases. A trial in a sexual harassment case can be an intensely frustrating experience, as the victim faces hostility and ignorance, not only from the defendant, but often from the judge. All in all, bringing suit is a major undertaking, with no guarantee of success.

Nevertheless, suing may well be the most appropriate response for many sexual harassment victims. Only thorough consultation with a competent attorney, discussion with individuals and groups with experience in sexual harassment cases, and careful consideration can tell a woman whether legal action is the right course for her.

FOOTNOTES

1. Claire Safran, "What Men Do to Women on the Job," *Redbook,* Vol. 148 (Nov. 1976), p. 217.

2. Peggy Crull, "The Impact of Sexual Harassment on the Job: A Profile of 92 Women" (New York: Working Women's Institute Research Series, Report No. 3, 1979), pp. 4–5.

3. U.S. Merit Systems Protection Board, *Sexual Harassment in the Federal Workplace: Is It a Problem?* (Washington, D.C.: U.S. Government Printing Office, 1981), pp. 5, 35.

4. Codified at 29 C.F.R. §1604.11 (1980).

5. *Barnes* v. *Train,* 13 FEP Cases 123, 124 (D.D.C. 1974), *rev'd sub nom. Barnes* v. *Costle,* 561 F.2d 983 (D.C. Cir. 1977).

6. Among the many cases in federal courts are *Barnes* v. *Costle,* 561 F.2d 983 (D.C. Cir. 1977) (office worker whose job was abolished by supervisor); *Williams* v. *Saxbe,* 413 F.Supp. 654 (D.D.C.), *rev'd on other grounds sub nom. Williams* v. *Bell,* 587 F.2d 1240 (D.C. Cir. 1978), *on remand, Williams* v. *Civiletti,* 487 F.Supp. 1387 (D.D.C. 1980) (office worker fired for refusing supervisor's sexual advances); *EEOC* v. *Sage Realty,* 24 FEP Cases 1521 (S.D.N.Y. 1980) (building lobby attendant forced to wear revealing uniform).

7. See, e.g., *Continental Can Co.* v. *Minnesota,* 297 N.W. 2d 241 (Minn. 1980).

8. Minnesota did so in the *Continental Can* case.

9. These states include Connecticut (Conn. Gen. Stat. §46a–60[8][1980]); Michigan (Mich. Comp. Laws §37.2102, 2103[h][1981 Supp.]); and Wisconsin (Wis. Stat. Ann. §111.32–5[g][4][1981 Supp.]). Moreover, in a number of states, e.g., Wisconsin, Wis. Stat. Ann. §108.04(7)(i)(1982 Supp.), unemployment compensation is available to women who have to leave jobs because of sexual harassment.

10. For example, *Monge* v. *Beebe Rubber,* 316 A.2d 549 (N.H. 1974) (holding that discharge because of sexual harassment is a breach of the employment contract).

11. U.S. Department of Labor, Office of the Secretary, Women's Bureau, *The Earnings Gap Between Women and Men* (Washington, D.C.: U.S. Government Printing Office, 1979), p. 14.

12. U.S. Department of Labor, Employment Standards Administration and Women's Bureau, *1975 Handbook on Women Workers* (Washington, D.C.: U.S. Government Printing Office, 1975), p. 90.

13. National Advisory Council on Women's Educational Programs, *Sexual Harassment* (Washington, D.C.: U.S. Government Printing Office, 1981), p. 63.

14. Crull, *op. cit.,* p. 6.

FURTHER READING

Backhouse, Constance; and Leah Cohen. *Sexual Harassment on the Job.* Englewood Cliffs, N.J.: Prentice-Hall, 1981.

Farley, Lin. *Sexual Shakedown.* New York: McGraw-Hill, 1978.

MacKinnon, Catharine A. *Sexual Harassment of Working Women.* New Haven: Yale University Press, 1979.

14
Health and Safety on the Job

JAMES CRAWFORD
LETITIA DAVIS
WITH JOAN LENNINGTON
EMILY NOVICK
ROBERT SCHWARTZ

James Crawford is a freelance writer who specializes in labor and regulatory issues and is the editor of Survival Kit, *the newsletter of the Massachusetts Coalition for Occupational Safety and Health.*

Letitia Davis is a doctoral candidate in occupational health at the Harvard School of Public Health and a co-chair of the Massachusetts Coalition for Occupational Safety and Health. She has taught health and safety at the Northeastern Regional Summer Institute for Union Women for several years.

The Massachusetts Coalition for Occupational Safety and Health (Mass-COSH) is a nonprofit, independent organization that unites workers, unions, and prolabor professionals fighting for better working conditions in New England. MassCOSH services include educational programs, technical assistance, medical and legal referrals, and exchange of information.

Attorneys Joan Lennington, Emily Novick, and Robert Schwartz are all members of the MassCOSH Legal Committee.

I had been handling mercury daily for eight years. When I found out I was pregnant, I became worried that it might harm the baby, and had my mercury levels checked. They were dangerously high, but I couldn't afford to quit, especially with the baby coming.

          —dental assistant

They started us on a new job where we had to weld over epoxy paint. We didn't know what was in the stuff, but we did know it was making us sick.

          —welder, shipyard

I never thought I'd have to deal with any health and safety problems when I got a job in an office. Then I started to work on a video display terminal.

          —clerical worker, bank

Are you worried about health and safety on the job? If so, you are not alone. In the past, occupational hazards were mainly thought of in terms of industrial accidents, explosions, and other obvious dangers. But today more is known about the hidden hazards of work, such as chemicals, radiation, and stress. Some of these cause subtle, everyday ailments like headaches, backaches, fatigue, and visual problems. Doctors and employers often ascribe such symptoms to life-styles or personal troubles, without considering the role of work. Too often, people end up blaming themselves for job-related illness.

Many hidden hazards don't affect the body immediately, but take their toll after years of exposure. Some cause chronic conditions like heart disease and cancer; others harm the reproductive system, affecting not only the worker, but future generations.

Workplace hazards should not simply be accepted as part of the job. Solutions exist to most problems. Conditions *can* and *should* be changed. What's more, you have a legal right to safe and healthful working conditions. While both men and women face health and safety risks on the job, some issues particularly affect working women.

Many jobs traditionally held by women—such as nursing, office work, and service work—are not as safe as once believed. Nurses, for example, are exposed to infections, radiation, anesthetic gases, and adverse effects of shift work. Clericals frequently face bad lighting, poorly designed chairs and equipment, and inadequate ventilation of fumes from photocopiers. Though less dramatic than those of heavy industry, these problems can just as seriously undermine workers' health. Traditional "women's jobs" rank low in pay and social esteem but often high as stress producers. Stress, the ultimate hidden hazard, increases workers' chances of hypertension, heart attack, stroke, and gastrointestinal illnesses.

Women entering traditionally male blue-collar jobs face the same, frequently dangerous conditions that men do. But discrimination can compound their problems. Pressure to prove themselves can keep women from lodging legitimate safety complaints. Or they may have trouble operating tools and machinery designed for the larger proportions of the average male. Only recently have respirators and other safety equipment been designed specifically to fit women.

On the other hand, women in nontraditional jobs often raise health and safety issues that affect everyone. Machinery and safety gear are sometimes designed improperly for *all* workers. And a job that's too heavy for a woman is probably too heavy for many men as well. Therefore, it's dangerous to let anyone frame health and safety as a "women's issue"; both women and men workers should be standing up for their rights.

The same can be said of reproductive hazards in the workplace, which interfere with workers' sex lives or keep them from conceiving and bearing healthy children. Today some employers are using these risks as reasons to ban women of childbearing age from certain jobs. Yet most reproductive hazards affect both sexes, and excluding women obscures the need to clean up the workplace for all workers. The practice also reinforces a view of women as secondary, dispensable members of the work force.

This is not to deny that women face special health and safety concerns during pregnancy. Some workplace exposures threaten the developing fetus, and changes in pregnant workers' breathing and blood volume may place them at higher risk. In late pregnancy, size and balance may pose problems as well, making it unsafe for women to continue in certain work. In such cases, the availability of pregnancy leaves and disability benefits becomes important.

This chapter summarizes your basic legal rights to a safe workplace; it tells how to use the Occupational Safety and Health Administration (OSHA), when to refuse hazardous work, and where to appeal a denial of pregnancy benefits. It also discusses the problem of sex discrimination on health and safety pretexts and outlines your rights when injured or made sick on the job. How and where to find more-detailed information is explained in a resource section on p. 534.

Understanding your options under the law is essential. But faced with a health and safety problem, you may want to consider other avenues as well. Workers' greatest victories (including their victories on this issue) have been won through collective action. Union contracts, for example, can set up procedures to deal with hazards, as well as provide for maternity and paternity rights, and adequate coverage for accident victims. Within unions, workers have formed health and safety committees and women's caucuses. Groups of nonunion clerical workers have used the media effectively to force improvements. Sometimes, direct action is called for. Often, several tactics can be used effectively at once.

Knowledge of the law will provide a basis for action, whatever tactics you decide on.

YOUR RIGHT TO A SAFE WORKPLACE

Lucy, a 30-year-old clerical worker, had always enjoyed excellent health. But that changed a few months ago, about the time she was transferred to a new office at the research and development firm where she worked. There she began operating a word processor. Soon her eyes became irritated and hard to focus, especially after work, and she had trouble reading at night or even watching TV. Finally, she visited an optometrist, who prescribed reading glasses. He warned that her symptoms might be due to staring into a video display terminal, with few breaks, for 7½ hours a day.

Also, Lucy started to experience frequent headaches and occasional dizziness at work. On investigation, she found similar complaints among her co-workers, some of whom blamed solvent vapors that came up from the lab downstairs. Although Lucy passed these findings along to management, she felt she wasn't taken seriously. One supervisor actually suggested the women's symptoms were "hysterical." No action was taken.

Determined not to let the matter drop, Lucy wondered if she should contact OSHA. She had heard of this federal agency but didn't know if it inspected offices. After all, everyone perceives offices as among the safest places to work.

In 1970, Congress passed the Occupational Safety and Health Act, with the intent of "assur[ing] so far as possible . . . safe and healthful working conditions [for] every working man and woman." The law established the Occupational Safety and Health Administration (OSHA) to set and enforce workplace standards, and defined employers' responsibility to maintain adequate safeguards. Under the law, OSHA is empowered to inspect workplaces, assess fines for violations, and order hazards corrected. Workers have the right to file complaints and initiate inspections by OSHA.

Before this federal statute was passed, state acts protected workers inadequately, if at all (10 percent of employees fell outside the jurisdiction of any law). Regulations varied considerably among the states, and enforcement was often haphazard. In a 1968 survey of 25 states, game wardens outnumbered safety inspectors by one and a half times.

Today, OSHA has jurisdiction over almost all workplaces. Twenty-four states still enforce health and safety rules, but with an important difference: they do so under federal supervision. To be approved, state programs must set regulations at least as stringent as OSHA's and hire enough trained inspectors to enforce them.

Are All Workers Now Covered by OSHA?

Unfortunately, no: Congress has not seen fit to extend the same protections enjoyed by private-sector workers to state, federal, county, and municipal employees. Some public workers, however, are covered under state OSHA plans. (Also, special federal legislation covers railroad workers and miners.)

What Are OSHA Standards and How Do They Work?

These fall into two categories: safety standards (e.g., machine guarding, fire prevention) and health standards (e.g., asbestos, vinyl chloride, noise). Both have the force of law. The bulk of these rules consist of "consensus standards"—industry groups' voluntary health and safety rules—which OSHA adopted in 1971. The agency also issues its own standards, but procedures are so cumbersome that it managed to regulate only twenty-two toxic chemicals in its first eleven years of existence.

Standards are supposed to reflect the "best available" scientific evidence, but in practice this is not always the case. Permissible exposure limits, for example, often do not protect against cancer or reproductive damage. For many hazards commonly faced by women—such as video display terminals, poor office lighting, and photocopier toners—no standards exist.

If No Standards Exist, How Are Workers Protected?

A mechanism of the Act known as the "general duty clause" applies in such situations. Its language clearly spells out the employer's obligation to provide "employment and a place of employment free from recognized hazards." If it is recognized, for example, that a workplace chemical causes reproductive harm, steps must be taken to control it—even if OSHA has not yet set a standard. Otherwise, OSHA may cite the employer for violating the general duty clause.

What if Workers Are Getting Sick, but No One Knows Why?

A mysterious ailment that affects several people on the same job could well be work-related. To find out for sure, you may request a "health hazard evaluation" by the National Institute for Occupational Safety and Health (NIOSH). This research agency has legal authority to enter a workplace and conduct a thorough investigation into a possible threat to workers' health. (NIOSH, however, has no power to cite employers for violations or order it to make changes; it can simply make recommendations.)

How Can I Request an OSHA Inspection?

Working through your union and dealing directly with your employer are often the fastest ways to resolve a health and safety problem. But if these methods don't work or seem impractical, you should file a complaint with

OSHA (see the resource section, p. 534, for the office in your area). Keeping your identity confidential if you wish, OSHA will contact the employer and may conduct a surprise inspection of the work site. ("Routine inspections" may be scheduled even though no complaint has been filed, although OSHA has only enough "compliance officers" to visit about 1 percent of workplaces each year.)

What Are My Rights During an Inspection?

A workers' representative has the right to accompany the OSHA inspector during a "walkaround tour" of the workplace. (In 1981, however, the federal government withdrew a rule requiring management to pay such employees regular wages during the walkaround.) The representative may be chosen by the union, the workers, or the inspector—never by the employer. During the inspection, the compliance officer may talk freely to employees, who have a right to privacy and confidentiality in these discussions. The most productive inspections result when workers and their unions are prepared to point out hazards.

What Should I Expect After the Inspection?

Citations, if any, must be prominently posted by the employer for three working days or until a violation is corrected (OSHA will set a deadline). If management decides to contest citations or fines—an increasingly common response—it does not have to "abate" a hazard until all appeals are exhausted. (This process can take years.) Workers have the right to be represented in all such proceedings, formal and informal, although exercising this right usually requires persistence. On the other hand, workers cannot formally challenge OSHA's failure to issue citations or fines—only the amount of time the employer is given to correct violations.

May My Employer Retaliate Against Me for Calling OSHA?

No. Section 11(c) of the Act forbids employers to fire, suspend, demote, or otherwise harass workers who exercise their health and safety rights. In addition to filing OSHA complaints, protected activities include assisting in inspections, filing health and safety grievances, complaining to management about hazards, and even talking to other workers about health or safety issues. *An important caution, however:* with a large case backlog, OSHA has limited ability to enforce this provision, and delays of two years are not uncommon. (For more on 11(c) procedures, see "Refusing Hazardous Work," below.)

What Are the "Right-to-know" Guarantees Under OSHA?

First, your employer must post information on workers' rights under the Act and provide copies of OSHA standards that apply to the workplace, on request. Second, it must give workers access to their personal medical files and exposure monitoring records. Third, it must make available *any information it has* on known hazards, such as data sheets on the effects of toxic substances. But there's a Catch-22. No federal regulation requires employers to keep accurate, complete information of this type on file. (At this writing, the federal government has proposed a very limited "Hazard Communication" standard which would obligate employers in manufacturing industries only to do so.) Some states and municipalities, however, have recently passed "right-to-know" statutes of their own.

REFUSING HAZARDOUS WORK

Katherine had enjoyed her job as an X-ray technician for a private hospital until she learned how hazardous it was. Because of poor maintenance, inadequate shielding, and some outdated equipment, both staff and patients were being exposed to unnecessarily large doses of radiation. She was especially concerned about the careless use of portable X-ray units in a nursery, because infants are especially at risk of radiation-induced cancer. But management brushed off her complaints and even implied she had a "bad attitude" as an employee.

So Katherine was torn. She felt it wrong to keep silent on the one hand, and she was fearful of losing her job on the other. She wondered if she had a legal right to refuse to use X-ray machines under what seemed to be dangerous conditions.

Work Refusals: What Should I Do If I'm Told to Perform Work That I Know Is Unsafe?

Certainly, your first step will be to try to convince your supervisor to delay or cancel the work assignment until corrective measures can be taken to eliminate the hazard. If you have a union contract with strong safety provisions, you may be able, through your union representative, to stop the job. But, too often, such intermediate steps are unsuccessful, and workers are left with the Hobson's choice of refusing the work outright or doing a job that may cause serious injury or even death. To many employers, a work refusal is the ultimate insubordinate act, and the usual response is immediate suspension or discharge. Fortunately, in this situation, there are legal remedies that may win back your job or restore lost pay.

If I Am Disciplined, What Rights Do I Have?

Workers have the legal right to refuse certain unsafe work assignments under two federal laws: the Occupational Safety and Health Act (OSHAct) and the National Labor Relations Act (NLRA). Both have qualifications that can be difficult to meet. If fired, you may win back your job, but be prepared for a long wait, perhaps as much as two years.

How Can OSHA Help?

The OSHAct forbids discipline for work refusals if:

1.   The employee has a reasonable and good-faith apprehension that the job presents "an imminent risk of death or serious bodily injury" (in the words of the U.S. Supreme Court's 1980 *Whirlpool* decision).*

2.   The employer has been informed of the hazard and has failed to correct it.

3.   There is insufficient time to correct the hazard by calling OSHA.

Procedure: The employee must file an "11(c) complaint" at the nearest OSHA office within 30 days of the date of discipline or discharge. After investigation, if the U.S. Department of Labor believes the case has merit, it will file a suit in federal court on the employee's behalf.

Expected time to a decision: Two years. The remedy may include reinstatement and back pay.

Weaknesses of the OSHAct: This protection does not apply to hazards, such as certain toxic substances, that have long-term effects but are not recognized as an "imminent" danger. Also, delays can be long. Employees may not sue on their own behalf, and of course, public employees are not covered.

Work Refusals: What Remedy Is Available Under the NLRA?

The NLRA protects work refusals under the following circumstances:

1.   The work refusal must be in good faith, although it does not have to involve a recognized or serious hazard. As long as the employee honestly believes the work is unsafe or unhealthful, she may refuse the job, whether or not it turns out to be as dangerous as first thought.

2.   The work refusal must be "concerted," that is, *it must involve more than one employee.* An individual's refusal, with the support of another worker or a union representative, is also considered concerted. Some decisions have protected individuals who refused to do work also performed by other employees.

3.   The work refusal must not be in violation of a no-strike clause in a union contract, unless the hazard poses an "abnormally dangerous" threat

---

*The Court unanimously upheld an OSHA regulation forbidding employers to discriminate against workers who refused unsafe job assignments under certain conditions. The regulation protects work refusals when a "reasonable person would conclude that there is a real danger of death or serious injury and that there is insufficient time, due to the urgency of the situation, to eliminate the danger through resort to statutory enforcement channels." Also, the employee must "have sought from his employer, and been unable to obtain, a correction of the dangerous condition."

of serious injury. (Brief work stoppages over a particular job hazard are not usually considered strikes.)

Procedure: Complaints must be filed at the nearest office of the National Labor Relations Board (NLRB) within 180 days of the discipline or discharge. If the NLRB thinks the case has merit, it will issue a complaint and schedule an administrative hearing.

Expected time to a decision: One year, but employers may then appeal to federal courts.

Weaknesses of the NLRA: Work refusals must be concerted, and the NLRA defers to no-strike clauses. Again, there can be delays, and the law provides no coverage for public employees.

What Other Avenues of Appeal Exist?

Unionized employees may contest disciplinary action through their grievance/arbitration process. Most arbitrators recognize the right to refuse unsafe work in certain situations, and this remedy is usually quicker than OSHAct or NLRA procedures. *Remember:* If you are disciplined for refusing a hazardous job, you should file a union grievance (if possible), as well as OSHA and NLRB charges. Even if you lose in two of these forums, you may win in the third.

PROTECTION AGAINST DISCRIMINATION: PREGNANCY AND REPRODUCTIVE HAZARDS

Maria was working as a spray painter in an auto assembly plant when she learned she was pregnant. Worried that solvents in the paint might harm her baby, she considered requesting a pregnancy leave. But she and her husband depended not only on her paycheck, but on her insurance benefits as well. (Besides, she felt fine and wanted to continue working.) So she asked her employer for a transfer to a less hazardous department.

The personnel office, however, rejected her request for alternative work. Maria seemed to be faced with an unfair choice: her baby's health versus her family's economic well-being. Did she have any other options under the law?

In October 1978, Congress amended Title VII of the Civil Rights Act of 1964 to prohibit discrimination on the basis of pregnancy. If you become disabled because of pregnancy, federal law now requires that you be treated the same as other temporarily disabled workers.

What Are My Rights if I Become Pregnant and My Job Could Harm Me or the Developing Fetus?

First, you need a medical determination that you are disabled. (Who determines pregnancy disability—your own physician or your employer's —depends on the procedure used to determine *all* disabilities where you work.) Then your rights would be the same as workers disabled for other reasons. Consider the following examples:

• If your employer allows workers to transfer to other jobs because of health problems, you, too, are entitled to a transfer if pregnancy prevents you from doing your regular job safely or if the fetus might be harmed by your continuing in that job.

• If employees where you work receive disability benefits when they are out because of illness, you have the same rights to those benefits when you are disabled by pregnancy. (Payment rates and maximum length of leave, for example, would have to be the same.) Medical insurance coverage may not be limited for pregnancy unless it is limited for other disabilities in the same way.

How Can I Qualify as "Disabled" on the Basis of Possible Harm to the Fetus?

A determination of disability is more often granted in late stages of pregnancy. But in early stages, when you have no trouble performing your job, the fetus may be at highest risk of harm from chemical hazards, or "teratogens." So it is important to investigate your workplace for such toxins. You will also need documentation to convince the appropriate doctor that potential hazards indeed exist. (When you know what you're talking about, a physician is less likely to clear you to work with reproductive hazards, for fear of future malpractice suits.)

Does Federal Law Guarantee Any Specific Employment Standards for Pregnant Workers?

No. It simply assures that, as an employee disabled by pregnancy, you may not be treated differently from other temporarily disabled employees. (Thus, if others have few rights, so will you.) You may, however, be afforded benefits under the laws of your state. In Massachusetts, for example, certain pregnant workers are guaranteed an eight-week unpaid maternity leave, without loss of seniority or accrued benefits. California requires that employees be granted, on request, up to four months of maternity leave. You may also be eligible for unemployment compensation if you are disabled only from doing your *regular job* and are laid off because your employer has no alternative work available. To find out your rights as a pregnant worker, contact the agency that enforces the state's antidiscrimination laws.

What Should I Do if I Am Discriminated Against?

If you believe your employer has violated a state or federal law in its treatment of your pregnancy, you should file a discrimination complaint, either with the federal Equal Employment Opportunity Commission (EEOC) or with your state's antidiscrimination agency. (*Note:* EEOC has jurisdiction only if your workplace has at least fifteen employees.) While you do not need a lawyer to file these complaints, it is certainly advisable to consult one before you do and throughout any proceedings that follow.

Your union grievance procedure may also provide a remedy if pregnancy rights are specified in contract language. Some union contracts guarantee longer pregnancy leaves than state laws do, or ensure that leaves be paid, or provide for child-care leaves.

May My Employer Exclude Me from a Job I Want Because of Potential Reproductive Dangers?

Legally, this remains an unresolved issue. In a much publicized 1979 case, five women employees of the American Cyanamid Company chose to be sterilized, rather than be excluded from their well-paid jobs, when management introduced a so-called "fetus protection policy." None were pregnant—the company simply wanted assurances they could not *become* pregnant, so it would not have to worry about liability for fetal damage due to lead poisoning. (Ironically, two years later, the women lost their jobs anyway when the company closed down its Lead Pigments Division for economic reasons.)

Litigation involving both EEOC and OSHA resulted from this case, but appeals are still pending in federal courts. In light of the legal uncertainties, a worker faced with this dilemma should file an EEOC complaint, but would also be well advised to fight the case through her union or one of various reproductive rights organizations.

THE RIGHTS OF INJURED WORKERS

At the age of 44, Shirley can work only part time as a secretary because of a disability she suffered while working for a previous employer. Eight years ago, she quit working for a large insurance company, where fumes from a photocopier had permanently damaged her lungs and sinuses. Shirley never filed for workers' compensation because she could not prove her illness was work-related. But, recently, the photocopier's manufacturer recalled its product after fumes produced by the machine were linked to respiratory impairments just like those Shirley suffered.

Now she plans to file for compensation and has an excellent chance of receiving it. But she has learned that her benefits will be based on a percentage of the wages she was earning eight years ago, when she left the insurance company. And the payments will be further reduced by her ability to work part time. So she may end up receiving less than twenty dollars a week, which hardly seems fair. Through no fault of her own, she can't walk up two flights of stairs without gasping for breath, much less pursue a normal career. Can't she sue her former employer for damages? What about the photocopier manufacturer?

Workers who suffer job injuries or illnesses are entitled to workers' compensation, which pays medical bills and makes up at least part of lost wages during a period of disability. No uniform federal workers' compensation exists. Most workers come under the jurisdiction of state acts (federal statutes cover certain groups, such as maritime, railroad, and federal employees). Each of these 50-odd acts has its own peculiarities, so it's important to acquaint yourself with the particular law that protects you. But since most are similar in principle, their provisions can be outlined in a general way.

At the outset you need to understand that the workers' compensation system is a compromise, essentially a trade-off between conflicting interests. Workers, on the one hand, do not have to prove their employer was negligent—which could be extremely difficult—only that their injury or illness resulted from work. In exchange for assuming no-fault responsibility for all workplace accidents, employers are protected from negligence suits by their employees. Also, benefits awarded under workers' compensation are considerably lower than those in personal-injury cases.

What Benefits Am I Entitled to Under Workers' Compensation?

Weekly cash benefits: These are usually equal to two thirds of your average weekly wage up to a fixed level. Some acts put a limit on the amount of money workers can collect for "temporary total disability." (After you have received that amount, payments will stop unless you prove *permanent* and total disability.) Many acts also compensate partial disability (e.g., if you can work but at a reduced earning capacity).

Medical coverage: This is for all reasonable medical expenses.

Loss-of-function benefits: These are for total or partial loss of use of body parts or senses.

Disfigurement benefits: These are for scars, burns, amputations, or other permanent disfigurements (provided by most states).

Rehabilitation expenses: These are payments for occupational therapy or retraining for workers unable to return to their former jobs.

Dependency benefits: This is an allowance (usually quite small) for supporting spouses and dependent children.

Death benefits: These are for survivors of workers who die from occupational accidents or disease.

What Illnesses and Injuries Are Covered?

Generally, those that "arise in and out of the course of work." This means that if employment *contributes in any way,* an injury or illness is compensable. For example, a disability would be covered that results when a preexisting back condition is aggravated at work—either by a specific accident or from a series of strains or movements.

In most states, occupational diseases are covered, but it is generally much harder to prove they are work-related.

When Should I File a Workers' Compensation Claim?

If you suffer a job-related illness or injury, report it immediately to your employer (although most statutes allow you a "reasonable" amount of time). You should start receiving payments from your employer (if it is a self-insurer) or its insurance carrier or, in a few cases, from state insurance funds. If your claim is contested—which is all too common with such long-term disabilities as back injuries and occupational diseases—you should file a claim with the appropriate state (or federal) agency. Each statute provides for a board or commissioners that hold hearings and rule on contested cases. Procedures and time limits vary among states.

What Is a Lump-sum Settlement?

Sometimes an insurance carrier or a self-insurer will offer an injured worker a "lump sum" of money as a final settlement of her case. But employees are not required to accept such settlements and should never do so without careful consideration and the advice of an experienced workers' compensation attorney. Such lump-sum agreements relieve the insurance company or self-insurer of *all* liability—including possible future medical and rehabilitation costs. Often what seems like a spectacular sum of money may be used up in a relatively short time and hence will fail to provide for a disabled worker's long-term needs.

May I Sue My Employer for Negligence Instead of Filing for Workers' Compensation?

No. Almost every state act shields the employer from such suits, regardless of whether the individual worker is willing to waive the right to compensation in exchange for the right to sue. Workers may, however, pursue product liability suits against manufacturers and distributors of poorly designed machines or toxic industrial chemicals. Such companies—provided they are still in business—are not immune to negligence actions. These "third-party suits," such as those filed against the asbestos manufacturers, can sometimes provide injured workers (or their survivors) with the only way to recover reasonable damages.

How Should I Select a Workers' Compensation Attorney?

Carefully. Representation by a competent attorney is usually a must in contested cases. But especially where a lump-sum settlement is being considered—a set percentage of which is deducted for legal fees—what is best for the attorney is not always best for the client. If possible, find a lawyer through your union or another referral you trust. That way, you're more likely to find one who will be both knowledgeable and ethical in representing your interests. Also, you needn't worry whether you can afford the best legal counsel. Workers' compensation cases are handled on a "contingent fee" basis—the attorney is paid only if you win; if you lose, you owe nothing (see also Chapter 21 on points to consider when hiring an attorney).

STRATEGIES

Workers' options for legal action on job safety and health have expanded enormously in recent years. But a knowledge of those options is only a starting point for those trying to improve conditions. Often, other strategies —such as organizing co-workers, attracting media attention, or a combination of legal and direct action—make more sense.

Purely legal strategies have several limitations that deserve mention. First, they are time-consuming, no matter how strong your case. In OSHA and NLRB proceedings, employers can stall a resolution for years. Second, even when a company loses, penalties are usually minimal. (The American workplace remains one of the safest places to commit negligent homicide.) Third, legal action is expensive, even if your attorney is willing to work for peanuts (few are). Fourth, employers who knowingly violate workers' rights are generally unintimidated by the law. Even a hard-fought legal victory may not deter further violations.

Consider the following examples of successful direct action, which have none of the above drawbacks:

• Office workers who were expected to stay on the job despite a malfunctioning heating system got together and agreed to wear snowsuits the next day. Management was so embarrassed by the spectacle that it corrected the problem without further delay.

• Assembly workers who experienced itching and rashes from fiberglass decided to stage a "nurse-out." When everyone visited the company first-aid room in a single day, the company realized production would go more smoothly if a substitute for the fiberglass could be found.

• Employees of a city health clinic, alarmed about asbestos being removed without precautions, drew up a leaflet explaining the threat to staff and patients alike. Responding to the mere *threat* that the leaflet would be made public, management gave in and instituted safe removal procedures.

FURTHER READING

U.S. Department of Labor, Occupational Safety and Health Administration. *General Industry Standards* (29 CFR 1910). Rev. ed., November 7, 1978. Washington, D.C.: U.S. Government Printing Office, 1979. (Single copies are available at regional OSHA offices.)

Stellman, Jeane M.; and Daum, Susan. *Work Is Dangerous to Your Health.* New York: Vintage Books, 1973. An excellent guide for working people on common chemical and physical hazards in the workplace.

Stellman, Jeane M. *Women's Work, Women's Health.* New York: Pantheon, 1977. Confronts some of the myths about women in the work force and outlines hazards in occupations where women are concentrated (e.g., clerical work, health care, service and domestic work, etc.).

Hricko, Andrea. *Working for Your Life: A Woman's Guide to Job Health Hazards.* Berkeley: Labor Occupational Health Project, University of California (2521 Channing Way, Berkeley, Calif. 94720), 1976. Describes particular workplace hazards for women and what can be done about them.

Urban Planning Aid. *How to Use OSHA: A Worker's Action Guide to the Occupational Safety and Health Administration.* Boston: Urban Planning Aid, 1975. Discusses the strengths and weaknesses of the OSHAct and how workers can best exercise their rights under the law.

Coalition for the Reproductive Rights of Workers. *Reproductive Hazards in the Workplace: A Resource Guide.* Washington, D.C.: CRRWO, 1980. Covers both the health/technical and political aspects of reproductive hazards in the workplace; provides an extensive discussion of legal remedies and strategies for action.

Women's Labor Project. *Bargaining for Equality.* San Francisco: Women's Labor Project, 1981. ($5 postpaid, P.O. Box 6250, San Francisco, Calif. 94101.) A guide to working women's legal rights, including sections on exercising rights to maternity benefits and fighting sexual harassment.

National Labor Law Center. "Safety & Health," Organizing Rights Series Shop-Sheet #2. (1982). $1.75 postpaid, National Labor Law Center, Suite 612, 2000 P Street, N.W., Washington, D.C. 20036. A pamphlet explaining how to use OSHA, NLRB, and union contract language to improve health and safety conditions on the job.

American Labor, no. 15 (1981). "Do-It-Yourself Tactics: Local Action on Job Safety." ($1.50 postpaid, American Labor Education Center, 1835 Kilbourne

Place, N.W., Washington, D.C. 20010.) Describes in detail various nonlegal options for action on job safety and health.

Warning: Health Hazards for Office Workers: An Overview of Problems and Solutions in Occupational Health in the Office. (April 1981). ($4, Working Women Education Fund, 1224 Huron Road, Cleveland, Ohio 44115.) Results of one of the few surveys of office workers' health, touching on stress, office air pollution, and video display terminals.

Makower, Joel. *Office Hazards.* Washington, D.C.: Tilden Press, 1981. A popular review of the scientific conclusions and controversies about health hazards in the modern office.

Radiation on the Job. (1981). ($2.75 postpaid, Low-Level Radiation Project, Coalition for the Medical Rights of Women, 1638B Haight Street, San Francisco, Calif. 94117.) A comprehensive pamphlet outlining hazards from ionizing radiation, especially those encountered in the health-care industry.

Health Protection for Operators of VDTs/CRTs. (1980). ($1 postpaid, New York Committee for Occupational Safety and Health, 32 Union Square, Room 404, New York, N.Y. 10003.) A booklet reviewing the broad range of health problems associated with video display terminals and suggestions for remedies.

15
Starting Your Own Business

RONA F. FEIT

Rona F. Feit is an attorney and small-business consultant in Washington, D.C. She is a former head of the women's business program at the U.S. Small Business Administration and was executive director of President Carter's Interagency Committee on Women's Business Enterprise. Prior to her government service, she practiced corporate law in New York City with the Wall Street law firm of Hughes, Hubbard & Reed. She is a graduate of Columbia Law School and Bryn Mawr College.

More women than ever before have been starting small businesses, and more than a few have built large and successful companies. Increasing numbers of women seem determined to follow their example. If you are one of these women, this chapter is for you.

Legal considerations are obviously only one aspect of starting a business, but knowing how the law affects your business and using this knowledge to advantage is an essential ingredient of entrepreneurial success. Since many laws vary from state to state, and each business situation presents a different set of facts for legal interpretation, no single chapter can provide this essential ingredient, nor can it be a substitute for the continuing "live" legal advice every entrepreneur needs.

This chapter aims, instead, to help you see why you need a lawyer when you are planning to start a successful small business and to give you enough information about the legal context in which a small business gets started to enable you to work more effectively with the lawyer you choose. To do this, the chapter will give you an overview of the few legal questions a female entrepreneur may face in business primarily because she is a woman;

it will discuss the most common legal issues facing any entrepreneur, male or female, showing how and when these issues arise.

You may be thinking that lawyers always say that lawyers are needed. Let me assure you that my views, far from being self-serving, spring from years of experience counseling hundreds of women entrepreneurs. I have seen too many of their businesses fail, too many of their dreams dashed, and too much suffering because they entered business thinking they could do it all by themselves.

Every entrepreneur must have a professional team (lawyer, accountant, insurance agent, and banker) if her small business is to survive in today's economic environment. The margin of error in small-business operations has grown increasingly narrow, and avoidable mistakes and failures to plan that might once have been tolerable are now likely to cause bankruptcy.

It is not easy to find professionals who combine technical competence with good business sense, and it is sometimes hard for a new business owner to judge whether or not she is getting either. The best course is to interview professionals recommended by successful business owners who have used them, and to pick those whose styles and attitudes suit you. Establish at the outset what their charges will be. Then give them a chance. Be polite and pay your bills. But trust your judgment. If you feel they give poor service, get in your way rather than facilitate your aims, are too expensive for what they accomplish or make mistakes, don't be afraid to act on your perceptions and replace them.

When picking a lawyer, look for someone who does not patronize you, who communicates clearly, hears what you say, relates legal advice to your business objectives, and, preferably, has considerable experience in dealing with businesses like yours. Your business lawyer should know what you are doing before, not after, the fact, and should act as a business adviser as you plan. She should be able to tap the expertise of legal specialists when necessary, and should be able to work well with your accountant, insurance agent, and banker. In my experience, having a creative accountant is usually more critical to business success than having a creative lawyer. On the other hand, because legal and accounting concepts overlap, a lawyer who really understands finance and taxes can compensate for a run-of-the-mill accountant who can set up good record systems and file adequate reports but has little sense of financial management and tax strategies. In any case, you will need both.

SPECIAL LEGAL ISSUES FACING WOMEN

The legal issues facing a woman starting a small business *because* she is a woman are few, because the main legal obstacles to women's business ownership have been eliminated. Both single and married women now have the legal right to make contracts, become owners of all kinds of business, borrow money in their own names, and keep and control the income they earn. While women as entrepreneurs still face sex discrimination from customers, suppliers, bankers, and trade and professional organizations, most of this discrimination, however unfair, is not illegal.

Sex Discrimination and Women Entrepreneurs

There have been significant efforts by women's groups, government, and some corporations to overcome the impact of sex discrimination on women business owners. Women's groups have lobbied government at all levels for help and have formed networks for mutual support. Since the mid-1970s, the federal government has responded by supporting efforts to increase public understanding of the past and potential contributions of women entrepreneurs to the economy and by promoting increased management assistance, better access to credit, and more government and private-sector contracts for women-owned businesses. Several states and cities have adopted laws or ordinances giving preference of one kind or another to woman-owned businesses seeking public contracts. A few large corporations have been making special efforts to do more business with women.

Women business owners, as a class, have no legal rights under federal law to special preference from government loan programs, from small-business contract set-aside programs, or from federal contracting officers. They do have the limited benefit of some performance goals in these areas and a national policy to assist woman-owned businesses to enter the economic mainstream. To be eligible for federal programs to assist businesses owned by the "socially and economically disadvantaged," women business owners must prove on an individual basis that they are thus disadvantaged. This has proved to be nearly impossible for nonminority women and nearly automatic for minority women, since these programs were intended to serve minorities when they were started. Even for those women who are declared eligible, the programs may make little difference. Resources are too small to help more than a few people.

You should keep track of special programs for women business owners. Consider joining a businesswomen's network in your area or one of the national organizations of women business owners. Such groups can help you keep informed, avoid the sense of isolation felt by many women in business, and give you practical and emotional support. For information about these groups and the current status of federal laws and programs, write to the Office of Women's Business Ownership, U.S. Small Business Administration (see p. 511 for address).

Credit

Credit is one area where discrimination against women business owners is illegal. Discrimination on the grounds of sex in the granting of both consumer and commercial credit is banned by the Equal Credit Opportunity Act (ECOA). Although ECOA has helped women in the consumer credit area, it offers little assistance in overcoming discrimination in commercial credit. As presently interpreted and enforced, it is inadequate in serving the woman business owner and implies protection where little or none exists in fact.

Marital Status: Problems for the Woman Entrepreneur

The other legal issues facing female entrepreneurs as women are not questions of illegalities, but of protecting interests endangered because they are or were married and became involved in business or property relationships with their husbands. The problems usually arise when the marriage ends, through either divorce or the husband's death, but some occur during the marriage. If you are a married woman planning to start a business, whether on your own, with others, or with your husband, you should learn how the property, inheritance, and domestic-relations laws in your state might affect your rights in the business, and take steps to avoid unwanted results. A good domestic-relations lawyer can advise you on most of these issues.

Some examples of the kinds of difficulties that may arise will help you understand why an unromantic, clear-eyed approach to legalities here is wise. Often, the only asset a married woman entrepreneur can put up as collateral for a business loan is the marital home or other property she owns jointly with her husband. Bankers will then require that both husband and wife sign the note, even if the husband will not be involved in the business in any way. Should there later be a divorce, there is apt to be a struggle over who is entitled to what property. In many states, contributions by a spouse to the acquisition of property during a marriage may give that spouse a claim to part of the property. The wife may find that a portion of her business is declared by the divorce judge to belong to her husband because he once signed a note on her business loan.

Married women who wish to obtain loans completely independently of their husbands may have problems if they hold property jointly with their husbands. Banks tend to ask for as much collateral as they can get and seek to include marital property even when a married woman has considerable property in her own name. Seeking a bank loan guaranteed by the U.S. Small Business Administration (SBA) will not help. The SBA, by statute, is a lender of last resort, and its loan guarantees are available only to those who cannot get credit elsewhere on reasonable terms. If a woman holds property with her husband and using it as collateral could get her a loan elsewhere, she cannot get an SBA-guaranteed loan. Similarly, she cannot refuse to put up such jointly held property as collateral if SBA requests it.

Judges in divorce cases may have considerable discretion in making awards of property between ex-spouses. Most judges are male, and the record is clear that some share sexist assumptions with the rest of society and apply these in court. Even in a community-property state, where, theoretically, property is split evenly between divorcing spouses, the application of the law can be uneven for a woman. In California, a community-property state, a woman and her husband shared equal ownership of a 10-year-old construction company. She was the force behind the success of the company and was the company president. Her husband, a carpenter, played only a minor role in management. The judge, noting that construction is a male-dominated industry and overlooking her role in the company, ordered her to sell her half of the company to her husband. The negotiations over the value of her half went badly (a common problem where a company's stock is not publicly traded and there is no agreed-upon evaluation formula between the owners). She received far less than her interest was worth. She then was unable to find a comparable job in another construction firm and had to start over, building a new company with few resources. Meanwhile, the business she had built was run into the ground by her former husband.

Many wives with less than a controlling interest in family businesses to which they have contributed years of sacrifice and toil gladly agree to their husbands' dominant ownership position as "appropriate" or "traditional." Frequently, they work with their husbands as equals and feel the legal arrangements to be merely technical. They are just as frequently rudely shocked by a husband's will that leaves his controlling interest to someone else (often a son) who does not treat the former wife as an equal and may indeed treat her shabbily.

A wife can protect her interests in her new business or in the new family business if she anticipates the problems and obtains written agreements settling in advance what might turn out to be an area of dispute. If your husband is willing to loan or give you money to start a business, put in writing what claims, if any, this gives him to your business, and be sure both of you sign the agreement. If you are in business together, be sure your ownership interests and rights are formalized in signed, written documents.

Agree at the outset, in writing, to a formula for determining the value of these interests should you divorce, die, or become disabled. Also agree in writing to restrict the transfer of your ownership interests in a manner each approves. Your lawyer may have other suggestions. These matters require tact, but they are easiest to accomplish before you start a business.

GENERAL LEGAL ISSUES FACING ALL ENTREPRENEURS

Except for the legal issues arising because of gender or marital status, the legal issues you, as a woman entrepreneur, will face grow out of the tasks involved in starting a business and the relationships you enter into due to these tasks. The remainder of this chapter will outline for you, roughly in the order they are likely to occur in reality, a representative selection of such tasks and relationships. It will point out which of these tasks and relationships might pose legal issues. Where the legal issues posed are common to many businesses, they will be discussed in somewhat greater detail.

If you consider the process of starting a small business to begin with your thinking about going into business, and to end when the business you have started becomes profitable, the process divides naturally into several phases:

1. The Research and Brainstorming Phase
2. The Choosing-how-to-start Phase
3. The Business Planning Phase
4. The Start-up Phase
5. The Early Operating Phase

THE RESEARCH AND BRAINSTORMING PHASE

In this phase, you are exploring if, how, and when to go into your own business. You will be firming up your personal and business goals; evaluating opportunities and looking for a winning business idea; reading business-for-sale ads; consulting business brokers; reading and studying about starting a business; seeking advice from business people and organizations; assessing your personality and experience to be sure entrepreneurship is for you; choosing the type of business you want to enter; getting as much working experience in such business as is feasible; estimating what such a business would cost to start; identifying potential cofounders or key members of a management team; brainstorming with them about your business idea; shopping around and finally picking a lawyer, accountant, and insurance agent; developing a relationship with a supportive banker; and finally, deciding when to move ahead. You should take plenty of time with this phase and you should be as thorough as possible. One of the biggest mistakes you can make is to be in a hurry to get into business.

Few legal issues surface in this phase. If your evolving business idea has unique aspects, an original concept, or information not generally available, be careful how much you tell to others, lest they steal your ideas. When brainstorming with potential cofounders or managers, where you must be open with your information, draw up separate preliminary nondisclosure agreements that each can date and sign. Each agreement should state that the signer understands three propositions: she is a candidate for the founders' team of your proposed business; she is to be given proprietary and confidential information to allow her to determine whether or not she wishes to join the team, and she agrees to treat the information as confidential and not to disclose it to anyone outside of the start-up group. Have a witness sign and date the agreement as well. If you will be needing a patent on an invention, be sure to start the patent application process as early as possible. It can take years to complete.

If you are interested in a business in a highly regulated industry such as broadcasting, or a recently deregulated industry such as trucking, find a lawyer who understands the industry and the impact that regulation or deregulation can have on it. Evaluate carefully with this lawyer the hassle, uncertainties, and costs you may have in such industry. Be sure you know what laws and regulations apply before you make a choice of any type of business. A woman I know spent time and money developing the plan for a sophisticated placement service before finding out that employment agencies in her state were regulated in such a way that her plan would not work.

Keep track of expenses incurred in organizing your business. You may be able to capitalize and amortize many of these expenses. Ask your accountant for details.

The Choosing-how-to-start Phase

In this phase, you have made the decision to go into a business of a certain kind but must decide how: whether to start your own or buy an existing business. Two common variations on these choices are buying a franchise, and becoming an independent sales representative of one or more direct selling companies.

The practical issues here include deciding which choice best matches your willingness and ability to take risks, your business sophistication, your financial ambitions, your desire for independence, your desired life-style, and your resources. The legal issues that arise with each choice vary, as always, with the circumstances.

Starting Your Own Business

Creating a new small business is the riskiest way to go into business. But though many fail, many are successful. Your first legal concern in starting your own business is to choose the legal business form that suits your purposes best. The basic legal forms are sole proprietorship, partnership, and corporation. All businesses come in one of the three categories, or are variations of these basic forms. Your choice of legal form is an important element in achieving your ambitions, whatever they may be. The form influences the policy and operating control you have over your business, your ability to get financing and to turn your ownership interest into cash someday, your protection from business-connected liabilities, the amount of taxes you pay, the fringe benefits you can take as business expenses, and the legal continuity of your business. One point to remember is that you may change from one form to another. No choice is irrevocable. Reorganizations can be costly, however, especially if there are tax consequences, and you should discuss any possible future changes with your lawyer and accountant so you understand the effects of these costs in advance.

Sole Proprietorships

A sole proprietor is a person who independently runs an unincorporated business for profit. Sole proprietorship is the cheapest and easiest way to start and run a business. This is its chief advantage. To get started, all you have to do is comply with local regulations on licensing and the use of a fictitious business name, if you use one. There may also be special local taxes on the income of an unincorporated business, but they are small. The simplicity and low cost of becoming a sole proprietor may account for the fact that the overwhelming majority of small businesses in the United States are sole proprietorships. There are other advantages: You have complete control of your business; there are no directors and no co-owners. Your business income and your personal income are taxed together, and you may deduct as a business expense personal expenses that are directly related to your business.

There are disadvantages as well. Since the business is legally identical with you, you are exposed to unlimited personal liability for debts and other obligations such as responsibility for damage to a customer's person or property through your negligence. Loans for business purposes will generally be treated as personal loans by your banker, and may be harder to get. You may find creditors, customers, or prospective employees unwilling to deal with you because of concern that you alone are the business and may disappear or die. You will not be able to deduct from taxes your expenses for such typical corporate fringe benefits as medical, disability, and life insurance. You will also not be able to get comparable coverage at comparable costs. There will be no corporate pension plan. You will pay taxes on all your business income at individual rates, not the lower, corporate rates. You will have no opportunity to report your business income to the tax collector in a different fiscal year from your personal fiscal year, as owners of corporations may do, thereby losing the possibility of reducing or spreading your tax burden more evenly over time. Finally, you will lose a number of other tax benefits available only to corporations. Unless you have a very small, marginally profitable business, incorporation is probably wiser than being a sole proprietor.

Partnerships

The legal concept of partnership covers a variety of unincorporated arrangements by which co-owners carry on a broad range of businesses. The most common varieties are general partnerships, limited partnerships, and joint ventures. Whichever variety seems right for you, remember the first rule of partnership: Do not enter a partnership unless your partners are people you respect, trust, and, preferably, like. In the partnership form, you and your partners are at each other's mercy.

A General Partnership: This is an association of two or more persons to carry on, as co-owners, a business for profit. (In some states, a corporation, which is an "artificial person," can be a partner.) General partnerships offer several advantages: They are easy to form. You can form one with a handshake, though a written agreement is generally preferable. This agreement, negotiated with the help of your lawyer, should spell out at least the nature and scope of the business; the duration of the partnership and what happens if one partner withdraws, retires, or dies; the capital contributions in money or property required of each (what and when); how each partner shares in the profits and losses and allocable expenses of the partnership; and each partner's rights and duties. If the terms of the oral or written agreement are not clear, the courts, following the Uniform Partnership Act, will presume that each partner has equal rights and obligations. There are few taxes, regulations, or fees associated with organizing a general partnership. You are usually required merely to register the partnership name and the names and addresses of the partners in your county seat. Partners are a source of money and talent. A general partnership allows you to pool assets and skills in a flexible manner. A partnership files a tax return, but pays no taxes itself. The partners pay its taxes individually. Allocated shares of profits, losses, and certain separable expenses such as premiums on group medical insurance "flow through" to partners in ways that can give them tax advantages. Professional advice and planning are required to do this properly and well. In a partnership, status problems between owners are minimized. All partners are "bosses" in the sense that each partner can legally bind other partners by her actions. This is true even though they may have unequal interests, responsibilities, and payouts. Finally, an advantage of a partnership is that the possibility of becoming a partner can motivate employees to better performance.

The disadvantages of general partnerships are also many. Probably the main disadvantage is that each partner is open to unlimited personal liability for her business acts and omissions and those of every other partner. Another problem is a partnership's uncertain life-span. It is technically dissolved when a partner dies or withdraws, or on the liquidation of a corporation that is a partner. This can be disastrous to a business deal, even though a dissolved partnership can be restructured and continued without the missing partner. Another disadvantage is the result of each partner's having so much power. Lines of authority can cross and there can be management chaos. If a business requires many ad hoc decisions that cannot easily be delegated by type to specific partners, it is probably dangerous to use the partnership form. Raising additional capital may require the addition of a new partner. Agreement by the partners to restructure their partnership to accommodate this can be difficult to obtain. Finally, since a new partner can be admitted only with the consent of all existing partners, it may be difficult to sell or otherwise transfer your partnership interest.

A Limited Partnership: This is a hybrid that combines some of the centralized-management features of a corporation with the tax features of a partnership. It has general partners and limited partners. The general partners have management control and unlimited liability for the acts and omissions of the partnership. The limited partners have essentially no management rights and their liability is limited to the extent of their dollar investment in the partnership. As in a general partnership, the profits, losses, and certain deductible expenses "flow through" to the partners as individuals under an agreed-upon allocation formula. Losses and deductions are commonly allocated mainly to the limited partners to enable them to offset taxable income.

The chief advantage of the limited partnership is its attractiveness to high-tax-bracket investors seeking tax advantages. It is, therefore, particularly popular in real estate, oil and gas, and research and development ventures in which large amounts of capital are required and the law allows substantial tax-deductible expenses.

The disadvantages include the problems of finding suitable partners; the need to master the technical complexities of the tax issues; the difficulties of negotiating a partnership agreement satisfactory to all parties; the need to comply with securities-law requirements (the selling of limited partnership interests is considered "an offering of securities," though certain offerings may be exempt); and the risk that limited partners may feel the partnership agreement has been violated by the general partners and may sue for rescission (cancellation) in an appropriate state court.

In organizing a limited partnership, the interests of general and limited partners are not identical; they should be represented by different lawyers. Once organized, the partnership as a legal entity should have its own lawyer.

A Joint Venture: This is a short-term general partnership of individuals, corporations, partnerships, or any combination of these. It is created to carry out a specific project, such as producing a Broadway play. In some states, a corporation is prohibited from becoming a "partner" but not from becoming a "venturer." When the project for which the joint venture was formed comes to an end, the venture ends.

Like a general partnership, the joint venture allows the pooling of skills and resources in a flexible manner but also limits the commitment of the parties to each other. Its other advantages and disadvantages are basically those of a general partnership.

Corporations

A for-profit corporation is a legal entity, separate and apart from its shareholder owners, that is chartered by a state to carry out legal corporate purposes. It is an artificial "person," liable for its own debts and taxes. Corporations are either public, or private (closely held). Public corporations have widely dispersed and numerous shareholders, while private corporations have only a few, often members of one family. The stock of public corporations is sold initially through public offerings regulated by the Securities and Exchange Commission and then traded on stock exchanges or sold "over the counter." The process of making a public offering of stock is legally complex and expensive, and public corporations are required to file many detailed reports on their operations with the government every year after they become publicly owned. A private, closely held corporation, on the other hand, sells its stock to a limited number of investors abiding by rules that exempt it from government securities regulation and reporting requirements. Certain private corporations may elect to become Subchapter S corporations, a special form permitted by the Internal Revenue Code, that has distinctive tax advantages.

The corporate form has much to recommend it and should be the choice of more entrepreneurs than it is. Statistics show that, taken together, small businesses that are corporations earn considerably more than those using other legal forms. It is unlikely that there is a direct cause-and-effect relationship between the corporate form and business success, but there may

be a relationship between the skill and sophistication of corporate entrepreneurs, their choice of the corporate form, and financial success.

A major advantage of the corporate form is the limited liability it offers
the owners of its corporate stock. A stockholder can lose only the amount
invested in the stock. A claim against the corporation cannot reach the
shareholder's personal assets. Limited liability will be of particular interest
to you if you are entering a business that carries more than ordinary risk
that property or persons might be injured by its operations. The concept of
limited liability will not, however, shield you from paying back loans to
your start-up business if it fails. Lenders consider loans to start-up corporations extremely risky, and they will insist that you pledge your personal
credit to back up such loans.

The corporate form offers tax benefits. Federal income tax rates on
corporate income are generally lower than the individual rates for a proprietor or a partner. You may choose a fiscal year for accounting and tax
purposes that will help your tax payments to occur at times least disruptive
to your cash flow. In addition, you may deduct from corporate income
many expenses not deductible for individuals, especially fringe-benefit costs
such as the premiums for employee life and medical insurance and corporate contributions to employee pension funds.

A corporation, as an artificial person, has a continuous life regardless of
what happens to its owners. This avoids sudden disruptions of the business.
A corporation's perpetual life also means that shares in the corporation will
have value even after the owner's death. Since shares can usually be freely
transferred to others, a corporate owner has great flexibility in estate planning.

The way corporations are structured promotes efficient, centralized management. Policy is made by a board of directors accountable to the shareholders, and officers with clear lines of responsibility are delegated to carry
out these policies. The benefits of corporate management structure are
especially clear in large enterprises with many employees, but they have also
proved useful to businesses involving only a handful of people.

Some entrepreneurs worry that they will lose control of their business if
they incorporate. This worry is unwarranted so long as they own a majority
of the voting shares, or own a large minority position when the rest of the
shares are dispersed in small holdings among many shareholders unlikely
to act together. Voting control can frequently be safeguarded by agreements
among shareholders who together constitute a majority, to vote as one on
key corporate matters. In a closely held corporation, an owner's control can
be as total as in any other form. Achieving this requires the owner to "wear
several hats" and observe the formalities of each role. An owner can be the
sole shareholder, the only or controlling director, and the president of the
company, all at once. With a little legal guidance, it is easy to keep the
records and comply with the legal requirements of each role.

A major benefit of the corporate form is the free transferability of ownership interests. Shares of stock can be sold, given away, put up as collateral, left to heirs, and generally dealt with like any other form of personal property. The transfer of stock will not affect corporate operations unless sufficient numbers of shares with voting rights change hands to shift the control of the corporation or significantly influence the composition of the board of directors. In closely held corporations, shareholders often agree to restrict the transfer of shares to ensure they are in business with people they know and approve. Frequently, these shareholders must offer any shares they wish to sell to existing shareholders before they can sell to others. Shares unregistered with the Securities and Exchange Commission also may not be sold freely to the public. Despite these common restrictions, the ownership interests in a corporation are more freely transferable than such interests in proprietorships or partnerships.

Corporations, as a rule, can raise money for operations more easily than the other forms of business organizations. Lenders and investors are more comfortable dealing with corporations and may and do work out with them a great variety of financing arrangements that would be impossible or awkward with proprietorships or partnerships.

The corporate form is not without disadvantages. It is the most expensive form to set up due to the legal procedures involved in clearing the corporate name, writing and filing the corporate charter, getting it approved, complying with various registration and capitalization requirements, drafting bylaws, and paying a number of related fees to government authorities. There are many published guides to incorporating, including some that are "do-it-yourself." Consult these for background if you wish, but don't do it yourself. Though incorporating is no mystery, it is not merely routine. Be aware that all kinds of slipups can occur in the incorporating process, the process differs from state to state, and failures to understand the significance of variations in charters can lead to reliance on standard approaches that may not fit your future operations and may require expensive changes later. You should have a lawyer's advice on such issues as where to incorporate (you do not have to incorporate in the state where you live and work, and there may be good reasons not to); how to state your corporate purposes; how to structure your shares to ensure future flexibility in getting financing and keeping control of the corporation; and what controls over the internal affairs of the corporation you wish to include in the charter as distinguished from the bylaws (which are easier to change).

A corporation is not only relatively expensive to set up, it is also more expensive and complex to maintain than a proprietorship or a partnership. As a creature of the state, it is more closely regulated than other forms, and these regulations require oversight and record keeping. Meetings of shareholders and directors must be held (even if only one person is a shareholder or a director) and formal minutes kept. A corporation must "qualify" to do business in each state in which it conducts intrastate business and have a registered office and agent there. Often these requirements can be met quite simply. They should not intimidate you.

"Double taxation" is a disadvantage of the corporate form. The corporation is taxed on its income and the shareholder is taxed on dividends which come out of corporate income. The same dollars are taxed twice. The practical consequences of this are usually minimized by the lower tax rates on corporate income and special tax treatment for dividend income. You must weigh how significant this disadvantage is in light of other advantages.

A Subchapter S Corporation: This is a corporation having the distinctive feature of not being subject to taxation at the corporate level. Instead, the taxes on earnings of the corporation, as in a partnership, are paid by the individual owners at individual rates. There is no "double taxation." S corporations are formed and maintained in compliance with Subchapter S of the Internal Revenue Code. As amended in 1982, the law provides that in any taxable year most small business corporations not members of an affiliated group may be eligible to elect S corporation status if the following conditions are present:

1. Only one class of stock is outstanding. (Differences in voting rights among shares of common stock do not create more than one class.)
2. There are 35 or fewer stockholders. (Husband and wife are treated as one stockholder.)
3. No partnerships, corporations, or nonresident aliens are shareholders, and all shareholders are individuals, estates, or certain types of trusts.

To elect S corporation status, you must follow detailed procedural rules, and all stockholders holding stock on the day of election must consent.

The advantages of the S form derive from the power to let profits, losses, deductions, and credits flow through to the owners while maintaining the other advantages of the corporate form. It is a particularly valuable form for the early, lean years of a corporation when there are corporate losses which can offset the owner/manager's salary and other personal income for tax purposes. It is also valuable for family-held corporations that desire to give income to certain family owners who, because of their age, infirmity, or lack of expertise, cannot justifiably be hired as employees. You can abandon S status whenever that becomes advantageous.

The chief disadvantage of S status is that its legalities must be carefully watched. Unintended terminations of status because of failure to meet eligibility requirements can and do occur and can be costly. Termination of status can also occur when passive investment income (such as royalties, rents, dividends, and interest) exceeds 25 percent of gross receipts for three consecutive taxable years and the corporation has earnings and profits. You should judge the risk that is involved here with the help of your lawyer. Inadvertent terminations can now be repaired within a reasonable period of time after the discovery of the event triggering termination. Another disadvantage is that deductions of losses are limited to the amount of the shareholder's "basis" in the corporation (the value of her capital contributions to the corporation for tax purposes). Keeping track of changes in your "basis" is technical, and it generally requires the help of your lawyer and accountant. You may find that the flow-through of losses is less advantageous to you than you expected. Yet another disadvantage is that shareholders, like partners, must pick up their share of corporate income for tax purposes even if that income has not been distributed to them but has been retained in the company to finance growth or for other reasons.

In starting your own business, the correct choice of legal form is the one that is suitable for your entrepreneurial objectives and your personal circumstances. Be sure your lawyer understands these objectives and circumstances and makes clear to you the practical connections between them and the features of each legal form. Then use your lawyer to set up your business in the manner most advantageous to you. Check with your lawyer when conditions change, and adopt a different form of doing business if your lawyer so advises.

Buying an Existing Business

Buying an existing business is generally less risky than starting a new one. Much is already in place, there is less to decide, less uncertainty, and hence less strain on the entrepreneur. There are two basic considerations in purchasing a business: evaluating its worth and getting it at the right price.

You will need professional help to evaluate a business. Your banker is in a good position to check out its reputation and problems. Your lawyer and accountant working together should scrutinize the business's records to give you a picture of the business's true financial condition and to uncover all existing and potential assets and liabilities. The seller should make available to you all the legal documentation of the business, including accounting records, tax returns, leases, contracts, deeds, evidences of debt, patents, trademarks, copyrights, any evidence of lawsuits, outstanding bids, employee benefit plans, and notices of liens or encumbrances on the business property or the property of others. The records of a business may be incomplete either as a result of deliberate intention or because of carelessness. You and your lawyer should review the way the business operated with the present owners to spot where there may be missing records or where there may be inaccurate or doctored records. Your lawyer must understand the government regulations affecting the business in order to be able to assess whether or not the business has been in compliance and what the burden of future compliance might be. Areas of concern here always include tax, labor, and workplace regulation and may include areas such as securities, antitrust, environmental, and consumer-protection regulations. Be skeptical and be thorough. Be sure you know the real reason the business is being sold.

To buy a business at the right price, you first have to know what a fair price is. Then you bargain for the best price you can get. Your lawyer, accountant, and banker can help you determine a fair price after you have checked out the condition and prospects of the business. There are various standard evaluation formulas. The price should reflect the value of a business's assets, the rate of return you can expect to earn on your investment, and sometimes the business's goodwill. You may want a professional appraisal. A major factor in determining the right price is knowing what to buy. You will need legal guidance to determine whether you should buy the entire legal entity, the business assets without the business obligations, the corporate stock, or a partnership interest. Similarly, how you buy the business helps determine what you should pay. The possibilities include paying cash, an installment purchase, a part purchase, part lease arrangement, a down payment plus future payments contingent on future earnings, a down payment plus hiring the seller in a management role and issuing notes to the seller for the remainder, an exchange of notes or shares, or whatever creative financing you and your lawyer and accountant can conceive.

You should tailor your terms of purchase to your financial needs, tax consequences, and practical concerns. Your lawyer should be able to outline options for you and be able either to negotiate a favorable deal for you or help you do so. Your purchase contract should hold the seller to a thorough list of representations and warranties about what you are getting, plus indemnification against your loss from any undisclosed liabilities.

In purchasing a business, be sure you know its profitability trend. Is it positive or negative, and why? You should know your objectives for the business and have a clear plan for reaching them, including reasoned estimates of the sales, cost, and time it will take to reach those objectives. Unless you know this, you cannot negotiate the right deal, and no lawyer can properly represent your interests.

Buying a Franchise

Buying a franchise is a way to start your own business but avoid some of the risks of a new venture. A franchise is a license from a franchising company (franchisor) permitting a franchisee (you) to market a product or service developed by the franchisor in a standardized manner and under conditions set by the franchisor. In return for your franchise fee and a percentage of your profits, as well as your compliance with the franchisor's operational requirements, you receive various kinds of practical assistance in making your franchise operations successful, usually including, at a minimum, both marketing assistance and training.

Buying a franchise is not risk free. Many franchisees fail, even though they have dealt with such well-known and reputable franchisors as McDonald's (fast food) or Baskin-Robbins (ice cream). You have enough control of the operations of your franchise to make mistakes. On the other hand, you do not have enough control really to be your own boss and you will have to share your profits with the franchisor forever. The chief advantage of buying a good franchise is the risk reduction that comes from selling a well-known product or service while being assisted in following a tested method of business management. The chief disadvantage is that you usually have to work as hard as if you had started your own business but cannot profit to the same extent if you are successful.

Every franchise opportunity is different and must be evaluated carefully. The field has been riddled with fraudulent operators promising the moon and gullible purchasers who have believed the promises without checking them out in advance. Because of abuses, the Federal Trade Commission (FTC) in 1978 issued a regulation setting up "Disclosure Requirements and Prohibitions Concerning Franchising and Business Opportunity Ventures." You and your lawyer should get a copy of this regulation and use it as a guide to finding out what you need to know about a franchise opportunity before you make any commitments or pay any money. A married woman should pay attention particularly to the rights of a franchisee's heirs or personal representatives upon the death or incapacity of a franchisee, if the franchisee is to be her husband. Some franchisors have made a rule of refusing to allow a husband's franchise to pass to a wife upon his death or disability, even if she has been working in the business and is well qualified to run it.

Buying a franchise is a complicated and frequently substantial investment; some cost hundreds of thousands of dollars. Get the disclosure the FTC requires. Then check up on what is disclosed. The FTC does not certify the accuracy of required disclosures. You and your lawyer should also go over the details of the franchise agreements you are offered, and be sure that you understand what they mean. Shop for the best deal. Talk to local franchisees of the companies you are considering. The companies are required to give you names and addresses of the franchises. Also check your state's franchising law if it has one. To get a clear sense of what the specific problems may be, write to the International Franchise Association (see p. 512 for address) for their free pamphlet *Investigate Before Investing: Guidance for Prospective Franchisees.* The public library should have one or more of several good books on franchising, and the local office of the U.S. Small Business Administration can direct you to its publications on the subject. See also the list of further reading on p. 370.

Becoming a Direct-sales Independent Contractor

Direct selling is a form of direct-to-consumer marketing through personal explanation and demonstration of products and services primarily in homes. The woman who sells Avon cosmetics, the Encyclopaedia Britannica, or Tupperware is a direct-sales independent contractor. She is in business for herself, acting as her own boss, keeping her own records, paying her own expenses, and controlling her own hours. Over 3 million women are in the direct-selling business, mostly part time but some full time.

There are three primary ways direct selling occurs:

Repetitive Person to Person: Door-to-door route sales, in which salespeople visit homes and sell products or services purchased frequently (e.g., cosmetics).

Nonrepetitive Person to Person: Door-to-door sales of products or services purchased infrequently (e.g., vacuum cleaners).

Party Plan: Salespeople offering products or services to groups at the home of a host or hostess (e.g., clothes).

The advantages of direct selling include the fact that you need little experience and money to start. Training is simple, usually free, and often on the job. The hours are flexible. High earnings (over $100,000 a year) are possible but depend on effort, personality, and the ability to build a sales organization of others you enlist to sell and who give you a percentage of the commissions they earn. Many salespeople earn less than $1,000 a year. Not every direct-sales company offers you the opportunity to build a sales organization. The ones that do are called "multilevel" companies, and some of these also offer the opportunity to become part of company management. There are tax advantages for independent salespeople, since many expenses can be claimed as business related and deducted from income. The Internal Revenue Service has shown some concern that direct-sales independent contractors may stretch the concept of business-related expenses too far, however, and is giving the area close scrutiny.

Direct selling has its disadvantages, too. Depending on the company, you may be required to do extensive paperwork, store inventory, make deliveries, and provide other services besides selling. It is generally thought to be a low-prestige business, though its image is improving. There are many direct-selling opportunities, and you should evaluate carefully the advantages and disadvantages of each.

You must look out for illegal pyramiding schemes (in which recruiting other salespeople brings rewards not tied to sales). You must also look out for companies that make fraudulent claims to consumers and do not deliver as promised, companies that require large initial payments of money before you receive anything in return, companies making promises of extraordinarily high or guaranteed profits, and companies showing reluctance to provide the disclosure required by the law and the Federal Trade Commission. Your lawyer should look over all the agreements you are given to sign before you commit yourself or pay any money.

Before you make any commitments, you should also check with local authorities to see how direct selling may be regulated. Some municipalities require you to register, and many limit door-to-door sales through licensing procedures. Some ban such sales altogether, while others require a fee. In a few places, the company may have been able to secure blanket registration for all its dealers. In some towns, local residents are exempt from registration requirements.

Like franchising, direct selling has its share of fraudulent operators. If you are interested in direct selling, you should contact the Direct Selling Association (see p. 511 for the address). It is a national trade association of leading direct-selling firms. It can help you identify firms that subscribe to its code of ethics and give you other information about the risks, opportunities, and features of direct selling.

The Business Planning Phase

The business planning phase of starting a small business overlaps the previous phases, since deciding the kind of business you want to enter, its legal form, and how you choose to start is part of business planning. With these decisions made, you still have to plan how to run your business. Even a simple direct-selling operation can profit from having a business plan.

A Business Plan: It is important that the plan be written. Only a written plan forces you to look at your business project objectively and thoroughly, to lay out goals for sales and cash-flow projections which, properly used, will help you to manage your business successfully, and to prepare a document that communicates to others (including financing sources, your lawyer, your accountant, and your insurance agent) all the basic information about your business and your plans for it. Putting the plan together with the help of your lawyer and your accountant can take as long as six months to a year, but the effort can save you from going into a business doomed to failure, as well as help you make the most of a good business.

Advice on preparing a business plan is available from the U.S. Small Business Administration and its publications both free and for sale. *The Business Planning Guide,* published by the Upstart Publishing Company, Inc., Portsmouth, New Hampshire 03801 (603-436-0219) is one of the most comprehensive and easily understood guides now available. Its principles apply to all start-ups, but it is aimed at the typical small business which starts modestly and plans for steady growth.

If you are considering starting a less typical small business, one that could expand rapidly to sales in the millions of dollars and yield a high return on invested capital in a short period of time (typically five years), then your business plan should address this challenge. It must not only be a blueprint for operations but also a sophisticated financing proposal. You will need a lot of money to grow this kind of business, and your business plan should show how and when you intend to raise and use this money. This is the kind of company that sooner or later considers a public offering of its stock.

For such a company, you will need to put together a highly qualified management team, and you should probably hire major national law and accounting firms, not only for their expertise but for the favorable impact such representation has on the financiers, investors, and lenders you will need to approach.

The Start-up Phase

In this phase, you are taking the practical steps necessary to open the doors of your business. You will be renting, buying, or constructing business facilities, furnishing them, setting up bank accounts, arranging financing, establishing office systems, setting up credit policies, hiring personnel, ordering supplies or inventory, planning advertising, and taking out insurance.

To accomplish these tasks, you will have to be concerned about complying with a host of relatively petty legal requirements and perhaps with a few of greater complexity. You will need to check federal, state, and local requirements for licenses, permits, and tax registrations. You may need to obtain a general business license or a special one for your type of business, an occupancy permit, or a certification that you have complied with fire, safety, and zoning restrictions. You will need to know what real estate, sales-and-use, employee withholding, self-employment, social-security, unemployment-compensation, personal-property, and federal, state, and local income taxes you may have to pay. You may need an employer registration number or other registrations. Your lawyer and your accountant can help with this and also with the setting up of a tax payment schedule.

In arranging your financing and setting up bank accounts, you will need your lawyer and your accountant to advise you on your options and help you negotiate with your banker or investors.

In hiring personnel and setting up salary structures and employee benefit programs, you may need legal advice on such issues as the need for employment contracts with managers, possibly including agreements not to compete if employment terminates; the legalities and tax ramifications of stock options, retirement, and pension plans; when to use independent contractors instead of employees; and compliance with myriad labor laws.

In setting up record-keeping systems, which you need primarily to operate your business efficiently, you will also need to keep records to substantiate your state and federal tax returns, and your rights under contracts, leases, insurance policies, and claims. Some records must be kept to meet legal requirements concerning employees and their rights.

If you lease, buy, or construct space for your business operations, you will need legal assistance with negotiating and drafting the agreements involved, and possibly with enforcing them. You may need special legal advice on financing real estate. If you need to buy expensive equipment, your lawyer and your accountant should advise you on alternative methods of purchase and their tax and other consequences.

Deciding on your credit policies toward customers, you will face problems of credit risk evaluation and the design of billing forms and collection processes. You will need to consider whether you wish to sidestep these problems by using a nationally recognized credit-card program, or whether it is better for you to develop and maintain your own credit forms that comply with the variety of laws regulating this area. You will need your lawyer's help with all of this.

Insurance planning is crucial to guard against risks that can hurt or destroy your business. You should use a competent insurance agent to work with you and your lawyer annually, to relate your risk-management needs to the financial position and objectives of your business, help you to decide where you should purchase insurance and when you should self-insure (bear the risk of loss yourself), and set up loss-prevention procedures.

The Early Operating Phase

As you begin operating your new business, protecting your interests and complying with applicable laws must be a constant concern. You may be faced with government inspections, penalties, and reports under a variety of laws, and may need to seek hearings, appeal rulings, or bring or fight lawsuits to protect your business interests. Every business is not affected by every law, but you should know which laws may affect you and take care to comply with those that do.

The following listing of specific areas of the law that can affect business operations is not exhaustive but should help you understand the legal context in which you may be doing business.

Labor Relations: A variety of federal laws prohibit discrimination in employment on the basis of race, creed, color, sex, national origin, age (40–65), and union membership; demand equal pay for equal work; set minimum wages, maximum hours, overtime-pay and record-keeping requirements, and child-labor limitations; prescribe a safe workplace; regulate the organizing of unions, and require collective bargaining with unions. There are also state laws that protect employees from losses due to industrial accidents, occupational diseases, and unemployment, and that may require you to make payments into insurance funds. You will need your lawyer's advice on compliance with these laws.

Taxes: Federal and state tax laws change regularly, so they and regulations issued under them must be closely monitored. Your lawyer and your accountant should help you take advantage of beneficial provisions and avoid the impact of the others.

Environment: Federal, state, and local governments have passed laws and regulations to decrease pollution to air, water, and other parts of the environment. You should know which of these affect your business and plan for compliance in your operational design.

Consumer Protection: Many federal laws are designed to protect the consumer from deceptive business practices and unsafe products. In addition, advertising is regulated to ensure that it does not tend to mislead or deceive either by picture or by word. Advertisers are held to their express and implied warranties and are liable for representations made by their advertising agencies. State laws pick up where federal laws leave off.

Fair and Open Competition: Federal antitrust laws seek to preserve fair and open competition. You must not unduly restrain others from competing freely, by boycotts, price-fixing, predatory price cutting, monopoly, or other restraints of trade, nor may others do this to you. You should know your rights and obligations generally, and if a problem arises, you should seek the help of a legal specialist in this area.

Protection of Intellectual Property: The law protects concrete expressions of a novel or useful idea or design with patents which exclude others from using, manufacturing, and selling your product without your authority. Business know-how, which qualifies as a trade secret, is protected by state laws and the common law. Common-law or federal statutory copyright protects literary and artistic property from unauthorized reproduction or performance. Certain words, symbols, or devices may be registered or protected under state and federal laws as trademarks. All these protections are limited and not automatic, and if you need such protection you may need a lawyer who specializes in patent, trademark, and copyright law to advise you.

Credit: Federal and state laws regulate the extension of credit (to whom, with what disclosures, at what interest rates, and under what conditions), how you investigate creditworthiness, and how you can collect what is owed you. Overzealous, oppressive collection practices are illegal. Collecting debts can require resort to the courts and the use of court orders to repossess what you have sold, to take a debtor's property or a portion of a debtor's wages to pay off the debt, or to tie up a debtor's bank account.

Export/Import: Exporting and importing businesses are subject to many laws, foreign and domestic, and are served by several government agencies (e.g., U.S. Department of Commerce's Industry and Trade Administration, U.S. Small Business Administration, U.S. Customs Service), and quasi-public institutions (e.g., the Overseas Private Investment Corporation [OPIC], the Export–Import Bank, the World Bank, regional development banks). You may need a specialist in international trade law to advise you on these laws and agencies. There are regulations about what you may import or export, with what countries you may deal and how you may deal, as well as many other matters.

Commercial Practices: Standards of commercial practice for all businesses are defined in the Uniform Commercial Code (UCC), which deals comprehensively with the legal problems that arise in the distribution of goods. Commercial transactions vary widely, given the complexity of the modern world, yet the UCC provides a legal guide for almost every situation from sales, contracting, methods of payment, banking practices, warehousing, and secured transactions to the use of the full range of commercial documents such as checks, letters of credit, bills of lading, and warehouse receipts. Some states have modified the UCC, and your lawyer should know how to interpret the statutes in the states in which you do business.

Financing: There are many ways to finance a business, and all of them have legal aspects. If you need to go beyond simple loans from bankers, family, and friends to raise money, you are likely to confront the securities laws and regulations designed to protect the public from fraud and dishonest dealings. You may borrow money (debt financing) or sell an ownership interest in your business (equity financing) or use a combination of both.

Debt or equity interests may be offered to restricted groups of investors or venture capitalists and be exempt from expensive registration and reporting requirements, or they may be offered to the public and not be exempt. Before you move in this area, be sure you have financial advisers who understand the options, and a lawyer who knows the securities laws. Despite recent federal efforts to simplify the requirements for small businesses, the issues remain complex and treacherous.

Many experienced business people have said that if you think you cannot afford a lawyer (and an accountant), you cannot afford to go into business, and you don't know enough to be in business. They are right.

This does not mean that you should put yourself passively in the hands of "experts" and just "let the meter run." In business, you must always be in charge. You must know what you want and insist on getting it at a fair price. Women seem to have a tendency to fall into a parent-child relationship with professional advisers, particularly if they are male. Avoid this trap by understanding your business thoroughly and keeping your business objectives foremost in your mind.

As a business owner, do not be intimidated by your awareness that legal questions surround everything you do. The law is there to preserve fair dealing, good-faith actions, open competition, honesty, and responsible behavior. If you follow your own decent instincts to tell the truth, not to take unfair advantage of others, and to be a good citizen, you can operate your business freely, boldly, and creatively without unreasonable risk. That is the secret of free-enterprise success and the fun of having your own business.

FURTHER READING

Bangs, David H., Jr.; and Osgood, William R. *Business Planning Guide.* Portsmouth, N.H.: Upstart Publishing.

Becker, Benjamin M.; and Tillman, Fred A. *The Family Owned Business.* Chicago: Commerce Clearing House. (Guidance on all aspects plus valuable sections on family conflicts and problems of widows.)

Finn, Richard P. *Your Fortune in Franchising.* Contemporary Books.

Honigsberg, Peter Jan; Beatty, Jim; and Kamoroff, Bernard. *We Own It: Starting and Managing Co-ops, Collectives and Employee Owned Ventures.* Laytonville, Calif.: Bell Springs, 1981.

Kamoroff, Bernard. *Small Time Operator: How to Start Your Own Small Business, Pay Your Taxes and Stay Out of Trouble—A Guide and Workbook.* Laytonville, Calif.: Bell Springs, 1981.

Lane, Marc J. *Legal Handbook for Small Business.* New York: AMACOM, 1978. (Some information is dated but still a useful guide.)

National Labor Relations Board. *A Layman's Guide to Basic Law Under the National Labor Relations Act.* Washington, D.C.: U.S. Government Printing Office.

Taylor, C. *Women and the Business Game: Strategies for Successful Ownership.* New York: Simon & Schuster.

U.S. Department of Commerce. *Basic Guide to Exporting.* Washington, D.C.: U.S. Government Printing Office.

U.S. Department of Commerce. *Franchise Opportunities Handbook.* Washington, D.C.: U.S. Government Printing Office.

U.S. Department of Labor. *A Handy Reference Guide to the Fair Labor Standards Act.* Washington, D.C.: U.S. Government Printing Office.

Warner, Ralph. *Everybody's Guide to Small Claims Court.* Reading, Mass.: Nolo Press/Addison Wesley, 1980.

FREE OR ALMOST FREE BOOKLETS AND BROCHURES

Lists of free and for-sale management assistance publications of the United States Small Business Administration are available from any SBA district office or from SBA, P.O. Box 15434, Fort Worth, Texas.

Bank of America publishes a useful Small Business Reporter series, free at branches or $2.00 per copy. Write Bank of America, Dept. 3120, P.O. Box 37000, San Francisco, Calif. 94137 for information about their *Business Profiles, Business Operations Reporters* and other publications, including *Franchising* and *How to Buy or Sell a Business.*

Federal Trade Commission, Washington, D.C. 20580 publishes *Advice for Persons Who Are Considering an Investment in a Franchise Business,* Consumer Bulletin No. 4. (Free)

Patent and Trademark Office, U. S. Department of Commerce, Washington, D.C. 20231: *General Information Concerning Trademarks; General Information Concerning Patents; Questions & Answers About Patents; Patents & Inventions: An Information Aid for Inventors.* (Free)

Internal Revenue Service, Department of the Treasury, publishes free the *Tax Guide for Small Businesses,* Publication No. 334 (revised annually). Available at any IRS office, it is complete and indispensable.

PERIODICALS

Inc. magazine, 38 Commercial Wharf, Boston, Mass. 02110 (focuses on growth-minded businesses with more than $1 million in annual sales).

In Business magazine, J. G. Press, Inc., Box 323, Emmaus, Pa. 18049 (directed to owners of smaller-scale businesses with under $1 million annual volume concerned about their businesses' impact on their communities and life-styles).

16
Planning for Retirement

MARTHA KEYS

Martha Keys, B.A., member, United States House of Representatives, 1975–79, special adviser to Secretary of Health, Education and Welfare, 1979–80, member, National Commission for Social Security Reform, Washington, D.C.

Retirement planning is a revolutionary concept for too many women. Younger women are generally disinterested; married women have traditionally left it to their husbands. Many facts of life in today's society make it essential to think ahead about retirement in a way that was much less necessary or even possible in the past.

Every woman, married or single, should start planning for her *own* retirement years as soon as she starts work, or when she is of an age to start work.

In the 1980s a large part of the work force of whole cities is out of a job because of the closing of a steel mill, a copper mine, or some other industrial plant that may never open again. In a family in which the husband is the main wage earner, it doesn't make sense for the couple to keep their fingers crossed and hope he will never get laid off in the course of his working life. The majority of working women are in low-paying occupations that will produce at best a tiny pension to supplement Social Security income; but, married or single, women still need to find ways to put away sufficient money in the course of their working lives to provide for themselves after they are 65 years of age. One of the best side effects of this is that by agreeing to take control of their own economic planning, women are taking an *active* role in their own present and future lives.

Planning is especially important for the woman who has decided to stay home while she raises her children. We give lip service to the importance of home and motherhood, but that's *all* we give. Social Security does *not* give credit to the homemaker for the work she performs in the home—although the estimated value of such work is around $20,000 a year. This makes it essential for even the full-time homemaker to earn at least a minimal amount of money from paid work each year if she is to qualify for Social Security benefits herself, rather than being solely dependent on her husband's Social Security benefits. A homemaker who, let's say, earns $1,000 a year typing at home not only can contribute and qualify for Social Security benefits, but can also, as a self-employed person, open a Keogh tax-deferred account and perhaps even deduct expenses for a home-based office from her income tax. (See pp. 511 for the address of the National Alliance of Home-Based Businesswomen.) However, if a woman *doesn't* earn any money from paid work, not only is she ineligible for her own individual Social Security benefits (as opposed to dependent or survivor benefits), and she cannot open either an IRA or a Keogh tax-deferred account.

The need for planning is underlined by the plight of older women in the 1980s. The following statistics are from the 1980 White House Mini-Conference on Older Women:

- Women retire on less than half the income that men retire on.
- Eighty percent of retirement-age women have no access to pensions other than Social Security.
- The average age of women at widowhood is 56.
- One third of all widows live below the official poverty line.
- Less than 10 percent of widows receive private-pension survivor benefits.
- Two thirds of widows live alone.
- Three fifths of all women over 65 are unmarried, while three fourths of men over 65 live with their spouses.
- At age 75, there are twice as many women as men.
- Women outnumber men in nursing homes more than two to one.
- Ninety percent of women are eligible for Social Security, and in 1980 more than 60 percent of those collecting had no other income.

What adds urgency to the situation is the fact that life expectancy for women has grown from 48 years at the turn of the century to 78 years today (7 years more than life expectancy for men). In spite of this, little public attention has been given to the unique needs and resources of older women. Thus, they are too often the victims of poverty, social injustice, and isolation. Younger women can escape this trap, but it takes both a healthy understanding of the institutions that govern the flow of income in later life and flexibility of mind and spirit, to take advantage of the opportunities that exist.

A good way to begin is to stop thinking of life as a series of neat and separate boxes: education, marriage, work, children, and retirement. Such a concept is entirely irrelevant to our world today, where learning opportunities are lifelong, work takes many forms from childhood throughout life, and retirement is only a time when income that has been set aside earlier can replace earnings from current full-time work. Retirement does not mean leaving the active arena of life. It can be the time to embark on a new career, or it can mean the time and freedom to pursue activities of interest.

Women must not delay beyond age 45 in thinking seriously about income at age 65 and beyond. Obviously, the earlier you start the better.

STEP-BY-STEP PLANNING

There are a number of steps all women should take if they are able to do so. These are small steps, but taken one at a time they can build up over a period of years to a measure of financial security.

Establish a Credit Record

Married and single women, whether they are full-time homemakers, students, or working, who do not have credit cards in their own names, and separate checking/savings accounts, should take steps to establish a credit identity without delay. Credit is an important asset, and it may be very hard to establish after divorce when you have an urgent need.

Individual Life Insurance

There are many types of life insurance available, and both married and single women can investigate this option to find out if it suits their individual needs. Women often rely on a spouse, or if they're single think that life insurance is not for "single people." However, there are many plans, and this is something a woman should investigate herself and make a personal decision.

Health Insurance

Women who are widowed or divorced in their fifties, especially if they have ever had a serious illness, may find it difficult or impossible to get health insurance. It is risky to rely on a spouse's insurance, especially in a time of high unemployment. If you are covered as a spouse by your husband's health insurance, you may not be able to continue your coverage if you divorce or your husband dies. An inquiry to the company should bring you the answers as to whether or not your coverage could be continued, that is, continued at the present level and continued at an affordable cost in either of these events. Obviously if you are covered by an individual policy, you do not have this problem.

Although health insurance is expensive on an individual basis, remember that if you are self-employed you may find it worth while to go into partnership with two other business people, because you would then be able to get the much lower group insurance rates.

IRAs and Keoghs

IRAs (Individual Retirement Accounts) are open to all employed women. If a woman with a full-time job does work at home, she may also qualify for a Keogh (for self-employed people). At the end of the chapter, you will find a list of books on IRAs and Keoghs; or you can check at your savings-and-loan or commercial bank for further information. In the case of Keogh tax-deferred accounts, there is quite a bit of flexibility in the type of account or accounts you can set up, so it pays to do some research beforehand.

The basic principle behind both IRAs and Keoghs is to defer taxes in the year in which you make a deposit. Then, at age 59½, when you are entitled to start withdrawing money, you may well be earning at a lower level than you did during your regular working life, and thus will pay tax at a lower rate on the withdrawals.

Job Training and Further Education

On pp. 385 you will find a list of free or inexpensive publications available from the Consumer Information Center. Before embarking on a program of job training or further education it is *essential* to check up on the job trends in your area. There's no use struggling to get qualified for work that isn't available within commuting distance. Since many of the "pink ghetto" jobs such as file clerk or secretary are poorly paid, women may want to investigate apprenticeships in such areas as construction, manufacturing, or service trades, which lead to much higher pay scales. (See pp. 385 for a pamphlet published by the Consumer Information Center.)

Whether you are entering a job-training program to get the skills to go to work for the first time, or whether you are going back to school to get a high school equivalency certificate or a bachelor's or master's degree in order to upgrade your present job, you are taking important steps toward future economic security.

The most encouraging feature of going back to school as an "older" student (that's anybody from the mid-twenties on!) is that you have a lot of company. Many women, from their twenties to their eighties, are deciding to go back to school to complete their education or start off on a new track. And don't forget: the sooner you get started, the better off you will be.

Miscellaneous Survival Tips

If you are already working and have been for some years, it is important to remember that a percentage of your annual earnings or take-home pay should be set aside in a savings account, mutual fund, Keogh or IRA (where applicable), or some other income-producing source. There are many excellent books available to introduce the beginning investor to the complexities of the market. There are also courses at local community colleges on investment. But remember: the stock market is not for novices. It is a form of gambling, and you should never invest more than you can afford to lose. The methods of saving money listed above are less glamorous but safer for those who can't afford to lose money.

Real Estate: If you are considering buying a home, whether you are single or married you may find that a two-family house is a good buy. The rent on the second unit can cover all or most of the mortgage and other costs, and when the mortgage is paid off you will still have money coming in to help defray property taxes and maintenance expenses.

If you're in your twenties, thirties, or forties and considering buying a one-family house, you may want to check first on zoning restrictions. When you are approaching retirement age, you may want to renovate your home into a two-family, rather than sell it and move to a smaller house or apartment—especially if you have grown children who no longer live at home. As mentioned above, rental income could cover maintenance and taxes after the mortgage is paid off.

Home sharing is another reason to check zoning regulations before you buy a home. The home-sharing movement is growing among people of all ages, and it is certainly worth considering for the retirement years when, statistically, a woman is likely to be on her own. (It is safer and more economical to have a housemate than to live alone.)

If you own your own home and have done so for three years or more and you or your spouse is 55 years old or over, you can now sell your home with up to $125,000 capital-gains tax free. This is a once-in-a-lifetime benefit, and you will need the advice of a lawyer or a real estate broker in order to estimate whether you stand to gain enough to make such a sale worthwhile.

Whatever preventive measures you take, it is essential to know the legal requirements of the retirement institutions that will provide most of your income after 65. Each is different; each will respond to you based on the decisions of others as well as your own decisions; probably none will adequately respond to the full and unique patterns of your life and productive work. You can avoid the pitfalls that lead to becoming a poverty statistic and preserve the basic plank of a good life in later years—a decent income —if you are lucky and if you understand the quirks of all pension systems which bar women from receiving adequate retirement benefits.

Definitions of three basic terms follow. They will appear often in the following discussion.

- **Worker benefit:** A primary benefit to which a person is entitled, based on a record of work, contribution, earned retirement credits, and age. Social Security and a company pension plan are examples of worker benefits.
- **Dependent benefit:** This is a derivative benefit usually for a spouse, based primarily on the record of work, contribution, earned retirement credits, and age of another person.
- **Survivor benefit:** This is a benefit for the surviving spouse of a worker. In the case of pensions other than Social Security, its existence will depend on election by the worker at the time of retirement to provide a survivor annuity.

SOCIAL SECURITY

Social Security is the most important source of retirement income for women today. In the 1980s, 90 percent of women over age 65 receive a Social Security benefit either as a retired worker, dependent, or survivor. At the time of writing, it is tax-free income and also is protected from inflation by an annual cost-of-living increase. But Social Security alone is not sufficient income for anyone's retirement needs. Nevertheless, it is the sole source of income for more than 60 percent of today's single (never-married, divorced, widowed) women over 65 years of age.

The Social Security law was passed in 1935 and, without question, it has served women better than any other system. However, it remains a system based on four assumptions that work to the *disadvantage* of women, namely that:

- men are the sole wage earners for the family,
- women are typically homemakers,
- there is no economic value to work in the home, and
- marriages last a lifetime.

Although these assumptions may have had some bearing on the society of the 1930s, it is easy to see how poorly they reflect the society of the 1980s, with the majority of married women in the paid work force earning an average of 39 percent of family income. The fact that one in two marriages ends in divorce is another significant change.

The following chart will show some of the ways that you might be treated by the Social Security system in the determination of your retirement benefit.

	AGE OF ELIGIBILITY	PERCENTAGE OF BENEFIT
As a worker	65	100%
As a worker	62	80%
As a dependent (wife of retired or disabled worker)	62	50%
As a widow	65	100%
As a widow	60	71.5%
As a disabled widow	50	71.5%

If You Are a Worker in the Labor Force

Social Security is designed to provide the best benefits to those workers who have been in the labor force on a continuing basis, and its benefits are higher for those who have earned higher incomes. Most other retirement systems work in the same way. If you work most of your life with little or no interruption, then your Social Security benefit will fairly reflect the credits you have earned by your work and will be based on the amount of your lifetime earnings and taxes paid.

Work Credits

You qualify for benefits by accumulating work credits. These are divided into "quarters of coverage" (check with your local Social Security office to see how much income you must earn in each quarter to qualify). For example, if you are self-employed you must earn at least $400 in a year before you acquire any coverage. Workers born in or after 1929 will need 40 quarters of coverage to qualify for retirement benefits. A quarter of coverage is obtained by wages in covered employment of more than $50 in a calendar quarter. Each year's earnings will be averaged together to reach an average annual earnings. The formula provided in the Social Security law will be applied to this figure to compute the level of benefit that you will receive each month.

However, if you choose to spend years out of the labor force, perhaps while your children are young or when special family needs arise, you will have a problem. Your decision will mean that years of zero earnings will be averaged into your annual earnings over your work life. As Marilyn Block put it, "Women are punished if they elect to drop out of the labor force to raise families." Many women find that they can never build up enough of a work record to make up for those years out of the labor force and thus qualify for a satisfactory benefit.

These zero years when coupled with low women's salaries account for the fact that last year more than 2 million women who had worked and paid taxes over enough time to qualify for Social Security instead received the 50 percent dependent benefit derived from their husband's work record, because it was higher than their own benefit. The dual-entitlement provisions of Social Security will automatically select the higher of the benefits to which you are entitled: your worker benefit or a dependent benefit (providing your husband has reached the appropriate age and made the decision to retire). However, this is inadequate compensation for continuous productive work for the family unit, whether inside the home as a full-time homemaker or outside in the labor force. This is occasionally referred to as the nonduplicative provision of Social Security, making it sound quite efficient and fair. However, this inability to combine periods of work at home with periods of work in the labor force for an earned retirement right is detrimental to women and very unfair.

If You Are a Dependent Spouse

As a 62-year-old wife of a worker, you will be eligible for a 50 percent benefit to be added to your husband's benefit at the time that he reaches an appropriate age (62 or 65) and decides to quit working and earning full wages (Social Security's retirement test prevents full benefits from being paid to a person under 72 earning more than $6,000 annually). The dependent benefit bears little relation to your own life or work other than that you must be age 62 to be eligible for it. It is almost entirely contingent upon the age, retirement decision, and work record of your husband, the primary worker.

If You Are Divorced

Marital status will not affect you as a worker with individual eligibility for Social Security. However, in order to have any rights to a dependent benefit based on your former husband's record, your marriage must have lasted at least ten years (reduced from twenty years in 1977). In addition, your benefit depends on several other factors:

• That you not remarry;
• Your former husband reaches retirement age (or becomes disabled or dies);
• Your former husband's obligations to a new dependent spouse and/or family do not cause the maximum family benefit to be reached, and
• You are the appropriate age also.

It is interesting to note that the benefit level would be different in the case of retirement, disability, or death of your former husband, although this would have no relation to your needs.

If You and Your Husband Are Retired

The unrealistic structure of Social Security will affect the level of income that you and your husband receive when both of you live in retirement; and it will affect the surviving spouse (statistically the widow) even more. Couples in which both husband and wife have worked and earned individual worker benefits will have lower combined benefits in retirement than couples in which one person alone has earned the same level of family wages over the years. The chart below shows the differences in both retirement benefits and survivor benefits for both types of couples. The larger retirement benefit for Couple A is caused by the dependent benefit available to the spouse who has not worked. The larger survivor's benefit for Couple A results from the widow's receipt of the full 100 percent benefit of her worker spouse. The widow of Couple B will receive only one worker benefit, either her own or her husband's, whichever is higher.

Average Family Earnings	*Couple A One Earner*	*Couple B Two Equal Earners*
$9,000	$6,336	$5,546
12,000	7,776	6,528
18,000	9,624	8,448
21,000	10,308	9,408
SURVIVOR A		SURVIVOR B
9,000	4,224	2,784
12,000	5,184	3,264

If You Are a Widow Before 60

Dependent benefits do not exist for widows until they are at least age 60, with two exceptions: the presence of children under 16 of the deceased worker and the disability of the widow, which would entitle her to receive a portion of a survivor benefit at age 50. Further, if a widow under 60 is receiving benefits, she will lose them if she remarries. This period of early widowhood, called by many the "widow's gap," is a very traumatic time. Employed women may well face prejudice on grounds of sex and age in addition to having to deal with personal grief. For women who have had little or no experience in the job market, it can be catastrophic. It is not an easy time of life to gain entry into the labor force for the first time, although it can be done. (See p. 385 for a pamphlet describing federal aid programs for those who are returning to work, and see p. 545 for a list of organizations aiding older women.)

It is essential that women face the possibility of finding themselves in the "widow's gap" and realize that income during the pre-60 years will have to come from *somewhere*—either from employment, assets, insurance, or investments. If you are approaching this age and have never worked or haven't worked for years, you should consider acquiring job skills your number one priority.

If you or a member of your family has become disabled, or a member of your family has died, you should check with your nearest Social Security office to see if you or anyone in your family is eligible for benefits. Many people miss out on benefits to which they are entitled, because they don't know they are eligible. Social Security benefits must be applied for; they won't come to you by magic.

Social Security Changes

The Social Security law has gone through many changes since 1935 regarding coverage, eligibility, taxes, and amount of benefit. Basic changes in the overall structure have not yet occurred, although they have been recommended many times and with increasing frequency since the mid-seventies. It is essential for all women to be aware of changes in the law, which are certain to occur in the future. It will be beneficial if there is an end to the treatment of the spouse as an adult dependent, so that all women will have the right to retirement income in response to their productive work, whether it is done in the home or in the workplace.

OTHER PUBLIC PENSIONS

Most federal employees and about one fourth of state and local employees are not covered by Social Security retirement benefits. As a worker in the federal civil, military, or foreign service, you will earn a benefit through those retirement systems based on your contribution, years of work, salary, and age. (Military personnel are also covered under Social Security.) Like Social Security, most federal pensions are adjusted each year based on the increased cost of living. However, unlike Social Security (at the time of this writing), these pensions are included in taxable income. Federal employees hired after 1983 will be covered by Social Security and an additional civil service plan. Although the specific provisions of this plan are not set at the time of this writing they will probably follow the general plan in effect before 1983. If you are affected by this new system you should obtain current information from the division of personnel where you or your spouse work. Few individual pension plans for state and local employees have any cost-of-living adjustments; if they do, they are adjusted at only a fraction of the increased cost of living, and all are taxable.

If You Are a Dependent Spouse of a Government or a Military Worker

The spouse of a federal worker will be treated very differently from the spouse of a Social Security retiree. Federal employees must elect to provide a survivor annuity at the time of their retirement. This means accepting a lower monthly retirement benefit in exchange for the continuation of that benefit to the surviving spouse. In the past, there have often been devastating consequences to the uninformed widow who suddenly stopped receiving her monthly retirement check and learned that her husband had decided not to provide a survivor annuity. As a result of a change in the law in 1980, the worker must at least have the written or witnessed acknowledgment of the spouse in order to refuse to provide the survivor annuity. This is a very important change.

The many plans covering the 28 percent of state and local government workers who are not covered under Social Security are all different. However, like other private pensions, they offer much less protection to the spouse as a survivor. A woman should know the particular provisions of her husband's plan and discuss with him the consequences for the survivor.

If your spouse is in either the Foreign Service or military service, or works for any government department you should investigate your rights specifically. In both areas recent court cases and legislation have contributed to specific differences in treatment. There has until recently been no coverage for divorced spouses in civil, foreign, or military service retirement; however, both the military and Foreign Service systems have acknowledged the court's right to divide benefits in certain cases in response to judicial decisions or legislative direction.

PRIVATE PENSIONS

Each year, more women are being covered by private pension systems. Yet in 1980 only 14 percent of women over 65 received any income from a private pension—either as a worker or as a survivor. If you are an employee who can participate in a private pension plan, or a spouse who depends on the private pension coverage of your husband, you need to know several facts.

Vesting in a Private Pension Plan

There are many reasons why few women have coverage under private pensions: industry, occupation, union membership, size of firm, etc. Nevertheless, as you may participate in a private pension plan, you should be aware of the several legal provisions that will make it difficult for you to gain vested rights to a pension. If you are vested, you have earned the right to receive a pension at retirement even if you leave the company beforehand.

Commonly, vesting requires 10 years of work for the same employer. If there is an interruption in this work, it cannot be longer than the term of previous work, or all rights are lost and the person must begin again to accumulate the 10 years required for vesting. Thus, if you work for 3 years, then remain at home for 3½ years and return to work for the same employer, you probably will have to begin again on the vesting period. Also, a pension plan does not have to be offered to a worker until age 25.

Childbearing, moving to accommodate husband's career changes, and other factors combine to make it difficult for women employees to meet this requirement of 10 years with the same employer. The vesting time and the lack of transferability of private pensions are much greater problems for women than for men. In fact, as recently as 1980, the average job tenure for women was 2.6 years.

If You Are a Spouse of a Worker with a Private Pension

Your protection as a spouse is much less sure in private pension plans. There are several reasons for this. First, the election of a survivor annuity must be made by the worker at the time of retirement. This is done simply by a signature. Unlike the new law for federal retirees, there are no requirements in law for joint signature or notification of the spouse of a private annuitant. The decision to provide a continuing benefit for the surviving spouse will mean taking a lower monthly benefit while both spouses are alive. Obviously this is a subject of discussion for you and your spouse.

Secondly, if the worker should die before actually reaching retirement age, ERISA (the federal law that sets minimum requirements for qualifying private pension plans) does not require any survivor annuity to be paid— and few plans provide such annuities. This could occur while the worker is still on the job or after resigning, but before reaching the appropriate age. This often happens even though the worker has worked for many more than the requisite number of years for vesting and has earned the right to a pension at retirement age.

Statistically, you are apt to be on your own during some of your aging years, like it or not. Contemplation should be given in advance to options of education, training for new employment, and new ventures that could give more excitement to your life in the future and bring more financial security as well.

Community services—colleges, state educational agencies, YWCAs, church groups, and women's centers—are expanding their interest and offerings for educational programs for midlife planning. This is a good way to open your mind to nontraditional and postretirement careers both paid and voluntary. Like many others, you will probably find hidden abilities that haven't been used for years, if ever. Many times, these are the basis of work alternatives that can add to your income as well. These approaches to planning—preventive approaches and strategies—are best for both health and income security.

Remember all of the possibilities of retirement income: social security, other pensions, employment, savings and investments, assets, new lifestyles. Several of these may add up to income security for you in retirement years.

FURTHER READING

The following publications are available from the Consumer Information Center, Department H, Pueblo, Colo. 81009. Write for their Consumer Information Catalog for the most recent prices and publications:

College Costs/1981–82. 204K.

Exploring Careers: The World of Work and You. 222K.

Federal Financial Aid for Men and Women Resuming Their Education or Training. 508K.

Job Openings. 510K.

Job Options for Women in the 80's. 123K.

The Job Outlook in Brief. 124K.

Know Your Pension Plan. 509K.

Matching Personal and Job Characteristics. 125K.

Merchandising Your Job Talents. 126K.

Occupational Outlook Quarterly. 127K.

Student Guide—Five Federal Financial Aid Programs. 512K.

Study and Teaching Opportunities Abroad. 128K.

A Woman's Guide to Apprenticeship. 228K.

A Woman's Guide to Social Security. 513K.

A Working Woman's Guide to Her Job Rights. 129K.

Your Social Security. 514K.

William J. Grace, Jr. *The ABCs of IRAs.* New York: Dell Publishing, 1982.

Guide to Retirement Planning. Available from Lord, Abbott & Co., Retirement, P.O. Box 666, Wall Street Station, New York, N.Y. 10005—free.

A Shopper's Guide to IRAs and Keogh Plans: Choosing a New Plan and Evaluating the One You Have. Available from NROCA Press, Box 12066, Dallas, Tex. 75225.

Part Four

WOMEN AND CRIME

Your Rights in the Criminal Legal System

17
What to Do if Arrested or Called to Testify

GERALDINE S. RUSSELL
JULIE E. O'CONNOR
THERESA J. PLAYER

Geraldine S. Russell is an attorney in private practice in San Diego, California. She is certified as a criminal law specialist by the State Bar of California and represents individuals accused of serious crimes.

Julie E. O'Connor is an attorney practicing criminal-defense and juvenile law in San Diego, California. She is active in bar and community organizations.

Theresa J. Player is Director of the Legal Clinic at the University of San Diego Law School. She was formerly in private practice in San Diego specializing in criminal-defense and family law.

IF YOU HAVE BEEN THE VICTIM OF A CRIME OR A WITNESS TO A CRIME

At some time in your life, you may be the victim of a crime. Or perhaps you may be a witness to a crime against someone else. Should you find yourself in such a situation, we offer these suggestions for ways to cope with some experiences you are likely to encounter.

What to Do Immediately
The first thing to keep in mind is that it is very important to remain as calm and clearheaded as possible. This may be extremely difficult, but the first few moments after a crime has occurred can be crucial.

In many cases, the first thing to do is to call the police. If you need more immediate help, call a neighbor. When you call the police, be sure to give all the pertinent information, especially the address, the time, and any information you have about the person who committed the crime. Listen carefully to the questions the dispatcher asks you and try to answer as completely as possible.

While it is still fresh in your mind, write down every single detail about the incident that you can remember. For example, if your house has been burglarized, these details would be important:

1. Exact time of day you noticed items missing.

2. Anything unusual in the premises (look for windows, doors, etc., that have been broken).

3. As complete a list as possible of the missing items. A list previously made for renter's or homeowner's insurance can be helpful. Serial numbers on the items are especially crucial in obtaining recovery. Photographs of the items might be the best evidence.

If the situation is one in which you actually saw the person who committed the crime (often called the "perpetrator"), write down as soon as possible a complete description of the individual(s), including:

Height (as nearly as possible; e.g., "tall");

Weight or build (approximate number of pounds or description of type: heavy, slim, muscular, etc.);

Hair (length, color, texture; e.g., short, dark, curly);

Age (as nearly as possible);

Color of eyes;

Color and texture of complexion;

Presence, color, shape, texture of facial hair (if any);

Clothing (color and type);

Shoes (type and color);

Whether a hat was worn and its description;

Voice (high, low, husky, etc.);

Any particular words or phrases used;

Any distinguishing marks or characteristics (scars, tattoos, a limp, etc.).

If you have any drawing ability or if you have access to someone who does, draw as complete a picture as possible while the image is still fresh. Many police departments now have artists who can draw from a verbal description.

Regardless of the crime involved, you should not change anything. For example, if you are the victim of a burglary, don't touch anything, don't open or close doors or windows, don't move furniture; you might erase valuable clues such as fingerprints; you could make it more difficult to determine how entry was gained. If you were personally assaulted, battered, or robbed, do not clean up or change your clothes before the police arrive. It is very helpful if the police can see and record everything, either in writing or with a camera, including cuts, bruises, torn clothing, etc.

This is especially true if you have been raped. Do not take a bath or douche—this will destroy important identifying information as well as crucial evidence of the crime. You will be asked to submit to a pelvic examination by a physician who will examine the pelvic area carefully and take samples. Some police departments now have personnel who have been trained to deal with rape victims in a sensitive and helpful manner. If the police person interviewing you is insensitive or discourteous, you have the right to request another person (see Chapter 19).

How to Deal with the Police

When a crime is reported, the police will be the first agency to take any action. Generally, one officer will be designated as the investigating officer and will ask questions of the victim and any available witnesses, search the area for evidence, and write up and file a report. If necessary, follow-up investigation will be conducted and supplemental reports will be filed. Remember, the main method of gathering information is to question witnesses, especially the victim.

Your role in this investigation is to give complete and detailed information about anything you perceived: basically, anything you saw, touched, heard, tasted, or smelled. In short, you should give them information from your own personal knowledge. Here are some suggestions for specific problems in dealing with the police:

1. Tell the police only what you actually remember. DO NOT GUESS. If you are not sure, don't be pressured into giving information just to answer the questions.

2. Do not let the police suggest any details to you. They may have someone in mind as a possible suspect, but don't try to make your description fit that person just to make the police happy. If you provide a description that includes details not from your actual memory, but from those which have been suggested by the police, this may come up in court and lessen your credibility.

3. One situation that arises frequently is that the police may ask you to try to identify the perpetrator from a group of people. Either this might be done at a lineup in the police station or you may be shown a series of pictures and asked if the suspect is among them. This is often difficult and frustrating. It is extremely important that you be as accurate as possible. If you don't know or you aren't sure, don't be afraid to say so. You may feel some pressure to pick one of the people just so you won't have wasted everybody's time. Do not succumb to this pressure.

4. Other techniques used include hypnosis. Though not all courts ac-

cept this as proper evidence, police have used hypnosis to help witnesses remember details they cannot remember consciously. You must rely on the advice of your lawyer or the prosecutor as to whether it is advisable in a given instance.

5. Lie detector tests (sometimes called "polygraphs") are also used, although the results of such tests are not universally accepted in court. The police may ask you to take a lie detector test; again, do not agree to it until after you have consulted with your own attorney or with the prosecutor. Such a test has serious implications for your credibility. There is nothing harmful, dangerous, or painful about a lie detector test; it simply measures certain bodily reactions to questions asked by the examiner. Just listen carefully to the questions and answer them as honestly as possible. (But read No. 6, below, very carefully *before* you agree to this test.)

6. It is not necessary for victims or witnesses to retain their own attorneys. The prosecutor generally will look out for the interests of the victim. The attorney who calls a witness to the stand (whether prosecution or defense) generally advises the witness on questions concerning her testimony. However, questions do arise from time to time that require the advice of independent counsel. If at all possible, you should consult with a lawyer experienced in criminal law. Examples of this type of question are whether or not a victim/witness should submit to hypnosis or a lie detector test. The most crucial situation involves whether or not a victim or witness should answer questions that may tend to incriminate her. You have the right to refuse to answer a question if the answer would tend to incriminate you. This is called "pleading the Fifth" or "asserting the privilege against self-incrimination." This is an extremely important decision, one that should be made only after talking to your own lawyer.

How to Prepare for Court

Once the police have finished at least the preliminary part of their investigation, they will decide whether or not to refer the case to the prosecuting agency. The prosecuting agency, often called the district attorney, the state's attorney, the city attorney (or the U.S. attorney if the charge involves a federal crime), has the responsibility for deciding whether or not to bring charges (to take the case to court). This is a legal decision. If the prosecuting agency decides not to file a complaint, inquire of that agency regarding the reasons. If the case does go to court, the prosecutor is the lawyer who represents the "People" or the "Government" against the "accused" or the "defendant." If the prosecutor decides to go forward with the case, you may be called to testify. If you are the victim, the prosecutor will call you, probably as the main witness. If you merely saw the crime or you have some knowledge, you may be called by either side, or maybe both.

The first step is to review any notes you made and to try to recall as accurately as possible everything about the incident. If necessary, go back to the scene, review anything else that will help you remember everything. Talk to others who may help you remember.

Make sure you talk, well ahead of time, to the attorney who has subpoenaed you. Review the facts with the attorney and find out what she is going to ask you when you get to court. If necessary, meet with her several times. Find out if there is anything you should bring with you to court, such as documents or other evidence.

If you have been subpoenaed by one side or the other, remember that you do not have to talk to anyone else about the incident. Very likely, investigators on both sides will want to talk to you. You may talk to either or both, but you are not *required* to talk with anyone unless you are subpoenaed into court and the judge instructs you to answer the question. If you have doubts about testifying for either side, you should consult an independent attorney to determine if there is any reason why you should not testify.

If the case is one with a great deal of notoriety, you may be pressured to speak with the press. You are not required to talk with them under any circumstances. If you have any doubts about speaking with the press, consult your attorney before you say anything. Sometimes the judge issues a "gag order," forbidding anyone involved in a case from speaking with the press. In that case you must not speak to the press. And in general it is not a good idea to talk to the press while a case is pending.

If you are unfamiliar with the court proceedings, go down to the courthouse ahead of time and watch a trial or a hearing. Talk to the clerks and other court personnel; they are usually very helpful.

Dealing with the Courtroom Situation

Whether it is a court hearing with just a judge, or a jury trial, you should try to appear as low-key as possible. You should dress tastefully and comfortably, but not too casually. Your dress should not be overly flamboyant, nor should you overdo your makeup or hairstyle. Jurors and judges form attitudes about witnesses at least partly based on their appearance, and you should keep that in mind when choosing your dress and hairstyle.

If you are in the courtroom but not testifying, you should be quiet and low-key. Many judges do not allow gum chewing or reading while in court. Smoking is generally not allowed. You should not make facial expressions while others are testifying. Basically you should be attentive and respectful. Remember: jurors pick up cues about witnesses from *all* their perceptions, not just from the witnesses' testimony on the stand. Most important, you must be very careful when you are in the courthouse or anywhere in the vicinity, as you may be near jurors. You must not communicate with them, say anything about the case near them, or do anything that might prejudice them about the case.

Whether you are a victim or a witness, the general rule is that you may testify only about something you actually saw or heard or something about which you have personal knowledge. The attorney who calls you to the stand should review this with you ahead of time. If not, ask her to go over it. If you are a witness, but not the victim, you may be required to wait in the hallway while others are testifying. You must stay near the courtroom; you may leave only if excused by the judge. If uncertain as to how far you may go, ask the bailiff.

Testifying in Court

The lawyer for the side that subpoenaed you to court will call you to the stand. The clerk will first ask you to swear to tell the truth. Then you will be seated in the witness box and asked to state your name and spell it. Remember that everything you say must be taken down by the court reporter, so it is very important to speak slowly and distinctly. You must also speak loudly enough so that the jury (or just the judge if there is no jury) can hear you.

The lawyer for the side that called you to the stand will then ask you a series of questions about the incident or about anything you might know about the case. This is called direct examination. The form of the question will usually be open-ended and narrative, to allow you the freedom to tell the story in your own words as much as possible. Listen *very carefully* to the questions, and answer completely and honestly, but only what is asked. If you do not hear or understand the question, ask to have it repeated. Your answer should be short and to the point, unless a longer answer is needed. Do not volunteer information; if the lawyer wants more information, she will ask more questions.

If the questioning is in an area that upsets you and you don't feel that you can continue, don't be afraid to ask for a recess. Courtroom people understand that sensitive areas may upset people, and they are used to it. Remember that you are not the person on trial and that you shouldn't take the proceedings or any of the questions personally.

When the lawyer for the side calling you has finished asking questions, the lawyer for the other side is allowed to ask questions of you. This is called cross-examination. The form of the questions is closed-ended and leading. This often means that the answer is suggested in the questions. The purpose of cross-examination is to test the truthfulness of what you testified to under direct examination. You should not feel intimidated by the questioner. If you can't answer the question yes or no, tell that to the court, and the judge will usually let you give the correct answer. It is very important that you listen very carefully to the question. One technique is to take a deep breath after the question and before the answer. This allows your lawyer to object if necessary, and gives you time to think about the answer.

It is important not to get irritated or lose your composure during cross-examination. The questions often seem trivial and repetitive; if so, don't worry: it reflects badly on the lawyer asking the questions, not on you. Simply answer the question as honestly as possible. Your credibility is important, and everything you do and say, as well as your attitude, reflect on that. Keep in mind that you are the only one who knows what happened. If the question suggests an answer you don't agree with, then say so. Also, if you don't remember, say so; that's better than guessing. The same is true if you don't know the answer.

Most states now have a victim compensation fund. Ask the prosecutor to give you information on this. It is important to keep track of any medical expenses and lost wages.

If you are the victim, you might consider a civil suit against the perpetrator of the crime. Another possibility is to make a claim against any available insurance.

The victim of a rape has the right to a female companion in court while testifying. Counseling is available to help with the trauma (see Chapter 19).

WOMEN AS PARENTS

As a parent, it is not unusual to come into contact with the juvenile justice system. Parents meet the system in one of two ways: as parents of a child in a dependency action or of a child in a delinquency action. Some of the trauma of these situations can be relieved if the parent has a general understanding of the system.

The purpose of the juvenile law is for the state to provide protection of children. In most states, a child is defined as any individual under the age of 18. However, some states do take juvenile action on individuals up to the age of 21 years. Juvenile proceedings are civil, as opposed to criminal, proceedings. Through interpretation of social welfare laws, the court may promote unification of the family, rather than punishment proceedings. Generally the hearings are closed to the public. However, in some states the press may cover a case, at the discretion of the judge. Recently the press has been permitted into juvenile proceedings by legislation under the theory that the public has the right to know what is happening. Such legislation generally covers major crimes only: murder, rape, or mayhem (willful and permanent crippling or mutilation—particularly of a limb—or disfigurement).

A Dependency Action

In a dependency action, the court conducts an investigation into allegations of child abuse, neglect, abandonment, or other welfare issues. The family is investigated by a social worker, and if the allegations are found to be true the court will give orders to protect the child. The burden of proof in these actions is the same as in a civil case: by a preponderance of the evidence; that is, by evidence sufficient to persuade the judge that the charge is more likely true than not.

A Delinquency Action

In a delinquency action, the court investigates allegations of criminal behavior by a child. An investigation is made by a probation officer, and if the allegations are found to be true the court will make appropriate orders. In a delinquency action, the burden of proof is greater: beyond a reasonable doubt.

Both parent and child can be considerably affected by court hearings in either dependency or delinquency proceedings. If allegations of delinquency or dependency petitions are found to be true, the court may remove parental control and act in loco parentis; that is, take over the legal aspects of the parental role. The child may be placed in a foster home, a group home, a hospital, or a penal institutional setting. The court may also order parents into counseling or other rehabilitative programs. If a parent fails to comply with such orders, the court may find her to be in civil contempt. More likely, the court will simply continue to act for the parent, thus further disrupting the normal parent-child relationship.

The Parent in a Delinquency Action

The arrest of a child is procedurally identical to that of an adult. The first notice a parent has of a delinquency action is usually a phone call from the child. This call has legal significance. If a child refuses to talk to the police until she has spoken to a parent, the child has exercised her right to remain silent. By asking to speak to her parent, the child is seeking "counsel" and cannot be questioned until she has spoken to that parent. Thus, when that fateful call comes, it is important for the parent to advise the child to remain silent. Do not ask the child to discuss the case with you over the phone. Tell the child you will be there as soon as possible, then go immediately.

What You Should Do at the Police Station: At the police station, again do not ask the child to explain. Ask the police what happened; be courteous but firm in your demand that no questioning occur until your child has counsel.

If the incident is minor, the police may advise that the child will be referred to either a police-operated or county-operated counseling program. Such a program is commonly called a diversion program and is used in cases of minor drug or alcohol violations, petty thefts, and fights. If the child is referred to counseling with the assurance no charges will be brought, then an attorney is not necessary and the child will be released immediately to the parent. If the incident is more serious, such as car theft or a burglary, the police may very well release the child to you if you show concern in supervising the child and in making a court appearance with the child. Such releases are discretionary judgment calls that any officer makes several times a day. If the child is released to you, then you will receive a notice when to appear in court. Finally, if the incident is serious and the officer does not think the child should be released, the child will be taken to the juvenile hall, the local juvenile detention facility.

How to Pick an Attorney: If charges are going to be filed, an attorney is necessary to your child's case. It is important to hire an attorney familiar with the juvenile court system. Do not hire your divorce or probate attorney unless that person is also familiar with juvenile law. If you are unable to get a referral, then contact your local bar association for a referral. Some juvenile courts maintain referral lists of qualified attorneys (also see Chapter 21).

The Detention Hearing: If the child is not released after arrest, she will have a detention hearing within forty-eight hours. Juveniles do not have the right to bail, since the proceedings are civil. At the detention hearing, the court will advise the juvenile of the charges and will consider several issues related to whether your child should be released: the risk of harm the child poses to the community, the likelihood that the child will make court appearances, and whether the child herself will suffer harm if not kept in a custodial setting. If counsel has not been secured for the child, the court will appoint counsel, for which the parents will be billed. The detention hearing is a very important stage of the proceedings, since your child's placement during the case is determined. Juvenile halls are basically penal institutions and a child is rarely better off locked up than at home. While the facts alleged in the case may be discussed, the parents should limit all remarks to the issues of supervision. The attorney will address the legal issues. The parents must demonstrate a clear program of security and supervision. This may require some major sacrifices on the part of the parents, such as leaving a job in order to be at home with the child.

The tone of the case is often set at the detention hearing. Do not take a position that the court, the prosecuting attorney, and the probation department are simply persecuting your child and your family. Rather than dwell on any perceived unfairness about the proceedings, try to emphasize in your statements a desire to cooperate, to reunify the family, and to teach the child responsibility. Do not argue even if baited by an unkind judge. Defer any argument to the attorney who is familiar with the cast of characters in the courtroom.

If the court will not release your child from custody, there are other alternatives to juvenile hall that should be discussed where appropriate. Some courts have home supervision programs, in which the child is under house arrest and is supervised by a court officer, usually a probation officer. Sometimes foster-home placement is considered in delinquency actions, particularly where the crime relates directly to the home environment. In situations in which the behavior indicates psychiatric problems, many courts will consider placement in a children's psychiatric hospital setting, usually in a locked ward. Most insurance policies offer such coverage, and arrangements may be made by the parents for such placement. The least desirable placement is the local jail. In some instances, particularly where the crime involves great violence and the child appears to be dangerous to other juveniles, the court may order a juvenile to be placed in a juvenile tank at the city or county jail. Such placement isolates the child from juveniles charged with lesser offenses.

A Fitness Hearing: The next court appearance in a juvenile action occurs only in a small number of cases. It is referred to as a fitness hearing. The court will receive evidence to determine whether the case should be heard in the juvenile court as a civil proceeding or in the adult court as a criminal proceeding. Again substantial rights are involved, since a minor found unfit for juvenile court will be subject to punishment as an adult, including state prison. The advantages of juvenile treatment are obvious not only in that the punishment may be considerably less, but a juvenile record can be sealed and expunged, the case will receive limited publicity, and the child will suffer none of the loss of rights due to a felony conviction.

The criteria in a fitness hearing are specific. The minor must be 16 years of age, although some states have lowered the age to 13. The court will evaluate the criminal sophistication of the crime, including the degree of planning and organization required to commit the crime (e.g., use of disguises or sophisticated equipment). The court will determine whether juvenile services exist to rehabilitate the minor under the juvenile system. For example, if a 16-year-old is convicted of murder as alleged, can she be rehabilitated within the statutory time she is still a minor? The court will look at the previous delinquency record of the minor and evaluate whether there has been an increasing seriousness of offenses. The court will look at the success by juvenile services in previous attempts to rehabilitate the minor. And the court will look at the gravity and circumstances of the offense as alleged.

At the fitness hearing, defense counsel may cross-examine prosecution witnesses on these issues and may present evidence. Frequently, defense counsel will introduce parents' testimony on the issue of ability to rehabilitate the minor. Also, psychiatric testimony is often given on that issue. The allegations are not tried at this hearing, and for purposes of the hearing, the allegations are presumed to be true. This is sometimes difficult for parents, since many times it seems more reasonable to present a defense to the charges at this early opportunity. Parents must not present an air of resentment at the operation of the system, and must allow counsel to orchestrate the hearing to the benefit of the minor.

Plea Bargaining: Assuming the minor is found to be fit for purposes of the juvenile court services, the next hearing is for case negotiations. This is confusing to parents, since plea negotiations have been much maligned. Often, plea negotiation is the most important stage of the proceedings. If counsel can convince the prosecution to reduce the charges, the minor may benefit by great leniency. Plea negotiation is a complicated procedure by which the prosecutor and the defense counsel evaluate the case in a friendly but adversary atmosphere. No information shared by either side may be used against the other at trial. In other words, if, during plea negotiations, counsel confirms that the minor does admit to committing the crime, the prosecutor must not use that information at trial. At plea negotiations, defense counsel may turn over defense investigative reports, psychiatric reports, and other information that is sympathetic to the minor. The prosecutor has the power to reduce or even dismiss charges prior to trial if in her mind the case does not warrant treatment at the level charged.

For example, assume a minor is charged with the theft of a neighbor's car. The crime is a felony and the minor could spend a considerable amount of time in custody if convicted. Defense counsel can show that the minor has an insignificant prior record of possession of marijuana (not a theft-related offense), gets good grades in school, has apologized to the neighbor and made restitution for damage to the car. The prosecutor, at her discretion, believes that the minor has accepted responsibility for her wrongfulness and that the expense of trial is not warranted if the minor is willing to admit guilt to a lesser offense: joyriding, a misdemeanor. The minor will still be subject to punishment by the court, but the plea bargain reflects an agreement by both sides that the case is substantially less serious than originally believed at the time of arrest.

Approximately 80 percent of cases are handled by plea negotiation. The procedure saves the defendant the embarrassment of trial and the risk of conviction on the more serious charges. The prosecution is saved the effort of presenting the witnesses and police officers. The court is saved the expense in time and money of a trial, thus clearing the way for cases in which there are real disputes as to the facts and issues.

If a plea bargain is not made in the case, then the minor proceeds to trial. In the juvenile court, the rules of evidence and procedure are the same as for an adult trial. However, the juvenile has no right to a jury, and the case will be decided by the judge. In some cases there will be extensive pretrial motions on legal issues. These are decided in conformity with adult criminal proceedings.

Disposition: If the minor is found guilty beyond a reasonable doubt, the case proceeds to disposition. Disposition is similar to a sentencing proceeding. A probation social study of the minor will be submitted to the court, recommending appropriate rehabilitative measures. The court will take other evidence before reaching a decision. Parents can greatly influence the court's decision. A clear show of concern and cooperation will make the best impression. Again, do not argue with the court's decision of the case. The attorney can argue the case on appeal. Once a conviction has occurred, the parents must accept this fact immediately and demonstrate the ability to engage the child in an appropriately structured environment that will assure no recurrence of delinquent behavior. Some major change in the structure of the family may be necessary to convince the court that the minor should return home. If the family is unwilling to make necessary changes, then the likelihood of incarceration increases. At disposition, the child may be placed in any of the wide range of settings previously discussed: foster home, group home, hospital, juvenile camp, or the juvenile penal facility. The stronger the demonstrated family ties, the less the sentence generally is. Parents do make a difference.

The Parent in a Dependency Action

As opposed to delinquency actions, which routinely begin with an arrest, dependency actions begin in many different ways. Medical and school personnel are required by law to report any evidence of abuse or neglect such as healed fractures, venereal disease, or unexplained bruises. Many urban areas have child-abuse hot lines by which incidents are reported by neighbors or children themselves. Incest is often reported by the victim through rape-crisis hot lines. Still other cases are reported by welfare workers and community outreach workers who are in the home routinely. And of course some cases are a result of police responding to domestic violence complaints.

Many dependency cases are handled informally, rather than by court action. Such diversion from formal proceedings typically occurs where the parent has never been referred previously, the incident is not severe (for example, a single incident of overdiscipline), and the parent seems willing and open to counseling and positive-parenting instruction. The quandary in every instance for the parent is whether to discuss the matter with authorities. Dependency cases can also result in prosecution under the penal code for numerous crimes: child abuse, battery, or various sex crimes. The parent should consult an attorney experienced in juvenile law immediately if an investigation begins. It is not wise for a parent to think she can handle the situation herself. Oftentimes, parents think they can talk their way out of the situation when it would have been far better to remain silent as to the cause of the injury.

If the child is removed from the home, the court must have a detention hearing within 48 hours. The court will appoint counsel for the child, to avoid pressure from parents to drop any charges. Parents will be billed for the child's attorney. Some states do not appoint attorneys for indigent parents. At the detention hearing, the parent is advised of the charges against her and the court determines where the child shall live during the case. The child's own home or the home of a close relative is preferred if a safe setting can be assured. You must show as a parent that the problem is remedied. For example, the molester of the child has been removed from the home, the house has been cleaned, or the abusing parent is actively involved in parenting counseling. If a family placement is not available, the child will be placed in a county receiving home or in a licensed foster home. If the child is showing particular problems, the court may place the child in a psychiatric hospital.

The next hearing is the regular hearing. The state's case will be presented by a prosecutor or a social worker. The parent's attorney may cross-examine the witnesses and present witnesses. The parent does have the right to remain silent. However, if the parent does make a statement at this hearing, it may not be used in a later criminal proceeding for impeachment. The department of social welfare will present a report based on interviews with witnesses, the child, and the parents. Parents must be circumspect in all interviews with social workers throughout and emphasize a willingness to cooperate and a concern for the child's welfare, without making admissions. The reports are presented at the regular hearing from interviews done prior to the hearing. You must keep in close contact with your attorney during the time period between the detention hearing and the regular hearing.

If the charges are found to be true, the court will make the child a dependent of the court and take jurisdiction over the child, acting in loco parentis. The court not only has the power to control where the child lives, but also has authority to order counseling, parenting classes, therapy, and visitation with the child by the parents. If the parents do not show a commitment to cooperate in providing for the safety of the child, a permanent disruption of the relationship with the child may result. But a reunification of the family is the primary objective of the juvenile law as to dependent children. If within a year the parents have not made an effort to comply with court orders, the state may begin freedom-from-custody proceedings, to release the child from the parents and make the child available for adoption. An example of this situation is an infant abandoned at the hospital after birth by a mother suffering from drug addiction who fails to appear at court or to visit the infant. The child will eventually be placed for adoption by the state.

If you become the subject of a dependency action, you must deal quickly and realistically with the situation. You must seek counsel familiar with that area of law and rely on her advice. You must rise above your personal involvement in the situation and take every step to ensure a safe and healthy environment for the child in your home. Such action requires the strength to deal with some harsh reality, and for that reason you are wise to seek the aid of professional counseling. Such counseling is available in most communities through the YWCAs and YMCAs, through family stress programs offered by government agencies, through health plans, and through the military. This is one time in your life you must not be too shy to seek help. Your family's welfare is at stake (see also Chapter 18).

WOMEN AS DEFENDANTS

The defendant in a criminal case is an individual charged with a criminal offense. In most jurisdictions, the plaintiff is the prosecuting agency that represents the state or federal government.

What Should You Do if Stopped by a Police Officer?
The United States Constitution, Fourth Amendment, states:

> The right of the people to be secure in their persons, houses, papers and effects against unreasonable searches and seizures shall not be violated, and no warrants shall issue but upon probable cause, supported by oath or affirmation, and particularly describing the place to be searched, and the persons and things to be seized.

Everyone is guaranteed this right as a minimal protection against unwarranted invasions of privacy. States may adopt more stringent standards to protect the rights of their citizens.

A police officer is any law enforcement agent empowered by law to stop and question any individual, or to arrest a person, suspected of criminal activity. While the term "police" usually includes local police forces, the county sheriff's department, state law enforcement agencies, and the FBI, it can also include private security guards who are employed by public and private businesses, such as those in sports arenas and department stores.

A stop by a police officer occurs when the officer makes contact with a pedestrian or an occupant of a vehicle. The stop may be lawful depending on all the circumstances, such as whether or not it is an emergency, the time of day or night, and age and physical appearance of the individual. In general, the officer must have a reasonable belief of suspected criminal activity to stop any individual.

If you are stopped, you may be requested to produce identification. You should do so by presenting a current driver's license, military identification card, or other valid identification that, preferably, contains a picture for easy recognition.

If you are in an automobile, you should be sure it is safely parked before presenting any identification. Do not panic or become upset. You may ask the officer why you are being stopped, in order to gain an understanding of the situation.

You should have a cooperative attitude if you are questioned, and you should ask why you are being stopped before deciding whether or not to answer any questions. Do not volunteer information.

A vehicle stop may occur in other situations, such as a roadblock or a border check. In either case, you should remain in the vehicle unless requested or ordered to do otherwise. Do not give consent to the officer to search or inspect your vehicle unless you are legally obligated to do so (such as in an emergency).

If you are stopped at an airport, you may be required to go through a checkpoint, due to federal and local regulations. In business establishments, security guards may contact and question you about activities in the store. Various laws allow security personnel to detain persons suspected of shoplifting, causing a disturbance, and other offenses.

Banking institutions are regulated by the federal government, but state and local agencies may gain access, by issuing a search warrant, to inspect your bank records. You should contact your bank to determine what the bank policy is concerning privacy of bank records.

Is It Lawful for the Police Officer to Conduct a Search?

A search occurs whenever your person or property is examined, regardless of whether any object is seized or taken from you. If you are stopped and subjected to a search, try to remain calm and remember the sequence of events as the search is being performed. Make a mental or written note of the officer's name and badge number.

A search may consist of a pat-down search to look for contraband (such as weapons); a body-cavity search (a full body search usually takes place when a suspect is booked into jail); automobile search (interior, glove compartment, trunk); or a house search (a general exploratory search, which may include rummaging through personal items in drawers and cupboards). Whether the search is lawful is a determination to be made in a court of law.

What Should You Do if You Are Questioned by a Police Officer?

Regardless of the situation, you should not volunteer information to any law enforcement agent if you are under suspicion of any criminal activity. If you are stopped and questioned, you should be cooperative, provide identification, and find out the reason for the detention. If you are suspected of criminal activity, it is your legal right not to incriminate yourself.

The Fifth Amendment to the United States Constitution provides in part:

> No person . . . shall be compelled in any criminal case to be a witness against himself. . . .

If you are interrogated about criminal activity, the officer is required by law to advise you of your right to remain silent and your right to have an attorney present at the time of questioning. You may ask to see an attorney before any questioning by law enforcement agents. Do not volunteer any information.

What Should You Do if You Are Arrested by a Police Officer?

Arrest means physical restraint by being placed in custody. You may be formally charged by the arresting or prosecuting authority with criminal offenses. Try to make a mental or written note of the arrest process, including the officer's name and badge number. If you are placed in custody, you should receive a copy of the charges and notice of the amount of the bail upon booking into jail.

While in custody, you should not discuss the case with law enforcement officials, jail staff, or other inmates. If you are interrogated, you should request to see an attorney before making any statements about the case. Do not be persuaded to converse with police officers if they make promises about helping you get out of custody or helping you with the case.

You may be released from custody by one of several methods. A bail bond may be posted through a bail bonding agency by paying approximately 10 percent of the bond in cash and satisfying the remainder by either real or personal property, or a combination of both. Cash bail may be posted, in some jurisdictions, directly at the jail or the court. The cash will be returned after the end of the court proceedings. A surety bond may be posted where real property (land) is secured as collateral, instead of posting cash.

A release on your own recognizance ("OR" release) may be obtained through the jail or the court depending on the charges, your ties to the community in which you are arrested, and any prior criminal record.

What Can You Do If You Believe the Police Action Was Unlawful?

Most communities have local bar associations, which can refer you to attorneys that handle police-related complaints (see p. 542 for lists of organizations that have attorney referral services). You should seek advice from an attorney if the case involves false arrest, police brutality, or excessive force by a police officer.

In order to file a complaint against a law enforcement agency, you may be required to obtain a form from the local government authority in charge of the police agency (the city, state, or federal authority). The complaint form may specify a certain period of time in which you are allowed to file the complaint, such as one hundred days or six months. You should include all details of the incident, all parties and witnesses to the action, and damages suffered due to the misconduct (loss of wages, medical bills, etc.).

Watchdog agencies have been established in many cities to monitor police activities. You may seek contact with these agencies through local bar associations and other community groups.

How to Contact an Attorney to Represent You

You will need legal representation if you are charged with a criminal offense. You should not attempt to represent yourself unless the charge is a very simple matter such as a traffic ticket. Even if it is only a traffic ticket, depending on your driving record you should still consult a lawyer.

The lawyer you hire should have an initial consultation with you to discuss the case and fee arrangements. Attorney fees vary a great deal from city to city. If you need to defer payment, consult with your attorney. Court-appointed counsel is normally available for individuals charged with criminal offenses who have little or no income and assets (see information on referral services, p. 542).

What Happens After Charges are Brought Against You?

The prosecuting agency is required to file a criminal complaint in court, usually within two to three working days, which states the name of the defendant, the specific charges, the date the offense was allegedly committed, and, in some cases, the name of the victim. A criminal complaint may list multiple defendants and multiple charges.

The initial appearance in court is the arraignment, which provides the defendant with notice of the charges and the opportunity to request release from custody. Additional court appearance dates are set at the time of arraignment.

CHART OF COURT PROCEEDINGS

FELONY

(punishable by death or imprisonment in prison)

ARRAIGNMENT

1. Receive advisal of constitutional rights.
2. Receive copy of complaint.
3. Enter plea of not guilty.
4. Appointment of counsel or request continuance to obtain own counsel.
5. Bail setting.

PRELIMINARY EXAMINATION

1. If complaint is filed, hearing is held to determine if probable cause exists to hold defendant to answer on the charges. (If grand jury indictment is filed, defendant may not be entitled to this hearing.)
2. Magistrate may dismiss case if evidence is insufficient. (Case may be settled prior to trial by plea bargain.)

TRIAL

(same general procedures as in misdemeanor cases)

SENTENCING

1. Court usually refers defendant to probation office for presentence report to include defendant's background, prior criminal record, and recommendation as to punishment.
2. Sentencing hearing usually occurs within 3–4 weeks after conviction either by plea bargain or guilty verdict rendered at trial.

MISDEMEANOR

(punishable by imprisonment in local jail and/or a fine)

ARRAIGNMENT

1. Receive advisal of constitutional rights.
2. Receive copy of complaint.
3. Enter plea of not guilty.
4. Appointment of counsel or request continuance to obtain own counsel.
5. Bail setting.

Case may be settled prior to trial by plea bargain.

TRIAL

1. Jury selection. (If court trial is conducted, jury waiver by defendant should be made.)
2. Opening argument by counsel.
3. Prosecution presents evidence through testimony of witnesses and physical evidence, such as clothing, documents and demonstrative objects.
4. Defense presents evidence (or may elect not to present any evidence).
5. Closing arguments by counsel.
6. Jury instructions given by trial judge to jury.
7. Verdict is rendered (guilty/not guilty) or a mistrial is declared.

SENTENCING

(same general procedures as in felony cases)

Please refer to the chart on page 406 for a general explanation of court procedures.

FURTHER READING

Brown, David. *Fight Your Ticket.* Occidental, Calif.: Nolo Press, 1982.

Cohn, Roy M. *How to Stand Up for Your Rights and Win.* New York: Simon & Schuster, 1981.

Helm, Alice K. *The Family Legal Advisor.* New York: Crown, 1981.

Howell, John C. *The Citizen's Guide to the Law.* Englewood Cliffs, N.J.: Prentice-Hall, 1979.

Invaw, Fred E.; Aspen, Marvin E.; and Margolis, Jeremy D. *Criminal Law for the Layman.* Radnor, Pa.: Chilton, 1977.

Reader's Digest. *Family Legal Guide.* Pleasantville, N.Y.: Reader's Digest, 1981.

Ross, Martin J.; and Ross, Jeffrey Steven. *Handbook of Everyday Law.* New York: Fawcett, 1981.

Weber, Robert. *Before You See a Lawyer.* Piscataway, N.J.: New Century Publishers, 1981.

18
Family Violence
Spouse and Child Abuse, and Abuse of the Elderly

JUDIANNE DENSEN-GERBER, J.D., M.D.
JEAN LOTHIAN

Judianne Densen-Gerber, psychiatrist, attorney, author, and mother of four children, is president of Odyssey Resources Inc., an international research and consultation firm. In the early 1970s, when Odyssey researchers assessed the families of drug addicts and their ability to protect and nurture their young, they found many patient backgrounds of severe child abuse, often sexual in nature, and neglect. So Dr. Densen-Gerber began to develop treatment methods for the abused and is most recognized for her expertise in treating the sexually abused and the addicted. She has documented and challenged the use of children in pornography and all forms of "sexploitation" since 1977. Dr. Densen-Gerber is a graduate of Bryn Mawr College, Columbia University School of Law, and New York University School of Medicine.

Jean Lothian is vice-president for public information at Odyssey Institute Corporation and has worked for 15 years in both counseling and administrative positions with voluntary agencies. She is the author of papers and educational material on child sexual abuse. She is a graduate of the University of Massachusetts and has trained to be an incest therapist with Odyssey and the Parents/Daughters/Sons United Program at the University of San Jose, California.

I tried to take too much until my mind snapped.

—*Francine Hughes**

Family violence is a common problem and a critical one everywhere in the United States. It occurs at all income levels and among all sorts of people . . . In my experience (these) situations between husband and wife end in one of two ways: the parties divorce and get out, or it will terminate in death.

—*Kenneth Preadmore†*

Victim or Survivor?

This chapter is based upon extensive work with victims of childhood physical and sexual abuse and with women whose partners have abused either them or their children or both. It also deals with abuse of the elderly. For very practical reasons, a distinction is made between victims and survivors: victims die or live in fear, and they often are unable to protect themselves or anyone else; survivors, on the other hand, know they can control the direction of their lives, and they actively choose to take any and all steps necessary to stop violence against themselves and their children.

It is important to understand how a victim moves to survivor status. This transformation is accomplished in part through knowledge about her rights; information about places and people who can offer her help; and permission to rage constructively against the abuser(s). Such steps permit victims to move away from a sense of helplessness toward safety. In particular, rage, when put into the service of positive action to help oneself, can give a woman the strength she needs to get herself out of the abusive household. This process involves the rechanneling of psychic energy. It has long been known to psychiatrists that victims employ large amounts of energy in order to maintain the status quo of bad situations. Yet they feel powerless, overwhelmed, and too exhausted to ward off the grave dangers of physical harm and emotional disruption. The same energies, when put toward positive action to free oneself from abuse, lead to feelings of strength, self-respect, and accomplishment.

ABUSE ADDS NOTHING OF VALUE TO ANYONE'S LIFE

We *do not recommend* that anyone act violently toward a spouse, parent, or child, and we know of no research to prove that violence corrects any

*Battered wife who was charged with the death by fire of her husband in 1977 (from *The Burning Bed,* by Faith McNulty).[1]
†Sheriff, Ingham County, Michigan (from *The Burning Bed*).

situation or has any positive value. We *do recommend* rational action and legal steps in defense of self and family. Any woman who believes she must suffer, or accept violence toward herself or her offspring, or who condones her own or another's violent behavior, will find no support in this chapter.

Those who work in the field of family violence repeatedly learn that failure to protect oneself and one's children from violence creates continuing generations of family disruption and more victims, who eventually act out destructively toward themselves or others. If you are a victim and you do not decide *now* to separate yourself and your children from the abuser, someone may murder and someone may die. This chapter will then not help you, and you will need to move back to Chapter 17. It is essential that you become a survivor!

Such a message may sound humorous or insensitive, but we do not mean it to be. Americans live in a complex society in which all women, at one time or another, come face to face with financial, emotional, and legal hurdles. Victims let such realities overwhelm them; survivors confront the complexities armed with the knowledge that there are others to help them and that, with such assistance, they can expect to accomplish whatever they need to do.

A FEW STATISTICS ABOUT FAMILY ABUSE

Of all murders in the United States, 40 percent of female homicide victims are killed by husbands and 10 percent of male homicide victims are killed by wives.[2] Estimates project that a minimum of 2.5 million wives are abused annually in America.[3] Each year, 1 million children are abused and 2,000 of them die, and 300,000 youngsters are sexually abused by someone known to them in a parenting role.[4] Abuse of the elderly is estimated at between 500,000 and 2.5 million persons.[5] While deaths do end in official records, usually only 10 percent of child abuse[6] and wife abuse incidents[7] ever reach the attention of those who can help.

We urge all who are being abused to take the first step right now: decide you will not allow anyone in your family, including yourself, to remain unprotected and at risk. Read this chapter and learn how you, too, today, can take control of your own destiny and that of your loved ones.

You Must Decide to Go Outside the Family for Help and Openly State That You or Your Children, or Both, Are Being Abused

While other people close to you, such as a brother or a sister or another relative, may offer you comfort, they rarely have the information or the objectivity to advise you properly. Immediately tell someone about an abusive incident and obtain medical care and proof of such care for later legal proceedings. You may need to *prove* abuse and will not be able to do so without substantiation from a witness or medical personnel. Photographs taken by a physician at the time of treatment may also be used as evidence later.

You Must Decide to Take Any and All Steps Necessary to Stop the Abuse, Including, if Necessary, the Decision to End Your Relationship with the Abuser
    Even someone in a position to help you will be unable to do so if you cannot or will not act in your own best interests or those of your children.

You Must Ask Yourself Some Questions About the Future and Decide When You Will Involve Attorneys or Other Officials
    Examples of the questions you need to answer are as follows:
    1.   Will I tell the abuser to leave?
    2.   Can I take legal action if no departure date can be mutually agreed upon?
    3.   Will I accept financial aid from friends, relatives, or welfare until I get a job?
    4.   Which is worse, accepting abuse for myself and children because we have no financial resources, or getting help so we can feel safe even if we face a loss of economic support from the abuser?

    The authors recommend you answer yes to the first three questions, because law enforcement officials seldom will help you as long as you remain with the abuser and refuse to press charges. Usually, the least disruption for you and your children is when the abuser agrees to leave. Often, trained persons can successfully counsel the abuser to leave and frequently to seek help for his or her problems. You also have the right to leave. In either case, you may need financial assistance to meet daily expenses and to obtain legal help. Don't be ashamed to ask. Agencies were created for this purpose.

    In most localities, you and your children and the elderly have the right to receive public aid for food, shelter, clothing, and medical care if you have no savings or earnings of your own. Most areas have emergency shelters for abused women and some have room for children; if not, they usually will aid you in finding a safe place to stay. (See p. 525 for information on how to locate shelters.)

IF YOU MUST LEAVE YOUR HOME

1. *Do not* leave without your children, because you may leave them in danger. In certain jurisdictions, your partner could later charge you with abandonment.

2. *Do not* stay, with or without your children, with a male friend who lives alone, because your partner could later charge you with adultery or with being an unfit mother.

3. No one benefits from abuse, and nothing in a future on your own can be worse than what you have already survived.

4. Remember that whenever there are children, the law holds you, as their mother, responsible for their safety.

> *Remember the dignity of your womanhood. Do not appeal, do not beg, do not grovel. Take charge, join hands, stand beside us, fight with us.*
> —*Christabel Pankhurst*
> *English Suffragette (1880–1958)*[8]

SOME BASIC FACTS ABOUT FAMILY ABUSE

Does a Family Member Have the Right to Abuse?

No one has the right to abuse anyone: Family members, or those who come close to the family, such as a boyfriend, girl friend, stepparent, or in-law, have no legal right to abuse any family member. Staff in institutions and foster parents also do not have the right to abuse children or the elderly. Violence teaches nothing but fear and creates still more violence. Each person in the household has the right to feel secure and protected within the home.

Parents of minor children (in most states, under age 18) have the legal responsibility to protect their children from abuse. Most states will consider the nonabusing parent *neglectful* if she/he does not intercede when the abusing parent endangers a child. Most courts will recommend that the nonabusing parent receive counseling. A mother does not have the right to allow anyone, including her partner, to abuse the children living in the home; nor, of course, does she have the right to abuse them herself. (The family law division of your local bar association should be able to describe child-protection laws to you.)

All states have enacted child-protection laws, and anyone, including a child or other family member, can report instances of child abuse or neglect without fear of a lawsuit. In some states similar laws exist to protect the elderly from abuse by family members. Many states also have laws to protect the elderly from institutional abuse. Some persons are mandated to report suspected abuse. (See p. 531 for information on how to report child abuse and what happens when you do.)

What Is Family Abuse?

The obvious kinds of abuse result in death or physical injury to any person living in the family, including assault, beating, stabbing, shooting, kicking, biting, burning, drowning, suffocating, punching, and/or hitting another family member. Abusive actions are those which place the recipient of the act at risk of injury. Abuse of the elderly also includes withholding or overdosing medication, abandonment, and theft or misuse of money or other property.

What Is Spouse Abuse?

Spouse abuse is deliberate assault by a partner which results in serious or repeated injury. Other types of abuse include threats of death or physical violence, emotional abuse, and sexual abuse.

Can the Elderly Get Protection from Family Abuse?

Yes, the elderly have the right to ask a women's center or a domestic-violence center, for protection. Many states require that health care personnel report elderly abuse in nursing homes, and some states have laws to protect the elderly from abuse at home.

States define abuse variously. On p. 525 you will find sources of information about laws in your geographic area.

What Is Marital Rape?

In general, forced sex, that is, sex without consent, is considered abuse. However, in forty-two states the law does not admit rape happens within marriage or between married people who live apart. (The eight states that do recognize marital rape are as follows: Louisiana, Maine, New Hampshire, New York, North Dakota, Ohio, Oregon, and Wisconsin. All require legal separation and orders of protection before a wife may press charges.)

Who May Press Charges?

Any wife may *ask* to press charges against a husband who rapes her, whether or not the husband and wife live together. You may, however, need to file assault charges instead. The following states do *not* recognize rape charges by a wife: Arizona, California, Colorado, Connecticut, Delaware, Illinois, Kentucky, Minnesota, Montana, New Mexico, Oklahoma, Pennsylvania, South Dakota, Texas, Utah, Vermont, Washington, West Virginia, and Wyoming.

Rape laws in each state are very complex. A woman who believes she has been raped by her husband will do best to:

1.   Move out or tell the husband to move out.

2.   Obtain an order of protection (see p. 525), which makes it a crime for a husband or partner to abuse her physically or sexually or threaten her or her children.

3.   Because unless a woman lives in a separate household and has a protection order, even the states that do recognize marital rape will not be able to help her.

WHAT TO DO ABOUT FAMILY ABUSE

Ask for Help

Few women or children who live in an abusive household can stop the abuse without the help of a third party.

Legal Assistance for the Abused Spouse

If you can afford a lawyer, hire one who will act in your best interests.

HOW TO CHOOSE AN ATTORNEY

1.   Ask people with similar problems who employed a lawyer, then make an appointment to see the lawyer who handled their case to their satisfaction; ask for referrals at an abuse crisis center (p. 526), or call a local bar association or law school (see also Chapter 21).

2.   When you meet the attorney, make sure she explains things in words *you* understand.

3.   If you do not understand something, ask that it be restated in simpler language; if the attorney refuses, or you still do not understand, find another lawyer; the law is complicated, and you have the right to an attorney who will do her job by explaining the legal process to you in words you understand.

4.   Ask the lawyer exactly what the fees are for the first visit and for the entire legal action; you have the right to know the charges; do not retain anyone until you know how much it will cost.

5.   If you cannot afford the fees, say so; ask if the lawyer does work for women's groups you might contact, or ask to be referred to someone you can afford; or seek free counseling services if you cannot afford legal fees. Above all, do not sign anything you do not understand.

You will save legal fees by doing as much work on your own as you can.

Ask counselors at the women's centers to help you make phone calls. Listen to the way they get information over the phone, so you can make the next call on your own. If you cannot afford an attorney or are unclear about what is happening, women's centers in your area can refer you to appropriate legal services. They will help you learn more about the process.

SOME LEGAL STEPS TO STOP ABUSE

Protection Order

The attorney will request a protection order from the family court (in most states). The temporary protection order instructs your husband or partner not to harm you and lasts until the date set for trial. You need to go immediately to family court to get the temporary order; often you may need witnesses and bruises as proof.

1. You don't need an attorney to request the protection order. You can go to family court yourself to obtain it.
2. If you are not married to the abuser but he is the father of your children, you need paternity papers to go to family court for protection. Women who have no children or no paternity papers for their children go to criminal court to obtain the order.

Both you and your partner must appear at the trial hearing at which you present proof of your claim and he can respond. The judge will then decide whether to issue a permanent order of protection. In some instances, with sufficient evidence, the judge may decide before a trial to issue an arrest order. You must then take the order to the police, who, if they can find your partner, will arrest him. Failure of one partner to appear at the hearing can result in denial of either partner's claim, or can cause a default judgment.

Sole Occupancy

In some states, you can obtain the right to bar your partner from your home; the protection order doesn't bar him from the house but orders him not to harm you or your children while he lives *with* you. (There are legal penalties if he does harm you or your children.) Until you obtain legal separation, only a sole occupancy order can prevent him from returning to live with you.

Legal Separation / Divorce

The authors strongly recommend legal separation and/or divorce for any woman whose partner repeatedly inflicts abuse upon her or her children. Psychologists and counselors have found that reconciliation counseling rarely works while the couple live together; and in child sexual abuse, the abuse stops soonest when legal action is initiated. (Chapter 8 discusses divorce and separation.)

What Happens When an Abused Woman Calls the Police?

1.   A police officer must respond to your statement that your partner has injured or threatened you or your children or has violated your order of protection.

2.   If you have obtained a protection order, the police must arrest your partner for violating it.

3.   You must agree to press charges before the police can remove or arrest the abuser for harm to an adult.

4.   The police must remain until a crime of injury or violation of the protection order is stopped or prevented.

5.   If your partner has left when the police arrive, you must follow the same procedures in order to obtain an arrest warrant. You then take the arrest warrant to a police station, so they can locate and arrest the abuser.

What if the Police Refuse to Arrest Your Partner?

You may arrest the abuser yourself, and the police must assist you in taking the abuser to the police station. If the police refuse to help you, write down their names and badge numbers and tell them you are doing this. Take your children and go to the police station and file a complaint against the officer(s) and an arrest charge against your partner.

Rights like those above vary from state to state. They also depend upon whether you are legally married to the abuser, whether you have children, and whether you have records to show that your boyfriend is the father of the children in the home. In most states, such distinctions determine whether family court or criminal court intervenes (see p. 525). Women will do best to contact a counseling center *before an emergency* or go to a battered-women's shelter in an emergency. The people who work in these places will help you learn about the local rules and will be able to think clearly and objectively when advising you of your rights. Fear, shame, and embarrassment keep victims from going outside the home to seek help. Many also do not believe that anyone can or will assist them. This impression is fortunately not true. Such beliefs only increase the power of the abuser. Many persons who act violently toward their families do so because they know neighbors won't "interfere" and the family will keep the abuse secret. Often, victims call the police but afterward refuse to press charges.

In this way, the victims, in fact, give power to the abuser to continue until some family member is seriously hurt or dies. The police, an attorney, and the courts can do nothing to stop a *spouse* from abusing his *partner* until the victim partner takes legal action. While adults must initiate and follow through on legal action in order to gain legal protection for themselves from an abuser, no action by the parent or family is necessary in order for the court to intervene to protect a child. Adults responsible for the care of children must ensure that those children are safe from harm.

WHAT IS CHILD ABUSE?

Child abuse is usually defined as physical and emotional abuse and neglect, and sexual abuse.

What Constitutes Physical Abuse of a Child?

Most states define an abused child as one under a certain age (in many states, 18) whose parent or other person usually responsible for the child's care:

1. Inflicts or allows physical injury to be inflicted upon the child, or
2. Creates or allows a substantial risk of physical injury to be created.

WHAT IS CHILD NEGLECT?

Most states usually consider a parent or other person responsible for the child neglectful when she/he fails to provide: support, education required by law, medical or remedial care required by law, or other care necessary to the child's well-being (examples are as follows: adequate food, clothing, housing, schooling, and hospital, dental, surgical, and other care, and proper supervision); or abandons the child; or subjects the child to an environment injurious to the child's welfare.

An example of a neglectful parent would be one who does not protect the child from physical or sexual abuse by a spouse. Another example of neglect would be a parent who leaves small children alone in the home without adult supervision; and some states, such as New York and Massachusetts, add parental drug abuse and alcohol abuse as conditions of neglect. When considering the damage of parental alcoholism or drug addiction to children, the following statistics are helpful:

- 2.5 million American children live in the sole custody of a drug-abusing parent;[9]
- 55 percent of child-abuse-related deaths occur in the homes of substance abusers;[10]

• 75 percent of spouse-abuse incidents occur when the abuser is intoxicated.[11]

WHAT IS MENTAL INJURY, OR EMOTIONAL CHILD ABUSE?

Mental injury to a child includes psychological abuse and emotional neglect. No generally accepted definition exists; each state has its own laws. (You may contact your local bureau of child welfare for specific laws in your geographic area.)

Usually the court demands proof that parental behavior has resulted in psychological damage or emotional neglect to the child. Since emotional abuse is very difficult to prove, experts from the fields both of child protection and child psychology will be needed to testify. Since most emotional abuse is verbal and most court decisions rely on *acts committed* as proof of harm, the legal process is quite complex; and it is often impossible to obtain legal relief or remedy in cases of emotional abuse or neglect. Nevertheless, emotional abuse and neglect do occur, and any woman who believes her child is so abused should make every attempt to separate the abuser from the child.

Example of Emotional Abuse

An 8-year-old child regularly was taken on swimming and fishing trips by her father. On these trips, he regularly talked to her about death and drowning and detailed the ways in which he could kill her if he chose. Since there were no witnesses to the conversations and he made no attempts to actually drown the child, this case could not be proved in court. Yet, most mental health workers agree that this type of threatening conversation by any adult, especially the one who holds emotional and financial control over the child, represents a betrayal of the child's trust and need for safety. It is the parents' responsibility to nurture and protect their children. Given these facts, many professionals would testify to the potential or actual damage that has occurred.

Example of Emotional Neglect

The child's mother, who knew of and refused to protect the child from situations in which the father engaged in these threatening conversations, represents a failure to recognize the child's need and right to security. This is emotionally neglectful.

Any parent who does not remove children from a physically or sexually abusive household fails to meet the child's emotional needs and rights. Such omissions are emotionally neglectful.

WHAT IS SEXUAL CHILD ABUSE?

The term "incest" now includes more relationships than previously. Sexual activity is defined variously in the several states; many set limits on what an adult may or may not do depending on the age and sex of the child. Since most children under the age of 16 do not have the emotional maturity to decide what sexual activity is not in their own best interests, any adult who engages a child in sexual activity has committed a crime. (States vary in their definitions of the age of consent for sexual intercourse, but 16 is the age the authors recommend.) Most states only look at the age of the victim when legal action occurs. Some states treat the offender differently when she/he is also a minor. Male or female children should be protected from sexual activity with any male or female adult. Sexual acts include: intercourse (vaginal or anal); fondling; manipulating the child's genitals; causing the child to fondle or manipulate the adult's genitals; oral sex performed on or by the adult; exposure of genitals; and acts of urination or defecation that are performed by the adult or child for purposes of sexual stimulation or gratification. Other kinds of sexual abuse include engaging a child or children in sexual exhibitions for performance or photographic reasons and, of course, paying a child or accepting payment for a child to perform sexual acts.

While the above information may disturb many readers and some activities have, unfortunately, not been included in the child protection laws in all states, legislators are beginning to recognize the above activities as sexually abusive to children. Sadly, work with sexual abuse victims has shown that all of the acts on the above list have been committed by adults who use children sexually. The youngest child known to have received treatment for sexual abuse is 3 months old.

WHAT IS INCEST?

Until very recently, incest meant marriage or sexual activity between blood-related or marriage-related persons. Most states made marriage or sexual activities illegal for certain persons. Today, incest usually involves activities defined under sexual abuse, above.

Is There a Difference Between Sexual Abuse of a Child by a Stranger and Sexual Abuse by a Family Member?

Yes, both emotionally and legally the effects upon the child depend in part upon the response of the family when they learn of the abuse. Usually, when a child receives protection and sees that the family will take action against the abuser, the child recovers with less long-term damage than the child whose family denies the abuse.

All children have the right to be protected by both parents from sexual abuse by anyone and to receive medical, psychological, and legal services if such abuse occurs. In most states, families who want to take action against a stranger child molester must notify the police. They must press charges in criminal court and the police must report such charges to child-protection authorities.

Families who want to take action against a family member or someone else known to the child may go to either family court or criminal court, or to the police or child-protection service. A lawyer or a child-protection agency can help you decide what is the most appropriate agency to intervene. The police, in some states, do not need to be notified when a family member is implicated.

Does the Family Have a Right to Keep the Name of a Sexually Abused Child Protected from Public Exposure?

Yes, most localities will protect the identity of a child who is sexually abused. However, no family member has the right to keep the child hidden from protection, for example, by failing to take action.

Must Authorities Maintain Confidentiality?

Yes, authorities may not release information about child-abuse reports or findings to anyone without authorization by the parents or guardians.

Are Children Responsible for Their Own Abuse?

No. While most abused children feel it is their fault, *no child* is responsible for the abuse she/he receives from an adult. Nor is any minor child responsible for protecting a parent from the abuse of another adult.

Who May File a Report of Child Abuse?

Anyone may file a report of suspected abuse.

ASSISTANCE FOR REPORTING CHILD ABUSE

Where to Report

You do not necessarily need an attorney to stop an abuser from harming your children. Anyone may report child abuse to the child welfare agency, the police, or the Society for the Prevention of Cruelty to Children.

How to Report

Most telephone directories list a hot-line number for child-abuse reports. You must give the child's full name if possible or at least a first or last name, an address and apartment number or other specific directions for locating the child, your reason for suspecting the child is abused or neglected, and your own name, address, and phone number.

Who Is Required to Report Suspected Child Abuse?

Certain professionals are required to report, and they face misdemeanor charges if they fail to do so. These include: doctors, nurses, teachers, guidance counselors, nursery-school personnel, dentists, social workers, Christian Science practitioners, police, and similar persons.

Who May Remove a Child from the Home?

In most jurisdictions, a parent or legal guardian, the police, the child-protection worker from the Society for the Prevention of Cruelty to Children, or a representative of the local governmental child-protection agency may remove a child immediately from an abusive home.

These officials must go to family court within twenty-four hours, or the next work day after a weekend or holiday, to prove the need to maintain custody of the child and to keep the child from being returned to the home. Since removal usually occurs only when the officials believe the child to be in serious danger, the courts usually allow for temporary placement of the child outside the home.

What Happens to a Report of Child Abuse or Neglect?

The police or others who receive a report and do not remove the child must register the report with the child-protection agency.

What Does the Child-protection Agency Do?

In most states, the child-protection agency maintains a computerized record of all reports that result in confirmation of abuse or neglect. Within

48 hours, a worker will visit the home. If the child is in serious danger of harm, the worker has the right to remove the child.

If abuse or neglect is confirmed but the child is not in immediate danger of repeated abuse, the worker will ask the family to cooperate in counseling to protect the child.

If the parents refuse, the worker will go to family court, report findings, and request the court to order the parents to accept counseling or place the child in temporary foster care. The agency then sees the child and family on a regular basis until such time as the agency reports to the court that the child may live safely in the home without expectation of repeated abuse.

If, upon initial investigation, the child-protection agency finds no abuse or neglect, the worker must so report within 48 hours, and the original suspected-abuse record must be erased from the computer file. Details regarding exact actions to be taken by a child-welfare agency in a particular state can be obtained by contacting the local child-welfare agency. You have the right to ask and understand what happens to a report.

What Happens to Reports of Sexual Child Abuse?

The process is similar except that physical evidence is difficult to obtain. When a report is filed immediately, a hospital examination can allow laboratory proof of oral or anal or vaginal semen findings.

Even when the abuse has not recently occurred, in all such suspected cases, the parents are responsible for obtaining medical care to assure that the child does not have venereal disease or other physical effects of the sexual abuse, such as pregnancy. Refusal to obtain medical care for a child constitutes neglect.

Psychological evaluations of the child are also a right and will help the child-protection worker and the court determine if the child has been sexually abused. Such medical and psychological tests will also be necessary to limit visiting privileges should the offender or the child leave the home, and custody privileges, should divorce occur.

Will the Family Know Who Made the Report?

You are protected from liability for making the report, and most local agencies will keep your name confidential, *if you request it to be,* unless a court case results. If court action is taken to protect the child, you may be summoned to appear and testify.

Will I Be Notified of the Results of the Report?

Unless you are the parent or guardian, most agencies, because of confidentiality, will not notify you of the outcome of your report. You should call back the following day and, if necessary, file the report again and again until you see the abuse has stopped, because in most child-abuse-related deaths, children were already known to two or more agencies when death occurred.

One way to avoid the embarrassment of strangers entering the home on a family-violence call is to ask for help from any of the following places *before* an emergency arises. Most groups will help you, your children, the elderly, and the abuser if you ask.

- *Church:* clergy, women's groups, or special people within the church who know about family problems and can help; on military bases you can see the chaplain;
- *Doctor:* psychologist, therapist;
- *School:* teachers, guidance counselors, nurses, or other personnel involved with the child;
- *Women's centers:* such as abused-women's shelters, rape centers, hot lines, domestic-violence centers;
- *Children's service or protection agencies:* family counseling centers; military personnel may contact The American Red Cross Service to military juvenile division;
- *Legal counseling centers;*
- *Senior citizens or groups such as the Gray Panthers;*
- *The Department of Health and Social Services Bureaus* should help if a child is in an institution or foster care.

Emergency Action
- Call 911, or
- Leave the scene of the abuse *and take your children with you.* If you or your child has been injured, go immediately to a hospital, obtain the necessary medical care, and tell the hospital that you want to file a police report immediately. You will need written proof of the hospital visit.
- Most telephone books print hot-line numbers for child abuse, rape, and senior citizens services. White pages and Yellow or Blue Pages carry headings like the list above. Call the operator if you cannot find these places in the telephone directory.
- These sources of help can tell you more about services in your area. Often they will make appointments for you at the places specifically designed to meet your needs.
- The people who work in these places understand very well the sad fact that you and your children are in real danger at home. Often, from experience, they understand the dangers even better than you do. Many who work there once were abused themselves.
- You have the *right* to talk freely, to expose the abuse. If your children also face danger, you and those you contact have the legal *responsibility* to report the child abuse to the police or child-protection service. Otherwise *you* and they, too, are guilty!

• Do not hesitate to ask for support services you need, such as child-care assistance, food, shelter, medical care, job placement, or a phone away from your house to receive or make calls.

• Most likely, you will need one or all of the above. In most jurisdictions, most of these items can be arranged, *if* you let someone know.

When women come together to solve problems that affect women, a sense of pride and self-respect develops. The strength gained from these feelings allows women to take action to ensure that they have a say in what happens to them and their children. While we recognize the anger that women experience when they realize the amount of effort still needed to achieve equality with men under the law, we know that angry energy can be used constructively. We can take action so that we allow no one to abuse us or our families, and all women benefit by the example of each woman's personal decision to refuse abuse. The authors thank those who shared their knowledge in preparing this chapter, and thank the former victims who, by exposing their problems, have identified the services and information other women need.

ABUSE OF THE ELDERLY

What Is Abuse of the Elderly?

Physical abuse, mistreatment, and neglect are problems faced by the elderly both from their families and from institutions.

Physical abuse means inappropriate contact such as striking, pinching, kicking, shoving, beating, bumping, biting, or sexual molestation. Mistreatment refers to inappropriate use of medication, isolation, physical restraints, or chemical restraints. Neglect means failure to provide timely, safe, consistent, adequate, and appropriate services, food, care, and treatment.[12] Abandonment, theft of money or property, and verbal abuse are also faced by the elderly. No one has the right to abuse the elderly; or to take the money or property of another without court action.

Who Has to Report Abuse?

Some states require health and social service personnel to report suspected institutional abuse of the elderly to the local department of health. Individuals may also make such reports.

Some states also protect the elderly (usually persons over 60) from abuse from within the family. Where they exist, laws are similar to those protecting children and follow steps like those listed earlier in this chapter for child abuse.

About half of the states carry some form of law to protect the elderly, or other adults who cannot protect themselves, from abuse. (They are Alabama, Arkansas, Kentucky, Minnesota, North Carolina, Tennessee, Utah, Connecticut, Florida, Missouri, Oklahoma, Vermont, Arizona, Colorado, Kansas, Maine, Maryland, Massachusetts, Michigan, Montana, New York, Pennsylvania, and Wisconsin.) Some of these states require health care personnel to report suspected abuse, and those who do not report face fines. Others require the department of welfare to investigate reports within 48 hours.

How to Report

When a person is being abused in an institution, a report can be made to the department of health or whatever agency is responsible for licensing the institution to operate.

When a person is being abused in the home, in some states the department of welfare accepts reports.

All states have departments for the aging which can assist you in reaching the best place for help.

When to Report

As soon as you suspect that you or an elderly person you know is being physically abused, neglected, mistreated, or economically abused, you should telephone the offices named above for help in making your report.

Who Can Help

Many organizations can help. Some have authority to take action by law; others will assist you in reaching such authorities if you wish.

In some states, guardians can be appointed by the state to make decisions for senior citizens. However, guardians must submit proof that the elderly cannot act on her/his own behalf.

If you feel someone has unfairly gained control of you or your property, ask your clergy, social worker, doctor, nurse, or others to obtain legal help for you to protest the guardianship. You have the right to challenge anyone who attempts to become your guardian. The kinds of help you can get may come from:

- Clergy
- National Council on the Aging
  600 Maryland Avenue
  Washington, D.C.
  (202) 479-1200
- Senior citizen centers
- Gray Panthers
- Department of welfare

- Department of health
- Offices for the aging
- Visiting Nurse Association
- Hospital social workers or doctors and nurses
- Battered women's centers.

In an emergency, call 911 and ask the operator for help. If physical violence is occurring, call the police.

ACKNOWLEDGMENTS

The following were of particular assistance: Barbara Shaffer, New York City Department for the Aging; William Koester, New York State Office for the Aging; Joan Ellenbogen, Esq.; Marcia Goldstein, Esq.; Candice Butcher; New York Department of Social Services Domestic Violence Program; Leslie Crocker-Schneider, Esq.; Marjorie Fields, Esq., Brooklyn Legal Services Corporation. A handbook written by Ms. Fields and Ms. Lehman is listed on p. 428 of this chapter and provided much of the information on police process. Ms. Sabra Wooley, National Center for the Control of Rape and the National Institute of Mental Health, has produced a listing of centers throughout the country and regularly updates them; she is also the author of *The Battered Woman,* which is listed on p. 426 of this chapter. The authors offer appreciation to all at the Center for Women's Policy Studies, whose excellent materials and immediate responses are invaluable resources.

FOOTNOTES

1. McNulty, Faith. *The Burning Bed.* New York: Harcourt Brace Jovanovich, 1980.

2. Hilberman, E. "The Wife Beater's Wife Reconsidered," *Amer. Journal of Psychiatry,* Nov. 1980.

3. Strauss, M.; Gelles, R.; and Steinmetz, S. *Behind Closed Doors.* Garden City, N.Y.: Anchor/Doubleday, 1980.

4. Giarretto, Henry. Training comments at Parents/Daughters/Sons United, 1980.

5. Pedrick-Cornell, Claire; and Gelles, Richard J. "Elderly Abuse: The Status of Current Knowledge." Paper presented at National Conference on Abuse of Older Persons, Boston, Mass., Mar. 23, 1981.

6. Strauss, M.; Gelles, R.; and Steinmetz, S. op. cit.

7. Leghorn, L. "Social Responses to Battered Women." Reprint of speech given in October 1976 to Wisconsin Conference on Battered Women.

8. Morgan, Robin, ed. *Sisterhood Is Powerful.* New York: Vintage Books, 1970.

9. Cuskey, Walter R.; Richardson, A.; and Berger, L. *Specialized Therapeutic Community Treatment Program for Female Addicts.* Washington, D.C.: DHEW Publication No. (ADM) 79-880, 1979.

10. Densen-Gerber, J. *Child Abuse and Neglect as Related to Parental Drug Abuse and Other Antisocial Behavior,* New York: Odyssey Institute, 1978.

11. Hilberman, E. op. cit.

12. New York State Office for the Aging. *A Guide to the Patient Abuse Reporting Law.*

FURTHER READING

Most of the resources listed on pp. 525–32 will mail you a reading list and most would appreciate a stamped, self-addressed envelope or a donation to cover the costs of printing, photocopying, and mailing. The following are particularly useful:

SPOUSE ABUSE

Center for Women's Policy Studies. *A Comprehensive Bibliography: Domestic Violence Crisis Intervention.* A listing of recent and valuable publications. (2000 P Street, N.W., Suite 508, Washington, D.C. 20036)

Fields, Marjorie D.; and Lehman, Elyse. *Handbook for Beaten Women.* (A small, practical guide available free, in English or Spanish, from: Brooklyn Legal Services Corporation B, 105 Court Street, Brooklyn, N.Y. 11201)

Strauss, M.; Gelles, R.; and Steinmetz, S. *Behind Closed Doors: Violence in the American Family.* Garden City, N.Y.: Anchor Press/Doubleday, 1980.

Wooley, Sabra R. *Battered Woman: A Summary.* Washington, D.C.: Women's Equity Action League. (805 15th Street, N.W., Suite 822, Washington, D.C. 20005)

CHILD SEXUAL ABUSE

Armstrong, Louise. *Kiss Daddy Goodnight.* New York: Hawthorn Books, 1978. Also in paperback, Pocket Books.

Bock, Richard D. *Got Me on the Run: A Story of Runaways.* Boston, Mass.: Beacon Press, 1973.

Bracey, Dorothy Heid. *Baby Pros.* New York: John Jay Press, 1979.

Brady, Katherine. *Fathers' Days.* New York: SeaView Books, 1979.

Burgess, Ann W.; et al. *Sexual Assault of Children and Adolescents.* Lexington, Mass.: Lexington Books, 1978.

Butler, Sandra. *Conspiracy of Silence.* New York: Bantam Books, 1978.

Chapman, Christine. *America's Runaways.* New York: Morrow, 1976.

Densen-Gerber, J. D.; and Benward, J. *Incest as a Causative Factor in Drug Abuse and Other Anti-Social Behavior.* New York: Odyssey Institute, 1976.

Fishman, Merle. *Just One Story.* Sherman Oaks, Calif.: M. Fishman, 1979.

Forward, Susan; and Buck, C. *Betrayal of Innocence.* Los Angeles: J. P. Tarcher, 1979.

Groth, Nicholas. *Men Who Rape.* New York: Plenum Press, 1979.

Janus, Sam; and Hirschman, Lisa. *Death of Innocence: How Our Children Are Endangered by the New Sexual Freedoms.* New York: Morrow, 1981.

Justice, Blair; and Justice, Rita. *The Broken Taboo; Sex in the Family.* New York: Human Sciences Press, 1979.

Linedecker, Clifford C. *Children in Chains.* New York: Everest House, 1981.

Lloyd, Robin. *For Money or Love: Boy Prostitution in America.* New York: Ballantine Books, 1976.

Raphael, Maryanne; and Wolf, Jenifer. *Runaways: America's Lost Youth.* New York: Drake Publishers, 1974.

Rush, Florence. *The Best Kept Secret: Sexual Abuse of Children.* Englewood Cliffs, N.J.: Prentice-Hall, 1980.

Sanford, Linda Tschirhart. *The Silent Children: A Parent's Guide to the Prevention of Sexual Abuse.* Garden City, N.Y.: Doubleday/Anchor Press, 1980.

Williams, Joy. *Red Flag, Green Flag People.* Fargo, N.D.: Rape and Abuse Crisis Center, 1980.

CHILD ABUSE: GENERAL

Caplan, Frank. *Parents Yellow Pages.* Garden City, N.Y.: Anchor Press/Doubleday, 1978. Easy-to-use guidebook to resources for parents.

Densen-Gerber, Judianne. *Child Abuse and Neglect as Related to Drug Abuse and Other Antisocial Behavior.* New York: Odyssey Institute. Includes recommendations for model laws, and cites case histories.

Gordon, Thomas. *Parent Effectiveness Training in Action.* New York: Bantam, 1976. A manual about positive parenting.

Hayden, Torey L. *One Child.* New York: G. P. Putnam's Sons, 1980. A schoolteacher's account of her personal work with a severely abused child.

Holmes, Beth. *The Whipping Boy.* New York: Jove Publications, 1978. An account of severe emotional abuse.

Hymes, James. *Understanding Your Child.* Englewood Cliffs, N.J.: Prentice-Hall, 1952.

———. *Behavior and Misbehavior.* Englewood Cliffs, N.J.: Prentice-Hall, 1955.

Kempe, C. H.; and Helfer, R. *The Battered Child.* Chicago: University of Chicago Press, 1974.

Mewshaw, Michael. *Life for Death.* Garden City, N.Y.: Doubleday, 1980. A personal account of a family and friend who attempted to help an abused adolescent when he was arrested and jailed for the murder of his parents.

National Institute of Mental Health (NIMH). The NIMH publishes a free, 19-page listing of books. Order from:
DHEW Publications (HSM) 73-9034
Public Health Service Mental Health Administration,
5600 Fishers Lane, Rockville, Md. 20852

Stone, J.; and Church, Joseph. *Childhood and Adolescence.* New York: Random House, 1957.

AUTHOR'S NOTE

Not long after I completed the first draft for this chapter on rape, I was assaulted while letting myself into my home. I fought back and chased the assailant away. Fortunately, I was not raped. But the incident remains with me: I am proud; I am more aware of my strength; but I am also angry and scared thinking about what could have happened.

So this chapter takes on a different meaning for me. My vision has never been so strong. Rape and violence are very real; they do not happen only to someone else.

Educating ourselves about the law—and working for law reform—is one step toward improving our society, but it is only a beginning. Now more than ever, I am convinced that we must strive to change our society's underlying values so they do not perpetuate a culture that allows sexual violence to continue.

L.A.M.

19
Rape

LYNN A. MARKS
KAREN KULP

Lynn A. Marks, an attorney, is the executive director of Women Organized Against Rape (WOAR) of Philadelphia and has served as the rape victim advocate in the Philadelphia District Attorney's Rape Prosecution Unit. She has drafted legislation to help rape victims, and she argued a case on the confidentiality of victim records that resulted in a landmark decision.

She is also the vice chair of the Philadelphia Bar Association's Women's Rights Committee, an Advisory Council member of Women's Alliance for Job Equity, which advocates against sexual harassment, and a member of the Philadelphia Mayor's Commission on Women. She is on the Steering Committee for the Lawyers' Committee for Reproductive Rights. She teaches a college course on justice and is a graduate of Skidmore College and the University of Pennsylvania Law School.

Karen Kulp, a photographer, writer, and feminist activist, works as public information coordinator for WOAR in Philadelphia.

Rape is one of the most violent, threatening, and disruptive experiences of a woman's life. The intimate nature of the crime leads to the mistaken belief that it is a sexually motivated act. On the contrary, it is a criminal act of violence and domination, motivated by anger and hostility and not by sexual need.

Each state has a separate statute classifying rape or sexual assault as a crime. In most states, rape is defined as forcible sexual intercourse, accomplished against the will of the victim. Many laws limit the definition of rape by relationship of the parties involved or by their gender. In most states, it is not against the law for a man to force his wife to have sex. Nor can men be raped, under most state laws.

Some acts of forced sexual conduct may not be considered rape under the law, yet the emotional effects can be the same or worse. For instance, the law limits rape to sexual intercourse committed by physical force or the threat of physical force; it does not include intercourse committed by means of psychological, social, or financial pressure. For example, if a woman has sex against her will with her doctor because she feels psychologically coerced, this is not usually considered rape unless she is also physically threatened. This means that women may be forced without physical violence into having sex to save their relationships, to save their jobs, or to save their lives.

Other offensive conduct in which a woman might "feel raped" includes obscene phone calls, pinches, grabs, or lewd remarks. These "little rapes" usually go unreported, unprosecuted, and unpunished. However, such conduct perpetuates a world in which women are victimized and objectified.

Furthermore, most women live to some extent in fear of rape. Consciously and unconsciously, this fear limits freedom of movement, pursuit of education, and choice of housing and jobs. Many women are brought up to believe that the world is not a safe place for a woman alone.

Historically, a woman needed the protection of a man to be safe. Rape was treated as a crime against property—a woman was no more than a man's property. A rape victim's father or husband was the injured party. A single woman was fair game for any man to make his property by raping her. In wartime, soldiers freely raped the enemy's women as part of their spoils.

Even today, people hold various stereotypes of rape. One image is of a perverted "psycho" who lurks in bushes, alleys, and elevators waiting for a victim. However, while some rapists may be psychotic, most are seemingly "normal" members of a community. Another stereotype is of a man so overcome by sexual passion that he cannot help himself and takes a woman by force. However, rapists are primarily motivated not by a sexual need but by a need to overpower someone weaker: usually a woman or a child, but sometimes another man.

People wrongly assume that the victim is young, attractive, and provocatively dressed, furthering the mistaken belief that rape is motivated by sexual desire. Victims, however, can be old or young, unattractive or pretty, disabled or physically fit. Rapists can be any age, race, economic status, religion, or occupation. They may be married and have normal sex lives. The rapist and the victim are usually the same race.

Furthermore, most people assume that rape happens between strangers. Statistics show, however, that in the majority of reported cases, women are raped by someone they know. If a woman is raped by an acquaintance or someone she trusts, she may doubt her judgment and question her trust in people even more than a woman who is raped by a stranger. In addition, others might question her actions.

Men are often socialized to be aggressive sexually, women to be passive. Accordingly, a woman's resistance is seen as part of the game of pretending reluctance while really wanting to engage in sex. A woman is in a double bind: a "good girl" supposedly says no when she means yes. So if a man rapes her, he is only fulfilling her real wishes. On the other hand, if a woman is sexually active and assertive, many feel that she cannot really be raped, because her life-style is seen as a provocation.

The extremes of women as either virgins or whores are reinforced all around us. On television, female leading characters are portrayed as either innocent, dependent, and ladylike, or as evil, independent, and masculine. The ladylike woman, who is good on the surface, uses manipulation to get what she wants. This manipulation may include having sex when she does not want to in order to get a man. The independent woman often gets punished, sometimes in the form of rape, to let her know she needs to be dependent on the protection of a man. If she remains independent, she is doomed to suffer a lonely and dangerous existence. If either "prostitute" or "virgin" is raped, too often our society holds her responsible for the attack.

Our society espouses contradictory values. Politicians, newscasters, and others decry the violence in our society. At the same time, movies, advertising, television shows, and song lyrics increasingly portray women in a context in which violence is seen as normal and expected.

In 1980, there were over 82,000 reported cases of sexual assault in the United States. Not surprisingly, rape remains one of the most under-reported crimes. A conservative estimate is that over 50 percent of all rapes go unreported. In this chapter, rape will be discussed within the context of the law. Yet rape happens with greater frequency and in more ways than the law defines.*

THE LAW

Rape

Most state statutes define a crime called rape; other states call the crime sexual assault, sexual battery, or unlawful sexual intercourse. Some state statutes list the crime in several degrees, according to its seriousness.

Several elements of the crime are common to almost all state statutes, even though they are worded in various ways:

*This chapter uses the feminine pronoun because rape happens most often to females. However, it should be noted that males can also be raped and may suffer reactions similar to those of female victims.

SEXUAL INTERCOURSE OR CARNAL KNOWLEDGE

Rape requires the penetration of one person's sex organs by another. Emission is not necessary. Some states also include as rape: nonconsensual anal intercourse, cunnilingus, fellatio, and/or intrusion of any object by force.

AGAINST ONE'S WILL OR WITHOUT CONSENT

1. Intercourse accomplished by force; or
2. Intercourse accomplished by threat of force; or
3. Intercourse accomplished if a person is incapable of consenting, such as if the person is unconscious, drugged, intoxicated, mentally incompetent, or under a stated age.

ABSENCE OF MARITAL RELATIONSHIP, IN MOST STATES

Most state laws do not recognize nonconsensual intercourse as rape when the parties are married, especially if they are living together.

Statutory Rape

In almost all states, sexual intercourse with a female under a stated age, *with or without her consent,* is a crime. Unlike rape, statutory rape is committed even if the female willingly participates. The objective is to protect girls from "illicit acts of intercourse" by making their consent legally impossible. Sex with underage boys is also usually a crime; however, the age of consent may differ from that of girls in some states.

Incest

Incest consists of either a sexual act or marriage between persons who are too closely related. Most state statutes restrict the crime to blood relatives, although many include some nonblood relatives as well.

Sexual Assault and Abuse of Children

Other kinds of sexual acts between children and adults, in addition to intercourse, are crimes in most states. There are a variety of crimes, with various names and definitions, depending on the state.

Sexual assault of children generally refers to rape or forced sodomy committed by someone who is not in a caretaking role to the child.

Sexual abuse of children generally refers to sexual contacts or interactions between a child and an adult who *is* in a caretaking role (e.g., parent, guardian, baby-sitter, other relative) perpetrated for the sexual stimulation of that adult or another adult. Examples include fondling, molestation, exhibitionism, using children in pornography, or showing pornography to children. Physical force is often not used. Rather, the adult tricks the child or takes advantage of the child's confusion about sex. Such acts are often repeated over time (also see Chapter 18).

MYTHS ABOUT RAPE PERMEATE THE LAW

Rape laws have grown out of and reflect our society's traditional beliefs, stereotypes, and myths about rape and its victims. In the crime of rape, unlike any other crime, the law may require supportive evidence, resistance, prompt complaint, and measures of victim credibility. Fortunately, as attitudes change, reforms are also being made in the laws and institutional practices. However, even though the laws have been reformed in many states, judges, jurors, prosecutors, and police may be biased against the rape victim because of these myths.

The following section shows how the law has incorporated some societal beliefs.

Belief: Women and Children Are Basically Untrustworthy. Their Word Alone Is Not Sufficient Proof.

Law:
Traditionally, the law requires supportive evidence (corroboration) to back up a victim's testimony, such as the presence of semen, physical injury, or a witness. This is not true for other crimes. The strictest state laws require corroboration of all parts of a rape victim's statement. Other states require that there be supporting evidence to document that there was penetration or that the victim did not consent. Still others have abolished special corroboration requirements altogether.

Another law in many states requires a rape victim to file a prompt police report. Thus, victims must often report a rape within three months. In other crimes, victims have two to five years to report. A prompt complaint can sometimes be used as corroboration.

Effects:
- Police may not believe a victim and not arrest a suspect if there is no corroborating evidence.
- Prosecutors may not take a case to trial without additional evidence.
- Even where a case does go to trial, judges and juries may not convict without additional evidence to support a victim's testimony.
- If a victim does not promptly report the attack, police, prosecutors, judges, and juries may assume that the assault was not committed.

Fact:
Often there is no corroborating evidence. There is usually no eyewitness. There is often no additional external physical injury, especially when a woman is threatened with a weapon and she submits, leaving no scars. There is often no evidence of sperm: Men do not always ejaculate; women often wash. Rape victims often do not report the crime immediately because of their emotional crisis.

Belief: Only a Virgin Can Be Raped. If a Woman Consented to Sex in the Past, Either with the Same Man or with Others, She Must Have Consented Again.

Law:
Traditionally, the law has allowed a woman's prior history to be introduced as evidence to question her credibility and to infer that because she consented to sex in the past, she must have consented this time. Many states, however, have revised their laws to forbid questioning of a victim's sexual past unless it involves the defendant on trial. These are known as "rape-shield" statutes. (Note that the alleged rapist's prior criminal record must not be brought out at trial.)

Effects:
• Women may be hesitant to report a rape for fear that their sexual experience will be made public.
• Judges and juries might make decisions based on a woman's sexual experience, rather than on the incident itself.

Fact:
Whether a woman is a virgin or a prostitute is irrelevant to whether or not she consents to any particular incident.

Belief: A Woman Who Does Not Resist Has Not Really Been Raped.

Law:
Traditionally, the law has required a woman to have "resisted to the utmost" in order to be able to make a charge of rape. This requirement is not necessary for other crimes. Some states no longer require physical resistance, and personal injury is no longer needed as proof. Nonetheless, a woman must be able to show that she did not consent—that the act was accomplished with force or threat of force.

Effects:
• A woman may blame herself for being raped unless she fought back.

• Family members, police, judges, and juries might not believe the woman if she did not fully resist and therefore did not incur injuries.

Fact:
Rape is a life-threatening situation. Often a weapon, threat of a weapon, or force is present. The victim is in an impossible situation: if she resists, she may be killed; if she does not, a charge of rape can often not be brought.

Belief: A Wife Cannot Be Raped by her Husband.

Law:
Most state laws do not recognize forced sexual intercourse as rape when the parties are married. These laws sometimes apply when unmarried persons cohabit. However, some states have revised their laws to make it a crime for a husband to rape his wife. In others, this is limited to cases in which the couple have a written separation agreement or a court order, and/or live apart.

Effects:
• Men often believe they have the "right to rape" their wives.
• Women themselves often do not view nonconsensual sexual relations with their husbands as rape, due to their own socialization.
• Police are hesitant to answer emergency calls regarding marital rape, reasoning that this is a domestic matter that should be handled privately.
• Even in cases where the law allows for marital-rape prosecution, judges and juries are not likely to see these cases as rape, especially if there is no outward physical injury.

Fact:
Many women report being repeatedly and brutally raped by their husbands. Even in states that permit marital-rape prosecution if there is a legal separation, women often cannot afford to move out, especially if there are children.

Belief: Men Cannot Be Raped.

Law:
Traditionally, the crime of rape meant only the penetration of the female sex organ by the male. Some state statutes now make it a crime for a man to be raped, as well as a woman. This is sometimes called involuntary deviate sexual intercourse or sodomy.

Effects:
• Men and boys may be reluctant to report being raped.
• Friends and family of a male victim may not believe that he could be raped. They may even joke about it.

- Police and prosecutors may lack sensitivity and experience in dealing with male victims.
- Judges and juries may carry into court their stereotypes of what a rape victim looks like and thus be hesitant to convict. This may be particularly true if the victim is large and tough-looking. If he is a homosexual, they may think he "asked for it" or "deserved it."

Fact:

Boys and men do get raped. This is almost always by another male. Twenty-five percent of the children under 12 who report being raped are boys. Adult men are raped, but rarely report it. Rapes in prison are common. When a male rapes another male, neither of them is necessarily a homosexual. There have been scattered reports of females raping males. When this does happen, it is generally an adult woman with a young boy.

Belief: False Accusations Are Likely to Be Made in Cases of Rape.

Law:

Judges may give "cautionary" instructions to the jury at the conclusion of the trial about the law they must apply to the particular case. For example, a judge tells the jury the charge of rape is "easily made and difficult to defend against." Thus the law requires them to examine the victim's testimony "with caution." Some state statutes now forbid this kind of instruction.

Effect:

- Through these instructions, judges can prejudice the jury against the victim.

Fact:

There is no documented evidence that a person makes false accusations for rape more than for any other crime.

THE AFTERMATH OF RAPE

What if You Are Raped?

- Do not wash or straighten things up.
- Get immediate medical attention.
- Call the rape crisis center, women's center, or victim advocacy organization in your community.

• Call the police.
• DON'T TRY TO COPE WITH IT ALL BY YOURSELF!

What Happens if You Decide to Report?

If there is a rape crisis center in your community, it can tell you what will happen if you call the police to report a rape. The following information will give you a general idea of what to expect during the medical examination (either in a hospital emergency room or by a physician) and from the police.

IT IS IMPORTANT TO GET PROMPT MEDICAL ATTENTION

• To check for and treat external and internal injuries; you may not be able to feel them.
• To protect against venereal disease.
• To check for possible pregnancy.
• To collect evidence to be given to police and used in prosecution if you decide to press charges.

WHAT WILL THE MEDICAL EXAMINATION INCLUDE?

• *Medical history:* You will be asked what happened. Be sure to show the doctor or nurse any place you were injured.
• *Pelvic examination:* to check for bruises on your outer genitals, any internal bruises or cuts in your vagina or anus, to take smears to check for the presence of sperm.
• *Blood test:* to check for venereal disease.
• *Penicillin injection:* to prevent venereal disease.
• *Morning-after pill (DES) or other contraceptive:* to prevent pregnancy if you were not using birth control.

Usually venereal disease does not show up in women and girls right away. It is important to see a doctor a month after the incident to check again for VD and pregnancy.

MEDICAL EXAMINATIONS: WHAT YOU SHOULD KNOW

• You may ask for an explanation of medical procedures.
• You can get pregnant from rape, although the likelihood is slight.
• The morning-after pill (DES) may have side effects. Ask your doctor.
• The hospital or doctor may be required by law to report a sexual assault to the police.
• You may ask the police to leave the examination room while you disrobe.
• Even if you choose not to report the incident to the police, it is important to receive medical attention.
• A counselor from a rape crisis center may be available to be with you in the hospital.

POLICE

A police officer is often the first contact you will have with the criminal justice system. The police, sheriff, or other designated law enforcement agency is responsible for investigating your case, apprehending a suspect, and gathering evidence to be used in prosecution.

In some cities, specialized units have been created to investigate sexual assaults. These units have been started so that officers can develop expertise in investigating sex offenses and sensitivity in treating victims.

Actual procedures differ from locality to locality. However, in most areas, the police perform the following functions:

- Answer emergency calls and dispatch patrol cars to the crime scene;
- Take you to get medical attention;
- Interview you and any other witnesses and write a report;
- Help you identify a suspect (if it was not an acquaintance) by (a) showing you "mug shots" of known and suspected sex offenders; and/or (b) making a composite sketch according to your description; and/or (c) arranging a lineup with the suspected assailant and others who look similar to him;
- Possibly ask you to take a polygraph (lie-detector) test before they arrest a suspect;
- Arrest a suspect;
- Testify at trial as to their findings.

What You Should Know About the Investigation

- You have the right to be treated with dignity. You are not the criminal.
- Even though you may feel in an emotional and physical crisis, it is important for the police to begin investigating the crime as soon as possible, to gather information.
- Rape crisis counselors might be available to offer emotional support during the police investigation.
- Everything you say to the police becomes part of a record that may be shared in court.
- You should give as much detailed information as you possibly can. Always tell the truth.
- You may be asked to take a polygraph (lie-detector or truth-telling) test. You might want to contact a rape crisis center to learn whether you must take it. In most states, the results of the test must not be presented in court, nor may the fact that you refused to take it.

• In many localities, if you are under 18, the police will notify your parents or guardian and tell them you were raped.

WHAT HAPPENS IF YOU DECIDE TO PRESS CHARGES AGAINST THE ASSAILANT?

In some localities, if you merely report the incident to law enforcement authorities, it will be assumed that you are prepared to press charges and an investigation will begin in order to arrest the assailant. In other places, you must sign a "complaint," which is a legal document declaring that you want to press criminal charges against your attacker.

If you decide to press charges and a suspect is arrested, you will become the main (or complaining) witness for the state in its prosecution of the alleged assailant. You will become involved in a process that begins with the police interview and ends with a trial.

The district attorney (DA) or prosecutor's office represents the interests of the state and thus will act as your attorney, free of charge, in the criminal lawsuit. Some prosecuting offices now have attorneys who specialize in handling sexual assault cases and receive special training. You may contact a private attorney, if you wish, to give you advice about the case, but the prosecutor is responsible for presenting the case in court.

Legal procedures vary from state to state and county to county. The following chart shows the common steps:

After the arrest and the filing of charges, the defendant (the accused) has a PRESENTMENT HEARING OR PRELIMINARY ARRAIGNMENT before a magistrate or judge: bail is set, he is advised of the charges against him and of his right to a lawyer. (You are not present.)

At the PRELIMINARY HEARING, a magistrate or judge must determine whether there is "probable cause" to believe that (a) a crime has been committed and that (b) the accused committed it. In some states GRAND JURY proceedings are held either instead of or after a preliminary hearing to determine probable cause. (You would testify at either of these proceedings.)

At the ARRAIGNMENT, the defendant pleads guilty or not guilty. (You are not present.) Plea bargaining may take place between the DA and the defense attorney to either dismiss charges or have the defendant plead guilty to a less serious offense and avoid the need for a trial.

If the defendant pleads "not guilty," a TRIAL proceeds. Either a judge alone or a twelve-person jury decides if the defendant is "guilty beyond a reasonable doubt." If he is, the judge will sentence him to a prison, mental institution, or probation.

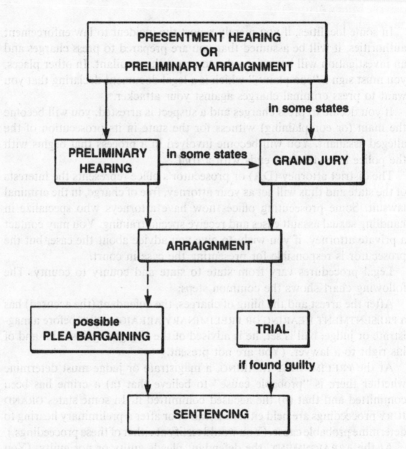

THE TRIAL ITSELF

Women's reactions to a rape trial range from feeling they have been raped a second time to feeling they have had the opportunity to vindicate themselves. Much depends on the facts of the case, the lawyers and judges involved, the support received from family and friends to go forward, and one's own attitude and personality.

You must be in the same room with the assailant; he has a constitutional right to hear all the charges and evidence brought against him. You will have to recount the specifics of the incident. You will probably have to return to court a number of times.

At trial, the district attorney/prosecutor will ask you questions about the incident, as well as what happened before and after the attack. The defense attorney (who represents the defendant) will cross-examine you for inconsistencies and try to show that either (a) you have identified the wrong man or (b) you consented and therefore were not raped.

Other people may also testify: the police, medical personnel, any witnesses, and perhaps someone you told about the attack. The defendant may testify, but he has the right to remain silent.

Sometimes women want to drop charges after they have reported the rape. But once a suspect has been arrested, it may be difficult to drop charges. However, since practices vary, you should check with your rape crisis center or prosecutor's office if you do not want to go through the trial.

The court experience can be the beginning of your healing process and a constructive way to channel your anger, humiliation, and frustration.

What You Should Know if You Decide to Press Charges
- You may request that the courtroom be closed to the public, except to people involved in the case. The judge may or may not honor your request.
- You may ask that your name and address not be given to the media. You need not give your address on the witness stand if you are afraid of retaliation or publicity. Just give your name and the prosecutor's office address.
- There is no standard length of time you will have to spend on the witness stand.
- If you are being harassed by the defendant or his family or friends, tell the prosecutor and the police immediately.
- You may request to be informed of any plea-bargaining arrangement.

- There is no standard term of sentence for a man found guilty of rape. It depends on the facts of the incident, his prior record, and the locality.
- You may ask to have input into the sentencing process. Sometimes you may tell the judge what effect the rape has had on your life. The judge may then consider this when determining the sentence.
- You should ask whether your state will compensate you by paying you.
- Parents of young victims should carefully weigh the advantages and disadvantages of putting their child through the legal system. Often, plea bargaining can be used to avoid courtroom testimony.
- In the case of rape by a stranger, if you choose not to press charges, a man who will potentially rape again will go free.
- In the case of incestuous or acquaintance rape, if you choose not to press charges, there may be nothing to prevent him from raping you again.
- Whether or not the assailant is found guilty, if you press charges, you are letting other rapists know that their crime does not go unrecognized.
- A verdict of "not guilty" does not mean the rape did not occur or that the judge/jury did not believe you. There may not be enough evidence to find him guilty "beyond a reasonable doubt."
- A rape crisis counselor or other victim advocate might be available to accompany you through the legal process.

FEELINGS AFTER A RAPE

Being raped is always traumatic. For many women, it is a major life crisis. You may experience many emotions following the attack: fear, anger, shame, guilt, anxiety, and helplessness.

Studies of rape victims have shown that reactions may come in phases. The period immediately following a rape is a time of crisis. It is a time of disorientation and disruption. It may be difficult to make even simple decisions. You may react to what has happened by crying, screaming, getting angry, or laughing. You may try to hide your feelings by remaining quiet and withdrawn or by acting calm and in control. No one reaction is more normal than any other. Many victims say that the most upsetting part of the attack was fearing that they would be killed.

A few weeks after the attack, you will probably have gotten back into your normal routine. However, you may remain fearful, irritable, moody; you may cry a lot, have trouble sleeping, lose your appetite, or have nightmares or phobias. You may have trouble concentrating at your job or in school. You may feel uncomfortable having sexual relations after rape. If you were not sexually active before the incident, the attack might be even more traumatic. In addition, you may experience a fear of men in general.

Months after the attack, you may find that you still dream about it or that you are still afraid or angry. Some women have chosen to move or change jobs to begin to get over it.

You may choose not to tell anyone what happened to you. You may feel that by not talking about it, you can forget it, and pretend the incident never happened. However, months or even years later, the memories may begin to haunt you. So, although no one should be forced to talk about what happened, it will be helpful to your recovery to do so.

Being raped can leave permanent emotional scars, but it is an experience most people get over sooner or later. How you cope will depend on how frightening the assault was, your own personality, and the kind of emotional support you get from others.

If a Woman You Know Has Been Raped

- You can help her recover. She will need you to understand that she has been through a frightening and painful experience.
- Listen to her. Encourage her to express her feelings. It may be difficult for you as well. But don't try to make her forget.
- Reassure her that the rape was not her fault, and that she is not dirty or ruined.
- Suggest she call a rape crisis center.
- Offer to accompany her through the court process if she chooses to press charges.

If Your Child Has Been Raped or Sexually Abused
(NOTE: This section refers to both sexes.)

- Even if you assume your child has never been abused, let her know in advance whom she can talk to if she is approached in an abusive way or if touching goes "too far."
- Encourage her to talk to you or another trusting adult about it.
- Tell her what sexual abuse is in words she can understand, and that it may be done by a stranger or by someone she knows well.
- Let her know that it is not her fault, even if she was acting affectionately toward the adult.
- Call a rape crisis center or other organization helping children and women for advice on how to deal with the situation.

Counseling Options

Not everybody who is raped will need long-term counseling, but most will need some immediate help in working out the emotional and physical pain that rape causes. Rape crisis centers were started to help sexual assault victims become sexual assault survivors. Many rape crisis centers were started by women who were victims, or who had friends who were victims, and who experienced firsthand the insensitivity of police, doctors, and mental health practitioners.

Rape crisis centers often provide 24-hour hot lines, and counselors in the emergency room and in court. Many centers offer only short-term counseling; others provide ongoing counseling services. Since it is helpful for many women to share their feelings with women who have been through similar experiences, victim support groups have been formed in some areas. Often these are facilitated by a woman who has worked out the trauma of her own assault.

Child victims may need special help, particularly if the offender is a family member.

Another option for counseling is private therapy. Most rape crisis centers can provide you with a referral to a therapist who has been trained in treatment issues concerning sexual assault. If you were in therapy before the assault, that is a good place for you to discuss the rape. But remember that therapists, like everyone else, may have their own stereotypes and myths about rape.

Often the family of the victim may want some counseling. In some areas, there are organizations that provide support to the lovers and husbands of victims.

Victim Compensation Programs

Victim compensation programs exist in many states to provide some monetary compensation for being raped, even if a suspect is not apprehended. Unfortunately, most programs cover only out-of-pocket expenses, rather than restitution for emotional stress, pain, and suffering. You should check the coverage in your state by contacting your police department or district attorney's office.

Civil Suits

A civil suit may be filed instead of, or in addition to, criminal prosecution and/or victim compensation.

A victim may *sue the assailant* in civil court to recover financial expenses and compensation for pain and mental suffering from the rape.

A victim may also *sue third parties* who may be held responsible for dangerous conditions that result in rape. Hotels, employers, universities, transit authorities, and landlords have been required to pay huge amounts to victims and are thereby induced to improve security to prevent future attacks and future lawsuits.

For more information, contact a private attorney or the district attorney's office.

Fighting Back

You may want to consider the option of fighting back if attacked. For years, women have been told that it is best to submit. Two 1981 studies, by Pauline Bart and by Jenny McIntirie, found that women who fought back often avoided being raped. Fighting back is not an option for every woman. However, you may want to think about what you would do if attacked. For some women, this thinking may result in taking a self-defense or martial-arts class. For others, it means carrying mace, tear gas, hat pins, or other weapons. Before you decide to carry a weapon, you should check with the police about its legality and about classes where you can learn to use the weapon effectively.

YOU SHOULD KNOW

- You may legally use force if you believe force is immediately necessary to protect yourself.
- You may use only the amount of force necessary to prevent or stop the attack.
- Some states allow you to use more force in self-defense, such as shooting to kill the attacker, if the incident takes place in your home. Check with your local police or district attorney's office for your state's laws.
- You may not legally use force as a warning, punishment, or retaliation.
- Every case will be judged individually to determine if "self-defense" was used legally.
- Weapons and protective devices such as mace can be taken away from you by an attacker and used against you.

PROGRESS AND GOALS

Fifteen years ago, rape was a private matter, with the burden borne alone by the victim and sometimes her family. Today, a rape victim has somewhere to turn. In many places she can call a twenty-four-hour crisis hot line and have someone with her in the hospital and court. She can expect more sensitive treatment from police, medical personnel, and prosecutors. The laws have been reformed in most states to make it easier for her to go through with criminal prosecution.

Rape has become a public issue spearheaded by the women's movement. Rape crisis centers have been largely responsible for the more sensitive treatment of victims. In addition to offering services to victims, rape crisis centers train police, medical personnel, prosecutors, and judges in sensitive and appropriate responses to rape and its victims. Education in the community is slowly erasing myths and stereotypes about rape.

The antirape movement has lobbied for fairer laws. Rape-shield laws protecting a woman's prior sexual history, laws decreasing corroboration requirements, and laws extending the period within which to file charges are some of the improvements.

Still needed are changes in the law that would broaden the definition of force to include psychological as well as physical force. In most states, it is still legal for a husband to rape his wife. Legislation is being advocated that would give rape crisis counselors a privilege of confidentiality with clients similar to that of doctors and lawyers.

The prevention of rape and other sexual assaults is now a priority for antirape activists. Women are training in self-defense and assertiveness. The traditional roles into which men and women have been socialized are being challenged. The role of pornography and violence in the media in promoting and condoning violence against women is being addressed. In some cities, men are organizing against rape to educate other men about their part in perpetuating rape. The sexual abuse of children, which has been largely unacknowledged, is now being recognized, as rape crisis centers start programs working with sexually abused children and prevention through education.

The seventies brought positive changes by medical personnel, police, and prosecutors in responding to the terrible toll that rape victims pay. Unfortunately, as a result of the changing political and financial climate of the eighties, rape crisis centers are in jeopardy. In the future, all of us must strive even harder to end the sexual victimization of women and children in our society.

FURTHER READING

Brownmiller, Susan. *Against Our Will: Men, Women and Rape.* New York: Simon & Schuster, 1973.

Burgess, Ann Wolbert; and Holmstrom, Lynda Lytle. *Rape: Crisis and Recovery.* Bowie, Md.: Robert J. Brady, 1979.

Griffin, Susan. *Rape: The Power of Consciousness.* New York: Harper & Row, 1979.

Groth, Nicholas. *Men Who Rape: The Psychology of the Offender.* New York: Plenum Press, 1979.

Sanford, Linda Tscheradt; and Fetter, Ann. *In Defense of Ourselves: A Rape Prevention Handbook for Women.* Garden City, N.Y.: Doubleday, 1979.

Taking Control, A Personal Safety Handbook. 1220 Sansom Street, Philadelphia, Pa. 19107: Women Organized Against Rape, 1982.

Part Five

HOW TO USE
THE LEGAL SYSTEM

20
Understanding the U.S. Court System

TONDA F. RUSH

Tonda F. Rush is a communications lawyer in Washington, D.C. A former newspaper reporter, she has pursued her interest in writing through a monthly article on legal affairs in Press Woman *magazine and through newspaper articles on law for laypersons. She is a graduate of the William Allen White School of Journalism and the School of Law at the University of Kansas.*

Have you noticed lately that the "repairman" who comes to fix your telephone is likely to be a woman or that the "stewardess" who served you drinks on the flight to Miami was a man; that you get more information nowadays when you deal with businesses; that you now see lawyers advertising on TV, though you never used to; that more people in wheelchairs seem to be out and about; that you hear more about people's rights?

A lot has changed in the past 30 years, and behind many of the changes are the courts, shaping and interpreting the laws that your elected representatives write.

Courts have ruled that employment discrimination is generally illegal. They have upheld laws requiring businesses to disclose more about themselves to consumers (the exact interest rates they intend to charge, for example). They have ruled that professional people may advertise and that public buildings must be accessible to the handicapped. They enforce rules to keep government from intruding needlessly upon private lives.

They lurk in the background in your daily life in more ways than you might ever imagine. You may encounter them in disagreeable situations,

Special thanks are due to Dorothy Rush of Kansas City, Kansas, whose suggestions for this chapter were invaluable.

such as bankruptcies or divorces; sad situations, such as the approval of a will or a lawsuit over an accident, and happy situations, such as the adoption of a child.

To many, they are as inscrutable as the weather and about as unpredictable. And in fact, some people have been heard to apply the weatherman's aphorism to the courts: if you don't like what they do, wait 24 hours and they'll change.

But courts generally are quite predictable and their rules understandable. Rather than assuming that only lawyers can work their way through the legal maze, you may discover that a few minutes' study will help you decide when and how you can use the courts to help you get what you want: your legal rights.

COURTS

There are 52 individual court systems in this country—50 state systems, the District of Columbia system, and the federal system. Sometimes these systems have the powers to decide exactly the same cases and settle the same disputes. Sometimes one is prohibited from venturing into another's territory. The issue depends upon who is in court and why she is there.

When the legal system began to blossom in this country, the states were colonies, each settled by a fiercely independent group of Europeans who clung to their own ideas of justice. Each colony, of course, became a state and brought into its statehood the history of the motherland's court system.

Most states followed the English lead in legal development, using the common-law system, which looks back to all decisions ever made by judges in recorded English legal history to dictate what should be the law in the future. (One state, Louisiana, remained true to its French heritage. It developed a slightly different system, based upon the Napoleonic Code, which was a compilation of French laws.)

In common-law countries, historically, the law was created as each dispute arose. Citizens who wanted to abide by the law looked backward to see what had been done before.

The English common law evolved out of the feudal system. Each lord had authority to govern his own fiefdom, as he saw fit, through manorial courts. Disputes went to the lord of the manor for resolution. Disputes among the nobility went to the king or his appointed chancellor for resolution. Decisions were based upon individual cases as they came along.

The principle of the common law was that it simply existed and was there to be discovered by the legal experts who governed. The "discoveries," however, were often rather arbitrary, providing no real guidance to law-abiding citizens. Courts began to realize that some consistency was needed. So the doctrine of *stare decisis* was established. The doctrine means simply that each decision sets the framework for the decisions that follow. Judges are bound to stay within the rules of the precedents.

Was William the Lesser fined ten chickens for stealing James the Least's rooster? Then Thomas the Bald must be fined ten cows for stealing Henry the Falconer's bull. But what to do when Richard the Chickenhearted steals Arthur the Round's saw? Is a saw like a rooster or a bull? How can Richard be fined ten saws, and of what use to Richard would they be? No, a new precedent must be made. When tools are stolen, new recompense must be devised. Perhaps Richard should provide one ox as payment. Henceforth, the fine for tool theft will be one ox, and the principle is established that when in-kind fines are practical, they will be ordered, but when they are not, other recompense will be permitted.

The example isn't meant to suggest that hens and cows were used for fines, as much as to illustrate that each case was used as an example for future judges to follow. As the cases proliferated, principles were established.

King Henry II was the first to nationalize the feudal courts. He created professional judges to decide local disputes. Their decisions were written down to become the law of the realm.

Eventually, Parliament was established to create laws also. Where it acted, its laws governed, but where it did not, common law was in force. The court acquired the power of interpreting Parliament's actions when it appeared a law might fit a certain crime or dispute, but not precisely.

The colonies followed English court rules until after the Revolution. The laws of Parliament and the English courts were the laws of the land. When independence was won and the colonial legislatures became state legislatures, the hold of Parliament was broken. But the spirit of the courts lived on. To this day, English rules about the use of property and the keeping of promises live among us, influencing our lives in ways we have come to take for granted. Where no legislated law exists, the time-worn English common law still governs. For example, the law by which you sue your neighbor if she damages your reputation, or slanders you, is rooted in the common law. Laws that keep others from trespassing on your property also hail from the common law.

Congress and state legislatures have taken the place of Parliament. They pass laws, which the courts interpret. Each state has a court system to interpret its own laws and to decide what its common law is.

State Courts

Each state has a supreme court. In some states it is called the Supreme Court; in others, such as New York and Maryland, it is the Court of Appeals. Those courts are presided over by justices, most of whom were judges at some point in their careers, but who were appointed to the state judiciary because of their respected scholarship, their political connections, or a combination of the two.

States may have a second level of court, the appellate, just under the state supreme court, that functions much like the state supreme court but in less-important cases. The purpose of an intermediate appellate system is to leave the high court free for only the most crucial cases, while ensuring that an appellate court exists to oversee what lower courts do.

At the bottom level are the trial courts. They are the ones you see most often on television and at the movies—both in the actual broadcasts recently made legal in many states and in fictional TV or movie dramas. Those courts are the first to hear most types of cases. They hear what witnesses and lawyers have to say about a particular dispute and they decide how the law should apply. They are the courts of record. It is the judges in the trial courts who have the first say about what a law means. Let's try an example.

The Bingo Case: A women's group had a meeting hall where family dinners were held each month. It was a serene place, a favorite community wateringhole, until a lottery agency opened up next door. Then all sorts of riffraff hung around, buying lottery tickets, drinking, and generally alarming the women and their families. So the women put pressure on their local politicians to do something about it.

Finally, the state legislature bowed to their demands and passed a law outlawing gambling in the state. The lottery shop closed its doors and the family dinners resumed, until one fateful night when the weekly bingo game was interrupted by several polite police officers stating that Ms. Right Just, the president, was under arrest for gambling.

The women were outraged. To have their friendly penny-ante bingo game demeaned as common gambling was the worst affront yet. They vowed to fight all the way to the Supreme Court. But their pleas were to no avail. Ms. Just was taken to the police station and booked on criminal charges.

Following some procedural formalities, she was brought into the trial court. Her lawyer and the lawyer for the state engaged in verbal fisticuffs about the meaning of the gambling law. Did it or did it not cover neighborhood games in which nothing but a few coins and a peck of corn were in use? The judge ruled that it did. She was put on trial.

A jury was called, a group of 12 citizens whose names were drawn out of a hat. (Or in this enlightened age, they were probably picked by computer.) Witnesses were called, including the police officers who testify that they saw her playing bingo. She testified on her own behalf, though the law permitted her to refuse to do so. She admitted that she was playing bingo but denied that she won any money.

The testimony ended, and the judge instructed the jury that she already had decided that bingo is a form of gambling if money changes hands. Because juries may not decide "legal" issues—in other words, what the law means—and may only decide "facts," the jury's sole duty was to determine whether she was playing bingo and whether money changed hands. The jury decided that it did and she was guilty.

She appealed to the next level, the state appellate courts. A copy of the transcript, or record, which tells exactly what was said in the trial, was presented to the judges in that court. (The higher courts rarely hear testimony on their own. They rely upon the lower courts to gather the proper information.)

The lawyers began their word battle again, arguing on two issues: First, is bingo gambling? And second, does the evidence show that Ms. Just was playing bingo?

The appellate court reviewed the documents before it. The lawyers made oral arguments, or speeches, about their cases, citing laws that went all the way back to the founding of the Republic in support of their positions. In six months or so, the court finally ruled: bingo is gambling if chance is involved, there is no element of skill required to win, the player pays money to play, and wins money if successful. Was Ms. Just playing for money? Alas, the jury (the fact finder) had said yes. The conviction was upheld.

This process could go on for years if the higher courts find they lack information to decide a case and kick it back to the lower-level court for more facts. But, as a rule, once around is sufficient, and twice almost always does it.

Eventually, the entire case could go to the state supreme court for a review.

In many states, that court has the right to refuse to review in most cases. Customarily in states where appellate courts exist, the highest court is reserved only for cases of great impact. Where no intermediate court exists, the state supreme court hears all appeals.

Here, because Ms. Just was challenging a new law and no one knew exactly what it meant yet, the court decided to review it. Its decision was that bingo is gambling.

Ms. Just's concern was not the fine, but the right to play bingo. Though she lost the battle, she won the war. Her group went back to the folks who put her in her predicament: the legislature.

The club asked the state legislature to change the law. Sure enough, the legislature had been following the whole case in the newspapers and had every civic-organization in the state breathing down its neck for not having foreseen what the courts would do. Next session, a new law was passed: no gambling would be permitted except bingo games by nonprofit organizations like the women's group. Back to the meeting hall the women went, a little poorer for the experience but victorious in the end.

State courts are financed by state tax money and supervised by judges elected by the citizens or appointed by the governor, and they do more than hold trials of alleged criminals. They also provide a forum for two persons to argue about the failure to perform a promise, or breach of contract. They oversee distribution of property after someone dies—through the probate court. They protect children from abuse—in juvenile or family court. They correct children who commit misdeeds—in juvenile court. They supervise adoptions. They provide a check against the abuse of power by elected officials by issuing orders against illegal actions when they arise. They are the front line for justice in the cities and states.

They have a counterpart on the federal level that closely resembles them, but in fact they are very different.

Federal Courts

There are 95 federal district courts in the United States, divided into 12 regions (circuits). They were created by Congress by authority of the United States Constitution.

They are presided over by federal judges. Unlike state judges, federal judges are never elected. They are appointed by the President, traditionally upon the advice of a senator of the same political party as the President. Once appointed, the Constitution says they will hold their offices during "good Behaviour." They may be removed only by resignation, retirement, death, or impeachment. Their appointments are made for life to prevent them from being influenced by changing political tides.

The independence of the judiciary is one of its most noted attributes. A former Supreme Court justice, David Brewer, describing his own, individualistic sense of the need for strong-minded judges on the bench, once said:

"If the Almighty should come and say to me that I must enter the kingdom of heaven, there is something in my Anglo-Saxon spirit which would stiffen my spinal column until it was like an iron ramrod and force from my lips the reply, 'I won't.' "

And in fact, the records of the judges indicate that they are rarely beholden to the politicians who appointed them. It was a court with a majority of President Nixon's appointees, for example, that eventually ordered that his tape-recorded office conversations, which he dearly wanted kept secret, had to be released to the public.

The powers of those judges are closely controlled by Congress, by authority of Article III of the Constitution. The powers are carefully defined to keep them from intruding more than necessary upon the powers of the individual states, in recognition of the principle of "federalism."

The federal courts, therefore, may preside over only certain kinds of cases. In legal language, it means they may try only cases over which they have "subject matter jurisdiction."

They are permitted to try only cases involving federal laws or the United States Constitution or cases involving state laws in which the persons involved are from different states.

Here are some examples:

A bank robbery trial—because the bank held federal deposit insurance.

An employment discrimination case—because federal laws guarantee equal opportunity in employment.

A claim for infringement of free speech—because the federal Constitution protects free speech.

A bankruptcy case—because a federal law permits overextended debtors to wipe out their debts and start over.

Air-pollution suits—because a federal law permits suits against industries that pollute the environment.

Each of those cases can reach a federal court, because each contains a "federal question."

Other kinds of cases, which deal only with state laws, also may go to a federal court, even though federal courts strongly prefer to let each state interpret its own laws. That preference is overcome by the courts' desire for fairness when the persons involved in a lawsuit live in different states.

The Fender-bender Case: Ms. Constance Sumer was on an automobile trip through a small town in a neighboring state. In a moment of inattention, she failed to notice a luxurious-looking sedan in front of her as it slid through a stop sign. She slammed on her brakes but—too late. A nasty-looking dent on the sedan and a ruined radiator on her car were the results.

In an actual case, the insurance companies probably would take over from here and she wouldn't worry about the causes of the accident any further. But, in her case, for one reason or another, the insurance companies did not become involved—perhaps she forgot to pay her premium.

She knew the accident was not her fault. She phoned the driver of the other car and demanded payment for the damage. To her chagrin, she discovered she was talking to the mayor of the little town where the accident happened. Not only did he refuse to pay, but he intimated the whole thing was her fault. You don't like it? So take me to court, he said flippantly. Where could she go to sue?

Her own state courts won't hear the case. Rules in every state require that, in most cases, a lawsuit must be handled in the home state of the person being sued or in the place where the cause of the lawsuit arose. The reason is simple: People could file groundless suits all over the country against people without the funds to travel to the filing court to defend themselves. By not showing up to fight a lawsuit, you lose. The basic unfairness of that truism led courts long ago to create a rule called personal jurisdiction. If the person isn't actually in the state (or if you're suing a corporation that doesn't do business in the state), you may not sue there.

So she had to go to the mayor's hometown or the place where the accident happened, which in this case were one and the same. Fat chance, she groused. It turned out the local judge, a political appointee, was the mayor's lodge brother. She wondered whether her side of the case would get the treatment it deserved from a politically elected judge in the small town.

Ideally, the judge's dedication to professional ethics would protect her from a biased trial. But the law wants to avoid even the appearance of improprieties. And enough examples of chauvinistic unfairness in communities have occurred in the past to cause Congress to make an exception to the "home court" rule.

When two people in a lawsuit are from different states, the lawsuit can be handled by a federal court. Congress's reasoning was that life-tenured judges would be more impartial and, perhaps, a cut above the local court in professionalism. The rule is called diversity jurisdiction and, despite its past success, is now being questioned by many lawyers who have noticed a flood of lawsuits in federal courts. With the quality of state courts improving constantly, many argue that the need for diversity jurisdiction has passed. Eventually, it may be abolished. But in this case, Ms. Sumer was able to sue the mayor in a federal court.

After a verdict is reached in a federal trial court, the lawyers for the losing side may believe the law was improperly applied. They may file an appeal with the circuit court.

The procedure is much the same as in the state. A written record of the trial court's activities is prepared for the appellate judges to read. Written "briefs" or arguments are prepared by the lawyers arguing their versions of the law's application. The judges weigh the arguments, listen to the lawyers in a court session in which they ask the lawyers questions about their interpretation of the case, and then they rule.

Because there is only one circuit court between each trial court and the highest court of the land, the U.S. Supreme Court, the opinions of the circuit courts carry great weight.

The Supreme Court may refuse to review most cases, but an appellate court may not. It must look at every case brought before it and, when it rules, its decisions become the law in that region until the Supreme Court sees fit to overrule it; that is, to change the law.

The outcome is that there may be a slightly different interpretation of the same federal law in Wyoming than there is in Florida if the circuit court there sees a case in a different light. Before relying upon a law, then, you must know not only its language, but what the courts have to say about it.

Often the regions hold such differing views about cases that some confusion results. One example was a recent debate about the circumstances under which police must have a search warrant to look inside your car. Another is about the circumstances in which certain kinds of government records must be open to the public.

Eventually, the confusion is generally resolved, by the only court that can tell these appellate judges when they are wrong: the U.S. Supreme Court.

The Supreme Court

The Supreme Court was created by the Founding Fathers. It is mentioned in the Constitution, which says, "The judicial Power of the United States, shall be vested in one supreme Court and in such inferior Courts as the Congress may from time to time ordain and establish."

Presiding over it are nine justices, all of whom are appointed for life by the President. Their appointments generally stir tremendous national interest, because their judicial inclinations can have a great effect upon the future of the nation.

The court has three functions: to ensure that the Constitution is upheld, to determine the proper interpretation of federal laws, and to oversee the lower courts.

You can't always go "all the way to the Supreme Court," as the members of the women's club threatened to do. If a case does not involve a constitutional right or a federal law, the Supreme Court has no power to hear it. If, as in the bingo case, the only issue involved was the interpretation of a state law, the word of the state court is final. An amazing number of cases, though, involve constitutional rights.

The Supreme Court currently accepts only about 200 of the 5,000 cases filed with it each year. To get a case before the court, a lawyer (or a layperson if it is her own case), prepares a petition for certiorari for the court. The petition will set out the facts of the case tried before the lower court, the rulings of the lower court, and all the reasons why the Supreme Court should devote some of its time to correcting the ruling. A winner in the lower court, of course, never brings a petition seeking review—she hopes the court will leave the decision alone, and usually will oppose a grant of certiorari.

Weekly, from October to July, the court holds a secret meeting to look over the petitions before it. In the past, the process of picking cases was shrouded in mystery. Recent journalistic feats have opened the process somewhat, to provide insights into the court's decision making.

Four justices must agree on a review before it will be granted. Generally those justices wish to grant review because they believe the lower court was wrong or they want to take the opportunity to resolve confusion among the various circuits. Their reasons are many and varied, some accounts say. But agreement for review is rare enough that by far the majority of petitioners go away disappointed. In those cases, the decision of the circuit court or state supreme court to rule on the issue is final.

After a petition is granted, however, the process begins again much as the processes in the other appellate courts. Generally, the Supreme Court doesn't pore over every word from a trial as a lower, appellate court might. Instead, the lawyers prepare a "statement of facts" about the case and their arguments about the application of the law. (Appeals rarely dispute the facts—it is the interpretation of the law that confronts the court.)

The Supreme Court accepts the attorneys' written arguments (briefs) and then hears their oral arguments in short sessions before the court. Customarily, attorneys go into the court with a prepared statement of their position but find they get to deliver only a portion of it, subject to frequent interruptions by the justices. The justices want to pick the attorney's brain a little, to find out whether the long-term effects of the suggested rulings have been thought through.

For example, in recent months, the Supreme Court considered whether the government is permitted to register only men for the draft, or whether such a policy unlawfully discriminates against the men. Because the registration was only for combat troops and women are barred by congressional dictates from combat, the government's lawyer was arguing it had a legitimate right to decide that military needs would be best served by registering only men. He was interrupted by Justice William Brennan:

"Could Congress decide to register only Negroes and no whites?"

The government's attorney, Solicitor General Wade McCree: "We would say that is not legitimate."

Brennan: "Could Congress include or exclude people based on religion?"

McCree: "That would not be legitimate either."

Brennan: "Only gender is legitimate. Is that what you're saying?"

McCree responded that the alleged inability of women to engage in combat made a difference in that case. (The case to question whether women truly are unable to engage in combat has yet to be tried.) Again he was pulled away from his argument, this time by Justice Thurgood Marshall:

"Women are being trained as astronauts. Can't they be trained for combat?"

And so on it went, with the justices interrupting both McCree and the attorney for the other side, with questions as they came to mind. At an hour's end, the attorneys were excused and the court retired to deliberate.

Its decision and a written opinion setting out the reasons for the decision were issued several months later. It decided that the discrimination was permissible. The opinion appeared in a volume of Supreme Court decisions for 1981, for legal researchers to consult for guidance on the law of sex discrimination.

The Supreme Court is the final word. Its ruling wisdom can radically change our lives, as illustrated in its 1972 opinion that the constitutional right to privacy prevented states from outlawing abortions in the early stages of pregnancy. Its decisions sometimes affect American life for decades after the justices who participated in the case have retired or died.

There are only two ways for the Supreme Court's opinions to lose their sway.

One is for Congress to change the law upon which the opinion is based, as some members of Congress have tried to do with the abortion ruling in the past few years. They could, for example, amend the Constitution to say that the right to privacy does *not* include the right to abortions or perhaps that there is no right of privacy in the Constitution.

The other is for the Court itself to change its mind. That rarely happens, so strongly do judges feel that stability is an essential element of government by law. Once in a while, though, society will so obviously outgrow a decision or the justices will become so profoundly convinced of the need for change, that a decision will forthrightly overrule an earlier one.

The most famous example is the reversal of the *Dred Scott* decision, issued when the courts ruled that blacks did not enjoy equal rights of citizenship. It took until 1954 to remove the last vestiges of that ruling, when the Court ordered desegregation of schools, but the Court eventually did come around to admitting it had been wrong. Usually, though, the decisions are indelibly stamped in the law, which is one reason why the appointment of a Supreme Court justice is cause for national deliberation and concern.

THE COURTS AT WORK

Criminal Cases

Both state and federal court systems include criminal courts, to enforce the respective state and federal criminal laws. The criminal court is the institution that comes to many people's minds when they think of the legal system. American schoolchildren learn the basics of criminal justice on cartoon shows, in school, on educational television, and in storybooks. A fascination with its processes has occupied novelists and authors for years, from Dickens's *Bleak House* to the tale of Alice's woes in the king's court in Wonderland.

A sense of fairness underlies the criminal system. You can't be sent to prison unless you have been found guilty of something. You can't be found guilty unless the government can prove you did something illegal. It can't prove you have done something illegal unless it follows rather rigid rules set up to keep the government from abusing its awesome power in its efforts to maintain law and order. Those rules, fashioned by courts as history unwound, are the source of hotly disputed legal controversies today.

Many are the stories in every community about a criminal set free because of a "technicality." Some people believe a smart lawyer can wangle a dismissal of a case regardless of a person's guilt. In fact, the "technicalities" are set up to protect the truth of evidence in a criminal case, not to protect the criminal. Their complexity is a measure of the difficulty of reaching the truth, which is often an elusive quantity indeed. Let's look back at Ms. Just to see why.

Before she was arrested, some behind-the-scenes preparation was necessary for the police. Since the days of the Crown's officers' disrespectful bursting into colonists' homes without warning, American law has prohibited police from crashing into private dwellings and businesses in search of criminal evidence. To arrest Ms. Just and search the meeting hall where the bingo game was played, therefore, the police needed a court order, or warrant, issued by a judge, usually a lower-level judge, who asked them why they thought a crime was being committed and why they believed Ms. Just was a suspect.

The judge's order is intended to provide a dispassionate analysis of the legal facts of a case. It might have been, for example, that the police officer on the meeting-hall beat simply didn't like Ms. Just and wanted to look in on the hall to find out whether he could catch her at some minor infraction of the law. Or it might have been that political pressure was applied to the police to embarrass a particular women's club. The judge's intervention is protection from personal vendettas as well as excess enthusiasm.

The requirement of a judge's order springs from the Fourth Amendment to the Constitution, which prohibits the government from seizing persons and their property without "probable cause," or a good reason for believing wrongdoing is afoot.

The Fourth Amendment applies both to people and to things. The police were neither permitted to take Ms. Just off to jail without a warrant nor to take possession of the bingo paraphernalia unless the judge had so ordered. Exceptions for the arrest rule are made when the officer happens to be present for another reason when a crime is committed and the person might escape before an identification or an arrest could occur. Persons seized in violation of the rule, however, may be able to escape trial. The judge may order their cases dismissed.

Exceptions for the property rule are made in cases in which the paraphernalia might have been destroyed before an order could be obtained or cases in which the police could have seen it from the street or in one of a few other narrow instances. But, basically, the rule protects the property. Property seized in violation of the order may be ruled by a later judge to be unavailable for use in court.

Requiring the police either to follow the rules for obtaining a judge's orders or risk losing the case has come under fire recently—particularly the so-called exclusionary rule, which prohibits use in court of improperly seized property.

That particular rule was established as a specific deterrent to police. The Supreme Court believed that police must be persuaded to respect privacy and that a good persuader would be the threat of lost cases. So the court fashioned the rule to encourage better police practices.

The rule is important in the 1980s, because it has fallen into disfavor in some sectors for excluding evidence that may have proved guilt but could not be used in court because of a misstep by the police. Its supporters argue that the exclusion of the evidence is an incentive for police to stay within the law. Its opponents argue that other incentives should be found that will permit the court to use the evidence at hand. No doubt, much public debate will precede any major changes. The results could significantly change the way criminal courts work in the future.

Let's assume that the police in Ms. Just's case followed the rules to the letter. They had proper warrants, obtained from a judge, to show up at the meeting hall.

The Arrest: When they knocked at the door to make the arrest, their first obligation was to determine that she was the person named in the warrant. Ms. Just, a disingenuous type, immediately confessed to her identity.

"You're under arrest," they responded. She just looked at them. They followed accepted procedures and placed handcuffs on her wrists. Had she resisted, they would have been permitted to use some force on her.

The police also are permitted to do a cursory pat-down to make sure no weapons are concealed. The extent to which body searches are allowed is a matter of current controversy, but most courts agree that some search is permissible.

While the police frisk Ms. Just or complete other formalities, she may well be chattering away nervously, to her later sorrow. "How can I be under arrest? All I was doing was playing bingo," she says in an unwitting confession.

Because nonplused suspects often rattle on to the police, who are jotting down everything for later use in court, the Supreme Court ruled in 1966 (the so-called Miranda ruling) that the police are required to inform arrested persons that they need not talk without an attorney.

The reading of the rights is almost as much a part of the common knowledge as the pledge of allegiance, so frequently is it heard in shoot-'em-up cop shows on television. The technique, every tube boob knows, is for the police officer to pull out a card from her wallet and read, "You have the right to remain silent. . . ."

The police-show portrayal is very close to real life. The language of the card is an embodiment of the 1966 court ruling. You have a right to know your constitutional rights when you are suspected of a crime. Among those rights are the right to remain silent, the right to have an attorney, and the right to stop talking to the police at any time, even if you have begun to answer their questions.

It is a good idea to call a lawyer immediately, before any questioning begins. If you cannot afford a lawyer, the law may require that one shall be provided for you at the expense of the government. Because an arrest is emotionally very upsetting, having someone around who knows the law and can provide some emotional support can keep you from making a bad situation worse. It is a good idea, also, to say as little as possible until the lawyer arrives.

The Bail-out: While Ms. Just was waiting for word to reach her lawyer that night, the police were hauling her off to jail. The police have the right to put suspects in jail for a short period of time while legal formalities are carried out—ranging from a few hours to a couple of days. After that, an opportunity to bail out of jail or to be brought before an impartial judge must be afforded.

The bail process is another right mentioned in the Constitution. Nowhere does it say a suspect has an absolute right to bail, but it does guarantee that bail shall not be "excessive."

The reasons for permitting bail-out are two: First, no jail could hold all the people awaiting trial at any given time. Second, statistics have shown that a person operating in the free world has a better chance of developing a good legal defense than someone behind bars—probably because she can gather evidence that busy lawyers might miss.

The bail process is a simple trade: your money or your life. Or, less dramatically, something of value as a guarantee of your intention to show up at court for the trial.

The government wants an assurance that the suspect won't leave town. Therefore, a sum of money high enough to be persuasive is usually set. Sometimes it is set by a judge. In most places, however, police have a list of established bail figures for minor crimes to keep from having to house suspects in jail at night until a judge can be found to set bail. The amount may be adjusted later by a judge, but often the police figure is continued by the judge for the duration of the case.

The bail sum is usually tied to the severity of the crime. Very high bail is set for very serious crimes—for the obvious purpose of making dangerous criminals unable to afford freedom. (It may be denied altogether if the criminal is thought to be a continuing danger to the community or to herself.)

The sum may be posted in any of several ways. The most common method is through a bail bondsman, someone who is in the business of putting up money as surety for a court appearance. The bondsman will sign a "bond" promising the court to pay the full amount of bail if the suspect doesn't show up at the appointed time. For the bond, the suspect has to pay the bondsman some percentage of the bail listed on the bond. The bondsman is a professional gambler, in a sense. If the suspect shows, the bondsman makes a profit. If the suspect does not, the court may require the entire sum of the bond to be paid and the bondsman takes a loss.

If the suspect has property, the value of the property may be pledged against the sum of the bail. Upon a failure to appear in court, the judge might then order the property sold and the bail paid to the court.

An increasingly common tool, the one used in the *Just* case, is the personal-recognizance bond. It means that the suspect signs a promise to appear. Her word is the bond.

Often, a good reputation in the community is the best insurance against having to post a bail bond. If a judge believes the suspect is good for the promise, unless the crime is very serious, a bond might not be required.

First Appearance: The government is required to bring a suspect before a judge. To set the court process in motion, the prosecutor will file a charge if one was not filed before the arrest. It will state the crime allegedly committed and the time and place of occurrence, as close to the truth as the government can determine.

The filing must be done quickly, before the time limits for custody have expired. For a person in jail, the time limits expire very quickly. For a person out on bail, the law permits a somewhat longer delay between the arrest and the court appearance. In both cases, however, the limits are strictly enforced, to protect citizens from being detained indefinitely without legal justification.

After the filing, haste remains important, for another constitutional right has intervened. Every person has the right to a speedy trial. Charges that sit untried are likely to be dismissed by a judge in the future, on the grounds that it is unfair to make someone defend herself against a charge whose evidence may have grown stale or even disappeared with the passage of time. The court appearance, then, becomes very important.

The first appearance is to hear the reading of the charges, to determine whether an attorney has been called into the case, and to set conditions for the pretrial release of the suspect. An unrepresented suspect has a right to demand an attorney at that point, if the charge she faces carries a possibility of a significant jail term—usually anything over six months.

For less-serious cases, in which no jail term is involved (usually a misdemeanor) the suspect will be asked at this proceeding to enter a plea—guilty or not guilty—and the case will move ahead to a trial. In a more serious case (a felony) another hearing date is set to complete the next step in the process.

Probable-cause Hearings: At this point the process varies from state to state. In some places, a grand jury will be convened. This is a group of citizens with investigatory powers used to determine whether a crime has been committed and to find a likely suspect upon whom to visit the full powers of the courts: a formal charge, or indictment.

If the state does not require a grand jury, the allegations made by the prosecutor may be enough until a judge has had an opportunity to test them. The probable-cause hearings, then, are to see whether enough evidence exists to move forward to the next step: the official charge.

The Arraignment: The charge—in the form of an indictment or another formal paper filed by the prosecutor called an information—is read publicly. At that point the accused felon is required to state whether she is guilty or not guilty. Silence will result in a not-guilty plea.

In a very few cases, a third sort of plea will be entered: a *nolo contendere,* or no contest. It amounts to the same thing as a guilty plea but is used occasionally in cases in which a lawsuit by the victim of the crime may be in the offing and the suspect wants to avoid admitting guilt in a courtroom, where the admission may later provide damaging evidence.

After the plea, a trial date is set.

The Trial: The trial is often romanticized as the stage for great drama. Most people have a general idea of how it works: a judge and jury hear evidence, a verdict is reached, and a sentence is pronounced. The actual process is often a plodding, painstaking affair, with great concern for operating by rather rigid rules.

The Constitution steps in again to provide some of the rules. For example, the Sixth Amendment of the Constitution provides that everyone has the right to a public trial. This prevents the government from using a technique that the French called *lettres de cachet,* which were sealed documents commanding citizens to go to prison without judicial hearings.

The same amendment holds fast to the requirement for the right to an attorney, even one paid by the government if the suspect is too poor to pay. (The suspect may be required to pay the government back later, but the important thing is to have legal help in place when it is needed.)

It is the suspect's right not to have an attorney. Judges will inquire very closely, however, to make certain the suspect understands what she is giving up.

The Fifth Amendment steps in to prohibit the government from forcing the suspect to testify at the trial. The amendment provides that you do not have to be a witness against yourself. Therefore, the government has the sometimes difficult task of proving its case without asking any questions of the person it would most like to question: the suspect. The suspect, of course, may choose to testify to be sure her side of the story gets told. In that case, the government has the right to ask its questions, because the suspect has "waived" her rights.

The Sixth Amendment intervenes again to require a right to a trial by jury. The extent of that right varies, but juries rarely have fewer than 12 persons—a figure considerably pared down since jury trial was first used in ancient Greece when a jury of 500 was required to try a criminal.

Not only must a jury be in place if requested, but it must be a jury of one's peers. That doesn't necessarily mean a blond-haired man of 30 has a right to a jury of Aryans, but it does mean the state may not prohibit blonds of 30 from being on the jury. The system used for picking the jury must be careful not to exclude any class of people.

The group chosen, the venire panel, is called from a large list of persons, usually a tax roll or a voters' roll or the two combined.

The panel shows up the day of the trial and waits for something to happen. If you have ever been called for jury duty, you know the truth of the old biblical saying "Many are called, but few are chosen."

The day of jury duty is a good day to start reading *War and Peace* or to knit an afghan, because it is sure to be a long one and not entirely productive. But it is an essential one, because jury duty is widely viewed as a civic duty, not to be shrugged off lightly. Judges look dimly upon lame excuses for not serving and often will refuse to grant a dismissal from jury duty. A refusal to serve could result in a jail sentence.

So the panel waits for the trial to happen. As it drains the coffeepot in the jury room, the lawyers, the judge, and others may be in the courtroom taking care of preliminary matters. The lawyer for the accused may be arguing that the judge should omit some piece of evidence because of the exclusionary rule or some other procedural problem. The judge's decision will affect the amount of evidence the jury will eventually hear and the rules under which the case will be tried.

A cast of characters will be scattered around the courtroom.

There is, of course, the judge. The judge is assisted by the bailiff, the person who heralds the judge's comings and goings with a trumpeted "All rise" and who calls the court to order with a "Hear ye, hear ye." Her duties are to assist the judge in whatever matters the judge chooses.

The judge may have several clerks present, whose job it is to take notes, notice irregularities in the trial, and be an additional set of eyes and ears for the judge. One clerk, the clerk of the court, is the person responsible for all official documents filed during the trial.

Sitting near the witness box will be an individual with a tape recorder if the court is very up to date, or more likely a contrivance that looks like an adding machine on a tripod. This is a stenotype machine, which the court reporter will use to record every word, sneeze, and hiccup that takes place among the trial participants. The recording will provide the official record for anyone who later wishes to review what went on—the most important "anyone" being the court of appeals.

Finally, there are the lawyers, at least one for the state and at least one for the suspect, now known as the defendant.

The trial begins. The jury hears some instructions. Its duty is to confine its deliberations to what is said in the court, to forget or disregard what they read or heard before they went into the court, to refrain from discussing the case outside the courtroom, and to avoid news accounts.

The jurors must undergo lengthy questioning about themselves, their knowledge of the case, and their acquaintance with the people involved in the case. Unlike early days of jury trials, when juries were chosen precisely for their knowledge of the defendant and the crime, today juries are sought who know as little as possible. Lawyers want jurors with minds like clean slates.

The purpose of the trial is to put forth evidence—either the spoken word or physical objects—to persuade the jury. They are the fact finders, the people who will decide what is true and what is not.

There are rules, as you might expect, governing what they might hear before they retire for their verdict.

They are allowed to hear only what is relevant to the facts at hand. The fact that Ms. Just, the bingo player, once learned to play canasta with her grandmother is not relevant to the case, because her tendency to be a gambler doesn't prove she was gambling on the night in question. The fact that she drives a dune buggy may be relevant if it can be shown that it was purchased with her bingo winnings. A thing is relevant if it tends to prove a fact pertinent to the case.

The juries may hear only evidence provided by persons with firsthand information or by paid expert witnesses who testify about matters familiar to their professions, such as ballistics or autopsies. Information provided second- or thirdhand to the witnesses usually may not be spoken by the witnesses, because it is "hearsay" and is considered too unreliable by the law to be heard in a matter as grave as a criminal trial. Exceptions are made when the person who initially provided the information is present to provide another view, but the rule generally excludes information from persons who can't be questioned in front of the jury.

The jury may hear only what goes on in court. It may not go out and visit the scene of the crime on its own. It may not ask around the neighborhood for versions of the events at issue from witnesses not brought before the judge. It may hear only the answers to the questions brought by the lawyers, and occasionally the judge.

As the trial begins, the jury is asked to take an oath to abide by the rules of the trial. When the oath is taken, the trial has officially begun.

The responsibility for proving the case rests with the government, represented by the prosecutor. Since she has the more difficult task, the government gets the first shot and the last shot at persuading the jury that the government's version of the facts is correct.

The trial opens with statements from first the prosecutor and then the defense, advising the jury of the sort of case at hand and what each side intends to prove.

Witnesses are called first by the prosecution. Each witness is asked to take an oath swearing to tell the truth. Most witnesses have been brought into court, most likely, by orders (subpoenae) from the court commanding them to appear. A failure to appear or a failure to answer the questions posed could result in a jail term.

The attorneys will have discussed the case with their own witnesses first, to minimize the chances of surprises in court. Each attorney will ask questions designed to cultivate favorable information for its side. The true test, then, comes in the cross-examination, when the other side gets to take a poke.

There was the case, for example, of John Sneed, on trial for drunk driving. The prosecution brought as its key witness Mr. Busy Body, known for his meddling in other people's affairs. He testified that he saw Sneed outside a liquor store on his street corner with a bottle of liquor under his arm and that Sneed opened the bottle, took a swig, and got into his car.

The defense counsel is doubtful.

"Mr. Body, how far is it from your house to the liquor store?"

"About 500 feet."

"And where were you standing when you saw Mr. Sneed open that bottle?"

"In my front yard."

"And what time of night was it?"

"About midnight."

"Are you in the habit of standing in your front yard at midnight? Why did you go out there?"

"Why, of course I'm not. I went out there to watch Mr. Sneed."

"And why were you watching Mr. Sneed?"

"He's a member of my church and we don't believe in spirits—the alcoholic sort, I mean."

"And you saw him pass your house on his way to the store and you went outside? You said you were in your bathrobe?"

"That's correct."

"What was the temperature outside that night, Mr. Body?"

"About 20 degrees, I believe. The ground was frozen."

"Isn't it true, Mr. Body, that you didn't go outside that night, because it was too cold, but that you watched Mr. Sneed from your window with your racetrack binoculars?"

"I take offense to that, sir. Those binoculars are for bird watching."

"And isn't it true that Mr. Sneed saw you standing there and waved to you, as he testified earlier?"

"Well, yes."

"And isn't it true that when he saw you in church the next day he asked why you didn't wave back and you said you couldn't see that far without your glasses on—even with your racetrack—excuse me, your bird-watching binoculars?"

"Well, yes."

"And isn't it true that if you couldn't see the wave of an arm, you couldn't see the top of a scotch bottle? Isn't it true that you don't know for a fact that he drank from that bottle?"

"No, that's not true. I stood in front of him in choir practice the next morning and he sang like a man awash in good fortune," Mr. Body said peevishly. "He surely didn't get to feel that good from the communion wine. A man that happy oughtn't to be in church."

"Your honor, I rest my case," said the defense counsel. "My client's only crime was his happiness. The night of the 'crime,' he became engaged to be married."

"You may step down," the judge advised Mr. Body, concealing a grin. The jury acquitted Mr. Sneed.

The stories are recited and examined. At the end of it all, the jury retires to a room apart to come to a decision: guilty or not guilty.

The jury is an impartial body to perform the serious task of sorting fact from fiction, of weighing the argument of the government against the rebuttal of the defendant. Most studies show that, once on duty, juries become solemn and dedicated bodies, determined to discharge their duties responsibly.

Before they retire to begin their function, the judge will inform them on some matters of the law. The judge in Ms. Just's case, you will remember, told the jury that it had already been decided as a matter of law that bingo was gambling. Their task was to find a fact: Was Ms. Just playing bingo?

The jury may take any physical evidence from the trial into a jury room with them. They may ask to have portions of the testimony reread by the court reporter. They may ask questions of the judge about legal definitions of things they do not understand. But they may not leave the room, except for eating and sleeping and other necessities, until they reach a decision.

What goes on in the jury room remains the secret of the jurors, unless one or another juror chooses to tell the story of the deliberations later.

When the verdict is reached, everyone reassembles in the courtroom and the jury announces its decision. In Ms. Just's case, the verdict is "Guilty, as charged, of gambling."

The judge thanks the jury and sends it off to receive jury pay (a nominal sum) and begins the next phase of the trial: the sentence.

The Sentence: In serious crimes, the advice of psychologists and other learned social scientists is often sought to help the judge make a decision about the need for incarceration to reform the criminal. Following the experts' report, which the judge is free to disregard, the sentence is pronounced.

It is limited by two considerations: First, the law defining the crime must set some penalty, usually a bracketed time, such as five to ten years. The judge may choose a specific time or may pronounce the sentence at five to ten years and leave it up to the prison authorities to decide when the proper time is served.

Second, the Constitution again intervenes. The Eighth Amendment provides protection against "cruel and unusual punishments." Sentences grossly out of proportion to the crime may not be tolerated. In the past, convictions have been erased for that reason. Recent Supreme Court decisions, however, have shown greater tolerance for exceedingly long sentences, indicating a reluctance to second-guess the trial judge. Some protection, however, remains.

The sentence often appears to the public to be the end of it all. But, in fact, it falls somewhere nearer the beginning.

After the prisoner goes off to jail, she has the various levels of appeal to explore, and if those fail, has yet another constitutional right.

The right of habeas corpus provides the constant scrutiny of the courts against incarceration in violation of one's rights. Any time a person is in jail, she may bring a habeas corpus petition to a judge, alleging a violation of rights, and get the conviction process, or some condition in the prison, examined by another judge.

Habeas Corpus: Habeas corpus petitions are both the bane and the blessing of the criminal justice system. While they provide an essential guarantee against inhumane imprisonment and unfair trials, some say they clog court calendars, as prisoners hopeful of finding a legal release from prison file their sometimes frivolous petitions for review. We won't belabor the point here but will recommend for the interested reader the true tale of one habeas corpus case: in *Gideon's Trumpet,* a book by Anthony Lewis.

Civil Cases

Going to court with a lawsuit is not unlike going to the dentist with an abscess. You're hard-pressed to decide which you dread the most, the cure or the disease. But when the pain is bad enough, the cure looks better and better.

Some of the frustrations from working within the civil court system are necessary, made so by complex rules to protect the rights of all involved. Some come from lack of understanding. The latter can be alleviated with a liberal dose of knowledge, taken with a spoonful of patience.

The chief problem of lawsuits is that they take a long time. Some are like the trial in *Bleak House, Jarndyce* v. *Jarndyce,* in which the unfortunate youths whose property was the object of the suit were born so long after the start of the legal proceedings that they didn't have the slightest idea what it was all about, except for some haggling over "costs."

Other suits, even though the product of hours of research and thought, seem to be over almost before they have begun, because settlements were reached.

The common knowledge of government often omits civil courts. Maybe it's because they lack the *Sturm und Drang* of criminal courts and their plodding progress doesn't attract the screenwriter or novelist as often as the dramas of prosecution do. Ever seen a dramatic presentation of a deposition hearing? read a story about the gripping interrogatories of the plaintiff in a contracts case? Probably not.

But the twists and turns of justice in a civil court can touch more lives than a criminal conviction. Class actions (lawsuits in which persons with a common complaint may join forces on behalf of nameless comrades) can bring an unexpected bit of cash and cause a change in government or business practices, as witness the many suits against employers who have exposed workers to health-endangering asbestos. An injunction could stop the construction of a new office building or a city sewer. The threat of a damage suit from an accidentally broken tooth could, as happened in an East Coast aquarium, cause removal of all the water fountains, leaving the visitors muttering to themselves about the drought among the oceans.

As with the courts in general, however, a bit of knowledge goes a long way. Though legalisms have proliferated on the civil side, making common parlance harder to grasp in civil cases than in criminal cases, with a little effort the system can be understood.

Civil courts grew out of the English traditions: the common-law rule, which began with the manorial system, discussed earlier; and the chancery courts, in which judges acting as representatives of the king meted out justice based upon the fairness of the situation as they saw it and were not bound by common-law precedents.

In today's civil courts, the distinctions between the two kinds of cases have blurred, but vestiges of each kind remain.

A court may, for example, rule from precedent that a landlord has a right to damages from a tenant who burned a hole in the floor from careless use of a candle, but it could restrain the landlord from collecting the damages after finding in equity that the tenant used candles for light because the landlord neglected to pay the electric bills. Equity, in other words, is used to inject fairness where the rigidity of precedent forbids it. All judges have equitable powers, but they use these powers sparingly for fear of creating disorder in an otherwise orderly judicial system.

Civil courts exist in both the state and the federal systems. The rules of play differ, but the basic sorts of suits—or causes of action—are the same. In those forums, parties to a contract may sue for failure to abide by contractual terms, persons injured in accidents may sue for medical costs, and citizens denied constitutional rights may petition the government for redress. All these matters take place in civil courts. In addition, civil courts handle adoption and divorce proceedings and probating of wills.

The content of those matters is taken up elsewhere in this book. The present chapter will focus upon the process of getting into court and emerging with a decision.

Before assuming that the principles discussed apply precisely to a particular court, however, it is advisable to seek the advice of a lawyer. Failure to observe correct procedures in this game is like showing up at the ball park with a tennis racket. In this park, however, one strike may send you to the showers, so it's worthwhile to proceed with caution.

Jurisdiction: In the sections on state courts and federal courts, subject-matter jurisdiction was discussed—the sort that determines whether the court has the authority to hear a certain kind of case.

Another type of jurisdiction was mentioned in the auto-accident illustration. It is called personal jurisdiction, and it means, simply, the degree of authority a court may exercise over an individual to make her show up to answer a complaint.

The court has no power over someone it may not legally reach, i.e., who is not physically present in its jurisdiction, though that presence may be a figurative presence, such as that of a corporation with business offices in many places or a magazine with readers throughout the country.

The long arm of the law has a few tricks up its sleeve to pull in those who would elude it, but for individuals the rule is that to be sued in a court you must be physically within its district. If you are not, you may not be sued unless you consent to it (which you may be likely to do, crazy as it sounds, to get an issue settled expeditiously), or unless there is a special state law requiring you to waive (give up) your jurisdictional protection. An example is a state law holding that driving on state highways is a tacit consent to be sued there if you do something on them that gives someone cause to sue you, such as causing a traffic accident.

If you doubt a court's jurisdiction over you, you may force it to rule on those objections before proceeding with the case. The rule may save untold legal expense. You may see a catch here: to come to court for a jurisdictional ruling you have to come to court, thereby putting yourself in harm's way for an order to appear in court for the rest of the case.

To ameliorate the unfairness, many courts permit what they call special appearances, in which you show up only to resolve the jurisdictional problems and are immune from the rest of the suit if the ruling is in your favor. It is wise to check before buying a plane ticket. You may arrive at the gate to be greeted by a summons server.

Complaint: All lawsuits begin with a complaint, or petition, which is a court document filed by the person who believes she has a right to sue.

To track the process, let's put Connie Sumer back behind the wheel of her car, run the film back a few hundred miles, and let her roll on down the highways of her own state.

A hapless lass, she finds misfortune there as well. She turns her attention briefly to the dial on her radio and while coasting accidentally onto the shoulder of the road, hits an enormous pothole, the kind that makes you hope we really do have good relations with China.

The pothole causes a tire to blow and the blown tire thumps along for a few feet before it stops, sagging hopelessly around the rim, at the road's edge.

As she sits fuming, however, Mr. Fatte Head putts along in his van, also fiddling with a musical contrivance of some sort, and plows into her. The back end of her car buckles and she bumps her head on the steering wheel.

Now, here is our hero with a dented trunk, a flat tire, and an angry knot on her head, to match the angry knot she feels welling up in her throat. She reaches for her handy "what to do when an accident happens" kit and finds, in despair, her insurance premium sitting right there with it, all sealed and ready to mail—a month ago.

Now her only hope for getting the car repaired is to sue someone for the damage done. And it seems as if a loose tooth was jarred right out of its socket by the bump. Visions of mounting bills rise before her. She's mad and ready for a fight. She calls her lawyer.

Now, the question is, What caused the accident? the pothole, or F. Head? Being an astute person, her lawyer advises that suing only one would result in one blaming the other and leaving them with a potentially important person absent from the court. Even though Ms. Sumer suspects the pothole was really at fault and she thinks Mr. Head was a nice guy, she wisely agrees to sue them both. Mr. Head, her lawyer advises, can always sue the pothole to get back whatever money he might have to pay her.

The pothole, a long-standing member of the community, will turn to its attorney, who also happens to represent the city that owns the right-of-way where the pothole lives. It knows it has particular advantages in a lawsuit that the other people don't have. It belongs to a city government, which can be sued only with its consent.

That doesn't mean that it has to agree to each suit. But it means that the government in question at some time must have passed a law making the pothole vulnerable to lawsuits in general.

The reason for the requirement is an old doctrine in the common law called sovereign immunity or, in lay terms, "The King can do no wrong." The King in England was the law and one couldn't sue the law. The belief that the government could not be held accountable for its wrongs carried across the Atlantic and became part of American law until recent history pointed to the need for a change.

As city governments became operators of hospitals, builders of streets, and managers of sewage systems, the numbers of accidents attributable to city actions grew (or state actions, as states likewise provided new services), and the citizen demand for a change in sovereign immunity grew. Now, in most places, governments may be sued for accidents they cause. (Their immunity remains intact, however, for some other things. It's best to check with a lawyer before suing a city or a state, in order to see whether your suit will be allowed.)

Suing the other driver is an easier proposition. All she must do is find him in the state or, possibly, invoke a special law that makes persons who drive through the state liable for their actions.

When they are sued, the defendants have a right to know exactly what they are accused of. The accusations come in the form of the complaint, or petition.

Ms. Sumer or her lawyer will draw up a legal-looking paper of a size and shape dictated by the court that may read roughly as follows:

In the Court of Mis-State
District of Wholey Streets

Complaint

The plaintiff, Ms. Sumer, is a resident of county Negligent in the state of Mis-State.

The defendant, Mr. Head, is a resident of county Negligence and can be found at 4220 No Street.

The defendant, city of Careless, can be found at City Hall, 10 & Intersection, Careless, Mis-State.

The defendant, city of Careless, owns and operates the street at 3rd & Pothole.

On May 17, Ms. Sumer was driving on Pothole Street and her vehicle struck a pothole on the navigable portion of the road with such force that the vehicle was rendered inoperable.

Within a few minutes, a car driven by defendant Mr. Head struck the plaintiff's car in the rear, causing $3,000 in damage.

The accident caused Ms. Sumer's head to strike the steering wheel of her car. The impact loosened one tooth to such a degree that medical attention was required.

The cost of the auto repair was $3,000.

The cost of medical bills was $4,000.

In addition, plaintiff endured pain and suffering from the injury in the amount of $5,000.

(Each of the paragraphs represents an allegation, something Ms. Sumer believes to be true. At the end, she will sign a statement to that effect. But, before it, she will include a request to the courts, known in some courts as a prayer.)

"Wherefore, plaintiff asks the court to order defendants jointly and severally to pay plaintiff property damages in the amount of $3,000, medical costs in the amount of $4,000, pain and suffering in the amount of $5,000, costs of this action and [remembering equity, she throws in a wild card], such other relief as the court finds just and equitable."

She signs the complaint and takes it to the clerk of a civil court in charge of lawsuits of the damage amount she seeks. With a filing fee of maybe $50 (higher in some places, lower in others) she has created a lawsuit. A file is opened in the courthouse and an entry on a list of suits, known as the docket, is made.

Service: The process begun, the rights of the defendants now intercede. They have a right to see the complaint if they are to be held accountable to respond to it. If they haven't received word of the suit properly, they may not be ordered to respond.

It is plaintiff's responsibility to provide the names, with proper spelling, and the addresses of the defendants.

The court may have officers (marshals or sheriff's deputies) who will serve the papers on the defendants. Or the plaintiff may hire a private process server to do it. The one rule is that the plaintiff may not do it herself.

For the city, service is easy. The city will have appointed a city officer, probably a clerk, to receive lawsuit summonses.

Serving Mr. Head may be harder, particularly if he doesn't want to be served. He may elude the process server (though they are crafty devils at times, jumping out of trunks and handing out papers over transoms). As long as he makes himself scarce, he may be able to avoid the suit altogether.

When he is found, he will receive a copy of the complaint and a notice from the court ordering him to respond to the suit within a certain number of days (usually 20 to 40) or risk a court ruling against him.

Answer: A failure to show up to respond could mean an automatic ruling for the plaintiff, so long as it can be proved that the defendant was served and simply neglected to answer.

Most defendants make a response, paragraph by paragraph, to the complaint, also on a legal-sized document pursuant to court rules. The answer will contain numbered paragraphs saying something like "The defendant admits the allegations in paragraph 1, has no knowledge of paragraphs 2 and 3 and denies all other allegations."

In this case, there are two defendants, each of whom wishes to protect herself/himself by shifting the blame to the other or to Ms. Sumer. So they will use Ms. Sumer's lawsuit as a vehicle to begin their own suits. Their answers will contain "cross claims" accusing each other of responsibility. They may decide to hold Ms. Sumer responsible also, so they will file a "counterclaim" against her.

The answers may also contain a request to the court in the form of a motion to dismiss Ms. Sumer's claims as legally improper.

Discovery: You may imagine that in order to get into court, you have to be able to prove your case. You may have talked yourself out of lawsuits in the past, mourning the paucity of proof to persuade a court. To ameliorate that problem, however, courts provide a process known as discovery, a tool for researching claims.

Consider the case of Susan E., a claims adjuster at an insurance agency. She did quite well at her company for a number of years, having worked her way up as a secretary. Then, one day, she noticed all the other claims adjusters, who happened to be male, departing for a weekend convention in a resort city. She complained at the exclusion.

Her complaints sparked a terrific controversy at the company. Her diligence had been rewarded with occasional pay raises, but nothing in the way of a promotion was even hinted at. As discussion of her complaint grew louder, she began to suspect that she was being held back from opportunities her male counterparts were offered. Sure enough, at the first of the year, they all went off again to a trade-association seminar, leaving her behind. When they returned, the office was reorganized and she found herself in a new cubicle, in the back of the building, with a larger case load and fewer co-workers to share the work.

She plugged away until May. Then she found out two men who had been hired after her had been promoted. She complained and was fired for being "uncooperative."

At home she fumed and steamed about the unfairness of it all. She had suspicions that the "reorganization" had carried a hidden message for her to keep quiet and accept her inferior status as a woman at a conservative company. She knew she had no formal proof but, bravely, visited a lawyer and filed a lawsuit.

Her lawyer surprised her six months later with a sheaf of papers she had received from the insurance agency in court-supervised requests for documents. In them were payroll slips for the men in Susan's department, all showing higher wages of at least 30 percent.

The crowning blow came one day when the department head was called to her lawyer's office for a court-supervised deposition, a formal questioning conducted under oath. The department head admitted that the management had a policy of promoting men over women, because "clients don't see women as carrying much authority and it's important for us to have a public image of competence."

With her discovered information, the lawyer negotiated a settlement with the company for that extra 30 percent of lost wages during Susan's tenure as an employee.

Discovery is a process not to be taken lightly. It determines, by and large, who will win a case. A defendant who sees a stream of negative information flowing into the plaintiff's hands is likely to offer a settlement to end a case before she winds up in court, where a jury could pull her into much greater losses.

Parties to lawsuits are required to share information with each other, unless it is protected by a recognized privilege (such as the priest-penitent privilege, forbidding a priest to testify to what he hears in a confessional, or the doctor-patient privilege, prohibiting doctors from revealing patient confidences). An order to be deposed or to produce documents carries the weight of the court with it. Failure to comply could mean any number of punishments meted out by the court in its broad powers—from automatic loss of the case to a fine or jail sentence.

Settlement: As discovery proceeds, the discomfort of the disadvantaged party will become evident. A defendant turning over incriminating evidence will try to buy her way out, in a perfectly acceptable manner, by offering some money short of the sum sought in the prayer in exchange for dismissal of the suit. Sometimes, even a defendant with a good case will offer some money to save the inconvenience and expense of trying a case in court. In that case, a plaintiff who has turned up little helpful information in discovery will be willing to settle out of court for much less than the requested sum. A plaintiff looking ahead to victory may want to hold out.

Settlements can be tricky. They usually are accompanied by agreements not to file any more lawsuits. Plaintiffs must be careful not to give away too much when they settle. For example, an unscrupulous defendant may ask them to waive any further right to sue, even for unrelated problems. By not reading the small print, the plaintiff may learn the hard way that legal documents mean what they say.

Settlement sometimes begins even before the lawsuit is filed. It is not uncommon for insurance companies faced with potential suits to send out claims adjusters immediately after an accident with an offer of money and a "release" for the injured person to sign, giving away any future right to sue. Beware! Check with a lawyer before signing. Or at the very least, read the release carefully and don't be tempted by easy money. An eager adjuster may be simply meticulous and forthright about compensating for injuries. Or she may be hoping to escape huge damages in court, damages the company rightfully should pay.

Motions: Various motions will be filed during the case. Most will have to do with the discovery of evidence. But several will be for dismissal of the case, filed by either side as they sense an advantage for their side that might convince the court the case should not go on.

Courts will not dismiss properly filed lawsuits with actual legal claims as long as disputes remain about the facts involved in the case. If there is a question, for example, that the pothole actually caused an accident, the court will not dismiss a case on Ms. Sumer's motion. On the other hand, if the city admits the pothole caused the accident but claims it is not responsible for the hole, Ms. Sumer may win a motion to hold the city responsible as a matter of law.

Whether the motion for a judgment is granted will depend upon the law governing city responsibility for potholes and the status of other issues still unresolved by the parties. If everything is over but the shouting (for example, everyone agrees the accident was caused by the pothole, but they disagree whether the city had a responsibility to repair it before an accident occurred), it will be left in the judge's hands to decide how the law applies. If the judge says yes, the case would end with a judgment against the city.

Trial: If various motions to end the case are heard and disposed of unsuccessfully, the matter goes to trial.

Unlike criminal cases, many civil cases are not tried by juries. The judge acts as the finder of fact, the entity responsible for sorting out the story and deciding who is telling the truth and who is not. In federal court, the right to a jury trial is guaranteed in most civil cases. The rules in state courts for jury trials depend partially upon the amount of money sought in the lawsuit.

But, as a practical matter, many persons prefer a trial by the judge, because jury trials can be twice as expensive and take twice as long.

Civil trials proceed otherwise much like criminal trials. The person bringing the suit begins by calling witnesses, who are cross-examined by the other side—or in this case, the other two sides. The witnesses are sworn to tell the truth. They testify only to the questions they are asked and only to their firsthand experience.

They may not testify to rumors or stories they heard from someone, only to their own personal knowledge. They may not testify to "hearsay."

Some witnesses will be "experts," paid by one side to give an informed opinion of the case. Expert witnesses are asked to use their expertise to assess many things: how fast a bullet travels, how far a car can skid, how often the sponge gets sewn up inside the patient, how a child will be affected by a divorce. Expert witnesses are the only witnesses who will be permitted to state their opinions and their conclusions. On the other hand, lack of firsthand knowledge about a case often prevents them from testifying to specifics about the case, which other witnesses will be expected to supply.

In a divorce court, a pair of witnesses were called to discuss the fitness of two parents, both of whom wanted custody of their child, 8-year-old Vicki.

The first witness was Mrs. Kline, a neighbor. Under examination by the wife's lawyer, she testified that she saw the husband, Robert, strike Vicki in public.

"How often did this occur?" the lawyer asked.

"It seemed every time I saw them in public the child did something to displease him. He would slap her across the face on those occasions—hard," Mrs. Kline said.

"And in your opinion was the father's behavior bad for Vicki? Did it make her afraid of him?" the lawyer asked.

"Objection!" cried Robert's lawyer. "This witness is being asked to state a conclusion."

"Sustained," said the judge, agreeing with Robert's attorney. "She may testify only to what she observed."

Then the expert witness, a child psychologist, was called. Having never seen Robert strike Vicki and having, in fact, been called into the case only after the divorce was filed, she could not testify to the particular damage to Vicki's psyche either. But as an authority on child rearing, about which the jury was told she had written many books, she was permitted to testify as follows:

"Dr. Bellows, you have observed the behavior of many 8-year-olds, have you not?" the wife's attorney asked.

"That is correct," she replied.

"You've heard testimony here today that Vicki was struck in the face by her father when she displeased him. Would you tell us what effect this behavior could have on an 8-year-old?"

"Aside from the obvious physical injury, I would be concerned about psychological damage. A child at that age is still very dependent upon parental approval. Constant physical or mental abuse would make her fearful of public performances of any kind, for fear of invoking the adverse opinion of the parent. It could very well make the child withdraw into herself."

"Then, in your opinion, should a parent who behaves in this manner be trusted with the custody of a young child?"

"Objection," Robert's attorney cried again.

"Overruled," the judge said, disagreeing with him this time. "This witness is a duly qualified expert in her field and she is answering only to the effect of abusive behavior on a typical 8-year-old. The jury may evaluate the evidence in that light." The psychologist responded in the negative. Robert lost the custody case.

One unusual element in this scene is that Dr. Bellows was permitted to hear the neighbor's testimony.

In many cases, witnesses are kept isolated from the courtroom while testimony is heard. The long wait for their turn is sometimes tedious, particularly since they are expected not to discuss the case that brought them all together. (One innovative court recently had video games installed in its waiting room to keep jurors and witnesses occupied. The machines brought such a windfall of quarters that the court was left with the unexpected problem of figuring out what to do with the added revenues.)

During court cases, every effort is made to keep the evidence before the jury as pristine as possible. That means not only excluding witnesses to keep them from tailoring their testimony as they hear each other's stories, but also shielding the jury from any information other than that heard under the judge's supervision. Juries may not hear news reports of a trial or discuss the case with anyone—neither families, friends, witnesses, nor even each other. Without such a rule, each juror might make a decision based upon independent information and each would, in a sense, be hearing a different case.

In jury cases, the opinions of those twelve (or in some cases eight or ten) citizens are the deciding force. Lawyers play to them as to a theater audience, wishing to make a good impression, to highlight favorable evidence, and discount the unfavorable.

The theatrics run high where stakes are large. Impassioned speeches, pitiful stories from the witness stand, and hostile attacks to discredit the other side are part of the play. Judges are responsible for seeing that none of the histrionics are overplayed to the detriment of the truth. Part of their unquestioned authority to control their courts is to see that lawyers stay within the evidence when they make closing speeches to the juries, that witnesses are not harassed beyond tolerance, and that juries are not senselessly exposed to inflammatory evidence.

A lawyer, for example, could be expected to bring his amputee client into the spotlight of an auto negligence suit over a lost arm in order to invoke the jury's sympathy. But a judge is highly reluctant to permit the introduction of the severed but preserved limb into the courtroom, unless the limb's condition itself is somehow an issue. Even the impassive court can be shocked. It has the right to protect itself when necessary.

Civil trials may go on for weeks or months, with volumes of testimony and exhaustive questioning. When they end, they end with a common refrain: Either the plaintiff gets what she wants or she doesn't. Either Ms. Sumer will go home with all or some of her medical costs and her auto damages or she won't.

The Verdict: Ms. Sumer's lawsuit is brought to redress a wrong done to her by the other driver and by the city's negligence in allowing the pothole to remain unfilled.

She had a number of options when she began her suit:

She could have asked for declaratory relief—an order by the judge that the hole be filled.

She could ask for the city or the other driver to be punished for behaving irresponsibly. The punishment would come in the form of money in her pocket.

She could ask for actual damages: her medical expenses, the repair to her car, her own pain and suffering.

She could ask for costs.

In the United States (unlike Britain), it is generally assumed each person will pay her own attorney. Attorney fees are not part of the costs, which include only filing fees and other incidentals. (In some special cases, where particularly important rights are involved, Congress encourages filing of suits to enforce those rights by allowing an award of attorney fees to the winning party. Civil-rights suits are the most notable example, a fact to keep in mind if you ever are looking for someone to represent you inexpensively in a civil-rights action.)

The conclusion will be in the hands of the jury.

During the trial, the lawyers will all have produced receipts for medical bills and the auto repair to substantiate the damage claims. They will have haggled over how much Ms. Sumer suffered. They will have quizzed witnesses over how bad the city's treatment of the pothole was. The jury will have facts and figures in front of it for a determination of damages.

And it will have evidence to guide it in assessing those damages to the two defendants: the city and F. Head.

But its decision is its own province, untouched by the judge unless it is totally outside the bounds of the law.

In this case, the jury concluded that the city was primarily responsible for the damages for leaving an unrepaired pothole in harm's way. It assessed 60 percent of the damages to the city.

It decided Mr. Head was following her too closely. It required him to pay 20 percent.

That leaves 20 percent unpaid. The jury decided, as it is permitted to do in most states, that Ms. Sumer was 20 percent at fault herself for having been fiddling with her radio when she should have been driving.

Whatever chagrin she may have felt at losing that 20 percent was adequately recouped when she heard the rest of the verdict. The jury, getting its chance to sock it to the city for all of its collective woes with potholes the previous winter, ordered the city to pay punitive damages of $5,000 for failing to perform its duty in maintaining streets.

After the Verdict: A judge may not make a wholesale revision of a jury's verdict unless she believes the jury was behaving dishonestly, was improperly influenced, or was entirely wrong in its judgment.

She may, however, force a reduction in the award.

One example occurred in a Wyoming court in 1981. A former Miss Wyoming sued *Penthouse* magazine for having run a fictitious story about a Miss Wyoming possessing magical sexual prowess. The jury found only about $1.5 million in actual damages. But, outraged over the slur to Wyoming, it assessed a $28-million punitive-damages award. The judge apparently decided the slur was worth only $14 million, so he cut the award in half.

Appeals: Appeals of civil-court decisions follow the same process as criminal appeals. Upon a decision within the legally permitted number of days, the losing party may take the case to a higher court.

Civil appeals, as in criminal appeals, are over the interpretation of the law. For example, appeals courts will not decide as a rule that actual damages should have been $4,500 instead of $5,000. But they will review questions about the degree to which cities may be sued. Judges' decisions are reviewable. Juries' decisions are less so.

An overview of the court system could not be complete without a caveat: Courts are operated by human beings. They are fallible. They are influenced by social mores and politics—philosophically if not monetarily, subtly if not overtly.

As Finley Peter Dunne once said: It doesn't matter whether the Constitution follows the flag. The Supreme Court follows the election returns.

But, politics aside, we have a government of laws, not of persons. Certain principles are inviolable. You may not be held in jail without a trial; you may not be deprived of freedom without a jury's finding. Police may not ransack your home without a court order. And you may not be silenced by the government for unpopular political views.

Those principles are embodied in the Constitution, a venerated document endowed with remarkable elasticity. It provides the basis for every law passed and for the protections against unjust laws.

Most of the rights in the Constitution are in the Bill of Rights and subsequent amendments. The first ten were added by popular demand after the body of the Constitution had already been written. The people were afraid of the King's tyranny, and they wanted to retain certain rights that would be safe from the government.

From time to time in American history, efforts have been made to change the Constitution. Six of those efforts (including the Equal Rights Amendment effort) have been unsuccessful.

Twenty-eight have passed. Such changes brought about and then repealed prohibition, gave women the right to vote, and gave citizens the right to vote for their senators, rather than relinquishing that right to their governors.

The changes can be made either upon a proposal by Congress, agreed to by three fourths of the states, or upon petition by the states themselves.

The latter technique has grown in favor in the 1980s as voters have become disenchanted with federal spending. As of 1982, only three more states' petitions may be needed to call a new constitutional convention for an amendment to balance the budget.

Controversies over the ways to keep the government in check are distinct from concern over the way to do it.

Many citizens feel that an amendment requiring Congress to control its spending is needed.

But the specter of a constitutional convention looms large. What if a Congress called to add a balanced-budget amendment got carried away by a few advocates to modify or repeal the Bill of Rights? Would delegates be above abolishing their own right to an attorney because they believe some defendants have gone scot-free because of the skills of their sharp lawyers? Would they give state police a figurative key to their homes by abolishing protection against search and seizure, because they believe some criminal has escaped prosecution by dint of the exclusionary rule? Would they give away their own right to speak freely about the government—a right that made possible the very campaign for a constitutional convention—because they disagree with their neighbors' views?

The dangers of a runaway convention have been much discussed. But they are not to be underplayed. A new Constitution could mean a new government, one in which the delicate balances and the concept of a constitutional shelter from powerful political winds would be mere reminiscences of a time when government was—excuse the expression—one of laws, not of men.

21
The Choices in Going to Court:
Going Lawyerless,
Hiring a Lawyer,
Mediation,
and Arbitration

TONDA F. RUSH

GETTING TO COURT

Q. What do you have when you have 1,000 lawyers at the bottom of the Indian Ocean?

A. A good start.

Heard any good lawyer jokes lately? No? How about this one?

Sally: Do you know how to save five lawyers on a boat in the middle of the ocean?

Sue: No.

Sally: Good.

Try that at a party and be a big hit. Lawyer jokes have replaced the light-bulb jokes that replaced the elephant jokes. The funny thing is . . . lawyer jokes predate them all.

Here's one from the sixteenth century: King Ferdinand admonished settlers in the New World against carrying along "law students, for fear lest lawsuits should get a footing in that new world." Or maybe Ferdinand wasn't kidding. Lawyers, for all their virtues, are a much criticized lot.

A woman friend recently said she was having a difficult time finding counsel to represent her in a suit for damages done to her car by a drunken lawyer whose car careened out of control. Somehow the police had let him get away without a blood-alcohol test to determine his level of intoxication. She wasn't sure whether a reluctance she found in many attorneys to handle her lawsuit was for lack of solid evidence or fear of the lawyer.

"I need a lawyer who isn't afraid to take on the law," she complained.

Sometimes things get bad enough, or lawyers are expensive enough, that you have to take on the law yourself.

The legal system belongs to everyone, not just the chosen few in the legal profession. (Did I say few? At last count, in 1981, there were 617,320 lawyers in the country according to the American Bar Association.) Court systems, in theory at least, are set up for laypersons as well as lawyers to use them. In practice, heading into court without a lawyer can be tricky business, but not impossible. It can be done.

Going Lawyerless

Having a lawyer is like keeping a life preserver in your canoe. You may never need it, but when you do, you really do.

For some sorts of disputes, lawyers may be a needless expense. For other cases, it is good to remember the old saw about the person who is her own lawyer having a fool for a client. There is a reason lawyers go to school for three years before they hang out their shingles. At 3 A.M., as you are buried in papers and books in preparation for your own lawsuit, you'll find out why.

To represent yourself in court, you have to know the issues you face, the facts of the case, and the rules of the court in resolving the dispute. And if you don't want to be outmaneuvered by the opposition, you need to know a little of what earlier courts have said about similar cases.

Before deciding whether you want to take on this behemoth of an institution, analyze the risks. Follow this rule of thumb: If it's a criminal case, ask yourself whether you could go to jail if you lose. If the answer is yes, get a lawyer, even if the jail stay is a remote possibility. A criminal record can cast a long shadow, and a jail sentence is no joke. It can interfere with social status, future jobs, bondability, and credit ratings. If the answer is no, read on.

Is a fine the probable outcome if you lose? If yes, find out how much. A clerk with the court that charged you should be able to tell you the fines permitted by law. If the law says you may be fined from $50 to $500, decide whether you can afford to lose $500. If you can't, see whether you can find a lawyer who will charge less than $500 to represent you. Balance the potential attorneys' fees against the potential fine. Which will cost the most?

If no, you're probably not in criminal court, where the customary penalties are fines and jail sentences. Read on.

If it's a civil case, are you bringing the case or is it being brought against you? If you are bringing the case, you are the plaintiff. If it is being brought against you, you are the defendant. If you are the plaintiff, are you asking for a lot of money or a very important court order? If so, get a lawyer. You will be sure to face considerable legal talent on the other side. If you are asking for a small sum, is it less than a lawyer would cost? If you are the defendant, what is being asked of you? Read the complaint served upon you very carefully. Can you afford to lose? If you lose, will the cost be greater than the cost of a lawyer?

In civil suits, once the stakes reach $1,000, the need for legal representation increases. When the stakes are under $500, it is sometimes difficult to find representation. In between, it's a judgment call.

These admonitions are not to imply that hiring a lawyer is hitching your wagon to a star. Even lawyers lose—one lawyer per case, at least. But getting a lawyer does increase protection against being thrown out of court on a technicality, which could ruin your chances of trying again.

Lawyerless in Criminal Court

Read Chapter 17. Then, if you decide to go ahead without a lawyer, ask the clerk in your local courthouse any questions that come to you about procedures: Where is the courtroom? Who is the judge? Who is the prosecutor? What is the potential penalty? Expect courteous and complete answers to factual questions.

While it is the clerk's duty to provide information about the court itself, it is illegal for nonlawyers to dispense legal advice. Therefore, to your solicitations for legal advice (can I bring my dog into court to prove she really didn't bark the night I was accused of disturbing the peace?), expect nothing more than a referral to the local bar association.

Ask to see the file on your case. Parts of it are public records. It will contain the complaint that brought you to court, as well as a notice from the sheriff or police officer who served you with a warrant for arrest, certifying that you were properly served. It may contain helpful information about search warrants or property that was seized from you. You may wish to contest the warrant or the seizure of property.

If you are going lawyerless because you can't afford a lawyer, you may have a right to a free lawyer. When you first appear in court, ask the judge whether that is true for your case, if she doesn't first ask you whether you want one. If the penalty does not involve a jail sentence, you have no right to a court-appointed lawyer.

If the penalty does involve a jail sentence, you may wish to check the local legal aid society, the local bar association, or the American Civil Liberties Union to see if they can provide you with counsel. If they do, you are likely to be supplied with a very busy lawyer who will appreciate all the help you can lend to your own cause. The demand for such services far exceeds the supply. If no one will represent you in court, perhaps you can find someone to "talk you through" the case so you can represent yourself more adequately.

If you fail to find a lawyer, or you choose not to use one, remember several important things:

1.   Always show up in court when you are summoned. When the judge gives you a trial date or a hearing schedule, be there. Failure to appear can result in a jail sentence.

2.   Follow any orders of the court, even if you believe they are wrong. Even an unconstitutional order must be followed, on penalty of a jail sentence. The propriety of the order may be subject to review in a higher court, but while it is in effect, it must be obeyed.

3.   Remember that the burden of proof is on the prosecutor. She will bring the first set of witnesses, and you will have an opportunity to question them. You may not use the right to question in order to state your own case. Your address to witnesses must be in the form of a question. At the beginning of the case, however, you will have a chance to state what your evidence will show and, at the end, why the prosecutor's evidence is too weak to prove its case and how your own evidence leads to the result you want. Remember that you do not have to prove yourself innocent. All the jury needs is a reasonable doubt as to your guilt.

4.   You have the right not to testify. It means, of course, that you will not get to tell your side of the story yourself and must rely on other witnesses to do so. But, by not testifying, you avoid questioning by the prosecutor. You must be careful when acting as your own lawyer not to lapse into testimony, but to stick to questioning.

At the end of the prosecutor's case, you are permitted to make a motion to the judge for dismissal of the case due to the prosecutor's failure to present sufficiently strong evidence. If the motion succeeds, you have won. If it fails, you get a second shot at victory with your own opportunity to bring evidence.

5.   If you object to something the prosecutor is doing (other than prosecuting you, to which you object most strenuously, of course), you must object to the judge as it happens. If a witness is testifying to something she does not have firsthand knowledge of, for example, you may believe the testimony is hearsay.

You should rise immediately and raise an objection with the judge and state your reason for objecting. (Object politely: the histrionics of television courtrooms are best left to the tube.) While it isn't advisable to continue to interrupt a trial with objections, it is also important not to let a big objection slip by. If you do, you may lose an opportunity to have an appeals court review a mistake in the trial court.

6.   If a jury returns a guilty verdict, you may ask to poll each member

of the jury to find out whether she voted for the verdict. Perhaps you will find the verdict was not unanimous and can be challenged in a higher court or overturned by the trial judge.

Though courts don't usually permit official inquiry into juries' reasons for their decisions, nothing prohibits jurors from speaking to you individually afterward if they wish to, to explain their findings. Often they wish to avoid such contact. The law protects them from harassment. But if they wish to talk (failing a direct order from the court to the contrary), they may.

7.   If you lose, consider an appeal. At that point, you again ought to explore getting a lawyer. If none materializes, consult the clerk of the trial court for the name of the clerk in the appellate court. The appellate clerk will provide a copy of the rules of that court to facilitate an appeal. Appeals are permitted only within a limited time after a conviction. The judge will advise you of the time limits.

8.   If you are in jail, heed the advice of other inmates only after doing your own research to confirm it. Though "jailhouse lawyers" are sometimes as familiar with the law as their professional counterparts, sometimes their legal interpretations are the subject of wishful thinking and can lead to an unfortunate outcome.

Lawyerless in Civil Court

Civil courts present such a plethora of situations that this short chapter is inadequate to cover them all. You could find yourself in a civil court for a divorce proceeding, an auto negligence suit, a challenge to taxes, an objection to the city's use of your land, or the contest of a will. The procedures of each are tailored to the issues involved.

This book is not meant to serve as a road map to success in a lawsuit. Civil lawsuits can be very complex. Persons contemplating prosecution of their own suits should consult an excellent laypersons' book on the law: Kantrowicz and Eisenberg, *How to Be Your Own Lawyer (Sometimes)* (New York: G. P. Putnam's Sons).

Before deciding to indulge in the expense of a full-blown lawsuit, consider the alternatives.

Negotiation

Litigation is expensive for everyone, even for (sometimes even more so for) large companies. Often it is cheaper to settle a case out of court than to hire a lawyer, a principle quickly learned by anyone who has negotiated with an insurance company.

Before going to court, you should always exhaust all means short of litigation. Often, a businesslike letter and a couple of phone calls will do the trick.

When Ms. Sumer first realized the expense of her auto repairs, she wrote to the city to advise it of her damages and to ask whether it would pay them. She discovered that the city was willing to talk to her about it and, indeed, that the law required her to file an official notice with the city of her damages before she could sue it, anyway. Her letter served that purpose. But, after several conversations, she realized the city would offer her only a fraction of her costs, so she decided to sue anyway.

But she used the lesson later when she got into a dispute with her dry cleaners'. Her favorite wool coat came back with a spot on it from the cleaning solvent. When she complained to the clerk, she got an insolent reply that the spot had probably been there for years. But she refused to leave the establishment without the name and address of the parent company.

She wrote the following letter:

> Spanking Cleaners
> 5549 Westwood
> Our Town, U.S.A.
>
> Attn.: Claims Department
>
> Gentlepersons:
>
> On May 1, 1982, I delivered a beige wool winter coat to your branch cleaners at 15th and Irving Streets. When I picked it up, three days later, I discovered a disfiguring spot on the back that was created during the cleaning process.
>
> I have consulted other dry cleaners and have been told nothing can be done to restore the garment to its original condition. Therefore, I am herewith filing a claim with your corporation for the replacement cost of the coat, which I estimate to be approximately $300.
>
> I will look forward to an immediate reply.
>
> Cordially,
> Constance Sumer

In return mail, she received a copy of a damage claim to be filled out and a form letter from the company stating that it did not consider itself responsible for the damage. Though some people would have given up the cause at that discouraging news, she was undaunted. She replied immediately:

> Gentlepersons:
>
> I received your reply of May 31 disclaiming responsibility for my damaged coat. I am attaching herewith copies of your letter and my original correspondence to you.

My coat was in fine shape when I first delivered it to you. When it came back to me, it was unwearable.

I have had the coat examined by several experts, who advise me that the cleaning solvent your company used to clean the coat is responsible for its present condition. I intend to hold you accountable for failing to fulfill your responsibility to clean the coat according to the standards of your industry.

This coat is worth a great deal to me. I believe its replacement value to be $300. If I do not receive satisfaction from your company within two weeks, I intend to represent myself in a lawsuit against you for the damage.

Cordially,
Constance Sumer

In a week and six days, an insurance adjuster appeared at her door.

Insurance adjusters can be charming people. You may discover that you like the one who handles your claim. It is best, however, to remember that you have a business relationship with that person. Your responsibility is to yourself; the adjuster's is to the company, to keep it out of court for as little money as possible. Adjusters know that they catch more flies with honey than hostility. They intend to bring back the most flies for the least honey, so to speak.

Ms. Sumer's adjuster was most reasonable. He certainly understood how important the coat was to her, and if it were up to him he'd pay her twice what it was worth for her trouble in having to replace it. But he had to answer to his company. Given the age of the coat, he said, the most he could offer was $200.

Ms. Sumer was adamant. She wanted $300 or nothing.

Back and forth they dickered, each refusing to budge. Finally, she grew weary of the process and announced she would discuss the issue with her lawyer. If necessary, she would sue.

The adjuster came around. A lawsuit would be expensive and time-consuming. He would offer her $250 in exchange for her promise not to sue.

She accepted. She figured the value of the months of good use plus her trouble in preparing for a lawsuit were worth $50. Besides, she wasn't entirely certain she wanted the trouble of a legal battle.

Insurance companies are good for their word. If they promise to send a check, they will. They want something for it, though, and that is the release.

The release represents a pitfall for the unwary. It buys the insurance company the assurance that it will be free from legal liability. A scrupulous company will limit its release to the terms of the original dispute. But the release is binding. It is important to read it carefully to be sure you are not giving away more than you sold.

In the case of the dry cleaners', Ms. Sumer promised that neither she, nor her heirs, nor anyone else with her power of attorney would sue the company or its successors for the damage done to that coat. She didn't promise never to sue the company for damage to any other garment it might clean. But she did commit herself forever not to sue for that coat.

Releases should be mutual. In her case, she had no fear of a suit from the dry-cleaning company. But suppose she had been asked to sign a release for Mr. Head's insurance company after the auto accident? If she got a settlement agreeable to her, should she agree not to sue Mr. Head? Of course.

But she very much needs to get Mr. Head also to agree not to sue her for the damage done to his car. Before signing, therefore, she exacted a promise from the insurance company that it would also prepare a release for Mr. Head to sign. Copies of both releases should be kept by both parties, as well as the insurance companies, just in case confusion arises in the future.

Small Claims Court

If the dry cleaners' negotiations had failed, Ms. Sumer would have had an extremely useful option. She could have sued the company in small claims court.

Until about ten years ago, suing for such small-potatoes cases was a practical impossibility. For the time it would take to find a lawyer and pay him or her for the trouble of drawing up a suit and prosecuting it, the eventual value of a suit would be nil.

The demands of consumer groups and a drive for court reform led to creation of small-claims courts in many states and the establishment of small-claims procedures in many already existing courts. These are layperson's courts. In some, lawyers are not only unnecessary, they are prohibited except when they are there to represent themselves.

These lower courts have "jurisdictional limits." They won't take a case for damages over the ceiling set by law. But damage ceilings may range from $500 to $1,500. Though your dispute may involve a higher sum, for many consumer problems you come out ahead if you accept the fact that possibly you won't receive full compensation. Balance the loss against the savings of attorneys' fees. A case in a civil court, for example, involving $1,700 may net a $300 lawyer's fee. It may be worthwhile to shoot for $1,500 and save the fee.

These courts are presided over by a judge who acts also as the jury. Complaints are filed as in the higher courts, but usually on a printed form provided by the clerk, to make sure you get all the right information before the court.

Summonses usually will be served by the court for a fee, just the same as summonses in any other sort of case. Witness fees are sometimes available. But, in both cases, those services cost money. It behooves you to try to get your witnesses to show up without court orders and to waive their witness fees if possible. Witnesses who don't want to come, of course, aren't likely to do so. You may use the power of the court to order them to come, but you will want to weigh the possible impact of their testimony. An angry witness has a powerful platform.

Once in court, the procedure follows the model of other courts. The plaintiff will call witnesses and the defendant will cross-examine. Then the defendant will call witnesses and the plaintiff will cross-examine. Each party will be allowed an opening and a closing statement. Then the judge will make a decision.

Judges often prefer to take a middle road in small-claims cases. The judge in the damaged-coat case might well have decided to give neither the $300 asked by the plaintiff nor the empty purse suggested by the defendant, but to take the age of the coat into account and grant $200.

The judge's decision in most courts is reviewable in a higher court, where, again, you are permitted a lawyer and may need a lawyer. The lion's share of small-claims cases are never appealed, however, for the very money-saving reasons that brought them to small claims in the first place.

Arbitration

Courts, even small-claims courts, have dockets (calendars) of cases that are packed to the top with unresolved disputes. A court case may take from six months to ten years to settle. It may draw unwanted publicity. It may involve numerous frustrating extensions of time and trips to the courthouse. For that reason, many are searching for alternatives to the system. A plethora of options are developing. One of the most popular is arbitration. Union members are familiar with the practice, because their employment contracts often call for arbitration in the event of an unresolvable dispute. Other kinds of contracts increasingly involve a mandatory arbitration. There is no reason many common consumer disputes couldn't follow the same path.

In arbitration, each party agrees to pick a person or team of persons to resolve their dispute. If one person is chosen, she is picked for neutrality. Often, arbitration requires three persons: one picked by each of the parties and one by the other two arbitrators.

Usually arbitration is binding. That is, the parties agree to accept the decision. Sometimes the result of an arbitration can be appealed to a higher court, but, like small-claims appeals, that defeats the purpose of doing arbitration in the first place.

A number of organizations offer arbitration services, including the American Arbitration Association. See p. 543 for address.

Mediation

A similar alternative is mediation. Mediators, like arbitrators, listen to both sides of an argument and try to find a middle ground. The difference is that they have to find a middle that both sides will agree to. Unlike arbitrators, they do not dictate an outcome.

Mediators can be extremely useful in sensitive cases, such as divorces, in which property has to be divided; or landlord-tenant cases, in which tempers might flare. Mediators tend to be single individuals, rather than teams, because it is important for that person to have good listening skills and be able to detect nuances in the parties' positions. Teamwork does not lend itself to compromise.

Mediators also can be found in a number of places. Or you may find your own mediator.

The important thing is to reach an agreement on how the discussion will be handled. Will each party get a set time to make arguments? May they question each other? Are there options that are simply outside the realm of consideration? Will you agree that if no decision is made within a certain number of hours another option will be tried? A good mediator will work with you to set the ground rules first. The key to conflict resolution is fairness. The rules protect that fairness and encourage the trust of the people involved.

Information about mediation also is available from the American Arbitration Association.

Working with a Lawyer

A friend of mine recently described a socialite's party she had attended. With food and decorations, the bill for the fete was $30,000. Her friends gaped at the sum, which was more than most of them earned in a year. How did a person come by that sort of money? they wondered. The host, my friend advised knowingly, is an ambulance chaser.

The term conjures up an image of a pet collie in hot pursuit of a squealing siren. But in fact, it refers to a breed of legal professional who makes a living off accidents and death by suing the people responsible for them.

In its worst sense, an ambulance chaser is an opportunist who hangs around emergency rooms and just happens to have a business card handy just as an accident victim leaves this life, suggesting to the grief-stricken families that they might feel better if they sue the *** who did this terrible deed. This sort of solicitation is not only distasteful, it is unethical and illegal. Therefore, it doesn't usually happen quite like that.

More common is the lawyer who simply has built a reputation as a hard-hitting litigator in accident suits. She gets the biggest settlements and the best verdicts for the client. She may be blustery and brash or sweet and sympathetic, but something in the technique has swayed enough juries to draw victories in court. The reputation as a winner draws business, and business begets business, and before anyone realizes it, the toughest and dirtiest cases fall at that person's feet.

There is nothing wrong with an ethical and competent ambulance chaser. if you happen to be a plaintiff in need of a good one. Newspapers and magazines are filled with accusations that they are responsible for big jury verdicts and, thus, higher insurance costs. That may be true. But the fact remains that when you need a life preserver in your canoe, you need a good one. You may get only one chance.

Shopping for a lawyer is not unlike shopping for a life preserver. You want to look for quality and price. A wise shopper is one who knows how to ask questions—and where to ask them.

Finding a Lawyer

Finding lawyers to ask questions of has been somewhat difficult until recent years. Only since the mid-1970s have lawyers been permitted to advertise in any way but the simple Yellow Pages listing. Advertising was once considered unethical and misleading to the public, and many practitioners still think it is. But due to pressure both from within and without the legal system, and a compelling court case, lawyers may advertise as long as they follow carefully drawn rules. Rules differ in the various states, but most states permit lawyers to advertise their names, locations, and telephone numbers, fees for initial consultation, and areas of practice that they generally work in.

The new practice eased the difficulty in lawyer-hunting considerably.

Lawyers advertise on television and radio, in the newspapers, and on billboards. Some write legal columns in local publications to get their names before the public. They may give simple legal advice in such formats, but they will always advise that the legal answer to each problem is determined by the problem. You will be warned—and you should heed the warning— not to follow advice in the newspaper without checking with a lawyer first.

It seems like a Catch-22—you can't follow a lawyer's advice without a lawyer. And in a way it is. Note the sections on going lawyerless in civil and criminal courts. Careful reading at a library and studying earlier chapters in this book will provide some guidance to legal questions yourself. But what to do when you decide you need a lawyer?

1. Ask friends. While buying a house, changing a name, divorcing a spouse, or opening a will, many people come into contact with lawyers. Ask for candid opinions of their lawyers' work.

2. Contact organizations set up to assist with legal problems like yours. Pick up the Yellow Pages and run down the column of associations. If you

see one that deals with subjects like the one you are handling, call it. A problem with a landlord, for example, may be a familiar one to a local tenants' union. A shelter for abused spouses will know lawyers who handle divorce and other domestic cases. Some communities have volunteer referral organizations who act as a clearinghouse for community organizations. If you can't find an organization through the telephone book, try to find the referral organization.

3.   That advice works well only for common problems—ones shared by many in the community, like landlord-tenant disputes. For other difficulties, try the local bar association.

You will see it listed with other associations, usually by the name of your state or county. If you can't find it that way, call the clerk of the local court to get the address and telephone number. The association will have a referral list of lawyers who are taking on new cases. Then you can choose your first candidate by whatever random method most suits you—perhaps you like the name, the address is near you, the firm sounds pretentious, it sounds earthy, or you closed your eyes and opened them right on that firm's name.

The Interview: Ask and It Will Be Given to You—for a Price: The great expansion of lawyers in the nation has created a greater sense of competition, especially among the young and struggling. A combination of competition and insistent consumers has led to a more open relationship between lawyer and client.

It is a business relationship. The lawyer works for you, bound by ethical considerations, the law, and your contract. The forming of that contract is the most important element of the case.

After picking the lawyer you think you may want to hire, call for an appointment. Ask, at the time, what the lawyer will charge for an initial consultation. If the fee is too high, look for another lawyer. If you can afford it, make a date.

At the first meeting, show up armed with facts and figures. Any documents that pertain to your case—sales slips, repair estimates, wills, or contracts—should go with you. Have a list in hand—or at least in your head—of things to bring up at that meeting.

Tell the lawyer, in as much detail as you can, exactly what your case is about and what you have done to resolve it. If you have already been in contact with an insurance adjuster or have already tried arbitration unsuccessfully, for example, the lawyer should know.

Take with you also the names and dates pertinent to the case: the names of other persons in your auto accident, the date your dog bit the neighbor child.

If you ever have dealt with another lawyer in regard to your case, be sure to tell your new lawyer about it. He or she may be accused of ethical violations for stepping into a case seemingly in the hands of a colleague. It is your right to fire your lawyer and hire a new one. But it isn't the lawyer's privilege to steal her colleagues' clients. Also, your new lawyer may be somewhat restricted legally by actions of the old.

Be prepared to answer many questions, possibly about things you didn't think were important. Don't give in to the impulse to put your own, favorable spin on the facts. Tell the bad with the good.

Trust the lawyer to keep information confidential. Especially in small communities, that trust is the linchpin of the legal relationship. If you have heard of that lawyer's indulging in cocktail party gossip about her cases, steer clear. The lawyer shouldn't have to be reminded of that trust, but if you are sharing particularly intimate information, it never hurts to remind her that you expect it to remain intimate.

Ask all the questions that come to your mind. If the lawyer is evasive or abrupt, think about finding a different one. You have a right to know what is happening with your case. A lawyer who is too taciturn or who is unapproachable with questions isn't anyone you want to hire.

Find out how long the case is expected to take. Find out how much time and effort you will be expected to put into it. Ask the lawyer how often you can expect progress reports. Don't accept a noncommittal "I'll let you know when something happens." Ask for regular updates. The fact is that lawyers sometimes get so busy they procrastinate with cases that have no deadlines. Your progress report will be a deadline that calls your case to mind.

Finally, get a firm understanding about costs. Ask:
• How much she charges per hour.
• How many hours the case should take.
• How you will be expected to pay—in a lump sum or in installments.
• Whether the case might net you attorneys' fees.
• What you can do to trim costs. For example, may you gather exhibits yourself instead of having the lawyer's clerk put them together?

And above all else, get the employment contract on paper, complete with a commitment for the progress reports.

If you expect to have trouble meeting the fees, be honest about your situation. Possibly a deferred payment will be acceptable. Treat the lawyer's bill like any other financial obligation, to be paid promptly for acceptable services rendered. Don't slough them off. Lawyers have a right to sue for their fees. And they will.

Fees are determined by the amount of time a case will take and the complexity of the case. An uncontested divorce can usually be handled for a set fee of several hundred dollars—if you shop around. The drawing of a simple will, without too many trusts, heirs, whereases, and wherefores, also can be done relatively cheaply.

The settling of a contract dispute will cost more. Likewise, a criminal case will be more expensive. Some lawyers will quote a set rate and some will simply state an hourly fee and give an estimate of the hours needed.

Some cases can be taken on a contingency-fee basis. That means the lawyer gets part of whatever you win. The fee will vary from a low percentage to a settlement before a court date, to a medium percentage for a settlement after trial begins, to the highest percentage for cases won in court. In any event, be wary of a lawyer who strays out of the 33–40 percent fee range. And if a lawyer offers to take a criminal case on a contingency-fee basis—in other words, you pay if you're found not guilty and you don't pay if you go to jail—make a beeline for the door. The lawyer is violating the profession's code of ethics.

If You're Not Satisfied

Talk to the lawyer. Explain why you are not satisfied and try to work out the differences. Try to avoid terminating the relationship. If you can salvage the one you have, it will save time and money.

If the lawyer has an associate whom you feel more compatible with, ask to have the case transferred.

If neither of those things works, fire your lawyer. You have a right to dismiss your employee-lawyer the same as you would have a right to dismiss any other employee. You have a right to your file when you leave the lawyer's office and you should take it so you will have the right information to pass on to the next lawyer.

If your dissatisfaction is grave enough to give you cause to doubt the lawyer's professionalism, make a complaint to your local bar association. If the association doesn't have a complaints committee, call your state supreme court clerk and ask about the procedure for complaining to the state bar. Lawyers are licensed by their states and they must continue to satisfy the state's requirements to remain in practice.

If you still are not satisfied, contact another lawyer about the possibility of a malpractice suit. Distasteful as they are, they are a fact of modern jurisprudence and sometimes they are the only tool a client has to ensure that justice is done.

When will you know that you should be dissatisfied?

If your lawyer refuses to talk to you about your case, you should get another lawyer.

If your lawyer misses court deadlines, you should get another lawyer. It behooves you to know when the deadlines are and to make sure your lawyer is on top of them. A missed court date sometimes means a lost case, and there's little you can do about that. If you are the victim of a lost case because of the lawyer's tardiness, a complaint to the state bar will be in order—and possibly a malpractice suit to boot.

If your lawyer abuses your confidences by sharing your information with persons outside her law office, get another lawyer.

If you suspect your lawyer is mixing your money with her personal or professional accounts, demand to see a ledger of the accounts. Clients' monies must be kept separately from all others to ensure that they are meticulously accounted for. Every year, the courts revoke the licenses of lawyers for failing to observe that rule. The legal profession considers it a most important one.

If your lawyer behaves in a less than professional manner, question her about the behavior and, if you are not satisfied, get another lawyer. It goes without saying that you, as the client, deserve respect. Your case deserves respectful handling. You have a right to expect your lawyer to show up in court well prepared, well dressed, and well mannered.

And the lawyer, by the way, has the right to expect the same from you.

FURTHER READING

Rudovsky, David; Bronstein, Alvin J.; Koren, Edward I. *The Rights of Prisoners.* New York: Avon Books, 1977.

Rosengart, Oliver. *The Rights of Suspects.* New York: Avon Books, 1974.

Gillers, Stephen. *The Rights of Lawyers and Clients.* New York: Avon Books, 1979. (Chapter 10 covers the rights of indigents, clients who represent themselves, and nonlawyers who sell law-related services.)

Glossary of Legal Terms

Administrator (administratrix)
A court-appointed estate representative charged with settling an estate where no will exists.

Adverse possession A common-law means of acquiring title to real property by continuous occupancy for a number of years.

Adultery Grounds for divorce based on the plaintiff's assertion that the defendant has had sexual relations with another person while married to the plaintiff.

Affidavit A sworn statement made in writing and witnessed by an official, such as a notary public, who has the power to administer oaths.

Annulment A court decree that formally invalidates a marriage by declaring it null from the beginning.

Amicus curiae (Latin for "friend of the court") A party, with no direct interest in a court proceeding, who has been allowed to introduce evidence or authority because of a particular expertise or general interest in the issue before the court.

Arrest The act of detaining a person pursuant to legal authorization, usually based on probable cause that a felony or a misdemeanor has been committed.

Attestation The witnessing and signing, by witnesses, of a document intended to have legal effect. Usually refers to witnessing a will.

Bench warrant A written authorization by a court for the arrest of a person charged with a crime.

Bequest (bequeath) A gift of personal property made by a will.

Beneficiary The person named in a will or trust to receive money or property.

Bond (bail) A written record of debt, public or private, usually in the form of an interest-bearing certificate. Sometimes a bond is used to secure the appearance at trial of a person under indictment, in which case it is called a bail bond.

Cause of action   The stated legal reasons for a civil lawsuit.

Codicil   A change or amendment to a will, executed with the same formalities as a will.

Community property   A system of property ownership in a marriage which gives title to the property to husband and wife equally, in most instances regardless of who acquired the property.

Complaint   A statement of the plaintiff's reasons for bringing a lawsuit. Sometimes called a petition, it includes the names of both plaintiff and defendant, and a statement of the basis of the suit and the damages or other remedy requested.

Connivance   A deliberate plot to facilitate grounds for divorce.

Conveyance   A transfer of an interest in property, usually real property, by means of a signed writing.

Child support   A periodic payment made pursuant to a court order for the maintenance of children in the custody of one parent by the noncustodial parent.

Cohabitation   Living together as husband and wife without being married.

Decedent   Person who is deceased, usually used in connection with the distribution and administration of the property of the deceased's (decedent's) estate.

Default judgment   The result of the failure of one party to a lawsuit to appear and offer a defense to the complaint. Usually the complaining party will be awarded no more than she has requested, which causes most complainants to seek maximum damages.

Defendant   The accused party in a lawsuit. (See Plaintiff.)

Descent   The term for inheritance of real property when the owner dies without leaving a will.

Devise   A gift of real property under a will.

Devisee   The recipient of a gift of real property as provided in a will.

Divorce nisi   Temporary judgment of divorce, which will be final unless one of the parties appears to defend the action, usually a no-fault divorce action.

Divorce a mensa et thoro   A limited divorce (by mutual agreement) effected by a separation decree by a court. Literally translated, it means divorce "from bed and board." The marriage is not dissolved by this type of divorce.

Divorce (a vinculo matrimonii)   The dissolution of a marriage that was validly entered into, often for cause (such as adultery) or because of irreconcilable differences between the parties.

Domicile The state of one's permanent, legal residence. A person may have several residences, but only one of them is her domicile.

Easement The right to use real property owned by another person for a particular, limited purpose, such as an easement for access to a body of water.

Emancipation Refers to the legal status of a child who has been freed from parental custody and control by virtue of employment or residence or other circumstances.

Escheat The legal process by which title to unclaimed property goes to the state.

Estate All the property owned by a person or in which the person has an interest at death, including real property, personal possessions, and intangibles.

Estate for years The term for a tenancy in real property measured by a specific period of time, often designated in a lease or a similar written agreement.

Estoppel A bar to the assertion of a fact or claim inconsistent with a previous claim or prior conduct, usually because the previous claim or conduct has been relied upon by others.

Executor The person appointed by a court to represent an estate and to administer and distribute estate property according to the decedent's will.

Fee-simple ownership Ownership of all interests in real property, usually by one person.

Felony A crime of such seriousness that a prison term or a substantial fine or both may be imposed. (See Misdemeanor.)

Fiduciary A person who has the legal responsibility to hold and manage property for another person. Guardians, executors, trustees, and custodians are said to have fiduciary duties.

Filiation order A judicial or other official determination that a man is the natural father of a given child, often required to enforce support or inheritance claims of the child.

Franchise A right conferred by written agreement to use, sell, or promote certain products or services in specific ways and places.

Full faith and credit A clause of the U.S. Constitution requiring recognition of the decisions in one state by the others under certain circumstances.

Garnishment (wage attachment) A legal procedure for taking the property of a debtor while it's in the possession of a third party, such as an employer, to pay the debt.

Guardian (ad litem) (either of the property or of the person)   A court-appointed representative with powers to protect the person or the property for a particular purpose or during a specified lawsuit (ad litem).

Habeas corpus   A Latin term which, literally translated, means "you should have the body," used to describe a legal proceeding for obtaining the release of a person in custody by seeking a court determination as to whether the person is legally detained.

Heir   The person who succeeds to the estate of another upon the death of that person, because of blood relation or statutory mandate.

Heir apparent   An heir who will succeed to property if he survives the current owner, his ancestor.

Heir presumptive   The person who would inherit should the ancestor die immediately. If other events occur, he might be precluded.

Holographic will   A will written, dated, and signed by the testator entirely in her own handwriting and often not witnessed.

Interrogatory   A set of questions, posed in a civil suit, that must be answered under oath.

Intervivos   A term indicating a transaction taking place during one's lifetime, while living. It is frequently used to refer to a trust for management of property during one's lifetime. (See Trust, intervivos trust)

Joint tenancy   A method of property ownership whereby two or more persons have equal interests in the same property, which passes automatically by operation of law to the survivor or survivors upon the death of any joint tenant.

Judgment   An official, final determination by a court of law.

Jurisdiction   The authority of a court to hear a particular case, based on where the parties live or choose to appear to do business, the type of action, and the amount of money involved.

Legacy   A gift in a will of personal property or money; often used interchangeably with the term "bequest."

Levy   The process by which authorities seize and sell property that is the subject of a judgment or garnishment.

Lien   The right of one person to enforce a claim for money against the property of another until the claim is paid or otherwise satisfied.

Life estate   An interest in real or personal property that lasts only so long as the life of the holder of the interest, known as a life tenant.

Marriage A civil contract requiring the consent of both parties and of the state.

Misdemeanor The violation of a public law, punishable by a fine or a short term of imprisonment.

Nineteenth amendment The amendment to the U.S. Constitution that prohibits the states from abridging, on account of sex, a citizen's right to vote.

Novation An agreement among three parties that substitutes a new party for one of the parties to a previous contract. The obligations of the original two parties are discharged, and the novation becomes a new contract.

Personalty Items of such tangible property as furniture and jewelry, as opposed to land, or real property.

Plaintiff Person who is bringing a civil action against a person or other entity against which she has a complaint. The accused party is the defendant.

Precedent The terms of a previous court decision, on the same law and similar facts, which should dictate the result of the present lawsuit.

Prima facie Evidence that is sufficient to determine the issue unless a persuasive defense is offered or the evidence is contradicted.

Probate The procedure by which a court determines that a document purporting to be a will is valid and properly executed and then supervises the administration of the estate.

Pro se proceeding A proceeding on behalf of oneself, in which one is acting as her own attorney.

Protection order A court order, usually issued by a family court or a criminal court, ordering a person not to harm or harass a specific other. It may be either a temporary or a permanent order.

Quitclaim deed A document transferring all the interest in real property a person may have. There is no warranty that the title is good or that any particular interest exists in that property.

Real property (realty, real estate) The legal term for land or interests in land, as opposed to tangible personal property, or personalty.

Remand To send a case back to a lower court, usually the one that first decided the case, for different or corrective action.

Rescission (rescind) The legal term for revoking, taking back, or canceling the legal effect of an agreement, contract, or decision.

Residuary estate The part of a decedent's property that remains after all gifts, legacies, debts, taxes, and administrative costs are paid.

Revocation Usually refers to an act, by a person who has made a will, which signifies that the will is to have no effect.

Separation (trial, legal) A court decree that does not dissolve a marriage but declares that the parties to the marriage are living apart usually for a cause similar to divorce grounds.

Statute A law passed by a local, state, or federal legislature.

Statute of frauds Requires that the terms of a contract or other agreement be in writing in order to be legally valid and enforceable. Most states have statutes reciting this requirement covering such agreements as sales of goods, land-sale contracts, contracts to answer for a debt of another, and contracts not to be performed within one year.

Statute of limitations A law that requires that certain claims be brought or lawsuits begun within a particular time period from the time the wrongdoing or other action occurred.

Summons A written notification to a defendant that a lawsuit has been started against her, requiring a court appearance within a certain time to submit an answer.

Surrogate The title often given the court or judge authorized to probate wills and administer estates.

Tenancy by the entirety The ownership of real property by a husband and wife, similar to a joint tenancy because the survivor obtains complete title by operation of law upon the death of either person.

Testator (testatrix) The man or woman who is signing a last will and testament.

Tort A civil wrong committed upon the person or property.

Trust An entity or responsibility to hold property and take title thereto for the benefit of another person or persons. A trust created by will is called a testamentary trust and becomes effective upon the death of the creator. A trust created by written agreement during the creator's life is called an intervivos trust.

Writ A court order directing a particular action by a public official.

Further Information: Hot Lines and Addresses

This listing of help organizations was up to date at the time of going to press, but readers should be aware that organizations bloom and wither away, and relocate, so the listings cannot be regarded as definitive. However, if you have a problem, we hope that you will at least find a place here to start solving it.

When you are searching for a solution to your problem, diligence and perseverance pay off.

Abuse
See Family Abuse for child and spouse abuse and abuse of the elderly.

Aid to Families With Dependent Children
Check with state welfare office for details.

Aliens and Citizens
The following organizations will provide information on immigration and citizenship questions:

American Baptist Home Mission Societies
Valley Forge, Pa. 19481
215-768-2425

American Civil Liberties Union
132 West 43rd Street
New York, N.Y. 10036
212-944-9800

American Committee on Italian Migration
42 E. 23rd Street
New York, N.Y. 10010
212-460-5600

American Council for Nationalities Service
15 E. 40th Street
New York, N.Y. 10016
212-532-4166

American Federation of Jews from Central Europe
570 Seventh Avenue
New York, N.Y. 10001
212-921-3860

American Federation of Musicians
1500 Broadway
New York, N. Y. 10036
212-869-1330

American Fund for Czechoslovak
Refugees
1790 Broadway
New York, N.Y. 10019
212-CO5-1919

American Jewish Joint Distribution Committee, Inc.
60 East 42nd Street
New York, N.Y. 10017
212-687-6200

Association of Immigration and Nationality Lawyers
127 John Street
New York, N.Y. 10038
212-952-0700

Board of Global Ministries of the United Methodist Church
475 Riverside Drive
New York, N.Y. 10027
212-870-2164

Christian Church (Disciples of Christ)
222 South Downey Avenue
P.O. Box 1986
Indianapolis, Ind. 46206
317-353-1491

Church of the Brethren World Ministries Commission
P.O. Box 188
New Windsor, Md. 21776
301-635-3131

Church World Service
475 Riverside Drive
New York, N.Y. 10027
212-870-2164

General Conference of Seventh-Day Adventists
6840 Eastern Avenue, N.W.
Washington, D.C. 20012
202-722-6000

Holt International Children's Services, Inc.
P.O. Box 2880
Eugene, Ore. 97402
503-687-2202

International Rescue Committee, Inc.
386 Park Avenue South
New York, N.Y. 10016
212-679-0010

Japanese American Citizens League
Japan Center—22 Peace Plaza
San Francisco, Calif. 94115
415-563-3202

Lutheran Immigration and Refugee Service
360 Park Avenue South
New York, N.Y. 10010
212-532-6350

Mexican American Legal Defense and Education Fund
28 Geary Street
San Francisco, Calif. 94103
415-981-5800

National Association for the Advancement of Colored People
1790 Broadway
New York, N.Y. 10019
212-245-2100

National Chinese Welfare Council
3912 West Church Street
Skokie, Ill. 60203
312-676-9725

National Conference of Catholic Charities
1346 Connecticut Avenue, N.W.
Washington, D.C. 20036
202-785-2757

National Council of Jewish Women
15 E. 26th Street
New York, N.Y. 10010
212-532-1740

National Council of La Raza
1725 I Street, N.W.
Washington, D.C. 20005
202-293-4680

National Immigration Project
National Lawyers Guild
712 So. Grand View Street
Los Angeles, Calif. 90057
213-380-3180

Polish American Immigration and
  Relief Committee
17 Irving Place
New York, N.Y. 10003
212-254-2240

Tolstoy Foundation, Inc.
250 West 57th Street, 10th Floor
New York, N.Y. 10019
212-247-2922

Travelers Aid Services
1465 Broadway
New York, N.Y. 10036
212-944-0013

United Hias Service, Inc.
200 Park Avenue South
New York, N.Y. 10003
212-674-6800

United Presbyterian Church in the
  U.S.A.
Committee on Health and Human
  Development
475 Riverside Drive—Room 1062
New York, N.Y. 10027
212-870-2465

United States Catholic Conference
Migration and Refugee Services
1312 Massachusetts Avenue,
  N.W.
Washington, D.C. 20005
202-659-6625

Also check with church groups in
your area, the Travelers' Aid Society, the American Civil Liberties
Union, legal aid societies, or the
Legal Services Corporation for information on local groups aiding
those in need of advice on immigration matters.

Business, Women in
The following organizations will
be of particular aid to the majority
of women-owned businesses that
are sole proprietorships:

National Association of Negro
Business and Professional
Women's Clubs
1806 New Hampshire Avenue,
  N.W.
Washington, D.C. 20009
202-483-4206

National Association of Women
  Business Owners
500 North Michigan Avenue
Chicago, Ill. 60611
312-661-1700

National Alliance of Home-Based
  Businesswomen
P.O. Box 95
Norwood, N.J. 07648

National Federation of Business
  and Professional Women's Clubs
2012 Massachusetts Avenue,
  N.W.
Washington, D.C. 20036
202-293-1100

Office of Minority Business Enterprise
U.S. Department of Commerce
Washington, D.C. 20230

Office of Women's Business Ownership
Small Business Administration
1441 L Street, N.W.
Washington, D.C. 20416

Direct Selling Association
1730 M Street, N.W.
Suite 610
Washington, D.C. 20036

International Franchise Association
1025 Connecticut Avenue, N.W.
Washington, D.C. 20036

OTHER HELPFUL
ORGANIZATIONS

Networks and Membership Organizations of Professional Women and Business Owners:

These networks and organizations exist as national and as local groups. Many are listed in the books *Networks,* by Carol Kleiman, and *Networking,* by Mary Scott Welch. New groups spring up continually. For complete up-to-date nationwide listings, mail $2.00 and a stamped self-addressed envelope to "Professional Connections," *Savvy* Magazine, 111 Eighth Avenue, New York, N.Y. 10011. For information about groups in your state, contact the women's business owner representative in any district office of the U.S. Small Business Administration or the Office of Women's Business Ownership in Washington.

American Women's Economic Development Corporation, 60 East 42nd Street, Suite 405, New York, N.Y. 10165. This nonprofit group gives short- and long-term help with start-ups and expansions. Fees range from $25 for individual counseling sessions to $350 for 18 months of classes and individualized assistance.

Trade Associations: Small business as an interest group is represented by several national and regional organizations. Every trade and line of business has at least one association that offers its members various kinds of practical information and assistance. Trade associations are listed in the Encyclopedia of Associations, which should be in your local library.

U.S. Small Business Administration: District offices of the SBA exist in every state. They offer assistance with starting and managing businesses, financing businesses, and getting government contracts for small businesses. The women's business owner representative in each office is responsible for outreach to and promotion of women's businesses in the local business community and for referring women business owners to SBA resources or other government or private-sector help. The Office of Women's Business Ownership, at SBA headquarters, 1441 L Street, N.W., Washington, D.C. 20416, leads the agency's efforts on behalf of women business owners and is a source of information about all federal programs in this area. Write to get on their mailing list.

Chambers of Commerce: These organizations exist in many communities and are voluntary associations of business people. Their activities vary, but many offer advice, services, and contacts to new business owners, including women.

Educational Institutions: A 45-hour course in entrepreneurship has been developed by the American Association of Community and Junior Colleges' Center for Women's Opportunities, One Dupont Circle, N.W., Washington, D.C. 20036. It is available at many community colleges and might be available at others if there is a demand for it. Small Business Development Centers are situated in over 15 state universities and offer free assistance in many areas to local businesses. Your nearest SBA office can direct you to SBDCs and also advise you of other resources available at nearby colleges and universities. Many have free Small Business Institute programs offering local business owners the assistance of graduate business students.

State and City Business Assistance Programs: Many states and cities offer special programs to assist or finance small businesses or to award them contracts. Check with your city's or state's department of commerce, office of economic development, or similar office, for information. The office of your state's attorney general and of your city or county clerk can help you determine and comply with state and local legal requirements.

Child Snatching

Child Custody Project
(Patricia M. Hoff, Director)
National Legal Resources Center for Child Advocacy and Protection
American Bar Association
1800 M Street, N.W.
Washington, D.C. 20036
202-331-2250

Child Find
P.O. Box 277
New Paltz, N.Y. 12561

Child Support

If you're having trouble collecting child support, contact one of the following organizations:

Federal Parent Locator Service
Office of Child Support Enforcement
Department of Health, and Human Services
Washington, D.C. 20201

National Organization to Insure Support Enforcement
12 West 72nd Street
New York, N.Y. 10023

CHILD SUPPORT ENFORCEMENT OFFICES

Region I (Connecticut, Maine, Massachusetts, New Hampshire, Rhode Island, Vermont)

Regional Representative, OCSE
John F. Kennedy Federal Building
Government Center
Boston, Mass. 02203

Region II (New York, New Jersey, Puerto Rico, Virgin Islands)

Regional Representative, OCSE
Federal Building—Room 4016
26 Federal Plaza
New York, N.Y. 10007

Region III (Delaware, Maryland, Pennsylvania, Virginia, West Virginia, District of Columbia)

Regional Representative, OCSE
3535 Market Street
Philadelphia, Pa. 19101

Region IV (Alabama, Florida, Georgia, Kentucky, Mississippi, North Carolina, South Carolina, Tennessee

Acting Regional Representative, OCSE
101 Marietta Tower, Suite 1801
Atlanta, Ga. 30323

Region V (Illinois, Indiana, Michigan, Minnesota, Ohio, Wisconsin)

Regional Representative, OCSE
300 South Wacker Drive, 18th
   Floor
Chicago, Ill. 60606
Region VI (Arkansas, Louisiana,
New Mexico, Oklahoma, Texas)
Regional Representative, OCSE
Office of Child Support Enforce-
   ment
Main Tower Building—Suite 1345
Dallas, Tex. 75202
Region VII (Iowa, Kansas, Mis-
souri, Nebraska)
Regional Representative, OCSE
601 East 12th Street—Room 1759
Kansas City, Mo. 64106
Region VIII (Colorado, Montana,
North Dakota, South Dakota,
Utah, Wyoming)
Regional Representative, OCSE
Room 11037, Federal Office Build-
   ing
19th and Stout Streets
Denver, Colo. 80202
Region IX (Arizona, California,
Hawaii, Nevada, Guam)
Regional Representative, OCSE
50 United Nations Plaza
Federal Office Building—Room
   270
San Francisco, Calif. 94102
Region X (Alaska, Idaho, Oregon,
Washington)
Regional Representative, OCSE
Arcade Plaza Building
1321 Second Avenue
Seattle, Wash. 98101

Consumer Information, General

Consumer Information Center
General Services Administration
Pueblo, Colo. 81009

You can obtain a list of their
publications by writing to the
above address.

INDUSTRY GRIEVANCE PANELS

APPLIANCES

Major Appliance Consumer Action Panel
20 N. Wacker Drive
Chicago, Ill. 60606
800-621-0477
   Handles individual complaints,
sends consumer literature

AUTOMOBILES

Autocap—National Automobile
   Dealers Association
8400 Westpark Drive
McLean, Va. 22102
   Handles individual complaints.
Dealer must belong to NADA

CEMETERY PLOTS

Cemetery Consumers Service
   Council
Box 3574
Washington, D.C. 20007
703-379-6426
   Handles individual complaints

ELECTRONIC PRODUCTS

Electronic Industries Association
2001 Eye Street, N.W.
Washington, D.C. 20006
202-457-4900
   Handles individual complaints,
sends consumer literature

FURNITURE

National Association of Furniture
   Manufacturers
8401 Connecticut Avenue
Suite 911
Washington, D.C. 20036
301-657-4442
   Handles individual complaints,
sends consumer literature. Manufacturer must be a member. Furniture must be less than one year old.

Furniture Industry Consumer Advisory Panel
Box 951
High Point, N.C. 27261
Handles individual complaints, sends consumer literature. Complaint must be about design defect, not wear and tear

MAGAZINE SUBSCRIPTIONS
Magazine Publishers Association
575 Lexington Avenue
New York, N.Y. 10022
212-752-0055
Handles individual complaints

TRAVEL SERVICES
American Society of Travel Agents
711 Fifth Avenue 6th Floor
New York, N.Y. 10022
212-486-0700
Handles individual complaints. Will tell you if complaints have been received about a particular company.

GOVERNMENT AGENCIES AND CONSUMER ACTION GROUPS
I *Groups handling specific products*

AIRLINES
Aviation Consumer Action Project
P.O. Box 19029
Washington, D.C. 20036
Provides do-it-yourself complaint kit. Sends free literature

AUTOMOBILES
National Highway Traffic Safety Administration
Traffic Safety Advice and Recall Information
Hot line: 800-424-9393
Provides referrals, sends free literature. Information on recalled automobiles

BANKS
The Federal Deposit Insurance Corporation:
800-424-5488
Receives complaints and provides consumer information on banking laws.

ENVIRONMENT
Environmental Protection Agency:
800-424-9346 (hazardous wastes);
800-531-7790 (pesticides)

FOOD, DRUGS, COSMETICS, MICROWAVE OVENS, SMOKE ALARMS
Food and Drug Administration
See phone book for local number.
Free microwave oven safety inspections. Provides referrals, sends free literature

FRAUD IN CREDIT (LENDING), FALSE LABELING OR ADVERTISING
Federal Trade Commission
Washington, D.C. 20580
202-523-3567
Helps individuals with complaints, sends free literature

HEARING AIDS
Better Hearing Institute
Hot line: 800-424-8576
Helps individuals with complaints, sends free literature

INSURANCE
Federal crime insurance for homes and businesses:
800-638-8780
Federal flood insurance:
800-638-6620

MAIL SERVICES
U.S. Postal Service Consumer Advocate
Washington, D.C. 20260
202-245-4514

Helps individuals with complaints

MOVERS (INTERSTATE), RAILROADS, BUSES

Interstate Commerce Commission
26 Federal Plaza
New York, N.Y. 10007
Hot line: 800-424-9312

Helps individuals with complaints

STUDENT LOANS

Student Information Center:
800-638-6700

Information on federal annual grants and loans

II *Groups handling general complaints*

DANGEROUS PRODUCTS

U.S. Consumer Products Safety
  Commission
Hot line: 800-638-8326
Maryland only: 800-492-8363
Alaska, Hawaii,
Puerto Rico, Virgin Islands:
800-638-8270

Provides referrals, sends free literature

ALL BUSINESSES AND CHARITIES

Better Business Bureaus
See phone book for local address

Helps individuals with complaints, provides referrals, sends free literature.

SELECTED PRODUCTS AND SERVICES

Consumers Union
256 Washington Street
Mount Vernon, N.Y. 10550
914-664-6400

Publishes *Consumer Reports* magazine. Will send copies of articles on particular products to you.

Consumer Information Center
General Services Administration
Pueblo, Colo. 81009

Publishes list of free or low-cost consumer publications put out by federal government.

ALL PRODUCTS AND SERVICES

Consumer Federation of America
1012 14th Street
Suite 901
Washington, D.C. 20005
202-387-6121

Helps individuals with complaints, provides referrals, sends free literature

III *Consumer Advocacy and Education Groups*

Consumer Federation of America
1012 14th Street, N.W.
Suite 901
Washington, D.C. 20005
202-387-6121

Promotes consumer education and advocacy

Consumer Research
P.O. Box 168
Bowerstown Road
Washington, N.J. 07882
201-689-3300

Publishes impartial laboratory tests on consumer goods.

Consumers Union
256 Washington Street
Mount Vernon, N.Y. 10550
914-664-6400

Publishes impartial laboratory tests on consumer goods.

Federation of Homemakers
P.O. Box 5571
Arlington, Va. 22205
703-524-4866

Grass-roots organization promotes consumer education and lobbies in Washington on consumer issues relating to food (e.g., labeling).

National Consumer League
1522 K Street, N.W.
Suite 406
Washington, D.C. 20005
202-797-7600

Promotes consumer education and advocacy.

Public Citizen
P.O. Box 19404
Washington, D.C. 20036

Funds lobbying, research, and legal action on behalf of consumers. Founded by Ralph Nader.

Credit

Complaints re refusal of credit, problems with getting credit, and credit counseling.

Credit Practices
Federal Trade Commission
Washington, D.C. 20580

Also check your phone book for regional offices of the FTC and the National Credit Union Administration.

Banking

GENERAL

American Bankers Association
1120 Connecticut Avenue, N.W.
Washington, D.C. 20036
202-467-4000

Electronic Fund Transfer
Contact the regional office of the Federal Reserve System.

Federally Chartered Banks
Comptroller of the Currency
Department of the Treasury,
or contact the regional office for your state.

State Chartered Banks
Contact state banking authority in your state.

Credit Unions (federally chartered)
Contact regional office for your state, or contact:

Credit Union National Association
1730 Rhode Island Avenue, N.W.
Washington, D.C. 20036
202-828-4500

Savings and Loan Institutions
Federal Home Loan Bank Board
Contact regional office for your state.

State Chartered Banks That Are Members of the Federal Reserve System
Federal Reserve System. Contact regional office for your state, or state banking authorities.

State banks not members of the Federal Reserve System.
Contact the regional office for your state of the Federal Deposit Insurance Corporation.

For the above regional offices, check your phone book or the Consumer's Resource Handbook, available in your library or from the Consumer Information Center, Pueblo, Colo. 81009.

Credit Counseling
Executive Director
National Foundation for Consumer Credit
8701 Georgia Avenue
Suite 601
Silver Spring, Md. 20910

Crime

(whether you are a victim of a crime or have been or are about to be arrested)
Within your local community you can locate a variety of legal organizations to assist you with your case or complaint. The following is a

basic list of agencies that provide legal services:

If you're a defendant:

City and county bar associations

City and county lawyer referral services

American Civil Liberties Union, local chapters

National Lawyers Guild, local chapters

City and county law libraries

Legal aid societies

Public defenders

If you're a victim:

Local district attorney

Local city attorney

National District Attorney Association

Day Care

Day Care and Child Development Council of America
1602 17th Street, N.W.
Washington, D.C. 20009
202-745-0220

National Child Day Care Association
1501 Benning Road, N.E.
Washington, D.C.
202-397-3800

Death

(legal problems relating to funeral homes, funerals, etc.)

Call the Better Business Bureau to report problems with a funeral home.

FUNERALS

Deceptive practices may be encountered in the funeral industry. At the time of going to press, the Federal Trade Commission was proposing regulations to enforce disclosure by funeral directors concerning such issues as embalm-ing, which is *not* required by law, and to require funeral homes to give prices over the phone, and to give itemized price lists, rather than follow a "package deal or else" policy. In the case of cremation, it would require funeral homes to provide less-expensive coffins.

Funeral societies may help you to avoid difficulties. For the name of a society near you, write to

The Continental Association of Funeral and Memorial Societies
1828 L Street, N.W. Suite 1100
Washington, D.C. 20036
202-293-4821

The Association of Retired Persons publishes *It's Your Choice; the Practical Guide to Planning Funerals* ($4.95, check or money order: write to It's Your Choice, 400 South Edward Street, Mount Prospect, Ill. 60056).

Displaced Homemakers

Displaced Homemakers Network
1531 Pennsylvania Avenue, S.E.
Washington, D.C. 20003
202-347-0522

Older Women's League
1325 G Street, N.W.
Lower Level
Washington, D.C. 20005

Pension Rights Center
1346 Connecticut Avenue, N.W.
Washington, D.C. 20036
202-296-3778

Women's Equity Action League
805 15th Street, N.W.
Washington, D.C. 20005
202-638-1961

League of Women Voters
1730 M Street, N.W.
Washington, D.C. 20036

National Women's Political Caucus
1411 K Street, N.W.
Washington, D.C. 20005

NOW Legal Defense and Education Fund
132 W. 43rd Street
New York, N.Y. 10036

Divorce
The following organizations will provide helpful information to women who are already divorced or who are contemplating divorce:

Children's Rights
3443 17th Street, N.W.
Washington, D.C. 20010
202-462-7573

National Association for Divorced Women
23 Exchange Place
New York, N.Y. 10004
212-344-8407

Organization of Women for Legal Awareness
94 Claremont Avenue
Maplewood, N.J. 07040
201-762-5208

Parents Without Partners International
7910 Woodmont Avenue
Bethesda, Md. 20014
301-654-8850

Education
GENERAL
American Association of University Women
2401 Virginia Avenue, N.W.
Washington, D.C. 20037
202-785-7700

American Federation of Teachers
Women's Committee
1816 Chestnut Street
Philadelphia, Pa. 19103
215-567-1300

Intercollegiate Association for Women Students
c/o American Association of University Women
2401 Virginia Avenue, N.W.
Washington, D.C. 20037
202-785-7700

National Coalition for Women and Girls in Education
Women's Equity Action League
805 15th Street, N.W.
Washington, D.C. 20005
202-638-1961

Office for Civil Rights
Department of Health, Education and Welfare
Washington, D.C. 20201

Office of Women in Higher Education
American Council on Education
1 Dupont Circle, N.W.
Washington, D.C. 20036
202-833-4692

Older Women's League
1325 G Street, N.W.
Washington, D.C. 20005
202-783-6686

Project on Equal Education Rights
NOW Legal Defense and Education Fund
425 13th Street, N.W.
Washington, D.C. 20005
202-347-2279

Project on the Status and Education of Women
Association of American Colleges
1818 R Street, N.W.
Washington, D.C. 20009
202-387-3760

National Women's Education Fund
1410 Q Street, N.W.
Washington, D.C. 10020
202-462-8606

Women Educators
P.O. Box 218
Red Bank, N.J. 07701

Women's Educational Equity Communications Network
Far West Laboratory
1855 Folsom Street
San Francisco, Calif. 94103
415-565-3032

WHERE TO SEND YOUR TITLE IX COMPLAINT

Region I (Connecticut, Maine, Massachusetts, New Hampshire, Rhode Island, Vermont)

Director, Office for Civil Rights, ED
140 Federal Street, 14th Floor
Boston, Mass. 02110
617-223-4248

Region II (New Jersey, New York, Puerto Rico, Virgin Islands)

Director, Office for Civil Rights, ED
Room 33-130
26 Federal Plaza
New York, N.Y. 10278
212-264-4633

Region III (Delaware, Maryland, Pennsylvania, Virginia, Washington, D.C., West Virginia)

Director, Office for Civil Rights, ED
3535 Market Street, P.O. Box 13716
Philadelphia, Pa. 19101
215-596-6771

Region IV (Alabama, Florida, Georgia, Kentucky, Mississippi, North Carolina, South Carolina, Tennessee)

Director, Office for Civil Rights, ED
101 Marietta Street, N.W.
Atlanta, Ga. 30323
404-221-2954

Region V (Illinois, Minnesota, Wisconsin)

Director, Office for Civil Rights, ED
300 South Wacker Drive, 8th Floor
Chicago, Ill. 60606
312-353-2520

—(Michigan, Ohio, Indiana)

Chief, Elementary and Secondary Education*
Office for Civil Rights, ED
55 Erieview Plaza, Room 222
Cleveland, Ohio 44114
216-522-4970

Region VI (Arkansas, Louisiana, New Mexico, Oklahoma, Texas)

Director, Office for Civil Rights, ED
1200 Main Tower Building, 19th Floor
Dallas, Tex. 75202
214-767-3951

Region VII (Iowa, Kansas, Missouri, Nebraska)

Director, Office for Civil Rights, ED
1150 Grand Avenue, 7th Floor
Kansas City, Mo. 64106
816-374-2474

*Please note: The Cleveland office handles complaints against elementary and secondary schools only. Complaints against colleges and universities anywhere in Region V should be sent to the Chicago office.

Region VIII (Colorado, Montana, North Dakota, South Dakota, Utah, Wyoming)

Director, Office for Civil Rights, ED
1961 Stout Street
Federal Office Building, Room 1194, 13th Floor
Denver, Colo. 80294
303-837-2025

Region IX (Arizona, California, Hawaii, Nevada)

Director, Office for Civil Rights, ED
1275 Market Street, 14th Floor
San Francisco, Calif. 94102
415-556-8592

Region X (Alaska, Idaho, Oregon, Washington)

Director, Office for Civil Rights, ED
1321 Second Avenue
M/S 624
Arcade Plaza Building
Seattle, Wash. 98101
206-442-2990

FOR ADDITIONAL INFORMATION AND PUBLICATIONS ON THE RIGHTS OF WOMEN AND GIRLS IN EDUCATION, CONTACT:

Project on the Status and Education of Women
Association of American Colleges
1818 R Street, N.W.
Washington, D.C. 20009
202-387-1300

The Project publishes a newsletter, *On Campus with Women,* and other topical publications relating to women and higher education.

Project on Equal Education Rights (PEER)
1413 K Street, N.W.
Washington, D.C. 20005

The Project publishes a newsletter as well as other publications dealing with women and girls in educational settings at all levels. Of particular interest is the pamphlet *Anyone's Guide to Filing a Title IX Complaint,* which can be obtained from the Project for $.75.

SELECTED FEDERAL LAWS PROHIBITING SEX DISCRIMINATION IN EDUCATIONAL INSTITUTIONS†

TITLE IX of the Education Amendments of 1972 as amended by the Bayh Amendments of 1974 and the Education Amendments of 1976.

TITLE VII (Section 799A) and TITLE VIII (Section 845) of the Public Health Service Act as amended by the Comprehensive Health Manpower Act and the Nurse Training Amendments Act of 1971.

†Based on a chart prepared in August 1979 by the Project on the Status and Education of Women, of the Association of American Colleges.

WHICH INSTITUTIONS ARE COVERED?

All institutions receiving federal monies by way of a grant, loan, or contract (other than a contract of insurance or guaranty). Noneducational organizations that receive or benefit from federal financial assistance and operate education programs are also covered.

All institutions receiving or benefiting from a grant, loan guarantee, or interest subsidy for health-personnel training programs or receiving a contract under Title VII or VIII of the Public Health Service Act.

WHAT IS PROHIBITED?

Discrimination against students and employees on the basis of sex.

Discrimination against students in admissions and against some employees on the basis of sex.

EXEMPTIONS FROM COVERAGE.

Religious institutions are exempt if application of the antidiscrimination provisions is not consistent with the religious tenets of such organizations. Military schools are exempt if their primary purpose is to train individuals for the military services of the United States or for the merchant marine. Discrimination in admissions is prohibited only in vocational institutions (including vocational high schools), graduate and professional institutions, and public undergraduate coeducational institutions.
Additional exemptions were enacted after Title IX's passage.

None.

HOW IS A COMPLAINT MADE?

U.S. Department of Education in your region.

By letter to U.S. Department of Education in your region.

WHO MAY MAKE A COMPLAINT?

Individuals and/or organizations on behalf of aggrieved party. Organizations may also file class or pattern complaints without identifying individuals.

Individuals and/or organizations on behalf of aggrieved party. Organizations may also file class or pattern complaints without identifying individuals.

TIME LIMIT FOR FILING COMPLAINTS.

Within 180 days from time of discriminatory act.

Within 180 days from time of discriminatory act.

MAY INVESTIGATIONS BE MADE WITHOUT COMPLAINTS?

Yes. Government may conduct periodic reviews without a reported violation, as well as in response to complaints.

Yes. Government may conduct periodic reviews without a reported violation, as well as in response to complaints.

ENFORCEMENT POWER AND SANCTIONS.

If voluntary compliance fails, Department of Education may institute administrative proceedings to suspend or terminate federal monies and to bar future awards, or it may refer the complaint to the Department of Justice with a recommendation for court action. Aggrieved individuals also may initiate suits. Court may enjoin the institution from unlawful activities and order equitable relief. Department of Education may delay new awards while seeking voluntary compliance.

If voluntary compliance fails, Department of Education may institute administrative proceedings to suspend or terminate federal monies and to bar future awards, or it may refer the complaint to the Department of Justice with a recommendation for court action. Court may enjoin the institution from unlawful activities and order equitable relief. Department of Education also may delay new awards while seeking voluntary compliance. Whether or not individuals have the right to sue institutions is not clear.

AFFIRMATIVE-ACTION REQUIREMENTS.
(THERE ARE NO RESTRICTIONS AGAINST ACTION THAT IS NONPREFERENTIAL.)

Affirmative action is not required but may be undertaken by an institution to overcome the effects of conditions that resulted in limited participation by persons of a particular sex. Department of Education may require remedial action if discrimination is found.

Affirmative action is not required but may be undertaken by an institution to overcome the effects of conditions that resulted in limited participation by persons of a particular sex. Department of Education may require remedial action if discrimination is found.

Is Harassment Prohibited?

Institutions are prohibited from discharging or otherwise discriminating against any participant or potential participant because she/he has made a complaint, assisted with an investigation, or instituted proceedings.

Institutions are prohibited from discharging or otherwise discriminating against any participant or potential participant because she/he has made a complaint, assisted with an investigation, or instituted proceedings.

Confidentiality of Names.

Individual complainant's name may be revealed during investigation. If court action becomes necessary, the identity of the parties involved becomes a matter of public record. The aggrieved party and the respondent are not bound by any confidentiality requirement.

Individual complainant's name may be revealed during investigation. If court action becomes necessary, the identity of the parties involved becomes a matter of public record. The aggrieved party and the respondent are not bound by any confidentiality requirement.

For Further Information and Relevant Documents, Contact:

Office of Civil Rights
Department of Education
Washington, D.C. 20201
or
regional Department of Education office

Office for Civil Rights
Department of Education
Washington, D.C. 20201
or
regional Department of Education office

NONSEXIST

If you are concerned about sexism or racism in books used by your child in school, one of the following organizations may be able to advise you:

Council on Interracial Books for Children
Racism and Sexism Resource Center for Educators
1841 Broadway
New York, N.Y. 10023
212-757-5339

Resource Center on Sex Roles in Education
National Foundation for the Improvement of Education
1156 15th Street, N.W.
Washington, D.C. 20036
202-833-4402

Women on Words and Images
P.O. Box 2163
Princeton, N.J. 08540

SPORTS

The following organizations are good information sources on sports and women in general, and on sexism in sports in particular.

Association for Intercollegiate Athletics for Women
1201 16th Street, N.W.
Washington, D.C. 20036
202-833-5485

Center for Women and Sport
White Building
Pennsylvania State University
University Park, Pa. 16802

National Association for Girls and Women in Sports
1201 16th Street, N.W.
Washington, D.C. 20036
202-833-5540

Project on the Status and Education of Women
1818 R Street, N.W.
Washington, D.C. 20009
202-387-1300

SPRINT
Women's Equity Action League Fund
805 15th Street, N.W.
Washington, D.C. 20005
(Call their toll-free number, 800-424-5162, for up-to-the-minute information on Title IX.)

Women's Sports Foundation
195 Moulton Street
San Francisco, Calif. 94125
415-563-6266

The Environment
The following is a listing of organizations involved in various aspects of environmental protection. If you have a pollution problem (air, water, or noise), check the Yellow or the Blue Pages of your phone book for the number of the state Environmental Protection Agency.

Environmental Action Coalition
417 Lafayette Street
New York, N.Y. 10003
212-677-1601

Institute for Environmental Action
530 West 25th Street
New York, N.Y. 10001
212-620-9773

National Audubon Society
950 Third Avenue
New York, N.Y. 10022
212-832-3200

National Center for Appropriate Technology
177 East 3rd Street
New York, N.Y. 10003
212-475-4840

Sierra Club
228 East 45th Street
New York, N.Y. 10017
212-687-2950

Environmental Protection Agency
Consumer Complaints
Washington, D.C. 20460
202-755-0707

Energy Action
1523 L Street, N.W.
Washington, D.C. 20005

Family Abuse
Where to call or write:
You may write or telephone the following for specific information and referrals in your geographic area. If you need immediate help, ask the operator to give you the telephone numbers of battered women's shelters or women's counseling centers or domestic violence centers or "victim's assistance bureaus," or call the police (911).

Odyssey Institute Inc.
817 Fairfield Avenue
Bridgeport, Conn. 06605
203-334-3488
    National listings and referrals

National Organization for Women
(NOW)
Task Force on Household Violence and Battered Women
425 13th Street, N.W.
Washington, D.C. 20004
202-347-2229

Abused Womens Aid in Crisis
AWAIC, Inc.
G.P.O. Box 1699
New York, N.Y. 10001
212-686-3628
    Nationwide listings re battered women

Family Violence Research Program
Sociology Department
University of New Hampshire
Durham, N.H. 03824
    Research papers on domestic violence

Women's Legal Defense Fund
2000 P Street, N.W.
Washington, D.C. 20036
202-887-0364
    Information on domestic violence

SPOUSE ABUSE

Center for Women's Policy Studies
2000 P Street, N.W., Suite 508
Washington, D.C. 20036
202-872-1770
    Nationwide listings and bibliographies and newsletter; also state-by-state charts and analyses of domestic-violence laws

National Clearinghouse on Domestic Violence
P.O. Box 2309
Rockville, Md. 20852
301-251-5172
    Listings for referrals and publications

Marjorie Fields
Brooklyn Legal Services Corporation B
105 Court Street
Brooklyn, N.Y. 11201
212-855-8003
    National listings, referrals, and information

ABUSED WOMEN'S SHELTERS

The following lists at least one resource, usually in the capital of each state, and was excerpted from "Domestic Violence Information Series Number 2, April, 1981." Staff at these centers can explain local laws to you.

You may call the shelter listed to find other resources in your state, or write National Clearinghouse on Domestic Violence, P.O. Box 2309, Rockville, Md. 20852.

ALABAMA

Birmingham/Jefferson   County
    Women's Center
2230 Highland Avenue
Birmingham, Ala. 35205
205-322-1915

ALASKA

Aiding Women in Rape and Emergency
P.O. Box 809
Juneau, Alaska 99802
907-586-6624

ARIZONA

Sojourner Center
P.O. Box 2649
Phoenix, Ariz. 95602
602-258-5344

ARKANSAS

Advocates for Battered Women
P.O. Box 1954
Little Rock, Ark. 72203
501-376-3219

CALIFORNIA

Mother's Emergency Stress Service
2515 J Street
Sacramento, Calif. 95816
916-446-7811 (crisis)
916-446-2791 (home)

Jenesse Center, Inc.
P.O. Box 73837
Los Angeles, Calif. 90003
213-582-4523

San Francisco Women's Center
63 Brady Street
San Francisco, Calif. 94103
415-431-1180

COLORADO

Columbine Center
1331 Columbine
Denver, Colo. 80206
303-399-0082 (crisis)
303-399-4555 (office)

CONNECTICUT

Hartford Interval House
Hartford, Conn. 06105
203-527-0550

DELAWARE

Child, Inc. / Family Violence Program
11th and Washington Streets
Wilmington, Del. 19801
302-652-8411 (crisis)
302-652-3547 (office)

DISTRICT OF COLUMBIA

House of Ruth
459 Massachusetts Avenue
Washington, D.C. 20001
202-347-9689

FLORIDA

Sexual and Physical Abuse Resource Center
P.O. Box 12367 University Station
Gainesville, Fla. 32603
904-377-8255 (crisis)
904-377-7273 (office)

Dade County Victims Advocates / Safespace
1515 N.W. 7th Street, Room #112
Miami, Fla. 33125
305-579-2915

Refuge House of Leon County, Inc.
P.O. Box 12304
Tallahassee, Fla. 32308
904-878-6089

GEORGIA

Council on Battered Women, Inc.
P.O. Box 54737
Atlanta, Ga. 30308
404-873-1766

HAWAII

Shelter for Abused Spouses and Children
c/o Kokua Kalihi Valley
1888 Owawa Street
Honolulu, Hawaii 96819
808-841-0822 (crisis)
808-841-3275 (office)

IDAHO

Emergency Housing Services, Inc.
P.O. Box 286
815 North 7th Street
Boise, Idaho 83701
208-343-7541

ILLINOIS

Gospel League
955 West Grand Avenue
Chicago, Ill. 60622
312-243-2480

Sojourn Women's Center
915 North 7th Street
Springfield, Ill. 62702
217-544-2484 (crisis)
217-525-0313 (office)

INDIANA

Salvation Army Family Violence
    Program
234 East Michigan
Indianapolis, Ind. 46205
315-637-5551

IOWA

Legal Service Corp.
315 East 5th Street
Des Moines, Iowa 50309
515-243-2151

KANSAS

Battered Women Task Force
P.O. Box 1883
Topeka, Kans. 66601
913-295-8499 (crisis)
913-233-1750 (office)

KENTUCKY

YWCA Spouse Abuse Center
604 East 3rd Street
Louisville, Ky. 40202
502-585-2331

LOUISIANA

Battered Women's Program
P.O. Box 2133
Baton Rouge, La. 70821
504-389-3001

YWCA Battered Women's Program
601 Jefferson Davis Parkway
New Orleans, La. 70119
504-486-0377 (crisis)
504-486-7666 (office)

MAINE

Spruce Run
44 Central Street
Bangor, Me. 04401
207-947-0496
207-947-6143 (evening & weekends)

MARYLAND

Good Neighbors Unlimited
208 Duke of Gloucester Street
Annapolis, Md. 21401
(No phone listed)

House of Ruth, Baltimore
2402 North Calvert Street
Baltimore, Md. 21218
301-889-7884

MASSACHUSETTS

Casa Myrna Vazquez
P.O. Box 18019
Boston, Mass. 02118
617-266-4305 (crisis)
617-262-9381 (office)

MICHIGAN

Battered Women's Program
YWCA of Metropolitan Detroit
2230 Witherall Street
Detroit, Mich. 48201
313-961-9220

Council Against Domestic Assault
P.O. Box 14149
Lansing, Mich. 48901
517-374-0818 (crisis)
517-484-1905 (office)

MINNESOTA

Harriet Tubman Shelter
30001 Oakland
Minneapolis, Minn. 55404
612-874-8867

MISSISSIPPI

Gulf Coast Womens Center, Inc.
P.O. Box 444
Biloxi, Miss. 39531
601-435-1968

MISSOURI

Women's Self-Help Center
27 North Newstead
St. Louis, Mo. 63108
314-531-2003 (crisis)
314-531-2005 (office)

MONTANA

Community Resources
1937 Florida
Butte, Mont. 59701
406-792-2616

NEBRASKA

People's City Mission
124 South 9th Street
Lincoln, Neb. 68508
402-432-5329

NEVADA

Advocates for Abused Women
P.O. Box 2529
Carson City, Nev. 89701
702-883-7654

NEW HAMPSHIRE

Concord Task Force on Battered
   Women
20 South Main Street
Concord, N.H. 03301
800-852-3311 (crisis)
603-228-0571 (office)

NEW JERSEY

Womanspace, Inc.
Mercer County Women's Center
P.O. Box 7182
Trenton, N.J. 08628
609-394-9000

NEW MEXICO

Battered Women's Project
P.O. Box 5701
Santa Fe, N.M. 87501
505-988-9731

NEW YORK

Mercy House
12 St. Joseph Terrace
Albany, N.Y. 12210
518-434-3531

Simple Gifts
80 Richmond Avenue
Buffalo, N.Y. 14222
716-884-5330

New York State Department of
   Social Services
Domestic Violence Program
2 World Trade Center
New York, N.Y. 10047
212-488-5012

Alternatives for Battered Women,
   Inc.
380 Andrews Street
Rochester, N.Y. 14607
716-232-7353 (crisis)
716-232-7379 (office)

Brooklyn Legal Services Corporation B
152 Court Street
Brooklyn, N.Y. 11201
212-855-8029

NORTH CAROLINA

Wake County Women's Aid:
Services for Abused Women, Inc.
718 Hillborough Street
Raleigh, N.C. 27603
919-832-4769

NORTH DAKOTA

Abused Women's Resource Closet
219 North 7th Street
Bismarck, N.D. 58501
800-472-2911 (crisis)
701-258-2240 (office)

OHIO

Choices for Victims of Domestic
Violence
P.O. Box 8323
Columbus, Ohio 43201
614-294-3381 (crisis)
614-294-7876 (office)

OKLAHOMA

YWCA Passageway—A Women's
Crisis Center
135 N.W. 19th
Oklahoma City, Okla. 73103
405-528-5508 (crisis)
405-528-5540 (office)

OREGON

Women's Crisis Service
P.O. Box 851
Salem, Oreg. 97308
503-399-7722 (crisis)
503-378-1572 (office)

PENNSYLVANIA

Women in Crisis
4th and Market Streets
Harrisburg, Pa. 17101
717-238-1068

Women Against Abuse
P.O. Box 12233
Philadelphia, Pa. 19144
215-386-7777 (crisis)
215-386-1280 (office)

Women's Center and Shelter of
Greater Pittsburgh
616 North Highland Avenue
Pittsburgh, Pa. 15206
412-661-6066

RHODE ISLAND

Sojourner House, Inc.
P.O. Box 5667, Weybosset Hill
Station
Providence, R.I. 02903
401-751-1262

SOUTH CAROLINA

Providence   Home—Women's
Shelter
3425 North Main Street
Columbia, S.C. 29203
803-779-4706 (crisis)
803-252-5264 (office)

SOUTH DAKOTA

Women and Violence, Inc.
P.O. Box 3042
Rapid City, S.D. 57709
605-341-4808

TENNESSEE

Oasis House
1013 17th Avenue South
Nashville, Tenn. 37212
615-327-4455

TEXAS

Center for Battered Women
P.O. Box 5631
Austin, Tex. 78763
512-472-4878 (crisis)
512-472-4879 (office)

Domestic Violence Intervention
Alliance
The Family Place
P.O. Box 19803
Dallas, Tex. 75219
214-521-4290 (crisis)
214-386-5055 (office)

Houston Area Women's Center,
Inc.
P.O. Box 20186, Room E401
Houston, Tex. 77025
713-527-0718 (crisis)
713-792-4411 (office)

UTAH

YWCA Program for Women in
Jeopardy and Their Children
322 East Third South
Salt Lake City, Utah 84111
801-355-2804

VERMONT

Vermont Legal Aid, Inc.
3 Summer Street
Springfield, Vt. 05156
802-885-5181

VIRGINIA

Women's Victim Advocacy Program / YWCA
6 North Fifth Street
Richmond, Va. 23219
(No phone number listed)

WASHINGTON

YWCA Women's Shelter Program
220 East Union
Olympia, Wash. 98501
206-352-2211 (crisis)
206-352-0593 (office)

The Battered Women's Project
City Attorney's Office
10th Floor, Municipal Building
Seattle, Wash. 98104
206-625-2119 (crisis)
206-625-2002 (office)

WEST VIRGINIA

Domestic Violence Center
31 Hillcrest
Charleston, W.Va. 25303
304-345-0848 (crisis)
304-346-9471, ext. 283 (office)

WISCONSIN

Family Service
214 North Hamilton Street
Madison, Wis. 53703
414-251-7611

WYOMING

Grandma's Safe House
P.O. Box 1621
Cheyenne, Wyo. 82001
307-632-2072

CHILD ABUSE

Most states handle child abuse matters through the welfare department's children's bureaus.

You may also telephone the Society for the Prevention of Cruelty to Children or Victims' Assistance Bureaus in your geographic area. The telephone operator should help you to locate such resources. IN AN EMERGENCY, CALL THE POLICE. The following will also provide information on child abuse:

National Center on Child Abuse and Neglect (NCCAN)
Department of Health and Human Services Administration for Children, Youth and Families
Washington, D.C. 20201

Odyssey Institute Inc.
817 Fairfield Avenue
Bridgeport, Conn. 06605
203-334-3488

Odyssey also has facilities in Louisiana, Maine, Michigan, New Hampshire, and Utah. Telephone the headquarters for more information.

Parents/Daughters/Sons United
P.O. Box 952
San Jose, Calif. 95108
408-295-0595

Project SEY (Sexually Exploited Youth)
Austin Child Guidance Center
612 West 6th Street
Austin, Tex. 78701
512-476-6015

Children's Hospital Medical Center
111 Michigan Avenue, N.W.
Washington, D.C. 20036
202-745-5682

American Bar Association
National Legal Resource Center
  for Child Advocacy & Protection
1800 M Street, N.W.
Washington, D.C. 20036
202-337-2250

Minnesota Program for Victims of
  Sexual Assault
430 Metro Square Building
St. Paul, Minn. 55101

Lloyd Martin Foundation for Sex-
  ually Exploited Children
P.O. Box 5835
Hacienda Heights, Calif. 91745

Family Violence Center
Department of Sociology, Univer-
  sity of New Hampshire
Durham, N.H. 03842

Children's Defense Fund
1520 New Hampshire Avenue,
  N.W.
Washington, D.C. 20036
202-483-1470

The Education Commission of the
  States
1860 Lincoln Street
Denver, Colo. 80295

MARITAL RAPE

Rape crisis centers, battered
women's shelters, and domestic violence centers can advise you.
Also, you may call or write:

National Clearinghouse on Marital Rape
Women's History Research Center
2325 Oak Street
Berkeley, Calif. 94708
415-548-1770

David Finkelhor, Ph.D.
University of New Hampshire
  Family Violence Research Pro-
  gram
Department of Sociology
Durham, N.H. 03842

Lisa Leghorn
46 Pleasant Street
Cambridge, Mass. 02139

Maria Green
New York County Lawyers Association
14 Vesey Street
New York, N.Y. 10007
212-267-6646

Family Planning
Check your Yellow Pages under
Family Planning or under Birth
Control Information Centers.

For further information contact:

Planned Parenthood Foundation
  of America
810 Seventh Avenue
New York, N.Y. 10019
212-777-2002

Or contact local planned parenthood affiliates.

Association for Voluntary Sterilization (AVS)
122 East 42nd Street
New York, N.Y. 10017
212-573-8322

Handicapped, General
Clearinghouse on the Handi-
  capped
Department of Education Services
Washington, D.C. 20202
202-245-0080

National Library Service for the Blind and Physically Handicapped
Library of Congress
1291 Taylor Street, N.W.
Washington, D.C. 20542
D.C.: 202-298-5100
Elsewhere: 800-424-8567

President's Committee on Employment of the Handicapped
1111 20th Street, N.W.
Washington, D.C. 20036
202-653-5044

National Center for a Barrier Free Environment
1140 Connecticut Avenue, N.W.
Suite 1006
Washington, D.C. 20036
202-466-6896
Elsewhere: 800-424-2809

Telecommunications Devices for the Deaf (TDD or TTY)
If you are hearing or speech impaired, call:

TDD/TTY Operator Services
800-855-1155 or 1(800)855-1155

The TDD operator will be able to help you make credit-card, collect, and third-number telephone calls. Also person-to-person calls and calls from a hotel/motel or from a coin phone.

Also call the TDD operator if you need help with a call or help with phone numbers not listed in the phone book, and also to report problems with your telephone.

The Consumer's Resource Handbook (available at your library or from the Consumer Information Center, Pueblo, Colo. 81009) has a listing of federal TDD numbers for all the major government agencies.

Handicapped, Equipment
For those in need of information about purchasing wheelchairs, electronic equipment to turn household appliances on and off, etc., contact one of the Centers for Independent Living, a nonprofit group specifically set up to aid the handicapped in New York State. For the names of Independent Living Centers, write:

The New York State Consumer Protection Board
99 Washington Avenue
Albany, N.Y. 12210.

Even if you are not a resident of New York State, you may still be able to get advice from this source on such matters as where to get the best prices for equipment, and information on insurance coverage.

The Center for Independence of the Disabled (New York City), 212-674-2300, has information on products used by the disabled in the home and office.

Handicapped, Organizations Aiding, General
Disability Rights Center
1346 Connecticut Avenue, N.W.
Washington, D.C. 20036
202-223-3304

Office for Handicapped Individuals
Department of Health and Human Resources
Washington, D.C. 20201

Health and Safety on the Job

REGIONAL OFFICES OF THE
OCCUPATIONAL SAFETY AND
HEALTH ADMINISTRATION

Region I (Connecticut, Maine, Massachusetts, New Hampshire, Rhode Island, Vermont)

JFK Federal Building, Room 1804
Government Center
Boston, Mass. 02203
617-223-6712

Region II (New York, New Jersey, Puerto Rico, Virgin Islands, Canal Zone)

Room 3445, 1 Astor Plaza
1515 Broadway
New York, N.Y. 10036
212-399-5754

Region III (Delaware, District of Columbia, Maryland, Pennsylvania, Virginia, West Virginia)

Gateway Building, Suite 2100
3535 Market Street
Philadelphia, Pa. 19104
215-596-1201

Region IV (Alabama, Florida, Georgia, Kentucky, Mississippi, North Carolina, South Carolina, Tennessee)

1375 Peachtree Street, N.E.
Suite 587
Atlanta, Ga. 30309
404-881-3573

Region V (Illinois, Indiana, Michigan, Minnesota, Ohio, Wisconsin)

230 South Dearborn Street
32nd Floor, Room 3263
Chicago, Ill. 60604
312-353-2220

Region VI (Arkansas, Louisiana, New Mexico, Oklahoma, Texas)

555 Griffin Square, Room 602
Dallas, Tex. 75202
214-767-4731

Region VII (Iowa, Kansas, Missouri, Nebraska)

911 Walnut Street, Room 3000
Kansas City, Mo. 64106
816-374-5861

Region VIII (Colorado, Montana, North Dakota, South Dakota, Utah, Wyoming)

Federal Building, Room 1554
1961 Stout Street
Denver, Colo. 80294
303-837-3883

Region IX (California, Arizona, Nevada, Hawaii, Guam, American Samoa, Trust Territory of the Pacific Islands)

450 Golden Gate Avenue
San Francisco, Calif. 94102
415-556-0586

Region X (Alaska, Idaho, Oregon, Washington)

Federal Office Building, Room 6002
909 First Avenue
Seattle, Wash. 98174
206-442-5930

NATIONAL ORGANIZATIONS
CONCERNED WITH WOMEN'S JOB
SAFETY AND HEALTH

Women's Occupational Health Resource Center
Columbia University School of Public Health
60 Haven Avenue, B-1
New York, N.Y. 10032
212-694-3464

A national clearinghouse for information about women's occupational safety and health. Also provides educational programs and conducts research on job hazards.

Committee for the Reproductive
 Rights of Workers
1917 I Street, N.W.
Washington, D.C. 20006
202-822-0061

An organization of labor unions, legal organizations, women's groups, and community organizations dedicated to defending the employment rights and reproductive freedom of workers exposed to hazards on the job.

Local Health and Safety Groups
"COSH" groups (committees for occupational safety and health) have been formed in over fifteen cities throughout the United States by unions, workers, and health and legal professionals. These organizations provide technical assistance, education programs, and political action on job safety and health.

CALIFORNIA

Bay Area Committee on Occupational Safety and Health (BA-COSH)
4135 Gilbert Street
Oakland, Calif. 94611

Los Angeles Committee on Occupational Safety and Health (LA-COSH)
P.O. Box 74243
Los Angeles, Calif. 90004

Santa Clara Committee on Occupational Safety and Health (SantaCOSH; includes Electronics Committee for Occupational Safety and Health, ECOSH)
361 Willow Street, #3
San Jose, Calif. 95110

San Diego COSH
P.O. Box 9901
San Diego, Calif. 92109

White Lung Association
P.O. Box 5089
San Pedro, Calif. 90733

CONNECTICUT

Connecticut Committee on Occupational Safety and Health (ConnectiCOSH)
P.O. Box 317
Farmington, Conn. 06032

ILLINOIS

Chicago Area Committee on Occupational Safety and Health (CACOSH)
542 South Dearborn, #502
Chicago, Ill. 60605

MARYLAND

Maryland Committee for Occupational Safety and Health (MaryCOSH)
P.O. Box 3825
Baltimore, Md. 21217

MASSACHUSETTS

Massachusetts Coalition for Occupational Safety and Health (MassCOSH)
718 Huntington Avenue
Boston, Mass. 02115

MassCOSH Western Region
134 Chestnut Street
Springfield, Mass. 01103

MICHIGAN

Southeastern Michigan Committee on Occupational Safety and Health (SEMCOSH)
c/o Labor Studies Department
Wayne State University
Detroit, Mich. 48202

MINNESOTA

Minnesota Area Committee on Occupational Safety and Health (MACOSH)
1729 Nicollet Avenue, South
Minneapolis, Minn. 55403

MISSOURI

St. Louis COSH
8909 Eager Road
St. Louis, Mo. 63144

NEW JERSEY

New Jersey Committee on Occupational Safety and Health
701 E. Elizabeth Avenue
Linden, N.J. 07036

NEW YORK

Allegheny Committee on Occupational Safety and Health (Allegheny COSH)
P.O. Box 184
Jamestown, N.Y. 14701

Central New York Committee on Occupational Safety and Health
119 Sherman Street
Watertown, N.Y. 13601

New York Committee on Occupational Safety and Health (NYCOSH)
32 Union Square East, #404-5
New York, N.Y. 10003

Oneida-Herkimer Committee on Occupational Safety and Health (OHCOSH)
Central New York Labor Agency
238 Genesee Street, Room 128
Utica, N.Y. 13501

Rochester Committee on Occupational Safety and Health (ROCOSH)
18 Wellington Avenue
Rochester, N.Y. 14611

Western New York Committee on Occupational Safety and Health (WNYCOSH)
343 Huntington Avenue
Buffalo, N.Y. 14214

NORTH CAROLINA

North Carolina Occupational Safety and Health Project (NCCOSHP)
P.O. Box 2514
Durham, N.C. 27705

OHIO

Central Ohio Committee on Occupational Safety and Health (COCOSH)
1187 E. Broad Street, Suite 21
Columbus, Ohio 43205

PENNSYLVANIA

Philadelphia Area Project on Occupational Safety and Health (PhilaPOSH)
1321 Arch Street, #607
Philadelphia, Pa. 19107

RHODE ISLAND

Rhode Island Committee on Occupational Safety and Health (RICOSH)
371 Broadway
Providence, R.I. 02909

SOUTH CAROLINA

Brown Lung Association
Greenville Chapter
P.O. Box 334
Greenville, S.C. 29602

TENNESSEE

Tennessee Committee for Occupational Safety and Health (TNCOSH)
705 North Broadway, Room 212
Knoxville, Tenn. 37919

WASHINGTON

Seattle Committee on Occupational Safety and Health (Sea-COSH)
2360 North 58th
Seattle, Wash. 98103

Washington Occupational Health Resource Center
Box 18371
Seattle, Wash. 98118

WEST VIRGINIA

Kanawha Valley Coalition on Occupational Safety and Health (KVCOSH)
P.O. Box 3062
Charleston, W.Va. 25331

WISCONSIN

Wisconsin Committee on Occupational Safety and Health (Wis-COSH)
2468 West Juneau
Milwaukee, Wis. 53233

CANADA

Windsor Council on Occupational Safety and Health (WCOSH)
824 Tecumseh Road, East
Windsor, Ontario N8X 2S3
Canada

Health Rights

ABORTION

Despite an amendment to the Constitution, the battle for abortion rights continues. Severe restrictions have been placed on the rights of poor women to obtain Medicaid-funded abortions. The following organizations are "pro choice":

American Civil Liberties Union Reproductive Freedom Project
22 East 40th Street
New York, N.Y. 10016

Catholics for a Free Choice
2008 17th Street, N.W.
Washington, D.C. 20002
202-638-1706

Rosie Jimenez Fund
711 San Antonio Street
Austin, Tex. 78701

National Abortion Federation
110 East 59th Street
New York, N.Y. 10022

National Abortion Rights Action League
1424 K Street, N.W.
Washington, D.C. 20005
202-347-7774

Planned Parenthood Federation of America
810 Seventh Avenue
New York, N.Y. 10019

Religious Coalition for Abortion Rights
100 Maryland Avenue, N.E.
Washington, D.C. 20002
202-543-7032

MENTALLY ILL PEOPLE

For information on patient support groups or organizations working for the rights of the mentally ill, contact your local bar association or the American Civil Liberties Union. The following organizations may be able to advise you on organizations in your area.

American Bar Association Commission on the Mentally Disabled
1800 M Street, N.W.
Washington, D.C. 20036
202-331-2200

National Committee Against Mental Illness
1101 17th Street, N.W.
Washington, D.C. 20002
202-296-4435

Project Release
130 West 72nd Street
New York, N.Y. 10025

Association for the Rehabilitation
of the Mentally Ill
853 Broadway
New York, N.Y. 10011
212-228-7240

MENTALLY RETARDED

The following is a listing of national organizations working for the rights of the mentally retarded:

American Association of Mental
Deficiency
5101 Wisconsin Avenue, N.W.
Washington, D.C. 20015
202-686-5400

American Bar Association
Commission on the Mentally Disabled
1800 M Street, N.W.
Washington, D.C. 20036

ACLU Juvenile Rights Project
22 East 40th Street
New York, N.Y. 10016

Center on Human Policy
Division of Special Education &
Rehabilitation
Syracuse University
Syracuse, N.Y. 13210

Child Welfare League of America,
Inc.
44 East 23rd Street
New York, N.Y. 10010

Children's Defense Fund
1520 New Hampshire Avenue,
N.W.
Washington, D.C. 20036
202-483-1470

The Council for Exceptional Children
900 Jefferson Plaza
1411 Jefferson Davis Highway
Arlington, Va. 22202

Institute for the Study of Mental
Retardation and Related
Disabilities
130 South First
University of Michigan
Ann Arbor, Mich. 48108

Joseph P. Kennedy, Jr. Foundation
1701 K Street, N.W.
Washington, D.C. 20006
202-331-1731

Mental Health Law Project
2021 L Street, N.W.
Washington, D.C. 20036
202-467-5730

National Association of Coordinators of State Programs for the
Mentally Retarded
2001 Jefferson Davis Highway
Arlington, Va. 22202

The National Association for Retarded Citizens
2709 Avenue E East
Arlington, Tex. 76010

National Center for Law and the
Handicapped
1238 North Eddy Street
South Bend, Ind. 46617

National Legal Aid & Defender
Association
1155 East 60th Street
Chicago, Ill. 60637

PATIENT'S RIGHTS

(Organizations Working on Behalf
of Patients)

CALIFORNIA

Charles Drew Health Rights Center
1621 East 120 Street
Los Angeles, Calif. 90059

National Health Law Program
2639 La Cunega Boulevard
Los Angeles, Calif. 90024
213-204-6010

DISTRICT OF COLUMBIA

Children's Defense Fund
1520 New Hampshire Avenue
Washington, D.C. 20056
202-483-1470

Committee on Health Law
American Public Health Association
1015 18th Street, N.W.
Washington, D.C. 20036
202-789-5600

Health Research Group
2000 P Street, N.W.
Washington, D.C. 20036
202-872-0320
(and local Public Interest Research Group affiliates—PIRGs)

National Urban Coalition
1201 Connecticut Avenue, N.W.
Washington, D.C. 20036
202-331-2400

MASSACHUSETTS

American Society of Law & Medicine
765 Commonwealth Avenue
Boston, Mass. 02215
617-262-4990

Center for Law and Health Sciences
Boston University School of Law
209 Bay State Road
Boston, Mass. 02215
617-353-2910

Joint Center for the Study of Law, Medicine & the Life Sciences
Boston College Law School—Tufts Medical School
Newton, Mass. 02158

NEW YORK

Health Policy Advisory Center
17 Murray Street
New York, N.Y. 10007

PHILADELPHIA

Health Law Project Library, University of Pennsylvania
133 South 36th Street, Room 410
Philadelphia, Pa. 19104
215-243-6951
Also contact the following in regard to health rights:

State Attorney General's Office
Department of Public Health
Insurance Commissioner
State Comprehensive Health Planning Agency

The following organizations were established to fight for women's health rights:

Coalition for Medical Rights of Women
16388 Haight Street
San Francisco, Calif. 94110
415-621-8030

Federation of Feminist Women's Health Centers
1112 South Crenshaw Boulevard
Los Angeles, Calif. 90019

National Women's Health Network
224 7th Street, S.E.
Washington, D.C. 20003
202-543-9222

Women's Occupational Health Resource Center
American Health Foundation
320 East 43rd Street
New York, N.Y. 10017
212-953-1900

Legal Department
Planned Parenthood Federation of America, Inc.
810 Seventh Avenue
New York, N.Y. 10019
212-541-7800

Reproductive Freedom Project,
and Women's Rights Project
American Civil Liberties Union
132 West 43rd Street
New York, N.Y. 10036
212-944-9800

National Women's Law Center
1751 N Street, N.W.
Washington, D.C. 20036
202-872-0670

Legal Defense Fund
National Organization of Women
1029 Vermont Avenue N.W.
Washington, D.C. 20045
202-332-7337

Women's Legal Defense Fund
2000 P Street, N.W.
Washington, D.C. 20036
202-887-0364

Homemakers
(see also Displaced Homemakers)

Homemakers are one of the groups
most discriminated against in this
country. Their daily contribution
to home and community is not
recognized as work for purposes of
unemployment compensation, social security based on their time
spent working, or workers' compensation. There are few if any of
the "job benefits," such as paid vacations, available to those who
have jobs. The following organizations offer information and ideas
on the role of homemakers.

Future Homemakers of America
2010 Massachusetts Avenue,
N.W.
Washington, D.C. 20036
202-833-1925

Martha Movement
1011 Arlington Boulevard
Arlington, Va. 22209

Wages for Housework
P.O. Box 830
Brooklyn, N.Y. 11202

Housing and Real Estate
The following organizations will
provide information for tenants or
homeowners with legal problems:

State department of community
affairs or other state offices with
responsibility for housing issues
County or municipal government office dealing with housing
affairs
American Civil Liberties Union
—local chapter
Legal Aid Society—local chapter
County or state bar association
local tenants organization

Job Discrimination
Check your local phone book for
district offices of the Equal Employment Opportunity Commission (EEOC) or the state human
rights commission. The following
is a general listing of organizations
involved in getting equal rights for
women in the job market.

American Association for Affirmative Action
c/o Betty Newcomb
Ball State University
Muncie, Ind. 47306

Coalition of Labor Union Women
386 Park Avenue South
New York, N.Y. 10010

Comparable Worth Project
488 41st Street, No. 5
Oakland, Calif. 94609

This is a clearinghouse for news on wage discrimination. Publishes a monthly newsletter and distributes a variety of materials on wage discrimination at modest cost.

Equal Employment Opportunity Commission
2401 E Street, N.W.
Washington, D.C. 20506

Federally Employed Women
1010 Vermont Avenue, N.W.
Washington, D.C. 20045
202-638-4404

Federation of Organizations for Professional Women
2000 P Street, N.W.
Washington, D.C. 20036
202-466-3544

National Commission on Working Women
2000 P Street, N.W.
Washington, D.C. 20036
202-892-1782

National Committee on Pay Equity
1201 18th Street, N.W.
Room 615
Washington, D.C. 20036

This is a national membership' advocacy group working in the area of pay equity which provides a number of publications for laypersons.

National Congress of Neighborhood Women
11-29 Catherine Street
Brooklyn, N.Y. 11211

Office for Civil Rights
Department of Health, Education and Welfare
Washington, D.C. 20201

Union Women's Alliance to Gain Equality
P.O. Box 462
Berkeley, Calif. 94701

United Auto Workers Women's Department
8000 East Jefferson Avenue
Detroit, Mich. 48214

Wider Opportunities for Women
1511 K Street, N.W.
Washington, D.C. 20006
202-638-3143

Women's Bureau
Office of the Secretary, Department of Labor
Washington, D.C. 20210

Women's Equity Action League
805 15th Street, N.W.
Washington, D.C. 20005
202-638-1961

Women Library Workers
P.O. Box 9052
Berkeley, Calif. 94709

Working Women, National Association of Office Workers
1258 Euclid Avenue
Cleveland, Ohio 44115

Insurance
National Women's Insurance Center
1015 20th Street, N.W.
Washington, D.C. 20036
202-333-1200

Lawyers
Before hiring a lawyer, you may find it useful to read Gillers, *The Rights of Lawyers and Clients* (New York: ACLU/Avon Books, 1979). (Chapter 10 has information on the rights of the poor, people who represent themselves without a lawyer, and do-it-yourself divorce kits.)

Bar associations very often run referral services, and in some cases the first interview with a lawyer may be free.

A number of states and cities have women's bar associations. For information, contact the National Conference of Women's Bar Associations

Officers

PRESIDENT

Timmerman Tepel Daugherty
32 Shangri La Drive, South
Lexington Park, Maryland 20653
(301) 862-2155
D.C. (202) 870-3514

VICE PRESIDENT

Carol Rabenhorst
1620 Eye Street, N.W.
Suite 1000
Washington, D.C. 20006
(202) 828-8237

VICE PRESIDENT

Pamela Harwood
15736 Munich
Detroit, Michigan 48224
(313) 965-3464

VICE PRESIDENT

Gill Freeman
2020 One Biscayne Tower
Miami, Florida 33139
(305) 371-6262

TREASURER

Janis McDonald
P.O. Box 1226
108 N. Columbus Street
Alexandria, Virginia 22313
(703) 836-6595

CORRESPONDING SEC.

Peggy LeBlanc
610 Poydras St.
Suite 318
New Orleans, Louisiana 70130
(504) 525-9538

RECORDING SEC.

Dolores Wilson
744 Broad Street
30th Floor
Newark, New Jersey 07102
(201) 648-3827

Directors

Susan Low
Suite 406
1101 17th Street, N.W.
Washington, D.C. 20036
(202) 296-0555

Joan Ellenbogen
888 Seventh Avenue
New York, New York 10106
(212) 245-3260

Pauline Weaver
Courthouse
1225 Fallon Street
Oakland, California 94612
(415) 874-5353

Debra Goodstone
3050 Biscayne Blvd.
Miami, Florida 33140
(305) 576-1500

Naomi Kauffman
100 Military Plaza
Suite 201
P.O. Box 486
Dodge City, Kansas 67801

Marjorie Holmes
300 Montgomery Street
Suite 700
San Francisco, California 94104
(415) 391-6055

Aldrinette Chapital
1310 Prairie
Suite 300 A
Houston, Texas 77002
(713) 223-1780

Sheila Birnbaum
Associate Dean
New York University School of
Law
40 Washington Square, South
New York, New York 10012
(212) 598-2501

Susan Ness
5505 Devon Road
Bethesda, Maryland 20814
(301) 654-2110

Helen Stone
1301 Spruce Street
Boulder, Colorado 80320
(303) 442-0802

Mary Ann Coffey
21st Floor
601 Poydras Street
New Orleans, Louisiana 70130

Judge Clarice Jobes
Recorders Court
1441 St. Antoine
Detroit, Michigan 48226

Jo Nelson
3210 Smith
Houston, Texas 77006

Arnette Hubbard
134 North LaSalle Street
Suite 300
Chicago, Illinois 60602

Ellen Fallon
Langrock, Sperry, Parker & Stahl
Drawer 361
Middleburg, Vermont 05753
    In addition, you may wish to
    contact the following organi-
    zations for information:

American Civil Liberties Union
(check the phone book for the
local chapter)

American Trial Lawyers Association

Women Trial Lawyers Caucus
1050 31st Street, N.W.
Washington, D.C. 20007
202-965-3500

National Women's Law Center
1751 N Street, N.W.
Washington, D.C. 20036
202-872-0670

Women's Legal Defense Fund
2000 P Street, N.W.
Washington, D.C. 20036
202-887-0364

American Arbitration Association
140 W. 51 Street
New York, N.Y. 10019
212-484-4000

Lesbians

Lesbian mothers, rights organizations:

Lesbian Mothers National Defense Fund
2446 Lorentz Place North
Seattle, Wash. 98109

National Gay Task Force
80 Fifth Avenue
New York, N.Y. 10011

Books for Lesbian mothers:

E. Carrington Boggan et al. *The
Rights of Gay People.* New
York: ACLU/Avon Books,
1975.

Hovell. *Lesbian Mothers Custody
Cases: Who to Call for What.*
(Order from: Mary Hovell, 2101
Smith Tower, Seattle, Wash.
98104.)

Lesbian organizations, general:

Daughters of Bilitis
1151 Massachusetts Avenue
Cambridge, Mass. 02138

Gay Rights National Lobby
Women's Caucus
750 7th Street, S.E.
Washington, D.C. 20002
202-546-1801

National Gay Task Force
80 Fifth Avenue
New York, N.Y. 10011
212-741-5815

National Lesbian Feminist Organization
P.O. Box 14643
Houston, Tex. 77021

The Task Force on Gay Liberation publishes A Gay Bibliography. (Order from: American Library Association [Task Force], P.O. Box 2383, Philadelphia, Pa. 19103.)

Parents
Support organization for single parents:

Parents Without Partners
7910 Woodmont Avenue
Bethesda, Md. 20014
301-654-8850

Minority Women, Organizations
ASIAN-AMERICAN WOMEN

Council of Asian-American Women
3 Pell Street
New York, N.Y. 10013

Organization of Chinese-American Women
1525 O Street, N.W.
Washington, D.C. 20005
202-328-3185

The Organization of Pan Asian-American Women
915 15th Street, N.W.
Washington, D.C. 20012
202-737-1377

BLACK WOMEN

Links
1522 K Street, N.W.
Washington, D.C. 20005
202-783-3888

National Alliance of Black Feminists
202 South State Street
Chicago, Ill. 60604
312-939-0107

National Association of Negro Business and Professional Women's Clubs
1806 New Hampshire Avenue, N.W.
Washington, D.C. 20009
202-483-4206

National Council of Negro Women
348 Convent Avenue
New York, N.Y. 10027
212-862-2035

National Hook-Up of Black Women
1522 K Street, N.W.
Washington, D.C. 20006
202-737-1172

National Organization on Concerns of Black Women
3958 Louise Street
Lynwood, Calif. 90262

National Association of Colored Women's Clubs
5808 16th Street, N.W.
Washington, D.C. 20011
202-726-2044

National Association of Negro Business and Professional Women's Clubs
1806 New Hampshire Avenue, N.W.
Washington, D.C. 20009

HISPANIC WOMEN

Comisión Femenil Mexicana Nacional
379 South Loma Drive
Los Angeles, Calif. 90017

Mexican-American Legal Defense and Education Fund
Chicana Rights Project
201 North St. Mary's Street
San Antonio, Tex. 78205

Mexican-American Women's National Association
P.O. Box 23656
L'Enfant Plaza Station, S.W.
Washington, D.C. 20024

National Chicana Foundation
1005 South Alamo
San Antonio, Tex. 78210

National Conference of Puerto Rican Women
927 15th Street, N.W.
Washington, D.C. 20008
202-393-1604

Native American Women
Cante Ohitika Win (Brave Hearted Women)
P.O. Box 474
Pine Ridge, S.D. 57770

Women of All Red Nations
c/o Lorelei Means
General Delivery
Porcupine, S.D. 57779

Names
The rights of women to use their own names after marriage are now generally accepted in most states. However, if you have a problem or a question about names, contact:

Center for a Woman's Own Name
261 Kimberley Street
Barrington, Ill. 60010

Offenders, Women
(These organizations do not generally provide legal assistance for individuals.)

Center for Women's Policy Studies
2000 P Street, N.W.
Washington, D.C. 20036
203-872-1770

Girls Clubs of America
205 Lexington Avenue
New York, N.Y. 10016

New Directions for Women
346 South Scott
Tucson, Ariz. 85701

Women's Prison Association
110 Second Avenue
New York, N.Y. 10003
212-674-1163

The NAACP Legal Defense Fund
10 Columbus Circle
New York, N.Y. 10023

READING

Rudovsky, Bronstein, and Koren. *The Rights of Prisoners.* New York: ACLU/Avon, 1977.

Older Women
The following organizations are working for the rights of older people·

American Association of Retired Persons / National Retired Teachers Association
1909 K Street, N.W.
Washington, D.C. 20049
202-872-4700

The Gerontological Society
1835 K Street, N.W.
Washington, D.C. 20036
202-466-6750

Gray Panthers
3700 Chestnut Street
Philadelphia, Pa. 19104
215-382-6644

National Action Forum for Older Women
Health Sciences Center
State University of New York
Stony Brook, N.Y. 11794

National Association of Retired Federal Employees
1533 New Hampshire Avenue, N.W.
Washington, D.C. 20036
202-234-0832

National Caucus of the Black Aged
1424 K Street, N.W.
Washington, D.C. 20036
202-637-8400

National Council on the Aging
1828 L Street, N.W., Suite 504
Washington, D.C. 20036
202-223-6250

National Council of Senior Citizens
925 15th Street, N.W.
Washington, D.C. 20005
202-347-8800

National Senior Citizens Law Center
1424 16th Street, N.W.
Washington, D.C. 20005
202-232-6570

Older Women's League Educational Fund
3800 Harrison Street
Oakland, Calif. 94611

Pension Rights Center
1346 Connecticut Avenue, Room 1019
Washington, D.C. 20036
202-296-3778

Transit, the National Institute for Transition
22 Monument Square
Portland, Me. 04111

Rape

Resources for rape victims/organizations offering guidance:

Feminist Alliance Against Rape
P.O. Box 21033
Washington, D.C. 20009

National Directory: Rape Prevention Treatment and Resources
Order from National Institute of Mental Health
5600 Fishers Lane
Rockville, Md. 20857

National Women's Health Network
2025 I Street, N.W., Suite 105
Washington, D.C. 20006

National Coalition Against Sexual Assault
P.O. Box 154
Edwardville, Ill. 62026

National Communications Network for Elimination of Violence Against Women
4520 44th Avenue, South
Minneapolis, Minn. 55406

National Organization for Victim Assistance (NOVA)
1757 Park Road, N.W.
Washington, D.C. 20010

Check Yellow Pages or call information in your area for:
Women's centers
National Organization for Women (NOW) chapter
Rape crisis center or domestic violence center
District attorney's office (prosecutor)

Runaways

HOT LINES

National Runaway Switchboard
1-800-621-4000

Operation Peace of Mind
1-800-231-6946

Rural Women

Council on Appalachian Women
P.O. Box 490
Mars Hill, N.C. 28754

Rural American Women
1522 K Street, N.W.
Washington, D.C. 20005
202-785-4700

Women Involved in Farm Economics
P.O. Box 172
Crook, Colo. 80726

Social Security

Pension Rights Center
1346 Connecticut Avenue, N.W.
Washington, D.C. 20036
202-296-3778

Sexual Harassment on the Job

Alliance Against Sexual Coercion
P.O. Box 1
Cambridge, Mass. 01239

Women Organized Against Sexual Harassment
2437 Edwards Street
Berkeley, Calif. 94702

Working Women's Institute
593 Park Avenue
New York, N.Y. 10021

There are numerous articles and other publications about sexual harassment. The above-listed organizations also maintain bibliographies that are periodically revised.

Tenant Aid Organizations

See Housing and Real Estate

Women's Organizations

Women's Action Almanac (New York: William Morrow, 1979) has a comprehensive listing of women's organizations.

Veterans

The following is a listing of Veterans' Assistance Centers, state by state:

ALABAMA

474 South Court Street
Montgomery, Ala. 36104

ALASKA

429 D Street, Suite 214
Anchorage, Alaska 99501

709 West Ninth Street
Juneau, Alaska 99802

ARIZONA

3225 North Central Avenue
Phoenix, Ariz. 85012

ARKANSAS

700 West Capitol Avenue
Little Rock, Ark. 72201

CALIFORNIA

101 South Willowbrook Avenue
Compton, Calif. 90220

11000 Wilshire Boulevard
Los Angeles, Calif. 90024

929 North Bonnie Beach Pl.
East Los Angeles, Calif. 90063

1250 Sixth Avenue
San Diego, Calif. 92101

211 Main Street
San Francisco, Calif. 94105

COLORADO

Denver Federal Center
Denver, Colo. 80225

CONNECTICUT

450 Main Street
Hartford, Conn. 06103

DELAWARE

1601 Kirkwood Highway
Wilmington, Del. 19805

DISTRICT OF COLUMBIA

25 K Street, N.E.
Washington, D.C. 20002

Black War Veterans of the U.S.
40 G Street, N.E.
Washington, D.C.
202-789-0330

FLORIDA

Post Office and Courthouse Building
Jacksonville, Fla. 32201

51 S.W. First Avenue
Miami, Fla. 33130

144 First Avenue South
St. Petersburg, Fla. 33731

GEORGIA

730 Peachtree Street, N.E.
Atlanta, Ga. 30308

HAWAII

680 Ala Moana Boulevard
Honolulu, Hawaii 96801

IDAHO

550 West Fort Street
Boise, Idaho 83707

ILLINOIS

2030 West Taylor Street
Chicago, Ill. 60612

INDIANA

575 North Pennsylvania Street
Indianapolis, Ind. 46204

IOWA

210 Walnut Street
Des Moines, Iowa 50309

KANSAS

5500 East Kellogg
Wichita, Kans. 67218

KENTUCKY

600 Federal Plaza
Louisville, Ky. 40202

LOUISIANA

701 Loyola Avenue
New Orleans, La. 70113

MAINE

Togus, Me. 04330

MARYLAND

31 Hopkins Plaza
Baltimore, Md. 21201

MASSACHUSETTS

John F. Kennedy Federal Building
Boston, Mass. 02203

MICHIGAN

801 West Baltimore Street
Detroit, Mich. 48232

MINNESOTA

Fort Snelling Federal Building
St. Paul, Minn. 55111

MISSISSIPPI

1500 East Woodrow Wilson Drive
Jackson, Miss. 39216

MISSOURI

601 East Twelfth Street
Kansas City, Mo. 64106

1520 Market Street
St. Louis, Mo. 63103

MONTANA

Fort Harrison, Mont. 59636

NEBRASKA

220 South Seventeenth Street
Lincoln, Nebr. 68508

NEVADA

1201 Terminal Way
Reno, Nev. 89502

NEW HAMPSHIRE

497 Silver Street
Manchester, N.H. 03103

NEW JERSEY

20 Washington Pl.
Newark, N.J. 07102

NEW MEXICO

500 Gold Avenue, S.W.
Albuquerque, N.M. 87101

NEW YORK

Executive Park
North Stuyvesant Plaza
Albany, N.Y. 12201

111 West Huron Street
Buffalo, N.Y. 14202

252 Seventh Avenue
New York, N.Y. 10001

100 State Street
Rochester, N.Y. 14614

809 South Salina Street
Syracuse, N.Y. 13202

NORTH CAROLINA

Wachovia Building
Winston-Salem, N.C. 27102

NORTH DAKOTA

21st Avenue & Elm Street
Fargo, N.D. 58102

OHIO

550 Main Street
Cincinnati, Ohio 45202

1240 East Ninth Street
Cleveland, Ohio 44199

360 South Third Street
Columbus, Ohio 43215

OKLAHOMA

Second & Court Streets
Muskogee, Okla. 74401

200 Northwest Fourth Street
Oklahoma City, Okla. 73102

OREGON

426 West Stark Street
Portland, Oreg. 97204

PENNSYLVANIA

5000 Wissahickon Avenue
Philadelphia, Pa. 19101

1000 Liberty Avenue
Pittsburgh, Pa. 15222

19–27 North Main Street
Wilkes-Barre, Pa. 18701

PHILIPPINES

1131 Roxas Boulevard
Manila, Philippines 96528

PUERTO RICO

G.P.O. Box 4867
San Juan, P.R. 09936

RHODE ISLAND

Federal Building, Kennedy Plaza
Providence, R.I. 02903

SOUTH CAROLINA

1801 Assembly Street
Columbia, S.C. 29201

SOUTH DAKOTA

2501 West Twenty-second Street
Sioux Falls, S.D. 57101

TENNESSEE

110 Ninth Avenue South
Nashville, Tenn. 37203

TEXAS

1100 Commerce Street
Dallas, Tex. 75202

2515 Munworth Drive
Houston, Tex. 77054

1205 Texas Avenue
Lubbock, Tex. 79401

410 South Main Street
San Antonio, Tex. 78285

1400 North Valley Mills Drive
Waco, Tex. 76710

UTAH

125 South State Street
Salt Lake City, Utah 84111

VERMONT

White River Junction, Vt. 05001

VIRGINIA

211 West Campbell Avenue
Roanoke, Va. 24011

WASHINGTON

915 Second Avenue
Seattle, Wash. 98174

WEST VIRGINIA

502 Eighth Street
Huntington, W.Va. 25701

WISCONSIN

342 North Water Street
Milwaukee, Wis. 53202

WYOMING

2360 East Pershing Boulevard
Cheyenne, Wyo. 82001

INDEX